M. J. WAY

WITHDRAWN
UTSA LIBRARIES

BIOLOGICAL BASIS OF ALCOHOLISM

Biological Basis of Alcoholism

YEDY ISRAEL

UNIVERSITY OF TORONTO AND
ALCOHOLISM AND DRUG ADDICTION
RESEARCH FOUNDATION, TORONTO
CANADA.

JORGE MARDONES

INSTITUTO DE INVESTIGACIONES SOBRE ALCOHOLISMO
UNIVERSIDAD DE CHILE, SANTIAGO

WILEY-INTERSCIENCE, a Division of John Wiley & Sons, Inc.
New York · London · Sidney · Toronto

PREFACE

In the last decade the emphasis of research in alcoholism has shifted to more biological aspects. Although alcoholism has been classically considered a problem of the soul, with implications in the soma, both soul and soma are known to be closely related to cellular properties of the biological system, and therefore separate distinctions can no longer be drawn. Thus, the kind of interaction of alcohol with the biological system, the genetic characteristics of the system, as well as the frequency of interaction, combine to project the image commonly referred to as alcoholism.

We have invited a selected group of researchers in this field to analyze the different approaches and recent findings and to offer their personal views in the context of their particular disciplines. These investigations begin at the subcellular and cellular levels and increase in complexity and level of integration to the organ, the individual, and the society.

It is our firm belief that only a multidisciplinary approach will combine the pieces of this puzzle and will clarify a solution to the age-old problem of alcoholism.

YEDY ISRAEL
JORGE MARDONES

June 1971

CONTENTS

Chapter 7   Effects of Alcohol on Cardiac and Muscular Function   183

Ralph M. Myerson

Chapter 8   The Importance of Congeners in the Effects of Alcoholic Beverages   209

Henry B. Murphree

Chapter 9   Tolerance to, and Dependence on, Ethanol   235

Harold Kalant, A. Eugene LeBlanc, and Robert J. Gibbins

BIOLOGICAL BASIS OF ALCOHOLISM

Chapter I

THE METABOLISM OF ALCOHOL

FRANK LUNDQUIST

DEPARTMENT OF BIOCHEMISTRY A
UNIVERSITY OF COPENHAGEN
COPENHAGEN, DENMARK

A. Introduction

The study of the biochemistry, physiology, and pharmacology of alcohol metabolism in man and animals has contributed significantly to a growing understanding of the pathological manifestation of alcohol abuse and also to an understanding of the role of ethanol as a nutrient that may provide a sizable part of the caloric requirements of the body.

It is becoming increasingly evident that the effects, metabolic and pharmacological—on the organism are very different at high and low levels of ethanol consumption. When consumed in moderate quantities, alcohol seems to be a relatively innocuous nutrient that can be tolerated without apparent harm to the organism. When consumed in quantities that constantly approach the upper limit of the mechanisms responsible for its metabolic elimination, however, it becomes a drug that may produce very serious metabolic derangements. Various aspects of alcohol metabolism are reviewed in a number of monographs [21, 37, 184, 229] and articles. The literature before 1959 is adequately handled by Jacobsen [83]. Recent reviews include papers on the problems of fat accumulation and liver diseases as a consequence of ethanol consumption [105, 110], on metabolic pathways [124], on the influence of ethanol on the metabolism of other substances [49], on the influence of hormones [176], and on the biochemical pharmacology of alcohol [47, 146, 211].

B.   Organs Responsible for Alcohol Metabolism

It is an old observation [8, 105] that ethanol can be oxidized in preparations of liver tissue, but the questions of how much of the total alcohol metabolism takes place in the liver and how much in other tissues and how completely alcohol is metabolized in the different organs of the animal body have proved difficult to answer. The experiments of Lundsgaard [133] show quite clearly that in the cat the liver is responsible for by far the largest part of alcohol metabolism, measured by the disappearance of ethanol from the blood. Later work shows that also in other species [39, 62, 63], including man [100, 213], more than 70% of alcohol metabolism is accounted for by oxidation in the liver. Larsen [101] measured alcohol oxidation in eviscerated cats before and after the removal of the kidneys. These organs were found to be responsible for about 5% of the total ethanol metabolism or one-third of the extrahepatic metabolism. Similar results were obtained in experiments with kidney slices [105].

Because muscle tissue constitutes a large part of the body weight, even a small alcohol-oxidizing capacity per unit mass may contribute significantly to the extrahepatic ethanol metabolism. In the experiments of Larsen [101] and Forsander et al. [51] on eviscerated cats and rat hindquarters respectively, some residual alcohol oxidation was observed. This may partly be caused by the skeletal muscle tissue. By means of radioactive ethanol, rat diaphragm has been found to produce $^{14}CO_2$ [7, 141]. Several other investigators [compare 83] have observed some ethanol metabolism in the perfused rabbit heart, but these experiments have apparently not been repeated with more specific analytical methods. In the intact human subject no net uptake of ethanol by the heart could be measured, i.e., less than 10 mg/hr of ethanol [116].

Many attempts have been made to measure the activity of alcohol dehydrogenase in different tissues from various animal species, but such measurements are difficult and uncertain when the level of enzyme activity is low. Kidney [17, 128, 150] and intestinal mucosa [187], however, have been shown to contain alcohol dehydrogenase; brain, smooth muscle, and other tissues contain no significant activity. Quantitatively there seem to be considerable interspecific variations. For instance, the content of alcohol dehydrogenase in kidney tissue from rat, mouse, rabbit, and pigeon was found to range from 20 to 90 μg/g of fresh tissue; kidney from cat, dog, horse, and cow contained only 1 to 10 μg/g [128]. In man and rat the results of alcohol dehydrogenase measurements are given in Table I. Results in various species are given in Table II.

TABLE I   Alcohol Dehydrogenase Activity in Various Mammalian Tissues

	Percentage of activity in liver		
	Man		Rat
	[187]	[150]	[97]
Liver	100	100	100
Gastric mucosa	5	3	5
Duodenal mucosa			2
Lung	3	1	
Lymph nodes	. . .	1	
Kidney	1		
Kidney cortex			10

TABLE II   Alcohol Dehydrogenase Activity in Liver from Different Animal Species[a]

	IU/100 g fresh weight
Man	200
Rhesus monkey	200
Horse	1540
Cow	110
Pig	320
Guinea pig	83
Rat	121
Mouse	115

[a] The reaction was measured in the direction of ethanol oxidation [150].

C.   Elimination of Alcohol

The absorption of alcohol from the digestive tract and its distribution in the body are not considered in this review, although these problems are of considerable practical importance [220]. It should be pointed out, however, that in studies on the elimination of alcohol it is important that sufficient time is allowed after the administration of alcohol in order to secure the complete absorption of alcohol from the gut or the peritoneal cavity and also for equilibration between tissues and blood.

Elimination of alcohol from the organism takes place largely through metabolic removal, but in some cases other routes cannot be neglected. The two most important processes in this category are elimination through the lungs and kidneys. The amount of alcohol lost in this way is proportional to the concentration in the blood. Therefore these routes may play a role mainly at high concentrations of alcohol. In man, pulmonary and renal elimination contributes 10 to 15% to the over-all elimination rate at blood alcohol levels of 200 to 300 mg/100 ml. In small animals in which the respiratory exchange is relatively high, measured per unit of body weight, elimination through the lungs should be correspondingly increased, but reliable measurements are not available.

1.   Elimination of Alcohol in Man

A.   OVER-ALL ELIMINATION. The type of experiment most often performed on human subjects involves the intake of a relatively small dose of ethanol followed after a suitable equilibration period by the removal of a series of venous or capillary blood samples. In nearly all cases the blood alcohol concentrations obtained are low, and the disappearance is therefore nearly exclusively caused by the metabolic conversion of ethanol. In some cases [12, 13, 79–81, 145, 147] the formation of labeled CO_2 from ^{14}C ethanol has been measured instead of the change in alcohol concentration [71, 83, 126, 188, 229]. Such measurements, however, do not estimate the rate of alcohol oxidation but indicate to what extent the primary oxidation products acetaldehyde and acetate are further oxidized in the body. The two procedures cannot be expected to give the same result, because the fate of acetate may be different under varying experimental conditions. Acetate may, for instance, be incorporated into lipids to a larger or smaller degree.

B.   HEPATIC ELIMINATION. The part played by the liver in alcohol metabolism may be evaluated through the catheterization technique, in which samples of arterial blood and blood from a hepatic vein are removed simultaneously and the blood flow through the liver is estimated in the usual way by measuring the clearance of a dye that is exclusively eliminated through the bile, such as bromsulphalein or indocyanine green. In this way the removal of alcohol per minute by the splanchnic organs is determined [131, 213, 232]. Values of about 1.6 mmoles/min were obtained, compared with a total rate of elimination of about 2.1 mmoles/min.

C.   KINETICS OF ALCOHOL ELIMINATION IN MAN. The careful work of Widmark in the twenties on the elimination of alcohol in man, and some experimental animals, established that the blood alcohol concentration after the completion of absorption and distribution in the body decreased at a constant rate that was found to be virtually independent of physiological factors, such as physical work [20, 103, 157]. The blood alcohol concentration attained in Widmark's experiments was, however, low (about 0.1%), and similar low concentrations have been used in nearly all later quantitative measurements of alcohol metabolism in man. The conclusions drawn from these numerous investigations [71, 83, 126, 188, 229] must therefore be limited to the statement that within experimental error the decrease in blood alcohol concentration approaches a straight line in the concentration range of 0.1 to 0.02%. At very low concentrations this relation cannot hold for two reasons. If it is accepted that the metabolism of alcohol takes place nearly exclusively in the liver, then when the ethanol concentration is so low that the liver removes from the blood virtually all the alcohol that flows through it, the rate of decline in blood alcohol concentration depends on hemodynamic relations, including the diffusion of alcohol from the peripheral organs to the blood. This results in an exponential decrease. The second factor is concerned with the enzymatic mechanism responsible for the removal of alcohol. Any such mechanism is concentration-dependent when the concentration of the substrate (alcohol) is sufficiently low. Analysis of the elimination curve at low alcohol concentration, which is made possible by the use of a sensitive enzymatic method for alcohol determination, has shown a definite retardation of alcohol elimination when the concentration falls below about 3 mM (or 0.015%). From this result a Michaelis constant for the rate-limiting step in alcohol metabolism was estimated to be about 2 mM, although such an estimate must necessarily be rather uncertain [126].

The question whether the rate of alcohol elimination (apart from the relatively insignificant amount eliminated through respiratory gases and urine) remains constant at higher concentration, has not been sufficiently clarified. A number of reports [143, 145, 146, 155], however, show quite convincingly that some subjects under controlled experimental conditions can metabolize considerably larger quantities of alcohol than can be calculated from the rate constants determined at low blood alcohol levels (compare Section E.3). A complete elimination curve covering the whole concentration range from, say, 0.3% to near zero has apparently never been published, and so there seems to be the possibility that at high concentrations alcohol is metabolized by a concentration-dependent mechanism. This problem is further discussed in Sections D and E.

2. Elimination of Alcohol in Experimental Animals

A. WHOLE ANIMALS. The rate of elimination of alcohol in a number of animal species has been determined. Examples are given in Table III.

TABLE III   Rate of Alcohol Metabolism in Different Animal Species

Animal species	Alcohol metabolism, mg/(kg body wt) (hr)	Range of blood alcohol concn, percent	Concn dependence	Ref.
Mouse	400–800	0.4–0.2	—	153
	500–1400	0.35–0.0	+	140
Rat	303 ± 77 (fed)	0.3–0.0	—	159
	176 (fasted 48 hr)			
	270 (fasted 18 hr)	. . .	. . .	4
Cat	120–210[a]	0.4–0.0	+	33, 34
	100	0.1–0.0	. . .	101
Dog	150	. . .	(+)	36
	180	0.25–0.02	—	121
	155 ± 25	?	. . .	152
	100–200[b]	0.3–0.0	+	139
Rabbit	137–203	0.1–0.03	—	45
Horse	52–78	0.1–0.0	. . .	106
Cow	63–133	0.12–0.03	. . .	54
Wether	180[a]	0.11–0.04	. . .	85
Man	100	0.1–0.01	—	Numerous authors

[a] Calculated from the decline in blood alcohol concentration, assuming a distribution factor of 0.75.
[b] Variations from hour to hour.

The variable influence of the expiration of alcohol has not been taken into account in any of these measurements.

B.   PERFUSED ORGANS.   A closer study of alcohol metabolism in the liver and of the metabolic changes caused by alcohol can be achieved with perfused liver preparations. So far few studies have, however, been published, but recently renewed interest in this technique is apparent [e.g., 53, 62, 63, 231].

C.   TISSUE PREPARATIONS.   Even simpler preparations, such as tissue slices [e.g., 55, 105, 174, 175, 209, 216] and homogenates [8, 67, 130] of liver and kidney, have been used in studies on alcohol oxidation. Such methods are, however, not suited for a quantitative evaluation, because quite considerable reduction in the elimination rate is observed, compared with the intact animal or perfused preparations. Dependence on the composition of the medium and the gas phase also introduces uncertainty [216]. For the study of metabolic details and of the influence of alcohol on other metabolic processes in the liver, however, such preparations seem suitable.

D.   KINETICS OF ALCOHOL ELIMINATION IN ANIMALS.   The shape of the elimination curve in some animal species has been followed in a considerable concentration range. With small animals, however, a number of difficulties are encountered. For instance, it is difficult to obtain a sufficient number of blood samples without interfering with the physiological state of the animal. Intravenous administration of alcohol, because of the faster distribution in the tissues, is much to be preferred to intraperitoneal injection or oral administration. This is not always possible in small animals, however. The difficulty was circumvented in an elegant manner by Lester et al. [107], who introduced a subcutaneous depot of air in rats. From this depot, which was found rapidly to attain equilibrium with the circulating blood, gas samples were removed and examined by means of gas chromatography.

As a result of these and other difficulties most of the published experiments on rats, which are by far the most commonly used experimental animal in this field, show a considerable spreading of the experimental points, which prevents any certain conclusions about the kinetics of the elimination process. It should be mentioned, however, that the work of Marshall and Owens [140] on mice shows a surprisingly close fit to linear elimination kinetics in the whole range of 0.4 to 0% blood alcohol.

In large animals, such as the dog, suitable curves have been obtained at low ethanol concentrations [139]. When measurements were made at high blood alcohol concentrations, however (see Table III), irregularities were found in the elimination rate.

In considering the results from various authors on different animal species, it should be kept in mind that species differences may exist in the predominant enzymatic mechanism of alcohol metabolism and also that the range of alcohol concentration and the nutritional state of the animals and other factors may change the kinetics radically (see Section E).

D.   Enzymology of Alcohol Metabolism

It is now apparent that the oxidative metabolism of alcohol takes place in several steps, each of which may be catalyzed by more than one enzyme. The quantitative evaluation of the role of the individual enzymes in a given species under physiological conditions cannot be achieved by in vitro studies alone, but an approach may be made by the application of suitable inhibitors in vivo (compare Section D.5).

1.   Oxidation to Acetaldehyde

The first oxidation step in the metabolism of alcohol is assumed to be oxidation to acetaldehyde. One could imagine also oxidation to ethylene glycol. Although no evidence is available for this pathway, it cannot be excluded that a hydroxylation reaction of this type could take place. By far the largest part of alcohol oxidation, however, results in the formation of acetate, or acetyl coenzyme A, which presumably must arise via acetaldehyde. The presence of acetaldehyde in the organism in increased concentrations during ethanol metabolism has been established, but the concentrations observed were very small. The analytical determination of acetaldehyde in blood is difficult, and surprisingly different results have been reported by various authors, ranging from 10 to 170 μM. Gas chromatography, when properly conducted, i.e., when the artifactual formation of acetaldehyde or substances that may be mistaken for acetaldehyde, such as acetone, was avoided, has shown a concentration of about 10 μM (0.4 μg/ml) in blood [6] and 4 to 6 μg/liter alveolar air in man [58]. These results are at variance with other reports [212], but they agree well with some enzymatic determinations on blood [126, 218]. Again it should be remembered that species differences may exist. The relative activity of the enzymes causing the formation and removal of acetaldehyde together with their Michaelis constant for this substrate determines the steady-state level of acetaldehyde in the tissues and blood. Relatively small changes in the parameters mentioned could result in appreciable differences in acetaldehyde concentration.

In the liver at least three enzymes are present that can oxidize ethanol to acetaldehyde, viz., alcohol dehydrogenase, catalase, and one or more mixed-function alcohol hydroxylases.

A. ALCOHOL DEHYDROGENASE. Among the three enzymes mentioned above, it is generally believed that the alcohol dehydrogenase requiring nicotinamide adenine dinucleotide (NAD) is the most important quantitatively, at least under conditions that may be characterized as physiological. The enzyme may be isolated from liver in amounts that can account for the metabolic activity observed. This is true with the horse and man [28, 106, 151, 224].

This enzyme has been known for a long time. Its properties were investigated in considerable detail by Lutwak Mann already in 1938 [135]. She observed that cozymase (now known as NAD) was required for its activity and also that alcohol dehydrogenase from liver was remarkably stable. Bonnichsen and Wassén [15] in 1948 prepared alcohol dehydrogenase from horse liver in the crystalline state, and this achievement made possible a large number of kinetic investigations, which has made liver alcohol dehydrogenase (L-ADH) one of the best-characterized enzymes from a kinetic point of view. Especially the penetrating studies of Theorell and his coworkers [190, 191, 196, 201–204], but also those of other groups [9, 193, 233], have contributed to the mechanistic understanding of this enzyme.

The following equilibrium is catalyzed by alcohol dehydrogenase:

$$NAD^+ + CH_3CH_2OH \rightleftharpoons NADH + H^+ + CH_3CHO \qquad (1)$$

The equilibrium constant has been measured repeatedly. At $20°$ and ionic strength 0.1 it was found to be 8×10^{-12} [5].

The position of this equilibrium is very unfavorable for the oxidation of ethanol. The change in free energy at physiological pH ($\Delta G'$, pH 7.4) is calculated to be $+4.9$ kcal/mole. If the concentration of the reduced and oxidized form of the coenzyme were equal, the equilibrium concentration of ethanol would be approximately 5000 times the aldehyde concentration. In the cytoplasm, the phase in which alcohol dehydrogenase is present, the concentration of free NADH is very much lower than that of NAD because of binding to enzymes. From measurements of lactate and pyruvate concentrations, which are assumed to be in equilibrium with NAD and NADH under most conditions, it is found that the NAD/NADH ratio is about 700 [230] under normal conditions. During ethanol metabolism the ratio is reduced about three times. The low concentration of NADH, as seen in (1), facilitates the reaction. Another major factor that keeps the reaction going is the constant and effective removal of acetaldehyde.

The concentration of this metabolite in the steady state is probably well below the equilibrium concentration. The oxidation of acetaldehyde to acetate has a large affinity ($\Delta G'$ about -13 kcal/mole) that furnishes the free-energy change needed to pull the dehydrogenation of ethanol.

Isoenzymes of alcohol dehydrogenase. Preparation of crystalline ADH from horse liver is relatively simple. By the improved procedure published by Dalziel [28] 2 g of enzyme is obtained from about 5 kg of liver. From human liver a very pure product was prepared in a yield of about 100 mg/kg of liver (or 10% of the activity of the crude extract) [151].

When crude preparations of ADH from various species are examined by gel electrophoresis, the presence of a number of isoenzymes has repeatedly been found [160, 164, 165, 205, 223]. Purification of one of the isoenzymes of horse liver ADH has resulted in a new crystalline enzyme with a slightly different amino acid composition and special affinity for hydroxy steroids, such as 3β-hydroxy-5β cholanic acid [205].

There can thus be no doubt that mammalian liver contains more than one enzyme capable of oxidizing alcohols by means of NAD. Further studies [134, 163, 165] indicate that the pattern of isoenzymes observed by electrophoretic procedures may arise by the combination of subunits in analogy to what has been demonstrated for lactate dehydrogenase. ADH consists of two subunits that can be separated after treatment with SH compounds and urea. The inactive subunits can be recombined to the active enzyme. The presence of two different subunits A and B may give rise to three different species of active enzyme AA, AB, and BB. In the horse [134] one or both of the subunits seem to exist in different forms, which can explain the larger number of isoenzymes in this species [163]. Differences with regard to the amino acid composition of the two subunits of horse L-ADH have been observed [86]. The presence of isoenzymes with different specificity and kinetic properties of course introduces difficulties in the interpretation of experiments on alcohol metabolism.

A special and remarkable case of "isoenzymes" was noted by von Wartburg [222], who found in some human subjects the presence of an "atypical" ADH that differed from the typical one in specific activity, pH optimum, and behavior toward thiourea and a number of inhibitors [223]. The atypical enzyme, however, had the same immunological and electrophoretic properties as the typical one. Purification of the atypical enzyme showed that during a step involving chromatography on carboxymethyl cellulose the enzyme apparently reverted to the normal form, as shown by the kinetic properties [148]. The nature of this interesting phenomenon awaits further investigations.

Properties of alcohol dehydrogenase. The molecular weight of horse liver ADH has been determined [35] to be 84,000 and the isoelectric point to be pH 6.8. Two atoms of zinc are present in the molecule and are essential for enzymatic activity. When zinc is removed by dialysis at pH 5.5, the activity is lost. Substances that form complexes with zinc inhibit the enzyme. The enzyme furthermore contains two active SH groups that react with iodoacetic acid, with loss of activity. The position of the two cysteine groups in the peptide chain is known [73], but the complete architecture of ADH has not yet been elucidated. Alcohol dehydrogenase has the ability to form well-defined crystalline complexes with a number of organic substances. Some heterocyclic compounds, especially pyrazole and derivatives of this substance, for instance, 4-iodopyrazole, have a considerable affinity to the enzyme and may thus be used as effective inhibitors [183, 200] both in vitro [200, 206] and in vivo [61, 107]. Other inhibitors are also known, for example, various substituted alcohols, SH reagents, and a number of anions [196], the action of which may be assumed to be rather unspecific.

The liver enzyme, in contrast to the corresponding enzyme from yeast, is very unspecific. A large number of alcohols and aldehydes apart from ethanol and acetaldehyde are quite effective substrates for the enzymes from horse liver and human liver (compare Tables IV and V). Of special

TABLE IV   Relative Activity of ADH Toward Different Alcohols[a]

	Horse L-ADH	Human L-ADH
Methanol	0.0	1.2[b]
Ethanol	1.0	1.0
1-Propanol	1.1	1.4
2-Propanol	0[c]	0.4
Allyl alcohol	1.4	
1-Butanol	1.6	1.7
Cyclohexanol	1.0	
Ethylene glycol	0	0.1[d]

[a] Substrate concentration about 10^{-3} M, velocities expressed as fraction of activity with ethanol. pH 8.8 for human enzyme, 9.5 for horse enzyme.
[b] Substrate concentration 0.5 M.
[c] Activity at higher substrate concentration.
[d] Substrate concentration 1.6 $\times$ 10^{-2} M.

TABLE V   Relative Activity of Horse Liver
Alcohol Dehydrogenase in the Reduction
of Aldehydes[a]

Formaldehyde	0.2
Acetaldehyde	1.0
Butyraldehyde	17
Cyclohexanone	0.2
Benzaldehyde	1.8
D,L-Glyceraldehyde	0.1

[a] In several cases the substrate concentration used was not sufficient to secure maximal velocity. Phosphate buffer pH 6.95, ionic strength 0.1. Substrate concentration 5×10^{-5} M. Velocities expressed as fraction of velocity for acetaldehyde.

interest is the observation that human liver ADH catalyzes the oxidation of methanol in contrast to the horse liver enzyme. This finding provides a rational basis for the empirical treatment of methanol poisoning by ethanol, which competes successfully with methanol for the enzyme and thus prevents the accumulation of the toxic products formate and formaldehyde.

The kinetic properties of ADH have been the subject of many studies by a number of different techniques. A considerable displacement in absorption maximum (from 340 to 325 nm) takes place when NADH or various analogs of this coenzyme are combined with ADH. Also the fluorescence of NADH is increased very markedly on binding to the enzyme. These optical properties permit a detailed description of all kinetic steps involved in the catalytic action.

The early studies of Theorell, Chance, and Bonnichsen [201, 202] led to the formulation of the so-called Theorell-Chance mechanism for the action of dehydrogenases. The reduction of acetaldehyde is believed to take place via the following steps:

$$E + NADH \rightleftharpoons E\text{-}NADH \tag{2}$$

$$E\text{-}NADH + \text{aldehyde} + H^+ \rightleftharpoons E\text{-}NAD + \text{alcohol} \tag{3}$$

$$E\text{-}NAD^+ \rightleftharpoons E + NAD^+ \tag{4}$$

E signifies one equivalent of enzyme, i.e., the amount that binds one molecule of coenzyme, which is one half molecule. Determination of the kinetic constant for the three reactions permits the calculation of the over-all equilibrium constant. The figure arrived at corresponds well with the directly measured equilibrium constant [203]. A somewhat more complicated mechanism seems to be involved with certain other substrates, various ketones, and secondary alcohols. The formation and conversion of ternary complexes of enzyme, coenzyme, and substrates in these cases may be important for the reaction velocity [29].

By means of the rapid-mixing stopped-flow spectrophotometric method it has been observed by means of certain aromatic aldehydes that exactly one-half of the limiting substrate or coenzyme is converted in a very fast reaction immediately after the mixing, followed by a slower reaction corresponding to the steady-state kinetics [9]. The most obvious mechanistic interpretation of this result is that the enzymatic sites on the two subunits are nonequivalent.

TABLE VI   Michaelis Constants for Horse and Human Liver
Alcohol Dehydrogenase[a]

	Horse L-ADH		Human L-ADH
	pH 7.15	pH 9.00	pH 9.3
Ethanol, mM	0.59	0.60	1.0
Acetaldehyde, mM	0.11	0.40	0.6
NAD, μM	10	11	
NADH, μM	10	3	

[a] Values from Refs. 204 and 11.

As seen in Table VI, alcohol dehydrogenase from horse and human liver has K_m values for alcohol in the same range, about 1 mM. This means that ethanol is effectively removed from the blood down to very low concentrations, provided that the reaction product acetaldehyde is efficiently removed.

Apart from the work published by Theorell's group several kinetic studies on liver ADH with different experimental approaches have been published [11, 59, 189, 193, 225, 232]. This enzyme is in fact one of the best known from a kinetic point of view.

B.   CATALASE. Already in 1936 Keilin and Hartree [89] suggested that catalase might be a factor in alcohol metabolism. By means of coupled enzyme systems consisting of catalase and an aerobic dehydrogenase, which produces hydrogen peroxide—for instance, xanthine oxidase + hypoxanthine—an increased oxygen uptake was observed when ethanol was added to the system. They suggested that catalase could function as an alcohol peroxidase under suitable conditions. This was later proved by Laser [102], who found that the efficient oxidation of ethanol took place when hydrogen peroxide was added to catalase and ethanol under conditions when the concentration of the peroxide was constantly kept at a very low level. Under in vitro conditions a cyclic oxidation can be established in which the hydrogen peroxide necessary for ethanol oxidation is provided by the oxidation of acetaldehyde by means of aerobic aldehyde dehydrogenase:

$$\text{Ethanol} + H_2O_2 \xrightarrow{\text{catalase}} \text{acetaldehyde} + 2H_2O \tag{5}$$

$$\text{Acetaldehyde} + H_2O + O_2 \xrightarrow{\text{aldehyde oxidase}} \text{acetate} + H_2O_2 \tag{6}$$

$$\text{Sum: ethanol} + O_2 \rightarrow \text{acetate} + H_2O \tag{7}$$

A high concentration of acetaldehyde (1 mM) was used to start the reaction, but the concentration of the aldehyde was unfortunately not followed during the reaction.

When the Michaelis constants for the various liver flavoproteins that catalyze acetaldehyde oxidation are considered, it seems unlikely that such a mechanism can be of any significance in vivo, because the concentration of acetaldehyde (see below) is not high enough to permit any significant oxidation by this pathway [129]. It is remarkable that the various peroxidases tested have no ability to catalyze ethanol oxidation; in fact catalase seems to be the only hemoprotein with this property [90]. In liver homogenates a definite increase in alcohol oxidation was observed when a hydrogen peroxide–producing system (glucose oxidase) was added, indicating that the catalase reaction might in fact play a role, provided that the supply of peroxide was sufficient [130]. Addition of substances that are believed normally to be oxidized with the formation of hydrogen peroxide—e.g., hypoxanthine—did not cause a significant increase in alcohol oxidation. In more or less artificial systems, erythrocytes, pigeon liver mitochondria under certain conditions, a coupled peroxidation of ethanol has been demonstrated [144, 198], but these reactions are not believed to be of physiological significance. Several attempts have been made to evaluate the role of catalase in alcohol metabolism by means of the inhibitor 3-amino-1,2,4-triazole. The results have been variable, but most authors [93, 154] find no significant inhibition in the rate of alcohol metabolism in rats and dogs. In rat liver homogenates no significant effect was observed, but o-phenantrolin, which inhibits ADH, caused nearly complete inhibition, which should exclude the catalase pathway under the conditions used, that is, low ethanol concentration [130].

TABLE VII   Effect of 3-Amino-1,2,4-Triazole on the Rate of Alcohol Metabolism in Liver Slices from Alcohol Chronically Treated and Glucose-Control Rats[a]

	Alcohol metabolism, μmoles/(g)(hr)	
Addition	Glucose controls	Alcohol chronically treated
...	(a) 25.5 ± 2.4 (6) $(p < 0.4)$	(c) 48.6 ± 4.2 (7) $(p < 0.01)$
3-Amino-1,2,4-triazole	(b) 22.7 ± 2.4 (6)	(d) 32.3 ± 3.3 (7)

[a] 3-Amino-1,2,4-triazole was used at a final concentration of 15 mM in the incubation medium. The values given represent the mean $\pm$ SEM. Gas mixture used: 18% O_2:77% N_2:5% CO_2. From Ref. 217; see Ref. 216 for experimental conditions.

Videla and Israel (Table VII) found that in rat liver slices under normal conditions aminotriazole had no effect on the rate of alcohol metabolism. In animals that have received chronic administration of alcohol for 3 to 4 weeks, however, the oxidation of alcohol by liver slices is increased 70 to 90%. This increase was markedly although not completely inhibited when the slices were incubated in the presence of 3-aminotriazole. In a preparation of rat liver "microsomes" that metabolizes ethanol (see Section D.1c) a significant inhibition was observed when the animals were pretreated with aminotriazole [179]. The inhibition of ethanol oxidation, however, was again less extensive than the inhibition of catalase activity measured separately.

These and other observations suggest that catalase may play a role in alcohol metabolism, although the exact mechanism and the quantitative significance are not known yet.

C. MIXED-FUNCTION OXIDASES. An increasing number of observations suggests that the smooth endoplasmic reticulum of liver cells, which is known to play an important part in drug detoxication, may also be a significant factor in alcohol metabolism under some circumstances. Orme-Johnson and Ziegler [158] studied preparations of the microsome fraction consisting partly of endoplasmic membranes from pig, rat, and rabbit liver and demonstrated an oxidation of alcohol to acetaldehyde, presumably according to the following scheme:

$$\text{Ethanol} + \text{NADPH} + \text{H}^+ + \text{O}_2 \rightarrow \text{NADP}^+ + \text{acetaldehyde} + 2\text{H}_2\text{O} \quad (8)$$

The reaction was most effective when methanol was the substrate; e.g., in the pig methanol was oxidized twice as fast as ethanol in this preparation. The enzyme may therefore be important for the elimination of methanol in organisms in which alcohol dehydrogenase does not react with methanol—e.g., the horse. Hydroxylases of this type would in general be inhibited by carbon monoxide, because cytochrome P 450 is thought to be a cofactor. Orme-Johnson and Ziegler found no inhibition, however, but observed inhibition by cyanide and azide. In a similar system (rat liver microsomes) Lieber and DeCarli [112–114] demonstrated ethanol oxidation to acetaldehyde, but in contrast to Orme-Johnson and Ziegler they state that carbon monoxide inhibits the system considerably. Unfortunately a quantitative comparison of the activity of the enzyme system studies by the two groups is not possible. Other workers [179] found that in microsome preparations of rat liver the requirement for NADPH, or an NADPH-generating system, might be abolished when a hydrogen peroxide–generating system (glucose-glucoseoxidase) was added. In agreement with earlier workers they found that direct additions of hydrogen peroxide were not effective. This finding suggests that catalase may be a factor in the system, and as mentioned above, catalase inhibitors in fact to some extent prevent the reaction. These authors also point out that hydrogen peroxide formed by the oxidation of NADPH together with catalase may explain the reaction. Further support for the belief that this is not a hydroxylating enzyme is found in the lack of inhibition by SKF-525A (diethyl-aminoethyl-diphenylpropylacetate). Tephly et al. [199] measured the formation of $^{14}\text{CO}_2$ from labeled ethanol in rat given SKF-525A. They found no significant effect of this inhibitor, which they take as evidence that the microsomal pathways are of little importance. The dose of alcohol used, however, was small (250 mg/kg rat), and this may be an important factor in the microsomal pathway. The dependence of the rate of alcohol oxidation in membrane preparations on the concentration of ethanol has been measured [114]. Some of the differences might be clarified, because the microsomal system has a considerably higher Michaelis constant for ethanol than the ADH system (cf. Section E.3).

If drug-detoxicating systems play a role in alcohol metabolism, it might be expected that factors that increase the smooth endoplasmic reticulum would also increase alcohol metabolism. That this is the case was in fact shown already in 1960 by Fischer and Oelsner [42, 45, 46], who observed that the rate of ethanol metabolism in rabbits treated for some weeks with barbiturates was about 50% higher than in the control group. The authors found no increase in the amount of alcohol dehydrogenase in the liver. Similar results have been obtained in work on isolated microsomal preparations [113]. Even treatment with carbon tetrachloride was found to accelerate alcohol metabolism [44]. Rubin and Lieber [181] and Rubin et al. [182] found that the chronic administration of alcohol might itself be a stimulus for the increase of the hepatic endoplasmic reticulum, observed by electron microscopy, and at the same time certain detoxicating enzyme systems showed enhanced activity, e.g., aniline hydroxylase (about three to eight times increase) and pentobarbital hydroxylase, which increase approximately twofold in both rats and human subjects. It was also observed that in vitro 50-mM ethanol inhibited significantly some of the drug-metabolizing enzymes. These interesting findings may to some extent explain the known resistance of alcoholics to certain drugs, e.g., barbiturates, and also the increased sensitivity to barbiturates of intoxicated nonalcoholics. The investigations mentioned were made on isolated preparations; Videla and Israel [216] studied the effect of chronic ethanol administration on the alcohol metabolism of liver slices. As mentioned in Section D.1b, they found a very pronounced increase (70 to 90%), which again slowly disappeared when alcohol administration was discontinued. A large part of the increment could be inhibited by the catalase inhibitor 3-amino-1,2,4-triazole, which had no significant influence on the rate of alcohol metabolism in liver slices from normal animals (Table VII). It is therefore still an open question whether there may be two types of "microsomal" alcohol metabolism. The preparations used may contain "peroxisomes," the catalase containing cell particles [179] that could be responsible for at least some of the extra alcohol oxidation. This possibility requires a sufficient production of hydrogen peroxide. Under certain conditions of increased drug metabolism NADPH is used, and produced, in increasing amounts. The possibility should therefore perhaps be investigated whether oxidations of NADPH by an aerobic microsomal oxidase [60] could account for some alcohol oxidation and whether the mixed-function oxidase system could be responsible for another part of the metabolism (compare Figure 1). It is noteworthy that in both cases a reaction is involved with NADPH and molecular oxygen. In considering such a mechanism, it should not be forgotten that the hydroxylating system is quite fragile, and so it could perhaps, if disorganized, show a preponderance of NADPH oxidase activity.

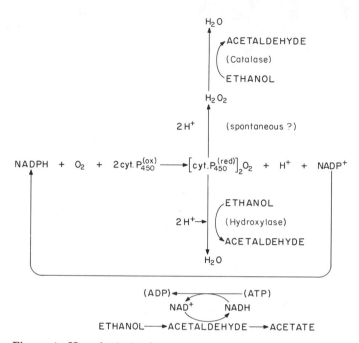

Figure 1. Hypothetical scheme of ethanol oxidation via NADPH requiring pathways in the endoplasmic smooth membranes. This scheme may explain why the inhibition of microsomal ethanol oxidation by inhibitors of catalase and the hydroxylase reactions is only partial. The existence of microsomal pathways in connection with a transhydrogenation of NADH to NADPH, which can take place by various reactions, may accelerate also the oxidation via the ADH reaction by removal of NADH, provided that this is the rate-limiting step under normal conditions (cf. Section E.2).

2. Oxidation of Acetaldehyde to Acetate

As previously mentioned, the equilibrium of the alcohol dehydrogenase reaction is situated unfavorably for alcohol oxidation. It is therefore necessary that the reaction product, acetaldehyde, is very effectively removed. That this is in fact the case is indicated by the low steady-state concentration of acetaldehyde in the blood (see Section D). Several enzymes present in the liver are known to catalyze the oxidation of a number of aldehydes to acids.

A. NAD-REQUIRING ALDEHYDE DEHYDROGENASES. In the early work on acetaldehyde metabolism in liver preparations Dixon and Lutwak-Mann

[30] observed a dismutation of acetaldehyde to ethanol and acetate. The reaction was dependent on catalytic amounts of NAD. Racker [167] showed that this reaction required two enzymes, alcohol dehydrogenase and an aldehyde dehydrogenase, which he prepared free from ADH with ox liver as the starting material. The enzyme, which is rather unspecific with respect to aldehyde substrate, catalyzes the following reaction:

$$NAD^+ + aldehyde \rightarrow carboxylic\ acid + NADH + H^+ \qquad (9)$$

The reaction product in the case of acetaldehyde was identified as free acetate and not acetyl coenzyme A, which has been found as the reaction product of some bacterial enzymes. The Michaelis constant for the enzyme toward acetaldehyde is extremely low (10^{-9} to 10^{-6} M) [167, 17]. A similar unspecific enzyme has been isolated from human liver [10, 95]. The Michaelis constant for acetaldehyde was about 0.5 μM, but the K_m for NAD was rather high, about 0.6 mM. Unfortunately the total activity in the liver toward acetaldehyde cannot be deduced from these papers.

In spite of attempts to fractionate the enzyme no indication was found for the presence of more than one NAD-requiring aldehyde dehydrogenase. Like the aldehyde dehydrogenases from other mammals the human enzyme is present mainly in the cytoplasm. Mitochondria, however, also seem to contain either the same or a very similar NAD-requiring aldehyde dehydrogenase [17, 219], and washed rat liver mitochondria in fact oxidize acetaldehyde quite readily [68]. Other organs than liver contain aldehyde dehydrogenase, e.g., erythrocytes [142] and kidney [17]. The quantitative importance of other organs than the liver, however, in the removal of acetaldehyde formed in alcohol metabolism has not been directly evaluated. The observation that in vivo more than 80% of the alcohol oxidized in the liver is recovered in the hepatic venous blood as acetate suggests, however, that only a small fraction of the acetaldehyde is metabolized outside of the liver.

B. FLAVOPROTEIN ENZYMES. An extensive literature exists on the isolation and characterization of flavoproteins, which catalyze the oxidation of aldehydes. Many of these enzymes also oxidize substances of a quite different nature, such as purines, pteridines, and quinine. Xanthine oxidase from liver is known to oxidize acetaldehyde, but a flavoprotein that oxidizes aldehydes but not xanthine has been isolated from rabbit liver [170–172]. It is still an open question whether these enzymes in vivo produce hydrogen peroxide or donate electrons to cytochrome either in the mitochondrial respiratory chain or in the cytoplasmic membrane system. To what extent flavoproteins are involved in aldehyde oxidation during alcohol metabolism is not known, but the enzymes so far examined all have a rather low affinity to acetaldehyde, the Michaelis constant being above 1 mM [129], that is, much higher than the actual concentration of acetaldehyde measured. Moreover the activity of these enzymes in the liver seems to be very modest.

3. Metabolic Fate of Acetate

The main end product of ethanol metabolism in the liver is acetate, which is released into the hepatic venous blood. This has been suggested already by Lundsgaard [133] and more convincingly demonstrated by chromatography [50] and enzymatically [123, 137]. More recent work [232] performed on patients with portacaval anastomoses, in whom the interpretation of the experiment is not complicated by the metabolic activity of the extrahepatic splanchnic organs, has shown that at least 85 to 90% of the acetate formed leaves the liver. Similar results were found in perfused rat liver [231] and in rat liver homogenates [130]. Acetate that is present in the blood in a concentration of 1 to 2 mM during alcohol metabolism is readily metabolized in peripheral organs [125]. Lindeneg et al. [116] measured the acetate utilization in the heart in human subjects given small quantities of alcohol. They observed that acetate, and lactate, were utilized roughly in proportion to their concentration in the arterial blood. Acetate consumption accounted for about 20% of the myocardial oxygen uptake. A measure of the complete combustion of alcohol to CO_2 is obtained in studies with ^{14}C-labeled alcohol. A series of papers describing this technique in human subjects has been published by a Swedish group [12, 13, 79–81].

4. Minor Pathways in Alcohol and Acetaldehyde Metabolism

Apart from the oxidative attack on alcohol the liver can also to a small extent incorporate the ethyl group into ethyl glucuronide [88] and ethyl sulfate [173], which are excreted in the urine.

Acetaldehyde is a highly reactive substance, which might be expected to enter into a number of reactions. Acetoin formation is one of these possibilities, which was studied by Stotz et al. [195] and Järnefelt [84].

The reaction

$$\text{pyruvate} + \text{acetaldehyde} \rightarrow \text{acetoin} + CO_2 \qquad (10)$$

was demonstrated but requires apparently a rather high aldehyde concentration and has not been found to take place to a significant extent during alcohol metabolism [64, 122]. The reaction probably occurs between acetaldehyde and "active" thiamine-bound acetaldehyde derived from pyruvate. A similar reaction between acetaldehyde and α-oxoglutarate was studied by Westerfeld and coworkers [14]. The reaction product 5-hydroxy-4-keto-n-hexanoic acid was identified, but also this reaction is quantitatively insignificant.

E.   Factors Which May Change the Rate of Alcohol Metabolism; Importance of Different Pathways

Since the work of Widmark the constancy of alcohol metabolism under different circumstances has been a widely accepted dogma, at least as far as man is concerned. As already mentioned, there may be reason to revise this point of view on the basis of a number of recent reports.

1.   Influence of Ethanol Concentration on the Rate of Alcohol Metabolism

Provided that ethanol itself does not activate or inhibit any enzyme in the liver cell, one would expect the rate of alcohol metabolism through the ADH pathway to be independent of the alcohol concentration above 5 mM (25 mg/100 ml). It is assumed that the reaction proceeds far from equilibrium. If the mechanisms discussed in Sections D.2 and D.3 play a role in the normal organism, however, it is conceivable that the process shows dependence on alcohol concentration. Some indications for such an assumption were found in experiments in which labeled ethanol was added to rat liver slices in different concentrations and the amount of label incorporated into acetate and other substances was measured [207]. At high concentrations (80 mM) the formation of acetate was more than 50% higher than at 4 mM (see Table VIII). Although the oxidation was nearly abolished by pyrazole at the low alcohol concentration the major part was resistant to this inhibitor at the high ethanol concentration, suggesting that another pathway is included when the alcohol concentration is sufficiently high.

TABLE VIII   Rate of Acetate Production in Dependence of Alcohol Concentration[a]

| Ethanol concentration, mM | Acetate production, μmoles/(g fresh wt) (hr) | |
	Control	Pyrazole (18 mM)
4	20.2 ± 1.1	3.6 ± 0.4
40	29.1 ± 1.5	14.6 ± 2.0
80	34.9 ± 1.6	23.9 ± 3.6

[a] Rat liver slices were used in Krebs-Henseleit buffer. In the presence of pyrazole the lactate/pyruvate ratio was decreased markedly, compared with the controls with ethanol only. Acetate was determined enzymatically and also as radioactivity fixed in the nonvolatile fraction after incubation with ^{14}C-labeled ethanol. Each group comprises 6 to 15 animals. From Ref. 207.

2.   Changes of the Rate of the Alcohol Dehydrogenase Reaction

The possibility of changing the rate of ethanol removal under the assumption that ADH is the sole catalyst responsible for the oxidation depends on which of a number of factors is rate-determining under normal conditions of pH, ionic composition, etc. These factors are (a) the amount of enzyme; (b) the capacity of the shuttle mechanism that is responsible for the transport into the mitochondria of reducing equivalents from NADH, produced in the cytoplasm by the dehydrogenase; (c) the rate of the oxidation of NADH in the mitochondria; and (d) the rate of the removal of acetaldehyde.

A.   AMOUNT AND ACTIVITY OF ADH. Several measurements have been published of ADH activity in liver preparations from animals under different conditions, such as fasting and prolonged treatment with alcohol. Smith and Newman (194) found that even fasting for 48 hr caused no change in the total ADH activity of the liver in rats. Attempts to demonstrate an increase in ADH activity after the chronic administration of alcohol in most cases have been negative [65, 112, 216, 221]. Prolonged administration of ethanol was found by some authors even to decrease the amount of ADH in the liver [27, 40, 149].

On the whole changes in the amount of ADH seem unlikely as a normal phenomenon. In human subjects who have the atypical ADH, which shows a much higher activity than normal ADH (compare Section D.1a) the rate of alcohol metabolism is not higher than normal [32]. This observation clearly suggests that the amount of enzyme (total ADH activity) is not normally rate-determining. The activity of ADH may, however, be influenced by factors such as the concentration of free fatty acids, which significantly inhibit ADH, even at low concentrations [175]. The effect of insulin on alcohol oxidation in liver slices has tentatively been ascribed to this effect [175].

B. THE TRANSFER OF REDUCING EQUIVALENTS FROM NADH INTO THE MITOCHONDRIA. More than 90% of the oxygen uptake of liver occurs in the mitochondria. NADH, however, cannot penetrate the mitochondrial membrane and therefore is not oxidized when added to carefully isolated intact mitochondria. Some carrier system is apparently needed.

The nature of this transport system is still uncertain. One possibility that has been suggested is that dihydroxyacetone phosphate is reduced in the cytoplasm by NADH and glycerophosphate dehydrogenase. The glycerophosphate readily penetrates mitochondria and can be reoxidized inside of them to dihydroxyacetone phosphate by a glycerophosphate oxidase system, which is a flavine enzyme closely connected with the respiratory chain. Although the enzymes are present in liver cells, this cyclic system seems not to be of major importance, as demonstrated by Hassinen [74, 75]. He found that in perfused rat liver oxidizing ethanol, the increased fluorescence from reduced flavoprotein [231] could be abolished by treatment with rotenone. Because the inhibitor prevents electron transport between NADH and flavoprotein, it seems likely that the glycerophosphate cycle does not contribute significantly to the hydrogen transport.

The other mechanism consists in principle of the system malate-oxaloacetate. Malate dehydrogenases are present in both cytoplasm and mitochondria. Reduction of oxaloacetate to malate by NADH in the cytoplasm followed by transport of malate into the mitochondria and reoxidation to oxaloacetate would constitute a suitable carrier system, provided that the permeation of the mitochondrial membrane by oxaloacetate or malate is not restrictive. Evidence has been produced [99] that this simple system requires modification in order to explain the actual transfer of reducing equivalents because the transport of oxaloacetate through the mitochondrial membrane seems to be slow. Borst [16] and others suggest that transaminase systems serve as an intermediary system in the reaction, as outlined in Figure 2.

The difficulty with this mechanism is that even if the permeability barrier is circumvented, there remains the fact that the concentration of NADH

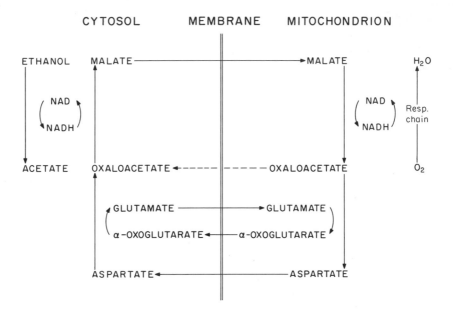

Figure 2. Possible mechanism for transport from the cytosol into the mitochondria of reducing equivalents formed through dehydrogenation of ethanol in the cytosol. The oxidation by means of molecular oxygen takes place in the mitochondria [99].

in the mitochondria is very much higher than in cytoplasm, which means that in order to bring about the transport of reducing equivalents, energy must be put into the system. How this is achieved is still an open question [66]. Hassinen [75] examined this reaction in liver mitochondria in combination with ADH, but the rates of oxidation seem to be too small to account for the processes in vivo.

The transport system may be rate-limiting, but two observations seem to make this unlikely.

1. The fact that the NADH concentration inside of the mitochondria, as measured by the hydroxybutyrate/acetoacetate ratio, is increased in approximately the same proportion as in the cytoplasm (compare Section F.1a).

2. The finding that NADH added to the complete system (mitochondria, malate, aspartate-α-oxoglutarate transaminase, malate dehydrogenase) is oxidized at a rate sufficient to explain the rate of alcohol oxidation observed

in vivo [68]. It must be concluded, however, that at the present time it has not been possible to construct an artificial system that can oxidize alcohol at a suitable rate.

C. THE OXIDATION OF NADH. The oxygen uptake of mitochondria is known to be strongly dependent on the supply of ADP, which depends on the rate of ATP utilization. When this is seen in connection with the observation that at low levels of blood alcohol the oxygen uptake of liver in vivo is not significantly changed from the control value [131, 232], it seems possible that in fact the NADH oxidation that is coupled to ATP formation may be rate-limiting. If this were the case, an acceleration of alcohol metabolism should be possible by means of uncouplers of oxidative phosphorylation. Early experiments with a number of experimental animals showed in fact an increased alcohol metabolism when dinitrophenol was administered [21, 72, 83]. The interpretation of these experiments was, however, made difficult by the general increase in metabolism of the animals, which could cause increased excretion of alcohol through the respiratory air. Recent experiments on liver slices [216] show that the addition of dinitrophenol or arsenate gives rise to a considerable increase (more than 100%) in alcohol oxidation. Oxidation of cytoplasmic NADH by other routes than through the respiratory chain would increase ethanol oxidation if both the transport mechanism and the mitochondrial oxidation were rate-determining. Infusion of pyruvate in dogs was found to increase ethanol metabolism considerably [227, 228]. Also the addition of pyruvate to liver slices produced an increased removal of alcohol [105, 194]. It was suggested that the oxidation of NADH by pyruvate with the formation of lactate might be responsible for these results. Other authors have, however, found no significant effect of pyruvate, possibly because too low concentrations were used [22, 92]. A similar mechanism may be involved in the effect of fructose (see below), because some fructose is reduced by NADH to sorbitol, which leaves the liver.

Gordon [62, 63] makes the interesting observation that when rat liver is perfused with blood equilibrated with 95% oxygen, the rate of alcohol metabolism increases very markedly, and the rate of oxidation depends on the alcohol concentration in contrast to experiments at normal oxygen tensions. This effect was, however, observed only at relatively high ethanol concentrations and therefore can hardly be caused by the direct aerobic oxidation of NADH by flavoprotein enzymes in the cytoplasm. Similar experiments on liver slices [216] also showed a higher rate of ethanol metabolism when oxygen was used as the gas phase. The initial concentration of ethanol was 10 mM. Whether this increase is caused by the oxidation of NADH or it is due to another pathway was not established with certainty (see Section D.1c).

The effect of fructose. This sugar has been shown to increase alcohol oxidation both in vitro [210, 216] and in vivo [127, 166, 213] when sufficiently high fructose concentrations are used. The mechanism suggested to explain this finding [82] is that D-glyceraldehyde formed from fructose-1-phosphate may oxidize the ADH-NADH complex directly without the liberation of the reduced coenzyme. Such a dismutation would accelerate the ADH reaction if the amount of enzyme were limiting, because the dissociation

$$ADH\text{-}NADH \rightarrow ADH + NADH$$

is the slowest reaction in the cycle (see Section D.1a).

If, however, the transport or oxidation of NADH determines the over-all velocity, it is apparent that fructose and glyceraldehyde should also in this case accelerate the process. The glycerol formed is phosphorylated, leading to increased concentrations of glycerophosphate [207, 210], which presumably is oxidized in the mitochondria (see above). In this way the oxidation of the extra reducing equivalents from the alcohol oxidation could be accounted for. The oxygen uptake of the liver *in situ* when ethanol and fructose are present in the blood is actually increased about 60% [213]. Glyceraldehyde was shown to have the same effect as fructose on slices of rat [210] and human liver [207].

Finally fructose may increase the requirement for ATP formation and hence facilitate NADH oxidation partly by the accumulation of fructose-1-P [76] but also because the net yield of ATP obtained by the anaerobic metabolism of fructose may be less than the two molecules obtained in the case of glucose.

D.   REMOVAL OF ACETALDEHYDE. If the metabolism of acetaldehyde were slower than the ADH reaction, a different situation would arise. The acetaldehyde concentration in this case would be expected to be in equilibrium with the ethanol concentration, and the rate of alcohol removal would then be determined by the activity of the aldehyde dehydrogenases. The consequences of such an assumption would be that the aldehyde concentration should increase roughly in proportion to the alcohol concentration and at the levels frequently encountered in intoxicated persons be considerably higher than found experimentally. Freund and O'Hollaren [58] found that the concentration of acetaldehyde in expired air in human subjects was nearly constant when alcohol was administered independent of the concentration of alcohol in the blood. The concentration corresponding to equilibrium in the ADH reaction when calculated on the assumption that the alcohol concentration is 60 mM and the NADH/NAD ratio about 1:500 should be about 0.3 mM, which is considerably higher than the values found experimentally. Another observation, which is hardly compatible with this possibility, is that the rate of alcohol metabolism is not reduced by Antabuse, which inhibits aldehyde oxidation and indeed causes an increase in blood acetaldehyde concentration.

It seems therefore on the basis of evidence available at present to be unlikely that the removal of aldehyde is rate-limiting in the over-all process of alcohol oxidation.

3. Evidence of Changes in Alcohol Metabolism Caused by Other Pathways than Alcohol Dehydrogenases

A number of observations point to the possibility that the rate of alcohol metabolism at least in some species, may be increased through an effect from the non-ADH system(s).

1. Factors that induce increases in the endoplasmic reticulum such as the chronic administration of alcohol [109, 112] and treatment with barbiturates [42, 45, 46, 113] and other drugs [44] or cortisol [43] seem to provoke an increase of alcohol elimination that may be quite sizable.

2. Oxygen, at least in vitro, may facilitate pathways for either the reoxidation of reduced coenzymes or the formation of hydrogen peroxide, which could catalyze alcohol oxidation via the catalase system.

3. High alcohol concentrations even in acute experiments may accelerate ethanol metabolism [207] by the non-ADH enzyme systems, because the Michaelis constant for alcohol of these enzymes is appreciable higher than for the ADH system [114]. Evidence in this direction was also published by Gordon [62, 63].

The following picture may tentatively be suggested regarding factors that influence ethanol metabolism.

At low alcohol levels and "normal" conditions the alcohol dehydrogenase system seems to be solely responsible for ethanol metabolism. Factors that permit an increased oxidation of NADH may increase the over-all rate under these conditions.

When the concentration of alcohol is increased, hydroxylating enzymes using O_2 and NADPH, and the peroxidation of alcohol by means of catalase may play a more important part. Activation of the endoplasmic reticular system by prolonged alcohol administration, treatment with drugs, such as barbiturates, or treatment with corticosteroids increases the amount of membrane-bound enzymes, including hydroxylases and NADPH oxidase, which produces hydrogen peroxide [60], which again permits a higher rate of ethanol oxidation. A quantitative estimate of the maximal increase in alcohol metabolism under these circumstances is not easy to obtain, but a near doubling of the rate is not unlikely. Oxidation of alcohol by either hydroxylation or catalase activity does not give rise to ATP formation, and so no utilizable energy is produced, in contrast to the breakdown via the ADH route, in which NADH is oxidized in the mitochondria. The consequence of this is that in order to keep up the production of ATP at the normal rate, the liver must use more oxygen. In other words a specific dynamic action of alcohol should be observable under these conditions. Scheggia et al. [186] in fact found a pronounced specific dynamic action of ethanol in certain alcoholics, compared with nonalcoholics given the same quantity of alcohol. Such an oxygen consumption without the production of utilizable energy is to be expected in order to explain the reported very high alcohol metabolism in some individuals [145, 147, 155]. Controlled consumption of alcohol for a 4-day period of 300 g/day, reported by Mendelsohn, would indicate nearly a doubling of the normal rate of metabolism (from 7 to about 12.5 g/hr of alcohol). The oxygen consumption of the liver necessary to oxidize this amount of ethanol to acetate is calculated to be 1.5 times the normal total oxygen consumption of the liver, measured *in situ* [232].

4.   Possible Influence of Hormones on Alcohol Metabolism

No attempt is made here to review the large number of partly contradictory reports on the effect of various hormones on alcohol metabolism, but a few pertinent observations should be mentioned. First, none of the hormones tested seems to have more than a marginal effect on alcohol elimination in vivo. A more pronounced response is sometimes observed in experiments with liver slices. Thyroid hormones have no significant effect on the ethanol metabolism of liver slices; neither the removal of the thyroid gland nor treatment with the hormone caused significant change in the rate [177]. This is in agreement with the most reliable experiments in intact animals and man [87, 94].

Insulin may have a small accelerating effect in vivo [23], although this has not always been found [91]. Experiments on liver slices [175] showed quite clearly an acceleration in livers from insulin-treated animals and a decrease in diabetic rats. Similar results were obtained with glucagon in small doses. This may have been caused by increased insulin secretion; higher doses of glucagon did not show this effect. The author suggests that these hormonal actions may be related to changes in plasma free fatty acids.

Glucocorticoids were found by Fischer [43] to accelerate alcohol metabolism in the rabbit, presumably by the proliferation of the endoplasmic reticulum.

On the whole there is no convincing evidence that any hormone under physiological circumstances influences the rate of alcohol breakdown appreciably.

F.   Metabolic Consequences of Ethanol Metabolism

1.   Primary Changes in Coenzyme Concentration

Many of the metabolic changes observed during alcohol metabolism seem to be closely connected with changes in the steady-state concentration of a few cofactors. Because these changes are highly reproducible and well defined, the use of ethanol has developed into a useful tool for the study of metabolic regulation in the liver cell.

A.   NICOTINAMIDE COENZYMES. The increase in the ratio of the reduced to the oxidized form of nicotinamide adenine dinucleotide (NAD) in the liver, which takes place after the ingestion of ethanol, is one of the earliest observations made on changes produced by even very small concentrations of ethanol. Direct determination of NAD and NADH in extracts from liver tissue showed a definite increase of NADH; the total amount of the coenzyme did not change [18, 51, 194]. A refinement of this observation was made when the ratio of the concentrations of the free, i.e., not protein-bound, coenzymes was determined by suitable substrate pairs, which are assumed to be in equilibrium via NAD. The reaction

$$\text{Lactate} + \text{NAD}^+ \rightleftharpoons \text{pyruvate} + \text{NADH} + \text{H}^+ \qquad (11)$$

is catalyzed by a powerful lactate dehydrogenase present exclusively in the extramitochondrial part of the cell. Because the equilibrium constant K is known, the following equation should hold:

$$[\text{NADH}] \times [\text{H}^+]/[\text{NAD}^+] = K \times [\text{lactate}]/[\text{pyruvate}]$$

Therefore measurements of the lactate and pyruvate concentration provide a measure of the redox state of the NAD-NADH pair in the cytoplasm.

Similarly NAD-dependent enzyme systems located exclusively in the mitochondria, such as β-hydroxybutyrate dehydrogenase, indicate the ratio inside of the mitochondria. A considerable number of measurements on intact human subjects and animals [53, 174] and on liver slices and perfused liver [48, 52] have been published. Good agreement was obtained that the cytoplasmic ratio in the intact organism increases about three times and the mitochondrial ratio perhaps somewhat less (cf. Table IX). When

TABLE IX   Effect of Ethanol Administration on NAD-Dependent Substrate Concentration Ratios in Rat Liver[a] [174]

	Control	Ethanol	Ethanol/Control
Lactate/pyruvate	10.8	33.9	3.1
Glycerol-P/DHAP	6.7	8.9	1.3
Hydroxybut./acetoacetate	2.7	5.3	2.0
Malate/oxaloacetate	54	98	1.8
Glutamate/oxoglut. $\times$ NH$_4^+$	43	75	1.8

[a] Liver tissue removed from anesthetized animals by the freeze-clamp technique.

ADH is inhibited by pyrazole in rat liver slices, the lactate/pyruvate ratio remains nearly unchanged in spite of the presence of even rather high alcohol concentrations [207], suggesting that the phenomenon is dependent on the alcohol dehydrogenase reaction.

In the perfused liver the increased reduction of NAD when alcohol is present in the perfusion medium has been observed by surface fluorescence [231]. The other nicotinamide coenzyme NADPH has not been so extensively studied. Measurements by Räihä and Oura [168] in rat liver showed no significant change in the concentration of NADPH. Because the reduced form is present in considerably higher concentration than the oxidized form, however, the ratio between reduced and oxidized coenzyme may still have been changed without the measurable alteration of the NADPH concentration. Williamson et al. [231] in the perfused rat liver observed a highly significant fall in the concentration of NADP that caused the NADPH/NADP ratio to increase about 50%. In view of the possible importance of NADPH in the auxiliary routes of alcohol oxidation a renewed study of this problem might prove valuable.

B.   ADENINE NUCLEOTIDES. The concentrations of the various adenine nucleotides (AMP, ADP, ATP, and cyclic AMP) are known to be important regulatory factors in intermediary metabolism. Administration of alcohol has been shown to increase the concentration of AMP in the liver; the concentrations of ADP and ATP show little variation either in vivo [208] or in perfused liver [231]. The mechanisms responsible for the change are not clear. Activation of acetate takes place with the liberation of AMP, and so this may be the source, although the amount of acetate metabolized in the liver is small, compared with the total alcohol oxidation. Another possible source of AMP may be the increased uptake of free fatty acids, which are activated with the liberation of AMP.

Similar changes in the AMP concentration are also seen after treatment with glucose, fructose, or acetate [169, 207]. The doubling of AMP concentration observed in the presence of ethanol probably produces changes in a number of metabolic processes. One consequence would be the increased breakdown of AMP and the oxidation to uric acid, which may explain the increased uric acid excretion of alcoholics. Similar but even more pronounced uricosuria is seen after fructose ingestion, which produces very high AMP concentrations in the liver [19].

c. COENZYME A DERIVATIVES. Changes in the distribution of this cofactor between the free form and acetyl or acyl, coenzyme A are not so well established as those mentioned above. Claims have been made that considerable reduction in the amount of coenzyme A should occur because of a reaction between the SH group and acetaldehyde [2, 234] but no significant concentration changes were found in any of the three forms in the perfused liver [231]. The changes observed in other parameters in this report were so similar to those found in intact rats that it seems likely that the distribution of coenzyme A compounds also depicts the physiological state.

Relatively small changes were observed in acetyl coenzyme A concentration in the liver of intact rats. It was found to increase when starved rats were given alcohol [117, 118] but to decrease in the case of normally fed rats [174]. However, it is too early to judge whether these changes have any decisive influence on the metabolic changes in the liver.

2. Effects of Alcohol Metabolism on the Tricarboxylic Acid Cycle

When ethanol is present in the blood or in the medium used for in vitro experiments, a very marked depression of the rate of CO_2 formation from the liver is observed [133]. In liver slices the RQ decreased from 0.74 to 0.02 without any change in the oxygen uptake [48]. In intact human subjects the measurement of the RQ of the liver is technically difficult, but very pronounced decreases were observed [131, 213]. Because nearly all CO_2 liberated arises from the citrate cycle, these findings must mean that the cycle is inhibited strongly during alcohol metabolism. In experiments on perfused rat liver Williamson et al. [231] measured the relevant parameters to decide the extent of inhibition when alanine was used as the substrate. Some assumptions must of course be made, but the figure arrived at, 75% inhibition, is in good agreement with the measurement of CO_2 output in the intact liver. The mechanism of this inhibition is discussed by Forsander [49], who points to three obvious possibilities: (a) decreased input of acetyl coenzyme A, (b) inhibition of citrate synthase, and (c) inhibition of some later reaction of the cycle. On the basis of a careful analysis of intermediates Williamson arrived at the conclusion that the inhibition of isocitrate dehydrogenase by the increased NADH concentration is a very likely mechanism. Because citrate does not accumulate under the experimental conditions used (medium depleted of fatty acid), however, the condensing enzyme must also be inhibited. The changes in the concentrations of adenosine nucleotides measured by these and other workers are compatible with increased ATP concentration intramitochondrially, a situation which would inhibit citrate synthase. The possibility that the intramitochondrial oxaloacetate concentration is reduced by the rise in NADH cannot be ruled out but on the other hand does not seem likely at least if malate is assumed to pass freely through the mitochondrial membrane [230]. A direct inhibitory effect of NADH on the synthase is a possibility that has been realized in the case of bacterial citrate synthase [226]. At present there is, however, no evidence of a similar mechanism in the mammalian enzymes.

Inhibition of the tricarboxylic cycle in itself would not seem to endanger the health of the cells, but at the same time the anaplerotic processes that place a constant drain on some of the individual members of the cycle are slowed down. Among these, the formation of the nonessential amino acids is a function that could well be vitally important for the organism.

3.   Effects on Carbohydrate Metabolism

A.   GLUCONEOGENESIS. A major function of the liver is to furnish glucose for the maintenance of the blood glucose concentration in times of need and to dispose of excess glucose when this sugar is present in abundance. Glucose formation may take place from a number of precursors, and the metabolic changes induced by ethanol may interfere to a different extent and even in opposite direction with different glucose precursors. Therefore the problem of the influence of alcohol on glucose production in the liver is somewhat complicated.

Under physiological conditions in the postabsorptive or fasting state lactate, glycerol, and amino acids are the most important sources of glucose. Various sugars (fructose and galactose) and other substances, however, are also converted to glucose when absorbed from the gut.

Gluconeogenesis from lactate. Perfusion experiments in which lactate was used as substrate for gluconeogenesis showed a pronounced reduction in the output of glucose when ethanol was added to the medium [96, 97]. This finding was explained by Krebs [97] by the diminished concentration of pyruvate, compared with control experiments without ethanol. The limiting step in gluconeogenesis from pyruvate may be carboxylation to oxaloacetate, which is a necessary step in order to reverse the glycolytic pathway (see Figure 3). Pyruvate carboxylase has a K_m for pyruvate (about

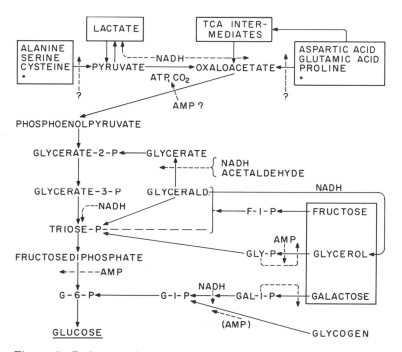

Figure 3. Pathways of gluconeogenesis. Activating and inhibitory influence of NADH, AMP, and other substances is indicated by dotted lines.

0.4 mM), which is above the usual concentration of this substance in the liver. A decrease in pyruvate concentration caused by the increased NADH concentration therefore reduces the rate of carboxylation proportionally. With increasing lactate concentrations the effects of ethanol should disappear as the pyruvate concentration, assumed to be in equilibrium with lactate, reaches a sufficiently high level if the explanation of Krebs is correct. This was in fact found to be the case [97]. Under physiological conditions the concentration of lactate in the blood increases during ethanol metabolism, because the uptake by the liver is reduced [213], but still the pyruvate concentration in the hepatic venous blood remains much lower than in control experiments. Changes in the concentration of acetyl CoA, which is a necessary activator of pyruvate carboxylase, might also be a factor in the ethanol effect on gluconeogenesis. Recent work [231] discourages, however, this possibility.

The increased concentration of NADH in the cytoplasm would be expected to accelerate the reduction of phosphoglyceric acid to triose phosphate, but apparently this reaction is not rate-limiting when lactate is the precursor of glucose.

Gluconeogenesis from pyruvate and amino acids. When pyruvate or other substances more oxidized than lactate are used as precursors of glucose, a net reduction is involved. This takes place at the conversion of phosphoglycerate to glyceraldehyde phosphate. Because this reaction is favored by the increased endoplasmic NADH concentration, it is to be expected that the rate of glucose formation should not be decreased but perhaps even increased. In the perfused rat liver it was in fact found that the initial rate of gluconeogenesis from pyruvate was unchanged by the ethanol [97]. In liver slices an increase was observed [56, 57].

In the perfusion study of Williamson et al. [231] alanine was used throughout. The effect of alcohol on gluconeogenesis was found to be dependent on the presence or absence of free fatty acids. When a fatty acid–depleted medium was used, a twofold increase was observed, but in the presence of 1-mM oleate the rate was reduced about 30%. The explanation offered for these findings, based on an analysis of the intermediates in the reaction sequence, is that in the absence of fatty acids the triose phosphate dehydrogenase step is rate-determining; in the presence of oleate another control point appears at the phosphofructokinase step. The observed decrease in citrate concentration, which would activate phosphofructokinase, is suggested to induce a recycling between fructose mono- and diphosphate, which would reduce the net formation of glucose.

The results of these workers are well documented, but it may be pointed out that the experimental situation used is highly unphysiological insofar as alanine is the only substrate furnished to the liver. In other words the liver must cover its own energy need from alanine at the same time that it converts some alanine to glucose. In this situation it is perhaps not surprising that the inclusion of a utilizable substrate, such as ethanol, can increase glucose formation.

Other workers, using somewhat different experimental procedures, found that gluconeogenesis from amino acids in the perfused rat liver decreased significantly when ethanol was present in the medium [17, 96, 97].

In the fasted dog Madison [137] found a pronounced decrease in glucose formation after the administration of alcohol, and this inhibition was further accentuated by glutamate or α-oxoglutarate. That the reduction in gluconeogenesis is in fact caused by the increased NADH/NAD ratio is suggested also by the observation that an infusion of methylene blue, which permits the reoxidation of NADH, abolishes the effect of alcohol on hepatic glucose production [137].

The observation [174] that in fed rats the glutamate concentration in the liver was increased about two times when alcohol was administered may be interesting in this connection, because the transamination of the various amino acids has to proceed predominantly with α-oxoglutarate to glutamate. If the transamination takes place near equilibrium, the increased concentration of glutamate reduces the level of keto acids. At the same time the inhibition of the tricarboxylic acid cycle reduces the rate of production of oxaloacetate, which constitutes the link between amino acid metabolism and glucose formation.

Glucose formation from other sugars. The formation of glucose from fructose was found to be increased after the administration of ethanol in man [213] and dogs [137] and in perfused rat liver [38]. Krebs et al. [97], however, found a decrease in the perfused rat liver preparation. In the absence of ethanol about half of the fructose metabolized in the human liver is given off in the hepatic veins as pyruvate and lactate [213]. In the presence of ethanol the amount of lactate and pyruvate is reduced, and glucose appears instead. One possible explanation of this phenomenon is that the increased NADH concentration in combination with the presence of acetaldehyde, which competes successfully with glyceraldehyde for the aldehyde dehydrogenase, inhibits the oxidation of glyceraldehyde, which is believed to be a key intermediate in the fructose metabolism of liver tissue.

The decreased oxidation of glyceraldehyde may lead either directly to increased triose phosphate formation by the action of triokinase or to the reduction to glycerol by alcohol dehydrogenase followed by phosphorylation and oxidation to triosephosphate by the mitochondrial glycerophosphate dehydrogenase system (see Section E.2b). In both cases glucose formation is favored. The metabolism of glyceraldehyde in rat and human liver may differ quantitatively [69]. In man the oxidative pathway seems to be more important than the phosphorylating pathway. During ethanol treatment the oxidative route is inhibited, and the metabolism of glyceraldehyde is forced toward gluconeogenesis. It is therefore quite possible that the action of ethanol on gluconeogenesis from fructose may be different in the two species.

Glucose formation from galactose is also reduced very markedly in the presence of ethanol in both human and rat liver. The mechanism in this case is very likely to be inhibition of UDP-galactose epimerase by NADH [143]. This block causes an accumulation of galactose-1-phosphate, which in turn has been shown to inhibit the first step in galactose metabolism, the phosphorylation by galactose kinase [26, 180].

When glycerol is used as the precursor of glucose, both the glycerol metabolism in the liver and the formation of glucose are inhibited in the presence of ethanol. The mechanism of the inhibition in this case seems to be at the level of glycerokinase, which is inhibited by AMP and by glycerophosphate [70, 180], the concentration of which has been shown to increase as a consequence of the increased NADH concentration [156, 209]. In man the uptake of glycerol in the splanchnic area is reduced to about half [132], and a very similar figure was found for the inhibition of glucose production from glycerol in the perfused rat liver when ethanol was present in the perfusion medium [97].

B. THE EFFECT OF ALCOHOL ON BLOOD GLUCOSE CONCENTRATION; ALCOHOL-INDUCED HYPOGLYCEMIA. Many and apparently contradictory results have been published regarding the influence of alcohol on the blood glucose concentration [see the review by Madison, 136]. Because apparently the influence of alcohol is very dependent on the nutritional state, it may clarify the picture if well-fed and starved organisms are considered separately.

Well-fed organisms. In man under most normal conditions and in well-nourished experimental animals ethanol causes a slight and transient increase in the blood glucose concentration [98, 131, 162]. In order to analyse this situation, it should be kept in mind that the blood glucose concentration in the postabsorptive state is the result of a considerable peripheral utilization and the hepatic production. Observed changes in the concentration of glucose may be the result of influence on either one or both processes.

There is some evidence that alcohol may cause a decreased peripheral utilization in starved dogs [136]. Whether this is also the case in the fed animals is not known with certainty. The extensive and preferential use of acetate in the peripheral tissues may, however, provide an explanation for such an effect. The hyperglycemia could also be caused by an increase in the breakdown of liver glycogen, for instance, by hormone action. Increased release of epinephrine by ethanol has, for instance, been claimed [1, 161], but this cannot be the whole explanation, because increased glucose production can be provoked by ethanol also in the isolated perfused liver [53]. The increase in AMP concentration mentioned earlier may be a factor in causing an elevation in the activity of glycogen phosphorylase or a decrease in the synthesis of glycogen by the inhibition of the reaction between ATP (uridine triphosphate) and glucose-1-phosphate [104]. A somewhat increased glucose-6-phosphatase activity has been observed in liver from ethanol-treated well-fed rats [174]. An increase in the hepatic fructose diphosphate concentration has also been observed under these conditions, and again the effect is compatible with the influence of the increased AMP concentration of the enzymes responsible for the synthesis and hydrolysis of fructose diphosphate [197, 214].

Starved organisms. In the starved organism the blood glucose concentration is derived exclusively through gluconeogenesis in the liver, and perhaps kidneys. The effect of ethanol on these processes, as discussed in Section F.3a, is therefore of decisive importance for the maintenance of the blood glucose concentration.

In animals that have been starved for a prolonged period (2 to 3 days) a pronounced fall in blood glucose concentration is invariably observed after the administration of alcohol [119, 120]. In man this phenomenon has attracted considerable attention, because the condition known as alcohol-induced hypoglycemia may be a serious and even fatal consequence of alcohol consumption. The problems are set out in detail in the excellent review by Madison [136], in which further references may be found. A considerable number of cases have been reported in the literature, mainly from areas in which malnutrition and starvation are common. Of the 101 cases reviewed by Madison 11 died from the complications of prolonged hypoglycemia. The clinical picture is that characteristic of hypoglycemic coma, including positive response to the intravenous administration of glucose. In cases of prolonged hypoglycemia severe damage to the central nervous system is frequently observed. The hypoglycemic syndrome in less severe cases may have a number of mental and neurological manifestations, some of which might be mistaken for ordinary drunkenness.

The alcohol-induced hypoglycemia is probably much more common than would be expected from the number of published reports. In the typical case the patient has been fasting for a considerable period before starting drinking. Often his general state of nutrition is bad, and vitamin deficiencies are common. Alcoholic intoxication may end in hypoglycemic coma, and so in the words of Madison, "The drunk one puts to bed at night may be the next morning's corpse from hypoglycemia."

Such patients and experimental animals are devoid of liver glycogen as verified by biopsy, and lack of response to glucagon administration [38, 56]. Furthermore it has been shown that the plasma insulin concentration is not increased, neither in man [56] nor in dogs [120].

Originally the hypoglycemic syndrome was ascribed to other substances in alcoholic beverages than alcohol, but it has been shown convincingly that even normal subjects, when fasted for a sufficient period (44 to 72 hr), develop hypoglycemia when pure alcohol is administered [3, 38]. The explanation of alcohol-induced hypoglycemia therefore now seems quite clear. Individuals who have no glycogen store left and in whom amino acids are scarce can barely meet the normal demand of the central nervous system for glucose. When gluconeogenesis is acutely inhibited by alcohol, glucose production declines below the compulsory need, and the blood glucose concentration drops to a level that may be dangerously low.

4. Effects of Ethanol on Amino Acid Metabolism

Relatively little work has been performed in this field. Changes in the concentration of some amino acids in the blood of human subjects have been recorded [192]. A reduction in the total concentration of free amino acids in blood was found when alcohol was given. In the case of serine, threonine, methionine, leucine, and alanine the difference was highly significant. A more detailed study of this problem might be of interest in connection with the role of the liver in the production of some amino acids. The role of transamination and the increased glutamate concentration in the liver was discussed in Section F.3.

The activation of methionine in rat liver was found to be increased when alcohol was given in both acute and chronic experiments [41]. The possible mechanism for this change in enzyme activity was not clarified.

5. Influence of Ethanol on Lipid Metabolism

The action of alcohol on the accumulation of fat in the liver is an important problem from a medical point of view in connection with the development of alcoholic liver disease. In a study by Edmondson et al. [31] as many as 96% of liver biopsy specimens from chronic alcoholics showed the picture of fatty liver.

The problems concerning alcoholic liver damage are discussed in Chapters IV and V; therefore only a short outline of the effect of ethanol on fat metabolism is given here. Thorough discussions of these problems are also to be found in the reviews by Lieber [108, 110].

The alcohol-induced changes in the metabolism of liver tissue may influence lipid metabolism in several ways:

1. The considerable reduction (about 75%) of the terminal oxidation of other nutrients, which is a consequence of the inhibition of the citrate cycle, mainly involves lipids, which normally furnish the largest part of the energy used by this organ. The dramatic decrease in fat oxidation has been demonstrated by the use of labeled palmitate [111, 178] and labeled chylomichrons in perfused rat liver [115]. Provided that the uptake of fatty acid by the liver and the output of lipids are unchanged, a rough calculation shows that about 80 g/day of fat should accumulate in the liver of a human subject during constant alcohol metabolism because of this "sparing action." No definite information is, however, available as to the correctness of the assumptions made.

2. The increased extramitochondrial concentration of NADH and NADPH may directly accelerate the rate of fatty acid synthesis, a contention for which there seems to be only circumstantial experimental evidence [111].

3. The increase in glycerophosphate concentration observed in the liver after the administration of alcohol, caused by the reduction of dihydroxyacetone phosphate by NADH, may be a factor that facilitates the esterification of free fatty acids to triglycerides.

Apart from these factors, which may all contribute to fat accumulation, other mechanisms may be of importance, e.g., decreased production or release of lipoprotein from the liver. The experimental evidence available, however, does not support such an assumption. Another possibility would be a change in the plasma free fatty acid concentration. Rather contradictory statements have been made concerning the change in the plasma free fatty acid concentration after alcohol intake. The work of Lieber and his associates seems now to have settled the question satisfactorily. At low blood alcohol concentrations a fall in the free fatty acid concentration is clearly observable [25], and an identical decrease could be produced by the infusion of acetate in concentrations comparable with those measured during alcohol metabolism. Therefore acetate seems to be the cause of the reduction in the plasma free fatty acid concentration. When larger doses of alcohol are given a definite increase in the concentration of free fatty acids is seen both in experimental animals [138, 176] and in man [110, 185]. Also the concentration of triglyceride in plasma shows a marked increase which may diminish again when alcohol intake is continued for a prolonged period. The explanation of the changes in blood lipid concentration is not clear at present.

6.   Influence of Ethanol on the Metabolism of Other Substances

In general it might be suggested that reactions in the liver that involve the oxidation of alcohol groups or the reduction of oxo groups are liable to be influenced by alcohol metabolism. The hexitol sorbitol is a good example. This alcohol is oxidized to fructose by means of the NAD-dependent sorbitol dehydrogenase. In the presence of alcohol the reaction is inhibited, as shown by the longer elimination time in man [215] and also in experiments on rats and liver slices [77, 78, 117].

Evidence of a change in the steady-state ratio of some keto/hydroxy steroids under the influence of an alcohol-induced rise in the NADH concentration has also been advanced [24].

Metabolism of serotonin has attracted considerable attention. Apparently the primary breakdown products, 5-hydroxyindole acetaldehyde may be either oxidized to the carboxylic acid or reduced to the corresponding primary alcohol. The rates of these pathways are changed by alcohol. For detailed discussion of this question and the similar problems regarding other biogenic amines reference is made to Chapter III.

REFERENCES

1. Abelin, I. V., C. Herren, and W. Berli, Über die erregende Wirkung des Alkohols auf den Adrenalin und Noradrenalin Haushalt des menschlichen Organismus, *Helv. Med. Acta,* **25,** 591 (1958).
2. Ammon, H. P. T., C.-J. Estler, and F. Heim, Inactivation of coenzyme A by ethanol: I. Acetaldehyde as mediator of the inactivation of coenzyme A following the administration of ethanol in vivo, *Biochem. Pharmacol.,* **18,** 29 (1969).
3. Arky, R. A. and N. Freinkel, Alcohol hypoglycemia: V. Alcohol infusion to test gluconeogenesis in starvation, with special reference to obesity, *New Eng. J. Med.,* **274,** 426 (1966).
4. Aull, J. C., W. J. Roberts, and F. W. Kinard, Rate of metabolism of ethanol in the rat, *Am. J. Physiol.,* **186,** 380 (1956).
5. Bäcklin, K. I., The equilibrium constant of the system ethanol, aldehyde, DPN+, DPNH and H+, *Acta Chem. Scand.,* **12,** 1279 (1958).

6. Baker, R. N., A. L. Alenty, and J. F. Zack, Toxic volatiles in alcoholic coma, *Bull. Los Angeles Neurol. Soc.,* **33,** 140 (1968).

7. Bartlett, G. R. and H. N. Barnet, Some observations on alcohol metabolism with radioactive ethyl alcohol, *Quart. J. Studies Alc.,* **10,** 381 (1949).

8. Batelli, F. and L. Stern, L'Alcoolase dans les tissus animaux, *Compt. Rend. Soc. Biol.,* **67,** 419 (1909).

9. Bernhard, S. A., M. F. Dunn, P. L. Luîsi, and P. Schack, Mechanistic studies on equine liver alcohol dehydrogenase: I. The stoichiometry relationship of the coenzyme binding sites active in the transient state, *Biochemistry* **9,** 185 (1970).

10. Blair, A. H. and F. H. Bodley, Human liver aldehyde dehydrogenase: Partial purification and properties, *Canad. J. Biochem.,* **47,** 265 (1969).

11. Blair, A. H. and B. L. Vallee, Some catalytic properties of human liver alcohol dehydrogenase, *Biochemistry,* **5,** 2026 (1966).

12. Blomstrand, R. and B. Holmström, Studies on the metabolism of ^{14}C-labelled ethanol in man: II. The expiratory $^{14}CO_2$ pattern after administration of ethanol-1-^{14}C and ethanol-2-^{14}C, *Arkiv Kemi,* **30,** 305 (1969).

13. Blomstrand, R., G. Carlberger, and B. Holmström, Metabolism of carbon-14-labelled ethanol in man: I. The expiratory carbon-^{14}C dioxide pattern after the administration of ethanol-1-^{14}C with different carrier doses, *Arkiv Kemi,* **30,** 291 (1969).

14. Bloom, R. J., P. G. Fuller, J. G. Westerfeld, and W. W. Westerfeld, The formation and determination of 5-hydroxy-4-ketohexanoic acid, *Biochemistry,* **5,** 3211 (1966).

15. Bonnichsen, R. K. and A. M. Wassén, Crystalline alcohol dehydrogenase from horse liver, *Arch. Biochem.,* **18,** 361 (1948).

16. Borst, P., Interrelation between cytoplasmic and mitochondrial diphospho-pyridine nucleotide in Ehrlich ascites tumour cells, *Proc. 5th Intern. Congr. Biochem.,* **2,** 233 (1961).

17. Büttner, H., Aldehyd- und Alkoholdehydrogenase-Aktivität in Leber und Niere der Ratte, *Biochem. Z.,* **341,** 300 (1965).

18. Büttner, H., F. Portwich, and K. Engelhardt, Der DPN$^+$- und DPN-H-Gehalt der Rattenleber während des Abbaues von Äthanol und seine Beeinflussung durch Sulfonylharnstoff und Disulfiram, *Arch. Exptl. Pathol. Pharmakol.,* **240,** 573 (1961).

19. Caraceni, C., M. Marugo, N. Scopinaro, and F. Minuto, Orotic acid and fructose-induced hyperuricemia, *Boll. Soc. Ital. Biol. Sper.,* **45,** 145 (1969).

20. Carpenter, T. M. and R. C. Lee, The effect of ingestion of alcohol on human respiratory exchange during rest and muscular work, *Arbeitsphysiologie,* **10,** 130 (1938).

21. Casier, H. and A. L. Delaunois, *L'Intoxication par l'alcool etylique,* Masson, Paris, 1947.

22. Clark, W. C. and H. R. Hulpieu, Comparative effectiveness of fructose, dextrose, pyruvic acid and insulin in accelerating the disappearance of ethanol from dogs, *Quart. J. Studies Alc.,* **19,** 47 (1958).

23. Clark, B. P., R. W. Morrissey, J. F. Fazekas, and C. S. Welch, The role

of insulin and the liver in alcohol metabolism, *Quart. J. Studies Alc.,* **1,** 663 (1940).

24. Cronholm, T. and J. Sjövall, Effect of ethanol metabolism on redox state of steroid sulphates in man, *European J. Biochem.,* **13,** 124 (1970).

25. Crouse, J. R., C. D. Gerson, L. M. DeCarli, and C. S. Lieber, Role of acetate in the reduction of plasma free fatty acids produced by ethanol in man, *J. Lipid Res.,* **9,** 509 (1968).

26. Cuatrecasas, P. and S. Segal, Mammalian galactokinase: Developmental and adaptive characteristics in the rat liver, *J. Biol. Chem.,* **240,** 2382 (1965).

27. Dajani, R. M., J. Danielski, and J. J. M. Orten, The utilization of ethanol: II. The alcohol-acetaldehyde dehydrogenase systems in the livers of alcohol treated rats, *J. Nutr.,* **80,** 196 (1963).

28. Dalziel, K., Purification of liver alcohol dehydrogenase, *Acta Chem. Scand.,* **12,** 459 (1958).

29. Dalziel, K. and F. M. Dickinson, The kinetics and mechanism of liver alcohol dehydrogenase with primary and secondary alcohols as substrates, *Biochem. J.,* **100,** 34 (1966).

30. Dixon, M. and C. Lutwak-Mann, Aldehyde mutase, *Biochem. J.,* **31,** 1347 (1937).

31. Edmondson, H. A., R. L. Peters, H. H. Frankel, and S. Borowsky, The early stage of liver injury in the alcoholic, *Medicine,* **46,** 119 (1967).

32. Edwards, J. A. and D. A. P. Evans, Ethanol metabolism in subjects possessing typical and atypical liver alcohol dehydrogenase, *Clin. Pharmacol. Therap.,* **8,** 824 (1967).

33. Eggleston, M. G., Determination of the metabolic rate of alcohol, *J. Physiol.,* **98,** 228 (1940).

34. Eggleston, M. G., Some factors affecting the metabolic rate of alcohol, *J. Physiol.,* **98,** 239 (1940).

35. Ehrenberg, A. and K. Dalziel, Molecular weight of horse liver alcohol dehydrogenase, *Acta Chem. Scand.,* **12,** 465 (1958).

36. Elbel, H., Tierexperimentelle Studien über die Alkoholverbrennung, *Experientia,* **14,** 255 (1958).

37. Elbel, H. and F. Schleyer, *Blutalkohol,* 2d ed., Thieme, Stuttgart, 1956.

38. Field, J. B., H. E. Williams, and G. E. Mortimore, Studies on the mechanism of ethanol-induced hypoglycemia, *J. Clin. Invest.,* **42,** 497 (1963).

39. Fiessinger, N., H. Benard, J. Courtial, and L. Dermer, Combustion de l'alcool éthylique au cours de la perfusion du foie, *Compt. Rend. Soc. Biol.,* **122,** 1255 (1936).

40. Figueroa, R. B. and A. P. Klotz, Alterations of liver alcohol dehydrogenase and other hepatic enzymes in alcoholic cirrhosis, *Gastroenterology,* **43,** 10 (1962).

41. Finkelstein, J. D. and W. E. Kyle, Ethanol effects on methionine metabolism in rat liver, *Proc. Soc. Exptl. Biol. Med.,* **129,** 497 (1968).

42. Fischer, H.-D., Der Einfluss von Barbituraten auf die Entgiftungsgeschwindigkeit des Äthanols, *Biochem. Pharmacol.,* **11,** 307 (1962).

43. Fischer, H.-D., Zum Einfluss von Hydrocortison auf die Entgiftungsgeschwindigkeit des Äthanols, *Biochem. Pharmacol.,* **15**, 785 (1966).
44. Fischer, H.-D., Zur Alkoholelimination bei Kaninchen nach CCl₄-Vergiftung, *Med. Pharmacol. Exptl.,* **17**, 60 (1967).
45. Fischer, H.-D. and W. Oelssner, Der Einfluss von Hexobarbital auf die Alkoholelimination bei Kaninchen, *Med. Exptl.,* **3**, 213 (1960).
46. Fischer, H.-D. and W. Oelssner, Der Einfluss von Barbituraten auf die Alkoholelimination bei Mäusen, *Klin. Wochschr.,* **39**, 1265 (1961).
47. Forney, R. B. and R. N. Harger, Toxicology of ethanol, *Ann. Rev. Pharmacol.,* **9**, 379 (1969).
48. Forsander, O. A., Influence of the metabolism of ethanol on the lactate/pyruvate ratio of rat-liver-slices, *Biochem. J.,* **98**, 244, (1966).
49. Forsander, O., Effects of Ethanol on Metabolic Pathways, *International Encyclopedia of Pharmacology and Therapeutics,* sec. 20, vol. 1, p. 117, Pergamon, New York, 1970.
50. Forsander, O. and N. C. R. Räihä, Metabolites produced in the liver during alcohol oxidation, *J. Biol. Chem.,* **235**, 34 (1960).
51. Forsander, O., N. Räihä, and H. Suomalainen, Oxydation des Äthylalkohols in isolierter Leber und isolierten Hinterkörper der Ratte, *Hoppe-Seylers Z. Physiol. Chem.,* **318**, 1 (1960).
52. Forsander, O. A., P. A. Mäenpää, and M. P. Salaspuro, Influence of ethanol on the lactate/pyruvate and β-hydroxybutyrate/acetoacetate ratios in rat liver experiments, *Acta Chem. Scand.,* **19**, 1770 (1965).
53. Forsander, O. A., N. Räihä, M. Salaspuro, and P. Mäenpää, Influence of ethanol on liver metabolism of fed and starved rats, *Biochem. J.,* **94**, 259 (1965).
54. Forsander, O. A., M. Lampila, and B. Westerling, The utilization of ethanol by dairy cows, *J. Sci. Agr. Soc. Finland,* **39**, 205 (1967).
55. Forsander, O. A. and J. J. Himberg, The share of ethanol in the total oxygen consumption by rat liver slices, *Scand. J. Clin. Lab. Invest.,* **21**, *Suppl.,* **101**, 18 (1968).
56. Freinkel, N., D. L. Singer, R. A. Arky, S. J. Bleicher, J. B. Anderson, and C. K. Silbert, Alcohol hypoglycemia: I. Carbohydrate metabolism of patients with clinical hypoglycemia and the experimental reproduction of the syndrome with pure ethanol, *J. Clin. Invest.,* **42**, 1112 (1963).
57. Freinkel, N., A. K. Cohen, R. A. Arky, and A. E. Foster, Alcohol hypoglycemia: II. A postulated mechanism of action based on experiments with rat liver slices, *J. Clin. Endocrinol.,* **25**, 76 (1965).
58. Freund, G. and P. O'Hollaren, Acetaldehyde concentrations in alveolar air following a standard dose of ethanol in man, *J. Lipid Res.,* **6**, 471 (1965).
59. Geraci, G. and Q. H. Gibson, The reaction of liver alcohol dehydrogenase with reduced diphosphopyridine nucleotide, *J. Biol. Chem.,* **242**, 4275 (1967).
60. Gillette, J. R., B. B. Brodie, and B. N. La Du, The oxidation of drugs by liver microsomes: On the role of TPNH and oxygen, *J. Pharmacol. Exptl. Therap.,* **119**, 532 (1957).

61. Goldberg, L. and U. Rydberg, Inhibition of ethanol metabolism in vivo by administration of pyrazole, *Biochem. Pharmacol.*, **18**, 1749 (1969).
62. Gordon, E. R., Effect of aeration on the consumption of ethanol by the isolated perfused rat liver, *Nature*, **209**, 1028 (1966).
63. Gordon, E. R., The utilization of ethanol by the isolated perfused rat liver, *Can. J. Physiol. Pharmacol.*, **46**, 609 (1968).
64. Greenberg, L. A., Acetoin not a product of the metabolism of alcohol, *Quart. J. Studies Alc.*, **3**, 347 (1942).
65. Greenberger, N. J., R. B. Cohen, and K. J. Isselbacher, The effect of chronic ethanol administration on liver alcohol dehydrogenase activity in the rat, *Lab. Invest.*, **14**, 264 (1965).
66. Greville, G. D., Intracellular Compartmentation and the Citric Acid Cycle, in *Citric Acid Cycle*, chap. 1, J. M. Lowenstein (ed.), Marcel Dekker, New York, 1969.
67. Griffaton, G. and R. Lowy, Oxydation de l'ethanol in vitro par un homogenat de foie de rat, *Compt. Rend. Soc. Biol.*, **158**, 998 (1964).
68. Grunnet, N., unpublished.
69. Grunnet, N. and H. I. D. Thieden, unpublished.
70. Grunnet, N. and F. Lundquist, Kinetics of glycerol kinases from mammalian liver and candida mycoderma, *European J. Biochem.*, **3**, 78 (1967).
71. Haggard, H. W. and L. A. Greenberg, Studies in the absorption, distribution and elimination of ethyl alcohol: III. Rate of oxidation of alcohol in the body, *J. Pharmacol. Exptl. Therap.*, **52**, 167 (1934).
72. Harger, R. W. and H. R. Hulpieu, The effect of certain drugs in the metabolism of ethyl alcohol, *J. Pharmacol. Exptl. Therap.*, **54**, 145 (1935).
73. Harris, I., Structure and catalytic activity of alcohol dehydrogenase, *Nature*, **203**, 30 (1964).
74. Hassinen, I., personal communication.
75. Hassinen, I., Hydrogen transfer into mitochondria in the metabolism of ethanol, *Ann. Med. Biol. Fenniae*, **45**, 35 (1967).
76. Heinz, F. and J. Junghänel, Metabolitmuster in Rattenleber nach Fructose-applikation, *Hoppe-Seylers Z. Physiol. Chem.*, **350**, 859 (1969).
77. Hillbom, M. E., Effect of ethanol on sorbitol oxidation in rats, *Scand. J. Clin. Lab. Invest.*, **21**, *Suppl.*, **101**, 18 (1968).
78. Hillbom, M. and P. Pikkarainen, Ethanol inhibition of sorbitol oxidation in liver slices of propyl thiouracil–treated and control rats, *Life Sci.*, **7**, 713 (1968).
79. Holmström, B., Studies on the metabolism of ^{14}C-labelled ethanol in man: III. The expiratory ^{14}CO$_2$ pattern after administration of ethanol-l-^{14}C in alcoholics, *Arkiv Kemi*, **30**, 311 (1969).
80. Holmström, B., Studies on the metabolism of ^{14}C-labelled ethanol in man: IV. The expiratory ^{14}CO$_2$ pattern after the administration of ^{14}C-labelled ethanol and ^{14}C-labelled acetate, *Arkiv Kemi*, **30**, 323 (1969).
81. Holmström, B., Metabolism of carbon-14-labelled ethanol in man: V. Synthesis of liver fatty acids, *Arkiv Kemi*, **30**, 333 (1969).

82. Holzer, H. and S. Schneider, Zum Mechanismus der Beeinflussung der Alkoholoxydation in der Leber durch Fructose, *Klin. Wochschr.,* **33,** 1006 (1955).

83. Jacobsen, E., The metabolism of ethyl alcohol, *Pharmacol. Rev.,* **4,** 107 (1952).

84. Järnefelt, J., *Studies on the Enzymatic Synthesis and Breakdown of Acetone in the Animal Organism,* thesis, Helsinki, 1955.

85. Johannsmeier, K., H. Redetzki, and G. Pfleiderer, Zur Frage der Beschleunigung des Blutalkoholabbaus, *Klin. Wochschr.,* **32,** 560 (1954).

86. Jörnvall, H., Differences in E and S chains from iso-enzymes of horse liver alcohol dehydrogenase, *Nature,* **225,** 1133 (1970).

87. Kalant, H., G. Sereny, and R. Charlebois, Evaluation of triiodothyronine in the treatment of acute alcoholic intoxication, *New Engl. J. Med.,* **267,** 1 (1962).

88. Kamil, I. A., J. N. Smith, and R. T. Williams, A new aspect of ethanol metabolism: Isolation of ethyl-glucuronide, *Biochem. J.,* **51,** 32 (1952).

89. Keilin, D. and E. F. Hartreé, Coupled oxidation of alcohol, *Proc. Roy. Soc. (London), Ser. B,* **119,** 141 (1936).

90. Keilin, D. and E. F. Hartree, Catalase, peroxidase and metmyoglobin as catalyst of coupled peroxidatic reactions, *Biochem. J.,* **60,** 310 (1955).

91. Kinard, F. W. and E. C. Cox, Effect of insulin on ethanol metabolism in normal and alloxan-diabetic dogs, *Quart. J. Studies Alc.,* **19,** 375 (1958).

92. Kinard, F. W., W. M. McCord, and J. C. Aull, The failure of oxygen, oxygen–carbon dioxide or pyruvate to alter alcohol metabolism, *Quart. J. Studies Alc.,* **12,** 179 (1955).

93. Kinard, F. W., G. H. Nelson, and M. G. Hay, Catalase activity and ethanol metabolism in the rat, *Proc. Soc. Exptl. Biol. Med.,* **92,** 772, (1956).

94. Kinard, F. W., M. G. Hay, and F. W. Kinard Jr., Effect of triiodothyronine on ethanol metabolism in the dog, *Nature,* **196,** 380 (1962).

95. Kraemer, R. J. and R. A. Deitrich, Isolation and characterization of human liver aldehyde dehydrogenase, *J. Biol. Chem.,* **243,** 6404 (1968).

96. Krebs, H. A., Effects of ethanol on the metabolic activities of the liver, *Advan. Enzyme Regulation* **6,** 467 (1968).

97. Krebs, H. A., R. A. Freedland, R. Hems, and M. Stubbs, Inhibition of hepatic gluconeogenesis by ethanol, *Biochem. J.,* **112,** 117 (1969).

98. Lange, K. and S. Kühne, Blutzucker und Blutalkoholspiegel bei weissen Ratten nach Alkoholbelastung und toxischer Leberschädigung, *Hoppe-Seylers Z. Physiol. Chem.,* **321,** 49 (1960).

99. Lardy, H. A., V. Paetkau, and P. Walter, Paths of carbon in gluconeogenesis and lipogenesis: The role of mitochondria in supplying precursors of phosphoenolpyruvate, *Proc. Nat. Acad. Sci. U.S.,* **53,** 1410 (1965).

100. Larsen, J. A., Determination of hepatic blood flow means of ethanol, *Scand. J. Clin. Lab. Invest.,* **11,** 340 (1959).

101. Larsen, J. A., Elimination of ethanol as a measure of the hepatic blood flow in the cat: II. The significance of the extrahepatic elimination of ethanol, *Acta Physiol. Scand.,* **57,** 209 (1963).

102. Laser, H., Peroxidatic activity of catalase, *Biochem. J.,* **61,** 122 (1955).

103. LeBreton, E., Demonstration directe de la non-utilisation de l'alcool éthylique comme source d'énergie pour le travail musculaire du rat, *Compt. Rend. Soc. Biol.,* **118,** 62 (1935).
104. Leloir, L. F., The biosynthesis of polysaccharides, *Proc. 6th Intern. Congr. Biochem.,* p. 15, New York, 1964.
105. Leloir, L. F. and J. M. Muñoz, Alcohol metabolism in animal tissues, *Biochem. J.,* **32,** 299 (1938).
106. Lester, D. and W. Z. Keokosky, Alcohol metabolism in the horse, *Life Sci.,* **6,** 2313 (1967).
107. Lester, D., W. Z. Keokosky, and F. Felzenberg, Effect of pyrazoles and other compounds on alcohol metabolism, *Quart. J. Studies Alc.,* **29,** 449 (1968).
108. Lieber, C. S., Metabolic derangements induced by alcohol, *Ann. Rev. Med.,* **18,** 35 (1967).
109. Lieber, C. S., Ethanol increases hepatic smooth endoplasmic reticulum and drug-metabolizing enzymes, *Science,* **159,** 1469 (1968).
110. Lieber, C. S., Metabolic effects produced by alcohol in the liver and other tissues, *Advan. Internal Med.,* **14,** 151 (1968).
111. Lieber, C. S. and R. Schmid, The effect of ethanol on fatty acid metabolism: Stimulation of hepatic fatty acid synthesis in vitro, *J. Clin. Invest.,* **40,** 394 (1961).
112. Lieber, C. S. and L. M. DeCarli, Ethanol oxidation by hepatic microsomes: Adaptive increase after ethanol feeding, *Science,* **162,** 917 (1968).
113. Lieber, C. S. and L. M. DeCarli, Effect of drug administration on the activity of the hepatic microsomal ethanol oxidizing system, *Life Sci.,* **9,** 267 (1970).
114. Lieber, C. S. and L. M. DeCarli, Hepatic microsomal ethanol oxidizing system: In vitro characteristics and adaptive properties in vivo, *J. Biol. Chem.,* **245,** 2505 (1970).
115. Lieber, C. S., A. Lefevre, N. Spritz, L. Feinman, and L. M. DeCarli, Difference in hepatic metabolism of long- and medium-chain fatty acids: The role of fatty acid chain length in the production of the alcoholic fatty liver, *J. Clin. Invest.,* **46,** 1451 (1967).
116. Lindeneg, O., K. Mellemgaard, J. Fabricius, and F. Lundquist, Myocardial utilization of acetate, lactate and free fatty acids after ingestion of ethanol, *Clin. Sci.,* **27,** 427 (1964).
117. Lindros, K. O., Interference of ethanol and sorbitol with hepatic ketone body metabolism in normal, hyper- and hypothyroid rats, *European J. Biochem.,* **13,** 111 (1970).
118. Lindros, K. O. and H. Aro, Ethanol-induced changes in levels of metabolites related to the redox state and ketogenesis in rat liver, *Ann. Med. Exptl. Fenniae,* **47,** 39 (1969).
119. Lochner, A. and L. Madison, The quantitative role of the liver and peripheral tissues in ethanol induced hypoglycemia, *Clin. Res.,* **11,** 40 (1963).
120. Lochner, A., J. Wulff, and L. L. Madison, Ethanol-induced hypoglycemia: I. The acute effects of ethanol on hepatic glucose output and peripheral glucose utilization in fasted dogs, *Metab. Clin. Exptl.,* **16,** 1 (1967).

121. Loomis, T. A., A study of the rate of metabolism of ethyl alcohol, *Quart. J. Studies Alc.*, **11**, 527 (1950).

122. Lubin, M. and W. W. Westerfeld, The metabolism of acetaldehyde, *J. Biol. Chem.*, **161**, 503 (1945).

123. Lundquist, F., The concentration of acetate in blood during alcohol metabolism in man, *Acta Physiol. Scand.*, **50**, *Suppl.*, **175**, 97 (1960).

124. Lundquist, F., Enzymatic Pathways of Ethanol Metabolism, in *Alcohol and Derivatives*, vol. 1, p. 95, *International Encyclopedia of Pharmacology and Therapeutics*, sec. 20, Pergamon, New York, 1970.

125. Lundquist, F., Production and utilization of free acetate in man, *Nature*, **193**, 579 (1962).

126. Lundquist, F. and H. Wolthers, The kinetics of alcohol elimination in man, *Acta Pharmacol. Toxicol.*, **14**, 265 (1958).

127. Lundquist, F. and H. Wolthers, The influence of fructose on the kinetics of alcohol elimination in man, *Acta Pharmacol. Toxicol.*, **14**, 290 (1958).

128. Lundquist, F. and P. H. Petersen, Alcohol dehydrogenase in kidney tissue, unpublished.

129. Lundquist, F., U. Fugmann, H. Rasmussen, and I. Svendsen, The metabolism of acetaldehyde in mammalian tissues: Reactions in rat-liver suspensions under aerobic conditions, *Biochem. J.*, **84**, 281 (1962).

130. Lundquist, F., I. Svendsen, and P. H. Petersen, The metabolism of ethanol in rat-liver suspensions, *Biochem. J.*, **86**, 119 (1963).

131. Lundquist, F., N. Tygstrup, K. Winkler, K. Mellemgaard, and S. Munck-Petersen, Ethanol metabolism and production of free acetate in the human liver, *J. Clin. Invest.*, **41**, 955 (1962).

132. Lundquist, F., N. Tygstrup, K. Winkler, and K. B. Jensen, Metabolism of glycerol in human liver: Inhibition by ethanol, *Science*, **150**, 616 (1965).

133. Lundsgaard, E., Alcohol oxidation as a function of the liver, *Compt. Rend. Trav. Lab. Carlsberg*, **22**, 333 (1938).

134. Lutsdorf, U. M. and J.-P. von Wartburg, Subunit composition of horse liver alcohol dehydrogenase isoenzymes, *FEBS Letters*, **5**, 202 (1969).

135. Lutwak-Mann, C., Alcohol dehydrogenase of animal tissues, *Biochem. J.*, **32**, 1364 (1938).

136. Madison, L. L., Ethanol-induced hypoglycemia, *Advan. Metab. Disorders*, **3**, 85 (1968).

137. Madison, L. L., A. Lochner, and J. Wulff, Ethanol-induced hypoglycemia: II. Mechanism of suppression of hepatic gluconeogenesis, *Diabetes*, **16**, 252 (1967).

138. Mallow, S., Effect of ethanol intoxication on plasma free fatty acids in the rat, *Quart. J. Studies Alc.*, **22**, 250 (1961).

139. Marshall, E. K. and W. F. Fritz, The metabolism of ethyl alcohol, *J. Pharmacol. Exptl. Therap.*, **109**, 431 (1953).

140. Marshall, E. K. and A. H. Owens, Rate of metabolism of ethyl alcohol in the mouse, *Proc. Soc. Exptl. Biol. Med.*, **89**, 573 (1955).

141. Masoro, E. J., H. Abramowitch, and J. R. Birchard, Metabolism of C^{14} ethanol by surviving rat tissues, *Am. J. Physiol.*, **173**, 37 (1953).

142. Matthies, H., Aldehyde dehydrogenase in non-nucleated erythrocytes, *Biochem. Z.,* **329,** 421 (1957).

143. Maxwell, E. S., The enzymatic interconversion of uridine diphosphogalactose and uridine diphosphoglucose, *J. Biol. Chem.,* **229,** 139 (1957).

144. McGuire, J., Coupled aldehyde dehydrogenase and catalase in mitochondrial extracts, *Arch. Biochem. Biophys.,* **110,** 104 (1965).

145. Mendelson, J. H., Ethanol-1-^{14}C metabolism in alcoholics and non-alcoholics, *Science,* **159,** 319 (1968).

146. Mendelson, J. H., Biochemical pharmacology of alcohol, *U.S. Public Health Serv., Publ.* 1836, p. 769 (1968).

147. Mendelsohn, J., S. Stein, and N. K. Mello, Effects of experimentally induced intoxication on metabolism of ethanol-1-C^{14} in alcoholic subjects, *Metabolism,* **14,** 1255 (1965).

148. Mezey, E. and P. R. Holt, Loss of the characteristic features of atypical human liver alcohol dehydrogenase during purification, *Life Sci.,* **8,** 245 (1969).

149. Morrison, G. R. and F. E. Brock, Quantitative measurement of alcohol dehydrogenase activity within the liver lobule of rats after prolonged ethanol ingestion, *J. Nutr.,* **92,** 286 (1967).

150. Moser, K., J. Papensberg, and J. P. von Wartburg, Heterogenität und Organverteilung der Alkoholdehydrogenase bei verschiedenen Spezies, *Enzymol. Biol. Clin.,* **9,** 447 (1968).

151. Mourad, N. and C. L. Woronick, Crystallization of human liver alcohol dehydrogenase, *Arch. Biochem. Biophys.,* **121,** 431 (1967).

152. Nelson, G. H. and F. W. Kinard, Effect of rate of intravenous injection on the metabolism of alcohol in the dog, *Quart. J. Studies Alc.,* **20,** 1 (1959).

153. Nelson, G. H., F. W. Kinard, and M. G. Hay, Rate of metabolism of ethanol in the mouse, *Am. J. Physiol.,* **190,** 169 (1957).

154. Nelson, G. H., F. W. Kinard, J. C. Aull, and M. G. Hay, Effect of aminotriazole on alcohol metabolism and hepatic enzyme activities in several species, *Quart. J. Studies Alc.,* **18,** 343 (1957).

155. Newman, H. W., Maximal consumption of ethyl alcohol, *Science,* **109,** 594 (1949).

156. Nikkilä, E. A. and K. Ojala, Role of hepatic L-α-glycerophosphate and triglyceride synthesis in production of fatty liver by ethanol, *Proc. Soc. Exptl. Biol. Med.,* **113,** 814 (1963).

157. Nyman, E. and A. Palmlöv, On the effect of muscular exercise on the metabolism of ethyl alcohol, *Scand. Arch. Physiol.,* **68,** 271 (1934).

158. Orme-Johnson, W. H. and D. M. Ziegler, Alcohol mixed function oxidase activity of mammalian liver microsomes, *Biochem. Biophys. Res. Commun.,* **21,** 78 (1965).

159. Owens, A. H. and E. K. Marshall, The metabolism of ethyl alcohol in the rat, *J. Pharmacol. Exptl. Therap.,* **115,** 360 (1955).

160. Papenberg, J., J.-P. von Wartburg, and H. Aebi, Die Heterogenität der Alkoholdehydrogenase aus Rhesusaffenleber, *Biochem. Z.,* **342,** 95 (1965).

161. Perman, E. S., Effects of ethanol and hydration on the urinary excretion of adrenalin and on the blood sugar of rats, *Acta Physiol. Scand.,* **51,** 68 (1961).

162. Perman, E. S., Effect of ethanol on oxygen uptake and on blood glucose concentration in anaesthetized rabbits, *Acta Physiol. Scand.*, **55**, 189 (1962).

163. Pietruszko, R. and H. Theorell, Subunit composition of horse liver alcohol dehydrogenase, *Arch. Biochem. Biophys.*, **131**, 288 (1969).

164. Pietruszko, R., A. Clark, J. M. H. Graves, and H. J. Ringold, The steroid activity and multiplicity of crystalline horse liver alcohol dehydrogenase, *Biochem. Biophys. Res. Commun.*, **23**, 526 (1966).

165. Pietruszko, R., H. J. Ringold, T. K. Li, B. L. Vallee, Å. Åkeson, and H. Theorell, Structure and function relationships in iso-enzymes of horse liver alcohol dehydrogenase, *Nature*, **221**, 440 (1969).

166. Pletscher, A., A. Bernstein, and H. Staub, Beschleunigung des Alcoholabbaus durch Fructose beim Menschen, *Experientia*, **8**, 307 (1952).

167. Racker, E., Aldehyde dehydrogenase, a diphosphopyridine nucleotide-linked enzyme, *J. Biol. Chem.*, **177**, 883 (1949).

168. Räihä, N. and E. Oura, Effect of ethanol oxidation on levels of pyridine nucleotides in liver and yeast, *Alkon Keskuslaboratorio, Report* 7123 (1961).

169. Raivio, K. O., M. P. Kekomäki, and P. H. Mäenpää, Depletion of liver adenine nucleotides induced by D-fructose: Dose-dependence and specificity of the fructose effect, *Biochem. Pharmacol.*, **18**, 2615 (1969).

170. Rajagopalan, K. V. and P. Handler, Hepatic aldehyde oxidase: II. Differential inhibition of electron transfer to various electron acceptors, *J. Biol. Chem.*, **239**, 2022 (1964).

171. Rajagopalan, K. V. and P. Handler, Hepatic aldehyde oxidase: III. The substrate binding site, *J. Biol. Chem.*, **239**, 2027, (1964).

172. Rajagopalan, K. V., I. Fridowich, and P. Handler, Hepatic aldehyde oxidase: I. Purification and properties, *J. Biol. Chem.*, **237**, 922 (1962).

173. Ramajorana, J., Elimination of ethyl alcohol in the urine in the form of the ether sulfate, *Nutr. Dieta*, **11**, 137, (1969).

174. Rawat, A. K., Effects of ethanol infusion on the redox state and metabolite levels in rat liver *in vivo*, *European J. Biochem.*, **6**, 585 (1968).

175. Rawat, A. K., Effect of hyper- and hypoinsulinism on the metabolism of ethanol in rat liver, *European J. Biochem.*, **9**, 93 (1969).

176. Rawat, A. K., *Influence of Hormones and Other Factors on Hepatic Alcohol Metabolism*, thesis, Copenhagen, 1969.

177. Rawat, A. K. and F. Lundquist, Influence of thyroxine on the metabolism of ethanol and glycerol in rat liver slices, *European J. Biochem.*, **5**, 13 (1968).

178. Reboucas, G. and K. J. Isselbacher, Studies on the pathogenesis of the ethanol-induced fatty liver: I. Synthesis and oxidation of fatty acids by the liver, *J. Clin. Invest.*, **40**, 1355 (1961).

179. Roach, M. K., W. N. Reese, and P. J. Creaven, Ethanol oxidation in the microsomal fraction of rat liver, *Biochem. Biophys. Res. Commun.*, **36**, 596 (1969).

180. Robinson, J. and E. A. Newsholme, Some properties of hepatic glycerol kinase and their relation to the control of glycerol utilization, *Biochem. J.*, **112**, 455 (1969).

181. Rubin, E. and C. S. Lieber, Hepatic microsomal enzymes in man and rat: Induction and inhibition by ethanol, *Science,* **162,** 690 (1968).

182. Rubin, E., F. Hutterer, and C. S. Lieber, Ethanol increases hepatic smooth endoplasmic reticulum and drug-metabolizing enzymes, *Science,* **159,** 1469 (1968).

183. Rydberg, U. S., Inhibition of ethanol metabolism *in vivo* by 4-iodo-pyrazole, *Biochem. Pharmacol.,* **18,** 2424 (1969).

184. Salaspuro, M. P., *Studies on the Influence of Ethanol on the Metabolism of the Normal and Pathological Liver,* thesis, Helsinki, 1968 (Alko).

185. Schapiro, R. H., R. L. Scheig, G. D. Drummey, J. H. Mendelson, and K. J. Isselbacher, Effect of prolonged ethanol ingestion on the transport and metabolism of lipids in man, *New Engl. J. Med.,* **272,** 610 (1965).

186. Scheggia, E., J. Trémolieres, and L. Carré, Actividad peroxidásica inducida por la administracion de etanol, *Rev. Asoc. Bioquim. Arg.,* **149,** 213 (1963).

187. Schmidt, E. and F. W. Schmidt, Enzym-Muster menschlicher Gewebe, *Klin. Wochschr.,* **38,** 957 (1960).

188. Schønheyder, F., O. S. Petersen, K. Terkildsen, and V. Posborg Petersen, On the variation of the alcoholaemic curve, *Acta Med. Scand.,* **109,** 460 (1942).

189. Shore, J. D., The rates of binding of reduced nicotinamide-adenine dinucleotide analogs to liver alcohol dehydrogenase, *Biochemistry,* **8,** 1588 (1969).

190. Shore, J. and H. Theorell, A kinetic study of ternary complexes in the mechanism of action of liver alcohol dehydrogenase, *Arch. Biochem. Biophys.,* **116,** 255 (1966).

191. Shore, J. D. and H. Theorell, Kinetics and dissociation constants of liver alcohol dehydrogenase with 3-acetyl pyridine NAD and NADH, *European J. Biochem.,* **2,** 32 (1967).

192. Siegel, F. L., M. K. Roach, and L. R. Pomeroy, Plasma amino acid patterns in alcoholism: The effects of ethanol loading, *Proc. Natl. Acad. Sci. U.S.,* **51,** 605 (1964).

193. Sigman, D. S., Interactions of substrates, inhibitors, and coenzymes at the active site of horse liver alcohol dehydrogenase, *J. Biol. Chem.,* **242,** 3815 (1967).

194. Smith, M. E. and H. W. Newman, Rate of ethanol metabolism in fed and fasting animals, *J. Biol. Chem.,* **234,** 1544 (1959).

195. Stotz, E., W. W. Westerfeld, and L. Berg, The metabolism of acetaldehyde with acetoin formation, *J. Biol. Chem.,* **152,** 41 (1944).

196. Sund, A. and H. Theorell, Alcohol Dehydrogenase, in *The Enzymes,* 2d ed., vol. 7, p. 25, P. D. Boyer, H. Lardy and K. Myrbäck (eds.) Academic, New York, 1963.

197. Taketa, K. and B. M. Pogell, Allosteric inhibition of rat liver fructose 1,6-diphosphatase by adenosine 5'-monophosphate, *J. Biol. Chem.,* **240,** 651 (1965).

198. Tephly, T. R., M. Atkins, C. J. Mannering, and R. E. Parks, Activation of a catalase peroxidative pathway for the oxidation of alcohols in mammalian erythrocytes, *Biochem. Pharmacol.,* **14,** 435 (1965).

199. Tephly, T. R., F. Tinelli, and W. D. Watkins, Alcohol metabolism: Role of microsomal oxidation *in vivo*, *Science*, **166**, 627 (1969).

200. Theorell, H., Recent Results on Complexes between Liver Alcohol Dehydrogenase Coenzymes and Inhibitors or Substrates, in *New Perspectives in Biology*, vol. 4, p. 147. B. B. A. Library, Amsterdam, 1964.

201. Theorell, H. and R. Bonnichsen, Studies on liver alcohol dehydrogenase: I. Equilibria and initial reaction velocities, *Acta Chem. Scand.*, **5**, 1105 (1951).

202. Theorell, H. and B. Chance, Studies on liver alcohol dehydrogenase: II. The kinetics of the compound of horse liver alcohol dehydrogenase and reduced diphosphopyridine nucleotide, *Acta Chem. Scand.*, **5**, 1127 (1951).

203. Theorell, H. and J. S. McKinley-McKee, Liver alcohol dehydrogenase: I. Kinetics and equilibria without inhibitors, *Acta Chem. Scand.*, **15**, 1797 (1961).

204. Theorell, H., A. P. Nygaard, and R. Bonnichsen, Studies on liver alcohol dehydrogenase: III. The influence of pH and some anions on the reaction velocity constants, *Acta Chem. Scand.*, **9**, 1148 (1955).

205. Theorell, H., S. Taniguchi, Å. Åkeson, and L. Skursky, Crystallization of a separate steroid-active liver alcohol dehydrogenase, *Biochem. Biophys. Res. Commun.*, **24**, 603 (1966).

206. Theorell, H., T. Yonetani, and B. Sjöberg, On the effect of some heterocyclic compounds on the enzymic activity of liver alcohol dehydrogenase, *Acta Chem. Scand.*, **23**, 255 (1969).

207. Thieden, H. I. D., unpublished work.

208. Thieden, H. I. D., The effect of ethanol on the concentrations of adenine nucleotides in rat liver, *FEBS Letters*, **2**, 121 (1968).

209. Thieden, H. I. D., The influence of ethanol on glycerol metabolism in liver slices from fed and fasted rats, *Acta Chem. Scand.*, **23**, 237 (1969).

210. Thieden, H. I. D. and F. Lundquist, The influence of fructose and its metabolites on ethanol metabolism *in vitro*, *Biochem. J.*, **102**, 177 (1967).

211. Trémolières, J., R. Lowy, and G. Griffaton, Physiologie de l'oxydation et de l'utilisation de l'éthanol à doses normales et toxiques, *Ann. Nutr. Aliment.*, **21**, 69 (1967).

212. Truitt, E. B. and G. Duritz, The Role of Acetaldehyde in the Actions of Ethanol, *Biochemical factors in Alcoholism*, pp. 61–69, Pergamon, New York, 1966.

213. Tygstrup, N., K. Winkler, and F. Lundquist, The mechanism of the fructose effect on the ethanol metabolism of the human liver, *J. Clin. Invest.*, **44**, 817 (1965).

214. Underwood, A. H. and E. A. Newsholme, Properties of phosphofructokinase from rat liver and their relation to the control of glycolysis and gluconeogenesis, *Biochem. J.*, **95**, 868 (1965).

215. Verron, G., Vergleichende Untersuchungen über den Sorbitstoffwechsel mit und ohne Alkohol zu satz, *Z. Ges. Inn. Med.*, **20**, 278 (1965).

216. Videla, L. and Y. Israel, Factors that modify the metabolism of ethanol in rat liver and adaptive changes produced by its chronic administration, *Biochem. J.*, **118**, 275 (1970).

217. Videla, L. and Y. Israel, to be published.
218. Wagner, H. J., Einfluss von Medikamenten auf den Acetaldehydspiegel in Blut nach Alkohol Zufuhr, *Deut. Z. Gerichtl. Med.,* **46,** 70 (1957).
219. Walkenstein, S. S. and S. Weinhouse, Oxidation of aldehydes by mitochondria of rat tissues, *J. Biol. Chem.,* **200,** 515, (1953).
220. Wallgren, H., Absorption, Diffusion, Distribution and Elimination of Ethanol: Effect on Biological Membranes, in *Alcohol and Derivatives,* vol. 2, *International Encyclopedia of Pharmacology and Therapeutics,* Pergamon, New York, 1970.
221. Wartburg, J.-P. v. and M. Rothlisberger, Enzymatische Veränderungen in der Leber nach langdauernder Belastung mit Aethanol und Methanol bei der Ratte, *Helv. Physiol. Acta,* **19,** 30 (1961).
222. Wartburg, J.-P. v., J. Papenberg, and H. Aebi, An atypical human alcohol dehydrogenase, *Can. J. Biochem.,* **43,** 889 (1965).
223. Wartburg, J.-P. v. and P. M. Schürch, Atypical human liver alcohol dehydrogenase, *Ann. N.Y. Acad. Sci.,* **151,** 936 (1968).
224. Wartburg, J.-P. v., J. L. Bethuen, and B. L. Vallee, Human liver alcohol dehydrogenase: Kinetic and physicochemical properties, *Biochem.,* **3,** 1775 (1964).
225. Weiner, H., Interaction of a spin-labeled analog of nicotinamide adenine dinucleotide with alcohol dehydrogenase: I. Synthesis, kinetics, and electron paramagnetic resonance studies, *Biochem.,* **8,** 526 (1969).
226. Weitzman, P. D. J., Reduced nicotinamide adenine dinucleotide as an allosteric effector of citrate synthase activity in E. coli, *Biochem. J.,* **101,** 44 C (1966).
227. Westerfeld, W. W., E. Stotz, and R. L. Berg, The role of pyruvate in the metabolism of ethylalcohol, *J. Biol. Chem.,* **144,** 657 (1942).
228. Westerfeld, W. W., E. Stotz, and R. L. Berg, The coupled oxidation-reduction of alcohol and pyruvate *in vivo, J. Biol. Chem.,* **149,** 237 (1943).
229. Widmark, E. M. P., Die theoretischen Grundlagen und die praktische Verwendbarkeit der gerichtlich-medizinische Alkoholbestimmung, Urban und Schwarzenberg, Berlin, 1932.
230. Williamson, D. H., P. Lund, and H. A. Krebs, The redox state of free nicotinamide adenine dinucleotide in the cytoplasm and mitochondria of rat liver, *Biochem. J.,* **103,** 514 (1967).
231. Williamson, J. R., R. Scholz, E. T. Browning, R. G. Thurman, and M. H. Fukami, Metabolic effects of ethanol in perfused rat liver, *J. Biol. Chem.,* **244,** 5044 (1969).
232. Winkler, K., F. Lundquist, and N. Tygstrup, The hepatic metabolism of ethanol in patients with cirrhosis of the liver, *Scand. J. Clin. Lab. Invest.,* **23,** 59 (1969).
233. Wratten, C. C. and W. W. Cleland, Kinetic studies with liver alcohol dehydrogenase, *Biochemistry,* **4,** 2442 (1965).
234. Zakim, D., Effect of ethanol on hepatic acyl-coenzyme A metabolism, *Arch. Biochem. Biophys.,* **111,** 253 (1965).

Chapter II

EFFECTS OF ALCOHOL ON THE NERVE CELL

Y. ISRAEL, E. ROSENMANN, S. HEIN, G. COLOMBO, AND M. CANESSA-FISCHER

DEPARTMENT OF PHARMACOLOGY
UNIVERSITY OF TORONTO, CANADA
LABORATORIES OF GENERAL BIOCHEMISTRY AND GENERAL PHYSIOLOGY
UNIVERSITY OF CHILE, SANTIAGO

A. Introduction

It is well recognized that one of the first steps toward an understanding of the problems underlying CNS tolerance to and dependence on alcohol should be the study of its basic mechanisms of action on nerve cells. This chapter describes the acute effects of alcohol on several cell functions related to excitability and electrogenesis.

Ethanol is classified as a general depressant. Among other compounds in this category are the higher alcohols, the volatile general anesthetics, and the inert gases. One property shared by these compounds is that of being lipid-soluble. The early studies of Overton [84] and Meyer and Hemmi

[77] show that the potencies of the different general depressants in vivo correlate well with their ability to dissolve in a lipid phase. These authors proposed that equal degrees of narcosis are obtained when equal concentrations of the general depressants are present in the lipid phase of the biological system. It has also been proposed that equal degrees of narcosis occur when an equal volume fraction of the cell membrane is occupied by the depressants [81]. Several studies have shown that there is a good correlation between the narcotic activity of the general depressants and the free energy of absorption of these compounds to a lipid phase [14, 28, 94].

Proteins have a lipophilic core in which the general depressants could also be solubilized, thus changing the molecular characteristics of the protein. In fact, several studies have shown that there is a good correlation between anesthetic properties and the ability of the depressants to bind to proteins and to alter their molecular structure [8, 95, 96].

Another property shared by most general depressants is their ability to increase the stability of microcrystals of hydrates so as to permit them to be formed at temperatures close to physiological temperatures [78, 86]. Pauling [86] suggests that the stability of these crystals may result from the van der Waals interaction between the entrapped molecules (depressants and side groups of proteins) and the water molecules of the framework, and also from the energy of the hydrogen bonds. These crystals may increase the rigidity of the protein molecules in the biological system. Cherkin [19] reviews the data for and against the lipid solubility and the microcrystal formation theories [24, 25].

Regardless of the type of mechanism responsible for the depressant effect, it is clear that ethanol should not be regarded as a special molecule. It is therefore important, when studying the possible mechanisms of action of alcohol on the nerve cell, to study at the same time the effect of other general depressants.

B.   Effects on Energy Metabolism

It is generally agreed that ethanol is not metabolized to a significant extent in the brain and that this tissue does not contain alcohol dehydrogenase activity [10, 65, 70, 87, 100, 105]. Work by Raskin and Sokoloff [88], using a very sensitive technique, nevertheless shows that the brain does contain an alcohol dehydrogenase but that its activity is markedly lower than that present in the liver. Since the depressant potency of the higher alcohols is much higher than that of ethanol—e.g., three orders of magnitude higher for n-octanol than for ethanol [14]—if a conversion of the alcohol to the homologous aldehyde were involved in the mechanism of depression, one would expect a marked dehydrogenase activity for the higher alcohols. Ferguson [29], however, using a histochemical technique, found no alcohol dehydrogenase activity for C_1–C_{13} normal alcohols in brain tissue. Furthermore since similar metabolic products are not to be expected from the large variety of general depressants, it is reasonable to assume that the acute effects of these compounds on that nervous system are due to direct interactions of the depressant molecules with the biological system. The problem in relation to tolerance to and dependence on alcohol might, however, be more complex (see Chapter III).

Studies by Battey et al. [9] in humans show that ethanol in concentrations of about 300 mg/100 ml of blood significantly reduces the brain oxygen consumption by about 30%. Subsequent studies by Wolpert et al. [108], Beer and Quastel [10], and De Gregorio et al. [22] show that ethanol in concentrations large enough to produce death if given in vivo does not modify the P/O ratio or the respiration of isolated brain mitochondria. Furthermore Wallgren and Kulonen [105] report that 0.4% ethanol does not inhibit the oxygen consumption by unstimulated rat brain cortex slices; rather a small activation was found. However, the respiration of the tissue is increased ("stimulated respiration") by electrical pulses [75] or depolarizing concentrations of KCl [5], ethanol in concentrations greater than 0.2% significantly inhibits the stimulated respiration [10, 31, 34, 71, 105]. Larrabe et al. [69] report that ethanol and several other general depressants inhibit the extra (stimulated) oxygen consumption in the superior cervical sympathetic ganglia in concentrations that do not affect the basal oxygen consumption. Similarly Matteo et al. [74] report that cyclopropane and diethyl ether inhibit the potassium-stimulated respiration of rat brain slices in concentrations that either increase or have no effect on the basal respiratory rate.

Studies by Machrowicz [72, 73] show that ethanol and the higher alcohols inhibit the utilization of glucose in KCl-stimulated brain cortex slices. In agreement with these data are the recent observations by Roach [89] that ethanol in small doses (2.5 g/kg) markedly inhibits the utilization of glucose in the brain of the hamster in vivo. The brain of animals sacrificed after the administration of ^{14}C glucose plus alcohol showed a 300% increase in the content of unchanged ^{14}C glucose with respect to control animals in which alcohol was not injected. Concomitantly ethanol inhibits the conversion of the carbon skeleton of glucose into glutamate, aspartate, glutamine, and γ-aminobutyric acid, thus suggesting an inhibition of the Krebs cycle turnover [89].

The processes leading to an increased oxygen and glucose consumption in the stimulated nerve cell can be summarized as follows:

1. A certain degree of depolarization produces changes in the nerve cell membrane that lead to the production of an action potential: sodium ions enter into the cell and potassium ions leak out [45, 49].

2. This is followed by an increased active transport of Na^+ and K^+ with a concomitant hydrolysis of ATP [20, 65, 76].

3. Thus, the availability of ADP to the mitochondria is increased and consequently (a) the oxygen consumption is increased. It is also to be expected that the oxidation of reducing equivalents provided by glucose and the Krebs cycle intermediates may increase, thus (b) increasing glucose utilization and Krebs cycle turnover [6]. (c) At the same time the steady-state level of creatine phosphate, a compound in equilibrium with ATP $(CrP + ADP \rightleftarrows ATP + Cr)$, is reduced [43, 104].

Wallgren [104] reported that 0.4% ethanol reduces by 50% the rate of creatine phosphate breakdown induced by electrical pulses in rat brain cortex slices (see Figure 1). In the absence of electrical stimulation ethanol

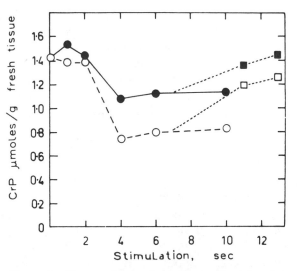

Figure 1. Changes in the level of creatine phosphate in rat cerebral cortex slices during and after brief periods of stimulation. Open circles, controls; black circles, 0.4% (87 mM) added. Dotted lines indicate resynthesis after termination of pulses at 7 seconds. From Wallgren [104]. (Courtesy of Pergamon Press and the author.)

did not alter the steady-state levels of creatine phosphate, ATP, ADP, or AMP. In vivo studies by Ammon et al. [3] show that ethanol increases the brain levels of ATP and creatine phosphate and reduces those of ADP.

The data accumulated with brain slices, isolated mitochondria, and experiments in vivo suggest that ethanol does not interfere with the synthesis of "high-energy" phosphates but that it inhibits their utilization. The effects of ethanol are thus probably exerted on the molecular processes that lead to the action potential or on the subsequent active transport of Na^+ and K^+.

C. Effects on Action Potential

Using the voltage-clamp technique, Moore et al. [79] and Armstrong and Binstock [4] showed that ethanol inhibits the action potential in the squid axon. The former report that 3% ethanol inhibits the maximum conductances for both Na^+ and K^+ by about 15 to 20%. The latter find that at these concentrations ethanol inhibits mainly the sodium conductance, and they report that 2.35% ethanol decreases the amplitude of the action potential by about 40%. Moore et al. [79], on the other hand, showed that 3.6% ethanol decreased the amplitude by only 5%. Rosenberg and Podleski [91] report that 3% ethanol has no effect on the amplitude of the action potential in the intact squid axon. We have confirmed these results in internally perfused squid giant axons (*Dosidicus gigas*). Ethanol added to either the perfusion fluid or the external solution to a final concentration of 2% has no effect on the amplitude of the action potential; 4% ethanol reduces the amplitude by about 10% when applied externally but produces no demonstrable effects when added to the perfusion fluid (see Figure 2). Thus the concentrations of ethanol necessary to inhibit the action potential in the squid axon are about one order of magnitude larger than those which produce marked effects on stimulated mammalian brain tissue. This may, nevertheless, reflect a species difference in sensitivity to alcohol. Gimeno et al. [35] report that 0.45% ethanol has no effect on several parameters of the action potential in the isolated rat heart atria. The only significant effect was a 10% reduction in spike duration, resulting from an increase in the rate of repolarization. Data by Houck [46] indicate that ethanol concentrations of about 5% are necessary to reduce by about 10% the amplitude of the action potential in the isolated lobster giant axon. In this system, however, ethanol inhibited rather than stimulated the rate or repolarization.

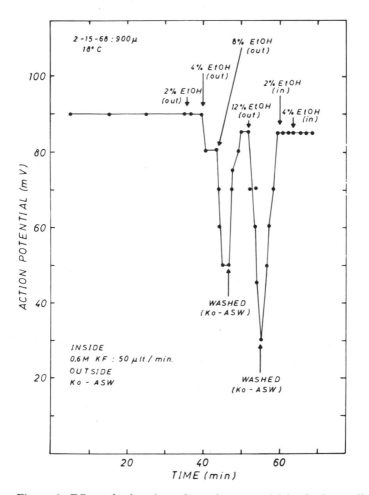

Figure 2. Effect of ethanol on the action potential in the internally perfused squid axon (Dosidicus gigas). The perfusion technique employed was that of Tasaki and Luxoro [98]. The internal perfusion fluid was 0.6 M KF and the flow of perfusion was 50 μlt/min. The external fluid was K⁺-free artificial seawater. Ethanol was added either to the internal or to the external fluids to the concentration desired.

D.   Effects on Active Transport of Na⁺ and K⁺ and (Na + K) ATPase

1.   Active Ion Transport

Ethanol in concentrations that are relevant to in vivo studies in mammals has been shown to inhibit the active transport of Na^+ and K^+ in several systems, including the mammalian brain. Streeten and Solomon [97] reported that 0.3% ethanol inhibits by about 20% the active transport of K^+ in red cells, without affecting the passive permeability to this ion. Israel and Kalant [53] have shown that ethanol inhibits the active transport of Na^+ in frog skin at concentrations as low as 0.1%. At 0.4% ethanol the inhibition was about 20%. The active transport of K^+ in rat brain seems to be more sensitive to alcohol. Ethanol at a concentration of 0.5% inhibits by 60 to 80% the initial rate of K^+ accumulation by rat brain cortex slices that have been depleted of K^+ [55] (see Figure 3). This effect was antagonized

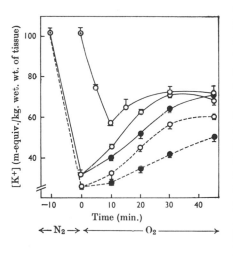

Figure 3. Effect of ethanol on K^+ content of rat brain-cortex slices incubated in modified Krebs-Ringer bicarbonate media. Anaerobic preincubation, where used, took place between −10 and 0 min.; aerobic incubation between 0 and 45 min. Continuous lines indicate the effect of incubation in a medium containing 6 mM K^+; broken lines indicate effects in 3.6 mM K^+. Mean initial value for unincubated samples: ⊙, slices incubated without ethanol; ○, slices incubated in the presence of 0.5% ethanol (108 mM), added at zero time; ●, vertical bars represent the standard deviation. From Israel et al. [55]. (Courtesy of The Biochemical Journal).

by K^+ in the incubation medium; if the concentration of K^+ is increased to about twice that normally present in the cerebrospinal fluid, the inhibitory effect of 0.5% ethanol is reduced to 30 to 40% [55]. (It is now believed that the composition of the cerebrospinal fluid corresponds to that of the brain extracellular compartment; see Tower [99] for general references.)

Since ethanol inhibits the action potential in the squid giant axon at rather high concentrations (see Figure 2), we felt that it would be important to know to what extent do these concentrations of ethanol inhibit the active transport of Na^+ or K^+ in the same preparation. To elucidate this problem, Na^{22} was microinjected into the squid giant axon, and the rate of efflux of the isotope was measured simultaneously with the action potential. Ethanol at a concentration that does not affect the amplitude of the action potential (3%) inhibits by about 30% the efflux of Na^{22} into the artificial sea water (10 mM K^+) bathing the axon. In the same

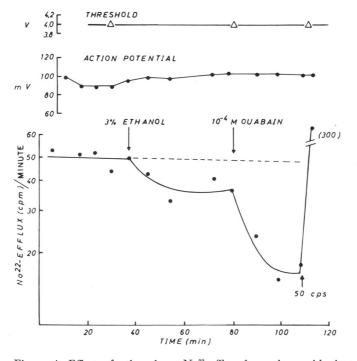

Figure 4. Effect of ethanol on Na^{22} efflux from the squid giant axon (Dosidicus gigas). Na^{22} was microinjected as described by Brady et al. [13]. The axon was bathed in artificial sea water (A.S.W.): 420 mM NaCl, 10 mK KCl, 10 mM $CaCl_2$, 50 mM $MgCl_2$, 5 mM Tris-Cl (pH 8.0). Action potentials were externally elicited with a S-4 Grass stimulator. Ethanol and ouabain were added to the A.S.W. to final concentrations of 3% (w/v) and 10^{-4} M respectively. The active transport properties of this system have been previously described by Cannesa-Fischer et al. [16].

system, ouabain 10^{-4} M produces a marked inhibition of Na^{22} efflux (see Figure 4). Baker and coworkers [7] report that ethanol in concentrations as low as 0.8% wt/v inhibits the efflux of Na^{22} from the squid giant axon. Unfortunately no actual data were given. Isobutanol 0.45% was found to inhibit the active (ouabain-sensitive) efflux of Na^{22} by about 80% [7].

Other general depressants, such as nitrous oxide [38] and cyclopropane [2] have also been shown to have a direct inhibitory effect on the active transport of sodium in frog skin and toad bladder respectively. It has been reported that ether and chloroform seem to have no effect on the active transport of Na^+ in red cells, unless lytic concentrations are used [40]. Unfortunately steady-state concentrations of Na^+ rather than actual Na^+ transport were measured, and thus the interpretation of this data is uncertain. Ethanol has been shown to inhibit the active (net) accumulation of K^+ in brain slices but not to change the intracellular steady-state concentration of this ion [55].

Data by Bennett and Hayward [11] suggest that an inhibition in the active ion transport might be involved in the production of high-pressure gas anesthesia in vivo. These authors report a reduction in the concentration of Na^+ in the cerebrospinal fluid of cats under argon or nitrogen anesthesia. Studies by Kalant et al. [63] show that ethanol produces an increase in intracellular Na^+ and a reduction in intracellular K^+ in most tissues of the rat, thus in agreement with an inhibitory effect of ethanol on the active transport of Na^+ and K^+.

Data by Chang et al. [17] and Israel et al. [58, 59] show that the active transport of amino acids, a process known to depend on the active transport of Na^+, is inhibited by ethanol. Concentrations of about 0.5% inhibit the active accumulation of L-phenylalanine in the everted rat intestine by about 60% [58].

2.   (Na + K) ATPase

A membrane-bound (Na + K)-activated ATPase is now believed to represent the carrier system in the active translocation of Na^+ and K^+ across the cell membrane (see Albers [1], Whittam and Wheeler [107], for general references). The enzyme is active only when both Na^+ and K^+ in addition to Mg^{++} are present in the incubation medium. The proposed mechanism for the (Na + K) ATPase involves the formation of a phosphorylated intermediate (E-P). Na^+ ions are necessary for the formation of the E-P compound; K^+ ions promote its hydrolysis, thus liberating inorganic phosphate. Ethanol in concentrations above 0.1 to 0.25% has been shown to inhibit the brain $(Na + K)$ ATPase [23, 54, 60]. The inhibitory effect of ethanol is antagonized by K^+, enhanced by Na^+ [54, 57], and it is of the uncompetitive type with respect to ATP [52]. These data suggest that ethanol interacts with the enzyme when it is in the E-P form. This is in agreement with data by Charnock and Opit [18], who have found that ethanol does not inhibit the formation of the E-P compound but prevents its hydrolysis. It is conceivable that when the enzyme is in the E-P form, lipophilic sites are exposed to which ethanol and other depressants could bind. These compounds might also displace phosphatidylserine, a phospholipid necessary for the ATPase activity [27, 51, 106].

Since the effect of alcohol on K^+ transport in brain slices, as well as on the $(Na + K)$ ATPase, is antagonized by K^+, the concentration of this ion present in the assay medium becomes very important. One percent ethanol inhibits the rat brain $(Na + K)$ ATPase by about 50% [54] when 2 mM K^+ is used. This concentration of ethanol is two to three times higher than that necessary to inhibit to about the same extent the active accumulation of K^+ in brain slices incubated in a medium containing 3.6 mM K^+ [55]. It seems, however, that when brain slices are used, the concentration of K^+ that reaches the sites for K^+ transport is only one-eighth to one-ninth of that in the extracellular medium, probably because of permeability barriers [55]. Thus the use of a K^+ concentration of about 0.4 to 0.5 mM for the ATPase assay might be more relevant to the work with brain slices (incubated in 3 to 3.6 mM K^+) and probably also to the in vivo situation.

Data by Ueda and Mietani [102], Trevor and Cummins [101], and Dahl [22] show that general depressants, such as diethyl ether, halothane, cyclopropane, and the short-chain fatty acids, also inhibit the brain $(Na + K)$ ATPase. The concentrations found necessary to produce significant inhibitions on the ATPase were about 10 times higher than those necessary to produce anesthesia in vivo. Unfortunately the concentrations of K^+ used for the ATPase assays were of about 10 to 20 mM. Using 4 mM K^+, Israel and Salazar [57] find that there is a good correlation between the concentrations of several general depressants necessary to inhibit the brain $(Na + K)$ ATPase and those which produce narcosis in vivo in tadpoles.

Data by Israel et al. [56] show that in rats the active ion transport and the $(Na + K)$ ATPase activity of brain tissue increase after the chronic administration of alcohol to the animals. These changes might constitute the basis for the acquired tolerance to alcohol (see Chapter IX).

E. Effects on Nerve Resting Potential

Several investigators have reported that ethanol in concentrations of 0.5% and higher has a depolarizing effect on the sciatic nerve, the sartorius muscle of the frog, and the tibial nerve of the rabbit [33, 66, 67, 85, 109]. Similar results have been reported for the squid [4] and the lobster [46] giant axons. Since it is known that the resting potential is a function of the concentration of K^+ in the cell—$V = (RT/F) \ln K^+_{in}/K^+_{out}$—a reduction in the intracellular concentration of this ion caused by an inhibition on the active transport of K^+ should lead to a depolarization. Houck [46] reports that the concentrations of ethanol necessary to produce noticeable changes in the resting potential of the lobster giant axon are higher than those necessary to produce changes in the action potential. Similar observations are reported by Inoue and Frank [50] for the frog sartorius muscle. This is, however, to be expected in a nerve or muscle having a small relation of membrane surface to nerve or muscle volume, since a marked inhibitory effect on active transport should occur before any significant change in the intracellular concentration of K^+ occurs. The problem seems to be more complex, however. In the squid axon, n-octanol, a powerful inhibitor of the $(Na + K)$ ATPase [57], has a hyperpolarizing effect [4]. It has also been reported that in the frog sciatic nerve the short-chain alcohols—methanol, ethanol, and propanol—have depolarizing effects and that the higher alcohols—pentanol to octanol—have hyperpolarizing effects [85]. Hurwitz et al. [47, 48] show that ethanol in concentrations of about 5% increases the passive efflux of K^+ in unexcited guinea-pig smooth muscle. If the efflux of K^+ promoted by ethanol were not accompanied by the efflux of an intracellular anion, one could expect a hyperpolarization of the membrane. It is not known, however, if this effect increases with an increase in chain length.

Another aspect that might also be involved in the depolarizing effects of ethanol is an increased permeability to Na^+ ions. Based on the observation that the depolarizing effect of ethanol in frog muscle fibers is markedly reduced when the fibers are incubated in a Na^+ free medium, Knutsson and Katz [67] suggest that the alcohol-induced depolarization is due to an increased influx of Na^+ into the fibers.

It seems, therefore, that the depolarizing effect of ethanol is due to a combination of several factors. It should be mentioned that in most of the studies in which the effects of alcohol on membrane resting potential have been investigated the concentrations of ethanol that had to be used to produce measurable changes were several times higher than those necessary to produce depression in vivo. This suggests that the thick peripheral nerves or the muscle fibers in the absence of repetitive electrical stimulation may not be adequate models for the study of the effects of ethanol on membrane resting potential or conversely that at low concentrations of ethanol no changes occur.

F.   Effects on Neurotransmitter Function and Metabolism

The reader is referred to Chapter III for the effects of alcohol on neuro-amine function and metabolism.

1.   Acetylcholine

Ethanol as well as higher alcohols has been shown to potentiate the effect of acetylcholine on frog rectus muscle [26, 82, 92, 93]. Ethanol in concentrations in the range of 1% increases the acetylcholine-induced muscle contraction by about 100%. This effect is also seen in eserinized preparations, thus suggesting that the effect is not due to an inhibition of acetylcholinesterase activity. This is in line with the findings that ethanol at these concentrations has no effect on acetylcholinesterase activity [62]. Using the longitudinal smooth muscle from guinea-pig ileum, Hurwitz et al. [47, 48] nevertheless report that 0.9% ethanol has no demonstrable effect on the acetylcholine-induced contraction but that higher concentrations are inhibitory.

Studies by Gage [32], Okada [83], and Inoue and Frank [50], using the isolated phrenic nerve diaphragm of the rat and the frog sartorius neuromuscular junction, show that ethanol potentiates the neuromuscular transmission both at the pre- and postsynaptic levels. Gage [32] reports that ethanol in concentrations as low as 0.037% has a demonstrable effect in increasing the quantal content of end-plate potentials without modifying the miniature end-plate potential (mepp) amplitude, thus suggesting a presynaptic effect of alcohol. At higher concentrations pre- and postsynaptic effects are seen. The presynaptic effects are, however, more marked [83]; 1% ethanol increases the mepp amplitude by 30% while increasing the mepp frequency by 200%. Larrabee and Posternak [68] report that ethanol (1 to 2%) facilitates synaptic transmission in the stellate ganglion of the cat. Since several factors, including an inhibition of the active transport of Na^+ and K^+ [12], are known to produce facilitation, it is not known whether this effect of ethanol is similar in mechanism to that in the neuromuscular junction. Data by Inoue and Frank indicate that the effects of ethanol on neuromuscular transmission cannot be extended to other general depressants. Ethyl ether was found to depress the amplitude of the end-plate potential [50]. Furthermore the effects of ether could be overcome in part by the subsequent addition of alcohol to the system. Okada [83] also reports that ether and chloroform do not increase the frequency or the amplitude of the mepp. Similarly Gissen et al. [36] report that halothane inhibits the amphibian neuromuscular junction pre- and postsynaptically. These results argue against a general mechanism of action for the general depressants involving cholinergic synaptic transmission.

Studies by Kalant et al. [61, 62] show that 0.5% ethanol reduces by 20 to 30% the spontaneous liberation of acetylcholine from nonstimulated rat and guinea-pig brain cortex slices. In nonstimulated slices the liberation of acetylcholine would conceivably correspond to the quantal liberation that is normally responsible for the production of mepp's. Furthermore data by Brossard and Quastel [15] show that 0.9% ethanol inhibits by about 35% the acetylcholine-stimulated incorporation of P^{32} into phospholipids in rat brain cortex slices. These studies suggest that in the brain ethanol inhibits, rather than stimulates, the acetylcholine synapse both at the pre- and postsynaptic level.

2.   Gamma-Aminobutyric Acid

Gamma-aminobutyric acid (GABA) is believed to be a negative feedback transmitter in the central nervous system as well as an intermediate in the normal metabolic pathways of the brain [90]. Therefore changes in GABA levels may reflect changes at the synaptic level as well as general metabolic changes.

Early studies by Hakkinen and Kulonen [41] show a 34% increase in the content of GABA in the brain of alcohol-intoxicated rats (4.3 g/kg of ethanol). This was confirmed by Mouton et al. [80], who found a 46% increase in GABA content in the brain of mice that have received 5 g/kg of ethanol. Several workers have nevertheless reported that alcohol has no effect on GABA levels or that it produces a small but not significant reduction [30, 39, 44]. In subsequent studies Hakkinen and Kulonen [42] reported that ethanol increases the GABA content of rat brain only if the animals are previously fasted. Using fasted hamsters, Roach [89] found that ethanol produces no significant effects on brain GABA levels. Gordon [37] studied the effects of ethanol in different areas of the brain in rats, apparently without a prior fasting period. Ethanol (4.3 g/kg) was found to produce a small reduction in the GABA content of cerebral hemispheres while lowering that in the cerebellum by about 60%. Further work at the cellular level is, however, necessary to determine if this effect is a reflection of changes in the general metabolic rate in the tissue or if the changes found are primarily changes at the synaptic level.

GENERAL CONCLUSIONS

The most marked effects of ethanol in the nerve cell seem to be exerted on the cell membrane on the action potential and on the active transport of Na^+ and K^+. Although ethanol at very low concentrations has activatory effects in the neuromuscular junction, these seem not to occur in the CNS. Further studies should be carried out to determine to what extent are the inhibitory effects produced on the action potential and on the active transport of Na^+ and K^+ responsible for the in vivo effects of ethanol as a depressant.

ACKNOWLEDGMENTS

We wish to thank the Foundations' Fund for Research in Psychiatry (United States), the Addiction Research Foundation (Ontario, Canada), and the United States Air Force (DAHC-19-68-6-0018) for their financial support.

REFERENCES

1. Albers, R. W., Biochemical aspects of active transport, *Ann. Rev. Biochem.*, **36,** 727 (1967).
2. Andersen, N. G., Synergistic effect of cyclopropane and epinephrine on sodium transport in toad bladder, *Anesthesiology*, **28,** 438 (1967).
3. Ammon, H. P. T., C. J. Estler, and F. Heim, Der Einfluss von Äthylalkohol auf den Kohlenhydrat und Energiestoffwechsel des gehirns wiesser Mause, *Arch. Int. Pharmacodyn.*, **154,** 108 (1965).
4. Armstrong, C. M. and L. Binstock, The effects of several alcohols on the properties of the squid giant axon, *J. Gen. Physiol.*, **48,** 265 (1964).
5. Ashford, C. A. and K. C. Dixon, The effect of potassium on the glucolysis of brain tissue with reference to the Pasteur effect, *Biochem. J.*, **29,** 157 (1935).
6. Atkinson, D. E., Regulation of enzyme activity, *Ann. Rev. Biochem.*, **35,** 85 (1966).

7. Baker, P. F., M. P. Blaustein, R. D. Keynes, J. Manil, T. I. Shaw, and R. A. Steinhardt, The ouabain-sensitive fluxes of sodium and potassium in squid giant axons, *J. Physiol.,* **200,** 459 (1969).

8. Balasubramanian, D. and D. B. Wetlaufer, Reversible alteration of the structure of globular proteins by anesthetic agents, *Proc. Nat. Acad. Sci. (U.S.),* **55,** 762 (1966).

9. Battey, L. L., A. Heyman, and J. L. Patterson Jr., Effects of ethyl alcohol on cerebral blood flow and metabolism, *J. Amer. Med. Ass.,* **152,** 6 (1953).

10. Beer, C. T. and J. H. Quastel, The effects of aliphatic alcohols on the respiration of rat brain cortex slices and rat brain mitochondria, *Canad. J. Biochem.,* **36,** 543 (1958).

11. Bennett, P. B. and A. J. Hayward, Electrolyte imbalance as the mechanism for inert gas narcosis and anesthesia, *Nature,* **213,** 938 (1967).

12. Bowman, W. C., M. J. Rand, and G. B. West, *Textbook of Pharmacology,* 2d ed., p. 700, Blackwell Scientific Publications, Oxford, 1969.

13. Brady, R. O., C. S. Spyropoulos, and I. Tasaki, Intraaxonal injections of biologically active materials, *Am. J. Physiol.,* **194,** 207 (1958).

14. Brink, F. and J. M. Posternak, Thermodynamic analysis of relative effectiveness of narcotics, *J. Cell Comp. Physiol.,* **32,** 211 (1948).

15. Brossard, M. and J. H. Quastel, Studies of the cationic and acetylcholine stimulation of phosphate incorporation into phospholipids in rat brain cortex in vitro, *Can. J. Biochem. Physiol.,* **41,** 1243 (1963).

16. Canessa-Fischer, M., F. Zambrano, and E. Rojas, The loss and recovery of the sodium pump in perfused giant axons, *J. Gen. Physiol.,* **51,** 162s (1968).

17. Chang, T., J. Lewis, and A. J. Glazko, Effect of ethanol and other alcohols on the transport of amino acids and glucose by everted sacs of rat small intestine, *Biochim. Biophys. Acta,* **135,** 1000 (1967).

18. Charnock, J. S. and L. J. Opit, personal communication.

19. Cherkin, A., Mechanisms of general anesthesia by nonhydrogen-bonding molecules, *Ann. Rev. Pharmacol.,* **9,** 259 (1969).

20. Cummins, J. T. and H. McIlwain, Electrical pulses and the potassium and other ions of isolated cerebral tissues, *Biochem. J.,* **79,** 330 (1961).

21. Dahl, D. R., Short chain fatty acid inhibition of rat brain Na-K adenosine triphosphatase, *J. Neurochem.,* **15,** 815 (1968).

22. De Gregorio, G., N. E. Lofrumento, A. Alifano, M. L. Manno, C. Serra, and R. Logoluso, Effetto dell'alcool sulla respirazione dei mitocondri di cervello, *Boll. Soc. Ital. Biol. Sper.,* **41,** 425 (1965).

23. Desci, L. and R. Rodnight, The phosvitin kinase enzyme of cerebral microsomes, *J. Neurochem.,* **12,** 791 (1965).

24. Eger, E. I., C. Lundgreen, S. L. Miller, and W. C. Stevens, Anesthetic potencies of sulphur hexafluoride, carbon tetrafluoride, chloroform and ethrane in dogs, *Anesthesiol.,* **30,** 129 (1969).

25. Eger, E. I. and R. O. Shargel, The lack of hydrate formation at a temperature of 0°C of methoxyflurane, halothane, diethyl ether and fluroxene, *Anesthesiol.,* **30,** 136 (1969).

26. Ettinger, G. H., A. B. Brown, and A. H. Megill, Potentiation of acetylcholine by alcohol and ether, *J. Pharmacol.*, **73**, 119 (1941).
27. Fenster, L. J. and J. H. Copenhaver, Phosphatidylserine requirements of (Na + K)-activated ATPase from rat kidney and brain, *Biochem. Biophys. Acta*, **137**, 406 (1967).
28. Ferguson, J., The use of chemical potentials as indices of toxicity, *Proc. R. Soc.*, **127**, 387 (1939).
29. Ferguson, M. M., Observations on the histochemical distribution of alcohol dehydrogenase, *Quart. J. Microscop. Sci.*, **106**, 289 (1965).
30. Ferrari, R. A. and A. Arnold, The effect of central nervous system agents on rat-brain γ-aminobutyric acid level, *Biochim. Biophys. Acta,* **52**, 361 (1961).
31. Fischer, E., The Counteraction of Weak Concentrations of Acid on the Depressing Effect of Alcohol on the Oxygen Consumption of Brain Slices, in H. E. Himwich (ed.), *Alcoholism: basic aspects and treatment*, 19, American Association for the Advancement of Science Publ. 47, Washington, D.C., 1957.
32. Gage, P. W., The effect of methyl, ethyl and *n*-propyl alcohol on neuromuscular transmission in the rat, *J. Pharmacol.*, **150**, 236 (1965).
33. Gallego, A., On the effect of ethyl alcohol upon frog nerve, *J. Cell. Comp. Physiol.*, **31**, 97 (1948).
34. Ghosh, J. J. and J. H. Quastel, Narcotics and brain respiration, *Nature, Lond.,* **174**, 28 (1954).
35. Gimeno, A. L., M. F. Gimeno, and J. L. Webb, The effects of ethanol on cellular membrane potentials and contractility of isolated rat atrium, *Amer J. Physiol.*, **203**, 194 (1959).
36. Gissen, A. J., J. H. Karis, and W. L. Nastuk, The effect of halothane on neuromuscular transmission, *Anesthesiology,* **28**, 252 (1967).
37. Gordon, E. R., The effect of ethanol on the concentration of gamma-aminobutyric acid in the rat brain, *Canad. J. Physiol. Pharmacol.*, **45**, 915 (1967).
38. Gottlieb, S. F. and S. V. Savran, Nitrous oxide inhibition of sodium transport, *Anesthesiology,* **28**, 324 (1967).
39. Hagen, D. Q., GABA levels in rat brain after prolonged ethanol intake, *Quart. J. Stud. Alcohol,* **28**, 613 (1967).
40. Halsey, M. J., E. B. Smith, and T. E. Wool, Effects of general anaesthetics on Na^+ transport in human red cells, *Nature,* **225**, 1151 (1970).
41. Häkkinen, H. M. and E. Kulonen, Increase in the γ-aminobutyric acid content of rat brain after ingestion of ethanol, *Nature, Lond.*, **182**, 726 (1959).
42. Häkkinen, H. M. and E. Kulonen, Comparison of various methods for the determination of γ-aminobutyric acid and other amino acids in rat brain with reference to ethanol ingestion, *J. Neurochem.*, **10**, 489 (1963).
43. Heald, P. J., Rapid changes in creatine phosphate level in cerebral cortex slices, *Biochem. J.,* **57**, 673 (1954).
44. Higgins, E. S., The effects of ethanol on GABA content of rat brain, *Biochem. Pharmacol.*, **11**, 394 (1962).
45. Hodgkin, A. L., The ionic basis of nervous conduction, *Science,* **145**, 1148 (1964).

46. Houck, D. J., Effect of alcohols on potentials of lobster axons, *Am. J. Physiol.,* **216,** 364 (1969).

47. Hurwitz, L., F. Battle, and G. B. Weiss, Action of calcium, cocaine and ethanol on contraction and potassium efflux of smooth muscle, *J. Gen. Physiol.,* **46,** 315 (1962).

48. Hurwitz, L., S. Von Hagen, and J. D. Joiner, Acetylcholine and calcium on membrane permeability and contraction of intestinal smooth muscle, *J. Gen. Physiol.,* **50,** 1157 (1967).

49. Huxley, A. F., Excitation and conduction in nerve: Quantitative analysis, *Science,* **145,** 1154 (1964).

50. Inoue, F. and G. B. Frank, Effects of ethyl alcohol on excitability and on neuromuscular transmission in frog skeletal muscle, *Brit. J. Pharmacol.,* **30,** 186 (1967).

51. Israel, Y., Phospholipid Activation of $(Na^+ + K^+)$-ATPase, in *The Molecular Basis of Membrane Function,* D. C. Tosteson (ed.), Prentice-Hall, Englewood Cliffs, N.J., 1969.

52. Israel, Y., G. Colombo, and S. Hein, to be published.

53. Israel, Y. and H. Kalant, Effect of ethanol on the transport of sodium in frog skin, *Nature, Lond.,* **200,** 476 (1963).

54. Israel, Y., H. Kalant, and I. Laufer, Effects of ethanol on Na, K, Mg-stimulated microsomal ATPase activity, *Biochem. Pharmacol.,* **14,** 1803 (1965).

55. Israel, Y., H. Kalant, and E. Le Blanc, Effects of lower alcohols on potassium transport and microsomal adenosine triphosphatase activity of the rat cerebral cortex, *Biochem. J.,* **100,** 27 (1966).

56. Israel, Y., H. Kalant, E. Le Blanc, J. C. Bernstein, and I. Salazar, Changes in cation transport and $(Na + K)$-activated-adenosine triphosphatase produced by chronic administration of ethanol, *J. Pharmacol. Expt. Therap.,* **174,** 330 (1970).

57. Israel, Y. and I. Salazar, Inhibition of brain microsomal adenosine triphosphatases by general depressants, *Arch. Biochem. Biophys.,* **122,** 310 (1967).

58. Israel, Y., I. Salazar, and E. Rosenmann, Inhibitory effects of alcohol on intestinal amino acid transport in vivo and in vitro, *J. Nutr.,* **96,** 499 (1968).

59. Israel, Y., J. E. Valenzuela, I. Salazar, and G. Ugarte, Alcohol and amino acid transport in the human small intestine, *J. Nutr.,* **98,** 222 (1969).

60. Jarnefelt, J., A possible mechanism of action of ethyl alcohol on the central nervous system, *Ann. Med. Exp. Fenn.,* **39,** 267 (1961).

61. Kalant, H. and W. Grose, Effects of ethanol and pentobarbital on release of acetylcholine from cerebral cortex slices, *J. Pharmacol.,* **158,** 386 (1967).

62. Kalant, H., Y. Israel, and M. A. Mahon, The effect of ethanol on acetylcholine synthesis, release, and degradation in brain, *Canad. J. Physiol. Pharmacol.,* **45,** 172 (1967).

63. Kalant, H., W. Mons, and M. A. Mahon, Acute effects of ethanol on tissue electrolytes in the rat, *Canad. J. Physiol. Pharmacol.,* **44,** 1 (1966).

64. Keesey, J. C. and H. Wallgren, Movements of radioactive sodium in cerebral-cortex slices in response to electrical stimulation, *Biochem. J.,* **95,** 301 (1965).

65. Kinard, F. W. and M. C. Hay, Effect of ethanol administration on brain and liver enzyme activities, *Amer. J. Physiol.,* **198,** 657 (1960).
66. Knutsson, E., Effects of ethanol on the membrane potential and membrane resistance of frog muscle fibres, *Acta Physiol. Scand.,* **52,** 242 (1961).
67. Knutsson, E. and S. Katz, The effect of ethanol on membrane permeability to sodium and potassium ions in frog muscle fibres, *Acta Pharm. Tox., Kbh.,* **25,** 54 (1967).
68. Larrabee, M. G. and J. M. Posternak, Selective action of anesthetics on synapses and axons in mammalian sympathetic ganglia, *J. Neurophysiol.,* **15,** 91 (1952).
69. Larrabee, M. G., J. G. Ramos, and E. Bulbring, Do anesthetics depress nerve cells by depressing oxygen consumption? *Fed. Proc. (Pt. 1),* **9,** 75 (1950).
70. Leloir, L. F. and J. M. Muñoz, Ethyl alcohol metabolism in animal tissues, *Biochem. J.,* **32,** 299 (1938).
71. Lindbohm, R. and H. Wallgren, Changes in respiration of rat brain cortex slices induced by some aliphatic alcohols, *Acta Pharm. Tox., Kbh.,* **19,** 53 (1962).
72. Machrowicz, E., The effect of aliphatic alcohols and corresponding aldehydes on glucose metabolism in rat brain cortex slices, *Federation Proc.,* **21,** 359 (1962).
73. Machrowicz, E., Effects of aliphatic alcohols and aldehydes on the metabolism of potassium-stimulated rat brain cortex slices, *Can. J. Biochem.,* **43,** 1041 (1965).
74. Matteo, B. C., G. P. Hoech, and F. C. G. Hoskin, The effects of cyclopropane and diethyl ether on tissue oxygen consumption and anaerobic glycolysis of brain in vitro, *Anesthesiology,* **30,** 156 (1969).
75. McIlwain, H., Metabolic response in vitro to electrical stimulation of sections of mammalian brain, *Biochem. J.,* **49,** 382 (1951).
76. McIlwain, H., *Chemical Exploration of the Brain,* Elsevier, Amsterdam, 1963.
77. Meyer, K. H. and H. Hemmi, Beiträge zur Theorie der Narkose: III, *Biochem. Z.,* **277,** 39 (1935).
78. Miller, S. L., A theory of gaseous anesthetics, *Proc. Nat. Acad. Sci. (U.S.),* **47,** 1515 (1961).
79. Moore, J .W., W. Ulbricht, and M. Takata, Effect of ethanol on the sodium and potassium conductances of the squid axon membrane, *J. Gen. Physiol.,* **48,** 279 (1964).
80. Mouton, M., C. Lefornier-Contensou, and J. Chalopin, Incidence de l'intoxication alcoolique sur la teneur en acide γ-aminobutyrique du cerveau de la souris, *C.R. Acad. Sci., Paris,* **264,** 2649 (1967).
81. Mullins, L. J., Some physical mechanisms in narcosis, *Chem. Rev.,* **54,** 289 (1954).
82. Nelemans, F. A., The influence of various substances on the acetylcholine contracture of frog's isolated abdominal muscle, *Acta Physiol. Pharm. Néerl.,* **11,** 76 (1962).
83. Okada, K., Effects of alcohols and acetone on the neuromuscular junction of frog, *Jap. J. Physiol.,* **17,** 245 (1967).

84. Overton, E., *Studien über die Narkose: zugleich ein Beitrag zur allgemeinen Physiologie,* Fisher, Jena, 1901.

85. Pasternak, J. and R. Mangold, Action des narcotiques sur la conduction par les fibres nerveuses et sur leur potential de membrane, *Helv. physiol. Acta,* **7,** 55 (1949).

86. Pauling, L., A molecular theory of general anesthesia, *Science,* **134,** 15 (1961).

87. Räihä, N. C. R. and M. S. Koskinen, Effect of a nonionic surface active substance on the activation of alcohol dehydrogenase of rat liver homogenates, *Life Sci., Oxford,* **3,** 1091 (1964).

88. Raskin, N. H. and L. Sokoloff, Brain alcohol dehydrogenase, *Science,* **162,** 131 (1968).

89. Roach, M. K., The effect of ethanol on the synthesis of amino acids from glucose in hamster brain, *Life Sci.,* **9,** part 2, 437 (1970).

90. Roberts, E., The Synapse as a Biochemical Self-organizing Cybernetic Unit, in O. Walaas (ed.), *Molecular Basis of Some Aspects of Mental Activity,* vol. 1, p. 37, Academic, New York, 1966.

91. Rosenberg, P. and T. R. Podleski, Ability of venoms to render squid axons sensitive to curare and acetylcholine, *Biochim. Biophys. Acta,* **75,** 104 (1963).

92. Sachdev, K. S., M. H. Panjwani, and A. D. Joseph, Potentiation of the response to acetylcholine on the frog's rectus abdominis by ethyl alcohol, *Arch. Int. Pharmacodyn.,* **145,** 36 (1963).

93. Sachdev, K. S., P. K. Rana, K. C. Dave, and A. D. Joseph, A study of the mechanism of action of the potentiation by aliphatic alcohols of the acetylcholine response on the frog's rectus abdominis, *Arch. Int. Pharmacodyn.,* **152,** 408 (1964).

94. Schneider, H., The intramembrane location of alcohol anesthetics, *Biochim. Biophys. Acta,* **163,** 451 (1968).

95. Schoenborn, B. P., Binding of anesthetics to protein: An x-ray crystallographic investigation, *Fed. Proc.,* **27,** 888 (1968).

96. Schoenborn, B. P. and R. M. Featherstone, Molecular forces in anesthesia, *Advanced Pharmacol.,* **5,** 1 (1967).

97. Streeten, D. H. P. and A. K. Solomon, The effect of ACTH and adrenal steroids on K transport in human erythrocytes, *J. Gen. Physiol.,* **37,** 643 (1954).

98. Tasaki, I. and M. Luxoro, Intracellular perfusion of Chilean squid axons, *Science,* **145,** 1313 (1964).

99. Tower, D. B., Inorganic Constituents, in *Handbook of Neurochemistry,* A. Laytha, (ed.), vol. 1, p. 1, Plenum, New York, 1969.

100. Towne, J. C., Effect of ethanol and acetaldehyde on liver and brain monoamine oxidase, *Nature, Lond.,* **201,** 709 (1964).

101. Trevor, A. J. and J. T. Cummins, Properties of sodium- and potassium-activated adenosinetriphosphatases of rat brain: Effect of cyclopropane and other agents modifying enzyme activity, *Biochem. Pharmacol.,* **18,** 1157 (1969).

102. Ueda, I. and U. Mietani, Microsomal ATPase of rabbit brain and effects of general anesthetics, *Biochem. Pharmacol.,* **16,** 1370 (1967).

103. Vernon, H. M., The action of homologous alcohols and aldehydes on tortoise heart, *J. Physiol.*, **43**, 325 (1912).

104. Wallgren, H., Rapid changes in creatine and adenosine phosphates of cerebral cortex slices on electrical stimulation with special reference to the effect of ethanol, *J. Neurochem.*, **10**, 349 (1963).

105. Wallgren, H. and E. Kulonen, Effect of ethanol on respiration of rat-brain-cortex slices, *Biochem. J.*, **75**, 150 (1960).

106. Wheeler, K. P. and R. Whittam, The involvement of phosphatidylserine in adenosine triphosphatase activity of the sodium pump, *J. Physiol.*, **207**, 303 (1970).

107. Whittam, R. and K. P. Wheeler, Transport across cell membranes, *Ann. Rev. Physiol.*, **32**, 21 (1970).

108. Wolpert, A., E. B. Truitt, Jr., F. K. Bell, and J. C. Krantz, Jr., Anesthesia: 1. The effect of certain narcotics on oxidative phosphorylation, *J. Pharmacol.*, **117**, 358 (1956).

109. Wright, E. B., The effects of asphyxiation and narcosis on peripheral nerve polarization and conduction, *Amer. J. Physiol,* **148**, 174 (1947).

Chapter III

EFFECT OF ETHANOL ON NEUROAMINE METABOLISM

VIRGINIA EISCHEN DAVIS AND
MICHAEL J. WALSH

METABOLIC RESEARCH LABORATORY
VETERANS ADMINISTRATION HOSPITAL
HOUSTON, TEXAS

A. Introduction

Much is now known about the fate and the peripheral effects of alcohol in the body. Most important though, alcohol also dramatically affects the function of the central nervous system, as reflected by euphoria, loss of motor control, lability of mood, unconsciousness, and a severe psychological and physical dependence. However, although alcohol is probably the oldest drug known to man, the precise biochemical mechanisms by which ethanol induces these effects have not been elucidated. Because ethanol is a central nervous system depressant, it is reasonable to look for ethanol-induced effects on amine metabolism as a basis for understanding the neuropharmacological actions of this drug.

Relevant to a possible interrelation between the central actions of ethanol

73

and the biogenic amines is the observation that the peripheral administration of normally innocuous amounts of biogenic amines markedly potentiates the hypnotic and toxic effects of ethanol [84]. Since peripherally administered neuroamines do not pass the blood-brain barrier in significant amounts, it is difficult to explain these phenomena solely on the basis of increased levels of the intact amines within the central nervous system.

What may also be pertinent is the additional observation that the pharmacological action of a number of other sedative-hypnotic agents, such as chloral hydrate, paraldehyde, and the barbiturates, is potentiated by the administration of biogenic amines. Additionally a biochemical explanation has not been offered to explain the efficacy of these drugs in the treatment of alcohol withdrawal or for the observation that dependency on alcohol can be shifted to these drugs. Therefore it seems possible that a common biochemical denominator involving neuroamines may underlie the action of such drugs in producing dependency.

The following discussion deals with the known interactions of ethanol and the neuroamines, presents some recent findings, and finally integrates these studies into a hypothesis speculating on the possible involvement of catecholamines in alcoholism.

B. Neurotransmitter Release

The excretion of tryptamine is markedly enhanced by ethanol in both normal and alcoholic subjects [88]. Similar reports of an effect of ethanol on other biogenic amine stores have appeared. Westerfeld and Schulman [107] report a release of serotonin (5-hydroxytryptamine, 5-HT) by alcohol. These investigators demonstrated a 40% decrease in the 5-HT content of the intestine after ethanol ingestion.

The majority of findings, however, has been concerned with the actions of ethanol on the storage and release of catecholamines. The urinary excretion of epinephrine and norepinephrine (NE) increases markedly in acutely intoxicated dogs [60]. These workers find that ethanol lowers the adrenal content of epinephrine and, after adrenalectomy, elevates only NE excretion. Subsequently ethanol has been shown by many investigators to increase the release and excretion of these amines in man [1, 9, 40, 75, 76]. Masse et al. [70] demonstrated an augmented total catecholamine excretion in rats. Catecholamines were elevated in the urine from 1.56 to 2.71 μg per 24 hr when rats drank a 1% alcohol solution *ad libitum,* compared with controls that drank water. Similar studies by von Wartburg and Aebi [99] also show that acute alcohol administration to rats produces marked elevations in the excretion of epinephrine and NE. Interestingly, however, a single challenging dose of ethanol to rats previously treated with ethanol for 50 to 200 days produces only small increases in the excretion of these neuroamines. Therefore the response to a challenging dose of ethanol seems to be related to previous long-term ingestion, and there seems to be a tolerance developed to this response.

Quite naturally these findings led to studies in alcoholic patients. One report [73] illustrates significant increases in the excretion of NE, epinephrine, normetanephrine, and metanephrine during alcohol ingestion by alcoholics. From these studies it seems that no difference exists between normals and alcoholics as far as the effect that ethanol has on neuroamine release. In the latter study, however, subjects who experienced withdrawal symptoms after cessation of drinking continued to show enhanced catecholamine excretion; asymptomatic patients had significantly lower levels. Other investigators [16] also found increases in plasma NE at 13 to 24 hr after the last alcohol consumption in 36 male alcoholics. They suggest that some of the excitatory symptoms of abstinence may be related to an increased sympathetic activity.

The realization that the release of neuroamines by ethanol might well be due to a metabolite rather than alcohol itself led to investigations of the mechanisms involved. Consequently Perman [77] and later Akabane et al. [2] and Schneider [84] investigated the effect of acetaldehyde, the proximate metabolite of ethanol, on the release of catecholamines. Using perfused adrenal preparations, these workers are able to show that acetaldehyde intensifies the secretion of both epinephrine and NE from the medulla. Similarly acetaldehyde increases the rate of secretion of catecholamines from isolated chromaffin granules [89].

The releasing action of acetaldehyde has also been studied with other isolated systems. Using concentrations of acetaldehyde ranging from 100 to 800 μg/ml, Kumar and Sheth [64] demonstrated positive inotropic and chronotropic effects on isolated rabbit atria. These findings were confirmed *in situ* with coronary sinus perfusion in dogs [54]. Later these same investigators [53] comprehensively studied the structure-action relationships of aliphatic aldehydes on the heart. Acetaldehyde had the greatest intrinsic activity as an indirect-acting adrenergic aldehyde (amine-releasing activity).

The indirect action of acetaldehyde on NE stores was also studied with the isolated guinea pig left atria [101, 105]. Acetaldehyde induced changes in the contractile force and transmembrane potential configuration similar to that produced by NE and tyramine. Positive inotropic effects were induced by acetaldehyde at concentrations ranging from 0.3 to 10 mM. These concentrations simultaneously altered the cell membrane action potential by increasing the velocity of the rising phase and the total area of the potential. The action of acetaldehyde most closely resembles that of the indirect-acting sympathomimetic amine, tyramine, because of the latency of maximum inotropy produced, reserpine-pretreatment elimination of the effect, and inhibition of inotrophy by the β-blocking drug, propranolol.

Finally the greater intrinsic activity of acetaldehyde compared with ethanol in the whole animal has been demonstrated [103]. After the administration of NE-H^3 in cats and rabbits, acetaldehyde produced a much larger and more immediate release of the neuroamine into the plasma from nerve terminals than did ethanol. These data have led many investigators to conclude that the elevated urinary excretion of catecholamines after the administration of ethanol is not a direct action but is mediated by the active metabolite, acetaldehyde.

Central nervous system stores of biogenic amines have also been studied in regard to ethanol's activity and in general have led to a similar conclusion. Gursey et al. [43] and later Gursey and Olsen [42] declare that the intravenous administration of ethanol produces a significant reduction in brain-stem 5-HT and NE. They feel that ethanol's effect resembles reserpine in action, because they find that the reduction in central amine stores lasts several days. Other investigators, however, have not found any effect of ethanol on the brain content of the amines [14, 21, 29, 31, 44, 78].

Duritz and Truitt [29] suggest that this discrepancy may be because acetaldehyde is responsible for this effect. Injection of acetaldehyde was shown to lower brain-stem NE markedly but not to alter 5-HT content. Ethanol after the administration of disulfiram [29] or α-methyl-p-tyrosine [21], however, caused significant decreases in brain-stem NE. These data can be explained by the fact that both compounds inhibit NE synthesis at different stages; α-methyl-p-tyrosine inhibits tyrosine hydroxylase, and disulfiram inhibits dopamine-β-oxidase as well as aldehyde dehydrogenase. In the presence of these inhibitors, acetaldehyde derived from ethanol released the amine, which was detectable as a decrease in total content, because the resynthesis of the amine was limited. Two studies have also shown that ethanol does not alter the brain concentration of another biogenic amine, dopamine [21, 44]. In general the many findings concerning the release of NE from both central and peripheral stores of this amine are in agreement with the idea that acetaldehyde is an indirect-acting adrenergic aldehyde.

C. Alterations in Biogenic Amine Metabolism

Ethanol has been reported to produce a pronounced decrease in the endogenous output of 5-hydroxyindoleacetic acid (5-HIAA) [83, 84] and 3-

methoxy-4-hydroxymandelic acid (VMA) in the urine of man [24] and dogs [56]. Studies with C^{14}-labeled serotonin [22, 34, 35] and norepinephrine [23, 90] further demonstrated a decreased excretion of 5-HIAA and VMA after ethanol. This aberration in the oxidative pathways of these biogenic amines was accompanied by an increased excretion of labeled 5-hydroxy-tryptophol (5-HTOH) and endogenous or labeled 3-methoxy-4-hydroxy-phenylglycol (MHPG).

Similar alterations in the metabolism of 5-HT have been shown to occur in liver homogenates from alcohol-treated rats to which substrate was added [36], but could not be shown to occur in rat brain after intracaudate injection of 5-HT-C^{14} to ethanol-treated rats [98]. Studies with tissue slices showed no effect of ethanol on the formation of 5-HIAA or 5-HTOH with brain slices, but a marked change occurred in 5-HT metabolism when liver slices were used [30].

1. Serotonin

Studies in our laboratory with serotonin-C^{14} in man [22] have given some insight into the conflicting reports. In man under normal conditions, only 2.3% of the radioactivity in the urine represented 5-HTOH, but 5-HIAA constituted 82% of the C^{14} excreted (see Table I). When the subjects were given ethanol, this normally minor reductive pathway assumed major proportions. The conversion of 5-HT-C^{14} to 5-HTOH was markedly enhanced to 42% of the excreted C^{14}; the amount of radioactivity as 5-HIAA was reduced to half (42%).

These observations in man are in marked contrast to what occurs in the rat (see Table I). In this species ethanol caused a significant reduction in the formation of 5-HIAA from 42 to 37% ($p < 0.001$). Concomitantly there was an almost equivalent elevation in the 5-HTOH formed that rose from 13 to 19%. The most striking comparison that is evident from these data is that the response in humans to a change in serotonin metabolism evoked by ethanol is much more sensitive. The dose of ethanol in the rat was seven times that given to man, but the alteration in 5-HT metabolism in man was eight times that produced in the rat. This relatively meager effect in the rat parallels quite closely the marked insensitivity of the rat to the pharmacological and intoxicating effects of ethanol.

Similar studies in the brain of the intact rat have used intraventricular injections of 5-HT-C^{14}. Ethanol pretreatment failed to alter the proportion of the acid in the brain and increased the amount of 5-HTOH only moderately but significantly, from 1.99 to 2.68% [25].

TABLE I   Effect of Ethanol on the Metabolic Disposition of Various Neuroamines in Both Humans and the Rat

Species	Amine	Metabolites	Percentage of C^{14} excreted	
			Control	Ethanol[c]
Human	Serotonin[a]	5-HIAA	82.3	42.2[d]
	(5-HT-C^{14})	5-HTOH	2.3	41.6[d]
	Norepinephrine	VMA	52.1	28.6[d]
	(NE-C^{14})	MHPG	11.6	26.7[d]
	Endogenous NE[b]	VMA	60.8	35.0[d]
		MHPG	32.1	55.5[d]
Rat	5-HT-C^{14}	5-HIAA	41.5	36.9[d]
		5-HTOH	13.0	19.1[d]
	NE-C^{14}	VMA	13.4	9.6[e]
		MHPG	21.2	25.1[e]
	Dopamine	HVA	41.4	31.7[d]
	(DA-C^{14})	MOPET	5.7	8.2 (N.S.)

[a] Serotonin was administered orally to humans and determined on an 8 hr urine collection, all other compounds were given i.v. and determinations made on a 24 hr urine in both humans and rats.
[b] Values represent percentage of the total O-methylated metabolites excreted.
[c] Humans received 60 ml of ethanol (0.65 g/kg) orally, rats received 4.5 g/kg, i.p. of ethanol for 5-HT and NE; and 6.0 g/kg, orally for DA.
[d] $p < 0.001$.
[e] $p < 0.03$.

2.   Norepinephrine

The observed alterations in serotonin metabolism by ethanol suggested that any biogenic amine that is a substrate for monoamine oxidase (MAO) would be subject to a similar perturbation in its metabolic disposition. Norepinephrine was particularly well suited for such an investigation because of its well established role in neurochemical transmission in both the central and peripheral nervous system. When NE-C^{14} was administered to humans, it was found that alcohol ingestion resulted in decreased excretion of the O-methylated acid metabolite VMA and a corresponding compensatory increased excretion of MHPG [23]. Additional experiments were performed to see if ethanol ingestion could modify the metabolic fate of endogenous epinephrine and NE. The primary effect of ethanol was again a reduction in the O-methylated acid derivative and an increase in the O-methylated glycol metabolite (see Table I). From indirect evidence [13] it seems that ethanol produces a similar alteration in the metabolism of NE in the CNS in man.

Again the rat was much less responsive to the effects of ethanol on NE-C^{14} metabolism despite the use of a dose that was seven times greater than that used in man. Ethanol evoked only a moderate, although significant, change in the O-methylated metabolites of this neurotransmitter (see Table I). Analysis of NE-C^{14} metabolites in the brain of rats (unpublished observations) after intraventricular injection of the amine did not show any change in the metabolic disposition of this amine after alcohol. The rat thus seems to be an unsatisfactory species for such biochemical analyses.

3. Dopamine

Dopamine (3,4-dihydroxyphenylethylamine, DA) is another biogenic amine that is a substrate for MAO and is also a neurotransmitter in the central nervous system [52]. Unfortunately the effect of ethanol on the metabolism of DA in man has not been studied. Results obtained with the rat, however, were quite interesting. The major metabolic product of this amine in the rat is 3-methoxy-4-hydroxyphenylacetic acid (homovanillic acid, HVA) and comprised 41% of the C^{14} excreted. After the administration of a larger dose of ethanol (6 g/kg p.o.), there was a diminution in HVA to 32% ($p < 0.001$). Unlike the effect of alcohol on the metabolism of other biogenic amines, however, there was no concomitant increase in the alcohol derivative (3-methoxy-4-hydroxyphenylethanol, MOPET). This seemingly incongruous finding led to a more detailed study of the metabolic fate of dopamine *in vitro* (see Section G.1).

D.   Mechanism of Modification in Neuroamine Metabolism

The precise mechanisms involved in the genesis of biogenic amine metabolic alterations evoked by alcohol are still unsettled. Various proposals have been suggested, however, to explain these findings. These effects have been attributed to a blockade of release of biogenic amines [56], to an inhibition of monoamine oxidase [83, 84], to a depletion of NAD with a resultant increased NADH/NAD ratio due to the oxidation of ethanol [34–36], and finally to a competitive inhibition between acetaldehyde derived from ethanol and the intermediate biogenic aldehydes for the active sites on aldehyde dehydrogenase [23, 66, 67, 102].

1. Effects of Cofactor Variation

Among the proponents of changes in nucleotide levels to explain alterations in neuroamine metabolism produced by ethanol have been Feldstein and coworkers [34, 35]. Their primary explanation of this effect involves the depletion of NAD by the oxidation of ethanol to acetaldehyde and acetate with concomitant generation of NADH. They propose that a lack of NAD is expected to block NAD-linked aldehyde dehydrogenase and cause a buildup of biogenic aldehydes. Conversely excess NADH facilitates the reductive pathway available to these aromatic aldehydes with conversion to their corresponding alcohol derivative by way of NADH-linked alcohol dehydrogenase. Indeed NADH added to rat liver homogenates produced a decrease in 5-HIAA formation and increased 5-HTOH [37]. Conversely the incorporation of NAD into incubation mixtures promoted the conversion of serotonin to 5-HIAA.

More recently Feldstein and Williamson [36] show that the administration of ethanol to rats decreases the *in vitro* conversion of 5-HT-C[14] to 5-HIAA with a concomitant increase in the formation of 5-HTOH in liver homogenates from these animals in the presence of excess NAD. These results are incongruous with their hypothesis that ethanol-evoked changes in biogenic amine metabolism are primarily mediated by alterations in ratios of reduced to oxidized pyridine nucleotides. Without cofactor, these workers found an increase in both the aldehyde and alcohol derivatives of 5-HT. They observed no change in the acid, 5-HIAA. But in the presence of excess NAD and ethanol, 5-HTOH did increase; 5-HIAA was decreased from the control. It seems premature to assume that NAD depletion by ethanol causes inhibition in 5-HIAA formation, when this acid is still decreased even when sufficient NAD is available. Similarly the concept that NADH generation promotes the production of 5-HTOH was not readily demonstrated in these experiments. The increase in 5-HTOH observed in incubation mixtures containing ethanol and NAD was equivalent to the increase that occurs with ethanol in the absence of any cofactor. These data [36] are contrary to their hypothesis that NAD/NADH ratio changes are solely instrumental in promoting these effects.

In vitro manipulation of amine metabolism by cofactor variation does not afford a strong basis for a singular role of these cofactors in ethanol-induced alterations in amine pathways. To make such an interpretation, it seems necessary for cofactor addition to promote restorative changes in the aberrations of amine metabolism evoked by alcohol either *in vivo* or *in vitro*. Another possible explanation of these data is that in the presence of NAD, ethanol is metabolized in liver to acetaldehyde, which competitively inhibits the oxidation of the aromatic aldehyde to 5-HIAA.

2.   Evidence of Competitive Inhibition

Several investigators have examined the role of acetaldehyde in mediating ethanol-evoked aberrations in biogenic amine catabolism. Recently evidence in support of this hypothesis has been provided. Lahti and Majchrowicz [67] investigated the *in vitro* metabolism of serotonin in rat liver homogenates. These workers find that acetaldehyde at concentrations ranging from 1.0 to 4.0 mM produces a marked decrease in the formation of 5-HIAA and concomitant increases in the production of neutrals (5-hydroxyindole-acetaldehyde and 5-HTOH). The addition of excess amounts of cofactor (7.5 mM NAD) does not overcome the alteration in 5-HT metabolism produced by acetaldehyde. The alteration of serotonin metabolism from a predominantly oxidative pathway to a reductive one with acetaldehyde occurs in the presence of adequate NAD. This result supports the role of acetaldehyde in causing this metabolic aberration. Furthermore these findings essentially preclude an effect of depletion of NAD as a requisite for this effect. The mechanism involved seems to be a competitive inhibition between acetaldehyde and 5-hydroxyindoleacetaldehyde as substrates for aldehyde dehydrogenase.

Evidence of this mechanism has since been provided by these same investigators [66]. Using rat brain mitochondria, they showed competitive kinetics with acetaldehyde and this same indolealdehyde as substrate. The K_i for acetaldehyde was twice the K_m for 5-hydroxyindoleacetaldehyde and agreed with the affinity of acetaldehyde for bovine aldehyde dehydrogenase that has been reported by others [32].

3.   Acetaldehyde Mediation in Vivo

The role of acetaldehyde in evoking a decrease in the oxidative pathway and a concomitant increase in the reductive one for NE metabolism *in vivo* has been examined [102, 104]. Rats were injected with NE-C^{14} i.v., and the urine was analyzed by the method of Davis et al. [23]. In the rat, MHPG is the major urinary metabolite; VMA is slightly less of the total radioactivity excreted. Administration of ethanol did not significantly alter the proportion of these two primary metabolites (see Table II). Acetaldehyde injections, however, caused a pronounced reduction in the

TABLE II   Effect of Ethanol and Acetaldehyde on the Metabolic Fate of Bound Norepi-nephrine-C^{14} in Rats and Comparison of 24 Hr and 12 to 16 Hr Metabolic Pattern in Urine

Compound	Total NE[a] 0–24 Hr	Bound NE[b] 12–16 Hr	Ethanol[b]	Acet-aldehyde[b]
Norepinephrine (NE)	14.33	4.87	3.99	5.36
Normetanephrine	21.94	5.49	6.92[c]	7.67[c]
Deaminated catechols	12.00	24.14	18.43	19.61
3,4-Dihydroxymandelic acid	5.20	12.16	8.71[c]	8.17[c]
3,4-Dihydroxyphenyl glycol	6.80	11.98	9.72	11.44
O-Methylated, deaminated metabolites	23.13	46.68	48.69	47.34
3-Methoxy-4-hydroxymandelic acid (VMA)	13.62	20.95	19.17	11.77[c]
3-Methoxy-4-hydroxyphenyl glycol (MHPG)	19.51	25.73	29.52	35.57[c]

[a] Values represent percentage of total C^{14} excreted in 24 hr.
[b] Values represent percentage of C^{14} excreted in 4 hr (bound NE represents the radio-activity in the urine 12–16 hr after i.v. injection of NE-C^{14}).
[c] Significant difference from control (bound NE), $p < 0.001$.

amount of VMA-C^{14} excreted and also increased the excretion of labeled MHPG (see Table II). This effect was also produced by the administration of two aldehyde dehydrogenase inhibitors, disulfiram and calcium carbimide. Combined administration of ethanol and these inhibitors enhanced this shift in NE metabolism. The blood levels of acetaldehyde were simulta-neously determined by an improved gas-chromatographic procedure [97], and the elevated concentrations of this potent metabolite of ethanol were well correlated with the magnitude of the alteration of NE metabolism.

These findings demonstrate that acetaldehyde is the quantitatively impor-tant mediator of the ethanol-evoked alterations in monoamine metabolism. The lack of an effect of ethanol alone on NE in the rat strongly implicates this mechanism. The ineffectiveness of ethanol on NE catabolism in these experiments as compared with others (see Table I) is due to the time period of analysis of NE.

The metabolites were assayed for the period of 12 to 16 hr after i.v. injection of NE, which more closely parallels the pattern of endogenous norepinephrine catabolism [61]. The radioactivity excreted during this time period (12 to 16 hr) represents NE-C^{14} that has been taken up into nerve endings, bound, subsequently released, and metabolized (see Table II).

The failure of ethanol to induce changes in NE metabolism in the rat finally demonstrates that changes that occur in man with ethanol cannot be attributed to a change in hepatic pyridine nucleotide levels as a result of ethanol oxidation. Although it has been demonstrated repeatedly that ethanol administration alters the NAD/NADH ratio in rat liver [11, 15, 18, 38, 51, 57, 74, 79, 91], ethanol does not modify neuroamine metabolism in the intact rat (see Table II). These findings could certainly explain why other workers have not demonstrated an effect of ethanol on biogenic amine metabolism in brain either *in vivo* [98] or *in vitro* [30]. Since ethanol administration does not produce changes in metabolism of peripherally administered NE-C^{14} in the rat, no effect on centrally administered amines would be expected. In liver homogenates, with high alcohol dehydrogenase activity and a high capacity to oxidize ethanol to acetaldehyde, ethanol-induced changes in amine metabolism have been found. Conversely with brain homogenates, ethanol would be ineffective in producing this action, since only a limited amount of alcohol dehydrogenase is present [80] and the generation of acetaldehyde from ethanol would be minimal. These data indicate that it would be preferable to study the pharmacology of alcohol and particularly the disease of alcoholism in a species other than the rat that might parallel man more closely to both the intoxicating effects and the addiction liability of the drug, alcohol.

E.   Biogenesis of Amine and Acetaldehyde Condensation Products

Chemically acetaldehyde is a very reactive substance. A reaction between acetaldehyde and various biochemical substrates has been demonstrated frequently [5–7, 106]. A condensation reaction has also been shown to occur between acetaldehyde with amino groups of aromatic amines to form Schiff's base intermediates [12, 82]. The Pictet-Spengler reaction, which is a special case of the Mannich reaction, involves the condensation of β-arylethylamines with carbonyl compounds. Subsequently the Schiff's base intermediate undergoes cyclization to form β-carbolines in the case of indolethylamines or tetrahydroisoquinolines in the case of phenylethylamines.

The synthesis of simple tetrahydroisoquinolines under physiological conditions that occur in plants has caused investigators to theorize such a mechanism to be involved in the biogenesis of plant alkaloids. Similarly since acetaldehyde is a reactive carbonyl agent, the possible formation of alkaloids in mammalian species after alcohol ingestion is an intriguing concept.

1.   Indolethylamines → β-Carbolines

Taborsky and McIsaac [93] performed extensive experiments in an attempt to synthesize β-carbolines from a vast number of tryptamine derivatives with acetaldehyde. These workers attempted to prepare 6-hydroxy-1-methyl-1,2,3,4-tetrahydro-β-carboline, the alkaloid formed from serotonin and acetaldehyde. They were unsuccessful in isolating a single purified product of this reaction. Instead they seemed to obtain a variety and mixture of products with this particular amine. The products proved, however, to be potent serotonin antagonists and additionally to cause aldosterone secretion, both of which are properties characteristic of the β-carbolines.

Additionally McIsaac [72] found that the indole alkaloid (β-carboline) of 5-methoxytryptamine, an amine prevalent in the pineal gland, and acetaldehyde could be formed *in vitro* under physiological conditions of temperature and pH. His interest in this compound arose from the fact that a stimulant for aldosterone secretion had been found in pineal tissue, and carbolines were known to produce this response. He also found that small amounts (0.5% of administered radioactivity) of this alkaloid were excreted when 5-methoxy-tryptamine-C^{14} was administered to rats pretreated with ethanol or acetaldehyde in the presence of an MAO inhibitor (Iproniazid) and an aldehyde dehydrogenase inhibitor (disulfiram) [72]. Therefore the possible formation of such alkaloids after alcohol ingestion does exist. Alkaloids of this type are closely related to harmaline in structure, a pharmacologically potent MAO inhibitor.

2.   Catecholamines → Simple Tetrahydroisoquinolines

It has been known for some time that formaldehyde can condense with catecholamines to form tetrahydroisoquinolines. The ready oxidation of these products to fluorescent materials is used in the localization of these amines in tissues. Cohen and Barrett [19] report the identification of tetrahydroisoquinolines in adrenals from animals given multiple injections of methanol. Cohen and Collins [20] also perfused bovine adrenal glands with high concentrations of acetaldehyde and isolated the 1-methyl-tetrahydroisoquinoline derivatives of NE and epinephrine. The new compounds found in these glands had R_f values on thin-layer chromatography identical with the reaction products of these amines with acetaldehyde in aqueous solution. They declare that the fluorescence behavior and infrared spectra of these compounds indicate tetrahydroisoquinoline formation.

Robbins [81] reports on the chemical reaction capability of several biogenic amines with acetaldehyde. He determined experimentally the second-order reaction rate constants (liter mole^{-1}min^{-1}) for alkaloid formation with dopamine (15.3), 1-dopa (6.1), and norepinephrine (1.9). Thus the facility of this reaction is appreciably retarded when the ethylamine moiety contains substituent groups. These data indicate that the addition of an alpha carboxyl (dopa) or a β-hydroxy group (NE) appreciably diminishes the velocity of the reaction compared with the unsubstituted dopamine. The ease with which dopamine and acetaldehyde react indicates that the possible endogenous formation of an alkaloid after alcohol administration is most likely with this amine, considering the rapid half-life of acetaldehyde *in vivo*.

We have examined this reaction by incubating rat brain-stem or liver homogenates with dopamine-C^{14} and acetaldehyde [108]. Acetaldehyde reacts with dopamine to form the alkaloid 1-methyl-6,7-dihydroxy-1,2,3,4-tetrahydroisoquinoline (salsolinol). The identity of this product was confirmed by thin-layer and gas chromatography. The structure of dopamine and salsolinol are shown in Figure 1. The formation of salsolinol in liver was proportional to the concentration of acetaldehyde (see Figure 1). The data are presented as the percentage of total radioactivity in the dopamine and salsolinol ion-exchange chromatographic fraction present as each compound. Addition of NAD to these incubation mixtures decreased the amount of salsolinol formed because of the oxidation of acetaldehyde by NAD-linked aldehyde dehydrogenase. Similar results were obtained using brain-stem homogenates. The amount of salsolinol formed in brain tissue when NAD was added was quite high and similar to liver without NAD. This is attributed to the limited capacity of the brain to oxidize acetaldehyde.

Salsolinol formation from dopamine was also observed when ethanol (100 mM) was incubated with either of these tissues. In liver, salsolinol formation was quite substantial and almost equivalent to that formed with 0.5 mM acetaldehyde. The addition of NAD to liver homogenates abolished salsolinol formation in the presence of ethanol. This occurred because NAD-linked alcohol dehydrogenase is the rate-limiting step, and acetaldehyde that was formed was rapidly oxidized by NAD-linked aldehyde dehydrogenase. In brain-stem homogenates with added NAD, however, significant formation of this alkaloid still occurred.

Therefore the ease with which this alkaloid is formed *in vitro* makes it a likely candidate for possible *in vivo* formation as a consequence of alcohol consumption. The formation of such an alkaloid in discrete areas of the brain where dopamine occurs in quite high concentrations, especially the basal ganglia, might contribute to some of the pharmacological and

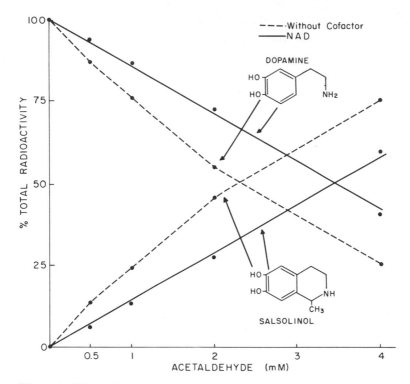

Figure 1. Effect of varying concentrations of acetaldehyde on the disappearance of dopamine-C^{14} and the formation of salsolinol-C^{14} as a percentage of the total radioactivity attributable to each compound in incubation mixtures of rat liver homogenates with and without exogenous NAD.

behavioral effects produced by either acute or chronic alcohol administration. Indeed alkaloids of this type have been shown to produce both central and peripheral pharmacological effects [33, 46, 47, 95].

F.   Inhibition of Monoamine Oxidase by Alcohol

As long ago as 1950 Heim [45] reported that ethyl and methyl alcohol inhibited monoamine oxidase (MAO), the enzyme that destroys norepinephrine, serotonin, dopamine, as well as other amines. No further mention was made of this until 1960, when Rosenfeld [83] measured serotonin metabolism and showed that there seemed to be an appreciable decrease in the formation of 5-HIAA after sublethal doses of alcohol. He suggested that the oxidation of alcohol, in all probability, competitively inhibited the oxidative metabolism of serotonin and perhaps in particular the oxidation of the aldehyde derived from it (see Section D.2). Perman [76] found no significant change with ethanol in man on the endogenous output of 5-HIAA. In 1964, however, Feldstein et al. [35] reexamined this effect by administering serotonin-C^{14} orally to six subjects. They were able to demonstrate that ethanol blocked the metabolism of serotonin to 5-HIAA. The alteration in metabolism showed a dose-response relationship, and the duration of the block was less than 24 hr. On the basis of these experiments it was not possible to detect which enzyme was altered by alcohol, MAO or aldehyde dehydrogenase.

Schenker et al. [88] noted increased tryptamine excretion after alcohol, which they attributed to MAO inhibition. They had previously examined the extent to which ethanol could be expected to inhibit MAO in rat tissues *in vitro* [71]. It was found that ethanol did inhibit MAO in mouse liver, using three substrates, but not in brain. They concluded, however, that the degree of inhibition found was relatively small, although significant, and could not account for the very marked increase in tryptamine excretion observed in their subjects. This led them to postulate a releasing of a bound form of the amine by ethanol (see Section B). Finally in 1964 Towne [96] demonstrated that acetaldehyde (0.12 M) inhibited both liver and brain MAO *in vitro* by 26 and 36% respectively. He explained the previously reported lack of effect of ethanol in brain to be due to the absence of alcohol dehydrogenase, so that little acetaldehyde was produced *in vitro*. Still the degree of inhibition with acetaldehyde was not very marked and the concentration required was rather high. Similarly inhibition of the enzyme (MAO) by ethanol (0.11 M) in liver was only 8%. In both of these reports [71, 96] substrate disappearance was used as the measure of MAO activity. The conclusion of these reports was that ethanol by way of its proximate metabolite, acetaldehyde, seemed to be a nonspecific inhibitor of MAO. One could rationalize this interpretation, because the high chemical reactivity of this two-carbon aldehyde could conceivably inactivate the enzyme.

In experiments performed in our laboratory on the *in vitro* metabolism of dopamine-C^{14} we have observed a similar phenomenon. In liver or brain homogenates, ethanol (50 or 100 mM) had an insignificant effect on the inhibition of dopamine deamination. This was essentially the finding of Towne [96] and our conditions of incubation were for 30 min., as were his. Maynard and Schenker [71] found 20 to 40% inhibition with ethanol, using various substrates and incubation of the samples for 70 min. This difference in procedure could well explain the diversity in experimental results. With acetaldehyde (2 to 4 mM) we observed a 20 to 40% inhibition of deamination in liver homogenates (50 mg of tissue) and a 30 to 45% inhibition in brain-stem homogenates (100 mg), as did Towne, using 120 mM acetaldehyde. We have found, however, the explanation for this effect to be more than a nonspecific protein binding of acetaldehyde.

As previously discussed (see Section E), acetaldehyde condenses with various amines to form alkaloids. The deamination rate varies markedly with the substrate concentration used. So at any given substrate concentration, when acetaldehyde is present, it essentially prevents the biogenic amine from being deaminated by condensing with it and forming the respective cyclic alkaloid derivative. This is definitely one of the contributing effects to the observed reduction in deamination rate with acetaldehyde. Rather than an actual inhibition of MAO, this phenomenon is due to substrate limitation resulting from condensation of the amine substrate with acetaldehyde.

There is an additional factor that may contribute to acetaldehyde's action on the oxidative deamination of biogenic amines. In the case of serotonin the resultant β-carboline derivative would in all probability be a potent inhibitor of MAO, as are the harmaline type of drugs. Similarly the tetrahydroisoquinoline derivative of dopamine and acetaldehyde, salsolinol, is also an inhibitor of MAO. We have found that salsolinol (2 to 4 mM) inhibits liver MAO by 25 to 33% and brain-stem MAO by 47 to 60%. Therefore the previously reported inhibition of MAO by acetaldehyde may well be due, first, to substrate limitation and, second, to the formation of alkaloids that inhibit this enzyme.

The effect of acetaldehyde is apparent and indirect rather than a nonspecific direct action on the enzyme. This response produced by acetaldehyde may not be of pharmacological significance, because of the high levels of acetaldehyde required to produce it *in vitro*. However, the endogenous synthesis of alkaloids after alcohol ingestion that are effective MAO inhibitors with greater intrinsic activity than acetaldehyde alone could still make this effect of alcohol an important one and will require further research in order to clarify this point.

G.   Aberrations in Dopamine Metabolism

A detailed knowledge of the metabolic disposition of dopamine is of considerable importance because of the neurotransmitter function of this amine. In addition to its essential role as the immediate precursor in norepinephrine biosynthesis, dopamine can be metabolized along several diverse pathways. As shown in Figure 2, the intermediate aldehyde derivative of dopamine,

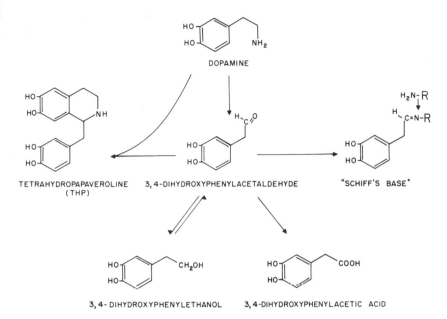

Figure 2. Possible divergent metabolic disposition of dopamine and its aldehyde (3,4-dihydroxyphenylacetaldehyde).

3,4-dihydroxyphenylacetaldehyde, represents the pivotal point from which several reactions ramify.

1. Alternate Metabolic Pathways

Most of the dopamine formed endogenously in the brain, for example, is first deaminated by monoamine oxidase to the intermediate aldehyde followed by oxidation to 3,4-dihydroxyphenylacetic acid (DOPAC), and the latter compound can then be *O*-methylated to produce 3-methoxy-4-hydroxyphenylacetic acid [8, 17]. In tissue preparations a major pathway for the metabolism of dopamine again is the direct amine-aldehyde-acid route leading to the formation of 3,4-dihydroxyphenylacetic acid (DOPAC). Alternatively reduction of the intermediate aldehyde to 3,4-dihydroxyphenylethanol also occurs to a small extent [41, 85]. Reduction of the aldehyde to the corresponding alcohol is probably a reversible process, and the alcohol may be easily oxidized back to the aldehyde.

It is also possible that 3,4-dihydroxyphenylacetaldehyde can be incorporated into protein, with a probable reaction being the formation of a Schiff's base from the intermediate aldehyde with amino groups of protein. Precedent for this suggestion is found in reports of the binding of the biogenic aldehydes derived from labeled serotonin and norepinephrine with protein [3, 58, 94]. The radioactivity bound to protein did not represent the intact labeled amine but a metabolite of the amine, because the binding was prevented by MAO inhibitors or carbonyl-trapping agents [4, 65].

In experiments in which labeled dopamine was incubated with rat brain stem or liver homogenates, a loss of radioactivity from the protein-free extracts of the reaction mixtures was consistently observed. The disappearance of radioactivity was proportional to the amount of tissue and to the time of incubation and directly related to the amount of dopamine deaminated. The loss of radioactivity was decreased on incorporation of the coenzyme for aldehyde dehydrogenase, NAD, or the carbonyl-trapping agent, semicarbazide, into the reaction mixtures. Thus the intermediate aldehyde of dopamine can also diverge from its major metabolic pathway and bind to tissue proteins [100].

The possibility of the formation of tetrahydroisoquinoline alkaloids during the metabolism of dopamine has received little attention. On incubation of dopamine with guinea pig liver mitochondrial preparations, Holtz and coworkers [48 50] found that the primary product of oxidative deamination, 3,4-dihydroxyphenylacetaldehyde, condensed with the unchanged parent amine to form the blood-pressure-lowering alkaloid, tetrahydropapaveroline (THP). These investigators isolated tetrahydropapaveroline by thin-layer chromatography in two different solvent systems. No quantitative information was given, however, on the relative magnitude of this alternative pathway for the metabolism of dopamine.

A. PHARMACOLOGY OF TETRAHYDROPAPAVEROLINE. In marked contrast to most metabolites of biogenic amines tetrahydropapaveroline is pharamcologically active, producing actions that are β-sympathomimetic in nature. This alkaloid derivative of dopamine evokes positive inotropic and chronotropic responses and a fall in blood pressure with an accompanying increase in peripheral blood flow. Relaxation of isolated smooth muscle preparations, such as uterus, intestine, and trachea, are produced by tetrahydropapaveroline. In addition the mobilization of lipids both *in vitro* and *in vivo* is enhanced by tetrahydropapaveroline. All the pharmacological effects reported for tetrahydropapaveroline can be prevented by β-adrenergic blocking agents [50, 62, 63, 68, 86, 87].

Although the acute pharmacological actions of tetrahydropapaveroline have received considerable attention, little consideration has been given to defining the conditions necessary for the metabolic formation of this alkaloid derivative of dopamine. Consequently we have investigated the relative magnitude of the alternative pathways available for the *in vitro* metabolic disposition of 3,4-dihydroxyphenylacetaldehyde derived from dopamine, with special reference to the formation of the alkaloid, tetrahydropapaveroline.

B. CONDITIONS MODIFYING TETRAHYDROPAPAVEROLINE FORMATION. Logically the amount of dopamine that would be converted to tetrahydropapaveroline should depend on the rate of aldehyde generation and more important on the rate at which the aldehyde is oxidized or reduced. The formation of tetrahydropapaveroline during the metabolism of dopamine by tissues, such as liver, having high aldehyde dehydrogenase activity should be insignificant. The amine-derived aldehyde would be rapidly oxidized to the acid if adequate exogenous cofactor, NAD, were present. In tissues, such as brain, however, with low aldehyde-oxidizing capacity [28] the aldehyde would be less readily converted to the acid, and condensation of the aldehyde with the parent amine to form tetrahydropapaveroline should be a predominant metabolic pathway.

The effect of NAD on the relative amount of 3,4-dihydroxyphenylacetaldehyde either oxidized to the acid or diverted to condensation with intact dopamine to form tetrahydropapaveroline was investigated by incubating labeled dopamine with either rat liver or brain-stem homogenates. In experiments with liver homogenates without added cofactor, tetrahydropapaveroline production represented 56% of the dopamine deaminated, and the acid metabolite comprised only 8%. Inclusion of NAD in the reaction mixtures unmasked the immense aldehyde-oxidizing capacity of liver. Under these conditions, tetrahydropapaveroline production was markedly depressed to only 0.6%, and acid formation represented 67% of the dopamine deaminated.

Marked quantitative differences were found in the metabolic disposition of dopamine by brain in comparison with liver. In the absence of exogenous NAD, tetrahydropapaveroline production by brain-stem homogenates comprised 70% of the dopamine deaminated, which was much higher than that found with liver (56%). Incorporation of NAD into incubation mixtures of brain-stem homogenates reduced the amount of tetrahydropapaveroline formed to only 47%. As with liver, incubation with NAD produced a concomitant increase in the acid metabolite that rose from 3 to 17% of the dopamine deaminated. Therefore the degree of modification of these metabolic products of dopamine by NAD addition was markedly attenuated in brain as compared with liver [100].

These data illustrate that marked differences in the aldehyde-oxidizing capacity of various tissues, whether due to enzyme content or cofactor availability, may have a pronounced effect on the localized disposition of the aldehyde arising from dopamine and other biogenic amines. Under conditions in which aldehyde oxidation is not limited, production of tetrahydropapaveroline may be of minor consequence. In the presence of compounds that inhibit aldehyde dehydrogenase, however, the formation of tetrahydropapaveroline may assume considerable proportions. Examples of frequently abused drugs or a metabolite of these drugs that inhibit aldehyde dehydrogenase include chloral hydrate and acetaldehyde, the primary metabolite of both paraldehyde and ethanol. Some of the pharmacological actions of these drugs might well be related to a possible enhancement of the production of tetrahydropapaveroline, a benzyltetrahydroisoquinoline alkaloid.

2. Effect of Alcohol and Acetaldehyde

Experiments were performed to determine the effect of ethanol and acetaldehyde on tetrahydropapaveroline production by rat liver and brain-stem homogenates in the presence of exogenous NAD (see Table III). The

TABLE III   Effect of NAD, Alcohol, and Acetaldehyde on the Metabolic Disposition of Dopamine-C^{14} by Rat Liver and Brain-Stem Homogenates

| | | Percentage of dopamine deaminated | | | |
| | | Liver | | Brain | |
Condition		DOPAC	THP	DOPAC	THP
Control	(−NAD)	8.34	56.43	2.88	70.02
Control	(+NAD)	67.37	0.64	16.78	46.65
Ethanol	(100 mM)			10.10[a]	55.98[b]
Acetaldehyde	(0.5 mM)	43.13[b]	2.45[b]	11.76[a]	58.44[a]
Acetaldehyde	(1.0 mM)	45.59[b]	5.37[a]	9.28[a]	63.67[a]
Acetaldehyde	(2.0 mM)	45.63[b]	9.32[a]	9.93[a]	65.00[a]
Acetaldehyde	(4.0 mM)	30.96[a]	14.61[a]		

[a] Significantly different from control (+NAD), $p < 0.001$.
[b] Significantly different from control (+NAD), $p < 0.01$.
DOPAC: 3,4-dihydroxyphenylacetic acid; THP: tetrahydropapaveroline, 1-(3′,4′-dihydroxybenzyl)-6,7-dihydroxy-1,2,3,4-tetrahydroisoquinoline.

cofactor was incorporated in order to simulate the *in vivo* situation and to allow the oxidation of ethanol to acetaldehyde.

Tetrahydropapaveroline production is of minor consequence in liver when adequate coenzyme is available (see Table III). Conversely the oxidation of 3,4-dihydroxyphenylacetaldehyde to DOPAC is the major pathway for disposition of dopamine, as would be expected for a tissue with large aldehyde-oxidizing capacity.

Acetaldehyde in concentrations ranging from 0.5 to 4 mM resulted in a marked response in this tissue with the increased generation of tetrahydropapaveroline. The enhanced production of tetrahydropapaveroline was proportionate to the amount of acetaldehyde added. Acetaldehyde, in all concentrations used, produced significant decreases in the acid metabolite, DOPAC. This is a consequence of the depressed oxidation of the aromatic aldehyde in the presence of the competitive inhibitor, acetaldehyde.

With the concentrations of substrate and cofactor used in these experiments, tetrahydropapaveroline constituted the predominant metabolite of dopamine in brain (see Table III). Incorporation of acetaldehyde at concentrations of 0.5 to 2 mM into the reaction mixtures produced incremental increases in the biogenesis of tetrahydropapaveroline ($p < 0.001$). Increased tetrahydropapaveroline formation occurred simultaneously with decreased conversion of dopamine to its oxidative metabolite, DOPAC ($p < 0.001$). The competitive inhibition of 3,4-dihydroxyphenylacetaldehyde, therefore, facilitated the diversion of the aromatic aldehyde to the alternate condensation route [27].

The formation of tetrahydropapaveroline by brain was also significantly potentiated by ethanol, 100 mM ($p < 0.01$). Addition of ethanol resulted in a decrease in the conversion of dopamine to DOPAC (see Table III). The significant reduction of DOPAC formation in the presence of ethanol from 16.8 to 10.1% of the dopamine deaminated is in agreement with the finding that rat brain has the capacity to oxidize ethanol to acetaldehyde [80]. The observed decrease in the conversion of the aromatic aldehyde to DOPAC could occur only if the active competitive inhibitor of aldehyde dehydrogenase, acetaldehyde, were formed under these conditions.

H. Speculations on the Possible Involvement of Neuroamines in Alcoholism

The significance of the alcohol-evoked and acetaldehyde-mediated blockade in the oxidation of the aldehyde derivatives of the neuroamines to any of the numerous neuropharmacological effects of alcohol has not been defined

There is, however, a possibility of a direct causal relationship between the striking ethanol-induced alterations in the metabolism of the intermediate aldehyde derivatives of the biogenic amines and the neuropharmacological effects of ethanol. The diversion of dopamine metabolism described above suggests that biogenic aldehydes derived from endogenous neuroamines or further reaction products of biogenic aldehydes or amines may play a role in some of the effects of ethanol. In this regard augmented biosynthesis of a benzyltetrahydroisoquinoline alkaloid formed by condensation of dopamine with its corresponding aldehyde has been demonstrated with both ethanol and acetaldehyde [27]. Similarly, acetaldehyde is known to condense directly with catecholamines and indolethylamines to form methyltetrahydroisoquinolines and β-carboline [20, 72, 108].

Acetaldehyde, the primary metabolite of alcohol, is a known inhibitor of the oxidation of aromatic aldehydes. Both ethanol and acetaldehyde significantly enhance tetrahydropapaveroline synthesis in brain-stem homogenates. These findings indicate that alcohol through acetaldehyde, its primary metabolite, might potentiate the biosynthesis of alkaloids derived from neurochemical transmitters by blocking the normal biochemical disposition of these substances.

It is possible that diversion of neuroamine metabolism with formation of biologically active alkaloid derivatives may be involved in the disease of alcoholism. Synthetic tetrahydroisoquinolines, chemically related to tetrahydropapaveroline, have been examined clinically [39] for their pharmacological effects. Furthermore, in plants tetrahydropapaveroline (THP, norlaudanosoline) is the natural biosynthetic precursor of a vast complex of alkaloids which includes the papaverine, tetrahydroberberine, aporphine, and morphine-type alkaloids [10, 59, 69, 92]. It is conceivable that tetrahydropapaveroline could be formed as a consequence of alcohol abuse and then undergo similar biotransformations in mammalian systems. A representation of one of these constructs is depicted in Figure 3. Inherent to this scheme is the conception that biotransformation of a drug (alcohol) results in the formation of an active metabolite (acetaldehyde), which in turn modifies the metabolism of a neuroamine (dopamine) to produce aberrant metabolites with unique pharmacological activity (alkaloids). In this instance the action of the drug (alcohol) is indirect. Its biotransformation is essential for the activation of a pathway available to neurotransmitter substances which may be normally inoperative [26, 27].

These considerations do not necessarily relate to the phenomena of tolerance and physical dependence on alcohol, since these aspects of addiction might be more directly related to other pharmacological actions of ethanol; for example, tolerance to alcohol seems to have both a meta-

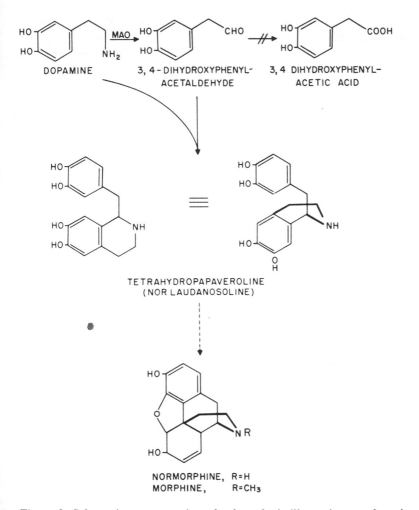

Figure 3. Schematic representation of a hypothesis illustrating an alteration in the metabolic disposition of dopamine produced by alcohol ($\not\to$) with the postulated resultant formation of complex alkaloid derivatives.

bolic and cellular component, and physical dependence as exhibited by an abstinence syndrome can be produced in animals pretreated with pyrazole, an alcohol dehydrogenase inhibitor. In the presence of pyrazole the production of acetaldehyde would be attenuated or nonexistent. The proposed sequence of events is probably also unrelated to the acute intoxicating actions of alcohol.

The direct condensation of acetaldehyde with neuroamines to form simple alkaloid derivatives may also contribute to some of the diverse pharmacological effects of ethanol. The formation of β-carbolines by condensation of acetaldehyde with indolethylamines has been demonstrated [93]. Some of these compounds are known to inhibit monoamine oxidase or to antagonize the actions of serotonin. Acetaldehyde also condenses with epinephrine and norepinephrine [20], as well as with dopamine [108]. These methyltetrahydroisoquinolines interact with neuroamine stores. Simple tetrahydroisoquinolines, as well as tetrahydropapaveroline, have been shown to cause a release of labeled norepinephrine from synaptosomal preparations and an inhibition of uptake of norepinephrine. In addition, salsolinol, the isoquinoline condensation product of dopamine and acetaldehyde, has been found to inhibit monoamine oxidase. Therefore formation of alkaloid derivatives of the amines may in turn alter biogenic amine activity or function and contribute to the central nervous system effects of ethanol. Further research into the formation and biological activity of aberrant biogenic amine metabolites is needed before a precise role for these compounds in the disease of alcoholism [55] can be established.

ACKNOWLEDGMENTS

This work was aided by U.S.P.H.S. Grant MH-15814 from the National Institute of Mental Health and by the Veterans Administration.

REFERENCES

1. Abelin, I., C. Herren, and W. Berli, Über die erregnede Wirkung des Alkohols auf den Adrenalin- und Noradrenalinhaushalt des menschlichen Organismus, *Helv. Med. Acta,* **25,** 591 (1958).
2. Akabane, J., S. Nakanishi, H. Kohei, S. Asakawa, R. Matsumura, H. Ogata, and T. Miyazawa, Studies on sympathomimetic action of acetaldehyde: II. Secretory response of the adrenal medulla to acetaldehyde: Experiments with the perfused cat adrenals, *Japan. J. Pharmacol.,* **15,** 217 (1965).
3. Alivisatos, S. G. A. and F. Ungar, Incorporation of radioactivity from labeled serotonin and tryptamine into acid-insoluble material from subcellular fractions of brain: I. The nature of the substrate, *Biochemistry,* **6,** 285 (1968).
4. Alivisatos, S. G. A., F. Ungar, and S. S. Parmar, Effect of monoamine oxidase inhibitors on the labeling of subcellular fractions of brain and liver by ^{14}C-serotonin, *Biochem. Biophys. Res. Commun.,* **25,** 495 (1966).

5. Ammon, H. P. T., C.-J. Estler, and F. Heim, Der Einfluss von Acetaldehyde auf Coenzym A-Aktivität und Atmung von Leber- und Hirnmitochondrien, *Biochem. Pharmacol.,* **16,** 769 (1967).

6. Ammon, H. P. T., C.-J. Estler, and F. Heim, Inactivation of coenzyme A by ethanol: I. Acetaldehyde as mediator of the inactivation of coenzyme A following the administration of ethanol *in vivo, Biochem. Pharmacol.,* **18,** 29 (1969).

7. Ammon, H. P. T., F. Heim, C.-J. Estler, G. Fickles, and M. Wagner, The influence of aliphatic alcohols and their halogen derivatives on the coenzyme A in the liver of mice, *Biochem. Pharmacol.,* **16,** 1533 (1967).

8. Andén, N.-E., B.-E. Roos, and B. Werdinius, On the occurrence of homovanillic acid in brain and cerebrospinal fluid and its determination by a fluorimetric method, *Life Sci.,* **2,** 448 (1963).

9. Anton, A. H., Ethanol and urinary catecholamines, *Clin. Pharmacol. Therap.,* **6,** 462 (1965).

10. Battersby, A. R., Alkaloid biosynthesis, *Quart. Rev.,* **15,** 259 (1961).

11. Baxter, R. C. and W. J. Hensley, The effect of ethanol and cyanide on NAD/NADH₂ ratios in rat liver, *Biochem. Pharmacol.,* **18,** 233 (1969).

12. Beck, R. A., C. C. Pfeiffer, V. Iliev, and L. Goldstein, Cortical EEG stimulant effects in the rabbit of acetaldehyde-biogenic amine reaction products, *Proc. Soc. Exp. Biol. Med.,* **128,** 823 (1968).

13. Bertani, L. M., S. E. Gitlow, S. Wilk, and E. K. Wilk, The influence of ethanol on catecholamine metabolism in the human subject, *Federation Proc.,* **28,** 543 (1969).

14. Bonnycastle, D. D., M. F. Bonnycastle, and F. G. Anderson, The effect of a number of central depressant drugs upon brain 5-hydroxytryptamine levels in the rat, *J. Pharmacol. Exp. Therap.,* **135,** 17 (1962).

15. Büttner, H., F. Portwich, and K. Engelhardt, Der DPN⁺- und DPN-H-Gehalt der Rattenleber während des Abbaues von Äthanol und seine Beeinflussung durch Sulfonylharnstoff und Disulfiram, *Naunyn-Schmiedeberg's Arch. Exp. Pathol. Pharmakol.,* **240,** 573 (1961).

16. Carlsson, A. and J. Häggendal, Arterial noradrenaline levels after ethanol withdrawal, *Lancet,* **ii,** 889 (1967).

17. Carlsson, A. and N.-Å. Hillarp, Formation of phenolic acids in brain after administration of 3,4-dihydroxyphenylalanine, *Acta Physiol. Scand,* **55,** 95 (1962).

18. Cherrick, S. R. and C. M. Leevy, The effect of ethanol metabolism on levels of oxidized and reduced nicotinamide adenine dinucleotide in liver, kidney and heart, *Biochem. Biophys. Acta,* **107,** 29 (1965).

19. Cohen, G. and R. Barrett, Fluorescence microscopy of catecholamine-derived tetrahydroisoquinoline alkaloids formed during methanol intoxication, *Federation Proc.,* **58,** 288 (1969).

20. Cohen, G. and M. Collins, Alkaloids from catecholamines in adrenal tissues: Possible role in alcoholism, *Science,* **167,** 1749 (1970).

21. Corrodi, H., K. Fuxe, and T. Hökfelt, The effect of ethanol on the activity

of central catecholamine neurones in rat brain, *J. Pharm. Pharmacol.*, **18**, 821 (1966).

22. Davis, V. E., H. Brown, J. A. Huff, and J. L. Cashaw, The alteration of serotonin metabolism to 5-hydroxytryptophol by ethanol ingestion in man, *J. Lab. Clin. Med.*, **69**, 132 (1967).

23. Davis, V. E., H. Brown, J. A. Huff, and J. L. Cashaw, Ethanol-induced alterations of norepinephrine metabolism in man, *J. Lab. Clin. Med.*, **69**, 787 (1967).

24. Davis, V. E., J. L. Cashaw, J. A. Huff, H. Brown, and N. Nicholas, Alteration of endogenous catecholamine metabolism by ethanol ingestion, *Proc. Soc. Exp. Biol. Med.*, **125**, 1140 (1967).

25. Davis, V. E., J. A. Huff, and H. Brown, Alcohol and Biogenic Amines, in *Biochemical and Clinical Aspects of Alcohol Metabolism*, V. M. Sardesai (ed.), chap. 12, Charles C Thomas, Springfield, Ill., 1969.

26. Davis, V. E. and M. J. Walsh, Alcohol, amines, and alkaloids: A possible biochemical basis for alcohol addiction, *Science*, **167**, 1005 (1970).

27. Davis, V. E., M. J. Walsh, and Y. Yamanaka, Augmentation of alkaloid formation from dopamine by alcohol and acetaldehyde *in vitro*, *J. Pharmacol. Exp. Therapy*, **174**, 401 (1970).

28. Deitrich, R. A., Tissue and subcellular distribution of mammalian aldehyde-oxidizing capacity, *Biochem. Pharmacol.*, **15**, 1911 (1966).

29. Duritz, G. and E. B. Truitt, Jr., Importance of acetaldehyde in the action of ethanol on brain norepinephrine and 5-hydroxytryptamine, *Biochem. Pharmacol.*, **15**, 711 (1966).

30. Eccleston, D., W. H. Reading, and I. M. Ritchie, 5-Hydroxytryptamine metabolism in brain and liver slices and the effects of ethanol, *Biochem. Pharmacol.*, **16**, 274 (1969).

31. Efron, D. H. and G. L. Gessa, Failure of ethanol and barbiturates to alter brain monoamine content, *Arch. Intern. Pharmacodyn.*, **142**, 111 (1963).

32. Erwin, V. G. and R. A. Deitrich, Brain aldehyde dehydrogenase: Localization, purification, and properties, *J. Biol. Chem.*, **241**, 3533 (1966).

33. Fassett, D. W. and A. M. Hjort, Some tetrahydroisoquinolines: II. Their action on blood pressure, respiration and smooth muscle, *J. Pharmacol. Exp. Therap.*, **63**, 253 (1938).

34. Feldstein, A., H. Hoagland, H. Freeman, and O. Williamson, The effect of ethanol ingestion on serotonin-C^{14} metabolism in man, *Life Sci.*, **6**, 53 (1967).

35. Feldstein, A., H. Hoagland, K. Wong, and H. Freeman, Biogenic amines, biogenic aldehydes and alcohol, *Quart. J. Studies Alc.*, **25**, 218 (1964).

36. Feldstein, A. and O. Williamson, The effect of ethanol and disulfiram on serotonin-C^{14} metabolism in rat liver homogenates, *Life Sci.*, **7**, 777 (1968).

37. Feldstein, A. and K. K. Wong, Enzymatic conversion of serotonin to 5-hydroxytryptophol, *Life Sci.*, **4**, 183 (1965).

38. Forsander, O., N. C. R. Räihä, and H. Suomalainen, Alkoholoxydation und Bildung von Acetoacetat in normaler und glykogenarmer intakter Rattenleber, *Hoppe-Seyler's Z. Physiol. Chem.*, **312**, 243 (1958).

39. Fraser, H. F., W. R. Martin, A. B. Wolbach, and H. Isbell, Addiction liability

of an isoquinoline analgesic, 1-(p-chlorophenethyl)-2-methyl-6,7-dimethoxy-1,2,3,4-tetrahydroisoquinoline, *Clin. Pharmacol. Therap.,* **2,** 287 (1961).

40. Giacobini, E., S. Izikowitz, and A. Wegmann, The urinary excretion of noradrenaline and adrenaline during acute alcohol intoxication in alcoholic addicts, *Experientia,* **16,** 467 (1960).

41. Goldstein, M., A. J. Friedhoff, S. Pomerantz, and J. F. Contrera, The formation of 3,4-dihydroxyphenylethanol and 3-methoxy-4-hydroxyphenylethanol from 3,4-dihydroxyphenylethylamine in the rat, *J. Biol. Chem.,* **236,** 1816 (1961).

42. Gursey, D. and R. E. Olsen, Depression of serotonin and norepinephrine levels in brain stem of rabbit by ethanol, *Proc. Soc. Exp. Biol. Med.,* **104,** 280 (1960).

43. Gursey, D., J. W. Vester, and R. E. Olsen, Effect of ethanol administration upon serotonin and norepinephrine levels in rabbit brain, *J. Clin. Invest.,* **38,** 1008 (1959).

44. Häggendal, J. and M. Lindquist, Ineffectiveness of ethanol on noradrenaline, dopamine, or 5-hydroxytryptamine levels in brain, *Acta Pharmacol. Toxicol.,* **18,** 278 (1961).

45. Heim, F., Über den Einfluss von Alkoholen auf den enzymatischen Abbau des Tyramins, *Naunyn-Schmiedeberg's Arch. Exp. Pathol. Pharmakol,* **210,** 16 (1950).

46. Hjort, A. M., E. J. deBeer, and R. W. Fassett, Some tetrahydroisoquinolines: I. Their relative toxicology and symptomatology, *J. Pharmacol. Exp. Therap.,* **62,** 165 (1938).

47. Hjort, A. M., E. J. deBeer, J. S. Buck, and L. O. Randall, Relative pharmacological effects of 1-methyl-3,4-dihydro and 1-methyl-1,2,3,4-tetrahydroisoquinoline derivatives, *J. Pharmacol. Exp. Therap.,* **76,** 263 (1942).

48. Holtz, P., K. Stock, and E. Westermann, Über die Blutdruckwirkung des Dopamins, *Naunyn-Schmiedeberg's Arch. Exp. Pathol. Pharmakol.,* **246,** 133 (1963).

49. Holtz, P., K. Stock, and E. Westermann, Formation of tetrahydropapaveroline from dopamine *in vitro, Nature,* **203,** 656 (1964).

50. Holtz, P., K. Stock, and E. Westermann, Pharmakologie des Tetrahydropapaverolins und seine Entstehung aus Dopamin, *Naunyn-Schmiedeberg's Arch. Exp. Pathol. Pharmakol.,* **248,** 387 (1964).

51. Horn, R. H. and R. W. Manthei, Ethanol metabolism in chronic protein deficiency, *J. Pharmacol. Exp. Therap.,* **147,** 385 (1965).

52. Hornykiewicz, O., Dopamine (3-hydroxytyramine) and brain function, *Pharmacol. Rev.,* **18,** 925 (1966).

53. James, T. N. and E. S. Bear, Cardiac effects of some simple aliphatic aldehydes, *J. Pharmacol. Exp. Therap.,* **163,** 300 (1968).

54. James, T. N. and E. S. Bear, Effects of ethanol and acetaldehyde on the heart, *Am. Heart J.,* **74,** 243 (1967).

55. Jellinek, E. M., *The Disease Concept of Alcoholism,* p. 113, College and University Press, New Haven, 1960.

56. Kahil, M. E., J. Cashaw, E. L. Simons, and H. Brown, Alcohol and the tolbutamide response in the dog, *J. Lab. Clin. Med.,* **64,** 808 (1964).
57. Kalant, H. and J. M. Khanna, Effects of Chronic Ethanol Intake on Metabolic Pathways, in *Biochemical and Clinical Aspects of Alcohol Metabolism,* V. M. Sardesai (ed.), chap. 7, Charles C Thomas, Springfield, Ill., 1969.
58. Keglević, D., S. Kveder, and S. Iskrić, Indoleacetaldehydes: Intermediates in indolealkylamine metabolism, *Advan. Pharmacol.,* **6A,** 79 (1968).
59. Kirby, G. W., Biosynthesis of the morphine alkaloids, *Science,* **155,** 170 (1967).
60. Klingman, G. I. and H. B. Haag, Studies on severe alcohol intoxication in dogs: I. Blood and urinary changes in ethanol intoxication, *Quart. J. Studies Alc.,* **19,** 203 (1958).
61. Kopin, I. J. and E. K. Gordon, Metabolism of administered and drug-released norepinephrine-7-H^3 in the rat, *J. Pharmacol. Exp. Therap.,* **140,** 207 (1963).
62. Kukovetz, W. R. and G. Pöch, Beta-adrenerge Effekte und ihr zeitlicher Verlauf unter Tetrahydropapaverolin und Isoprenalin am Langendorff-Herzen, *Naunyn-Schmiedeberg's Arch. Pharmakol. Exp. Pathol.,* **256,** 301 (1967).
63. Kukovetz, W. R. and G. Pöch, Die Hemmung mechanischer und metabolischer Katecholaminwirkungen durch Isopropylmethoxamin und Kö 592 am Herzen, *Naunyn-Schmiedeberg's Arch. Pharmakol. Exp. Pathol.,* **256,** 310 (1967).
64. Kumar, M. A. and U. K. Sheth, The sympathomimetic action of acetaldehyde on isolated atria, *Arch. Intern. Pharmacodyn.,* **138,** 188 (1962).
65. Kveder, A., S. Iskrić, and L. Stančić, Association of radioactivity from ^{14}C-labelled 5-hydroxytryptamine with proteins of rat liver mitochondria, *Croat. Chem. Acta,* **39,** 185 (1967).
66. Lahti, R. A. and E. Majchrowicz, Acetaldehyde: An inhibitor of the enzymatic oxidation of 5-hydroxyindoleacetaldehyde, *Biochem. Pharmacol.,* **18,** 535 (1969).
67. Lahti, R. A. and E. Majchrowicz, The effects of acetaldehyde on serotonin metabolism, *Life Sci.,* **6,** 1399 (1967).
68. Laidlaw, P. P., The action of tetrahydropapaveroline hydrochloride, *J. Physiol.,* **40,** 480 (1910).
69. Leete, E., The biogenesis of morphine, *J. Am. Chem. Soc.,* **81,** 3948 (1959).
70. Masse, G., R. Herbeuval, and M. L. Chollot, Etude de l'élimination urinaire des catécholamines chez le Rat au cours de la diurèse provoquée par l'alcool éthylique, *Compt. Rend. Soc. Biol.,* **155,** 1528 (1961).
71. Maynard, L. S. and V. J. Schenker, Monoamine oxidase inhibition by ethanol *in vitro, Nature,* **196,** 575 (1962).
72. McIssac, W. M., Formation of 1-methyl-6-methoxy-1,2,3,4-tetrahydro-2-carboline under physiological conditions, *Biochem. Biophys. Acta,* **52,** 607 (1961).
73. Mendelson, J. H., M. Ogata, and N. K. Mello, Catecholamines and cortisol in alcoholics during experimentally induced intoxication and withdrawal, *Federation Proc.,* **58,** 18 (1969).
74. Mirone, L., Effect of prolonged ethanol intake on body weight, liver weight

and liver nitrogen, glycogen, ADH, NAD and NADH of mice, *Life Sci.,* **4,** 1195 (1965).

75. Perman, E. S., Effect of ethyl alcohol on secretion from adrenal medulla in man, *Acta Physiol. Scand.,* **44,** 241 (1958).

76. Perman, E. S., Observations on the effect of ethanol on the urinary excretion of histamine, 5-hydroxyindole acetic acid, catecholamines and 17-hydroxycorticosteroids in man, *Acta Physiol. Scand.,* **51,** 62 (1961).

77. Perman, E. S., The effect of acetaldehyde on the secretion of adrenaline and noradrenaline from the suprarenal gland of the cat, *Acta Physiol. Scand.,* **43,** 71 (1958).

78. Pscheidt, G. R., B: Issekutz, Jr., and H. E. Himwich, Failure of ethanol to lower brain stem concentrations of biogenic amines, *Quart. J. Studies Alc.,* **22,** 550 (1961).

79. Räihä, N. C. R. and E. Oura, Effect of ethanol oxidation on levels of pyridine nucleotides in liver and yeast, *Proc. Soc. Exp. Biol. Med.,* **109,** 908 (1962).

80. Raskin, N. H. and L. Sokoloff, Brain alcohol dehydrogenase, *Science,* **162,** 131 (1968).

81. Robbins, J. H., Possible alkaloid formation in alcoholism and other diseases, *Clin. Res.,* **16,** 554 (1968).

82. Romano, C., F. H. Meyers, and H. H. Anderson, Pharmacological relationship between aldehydes and arterenol, *Arch. Intern. Pharmacodyn.,* **99,** 378 (1954).

83. Rosenfeld, G., Inhibitory influence of ethanol on serotonin metabolism, *Proc. Soc. Exp. Biol. Med.,* **103,** 144 (1960).

84. Rosenfeld, G., Potentiation of the narcotic action and acute toxicity of alcohol by primary aromatic monoamines, *Quart. J. Studies Alc.,* **21,** 584 (1960).

85. Rutledge, C. O. and J. Jonason, Metabolic pathways of dopamine and norepinephrine in rabbit brain *in vitro, J. Pharmacol. Exp. Therap.,* **157,** 493 (1967).

86. Santi, R., A. Bruni, S. Luciani, C. E. Tóth, M. Ferrari, G. Fassina, and A. R. Contessa, Pharmacological properties of tetrahydropapaveroline and their relation to the catecholamines, *J. Pharm. Pharmacol.,* **16,** 287 (1964).

87. Santi, R., M. Ferrari, C. E. Tóth, A. R. Contessa, G. Fassina, A. Bruni, and S. Luciani, Pharmacological properties of tetrahydropapaveroline, *J. Pharm. Pharmacol.,* **19,** 45 (1967).

88. Schenker, V. J., B. Kissin, L. S. Maynard, and A. C. Schenker, The Effect of Ethanol on Amine Metabolism in Alcoholism, in *Biochemical Factors in Alcoholism,* R. P. Maickel (ed.), p. 39, Pergamon, New York, 1967.

89. Schneider, F. H., Acetaldehyde-induced catecholamine secretion from the cow adrenal medulla, *J. Pharmacol. Exp. Therap.,* **177,** 109 (1971).

90. Smith, A. A. and S. Gitlow, Effect of Disulfiram and Ethanol on the Catabolism of Norepinephrine in Man, in *Biochemical Factors in Alcoholism,* R. P. Maickel (ed.), p. 53 Pergamon, New York, 1967.

91. Smith, M. E. and H. W. Newman, The rate of ethanol metabolism in fed and fasting animals, *J. Biol. Chem.,* **234,** 1544 (1959).

92. Spenser, I. D., Biosynthesis of the akaloids related to norlaudanosoline, *Lloydia,* **29,** 71 (1966).

93. Taborsky, R. G. and W. M. McIssac, The synthesis and preliminary pharmacology of some 9H-pyrido (3,4-b) indoles (β-carbolines) and tryptamines related to serotonin and melatonin, *J. Med. Chem.*, **7**, 135 (1964).
94. Titus, E. and H. J. Dengler, The mechanism of uptake of norepinephrine, *Pharmacol. Rev.*, **18**, 525 (1966).
95. Tóth, E., G. Fassina, and E. S. Soncen, Cardiovascular and lipid mobilizing effects of tetrahydroisoquinoline, *Arch. Intern. Pharmacodyn.*, **169**, 375 (1967).
96. Towne, J. C., Effect of ethanol and acetaldehyde on liver and brain monoamine oxidase, *Nature*, **201**, 709 (1964).
97. Truitt, E. B., Jr., Ethanol-induced release of acetaldehyde from blood and its effect on the determination of acetaldehyde, *Quart. J. Studies Alc.*, **31**, 1 (1970).
98. Tyce, G. M., E. V. Flock, and C. A. Owen, 5-Hydroxytryptamine metabolism in brains of ethanol-intoxicated rats, *Mayo Clin. Proc.*, **43**, 668 (1968).
99. von Wartburg, J. P., and H. Aebi, Der Einfluss langdauernder Äthylalkoholbelastung auf die Katecholaminausscheidung im Harn der Ratte, *Helv. Med. Acta*, **28**, 89 (1961).
100. Walsh, M. J., V. E. Davis, and Y. Yamanaka, Tetrahydropapaveroline: An alkaloid metabolite of dopamine *in vitro, J. Pharmacol. Exp. Therap.*, **174**, 388 (1970).
101. Walsh, M. J., P. B. Hollander, and E. B. Truitt, Jr., Sympathomimetic effects of acetaldehyde on electrical and mechanical properties of cardiac muscle, *J. Pharmacol. Exp. Therap.*, **167**, 173 (1969).
102. Walsh, M. J. and E. B. Truitt, Jr., Acetaldehyde mediation in the mechanism of ethanol-induced changes in catecholamine metabolism, *Federation Proc.*, **28**, 543 (1969).
103. Walsh, M. J. and E. B. Truitt, Jr., Release of 7-H^3-norepinephrine in plasma and urine by acetaldehyde and ethanol in cats and rabbits, *Federation Proc.*, **27**, 601 (1968).
104. Walsh, M. J., E. B. Truitt, Jr., and V. E. Davis, Acetaldehyde-mediation in the mechanism of ethanol-induced changes in norepinephrine metabolism, *Molec. Pharmacol.*, **6**, 416 (1970).
105. Walsh, M. J., E. B. Truitt, Jr., and P. B. Hollander, Adrenergic effects of acetaldehyde on mechanical and electrical properties of cardiac muscle, *Pharmacologist*, **10**, 183 (1968).
106. Westerfeld, W. W., R. J. Bloom, L. M. Shaw, and P. G. Fuller, The Acetaldehyde Condensation Reaction with Alpha-Ketoglutarate, in *Biochemical and Clinical Aspects of Alcohol Metabolism,* V. M. Sardesai (ed.), chap. 8, Charles C Thomas, Springfield, Ill., 1969.
107. Westerfeld, W. W. and M. P. Schulman, Some biochemical aspects of the alcohol problem, *Quart. J. Studies Alc.*, **20**, 439 (1959).
108. Yamanaka, Y., M. J. Walsh, and V. E. Davis, Salsolinol, an alkaloid derivative of dopamine formed *in vitro* during alcohol metabolism, *Nature*, **227**, 1143 (1970).

Chapter IV

THE EXPERIMENTAL APPROACH TO ALCOHOLIC LIVER DAMAGE

W. STANLEY HARTROFT

UNIVERSITY OF HAWAII SCHOOL OF MEDICINE, HONOLULU

A. Introduction

The association of hepatic damage with the chronic consumption of alcoholic beverages by man has been recognized for centuries [1, 3]. One of the earliest reports of the pathologic appearance of the alcoholic liver is that of Rokitansky [74], who described an "exquisitely fatty liver" in a young woman whose bibulous nature seemed to have been apparent to all, including her physicians. From the very start, students of the problem have been divided as to whether ethanol acts as a direct hepatotoxin analogous to ones such as carbon tetrachloride or whether the deleterious effect on the liver is the result of the disruption of the normal balance of the accompanying diet. The controversy continues with considerable intensity to the present day.

Even a brief theoretical consideration of the circumstances under which chronic liver damage occurs in alcoholic man emphasizes the nutritional aspects. Surveys [20, 39] have indicated that the chronic alcoholic often consumes on the daily average a quart or more of commercially available spirits. These beverages (whiskey, gin, etc.) all contain about 50% of ethanol v/v. Immediately two significant differences between alcohol and established hepatotoxins become apparent. The amount of alcohol required to produce liver damage is much, much greater—over several years hundreds of gallons may be consumed—than the comparably minute amounts needed in the case of the hepatotoxins. Second, alcohol has a large caloric content, absent in the case of the evident toxins. The calories[1] derived from the alcohol consumed by the chronic alcoholic, in most cases, exceed those obtained from his diet, because a quart of whiskey provides over 2000 kcal, nearly all of which are readily absorbed and metabolized. (Only a small percentage of ingested alcohol is lost via the breath or urine.) These calories,[1] whether taken in the form of beer, wine, or spirits, are virtually devoid of any significant content of essential food factors, amino acids, lipotropes, vitamins, and trace metals. It is almost certain that such an intake of "empty" calories disrupts the balance of an ordinary diet and imposes a catastrophic stress on the liver and other vital organs (such would be the case even if the calories were derived from nonalcoholic sources, such as fat or carbohydrate). This consideration must be constantly born in mind in planning and interpreting relevant animal experiments and in evaluating the situation in the patient. In this light it is a remarkable fact that only a small percentage of alcoholics[2] admitted to sanatoria for treatment of socioeconomic difficulties brought about by their alcoholism reveal any detectable impairment of liver function by currently used laboratory tests. The incidence of cirrhosis in proven alcoholics is only about 1 in 12, according to Sherlock [79]. This finding alone is strongly suggestive that factors other than the intake of alcohol per se are crucial in the production of liver damage, thereby pointing to the probable importance of others, namely, nutritional and, of course, constitutional or genetic ones.

It soon became readily apparent to investigators approaching the problem in the present century that the answer to the mechanisms of the production

---

[1] In this chapter the use of the term *calories* throughout always indicates kilocalories.
[2] The definition of the term *alcoholic* is difficult. Attempts to describe such an individual in terms of daily average amount and duration of his intake of alcohol have failed. In this communication we use the term to refer to an individual whose chronic consumption of alcohol has led him into socioeconomic difficulties (loss of friends, family, or earning power).

of liver damage with alcohol in man must be sought by animal experimentation. But not until the thirties or forties did it begin to be suspected that the dietary background of the animals receiving the alcohol must be carefully controlled, because the problem might well be more of a nutritional than a toxicologic matter. As an example, the late Mallory, Sr., made many unsuccessful attempts [52] to reproduce the lesion of intracellular hyaline within hepatocytes (Mallory bodies) that he discovered in livers of human alcoholics [51]. It is apparent now that at least one important reason for his failure was that he administered the alcohol to rabbits that were allowed to consume a completely normal diet. We now know that the latter largely protects the mitochondria of such alcohol-consuming animals to the extent that Mallory bodies do not form, although mitochondria undergo other changes in such a circumstance, evident only with the electron microscope.

A second obstacle to the experimental production of hepatic damage with the chronic consumption of alcohol is that most animals do not readily consume amounts of alcohol comparable with those regularly enjoyed daily by alcoholics. Many of the earlier attempts to reproduce the fatty, fibrotic and cirrhotic lesions in livers of animals offered alcohol failed, simply because it has now been established that the amounts of ethanol consumed were quite inadequate to produce significant degrees of liver damage.

In this review we make no attempt to deny all possibility of a theoretically direct hepatotoxic action of alcohol. We summarize data that indicate that even if such a toxic action existed, it would be under the usual circumstances which surround the habitual consumption of alcohol and which are such that any toxicity would be so overwhelmed by the effect of the quality of the accompanying solid diet that the latter would be the crucial factor determining the effect of the alcohol on the liver. It is now quite evident that in the rat even large amounts of alcohol ingested daily for many months do not impair hepatic function if the accompanying food mixture is optimally designed to compensate for the caloric stress imposed by the alcohol. Further the continued intake of alcohol does not inhibit in animals an astonishing degree of recovery of hepatic structure and function from previously established liver injury, even advanced cirrhosis, as long as the therapeutic diet is formulated to allow for the alcohol calories ("superdiet"). The question of whether or not such a superdiet protects the animal from a so-called "hepatotoxic action" of alcohol or more specifically corrects a harmful dietary imbalance induced by large numbers of nutritionally "empty" calories provided by the alcohol seems at this moment to be more a matter of semantics than one of practical importance. The experiments of Reynolds et al. [73] with human alcoholics certainly give the nutritional view gained from the animal studies considerable relevance to the situation in man.

In the following account we deal mainly with the experimental approach to the study of chronic consumption of alcohol by animals. Many publications have appeared concerning the effects on the liver of the administration of a single, massive dose of ethanol to rats. This acute model is dealt with only briefly, because there is little evidence that single doses of alcohol are associated with significant degrees of hepatic disease. These acute studies have, however, provided useful basic information.

B.   Methods of Alcohol Administration in Chronic Experiments

The simplest way of administering alcohol to animals in experiments designed to imitate the chronic consumption of spirits by man is by adding ethanol to the drinking water. This technique of course forces the rat either to consume the alcohol or to die of thirst. It was soon found by all investigators who tried the method [2, 6, 35, 88] that the maximum concentration of alcohol in the drinking water that would be tolerated by the animal was about 15% v/v. If more was added, the animals simply drank less, so that the absolute amounts of alcohol taken in were no greater and usually less than when offered in the lower concentration [88]. When alcohol was so given along with most solid diets, the percentage of total calories obtained from the alcohol was only about 25%[3] [6]. This quantity is much less than that consumed by victims of alcohol-associated liver damage. It would be more pertinent to the human situation if the proportion in the animal studies could be doubled. Certainly when a relatively small amount of alcohol (25% of total calories) is consumed by rats given most stock diets, even fatty livers—let alone fibrosis or cirrhosis—do not develop [88]. It later became evident that probably the levels of protein and lipotropes present in stock rations were protecting the livers of rats given ethanol by this technique and only when these factors were reduced by the appropriate formulation of semisynthetic diets did this intake of ethanol produce fatty livers and some fibrosis, but not cirrhosis [6].

Still a certain amount of useful information was acquired with the simple dilute ethanol solutions in place of drinking water. But it was not until the Lieber fluid diet was introduced that it was possible to persuade rats to consume large amounts of alcohol. Lieber et al. [44] devised a totally fluid diet from which the animal obtained not only his alcohol and water

[3] The percentages of the various sources of energy in all the diets throughout this chapter are in terms of the percentage of total calories provided by the diet unless indicated otherwise.

but also the rest of his dietary needs. Protein was supplied in the form of soluble amino acids, and fat was incorporated with the aid of an emulsifier as oils from corn or cotton. Rats offered this Lieber mixture regularly consumed 36% of their total calories in the form of alcohol. But if the concentration of ethanol in the mixture was increased—to 50%, for example—the rats simply consumed a smaller total amount of the fluid, lost weight, and their livers remained normal [63]. In experiments involving alcohol, as with all nutritional studies, it is essential that animals at least maintain their initial body weight, and best if they grow. But if they lose weight, they do not develop any evidence of hepatic damage, no matter how imbalanced the dietary regimen with or without alcohol.

The Lieber fluid is made up to provide 1 cal/ml of the mixture. The technique offers many advantages, and at the time of its introduction, represented a significant methodologic advance in the alcohol field. The total caloric intake can be readily metered, and the calculation of the percentage of calories derived from alcohol is a matter of simple arithmetic. It is much easier to obtain the latter ratio with Lieber's model than when the alcohol and the solid diet are offered separately, because with the latter technique individual records of the intake of fluid and of food must be kept. The calculations of the calories derived from each source are laborious. Groups given sucrose instead of alcohol can be very readily controlled isocalorically by the Lieber device.

The disadvantages of Lieber's technique are chiefly related to its expense, because of the high cost of the amino acids used in place of protein derived from natural sources—in our hands it took just about a dollar a day per rat—and because one is limited in the sources of fat that one can use (solid fats, such as butter, do not suspend well). Most important, although the fact that rats would consume a greater amount of alcohol when given the Lieber fluid than ever achieved before represented a significance advance over the simple dilute alcohol-drinking model, 36% of total calories from alcohol was still unfortunately less than that consumed by most patients who develop associated hepatic damage.

In our laboratories my colleague, Dr. E. A. Porta, was able to overcome some of these limitations of the Lieber fluid. He made the relatively simple discovery that by taking advantage of the "sweet tooth" of the rat, it was possible to go back to the less expensive and more flexible approach of administering the alcohol in the drinking water separately from the other dietary ingredients [60]. (The rat might be said to prefer a sweet martini to a dry one.) After trials of various proportions of alcohol to sucrose in the drinking water he found that the optimal mixture to achieve the maximum intake of alcohol under most dietary conditions was 32%

alcohol and 25% sucrose v/v. The percentage of total calories (diet plus drinking fluid) consumed by rats in the form of alcohol varies under these conditions with the quality of the solid food simultaneously offered, but it ranges from 40 to as high as 60%. We found [67] that the vitamin content of the solid diet did not influence the amount of alcohol consumed as reported in a somewhat related experiment previously [4]. Growth is maintained, thus satisfying this all-important nutritional requirement. Because of the saving in cost (amino acids need no longer be used) and the flexibility of the model (one is free to design any type of semisynthetic solid diet desired), in our laboratory we have now abandoned the Lieber model in favor of sweetened alcoholic drinking fluid. Furthermore of course this method of administration more closely mimics the conditions under which man consumes alcohol, because it allows the rat a free choice, in satisfying his energy needs, between alcohol and food.

It is possible that by supplying some of the vitamins in the alcohol-sucrose drinking fluid rather than in the solid diet, the intake of alcohol would be even further increased. Such modifications have not yet been explored. They offer promising pathways for studying the effect of specific factors that may influence significantly the amount of alcohol desired by test animals.

C.   Species of Choice

It is the rat, although rabbits [53], dogs [11], and even nonhuman primates [12] have been used in the experimental approach to the relation of alcohol to the liver. More complete knowledge of the nutritional requirements of this animal has been accumulated during the past several decades than for any other species, including man, since the introduction of the rat into the study of nutrition by McCollum. The omnivorous habits of the rat and its willingness to consume almost any food mixture, no matter how esoteric, distinguish it from all other common laboratory animals. It has been objected that the liver of the rat contains more choline oxidase than does that of man and therefore the rat should be more susceptible to the production of fatty liver and its sequelae (fibrosis and cirrhosis) than man [80]. But the difference would make the rat an even more sensitive test subject, because if it is possible to protect the rat's liver from the lipogenic effects of alcohol, the human liver with less choline-inactivating enzyme should also be protected and even more readily. Debate along these theoretical lines, however, is probably irrelevant, because results of rat experiments have now been confirmed in man [73].

D. Nutritional Effects of Chronic Consumption of Alcohol

During the early part of this century much of the experimental approach to alcohol and the liver was based on a hypothesis that commercially available spirits might contain harmful levels of substances, such as phosphorous, copper, or iron [52]. There are currently little data available to support this notion, and it is not considered further here, although MacDonald [50] restudied the possible cirrhogenic effects of iron, which in some wines is present in relatively large amounts. Others have postulated that the alcohol interferes with the absorption of essential food factors, thus producing a secondary malnutrition [32]. This hypothesis has in the past few years been given new support by the investigations of Leevy [40], which indicate that vitamin B_{12} and folic acid are not absorbed well by the chronic alcoholic.

During the thirties and the forties the hypothesis that alcohol exerted a direct hepatotoxic action was strongly advocated [2, 56]. But the concensus of current investigations has increasingly focused on the role of alcohol in disrupting the nutritional requirements for maintaining a healthy liver and by this route producing the damage. The view that alcohol exerts a direct hepatotoxic action is, however, still held by a few [46]. Our criticisms of the data that seem to support the latter notion are indicated below.

One of the first nutritional experiments with alcohol was carried out in dogs by Connor and Chaikoff [11]. By feeding the animals a low-protein, high-fat diet and administering large amounts of alcohol by tube, they produced fatty livers. Restoring the level of protein to the food of other animals given alcohol and low levels of dietary fat protected the liver. In later experiments these investigators demonstrated that high levels of fat alone in the absence of adequate protein produced the same changes even without added alcohol [8]. With the discovery of the lipotropic action of methionine-containing protein [5, 9, 89] it seemed that the results of the experiments of Chaikoff and Connor could be explained on the basis that the high alcohol or fat intake had increased the animals' lipotropic requirements that were insufficiently met when the low-protein diet was fed. Lowry et al. [49] later confirmed these findings in choline-deficient rats fed alcohol.

In 1947 Ashworth [2] reported that an adequate diet consumed by rats given a drinking fluid containing 15% ethanol v/v would not prevent their livers from becoming fatty. But livers of rats that consumed the basal diet designed by Ashworth and offered only water to drink did not become fatty. He concluded therefore that alcohol acted as a direct hepatotoxin.

But Ashworth's protocol did not permit him to determine whether or not the incorporation of additional lipotropic factors into the basal diet of the alcohol-consuming rats would have prevented the liver damage. It seemed quite possible that a basal diet that was adequate for the liver when consumed alone might not have contained sufficient lipotropes to compensate for the additional calories provided by alcohol. In Toronto in the laboratories of Professor C. H. Best an experiment was therefore carried out [6] to test the validity of this criticism of the Ashworth experiment.

The Toronto protocol permitted the evaluation of the effect of the calories per se provided by the alcohol on the lipotropic requirement. The leading group of rats was offered 15% alcohol in the drinking water v/v, just as Ashworth had done, but the accompanying solid semisynthetic diet contained just barely that amount of total lipotropic factors (choline plus the methionine in the casein that was used as the source of protein) to prevent a fatty liver in rats consuming the solid diet alone. All rats grew well, even the ones that derived some 25% of their total calories from the alcohol in their drinking water. Fatty livers with early fibrosis developed in the alcohol-fed animals as well as in others given an amount of sucrose isocaloric with the amount of ethanol consumed by the leading group. High supplements of choline chloride mixed with the basal diet of rats of still other groups consuming either alcohol or isocaloric amounts of added sucrose completely protected the liver. The data clearly established that under these conditions it was the result of the caloric stress which was responsible for significant degrees of liver damage and which had been imposed by either alcohol or sugar. Liver injury produced by either the sugar or the alcohol was completely prevented by adequate supplies of lipotropic factors added to the accompanying solid diet to compensate for the superimposed caloric burden.

It was stated at the time by the Toronto group that choline might well not be the only food factor capable of so protecting the liver from the threat of alcohol-derived calories. Indeed in quite recently reported experiments (*vide infra*) we have been able to support this speculation. Protein, vitamin B_{12}, and folic acid all exert varying degrees of protection with and without additional choline supplements, but the lipotropic content is the most essential and the only factor to be effective by itself [62].

The results of the group headed by Best were speedily confirmed. Klatskin [35] found that although his data indicated that calory for calory more choline was required to inhibit the effects of alcohol on the liver than for sugar, sufficient lipotropes would still protect in both situations. His quantitative data have not been confirmed by others. In fact in recent experiments the writer and his colleagues have consistently found the opposite (sugar is more harmful than alcohol in the absence of adequate choline). But throughout the 1950s there was general agreement that high supplements of lipotropes (choline, betaine, methionine-containing protein and methionine itself, alone or in various combinations) would protect the livers of rats receiving some 25% of their total calories in the form of alcohol.

From about the mid-1950s until the early '60s little new on the subject appeared. Although it was generally recognized that the amount of alcohol consumed by rats in this type of experiment was appreciably less than that consumed by the chronic alcoholic with cirrhosis, most investigators of the subject considered the controversy settled to the effect that alcohol could not be demonstrated in animals to act as a direct hepatotoxin and that its hepatolipogenic and cirrhogenic effects were the result of its producing relative dietary deficiencies. Clinicians, however, reported conflicting results in their attempts to treat patients with alcoholic cirrhosis by high doses of lipotropic pharmaceuticals [13].

Probably from some of these reasons the problem was reopened and received a fresh stimulus by the report in 1963 by Lieber and his colleagues [44] that when rats consumed 36% of their total calories in the form of ethanol, fatty livers resulted that could not be completely prevented by a diet adequate in protein and choline. These investigators achieved the hitherto unprecedented high intake of alcohol with their rats by devising the totally fluid diet already described. Their results touched off anew the controversy between the "nutritionalists" and the "toxicolists" regarding the pathogenesis of alcohol-induced liver damage. The controversy is not yet fully settled [42].

With Lieber's new method his group was able to report that when 36.0 cal per 100 of the total diet was provided by alcohol, 41.3 by fat, 18.8 by protein (as amino acids), and the remainder—only 3.9—from carbohydrate, rats developed fatty livers even with an adequate supplement of choline. It is important to note that the nonalcoholic portion of this mixture is a very high-fat, low-carbohydrate imbalanced diet. Controls fed a comparable liquid in which isocaloric amounts of sucrose had been substituted for the alcohol did not develop fatty livers. These findings led Lieber et al. to resurrect Moon's and Ashworth's earlier views that the hepatic fatty changes were caused by a direct toxic effect of the alcohol [78]. He extended these experiments in comparable short-term ones on man [41, 43, 45].

In the writer's laboratory we carefully duplicated all the experimental conditions of the Lieber experiment and obtained exactly the same results. But a consideration of the experimental design along with data derived from extensions of this approach with his liquid diet forced our group to draw diametrically opposed conclusions.

Although the lipotropic value[4] of the Lieber mixture is probably adequate to prevent fatty livers in rats fed normally balanced diets, there is a gross imbalance of the fat, carbohydrate, protein ratio present in this experimental alcohol regimen that is fully corrected in the sucrose control. Animals receiving the latter consumed a mixture consisting of 41.3% fat, 39.7% carbohydrate, and 18.8% protein (amino acids). This fat/carbohydrate/protein ratio is ideal for the rat as established by many nutritional experiments reported between the two wars. But by substituting ethanol to provide 36% of calories at the expense of a corresponding amount supplied by the carbohydrate in the control mixture, the rats drinking the alcohol liquid diet received only 3.7% of their calories as carbohydrate. There is evidence that at least some of the calories provided by alcohol eventually enter the same metabolic pathway as does fat [47]. It is likely that the alcohol liquid diet was somewhat analogous to an extremely high-fat diet (nearly 80% of calories coming from fat plus alcohol). But as noted, the controls enjoyed a nearly ideal balance of nutrients that resulted when sucrose replaced the alcohol as the source of calories in the liquid. In a series of experiments [63] we were able to show that such high-fat mixtures and, particularly, high-carbohydrate diets, without any added alcohol, would produce fatty livers even when the lipotropic value was adequate. When the calories from alcohol were incorporated into the experimental diets at the expense of both the carbohydrate and fat present in the control diet, so that the disturbance of the basic ratios was minimal, fatty livers were prevented [25, 36, 64]. The importance of a well-balanced diet in terms of the fat/carbohydrate/ protein ratios established nothing new of course, because the production of fatty livers in a number of species by very high-fat or very high-carbohydrate diets was already widely recognized. Alcohol apparently enhances such imbalances, a point that is quite relevant to the situation in man. Leevy [39] reports that the intake of carbohydrate is frequently abnormally high in alcoholic patients who develop cirrhosis, confirming an early survey by Figieroa et al. in Kark's laboratory [20].

In comparing the effects on the livers of rats fed various ratios of fat, carbohydrate, and protein in these fluid mixtures containing alcohol, we unexpectedly encountered some highly interesting correlations with the lobular distribution of the stainable lipid [63]. When the protein was low, the

---

[4] The lipotropic index represents the content of choline or its precursor methionine expressed as milligrams per 100 cal of diet. Methionine is considered to have one-third of the lipotropic activity [90] of choline, milligram per milligram, because the former has only one labile methyl group compared with choline's three.

fat appeared in periportal positions; when the carbohydrate was high, the fat was again periportal with the formation of fatty cysts. When the lipotropic factors were inadequate, the fat first appeared centrolobularly. Therefore the dietary composition controlled the anatomic distribution of the stainable fat, not the alcohol.

The original experiments conducted by Lieber's group were terminated after 6 weeks. In our hands, when the rats were maintained on the same regimen (alcohol liquid diet) for 3 months, we discovered that the fatty livers disappeared [36]. These data suggest that a sufficiently long period of adaptation permits the animal to compensate to a considerable extent for the alcohol being consumed and for the imbalance of fat and carbohydrate.

All these conclusions have now been confirmed and extended in similar experiments conducted in our laboratory using the Porta-sweetened alcoholic drinking fluid to provide the alcohol calories along with a solid semi-synthetic diet offered separately and in which the protein, lipotropic, and vitamin contents could be varied at will. The percentage of calories derived from alcohol in these experiments was higher than with the Lieber mixture and usually ran about 45% [60].

Results from this series of experiments [25, 36–38, 60, 67, 68] afforded the following conclusions. Livers of rats that consumed 46% of their calories as alcohol in the sweetened water and given a solid semisynthetic diet of 18.5% protein, 31% fat, and, 50.5% carbohydrate with a lipotropic value of 162 in the final total mixture (diet plus fluid) did not develop fatty livers, nor of course fibrosis or cirrhosis, after 5 months [36]. But both pair-fed and ad libitum controls, in which the calories from alcohol in the diet of the leading group had been replaced with either carbohydrate or fat, developed fatty livers. In all groups, including that receiving alcohol, mitochondrial enlargement and even Mallory bodies were encountered. It is of particular interest that the bodies were seen in the nonfatty livers of the leading alcohol group. Rats in all groups grew well.

When the calories derived from alcohol by rats in the leading group were replaced by a judicious mixture of fat, protein, and carbohydrate, so that the final ratio of calories was 62:24:14 respectively, the livers of these rats were normal by all parameters studied (histochemical, biochemical, ultrastructural). These results emphasize the importance of the ratio of the main sources of energy in the solid diet when consumed even alone and particularly when accompanied by a high intake (46%) of alcohol over a prolonged period (5 months).

In these experiments and in others in which the level of protein was lower (5.7% calories/total calories) [25] and that of carbohydrate high

(85% calories/total calories), the livers of rats consuming such food mixtures developed significant degrees of hepatocellular necrosis. In livers of other rats consuming similar diets in which the level of fat was high, instead of carbohydrate, necrotic foci were rare and scattered. But in rats consuming alcohol (46% of total calories) foci of necrosis were never found, although hepatocytic swelling was present when the level of dietary protein was this low (5.7%). The latter change was completely prevented in alcohol-consuming rats when the level of protein was raised to 9.0% of total calories. It seemed from all these findings that alcohol, compared with fat and carbohydrate, even offered a measure of protection against the hepatic necrosis induced by certain low-protein diets.

These findings are significant when it is recalled that many alcoholic patients who develop cirrhosis gave histories of consuming high levels of carbohydrate in their solid food [20].

The series of experiments summarized above, involving hundreds of rats and using both the liquid diet of Lieber and the sweetened alcoholic drinking fluid of Porta, demonstrated without exception that significant alterations in hepatic structure and function could never be correlated with either the level of alcohol consumption (up to 60%) or with the duration (up to 6 months) of its administration. Hepatic damage evaluated by liver function studies during the animals' lives and biochemical estimations of hepatic lipid, hydroxyproline, DNA, RNA, and collagen at autopsy was found only when the alcohol had been consumed along with a diet deficient in protein or lipotropic factors and when the carbohydrate/fat ratio was grossly distorted, especially when the level of sucrose was high and that of fat low. When all these factors were carefully controlled and an abundance of all vitamins and lipotropes were present in the solid food mixture (superdiet [37]), the livers of rats so treated remained essentially normal even when the animals had taken nearly half of their total calories as alcohol for periods of 4 and 6 months.

E.   Production of Cirrhosis in Experimental Animals with Alcohol

Aside from the initial report of the appearance of hepatofibrosis only, not cirrhosis, in the rats of the experiments by Best et al. [6] the production of true cirrhosis had not been achieved with alcohol in any experimental model before the advent of the Porta model. In our laboratories it enabled us to attempt this objective at reasonable expense; the Lieber fluid is too costly for well-controlled, long-term experiments. Because the rats could thereby be induced to consume some 45% of their total calories as alcohol during a period of months, it seemed reasonable to us to hope that this method would be successful, although all previous attempts by other investigators and by us had failed.

The leading group of rats was given a semisynthetic basal diet containing adequate amounts of protein and lipotropic factors, which when diluted by the alcohol and sucrose in the Porta drinking fluid provided a final caloric pattern of 5% protein, 16% fat, 35% carbohydrate, and 46% alcohol [67]. The lipotropic value was low (only 12). Three control groups were included in the design. In one the alcohol was replaced isocalorically with sucrose; in another, with fat; and in the final group the alcohol was replaced by a mixture of protein, fat, and carbohydrate giving a well-balanced ratio and a high lipotropic value. After 6 months, cirrhosis had developed in all the first three groups. In the alcohol-consuming animals, however, only a monolobular stage had been reached; in the fat and especially in the sucrose controls a more severe degree of hepatic damage had resulted, attaining the stage of frank multilobular nodular cirrhosis in the sucrose group. The livers of the rats in the fourth group (alcohol replaced by a balanced mixture of fat, protein, and carbohydrate) were completely normal by all parameters used; liver function studies were unaltered.

In other experiments the protective effects of protein versus lipotropic factors in rats placed on the alcoholic cirrhogenic regimen were compared [67]. Adequate levels of protein without a choline supplement prevented cirrhosis. High supplements of choline, without raising the low-protein level, completely protected the livers of rats consuming the Porta drinking fluid, but the growth rates were low, as for any animal given a low-protein diet. In other groups of rats the effect of giving 10 times the usual level of a complete vitamin mixture (without choline) was tested [67]. Cirrhosis was prevented, but protection from fatty hepatic changes and mitochondrial enlargement was not complete with the large dose of multivitamin preparation. Subsequent experiments demonstrated that folic acid and vitamin B_{12} were probably the responsible ingredients in the complete mix [65].

These results provided a firm basis for the earlier speculation by Best et al. [6] that choline, although highly effective by itself in preventing the fatty liver and fibrosis that otherwise developed in their rats consuming 25% of total calories as alcohol, was probably not the only dietary ingredient in most natural foods that could exert some degree of protective action under these conditions. It is of considerable potential practical importance that choline by itself is so effective [6, 67]. The chemical is cheap, and it would be perfectly feasible to add sufficient choline, as choline citrate because of its bland taste, to commercial alcoholic beverages in quantities sufficient to raise their lipotropic indices to well above the critical level of 40 (for rats). All the data available from the numerous animal experiments described herein, as well as Reynolds' experiment in human cirrhotics, strongly suggest that such a measure carried out on a national scale might be of considerable value in the prevention of chronic hepatic injury in alcoholics. The expense would be little, the effect on taste undetectable, and the benefits potentially great. If choline were so incorporated into spirits, the more consumed, the more choline taken; and protection might thereby be automatically provided independently of the well-documented erratic dietary habits of the alcoholic.

F.   Curing Cirrhosis with Alcohol

Having demonstrated that alcohol would not impair the functions of the liver when the consumption was accompanied by a suitable (superdiet), solid food mixture, a more severe test of the idea that ethanol lacked any direct hepatotoxic potential was conceived. In these experiments [68, 84, 85], first carried out with Lieber liquid model and later with the Porta sweetened alcoholic drinking fluid, advanced cirrhosis was produced and then the effect of feeding alcohol to these rats tested. Our hypothesis was based on the notion that, if alcohol per se were truly capable of directly producing liver injury, it should surely be capable of rendering a *coup de grace* to animals with such severe cirrhosis that hepatic coma threatened. To the contrary we found that such animals given 36 to 45% of their calories as alcohol along with a superdiet, far from being sicker, recovered completely in all measured parameters of liver function. At the end of 3 months of treatment, when autopsied, their livers revealed an astonishing degree of anatomic reversal toward structural normality.

In the first of these experiments [84] an advanced stage of multilobular nodular cirrhosis was produced by feeding the animals a low-choline, low-protein cirrhogenic diet for 7 months. The existence of such advanced degrees of cirrhosis in each rat was confirmed by inspecting the gross appearances of livers at laparotomy. Any animals that had not developed multilobular nodules were discarded at this stage. The remainder was then distributed among three groups, so that the average and the range of body weights in all were similar (the animals had lost weight because of their cirrhosis). One group was continued on the cirrhogenic diet as a "negative control"; many of them died before the conclusion of the experiment, 3 months later. Those in the second group were given a superdiet (35% protein in the form of amino acids) along with five times the normal requirement of rats for all vitamins. This group constituted the "positive control." The third was the experimental group, and it received the superdiet diluted, however, with an amount of pure ethanol sufficient to supply 36% of the total calories. Although this amount of alcohol significantly reduced the amount of protein and lipotropic factors in the final mixture, levels were still more than adequate, just as planned. When killed after 3 months, the survivors of the negative control group all exhibited extreme degrees of multilobular nodular cirrhosis; the livers of the second group (positive control) had regressed toward normal to the extent that only thin, compressed, and relatively acellular bands of fibrous tissue surrounded persistent clumps of ceroid pigment. But the livers of the third group (alcohol plus superdiet) had reversed even further toward normal, although the different parameters used for this evaluation (hepatic hydroxyproline, soluble and insoluble collagen, DNA/RNA ratios, etc.) did not differ statistically from those determined for rats of the second group.

Ultrastructurally mitochondria in livers of rats of the alcohol group still showed a degree of enlargement that, however, was less than in the negative control group of cirrhotics. This degree of persistent alteration of organelles could be attributed to the alcohol, because it was not seen at all in members of the positive control group (superdiet alone). But Mallory bodies present in all cirrhotic rats had completely disappeared from the livers of rats consuming the superdiet alone or with alcohol. In a few rats in both these groups killed 1 month after treatment, Mallory bodies had already vanished. The ready reversibility of these inclusions is of considerable relevance to the fact that they are so commonly found in admission liver biopsies of alcoholics and are often few or absent in cirrhotic livers of alcoholics who have died after a considerable stay in hospital (and therefore denied alcohol for a comparably long period).

In the second therapeutic experiment [68] two important modifications were made in the experimental design used in the first. The object here was to answer the question whether cirrhosis produced in rats with alcohol, rather than a low-protein, low-choline diet alone, could be cured with alcohol and a superdiet taken separately, as man does, rather than with alcohol and food administered together as in the first experiment. The data clearly indicated that it could.

Cirrhosis was produced in rats with alcohol by giving them the Porta fluid and providing them with a basal diet in which both the lipotropic content and the protein level were sufficiently low so that in the final caloric pattern 40% alcohol and 6% protein were combined. After 7 months, cirrhosis of the advanced multilobular nodular type had developed in those rats selected entirely at random and killed. These cirrhotic animals were then distributed among positive and negative control groups and an experimental one which continued to receive ethanol as before but which was offered the superdiet in solid form along with the Porta fluid. After 4 months all rats were killed. Results were the same as those of the first experiment. Hepatic function had been completely restored in all previously cirrhotic rats that had received the superdiet with or without alcohol along with nearly complete reversion to normal of all structural abnormalities. This experiment demonstrated that when alcohol was involved in the production of cirrhosis, the resulting lesions were just as capable of reversal as when the cirrhosis had been produced without alcohol and that successful treatment of the disease was possible when the alcohol and the superdiet were consumed separately, just as patients would do.

If the only available data concerning reversal of cirrhosis with alcohol were those obtained from animal experiments, we should have to be cautious in extrapolating the conclusions to alcoholic cirrhotic man. But essentially the same experiment was done successfully in the latter. Reynolds [73] treated a group of cirrhotics with alcohol in fruit juice and an excellent hospital diet, quite comparable with our superdiet, and in a double-blind design treated others with the same diet and the fruit juice alone. In order to maintain significant levels of blood alcohol in the leading group, Reynolds found he had to increase the intake of alcohol by the subjects as the diet effected recoveries of liver function and the ability to metabolize the ethanol at a normal rate. By the end of the experiment some of the patients were receiving nearly 500 ml of alcohol daily. Despite this large amount their hepatic function studies were normal at the conclusion of the treatment, and hepatic structure as evaluated in liver biopsies had reverted to a remarkable degree toward the normal.

Probably no one would recommend that a cirrhotic patient in socioeconomic difficulties as a result of his alcoholism be deliberately allowed to continue drinking. Treatment with a superdiet would probably do little for other than the liver of such a victim. But if he cannot be weaned from his alcohol, surely even his psychiatric troubles have a better prognosis if his liver disease can be improved than if his cirrhosis continues unabated. Both the experimental and clinical data presented above indicate that continued alcohol intake does not inhibit the regression of nodular cirrhosis if a suitable dietary regimen is insisted on and effectively implicated.

G.   Pathogenesis: Light and Electron Microscopy

In both animals [26, 30] and man [10] the liver damage produced under suitable conditions by alcohol is preceded and accompanied by the abnormal accumulation of fat. Again in both species the amount of fat reaches its highest levels at the onset of cirrhosis and falls as the latter condition progresses [10]. This phenomenon we regard as the biochemical reflection of the escape of lipid from ruptured fatty cysts or the lipodiastaemata, which we have called the cytometaplastic link between the fatty and fibrotic liver [30]. Certainly in both our animal models and in alcoholic cirrhosis in man, fatty cysts are a prominent feature.

Frank hepatocellular necrosis in the rat models is a variable and apparently unessential step in the pathogenesis of cirrhosis. It is only prominent when the accompanying diet is low in protein [25]. This finding probably has relevance to the necrotic foci encountered in acute alcoholic hepatitis in man [55, 59]. When present, these foci doubtless contribute to the architectural distortion and act as stimuli to the nodular regeneration that are the cardinal features of cirrhosis.

The first appearance of fibrosis is around remnants of ruptured fatty cysts [30]. Eventually these small islands join together to form annuli that surround the structural units of Rappaport [70]. Without Rappaport's conception of the hepatic acinus the pattern of the fibrosis in both animals and man seems paradoxical. It was described in the older literature [56] as "lobule-splitting," because the trabecular paths seemed to disregard the boundaries of the classic hexagonal lobule.

The first evidence of nodular regeneration can be seen within these isolated Rappaport units in which it is manifested by the appearance of frequently encountered mitotic figures in liver cells near the trabeculae [62]. Rather equal and uniform growth at all such sites leads to compression of the annuli with the eventual emergence thereby of the picture of a classic monolobular (Laennec) cirrhosis. The originally loose, cellular makeup of the fibrous bands becomes compressed by the expanding nodules of parenchyma into thinner bands of denser collagen. At this stage the trabeculae stain more deeply with the classic tinctorial methods for demonstrating collagen (anilin blue: light green) than before their compression [30]. Liver cells newly formed by mitotic division have less cytoplasm than normal ones, and there is also infiltration in and around the fibrous trabeculae of small oval cells with scanty cytoplasm that eventually proved by electron microscopy to be proliferating bile ductules [25, 29]. A fall in the DNA/RNA ratio of liver homogenates at this stage is a biochemical reflection of these alterations in cellular patterns [84].

In the last stages of the experimental models and for reasons not clearly understood, some nodules grow more rapidly than others. They thereby become compressed between the large, expanding ones. When a certain critical size has been attained—and it has never been determined just what this size is—the rapidly growing nodule is invaded by small triads containing bile ducts and branches of the hepatic artery. In this manner the nodule becomes split into several abnormal lobules, and its blood supply becomes primarily arterial. With completion of this step very large multilobular nodules (greater than 0.5 cm in diameter in man) are produced, and the intervening small ones become compressed, undergoing atrophy and fibrotic replacement. The latter development adds to the width of the trabeculae. At this stage, ascites may develop, presumably because of compression of blood vessels by the expanding nodules. The end result now fulfills all the criteria of a multilobular nodular cirrhosis of Marchand. In most of its features it is indistinguishable from postnecrotic cirrhosis.

Rupture of fatty cysts is a constant accompaniment to all stages in the development of fibrosis and cirrhosis [30]. Some of the fat is released into hepatic sinusoids and reaches lungs, kidneys, and brain as embolic fat [26]. The presence of large numbers of fat emboli has been considered the cause of sudden death in some alcoholics with acutely fatty livers [18, 24].

In our references thus far to the ultrastructural changes in the fatty and cirrhotic livers of rats given alcohol we have emphasized the mitochondrial changes [58]. In any case the enlarged and bizarre forms that these organelles assume are eye-catching [33, 34, 83]. Eventually they become sufficiently large so that they are visible by the light microscope as Mallory bodies (*vide infra*). This change, dramatic as it is, is not the only one. Both in the acute model and even in the early stages of the chronic ones the mitochondrial changes are accompanied by dilation of ergastoplasm and dispersion of ribosomes. Still later glycogen granules become sparse. In advanced stages the dilation of ergastoplasm becomes so extreme that a lacelike pattern is imparted to the entire hepatic cytoplasm under low magnification of the electron microscope [62].

Rubin and Lieber (75–77) report not only vacuolation of ergastoplasm but also its proliferation. They interpret this apparent hyperplasia as a morphologic manifestation of the induction of certain detoxifying enzymes by the alcohol and use this conclusion to support their hypothesis that ethanol is a toxin for the liver. They do not report actual micromensurational measurements of the ergastoplasmic membranes. In our material [69] obtained from livers of rats in experiments involving both the acute and chronic models of alcohol consumption, measurements of ergastoplasm by the method of Loud [48] have failed to confirm the reports by Lieber's group.

As liver cells undergo prenecrotic and necrotic changes, autophagic lysosomes and dense bodies become prominent. Numerous lysosomes contain ceroid pigment. These features are, however, common to all forms of cirrhosis and are not particularly associated with the effects of alcohol.

Probably the most characteristic, but not pathognomonic, finding in alcohol-associated cirrhosis in both experimental animals and man is the Mallory body (megamitochondrion).

H. The Mallory Body

Frequent allusions to this intracellular inclusion body that stains with most acid dyes (eosin, phloxine, chromotrope-2R, Luxol fast blue) have been already made. First described by Mallory [51], he initially believed its presence in either liver biopsies or autopsy specimens to be pathognomonic of the excessive consumption of alcohol. Subsequently Mallory himself and others encountered these curious bodies in cases of nutritional hepatic injury unassociated with any demonstrable history of alcohol consumption [54, 55]. Smetana et al. [81] describe numerous Mallory bodies in the cirrhotic livers of malnourished children in certain parts of India. These patients did not receive any alcohol of course but had consumed diets low in protein and lipotropic factors and high in carbohydrate.

In our laboratories the writer first encountered intracytoplasmic inclusions that corresponded to Mallory bodies in cirrhotic livers of choline-deficient rats [27]. By electron microscopy [28] they proved to be giant mitochondria, exceeding the size of the nucleolus and even attaining diameters equal to half or more of those of nuclei nearby in the same sections. Subsequently these megamitochondria have been produced at will by my colleague, Dr. E. A. Porta, in many experiments [58]. From his studies we have learned that the Mallory bodies when first formed consist exclusively of megamito-chondria of sufficient size so that they are visible with the light microscope. Like the Mallory bodies of man they stain with all the classic tinctorial methods originally devised to demonstrate normal mitochondria [57]. In hepatocytes of alcohol-consuming rats a continuous spectrum in the shape and size of mitochondria can be observed ranging from the normal to the huge megamitochondrion [33, 58]. We reserve the latter term for those mitochondria which have reached sufficient size to be visible by light microscopy as Mallory first described them. Their eventual fate is to be engulfed by autophagic lysosomes in which they may be observed in frag-ments along with remnants of other organelles, such as ergastoplasmic arrays.

Enlargement of mitochondria, even up to and including the stage of actual Mallory body formation, is a constant accompaniment to the con-sumption of large amounts of alcohol by rats. The inclusions were present in livers of rats of both the progressive and regressive experiments already described. Even when sufficient amounts of lipotropes and protein are in-cluded in the basal diets of alcoholic rats, so that fatty, fibrotic, and cirrhotic

changes were completely prevented, mitochondrial enlargement and sometimes even Mallory bodies formed [36]. They are particularly prominent
when the levels of protein are adequate. These findings have tempted us
to conclude that the mitochondrial enlargement may not be a true degener-
ative change, as Kiessling and Tobe report [34], but may in fact represent
a morphologic manifestation of successful enzymatic adaptation to caloric
stress, particularly facilitated when there is no shortage of the building
blocks of amino acids from adequate intakes of protein.

Just as in the human situation, so also in our animal experiments, Mallory
bodies were found in control groups of rats given isocaloric amounts of
carbohydrate in place of alcohol [36]. Here the resulting food mixture of
low protein, low choline, and high carbohydrate mimics the situation in
the Indian children described by Smetana et al. [81]. The resulting pattern,
complete with Mallory bodies, seen in our rats duplicates to a remarkable
extent the lesions they described.

Biava [7] and Smuckler [82] emphasize the nonmitochondrial component
of Mallory bodies in livers of man, but we have only been able to demonstrate elements other than mitochondrial in the late stages of their natural
history when found engulfed in lysosomes [58]. Certainly when first formed,
in both animals and man, the inclusions consist of megamitochondria.

I.   The Acute Model of Alcohol Administration

In 1958 Di Luzio [14] devised a model for the purposes of studying the acute effect
of alcohol on the liver. Six milliliters of ethanol per kilogram of body weight diluted with an equal quantity of water is introduced by gavage into animals starved
for 12 hr. They develop evident signs of acute intoxication (staggering gait and
semicoma). By both biochemical and histochemical parameters, 8 hr after giving
the alcohol, triglycerides attain their peak values (69.4 to 103.2 mg/100 g of wet
weight of liver). They disappear another 6 to 12 hr later. Administration orally or
by injection of relatively large amounts of choline before, with, or after the ingestion of alcohol does not prevent the accumulation of hepatic fat in the model [66].

In our laboratories [31, 66] we were able not only to confirm but also to extend
these findings of Di Luzio. Electron microscopy studies showed that the droplets of
abnormal lipid (centrolobular) were not membrane-bound. Their appearance was
accompanied by an alteration of the shape and size of the mitochondria; initially
they changed from oval in outline to spherical, and later many assumed bizarre
elongated or curved shapes partially enclosing fat droplets. Mitochondria returned
to normal as the fat disappeared.

Later Di Luzio discovered that various antioxidants, both the naturally occurring
alpha tocopherol and several synthetic ones, given with the alcohol prevented the
accumulation of hepatic fat and an increase of diene conjugation [15, 16]. Again
we were able to confirm his findings and in addition found that alpha tocopherol

also largely prevented, and synthetic oxidants completely prevented, the alterations in size and shape of mitochondria as well as the increase in hepatic fat.

Di Luzio [17] found that large doses of antioxidants given to rats chronically consuming a liquid diet that provided about 30% of calories as alcohol prevented a fatty liver. We have not been able to confirm this finding in our laboratories [60].

From this it can be concluded that when alcohol is given in large, intoxicating doses, a degree of lipoperoxidation is induced, as indicated by the increase in the level of diene conjugation and the protective effect of antioxidants. The mechanisms involved are doubtless similar to those following the administration of carbon tetrachloride and phosphorous [21–23, 71, 72] in which diene conjugation also rises and antioxidants exert protective actions. The failure of choline to prevent fatty livers in this model indicates here that the nutritional factors, other than antioxidants, are not the ones of primary importance. The blood levels of alcohol in these rats reach high levels (over 200 mg/100 ml of blood) within a few hours of its administration. This fact along with the data presented above may indicate under these extreme conditions that alcohol may in this instance be behaving somewhat like an hepatotoxin. It is of interest that under the conditions of the chronic administration of alcohol, both Lieber and Porta models, the total amount of alcohol consumed daily is appreciably greater than that given in the single, acute dose. But the blood levels of alcohol in the rats chronically consuming the alcohol along with food do not reach more than half of that found at the peak of the rise in Di Luzio's acute model [14].

If the dose of alcohol used by Di Luzio is accompanied by food, using amino acids for protein, a fatty liver does not result [19]. The blood levels of alcohol in this situation rise to only half of those attained when the ethanol is given to the fasted animal. This fact probably explains the absence of fat accumulation in the liver. Furthermore measurable amounts of alcohol in the blood of the fed rats disappear within 6 to 8 hr after gavage, less than half of the time needed for detectable amounts to disappear from the blood of the starved animals. Both protein and fat when either are fed alone to the alcohol-treated rats produce this effect; carbohydrate does not. Oral administration of fiber alone (alpha cell®) also prevents the steep rise in levels of blood alcohol and the development of a fatty liver, thereby indicating that the mechanism is the result of the bulk of the food or fiber, rather than some specific action of the protein or fat, acting to slow the rate of alcohol absorption. The delay in absorption permits a more efficient clearance of alcohol from the blood by the liver. The effect of bulky food other than carbohydrate in slowing the rate of absorption of alcohol has of course been recognized for years, even among lay drinkers.

If some toxic action of alcohol seems to be apparent in the acute model, is it logical to question or minimize such in the chronic experiments or in patients habitually consuming spirits? We believe it is, because it seems here that we are dealing with a matter of dose response as related to the height of blood levels of alcohol. Food accompanying the alcohol keeps the levels low in both acute and chronic circumstances. Further the fatty liver of acute ethanol intoxication is readily reversible within a matter of a few hours.

Relevant to this question, however, are the recently reported experiments of Takeuchi et al. [86, 87]. These Japanese investigators have administered massive, single doses of alcohol to rats in which dietary injury had previously been induced by low-choline, low-protein diets. They report the rapid development of frank necrosis in the previously fibrotic or cirrhotic livers of the acutely intoxicated rats. Their results have obvious relevance to acute alcoholic hepatitis in man.

CONCLUSIONS

It is not possible to produce disturbances of liver function or more than minor alterations detected ultrastructurally in liver structure by the administration of large amounts (36 to 50%) of alcohol to rats that consume suitably designed and well-balanced diets containing an abundance of protein, lipotropic factors, and vitamins (superdiet).

Rather remarkably the replacement of large amounts of alcohol calories by either carbohydrate or fat produces some fatty lesions even when the remainder of the dietary pattern resembles that of the protected alcohol-consuming rats.

When the dietary intake of rats drinking alcohol is inadequate in protein and lipotropic factors particularly or when the food mixture is inordinately rich either in fat or especially in carbohydrate, fatty livers, fibrosis, and cirrhosis develop. Alcohol under these adverse conditions, however, has no more of a cirrhogenic action than high levels of dietary fat and less than high dietary carbohydrate.

These results have been successfully applied to man. They explain the otherwise paradoxical fact that only a small minority of patients who consume sufficient alcohol so that they end up in sanatoria for the treatment of their psychiatric problems suffers from disturbed liver function. Leevy's excellent study of the habits of cirrhotics revealed no correlation between the degree of liver disease and either the amount or the duration of drinking. But those who developed the most advanced cases of cirrhosis were the alcoholics with low intakes of protein and high intakes of carbohydrate. This picture is just that which one would predict if one had deliberately carried out in man experiments designed to imitate our animal studies. The converse is the case, because the design of many of our protocols was formulated with Leevy's data in mind.

Similarly our therapeutic experiments with rats correspond closely to Reynolds' elegantly designed study of cirrhotics. The data from each reinforce the other. The parallel between the results of the therapeutic human studies and the animal work is close.

Results from all studies clearly indicate to this writer that the association between alcohol and hepatic injury in man is largely if not entirely attributable to the high caloric content and the attendant caloric stress with dietary imbalance imposed on livers when spirits are consumed in the amounts habitually resorted to by alcoholics and prealcoholics. In animals equally large caloric burdens derived from either fat or especially carbohydrate produce degrees of hepatic injury comparable or even greater under similar dietary conditions. Conversely alcohol cannot produce liver disease in animals when accompanied by a suitably designed food mixture either given with the alcohol in liquid form (Lieber model) or offered separately in solid form (Porta model). Even more dramatically, alcohol when consumed in large amounts does not inhibit the success of appropriate dietary treatments of cirrhotic rats and man.

If nobody consumed any alcohol or if all alcoholics took their physicians' advice and ceased drinking, the prevention and treatment of the associated liver disease would be no problem. To some it may still seem the method of choice for both purposes. But as a practical general prophylactic measure or an individual one for the treatment of a patient, denial of alcoholic beverages has not proved realistic. If these facts are faced, then as far as the hepatic health of our nation is concerned, it is a rather urgent matter that the general physician, and the public as well, be educated to realize that alcohol contains nearly as many calories as fat and that caloric stress can be easily induced by drinking. Only by appropriately modifying the accompanying diet can danger be averted, so that sufficient protein, lipotropes, and vitamins are provided to maintain a proper ratio of these factors to not only the calories from food but also those from alcohol.

All conventional portions of alcoholic beverages, whether a bottle of beer or a small glass of liqueur, contain approximately 200 cal in the form of alcohol. This amount is more than that provided by two slices of bread. The public should learn to eat equally less carbohydrate and fat on a calory per calory basis to match the extra energy from their drinks.

We firmly believe that the success of such an educational program would be marked by an accompanying decrease in the frequency of alcohol-associated cirrhosis, now sixth or seventh as a cause of death in adults. Failing this ideal approach, serious consideration should be given to the idea of supplementing alcoholic beverages with choline.

ACKNOWLEDGMENTS

We thank Professor E. T. Nishimura, Chairman of the Department of Pathology of the School of Medicine, University of Hawaii, Honolulu, for his assistance in editing this chapter; and Professor Eduardo A. Porta, Chairman of the Department of Pathology of the School of Medicine, University of Buenos Aires, Argentina, for helping with the bibliography.

REFERENCES

1. Addison, T., Observations on fatty degeneration of the liver, *Guys Hosp. Rep.*, **1,** 476 (1836).
2. Ashworth, C. T., Production of fatty infiltration of liver in rats by alcohol in spite of adequate diet, *Proc. Soc. Exper. Biol. & Med.*, **66,** 382 (1947).
3. Baillie, M., *The Morbid Anatomy of Some of the Most Important Parts of the Human Body,* p. 141, J. Johnson, St. Paul's Churchyard and G. Nicol, Pall Mall, London, 1793.
4. Beerstecker, E., Jr., J. G. Reed, W. D. Brown, and L. J. Berry, The effects of single vitamin deficiencies on the consumption of alcohol by white rats, *Univ. Texas Publ.* S109, 115 (1951).
5. Best, C. H., H. J. Channon, and J. H. Ridout, Choline and the dietary production of fatty livers, *J. Physiol. London,* **81,** 409 (1934).
6. Best, C. H., W. S. Hartroft, C. C. Lucas, and J. H. Ridout, Liver damage produced by feeding alcohol or sugar and its prevention by choline, *Brit. Med. J.* **2,** 1001 (1949).
7. Biava, C., Mallory alcoholic hyaline: A heretofore unique lesion of hepatocellular ergastoplasm, *Lab. Invest.,* **13,** 301 (1964).
8. Chaikoff, J. L. and C. L. Connor, Production of cirrhosis of liver of normal dog by high fat diets, *Proc. Soc. Exper. Biol. & Med.,* **43,** 638 (1940).
9. Channon, H. J. and H. Wilkenson, Protein and the dietary production of fatty livers, *Biochem. J.,* **29,** 350 (1935).
10. Connor, C. L., Cirrhosis of the liver, *Quart. J. Studies on Alcohol,* **1,** 95 (1940).
11. Connor, C. L. and J. L. Chaikoff, Production of cirrhosis in fatty livers with alcohol, *Proc. Soc. Exper. Biol. & Med.,* **39,** 336 (1938).
12. Cuedo, J., Production of liver damage in subhuman primates with alcohol, *(Discussion) Federation Proc.,* **26,** 1444 (1967).
13. Davison, C., Cirrhosis of the liver, *Am. J. Med.,* **16,** 863 (1954).
14. Di Luzio, N. R., Effect of acute ethanol intoxication on liver and plasma lipid fractions of the rat, *Am. J. Physiol.,* **194,** 453 (1958).
15. Di Luzio, N. R., Prevention of the acute ethanol-induced fatty liver by the simultaneous administration of antioxidant, *Life Sci.,* **3,** 113 (1964).
16. Di Luzio, N. R., The role of lipid peroxidation and antioxidants in ethanol-induced hepatic alterations, *Exp. Molec. Path.,* **8,** 394 (1968).
17. Di Luzio, N. R. and A. D. Hartman, Modification of Acute and Chronic Ethanol-induced Liver Injury and the Role of Lipoperoxidation in the Pathology of Ethanol Induced Fatty Acids, in *Biochemical and Clinical Aspects of*

Alcohol Metabolism, Y. M. Sardices (ed.), chap. XVI, p. 133, Charles C Thomas, Springfield, Ill., 1969.

18. Durlacher, S. H., J. R. Meier, R. S. Fisher, and W. V. Lovett, Jr., Sudden death due to pulmonic fat embolism in persons with alcoholic fatty liver, *Am. J. Path.,* **30,** 633 (1954).

19. Fardel, C., W. S. Hartroft, and E. A. Porta, The effect of meals on the fatty liver induced by acute alcoholism in rats, unpublished data.

20. Figieroa, W. G., S. Sergeant, L. Imperiale, G. R. Morey, C. R. Paynter, L. J. Vorhaus, and R. M. Kark, Lack of avitminosis among alcoholics: Its relation to fortification of cereal production and the general nutritional status of the population, *J. Clin. Nutr.,* **1,** 179 (1956).

21. Ghoshal, A. K., E. A. Porta, and W. S. Hartroft, The role of lipoperoxidation on the pathogenesis of fatty liver induced by phosphorous poisoning in rats (Abstr.), *Gastroenterology,* **56,** 414 (1969).

22. Ghoshal, A. K., W. S. Porta, and W. S. Hartroft, The role of lipoperoxidation in the pathogenesis of fatty livers induced by phosphorous poisoning in rats, *Am. J. Path.,* **54,** 275 (1969).

23. Ghoshal, A. K., E. A. Porta, and W. S. Hartroft, Studies on the hepatotoxic action of phosphorous (Abstr.), *Federation Proc.,* **29,** 755 (1970).

24. Goldberg, M. and C. M. Thompson, Acute fatty metamorphosis of the liver *Ann. Intern. Med.,* **55,** 416 (1961).

25. Gomez-Dumm, C. L. A., E. A. Porta, W. S. Hartroft, and O. R. Koch, A new experimental approach in the study of chronic alcoholism: II. Effects of high alcohol-intake in rats fed diets of various adequacies, *Lab. Invest.,* **18,** 365 (1968).

26. Hartroft, W. S., Accumulation of fat in liver cells and in lipodiastaemata preceeding experimental dietary cirrhosis, *Anat. Rec.,* **106,** 61 (1950).

27. Hartroft, W. S., Intracellular ("pseudoalcoholic") hyalin in experimental dietary cirrhosis of rats and mice (Abstr.), *Am. J. Path.,* **34,** 603 (1958).

28. Hartroft, W. S., Some Electron Microscopic Features of the Liver in Experimental Choline Deficiency, in *Aktuelle Probleme der Hepatologie,* G. A. Martini (ed.), p. 53, Thieme, Stuttgart, 1962.

29. Hartroft, W. S., Electron Microscopy of Liver and Kidney Cells in Dietary Deficiencies, in *Ciba Foundation Symposium on Cellular Injury,* A. V. S. De Reuch and J. Knight (eds.), p. 248, Little, Brown, Boston, 1964.

30. Hartroft, W. S., Experimental Cirrhosis, in *The Liver, Morphology, Biochemistry, Physiology,* C. Rouiller (ed.), vol. 2, pp. 477–514, Academic, New York, 1969.

31. Hartroft, W. S. and E. A. Porta, Ultrastructural hepatic changes in acute ethanol-treated rats (Abstr.), *Gastroenterology,* **46,** 304 (1964).

32. Himsworth, H. P., *Lectures on the Liver and Its Diseases,* Harvard, Cambridge, Mass., 1947.

33. Kiessling, K. H., H. Lindgren, B. Strandberg, and U. Tobe, Electron microscopic study of liver mitochondria from human alcoholics, *Acta Med. Scand.,* **176,** 595 (1964).

34. Kiessling, K. H. and U. Tobe, Degeneration of liver mitochondria after prolonged alcohol consumption, *Exp. Cell. Res.,* **33**, 350 (1964).
35. Klatskin, G., H. M. Gewin, and W. A. Krehl, Effects of prolonged alcohol ingestion on liver of rat under conditions of controlled, adequate dietary intake, *Yale J. Biol. & Med.,* **23**, 317 (1951).
36. Koch, O. R., E. A. Porta, and W. S. Hartroft, A new experimental approach in the study of chronic alcoholism: III. Role of alcohol *versus* sucrose or fat-derived calories in hepatic damage, *Lab. Invest.,* **18**, 379 (1968).
37. Koch, O. R., E. A. Porta, and W. S. Hartroft, A new experimental approach in the study of chronic alcoholism: V. "Superdiet," *Lab. Invest.,* 298 (1969).
38. Koch, O. R., E. A. Porta, and W. S. Hartroft, A new experimental approach in the study of chronic alcoholism: VII. Implications of dietary protein, in preparation (1970).
39. Leevy, C. M., Fatty liver. A study of 270 patients with biopsy-proven fatty liver and a review of the literature, *Medicine,* **41**, 249 (1962).
40. Leevy, C. M., Clinical diagnosis, evaluation and treatment of liver disease in alcoholics, *Federation Proc.,* **26**, 1474 (1967).
41. Lieber, C. S., Chronic alcoholic hepatic injury in experimental animals and man: Biochemical pathways and nutritional factors, *Fed. Proc.,* **26**, 1443 (1967).
42. Lieber, C. S., Metabolic derangements induced by alcohol, *Am. Rev. Med.,* **18**, 35 (1967).
43. Lieber, C. S., D. P. Jones, and L. M. De Carle, Effects of prolonged ethanol intake production of fatty liver despite adequate diets, *J. Clin. Invest.,* **44**, 1009 (1965).
44. Lieber, C. S., D. P. Jones, J. Mendelson, and L. M. De Carli, Fatty liver, hyperlipemia and hyperuricemia produced by prolonged alcoholic consumption despite adequate dietary intake, *Trans. Assn. Am. Physicians,* **76**, 280 (1963).
45. Lieber, C. S. and E. Rubin, Alcoholic fatty liver in man on a high protein and low fat diet, *Am. J. Med.,* **44**, 200 (1968).
46. Lieber, C. S. and E. Rubin, Ethanol: A hepatotoxic drug, Gastroenterology, **54**, 642 (1968).
47. Lieber, C. S. and R. Schmid, The effect of ethanol on fatty acid metabolism: Stimulation of hepatic fatty acid synthesis *in vitro, J. Clin. Invest.,* **40**, 394 (1961).
48. Loud, A. V., A quantitative sterological description of the ultrastructure of normal rat liver parenchymal cells, *J. Cell. Biol.,* **37**, 27 (1968).
49. Lowry, J. V., L. L. Ashburn, F. S. Daft, and W. H. Sebrell, Effect of alcohol in experimental liver cirrhosis, *Quart. J. Studies Alc.,* **3**, 168 (1942).
50. MacDonald, R. A., Human and Experimental Hemochromatosis and Hemosiderosis, in *Pigments in Pathology,* Moshe Wollman (ed.), chap. V, pp. 115–149, Academic, New York, 1969.
51. Mallory, F. B., Necrosis of the liver, *J. Med. Res.,* **6**, 264 (1901).
52. Mallory, F. B., Cirrhosis of the liver: Five different types of lesions from which it may arise, *Bull. Johns Hopk. Hosp.,* **22**, 69 (1911).

53. Mallory, F. B., Cirrhosis of the liver, *New Eng. J. Med.,* **206,** 1231 (1932).
54. Mallory, F. B., Phosphorous and alcoholic cirrhosis, *Am. J. Path.,* **9,** 557 (1933).
55. Mallory, G. K., Liver diseases associated with chronic alcoholism, *Lab. Invest.,* **9,** 132 (1960).
56. Moon, V. H., Experimental cirrhosis in relation to human cirrhosis, *A.M.A. Arch. Path.,* **18,** 381 (1934).
57. Norkin, S. A., R. Wertzel, D. Campagna-Pinto, R. MacDonald, and K. G. Mallory, "Alcoholic" hyaline in human cirrhosis: Histochemical studies, *Am. J. Path.,* **37,** 49 (1960).
58. Porta, E. A., Electron Microscopy of Liver in Experimental Chronic Alcoholism, in *Biochemical and Clinical Aspects of Alcohol Metabolism,* V. M. Sardesen (ed.), Charles C Thomas, Springfield, Ill., p. 189, 1969.
59. Porta, E. A., B. J. Bergman, and A. A. Steen, Acute alcoholic hepatitis, *Amer. J. Path.,* **46,** 657 (1965).
60. Porta, E. A. and C. L. A. Gomez-Dumm, A new experimental approach in the study of chronic alcoholism: I. Effects of high alcoholic intake in rats fed a commercial laboratory diet, *Lab. Invest.,* **18,** 352 (1968).
61. Porta, E. A., and W. S. Hartroft, Effect of Vitamin E on Ultrastructural Changes of the Liver in Acute Ethanol Intoxication, in *Symposium on Therapeutic Agents and the Liver,* S. Sherlock (ed.), Davis, Philadelphia, pp. 145–164, 1965.
62. Porta, E. A., W. S. Hartroft, and F. A. de la Iglesia, Hepatic changes associated with chronic alcoholism in rats, *Lab. Invest.,* **14,** 1437 (1965).
63. Porta, E. A., W. S. Hartroft, F. A. de la Iglesia, and C. L. A. Gomez-Dumm, Implications of the dietary constituents on the lobular distribution of hepatic lesions in experimental chronic alcoholism, *Am. J. Path.,* **48,** 39a (1966.)
64. Porta, E. A., W. S. Hartroft, C. L. A. Gomez-Dumm, and F. A. de la Iglesia, Role of dietary constituents in experimental chronic alcoholism, *Proc. VIIth Internat. Congress Nutr.,* **5,** 223–226 (1966).
65. Porta, E. A., W. S. Hartroft, and O. R. Koch, Effects of Folic Acid and Vitamin B_{12} in Experimental Chronic Alcoholism, in *Biological Aspects of Alcohol,* M. Roach and P. J. Creaven (eds.), Texas Research Institute of Medical Science. In Press (1970).
66. Porta, E. A., W. S. Hartroft, and M. Suzuki, Effects of choline chloride on hepatic lipids after acute alcohol intoxication, *Quart. J. Studies Alc.,* **25,** 427 (1964).
67. Porta, E. A., O. R. Koch, and W. Stanley Hartroft, A new experimental approach in the study of chronic alcoholism: IV. Reproduction of alcoholic cirrhosis in rats and the role of lipotropes *vs.* vitamins, *J. Lab. Invest.,* **20,** 562 (1969).
68. Porta, E. A., O. R. Koch, and W. S. Hartroft, A new experimental approach in the study of chronic alcoholism: VI. Recovery of chronic hepatic lesions in rats fed alcohol and a solid superdiet. In preparation.
69. Porta, E. A., J. G. Sugioka, and W. S. Hartroft, Quantitative morphologic

changes in hepatocytic mitochondria and SER of rats in acute and chronic alcoholism, *Acta Gastroenterologica Latino-Americana*, **1**, 63–73 (1969).

70. Rappaport, A. M., Anatomic Considerations, in *Diseases of the Liver*, L. Schiff (ed.), 2d ed., chap. 1, pp. 1–46, Lippincott, Philadelphia, 1956.

71. Recknagel, R. O., Carbon tetrachloride hepatotoxicity, *Pharm. Rev.*, **19**, 145 (1967).

72. Recknagel, R. O. and A. K. Ghoshal, Lipoperoxidation as a vector in carbon tetrachloride hepatotoxicity, *Lab. Invest.*, **15**, 132 (1966).

73. Reynolds, S. B., A. G. Redeker, and O. T. Kuzman, Role of Alcohol in Pathogenesis of Alcoholic Cirrhosis, in *Symposium on Therapeutic Agents and the Liver*, S. Sherlock (ed.), Blackwell Science Publication, Oxford, 1965.

74. Rokitansky, K., *Manual of Pathologic Anatomy, vol.* 2, p. 145, Syndenham Society, London, 1849.

75. Rubin, E. and C. S. Lieber, Early fine structural changes in the human liver induced by alcohol, *Gastroenterology*, **52**, 1 (1967).

76. Rubin, E. and C. S. Lieber, Experimental alcoholic hepatic injury in man: Ultrastructural changes, *Federation Proc.*, **26**, 1455 (1967).

77. Rubin, E. and C. S. Lieber, Alcohol-induced hepatic injury in nonalcoholic volunteers, *New Eng. J. Med.*, **278**, 869 (1968).

78. Rubin, E. and C. S. Lieber, Effect of alcohol on liver, *New Eng. J. Med.*, **279**, 46 (1968).

79. Sherlock, S., *Diseases of the Liver and Biliary System*, 4th ed., p. 412, Davis, Philadelphia, 1968.

80. Sideranski, H. and E. Farber, Liver choline oxidase activity in man and several species of animals, *Arch. Biochem. & Biophysic.*, **87**, 129 (1960).

81. Smetana, H. F., G. G. Hadley, and S. M. Sirsat, Infantile cirrhosis: An analytic review of the literature and a report of 50 cases, *Pediatrics*, **28**, 107 (1961) .

82. Smuckler, E. A., The ultrastructure of human alcoholic hyalin, *Am. J. Clin. Path.*, **49**, 790 (1968).

83. Svoboda, D. and R. T. Manning, Chronic alcoholism with fatty metamorphosis of the liver: Mitochondrial alterations in hepatic cells, *Am. J. Path.*, **44**, 645 (1964).

84. Takada, A., E. A. Porta, and W. S. Hartroft, Regression of dietary cirrhosis in rats fed alcohol and "superdiet": Evidence of the nonhepatotoxic nature of alcohol, *Am. J. Clin. Nutr.*, **20**, 213 (1967).

85. Takada, A., E. A. Porta, and W. S. Hartroft, The recovery of experimental dietary cirrhosis: I. Functional and structural features, *Am. J. Path.*, **51**, 929

86. Takeuchi, J., A. Takada, and K. Ebata, Effect of alcohol on the livers of rats: I. Effect of a single intoxicating dose of alcohol on the livers of rats fed a choline-deficient diet or a commercial ration, *Lab. Invest.*, **19**, 211 (1968).

87. Takeuchi, J., A. Takada, R. Kunaya, N. Okata, and Y. Okamura, Effect of alcohol on the liver of rats: II. Factors contributing to elevations of plasma transaminase activities and hepatocellular necrosis following a single administration of alcohol in rats, *Lab. Investig.*, **21**, 398 (1969).

88. Thorpe, M. E. C. and C. D. Shorey, Long-term alcohol administration: Its

effects on the ultrastructure and lipid content of the rat liver cell, *Am. J. Path.*, **48,** 557 (1966).

89. Tucker, H. F. and H. C. Eckstein, The effect of supplementary methionine and cystine on the production of fatty livers by diet, *J. Biol. Chem.*, **121,** 479 (1937).

90. Young, R. J., C. C. Lucas, J. M. Patterson, and C. H. Best, Lipotropic dose-response studies in rats: Comparisons of choline, betaine and methionine, *Canad. J. Biochem. Physiol.*, **34,** 713 (1956).

Chapter V

MECHANISMS OF LIVER AND PANCREAS DAMAGE IN MAN

GUILLERMO UGARTE AND JORGE VALENZUELA

DEPARTMENT A OF MEDICINE (HOSPITAL SAN FRANCISCO DE BORJA)
UNIVERSITY OF CHILE, SANTIAGO
PROGRAM FOR ALCOHOL PREVENTION RESEARCH AND MANAGEMENT CENTRAL
AREA OF SANTIAGO, NATIONAL HEALTH SERVICE, CHILE

Liver disease associated with heavy alcohol[1] intake or alcoholism is in many areas of the world a serious public health problem [86]. The mechanism through which excessive ethanol intake produces liver damage has received increasing attention in the last years. Although considerable progress has been obtained, the matter is still the subject of much controversy.

Acute and chronic pancreatitis, although a less frequent complication of alcoholism, is probably next to alcoholic cirrhosis the most serious gastro-enterological derangement observed in alcohol abusers and is presently the subject of much interest regarding its pathogenesis.

[1] Alcohol and ethanol are used synonymously in this chapter.

Selected clinical, pathological, and biochemical aspects of the basic mechanisms probably involved in alcoholic liver and pancreas damage in man are discussed, and the areas are pointed out in which controversy exists or more data are needed to solve the pathogenic riddles.

A.   Alcohol and Liver Damage

1.   Relationship between Alcoholism and Liver Damage

The association of alcoholism and hepatic damage has long been known; Vesalius is said to have recognized this relationship, and Addison observed that patients who died of liver failure after overindulgence in drinking showed at autopsy a fatty liver [72].

The most serious type of hepatic damage associated with prolonged excessive drinking is liver cirrhosis. A high incidence of cirrhosis of the liver, associated with the high prevalence of problem drinking has been observed in several countries. In England, back in 1927, a high correlation between death rates due to alcoholism and cirrhosis was reported [92]; in the United States an increased mortality due to cirrhosis followed the repeal of Prohibition [53].

Chile has a high prevalence of problem drinking revealed by field survey, indicating that 5% of the adult population are addicts and 14% excessive drinkers [68].

The mortality rate in Santiago due to cirrhosis is the highest in several cities studied [86], and 86% of the cirrhotic patients who die in our medical unit are alcohol abusers [117].

These facts clearly indicate a link between alcoholism and chronic liver disease. The exact mechanism by which the excessive intake of ethanol produces liver damage has not been fully clarified. Research in the last quarter of a century has placed considerable emphasis on the role of malnutrition and more recently on the toxic effects of ethanol in the liver. Nevertheless the pathogenesis of alcoholic liver damage remains controversial and recent clinical-epidemiological and experimental studies suggest that other factors do conjugate with protein malnutrition and ethanol metabolic effects to produce liver disease.

2.   Clinical Incidence of Alcoholic Liver Disease and Related Pathogenic Problems

Most of the numerous studies of Laennec cirrhosis in the past, although very helpful in clarifying many clinical, metabolic, and pathological problems of the disease, have contributed little to unravel its pathogenesis. A great number of these studies have dealt with far advanced stages of a chronic progressive process in which Laennec cirrhosis with liver failure is the terminal episode.

A better insight into the pathogenesis of alcoholic liver disease, besides the experimental approach, has been obtained clinically in recent years by studying alcoholic patients without important signs of liver failure, from a clinical, nutritional, alcohol-history, metabolic, and pathological point of view [42, 56, 57, 114].

In 200 biopsied cases admitted to our unit for alcohol treatment we have encountered a high incidence of hepatic morphological abnormalities without significant difference between gamma and delta alcoholics [42]. See Table I.

Alcohol intake, mainly as wine, in these patients ranged from 200 to 700 g/day for periods lasting from 6 to 40 years. Protein intake was low, but no clear-cut difference in protein nutrition could be observed when grouped according to the type of liver damage [42]. A prolonged history of excessive drinking lasting more than 15 years was present in 60% of the cases.

In these cases, as in a group belonging to a different ethnic and socio-economical level reported by Lelbach [56, 57], it is interesting to note, on one hand, that the duration of alcoholism correlated only with the incidence of cirrhosis and, on the other, that approximately 25% of the patients had a normal liver histology or slight unspecific abnormalities after many years of alcohol abuse (see Figure 1). It is also remarkable that in spite of a prolonged history of alcoholism and protein malnutrition a

TABLE I   Histological Findings in 200 Biopsies from Alcoholics

Histology	Inveterate δ alcoholics, %	Intermittent γ alcoholics, %	Total, %
Normal	6	7	6
Nonspecific abnormalities	2	17	19
Steatosis[a]	62	64	63
Fibrosis[b]	37	44	39
Alcoholic hepatitis	14	7	11
Cirrhosis	12	13	12

[a] Cases with well-established cirrhosis excluded.

[b] Included cases with cirrhosis.

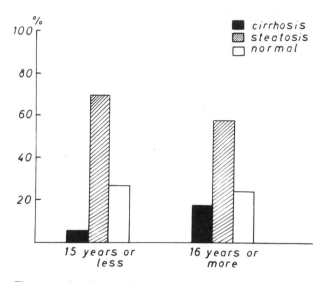

Figure 1. Incidence of hepatic abnormalities and duration of excessive drinking in alcoholics.

small proportion of cases progress from hepatic steatosis to cirrhosis of the liver.

3. Relationship among Fatty Liver, Necrosis, and Cirrhosis

Since the early studies of Best et al. [4] fatty liver was considered a precursor of alcoholic cirrhosis, extrapolating to man the results obtained with experimental models on choline-deficient diets [38]. Different mechanisms were postulated to explain the transition of fatty liver into cirrhosis, e.g., collapse of reticulum after the escape of fat from fatty cysts [37] or fibrosis produced on the site of parenchymal fissures resulting from an uneven distribution of the fat [78]. Although these mechanisms may operate in some circumstances, some other facts must be considered.

Experimentally induced fatty livers do not always progress into cirrhosis. In chronic carbon tetrachloride intoxication in which, besides the fat, there is marked necrosis, the cirrhotic stage is easily reached [6, 93]; the same is true for choline deficiency in which necrosis has been clearly demonstrated in radioautographic studies [91]. In chronic ethionine administration, in which necrosis is less severe, cirrhosis is difficult to obtain [77]. Orotic acid–induced fatty livers, conversely, do not show signs of necrosis, and they may persist for long periods without becoming cirrhotics [35].

Necrosis in alcoholic livers may conform several pictures, the best known of them is the so-called acute alcoholic hepatitis [3, 34, 80, 102]. This disorder usually appears after a massive and prolonged ingestion of alcohol. It is characterized by an episode of liver failure of varying severity, abnormal laboratory tests, fever, nausea, vomiting, and abdominal pain. Pathologically there are cellular degeneration, focal necrosis, inflammatory reaction with polymorphonuclear leucocytes, and steatosis. Presence of Mallory bodies is very common and seems to correspond to severe changes in mitochondria or megamitochondria [80], although this interpretation has been questioned [89].

Acute alcoholic hepatitis may take place in previously normal livers, fatty livers, or livers with fibrosis or cirrhosis.

As a variety of acute alcoholic hepatitis the picture of sclerosing hyaline necrosis [24] should be mentioned. In these cases lesions predominate in central areas and are associated with fibrosis, extending from the central veins.

Although the liver can recover completely even after an episode of severe necrosis [16], several observations have pointed out a worse prognosis in these patients [73]. Progression into cirrhosis in fatty livers with necrosis has been observed [78]. Active cirrhosis without fat, but with necrosis, has also been reported [106].

The facts mentioned above indicate that necrosis is probably more important than steatosis in the pathogenesis of cirrhosis, as it has been already suggested by others [79].

The presence of cirrhosis in asymptomatic individuals without a history of liver disease is not in contradiction with the necessary existence of previous necrosis, since this phenomenon, even in the form of acute alcoholic hepatitis without jaundice [3], may be clinically nonapparent [48, 114].

4. Role of Alcohol and Malnutrition in Liver Damage

The hypothesis that Laennec cirrhosis is due to protein malnutrition induced by chronic problem drinking has been widely accepted in the last decades. Data supporting this view have been given in numerous animal studies in which cirrhosis has not been reproduced with ethanol but with protein or lipotropic deficient diets, and recently in experiments showing that alcohol administration to cirrhotic rats receiving a high-protein diet does not prevent or slow recovery [110]. Clinical observations have pointed out too the importance of malnutrition showing a high incidence of protein deficiency in diets consumed by alcoholics [42] and demonstrating the effectiveness of high-protein diet in the treatment of alcoholic fatty liver and cirrhosis, even when moderate amounts of ethanol are simultaneously given [28, 107, 88].

If we consider this accepted evidence, there is little doubt that nutritional imbalance plays a very important role in chronic alcoholic liver disease. The assumption, however, that it is the most significant pathogenic factor leading to steatosis and cirrhosis in alcoholics is highly controversial. Although protein-calorie imbalance is the rule among the alcoholics seen in our unit, not only a small percentage (17%) develop cirrhosis after 16 or more years of alcohol abuse, but approximately 25% have a practical normal liver under the light microscope [42, 114]. Children with severe protein malnutrition do not develop cirrhosis [12], and this disease in adults seems to correlate better with the amount and duration of excessive drinking than with dietary protein deficiency. Because of the complex etiology and pathogenesis of liver cirrhosis it seems difficult to assess comparatively in this disorder the importance of malnutrition and alcohol effects per se.

A better approach seems to be the study of the acute and early chronic effects of excessive alcohol intake both in humans and experimental animals.

Human alcohol abusers show mainly two general patterns of alcohol intake. One group experiences intermittent ingestion crises or alcoholic sprees (gamma alcoholics), and the others drink continuously excessive amounts (delta alcoholics) [50].

In rats high amounts of alcohol given in a single high dose induce steatosis and ultrastructural changes in the liver [20, 82]. These changes are most probably due to alcohol itself and difficult to attribute to malnutrition. Fat mobilization has been demonstrated in this condition [5, 67], but no increase in circulating fatty acids has also been reported [25, 76]. Fatty acid composition of liver triglycerides has been found similar to fat depot [40], and so a decreased hepatic triglyceride utilization has been suggested [20].

Lipid peroxidation has been also postulated [20] and denied [36] as a pathogenic mechanism in alcoholic hepatic steatosis induced by ethanol, and its prevention with antioxidants demonstrated [20, 21].

These acute animal experiments may have their clinical counterpart in intermittent alcoholics in whom intake of 400 to 600 g of alcohol in few hours resulting in an increase in S-GOT levels have been observed [42, 117].

Chronic alcohol administration in high doses (36 to 45% of total daily calories) but usually somewhat inferior to the intake of an average alcoholic has been shown in human volunteers, either alcoholics with a previous history of hepatic steatosis [94, 95] or healthy individuals [96], to produce fatty and ultrastructural changes despite normal or high protein intake [63, 96]. Source of liver fat in this condition is mainly dietetic or originated in an enhanced fat synthesis in the liver [58, 61, 62, 105].

Human results have been reproduced in rats by different dietary methods that permit a high alcohol and adequate protein intake [2, 18, 60, 81].

Steatosis observed in some of these animal experiments, however, has been transient, disappearing after 4 weeks while on the alcohol diet. The adequacy of these diets has been questioned too, based on a supposed higher protein requirement when alcohol is consumed in high amounts [82–84, 33]. Rats fed a so called "superdiet" that contains besides alcohol a higher amount of protein and more balanced ratio of fat and carbohydrates show no substantial difference in liver fat deposition compared with controls [83, 84].

In human volunteers, however, high-protein and -alcohol diets (25% protein and 46% alcohol of total daily calories) determined liver changes identical with those produced by diets with a lower protein content [63, 96].

These controversial results probably suggest that besides a direct hepatotoxic effect of alcohol, other ethanol-induced metabolic abnormalities, such as impairment in amino acid absorption [44, 45] discussed below, should be considered in the interpretation of these nutritional-oriented experiments. Whatever is the relative importance of alcohol hepatotoxicity and protein malnutrition, there is no explanation for the existence of 25% of chronic alcoholics without visible fat in the liver biopsy performed during the first 5 days of abstinence [42, 114] (see Table I and Figure 1).

We have observed in some of these alcoholics without fatty liver after prolonged alcohol abuse that alcohol administration (46% of daily caloric intake) and adequate protein (16%) and fat intake (32%) do not induce histological or histochemical signs of hepatic steatosis after 10 to 14 days on this alcohol diet; fatty infiltration of the liver was reproduced in alcoholics with a previous history of steatosis [47, 114]. These observations indicate a different susceptibility to develop hepatic steatosis possibly constitutional or genetically determined in some alcoholics.

Different metabolic pathways for ethanol or some adaptive phenomena should be explored to explain the low susceptibility to alcoholic steatosis in these cases.

Facts heretofore discussed strongly indicate that hepatic damage in alcoholics results from the association of alcohol-dependent metabolic derangements and protein malnutrition plus a suggestive constitutional or genetic factor.

5.   Genetic Factors

The presence of a constitutional factor in the pathogenesis of Laennec cirrhosis has been long suspected since Chvostek described a particular somatotype often found in cirrhotics [27].

The association between a disease and a genetic marker suggests the presence of an inherited component [10]. A significant association has been reported between color blindness and alcoholic cirrhosis [13, 14]. Cruz-Coke presents evidence that this association is restricted to alcoholism and alcoholic liver disease and is not present in other types of liver damage despite liver failure [13, 14].

The association between color blindness and alcoholism seems clear, and the matter is extensively discussed by Cruz-Coke in this book.

The possibility that color blindness is also associated with an increased susceptibility of some alcoholics to develop cirrhosis has been studied in 140 biopsied alcohol addicts in our unit. Results, although confirming the

TABLE II   Distribution of Color Vision Disturbances Revealed by the Farnsworth-Munsell 100 Hue Test (FM), According to the Results of Liver Biopsy in 140 Alcoholics

| | FM, errors per cap | | | | | |
| | Red-green | | | Blue-yellow | | |
Liver biopsy	≤ 1.5	>1.5	p	≤ 1.5	>1.5	p
Normal and nonspecific alterations	17	7	...	16	8	
Steatosis	64	13	>0.2	46	31	>0.7
Cirrhosis	6	3	>0.8	5	4	>0.8
Steatosis + cirrhosis	14	6	>0.7	12	8	>0.8
Steatosis + necrosis	8	3	>0.7	7	4	>0.8
Steatosis + cirrhosis + necrosis	2	0	...	2	0	
Any specific lesion	94	25	>0.5	77	4	>0.7

Statistical analysis according to chi-square test; Yates correction was introduced when pertinent.

high correlation between color blindness, especially in the blue-yellow zone, and alcoholism, showed no difference between alcoholics with and without hepatic damage (see Table II). This finding rather indicates that the increased incidence of color blindness earlier reported by Cruz-Coke in patients with alcoholic cirrhosis is related to alcoholism and not to the liver cirrhosis.

6.   Alcohol Effects and Liver Damage

The mechanism by which ethanol may induce by itself liver damage is probably the chronic repetition of cellular derangements dependent on a direct chemical action or resulting from changes in biochemical pathways related to ethanol metabolism.

A direct cellular effect of ethanol is the impairment of amino acid transport observed in rats both in vitro and in vivo [7, 44]. This inhibition in amino acid transport by ethanol in physiological concentrations has been recently demonstrated by us for methionine in humans [45] (see Figure 2).

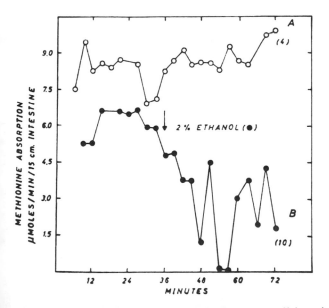

Figure 2. Methionine absorption in the human small intestine. The points represent the average for 4 subjects in curve A and 10 in curve B. The arrow shows the time at which alcohol was added to the perfusion fluid. No alcohol was added to the subjects in curve A throughout the experiments [45].

This derangement in intestinal absorption may explain the lower weight gain of rats given alcohol on a so-called adequate diet when compared with their pair-fed controls and may enhance both in animals and humans the effects on the liver of a low-protein intake.

The most significant effects of ethanol on the liver related to hepatic damage seem, however, to be indirect and related to alterations in other biochemical pathways resulting from alcohol metabolism.

A number of excellent reviews dealing with metabolic derangements induced by ethanol oxidation have appeared in the last years [46, 51, 59], and only some selected aspects are discussed here.

The most important change secondary to alcohol oxidation is the accumulation of NADH in the cytoplasmic soluble fraction [51, 59]. The increase in the NADH/NAD ratio favors the conversion of dihydroxyacetone phosphate to alpha-glycerophosphate. Dependent on NADH accumulation are also decreased mitochondrial oxidation of fatty acids [87], increased synthesis of fatty acids [58], and increased microsomal esterification of fatty Acyl-CoA compounds to triglycerides [134].

The significant alterations observed in mitochondrial morphology in alcoholics and alcohol-treated rats are probably the structural counterpart of the decreased activity in mitochondrial oxidative enzymes [52].

A mitochondrial impairment in alpha-glycerophosphate oxidation recently reported [101] probably enhances further accumulation of cytosol NADH in hepatic damage [55] and favors hepatic steatosis.

These abnormalities secondary to ethanol and acetaldehyde oxidation probably not only contribute to hepatic steatosis but also induce adaptive phenomena, such as increase of the smooth endoplasmic reticulum (SER) [94, 97] and peroxisomes [81, 94].

The relationship of mitochondrial abnormalities to ethanol oxidation is also suggested by the absence of mitochondrial changes after alcohol treatment in tissues lacking alcohol dehydrogenase activity, such as fetal livers or the brain [74].

The importance of ethanol oxidation in the pathogenesis of liver damage suggested by the data previously discussed induced us to study alcohol metabolism in human alcohol addicts with and without histological signs of liver damage.

A low liver alcohol dehydrogenase activity (alcohol:NAD oxidoreductase 1.1.1.1.E.C.) at pH 9.6 was observed both in patients with alcoholic liver disease and in alcoholics without histological signs of liver damage [116] (see Table III). Similar results had been reported elsewhere both in human alcoholics and in rats chronically treated with ethanol [1, 31, 30].

In spite of the decreased activity of liver alcohol dehydrogenase (LADH)

TABLE III   Hepatic ADH Activity, Rate of Blood Ethanol Elimination After Alcohol Infusion[a]

	Patients, N	ADH, μM/(hr)(mg)	Rate of alcohol removal (β), mg/(100 ml)(hr)
Moderate drinkers	8	0.37 ± 0.12	18 ± 6
Alcoholics:			
Without liver damage	18	0.18 ± 0.13	19 ± 8
With steatosis	18	0.12 ± 0.07	24 ± 11
With cirrhosis	10	0.11 ± 0.08	23 ± 7

[a] Alcohol (1.2 g/kg) infused intravenously.
Mean $\pm$ SD, ADH: alcohol dehydrogenase.

there was no impairment in the removal of ethanol from the blood when alcohol (1 g/kg b.w.) was infused intravenously to alcoholics without signs of important liver failure after 15 or more days of abstinence [115] (see Table III). Furthermore a moderate but significant increase in alcohol metabolic rate was observed in alcoholics with asymptomatic steatosis or cirrhosis when compared with drinkers without liver damage [115] (see Table IV). This finding induced us to study the prevalence of the hyperactive atypical variant of LADH described by Von Wartburg et al. [129, 130] in liver biopsies of alcoholics with and without hepatic damage, using the Q_{pH} screening method described by Von Wartburg [129, 130]. The

TABLE IV   Blood Ethanol Disappearance Rate in Subjects With and Without Hepatic Damage

	N	Rate of alcohol removal (β), mg/(100 ml)(hr)	SE
Moderate drinkers and alcoholics without hepatic damage	29	18.0	1.72
Alcoholics with steatosis or cirrhosis[a]	33	24.5	1.54

Subjects studied after 15 days of abstinence.
[a] Without signs of liver failure.
$2p < 0.01$.

ratio between activities assayed at pH 8.8 (atypical) and 10.8 (normal) showed a trimodal distribution of normal and atypical LADH in Chilean alcoholics [118], differing from the bimodal distribution observed in Switzerland and London [130] (see Figure 3).

This distribution showed overlapping of normal and atypical LADH with Von Wartburg screening test. Thus the Q_{pH} ratio was compared with the specific activity and samples with a high specific activity were considered atypical [118] (see Figure 4). According to this criterium liver homogenates showing a $Q_{pH} \leqslant 0.60$ were considered carriers of the atypical LADH (see Figure 4).

The correlation of the atypical LADH with the histological diagnosis demonstrated a significant higher prevalence of the atypical LADH among alcoholics with steatosis or cirrhosis considered as one group [118] and compared with alcoholics with normal liver histology (see Table V). We do not consider it prudent yet to reject the null hypothesis because a small shift in the Q_{pH} limit for the atypical LADH from 0.60 to 0.70 changes the significance from $p < 0.05$ to $p > 0.6$.

Although the significance of the increased prevalence of atypical LADH

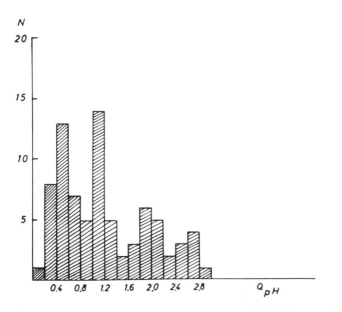

Figure 3. Frequency distribution pattern of LADH according to the Q_{pH} ratio in liver samples from 80 Chilean alcoholics; the Q_{pH} ratio is enzyme activity 10.8/8.8 pH (< 1 atypical LADH, > 1 normal) [118].

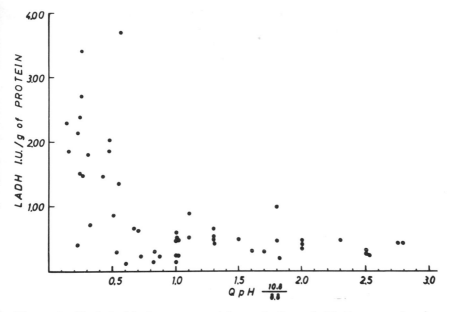

Figure 4. Alcohol dehydrogenase activity and Q_{pH} of 56 liver samples from alcoholic activities expressed in international units (IU) per gram of protein; Q_{pH} = ratio of activity at pH 10.8 to pH 8.8.

is questionable, it may explain the augmented blood ethanol disposal in alcoholics with hepatic damage and not in liver failure. This increase in blood alcohol removal, however, is much less than what would correspond to the activity of this enzyme in vitro [130]. This discrepancy between the fivefold increase in vitro of ethanol oxidation by the atypical enzyme and 30 to 50% increase in blood alcohol disappearance rate has been attributed to a probable rate-limiting factor in NADH oxidation [130].

Our study on blood alcohol removal in alcoholics [115], as most similar investigations [1, 8, 69] of alcohol metabolism rate in man showing no differences between alcoholics and normal individuals, has been carried after rather prolonged periods of abstinence. These results do not explain through an augmented ethanol metabolism the increased tolerance to alcohol effects that alcohol abusers often report to experience after some time of excessive drinking.

Recent experiments [127] with rat liver slices showing that uncouplers of the oxidative phosphorylation, such as dinitrophenol (DNP) and arsenate, greatly increase the rate of ethanol metabolism indicate that mitochondrial NADH oxidation is the important rate-limiting factor in alcohol

TABLE V   Correlation Between LADH, Q_{pH} and Histological Diagnosis in 80 Cases[a]
Distribution of atypical enzymes expressed as Q_{pH} in 80 liver biopsies of alcohol addicts.

Liver biopsy	Atypical $Q_{pH} \leq 0.60$	Normal $Q_{pH} \geq 0.61$
Normal	3	13
Steatosis	24	32
Cirrhosis	1	7

[a] X^2 with Yates correction 4.04; $p < 0.05$.

metabolic velocity. The same study [127] shows that chronic alcohol administration to rats for 3 to 4 weeks increases by 70 to 90% the ability of the liver to metabolize alcohol; DNP looses its effect in this condition [127]. The effect of chronic alcohol administration in the rat disappears after 2 weeks of alcohol abstinence. These results thus indicate that, in the rat, chronic alcohol administration produces adaptative changes that increase alcohol metabolism by liver slices.

The remarkable increase in blood alcohol disposal recently observed in human alcoholics studied shortly after the last drinking episode, while they were experiencing the abstinence syndrome, and the corresponding decrease in alcohol metabolic rate after weeks of abstinence indicate that adaptative changes in ethanol metabolism that are comparable with those observed in rats probably occur also in human drinkers [41, 119] (see Table VI).

The enhanced alcohol metabolism observed in alcohol-treated rats and human alcoholics may be related to other biochemical pathways for alcohol oxidation or NAD regeneration. Hepatic catalase represents another ethanol-oxidizing system not requiring NAD that may operate in individuals subjected to prolonged excessive alcohol intake. This possibility is supported by the enhanced activity of this enzyme in the liver of chronic ethanol-treated rats [120, 128] and by the increased number of peroxisomes observed in alcoholic subjects [81, 94] (see Table VII).

Alcohol metabolism could be increased by NADH oxidation by a peroxisomal lactate oxidase electron shuttle or an augmented ethanol metabolism by catalase in the presence of hydrogen peroxide formed after lactate or urate oxidation [19].

The lack of galactose metabolism impairment by NADH accumulation after alcohol intake in patients with alcoholic steatosis in contradistinction

TABLE VI   Duration of Alcohol Abstinence and Rate of Blood Ethanol Disappearance in Alcoholics

	Cases	Abstinence period, days	Rate of alcohol removal (β), mg/(100 ml)(hr) mean	SE
1	13	1	35.7	3.5
2	20	6–14	25.6	2.5
3	23	15–30	18.6	1.7

Difference between 1 and 2 = $t \cdot 2.46 \; p < 0.01$.
Difference between 1 and 3 = $t \cdot 4.90 \; p < 0.0005$.
Difference between 2 and 3 = $t \cdot 2.39 \; p < 0.0125$.

with normal individuals also suggests the existence of adaptative alcohol-metabolizing systems that may not accumulate NADH [99].

A new alternative mechanism for alcohol oxidation has been described in the microsomal fraction, with the same requirements of drug-metabolizing enzymes [64]. This finding seems to be connected with the increase in some drug-detoxifing enzymes and the hypertrophy of SER reported in alcoholic subjects [97]. The possible role of this metabolic system in vivo seemed supported by the prolonged alcohol sleeping time observed in mice when Proadifen, an inhibitor of microsomal enzymes, is administered before ethanol [65] and by the augmented alcohol elimination in rabbits and mice pretreated with drugs that induce hypertrophy of SER like hexobarbital [32].

TABLE VII   Hepatic Catalase Activity in Rats After 4 Weeks Submitted to an Alcohol Diet[a]

Group	N	Kat. F. units per total liver per 100 g b.w. Mean	SE
Alcoholics	8	589.3	51.8
Controls	8	331.4	15.4

[a] $p < 0.001$.

Recent studies have questioned the significance of a NADPH-dependent microsomal ethanol-oxidizing system (MEOS) in the oxidation of ethanol in vivo. Pretreatment of rats with phenobarbital does not enhance subsequent oxidation of ethanol-1-^{14}C in vivo; SKF 525-A has no inhibitory effect on alcohol oxidation [111]. If ethanol is oxidized significantly by a microsomal mixed oxidase reaction similar to that described for other drugs, it would be reasonable to expect as it is usually observed for other drugs, that phenobarbital would enhance and SKF 525-A would inhibit alcohol metabolism. That MEOS would at best account for no more than 7% of the total ethanol oxidized by alcohol-pretreated rats has been also suggested, based on the calculation of total microsomal protein in the liver of these rats [111].

Microsomal alcohol oxidation may be carried out also by catalase present in microsomal preparations, as it has been suggested, after the observation that 3-amino-1,2,4-triazole inhibits its oxidation by microsomes and that NADPH can be replaced by H_2O_2 [90].

To what extent these adaptative metabolic conditions observed in chronic alcohol drinking favor progression of liver damage or induce resistance to ethanol hepatotoxicity in man remains to be determined.

B.   Alcohol and the Pancreas

The relationship between alcohol and pancreatitis is generally acknowledged. Acute excessive ingestion of ethanol preceeds or seems to precipitate episodes of acute pancreatitis, while the incidence of chronic alcoholism and chronic pancreatitis are frequently related [9]. The mechanism by which alcohol damages the pancreas, although studied for many years, has not been fully elucidated yet [22, 103]. Some of the known effects of alcohol on the pancreas will be reviewed.

1.   Acute Effects of Alcohol on the Pancreas

A.   STIMULATION.   Ethanol, after ingestion, reaches the stomach, where it is partially absorbed through the mucosa of the body and fundus [133]. Alcohol in the bloodstream is able to stimulate the parietal cell secretion even when vagal, antral, or intestinal mechanisms of gastric secretion have been suppressed [133]. By topycal action on the pyloric gland area of the stomach, ethanol causes potent release of gastrin, which in turn increases gastric as well as pancreatic secretion [85, 104]. The property of ethanol of liberating gastrin is related to its chain length, as it is also observed with propanol but not with methanol or butanol [26]. Acid secretion enters the duodenum, where secretin and cholecystokinin-pancreozymin are released. As a result of all this hormone liberation, pancreatic secretion is strongly stimulated. The importance of the stomach on the stimulation effect of alcohol on the pancreas was emphasized in experiments of Walton et al. [131]. Dogs prepared with Thomas cannula had an increase in pancreatic juice flow after oral or intravenous alcohol. This effect was abolished, however, by total gastrectomy [131].

The stimulatory effect of intravenous alcohol on the human pancreas has been shown by Lowenfels et al. [66] in a patient with pancreatic fistula. A sustained increase in volume and amylase secretion was observed after intravenous administration of alcohol.

This effect, however, seems to be dependent on the presence of HCl in the duodenum. In a 60-year-old nonalcoholic woman, with achlorihidria resistant to augmented doses of histamine studied in our unit, alcohol was given intravenously (1 g/kg) (see Figure 5). The volume of duodenal aspirate and amylase concentration showed a tendency to decrease rather

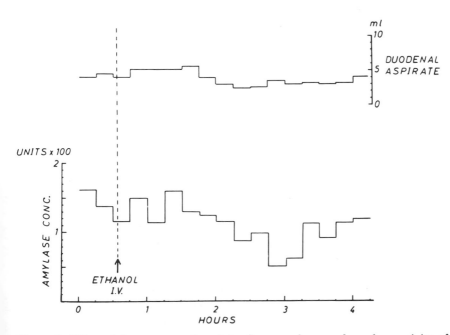

Figure 5. Effect of intravenous ethanol 1 g/kg on volume and amylase activity of duodenal aspirate from a patient with histamine-resistant aclorhidria.

than to increase after ethanol. The lack of pancreatic response might be interpreted in relation to the gastric anacidity previously demonstrated in this patient [121]. The importance of the stimulatory effect of ethanol on the pancreas through the gastric mechanism in the pathogenesis of alcohol pancreatitis is also suggested in experiments by Cueto et al. [15]. These authors reproduced some of the metabolic and morphological features of pancreatitis in two groups of dogs. In one group, HCl reached the first part of the duodenum, and in the other, the acid was derivated to the jejunum. Alcohol was administered through a gastrostomy or duodenostomy. Elevations of the serum enzymes, serum lipids, and pancreatic inflammatory reaction were observed only in animals with acid bathing the duodenum. In these experiments the increased production of acid and the presence of this stimulus in the intestinal mucosa seemed necessary for the production of the mechanism.

B.   PANCREATIC DUCT FLOW AND DUCTED PRESSURE. Menguy et al [70] and Walton et al. [132] studied the effect produced by different alcohol solutions that ranged from 10 to 90%, placed in contact with the duodenal mucosa on the biliary and pancreatic ductal pressure. A rapid and sustained increase in ductal pressure was observed. These findings were interpreted as evidence that alcohol produces obstruction of the pancreatic duct system. A similar finding is reported by Davis and Pirola [17] in subjects that received 20% alcohol intraduodenally. Alcohol in the concentrations used in these experiments, however, is rarely obtained in the human duodenum after beverages of common use. In experiments in our laboratory 40 g of ethanol was given orally to volunteers in solutions of 10 and 20%, and the maximal concentration reached at the intestinal level was 2.5 to 3% [45].

It seems, therefore, reasonable to conclude that alcohol intraduodenally may elevate the ductal pressure. The effectiveness of ethanol, however, on the sphincteric mechanism at the concentration it usually reaches the duodenum in man is uncertain.

Pirola and Davis [75] report that intravenous alcohol administration was followed by a rise in the common bile duct pressure that was associated with an increased sphincteric tone mechanism at the choledochoduodenal junction. This effect was found to be related to the level of alcohol in the blood rather than to the route of administration. Increased sphincteric tone seems to be the alcohol-induced mechanism that diminishes the volume of duodenal aspirate after continuous stimulation with secretin [17]. A similar effect has been observed by us when the pancreas was continuously stimulated with Pentagastrin [122, 124, 125]. From the data of Davis and Pirola

[17] and from our own findings it may be deduced that, although intravenous alcohol may diminish the pancreatic flow, the magnitude of this effect is moderate and would seem unable to suppress the response to a vigorous stimulation of the gland such as it is observed after oral ingestion of alcohol.

Finally Ridderstap and Bonting report that pancreatic fluid secretion in the dog is mediated by the $(Na + K)$-activated ATPase system [98]. Studies by Järnefelt [49] and Israel and Salazar [43] show that ethanol inhibits the $(Na + K)$-activated ATPase. The possibility that alcohol might reduce the volume of duodenal content also by inhibition of this enzymatic activity cannot be excluded.

C. PANCREATIC ENZYME SECRETION. Studies from our laboratory on nonalcoholic volunteers whose pancreatic secretion was continuously stimulated by Pentagastrin infusion demonstrated that ethanol intravenously diminished the amylase concentration of duodenal aspirate [122, 124]. Subsequently Orrego et al. [71] reported a reduction of the incorporation of P^{32} in vivo into the pancreatic phospholipids of rats that received 4.8 g/kg of ethanol in a single dose. This effect disappeared after 7 days in the acute experiment. Interestingly enough, vagotomy produced a similar effect. The possibility that ethanol could interfere with cholinergic stimulation necessary for normal P^{32} incorporation was suggested. Interference with normal cholinergic basal stimulation might help to explain our findings. When we studied this effect on one vagotomized patient, however, it was found that alcohol again decreased the volume and amylase concentration of duodenal content [125]. Another mechanism could be postulated. Large doses of ethanol may produce an increased liberation of catecholamines from the adrenal glands [54]. It has been suggested that epinephrine and other hormones accelerate the conversion of adenosine triphosphate (ATP) to cyclic 3',5'-AMP by the activation of adenyl cyclase [109]. Cyclic 3',5'-AMP has been proposed as a mediator of the inhibitory effect of glucacon on pancreatic secretion [23]. Therefore the inhibitory effect of alcohol on the enzyme secretion might be mediated by the adenyl cyclase system. This possibility remains to be investigated.

Phospholipids are known to participate in the mechanism of zymogen extrusion, probably incorporated to the lipoidal membrane of the granules [39]. Based on the findings of Orrego et al. [71], it might be proposed that alcohol interferes with the formation of zymogen membranes within the acinar cell. The alcohol pathogenic mechanism of pancreatitis might be then the result of the strong stimulatory effect of alcohol on the pancreas and the alteration of zymogen membranes. Pancreatic enzymes in this condition could become active within the cell, leading to inflammation and necrosis. This hypothesis does not seem to be supported by experiments by Sardesai and Orten [100]. These authors did not find increased free tryptic activity in the pancreas of animals that had received a prolonged treatment with ethanol. This subject, however, deserves further study.

D.   PROTEIN SYNTHESIS. The acute effect of alcohol on pancreatic protein synthesis has been studied by Tsuzuki et al. [112]. These authors did not observe an effect on the incorporation of DL-leucine-1-^{14}C into pancreatic proteins of the rat after two high doses of alcohol. A short period of protein-deficient diet combined with acute alcohol intake also failed to decrease protein synthesis. Thus it seems evident that acute alcohol administration does not interfere with pancreatic protein synthesis.

2.   Chronic Effects of Alcohol on the Pancreas

In contrast with the many studies devoted to investigate the acute effects of alcohol on the pancreas, the experimental work available on the chronic effects is scanty. Even more, in their results it is difficult to separate the alcohol effects from the ones produced by the dietary protein deficiency that is frequently associated.

A.   PANCREATIC FLOW. Studies of Feres et al. [29] in rats that received 1.5 ml/100 g of 40% ethanol daily for 10 weeks showed that the volume of bile-pancreatic flow augmented significantly at the end of the 10-week observation period. Because no hepatic abnormalities were observed, the authors concluded that the increased volume was due to the alcohol effect on the pancreas. These findings are in agreement with the general observation that the volume of pancreatic secretion is elevated in alcoholic cirrhosis [108, 126]. In our laboratory we have had the opportunity to study the volume of duodenal content after secretin (1 u/kg) in a group of alcoholic patients without history of pancreatitis and without overt hepatic insufficiency. Five patients with normal liver histology as well as 9 out of 10 cases with fatty liver had a volume of secretion that was within our normal range (1.34 ± 0.28 ml/kg 30 min). The remaining case with moderate fatty liver had a low volume 0.36 ml/kg 30 min. Five out of the 7 patients that were shown to have cirrhosis on the liver biopsy had a volume of secretion that was above our normal range, reaching in one case to 7.56 ml/kg. The volume of the other two was normal [123]. Thus some discrepancy is found between experimental data and studies in humans. From our results it seems that chronic alcoholism per se does not modify significantly the volume of pancreatic secretion after secretin. When hepatic

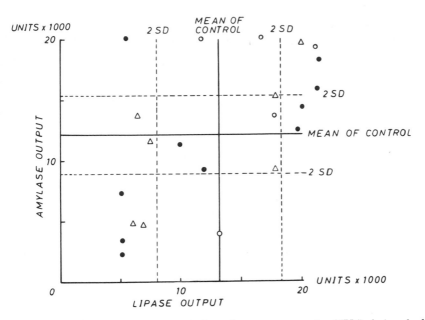

Figure 6. Pancreatic enzyme secretion after pancreozymin (IU/kg) in alcoholic patients with normal hepatic histology: (◯) fatty liver (●) and liver cirrhosis (△).

damage is associated, the volume may increase and reach sometimes considerably high values.

B. PANCREATIC ENZYME SECRETION. Experimental data from Feres et al. [29] showed that the protein content of bile-pancreatic secretion of rats that received ethanol for 10 weeks was higher than a control group. We have studied pancreatic enzyme output after pancreozymin (1 U/kg) in a group of alcoholic patients with variable degree of liver damage and without signs of liver failure or pancreatitis (see Figure 6). Decreased enzyme secretion was observed in three patients with fatty liver and in two with liver cirrhosis. All the remaining patients secreted amylase and lipase in amounts that correspond to our normal range [123]. From these results it may be concluded that, although deficient pancreatic enzyme output seems more frequent in alcoholic patients with advanced liver dysfunction, no parallelism may be established between liver alteration and pancreatic insufficiency.

C. PANCREATIC PROTEIN SYNTHESIS. Two groups of investigators have studied this problem with apparent contradictory results. Feres et al. [29]

observed that the administration of ethanol for 10 weeks did not modify the incorporation of ^{14}C-labeled amino acids into the protein of rat pancreas. Sardesai and Orten [100], however, report a decreased pancreatic protein synthesis in rats after a 46-week period of observation. The differences in results between these two groups of workers are probably related to the different duration of the period of study.

REFERENCES

1. Asada, M. and J. T. Galambos, The relationship between liver disease, hepatic alcohol dehydrogenase and alcohol metabolism in human, *Gastroenterology,* **45,** 67 (1963).
2. Ashworth, C. T., Production of fatty infiltration of liver in rats by alcohol in spite of adequate diet, *Proc. Soc. Exp. Biol. Med.,* **66,** 382 (1947).
3. Beckett, A. G., A. V. Livingstone, and K. R. Hill, Acute alcoholic hepatitis, *Brit. Med. J.,* **2,** 1113 (1961).
4. Best, C. H., C. C. Lucas, and J. H. Ridout, The lipotropic factors, *Ann. N.Y. Acad. Sci.,* **57,** 646 (1954).
5. Brodie, B. B., W. M. Butler, Jr., M. G. Horning, R. P. Maickel, and H. M. Maling, Alcohol induced triglyceride deposition in liver through derangement of fat transport, *Amer. J. Clin. Nutr.,* **9,** 432 (1961).
6. Cameron, G. R. and A. E. Karunaratne, Carbon tetrachloride cirrhosis in relation to liver regeneration, *J. Path Bact.,* **42,** 1 (1936).
7. Chang, T., J. Lewes, and A. J. Glayks, Effect of ethanol and other alcohols on the transport of amino acids and glucose by everted sacs of small intestine, *Biochim. Biophys. Acta,* **135,** 1000 (1967).
8. Clark, C. G. and J. R. Senior, Ethanol clearance and oxidation of ethanol to carbon dioxide in persons with and without liver damage, *Gastroenterology,* **55,** 670 (1968).
9. Clark, E., Pancreatitis in acute and chronic alcoholism, *Amer. J. Dig. Dis.,* **9,** 428 (1942).
10. Clark, C. A., *Genetics for the Clinician,* Oxford, London, 1962.
11. Connor, C. L., Fatty infiltration of the liver and the development of cirrhosis in diabetes and chronic alcoholism, *Amer. J. Path.,* **14,** 347 (1938).
12. Cook, G. C. and M. S. R. Hutt, The liver after Kwashiorkor, *Brit. Med. J.,* **3,** 454 (1967).
13. Cruz-Coke, R., Asociación de defectos de visión de colores y cirrosis hepática, *Rev. Med. Chile,* **93,** 519 (1965).
14. Cruz-Coke, R., Colour blindness and cirrhosis of the liver, *Lancet,* **1,** 1131 (1965).
15. Cueto, J., N. Tajen, and B. Zimmermann, Studies of experimental alcoholic pancreatitis in the dog, *Surgery,* **62,** 159 (1967).
16. Davidson, C. S. and R. A. MacDonald, Recovery from active hepatic disease of the alcoholic, *Arch. Intern. Med.,* **110,** 592 (1962).

17. Davis, A. E. and R. C. Pirola, The effects of ethyl alcohol on pancreatic exocrine function, *Med. J. Australia,* **2,** 757 (1966).
18. De Carli, L. M. and C. S. Lieber, Fatty liver in the rat after prolonged intake of ethanol with a nutritionally adequate new liquid diet, *J. Nutr.,* **91,** 331 (1967).
19. Duve, de C. and P. Baudhuin, Peroxisomes (microbodies and related particles), *Physiol. Rev.,* **46,** 323 (1966).
20. Di Luzio, M. R. and M. Poggi, Pathogenesis of the Acute Ethanol Induced Fatty Liver, in *Biochemical Factors in Alcoholism* R. P. Maickel (ed.), Pergamon, New York, 1966.
21. Di Luzio, N. R. and A. D. Hartman, Role of lipid peroxidation in the pathogenesis of the ethanol-induced fatty liver, *Fed. Proc.,* **26,** 1436 (1967).
22. Dreiling, L. A., A. Richman, and N. F. Fradkin, The role of alcohol in the etiology of pancreatitis: Study of the effect of intravenous ethyl alcohol on the external secretion of the pancreas, *Gastroenterology,* **20,** 636 (1952).
23. Dyck, W. P., J. Rudick, B. Hoexter, and H. D. Janowitz, Influence of glucagon on pancreatic exocrine secretion, *Gastroenterology,* **56,** 531 (1969).
24. Edmonson, H. A., R. L. Peters, T. B. Reynolds, and O. T. Kuzma, Sclerosing hyaline necrosis of the liver in the chronic alcoholic: A recognizable clinical syndrome, *Ann. Intern. Med.,* **59,** 646 (1969).
25. Elko, E. E., W. R. Wooles, and N. R. Di Luzio, Alterations and mobilization of lipids in acute ethanol treated rats, *Amer. J. Physiol.,* **201,** 923 (1961).
26. Elwin, C. E. and B. Uvnäs, Distribution and Local Release of Gastrin, in *Gastrin, Proceedings of a Conference,* M. I. Grossman (ed.), University of California Press, Los Angeles, 1966.
27. Eppinger, H., "Enfermedades del Hígado". Ed. Labor. Bs. Aires 1945.
28. Erenoglu, E., J. C. Edreira, and A. J. Patek, Jr., Observations on patients with Laennec's cirrhosis receiving alcohol while on controlled diets, *Ann. Intern. Med.,* **60,** 814 (1964).
29. Feres, A., H. Orrego, E. Navia, and L. Costamaillere, Effect of chronic administration of ethanol on the incorporation of 14 C-amino acids into pancreatic proteins, *Arch. Biol. Med. Exper.,* **5,** 62 (1968).
30. Figueroa, R. and A. P. Klotz, Alterations of liver alcohol dehydrogenase and other hepatic enzymes in alcoholic cirrhosis, *Gastroenterology,* **43,** 10 (1962).
31. Figueroa, R. and A. P. Klotz, Alterations of alcohol hepatic dehydrogenase and other enzymes following oral alcohol intoxication, *Am. J. Clin. Nutr.,* **11,** 235 (1962).
32. Fischer, H. D., Der Einfluss von Barbituraten auf die entgiftungsgeschwindigkeit des Athanols, *Biochem. Pharmacol.,* **11,** 307 (1962).
33. Gómez-Dumm, C. L. A., E. A. Porta, W. S. Hartroft, and O. R. Koch, A new experimental approach in the study of chronic alcoholism: II. Effects of high alcohol intake in rats fed diets of various adequacies, *Lab. Invest.,* **18,** 365 (1968).
34. Green, J., S. Mistilis, and L. Schiff, Acute alcoholic hepatitis: A clinical study of 50 cases, *Arch. Intern. Med.,* **112,** 67 (1963).

35. Handschumacher, R. E., W. A. Creasey, J. J. Jaffe, C. A. Pasternak, and L. Hankin, Biochemical and nutritional studies on the introduction of fatty livers by dietary orotic acid, *Proc. Nat. Acad. Soc. U.S.A.*, **46**, 178 (1960).
36. Hashimoto, S. and R. O. Recknagel, No chemical evidence of hepatic lipid peroxidation in acute ethanol toxicity, *Exp. Med. Path.*, **8**, 225 (1968).
37. Hartroft, W. S., Pathogenesis of cirrhosis produced by choline deficiency: Escape of lipid from fatty hepatic cysts into biliary and vascular systems, *Amer. J. Path.*, **27**, 951 (1915).
38. Hartroft, W. S., Experimental Cirrhosis, in *The Liver: Morphology, Biochemistry, Physiology*, C. Rouiller (ed.), vol. II, Academic, New York, 1964.
39. Hokin, L. E. and M. R. Hokin, Changes in phospholipid metabolism on stimulation of protein secretion in pancreas slices, *J. Histochem. Cytochem.*, **13**, 113 (1965).
40. Horning, M. G., E. A. Williams, H. M. Mailing, and B. B. Brodie, Depot fat as source of increased liver triglycerides after ethanol, *Biochim. Biophys. Res. Commun.*, **3**, 635 (1960).
41. Iber, F. L., N.Carulli, and R. M. H. Kater, The kinetics of alcohol removal from the blood of man: Comparison in recently drinking alcoholics and non-alcoholics, *Fed. Proc.*, **28**, 626 (1969) (Abstr.).
42. Insunza, I., H. Iturriaga, G. Ugarte, and H. Altschiller, Clinical and histological liver abnormalities in alcoholics, *Acta Hepato-Splen.*, in press.
43. Isracl, Y. and I. Salazar, Inhibition of brain microsomal adenosine triphosphatases by general depressants, *Arch. Biochem. Biophys.*, **122**, 310 (1967).
44. Israel, Y., I. Salazar, and E. Rosenmann, Inhibitory effects of alcohol on intestinal aminoacid transport in vivo and in vitro, *J. Nutrition*, **96**, 499 (1968).
45. Israel, Y., J. E. Valenzuela, I. Salazar, and G. Ugarte, Alcohol and aminoacid transport in the human small intestine, *J. Nutrition*, **98**, 222 (1969).
46. Isselbacher, K. J. and N. J. Greenberger, Metabolic effects of alcohol on the liver, *New Eng. J. Med.*, **270**, 351 (1964).
47. Iturriaga, H., G. Ugarte, and I. Insunza, Resistencia del Hígado humano al depósite de grasa a pesar de ingesta excesiva de alcohol, *Rev. Med. Chile*, **97**, 595 (1969).
48. Iturriaga, H., I. Insunza, and G. Ugarte, Hepatitis alcohólica, *Rev. Med. Chile*, in press.
49. Järnefelt, J., A possible mechanism of action of ethyl alcohol on the central nervous system, *Ann. Med. Exp. Fenn*, **39**, 267 (1961).
50. Jellinek, E. M., *The Disease Concept of Alcoholism*, Hillhouse, New Haven, 1960.
51. Kalant, H. and J. M. Khana, Effects of Chronic Ethanol Intake on Metabolic Pathways, in *Biochemical and Clinical Aspects of Alcohol Metabolism*, V. M. Sardesai (ed.), Charles C Thomas, Springfield, Ill., 1969.
52. Kiessling, K. H., and Pilström, L., Effect of ethanol on rat liver: I. Enzymatic and histological studies of liver mitochondria, *Quart. J. Stud. Alcohol*, **27**, 189 (1966).

53. Klatskin, G., Alcohol and its relation to liver damage, *Gastroenterology,* **41,** 443 (1961).
54. Klingman, G. J. and Mc C. Goodall, Urinary epinephrine and levarterenol excretion during acute sublethal alcohol intoxication in dogs, *J. Pharmacol. Exp. Therap.,* **121,** 313 (1957).
55. Leevy, C. M., Clinical diagnosis, evaluation and treatment of liver disease in alcoholics, *Fed. Proc.,* **26,** 1474 (1967).
56. Lelbach, W. K., Leberschäden bei chronischem Alkoholismus: Ergenbnisse einer klinischen, klinisch-chemischen und bioptisch histologischen Untersuchung an 526 Alkoholkranken während der Entzichungskur in einer offenen Tinkerheilstatte, Teil I-II, *Acta Hepatosplen.,* **13,** 321 (1966).
57. Lelbach, W. K., Leberschäden bei chronischem Alkoholismus: Ergenbnisse einer klinischen, klinisch-chemischen und bioptisch histologischen Untersuchung an 526 Alkoholkranken während der Entzichungskur in einer offenen Tinkerheilstatte, Teil III, *Acta Hepatosplen.,* **14,** 9 (1967).
58. Lieber, C. S. and H. Schmid, The effect of ethanol on fatty acid metabolism: Stimulation of fatty acid synthesis in vitro, *J. Clin. Invest.,* **40,** 392 (1961).
59. Lieber, C. S., Alcohol and the Liver, in *Progress in Liver Diseases,* H. Popper and F. Schaffner (eds.), vol. II, Grune and Stratton, New York, 1965.
60. Lieber, C. S., D. P. Jones, and L. M. De Carli, Effects of prolonged ethanol intake: Production of fatty liver despite adequate diets, *J. Clin. Invest.,* **44,** 1009 (1965).
61. Lieber, C. S., N. Spritz, and L. M. De Carli, Role of dietary adipose and endogenously synthesized fatty acids in the pathogenesis of the alcoholic fatty liver, *J. Clin. Invest.,* **45,** 51 (1966).
62. Lieber, C. S. and N. Spritz, Effects of prolonged ethanol intake in man: Role of dietary, adipose and endogenously synthesis of fatty acids in the pathogenesis of the alcoholic fatty liver, *J. Clin. Invest.,* **45,** 1400 (1966).
63. Lieber, C. S. and E. Rubin, Alcoholic fatty liver in man on a high protein and low fat diet, *Amer. J. Med.,* **44,** 200 (1968).
64. Lieber, C. S. and E. Rubin, Ethanol. A hepatotoxic drug, *Gastroenterology,* **54,** 642 (1968).
65. Lind, N. and M. W. Parkes, Effects of inhibition and induction of the liver microsomal enzyme system on the narcotic activity of ethanol in mice, *J. Pharmacol.,* **19,** 56 (1967).
66. Lowenfels, A. B., B. Masih, T. C. Y. Lee, and M. Rohman, Effect of intravenous alcohol on the pancreas, *Arch. Surg.,* **96,** 440 (1968).
67. Mallow, S., Effect of ethanol intoxication on plasma free fatty acids in the rat, *Quart. J. Stud. Alcohol,* **22,** 250 (1961).
68. Marconi, J., A. Varela, E. Rosenblat, G. Solari, I. Marchese, A. Alvarado, and E. Enriquez, A survey on the prevalence of alcoholism among adult population of a suburb of Santiago, *Quart. J. Stud. Alcohol,* **16,** 438 (1955).
69. Mendelson, J. H., Ethanol-1-C^{14} metabolism in alcoholics and non-alcoholics, *Science,* **159,** 319 (1968).
70. Menguy, R. B., G. A. Hallenbeck, J. L. Bollman, and J. H. Drindlay, Intra-

ductal pressures and sphincteric resistance in canine pancreatic and biliary ducts after various stimuli, *Surg. Gynecol. Obstet.,* **106,** 306 (1958).

71. Orrego-Matte, H., E. Navia, A. Feres, and L. Costamaillere, Ethanol ingestion and incorporation of ^{32}P into phospholipids of pancreas in the rat, *Gastroenterology,* **56,** 280 (1969).

72. Patek, A. J., Portal Cirrhosis (Laennec Cirrhosis), in *Diseases of the Liver,* L. Schiff (ed.), 2d ed., Lippincott, Philadelphia, 1963.

73. Phillips, C. B. and C. S. Davidson, Acute hepatic insufficiency of the chronic alcoholic (clinical and pathological study), *Arch. Intern. Med.,* **94,** 585 (1954).

74. Pilström, L. and K. H. Kiessling, Effect of ethanol on the growth and on the liver and brain mitochondrial function of the offspring of rats, *Acta Pharmacol. Toxic.,* **25,** 225 (1967).

75. Pirola, R. C. and A. E. Davis, Effects of ethyl alcohol on sphincteric resistance at the choledocho-duodenal function in man, *Gut,* **9,** 557 (1968).

76. Poggi, M. and N. R. Di Luzio, The role of liver and adipose tissue in the pathogenesis of the ethanol-induced fatty liver, *J. Lipid. Res.,* **5,** 437 (1964).

77. Popper, H., J. de la Huerga, and C. Yasmick, Hepatic tumors due to prolonged ethionine feeding, *Science,* **118,** 80 (1953).

78. Popper, H., P. B. Szanto, and H. Elias, Transition of fatty liver into cirrhosis, *Gastroenterology,* **28,** 183 (1955).

79. Popper, H., What Are the Major Types of Hepatic Cirrhosis? in *Controversey in Internal Medicine,* F. J. Ingelfinger, A. S. Relman, and M. Finland (eds.), p. 239, Saunders, Philadelphia, 1966.

80. Porta, E. A., B. J. Bergman, and A. A. Steni, Acute alcoholic hepatitis, *Amer. J. Path.,* **46,** 657 (1965).

81. Porta, E. A., W. S. Hartroft, and F. A. de la Iglesia, Hepatic changes associated with chronic alcoholism in rats, *Lab. Invest.,* **14,** 1437 (1965).

82. Porta, E. A., W. S. Hartroft, and F. A. de la Iglesia, Structural and Ultrastructural Hepatic Lesions Associated with Acute and Chronic Alcoholism in Man and Experimental Animals, in *Biochemical Factors in Alcoholism,* P. Maickel (ed.), p. 201, Pergamon, New York, 1967.

83. Porta, E. A., W. S. Hartroft, C. L. A. Gómez-Dumm, and O. R. Koch, Dietary factors in the progression and regression of hepatic alterations associated with experimental chronic alcoholism, *Fed. Proc.,* **26,** 1449 (1967).

84. Porta, E. A., O. Koch, C. L. A. Gómez-Dumm, and W. S. Hartroft, Effects of dietary protein on the liver of rats in experimental chronic alcoholism, *J. Nutr.,* **94,** 437 (1968).

85. Preshaw, R. M., A. R. Cook, and M. Grossman, Stimulation of pancreatic secretion by a humoral agent from the pyloric gland area of the stomach, *Gastroenterology,* **49,** 617 (1965).

86. Puffer, R. R. and G. W. Griffith, Pattern of urban mortality, *PAHO Scientific Publication* 151, 1967.

87. Reboucas, G. and K. J. Isselbacher, Studies on the pathogenesis of ethanol

induced fatty liver: I. Synthesis and oxidation of fatty acids by the liver, *J. Clin. Invest.,* **40,** 1355 (1961).

88. Reynolds, T. B., A. G. Redeker, and O. T. Kuzma, Role of Alcohol in the Pathogenesis of Alcohol Cirrhosis, in *Therapeutic Agents and the Liver,* N. McIntyre and S. Sherlock Davis, Philadelphia, 1965.

89. Rice, J. D. and R. Yesner, The prognostic significance of so-called Mallory bodies in portal cirrhosis, *Arch. Intern. Med.,* **105,** 99 (1960).

90. Roach, M. K., W. S. Reese, Jr., and P. J. Creaven, Ethanol oxidation in the microsomal fraction of rat liver, *Biochem. Biophys. Res. Commun.,* **36,** 596 (1969).

91. Rogers, A. E. and R. A. Mac Donald, Hepatic vasculature and cell proliferation in experimental cirrhosis, *Lab. Invest.,* **14,** 1710 (1965).

92. Rowntree, L. G., Considerations in cirrhosis of the liver, *JAMA,* **89,** 1590 (1927).

93. Rubin, E., F. Hutterer, and H. Popper, Cell proliferation and fiber formation in chronic carbon tetrachloride intoxication: A morphologic and chemical study, *Amer. J. Path.,* **42,** 715 (1963).

94. Rubin, E. and C. S. Lieber, Early fine structure changes in the human liver induced by alcohol, *Gastroenterology,* **52,** 1 (1967).

95. Rubin, E. and C. S. Lieber, Experimental alcoholic hepatic injury in man: Ultrastructural changes, *Fed. Proc.,* **26,** 1458 (1967).

96. Rubin, E. and C. S. Lieber, Alcohol-induced hepatic injury in non-alcoholic volunteers, *New Eng. J. Med.,* **278,** 869 (1968).

97. Rubin, E., F. Hutterer, and C. S. Lieber, Increase of smooth endoplasmic reticulum and hepatic drug metabolizing enzymes by ethanol, *Science,* **159,** 1469 (1968).

98. Ridderstap, A. S. and S. L. Bonting, Na-K, activated adenosine triphosphatase and pancreatic secretion in the dog, *Amer. J. Physiol.,* **216,** 547 (1969).

99. Salaspuro, M. P., Application of the galactose test for the early diagnosis of fatty liver in human alcoholics, *Scand. J. Clin. Lab. Invest.,* **20,** 274, (1967).

100. Sardesai, V. M. and J. M. Orten, Effect of prolonged alcohol consumption in rats on pancreatic protein synthesis, *J. Nutrition,* **96,** 241 (1968).

101. Sardesai, V. M. and A. J. Walt, Effect of Ethanol on Tissue Carbohydrate and Energy Metabolism, in *Biochemical and Clinical Aspects of Alcohol Metabolism,* V. M. Sardesai (ed.), Charles C Thomas, Springfield, Ill., 1969.

102. Schaffner, F., A. Loebel, H. A. Weiner, and T. Barka, Hepatocellular cytoplasmic changes in acute alcoholic hepatitis, *JAMA,* **183,** 342 (1963).

103. Schapiro, H., L. D. Wruble, and L. G. Britt, The possible mechanism of alcohol in the production of acute pancreatitis, *Surgery,* **60,** 1108 (1966).

104. Schapiro, H., L. D. Wruble, J. W. Estes, and L. G. Britt, Pancreatic secretion stimulated by the action of alcohol on the gastric antrum. *Amer. J. Dig. Dis.,* **13,** 536 (1968).

105. Scheig, R. and K. J. Isselbacher, Pathogenesis of ethanol-induced fatty liver:

III. In vivo and in vitro effects of ethanol on hepatic fatty acid metabolism in rat, *J. Lipid Res.,* **6**, 269 (1965).

106. Shorter, R. G. and A. H. Baggentoss, Observation on the histogenesis on cirrhosis of the liver in chronic alcoholism, *Amer. J. Clin. Path.,* **32**, 422 (1959).

107. Summerskill, W. H. J., S. J. Wolfe, and C. S. Davidson, Response to alcohol in chronic alcoholics with liver disease: Clinical, pathological and metabolic changes, *Lancet,* **1**, 335 (1957).

108. Sun, D. C. H., R. A. Albacete, and J. K. Chen, Malabsorption studies in cirrhosis of the liver, *Arch. Intern. Med.,* **119**, 567 (1967).

109. Sutherland, E. W. and T. W. Rall, The relation of adenosine 3'5'-phosphate and phosphorylase to the actions of catecholamines and other hormones, *Pharmacol. Rev.,* **12**, 265 (1960).

110. Takada, A., E. A. Porta, and W. S. Hartroft, Regression of dietary cirrhosis in rats fed alcohol and a "super diet": Evidence of the nonhepatotoxic nature of ethanol, *Amer. J. Clin. Nutr.,* **20**, 213 (1967).

111. Tephly, T. R., F. Tinelli, and W. D. Watkins, Alcohol metabolism: Role of microsomal oxidation in vivo, *Science,* **166**, 627 (1969).

112. Tsuzuki, T., N. Watanabe, and S. P. Thal, The effect of obstruction of the pancreatic duct and acute alcoholism on pancreatic protein synthesis, *Surgery,* **57**, 724 (1965).

113. Tygstrup, N., K. Winkler, and F. Lundquist, The mechanism of the fructose effect on the metabolism of the human liver, *J. Clin. Invest.,* **44**, 817 (1965).

114. Ugarte, G., H. Iturriaga, and I. Insunza, Some effects of Ethanol in Normal and Pathological Livers, in *Progress in Liver Diseases,* H. Popper and F. Schaffner (eds.), vol. III, Grune and Stratton, New York, 1970.

115. Ugarte, G., T. Pereda, M. E. Pino, F. Lorca, y F. Sepúlveda, Metabolismo del etanol en pacientes alcohólicos con y sin daño hepático: II. Velocidad metabólica del etanol y aumento de la lacticidemia, *Rev. Med. Chile,* **95**, 67 (1967).

116. Ugarte, G., M. E. Pino, and I. Insunza, Hepatic alcohol dehydrogenase in alcoholic addicts with and without hepatic damage, *Amer. J. Dig. Dis.,* **12**, 589 (1967).

117. Ugarte, G. H., Iturriaga, I. Insunza, and H. Atlschiller, Clinical and metabolic disorders in alcoholic hepatic damage, *Proc. Int. Symposium Alcohol and Alcoholism,* August, 1966, Santiago, Chile, University of Toronto Press, in press, and *Arch. Biol. Med. Exp. Supl.,* **3**, 203 (1969).

118. Ugarte, G., M. E. Pino, H. Altschiller, and T. Pereda, Prevalence of atypical liver alcohol dehydrogenase in alcoholics, *Quart J. Stud. Alcohol,* **31**, 571 (1970).

119. Ugarte, G., T. Pereda, M. E. Pino, Influence of alcohol intoxication and abstinence on blood alcohol clearance in alcoholics, *Quart. J. Stud. Alcohol,* in press.

120. Ugarte, G., T. Pereda, and H. Iturriaga, Influence of chronic alcohol feeding on catalase activity of rat liver, *Arch. Biol. Med. Exp.,* **16**, 56 (1969).

121. Valenzuela, J. E., unpublished observation.

122. Valenzuela, J., M. Petermann, G. Ugarte, A. Silva, and F. Lorca, Efecto del etanol sobre la secreción pancreática estimulada por un pentapeptido similar a la gastrina (I.C.I. 50,123), *Rev. Med. Chile*, **97**, 601 (1969).

123. Valenzuela, J. E. and M. Petermann, unpublished observations.

124. Valenzuela, J. E., G. Ugarte, and M. Petermann, Effect of intravenous ethanol on pancreatic secretion, *Gastroenterology*, **56**, 1203 (1969) (Abstract).

125. Valenzuela, J. E., G. Ugarte, and M. Petermann, Effect of ethanol on pancreatic secretion stimulated by Pentagastrin, to be published.

126. Van Goidsenhoven, G. E., W. J. Henke, J. B. Vacca, and W. A. Knight, Jr., Pancreatic function in cirrhosis of the liver, *Amer. J. Digest. Dis.*, **8**, 160 (1963).

127. Videla, L. and Y. Israel, Factors that modify the metabolism of ethanol in rat liver and adaptative changes produced by its chronic administration, *Biochem. J.*, **118**, 275 (1970).

128. Von Wartburg, J. P., and M. von Röthlisberg, Enzymatishe voränderungen in der leber nach langdauernder belastung mit aethanol und methanol bei der ratte, *Helvet. Physiol. Pharmacol. Acta*, **19**, 30 (1961).

129. Von Wartburg, J. P., J. Papenberg, and H. Aebi, An atypical alcohol dehydrogenase, *Canad. J. Biochem.*, **43**, 889 (1965).

130. Von Wartburg, J. P. and P. M. Schürch, Atypical human liver alcohol dehydrogenase, *Ann. N.Y. Acad. Sci.*, **151**, 936 (1968).

131. Walton, B. E., H. Schapiro, and E. R. Woodward, The effect of alcohol and histamine on pancreatic secretion, *Amer. Surgeon*, **28**, 443 (1962).

132. Walton, B. E., H. Schapiro, T. Yeung, and E. R. Woodward, Effect of alcohol on pancreatic duct pressure, *Am. Surgeon*, **31**, 142 (1965).

133. Woodward, E. R., C. Robertson, H. D. Ruttenberg, and H. Schapiro, Alcohol as a gastric secretory stimulant, *Gastroenterology*, **32**, 727 (1957).

134. Zakim, D., Effect of ethanol on hepatic acyl coenzyme A metabolism, *Arch. Biochem. Biophys.*, **111**, 253 (1965).

Chapter VI

INFLUENCE OF ETHANOL ON THE METABOLISM OF THE PATHOLOGICAL LIVER

MIKKO P. SALASPURO

RESEARCH LABORATORIES OF THE STATE ALCOHOL MONOPOLY (ALKO)
THIRD DEPARTMENT OF MEDICINE, UNIVERSITY OF HELSINKI, FINLAND

A. Introduction

Although the most conspicuous effects of alcohol are the functional changes affecting the central nervous system, the majority of studies of the pathologic alterations induced by ethanol are concerned with liver pathology. The influence of ethanol on the metabolism of the normal liver has recently been reviewed by many authors [37, 43, 52–54, 89]. It can be stated that most of these studies deal with the acute effects of ethanol on liver metabolism. The part played by the chronic consumption of alcohol, whether or not accompanied by various dietary deficiencies, in the pathogenesis of alcoholic cirrhosis has also been very well documented in these reviews.

But there is surprisingly little information about the metabolic or structural effects of ethanol on the previously diseased liver.

Lieber and associates [54] emphasize the role of ethanol as a direct hepatotoxic agent. Subsequent reports are somewhat controversial, however, because it has been shown that even in large amounts alcohol does not damage the liver if given in certain conditions of dietary intake [1, 32, 45, 72]. It looks as if both the direct toxic effect of ethanol and various nutritional deficiencies play important roles in the development of hepatic lesions during prolonged alcohol consumption. The relative significance of these etiologic factors in liver pathogenesis cannot be assessed in the light of present knowledge. There are alcoholics who consume a fairly adequate diet with regard to protein and vitamins and alcoholics whose food consumption has for long periods been grossly inadequate, so that they have grave nutritional deficiencies.

Since it has been shown that the effects of ethanol on liver metabolism differ considerably in normal and protein-deficient fatty livers [79, 80, 83], it may be conjectured that differences in the various metabolic alterations caused by ethanol and in all the structural changes in liver morphology occurring during the course of the development of liver cirrhosis depend on the nutritional status of the experimental animal or alcoholic patient. This point ought to be borne in mind when metabolic or other derangements directly attributable to ethanol are interpreted.

The purpose of this chapter is to consider the major metabolic changes in liver metabolism caused by ethanol, and all possible differences between the biochemical pathways of the normal and pathological liver are especially emphasized. By a pathological liver is meant almost exclusively a fatty and cirrhotic liver caused by protein deficiency because of the dominating role of nutritional factors in liver pathology. No attempt has been made to include all possible liver alterations or liver diseases. Since an understanding of alcohol metabolism in the normal liver is necessary, this is first briefly described.

B. Oxidation of Ethanol and Some of Its Effects on the Intermediary Metabolism of the Normal Liver

The liver is the chief organ concerned in the oxidation of ethanol [16, 51]. The first step in alcohol breakdown is its oxidation to acetaldehyde. This reaction is catalyzed by a zinc-containing enzyme [96], alcohol dehydrogenase, which is mainly located in the liver cytoplasm [70]. Nicotinamide adenine dinucleotide NAD functions as the coenzyme and hydrogen acceptor (see Figure 1). The next step is that in which acetaldehyde is further

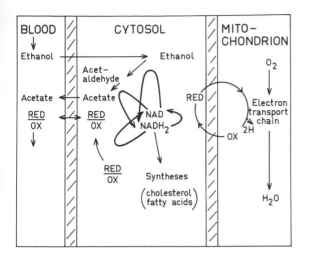

Figure 1. Hepatic oxidation of ethanol with some of its metabolic effects

oxidized by the NAD-dependent aldehyde dehydrogenase. This enzyme is mainly located in the cytoplasm, but an appreciable amount is also present in the mitochondria [8]. In liver perfusion experiments it has been demonstrated that the main product of acetaldehyde breakdown is acetate [24, 25]. This has also been confirmed in human subjects by means of hepatic vein catheterization [60]. Acetate is further metabolized via the citric acid cycle mainly in the extrahepatic tissues [26].

The oxidation of ethanol to acetaldehyde and acetaldehyde to acetate leads to the transfer of hydrogen to NAD, which is reduced to $NADH_2$ [60, 98]. Therefore the redox potential of the extramitochondrial compartment of the liver cells is shifted toward a more reduced state, manifested as an increase in the $NADH_2/NAD$ ratio. This change cannot be measured directly, because a very large part of the NAD is bound in various enzyme-substrate complexes, but it can be assessed indirectly from the ratios of metabolites, such as lactate/pyruvate, which reflects the redox state of the extramitochondrial cytoplasm, and β-hydroxybutyrate/acetoacetate, which is assumed to be in equilibrium with the intramitochondrial redox state [6, 35]. The influence of ethanol on the ratios of these "redox pairs" has been demonstrated by many investigators [7, 25, 60, 88].

The most important system for $NADH_2$ oxidation, the flavoprotein-cytochrome system with oxygen as the final hydrogen acceptor, is localized within the mitochondria [31]. The mitochondrial membrane, however, is highly impermeable to $NADH_2$ [73], and therefore some other hydrogen acceptor must serve as an intermediate carrier of the hydrogen across the mitochondrial membrane. Substrate pairs, such as the dihydroxyacetone phosphate/α-glycerophosphate [6] and malate/aspartate cycle [33], are perhaps the most important hydrogen carriers. By means of surface fluorometry and metabolite analysis in perfused livers it has been shown that the more reduced state shifts from the cytoplasm into the mitochondria in less than 1 sec [87].

When ethanol is oxidized in the intact organism, the breakdown of other substances decreases in proportion to the energy liberated from the ethanol [5]. Carpenter and Lee [10] observed that the oxidation of carbohydrate and fat was depressed by ethanol but that protein metabolism was very little affected. This alteration in the over-all metabolism of the body is one of the many changes that can be directly or indirectly attributed to the altered redox state of the liver. Other such changes are the following: during the oxidation of ethanol the citric acid cycle is blocked almost entirely [25, 51, 61]. The oxidation of fatty acids is suppressed [57, 63, 64, 76], and hepatic fatty acid synthesis [57, 68, 69] and the incorporation of acetate-C^{14} into cholesterol, cholesterogenesis [55], increases. Hepatic gluconeogenesis from various precursors is inhibited by ethanol [47], and increased $NADH_2$ leads to the dissociation of glutamic dehydrogenase into inactive subunits [28], so that a reduction of gluconeogenesis from amino acids also occurs. The increased lactate concentration during ethanol oxidation diminishes urinary uric acid output and may lead to hyperuricemia in subjects consuming alcoholic beverages [56]. Addition of ethanol has been reported to diminish the galactose-oxidizing capacity of rat liver homogenate [38]. Pronounced impairment of galactose elimination caused by ethanol has also been observed in rats and in normal human subjects [80, 84, 92, 94, 95]. Ethanol administration also inhibits serotonin oxidation, leading to diminished urinary excretion of 5-hydroxyindole acetic acid, 5-HIAA [78].

From the preceding summary it can be concluded that the major alteration in hepatic metabolism brought about by ethanol is the change in the redox state of the liver cells. A number of differences in metabolism, some expected and others surprising, between the normal and the pathological liver during ethanol oxidation are discussed in the following sections.

C. Influence of Ethanol on the Redox State of the Normal and Pathological Liver

In experiments with human subjects and rats, ethanol has repeatedly been observed to raise the normal lactate/pyruvate concentration ratio [7, 25,

88] (see Figure 2). The ratio between β-hydroxybutyrate and acetoacetate also increases during ethanol oxidation [25, 60, 88] (see Figure 3). The former is stated to reflect the oxidation-reduction equilibrium of the extramitochondrial cytoplasm; the latter, the β-hydroxybutyrate/acetoacetate substrate pair, is assumed to be in equilibrium with the NAD-dependent redox systems of the mitochondria [44, 46, 99].

In sharp contrast with the situation in normal and starved livers, ethanol only slightly increased the concentration ratios, lactate/pyruvate and β-hydroxybutyrate/acetoacetate in perfusion experiments with protein-deficient fatty rat livers [83] (see Figs. 2, 3). Maintenance on the high-fat, low-protein and choline-deficient diet had altered the capacities of the liver cells to metabolize the extramitochondrial reducing equivalents, and no change in the redox state of the liver cells toward greater reduction could be observed. This phenomenon can be attributed to a decreased rate of ethanol oxidation in proportion to oxygen consumption or to an increased capacity of the liver cells to transport hydrogen from the cytoplasm into other metabolic pathways.

It has been reported that rats with fatty livers and minimal cirrhotic changes maintain almost normal rates of ethanol metabolism [67], and in

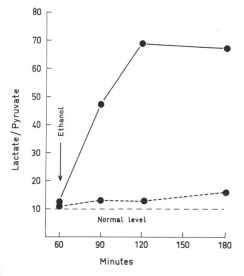

Figure 2. The influence of ethanol on the lactate/pyruvate concentration ratio in the medium during perfusion of normal and fatty livers of the rat. Ethanol was added to the perfusion medium immediately after sampling a 60 min: ●——● normal liver; ●- - -● fatty liver.

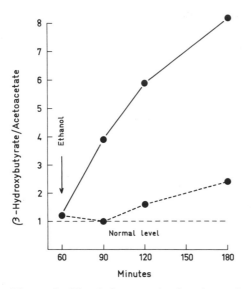

Figure 3. The influence of ethanol on the β-hydroxybutyrate/acetoacetate concentration ratio in the medium during perfusion of normal and fatty livers of the rat. Ethanol was added to the perfusion medium immediately after sampling at 60 min: ●———● normal liver; ●- - -● fatty liver.

human alcoholics lower rates of ethanol elimination have been observed only in severe liver cirrhosis [58, 101]. The relation of the rate of ethanol metabolism to various pathologic liver conditions is discussed at greater length later on, but it can be concluded that the oxidation of ethanol is impaired only in severe liver disease, and therefore the unchanged redox state of the fatty liver during ethanol oxidation can hardly be attributed to a decreased rate of ethanol oxidation.

Since the rate of ethanol breakdown obviously is not decreased in fatty livers, the amount of extramitochondrial reducing equivalents must be similar to that present in the normal liver. The almost unchanged ratio of $NADH_2$ to NAD indicates that the extra hydrogen must be transported to other pathways. The mitochondrial flavoprotein-cytochrome system represents a major system for $NADH_2$ oxidation, with oxygen as the final hydrogen acceptor (see Figure 1). An increase in the rate of this pathway could explain the unchanged redox state during ethanol oxidation. Ethanol did not increase the oxygen consumption of perfused fatty livers [83], however, and hence it is improbable that the extra hydrogen is consumed in oxidation in the cytochrome system.

A third possibility is that the liver cells use reducing equivalents in various syntheses, e.g., fatty acid and cholesterol syntheses (see Figure 1). Normally the mitochondrial flavoprotein–electron transport system reoxidizes $NADH_2$ originating mainly from the citric acid cycle. In normal livers carbon dioxide formation is greatly decreased during ethanol oxidation, indicating some block in the citric acid cycle [25, 57, 61, 63]. In sharp contrast with normal and starved livers, ethanol caused only a slight decrease in carbon dioxide production in experiments with choline-deficient fatty rat livers [83]. This means that in fatty livers $NADH_2$ is formed both extramitochondrially from alcohol breakdown to acetate and intramitochondrially in the citric acid cycle and that the total amount of reducing equivalents must be markedly greater in protein-deficient fatty livers than in normal or starved livers. The only possible pathway for this extramitochondrially derived hydrogen must be various syntheses, but this still remains to be proved.

The extent to which ethanol influences the redox state of cirrhotic livers cannot be exactly stated in the light of present investigations. In perfusion experiments with cirrhotic rat livers it has been shown that ethanol increases only slightly the lactate/pyruvate and β-hydroxybutyrate/acetoacetate ratios [82]. Because of technical difficulties in the performance of the experiments and possibly a slight degree of hypoxia the results are not quite reliable. The observations above, however, are consistent with the indirect results of Tygstrup and Lundquist [94], who report that ethanol does not decrease galactose elimination in cirrhotic patients (to be discussed later).

Very little is known about the influence of ethanol on the redox state of the liver in other pathological conditions. In experiments with liver slices, however, it has been shown that the influence of ethanol on the lactate/pyruvate ratio is decreased during thyroxine treatment [102]. This observation is confirmed by the results of Wilson [100], who reports that the ethanol-induced decrease of the mouse liver $NAD/NADH_2$ ratio is prevented by triiodothyronine treatment. Variations in the capacity of the liver to handle the extramitochondrially derived hydrogen during thyroid hormone treatment are, perhaps, correlated with changes in the over-all metabolism of the liver in this situation.

D.   Influence of Ethanol on Oxygen Consumption and Carbon Dioxide Production

Ethanol does not influence the oxygen consumption of normal livers in experiments with human subjects [57] or with liver slices of rats [20]. In perfusion experiments with starved, choline-deficient fatty and cirrhotic livers [25, 83], liver oxygen consumption also remains unchanged during ethanol breakdown.

It has been estimated that about three-quarters of the oxygen consumed by the liver may be used for the oxidation of ethanol to acetate [51, 60]. Since the oxygen consumption of the liver is not affected by the breakdown of ethanol, the oxidation of other substrates must decrease in proportion to the amount of ethanol oxidized. Normally the primary sources of hepatic metabolism are fatty acids, which are oxidized to carbon dioxide [29]. The metabolism of glucose plays a minor role in hepatic oxidation [64]. Thus during ethanol oxidation the further breakdown of acetate, normally derived mainly from fatty acids, is blocked in the citric acid cycle, as seen from the strong suppression of the production of carbon dioxide mentioned earlier [25, 51, 59, 61]. This is confirmed by the observation that carbon dioxide formation from labeled palmitate is inhibited during ethanol oxidation [57]. Likewise the decreased output of $^{14}CO_2$ from labeled glucose, fructose, and acetate in experiments with liver slices and the diminished incorporation of ^{14}C from labeled glucose and fructose into other compounds during ethanol oxidation must be due to the suppression of the citric acid cycle [13, 57, 63, 74, 76, 97]. Forsander [22] compared the effect of several aliphatic alcohols on the redox potential and carbon dioxide production of rat liver slices and found a strong negative correlation between the increase in the ratio of lactate to pyruvate and the production of carbon dioxide. The exact mechanism by which ethanol inhibits the citric acid cycle has not been elucidated, but increased $NADH_2$ generation and the change in the redox state of the liver during ethanol oxidation are probably the major factors [23, 54].

In fatty and cirrhotic rat livers, in contrast with normal and starved livers, ethanol only slightly decreases carbon dioxide production [83]. This indicates that protein deficiency alters the metabolic response of the liver in this respect as well. The primary cause is probably the unchanged redox potential of the liver cells, but it can also be assumed that all the events mentioned above in normal liver metabolism ensuing from an ethanol-induced decrease in the citric acid cycle are retarded in protein deficiency to some extent at least. At any rate, new efforts are called for to resolve the metabolic differences between normal and fatty livers.

E.   The Rate of Ethanol Metabolism

Since 1919 it has been known that ethanol normally is oxidized at a constant rate [66]. The liver plays a dominating role in the metabolism of ethanol. It is believed that the first step in the breakdown of ethanol, the conversion of ethanol to acetaldehyde, is the rate-limiting reaction. As previously mentioned, this reaction is catalyzed by an NAD-dependent enzyme, alcohol dehydrogenase. Since some correlation between the rate of alcohol metabolism and hepatic alcohol dehydrogenase activity has been demonstrated in animals, it has been suggested that the level of this enzyme limits the rate of ethanol metabolism [67, 86]. The assay of the activity of this enzyme, however, is fraught with difficulties, and exact comparisons between the rate of alcohol elimination in vivo and enzyme activities calculated from data obtained in vitro are rather questionable [8, 45]. It has also been suggested that both ethanol and oxidized nicotinamide adenine dinucleotide NAD ought to be considered substrates and that the rate-limiting step is the dissociation of enzyme and the reduced nicotinamide adenine dinucleotide $NADH_2$ [93]. According to this argument the availability of NAD during oxidation and further the $NAD/NADH_2$ ratio would regulate the rate of ethanol metabolism. This is rather improbable, however, since in protein-deficient fatty livers, in which the $NAD/NADH_2$ ratio is unchanged during ethanol oxidation, the rate of ethanol metabolism does not differ from normal. From all available data it can be concluded that the exact mechanism regulating the rate of ethanol oxidation in the intact organism has so far remained unknown. Most probably it is connected with the general energy-coupled regulation of oxidation.

The influence of various liver diseases on the rate of ethanol elimination has been studied extensively during recent years in both experimental animals and human beings. It has been reported that the rate of alcohol oxidation is decreased in liver fibrosis, owing to dietary deficiency [67]. In experiments with rats Horn and Manthei [36] demonstrated that after 2 months' feeding of a protein-deficient diet to growing rats both the activity of alcohol dehydrogenase and the oxidation of ethanol by liver slices were significantly lower than in controls. The diet they used, however, was not supplemented with cystine, and consequently their results are not comparable with our liver perfusion experiments [83], in which the rate of ethanol elimination was more or less the same in both normal and fatty livers. On the other hand it has been reported that in cystine deficiency it is hepatic cell necrosis rather than diffuse hepatic fibrosis ("portal cirrhosis") that develops [30]. Our observation is confirmed by studies on human alcoholics. Kulpe and Mallach [48] found no difference in alcohol elimination rates between 15 cirrhotic patients and normals. According to Lieberman [58] cirrhotic patients have lower rates of ethanol elimination than normal controls only when the disease process is far advanced. These observations are still corroborated by the results of several other investigators [4, 17, 18, 71, 101]. Leevy [50] shows that both the rate of ethanol elimination and the activity of liver alcohol dehydrogenase decrease as the liver gradually progresses from normal to fatty to cirrhotic. He has used, however, only one determination of blood alcohol concentration obtained 1 hr after administration, and this cannot be considered sufficient for the calculation of the rate of ethanol oxidation. It can be concluded that ethanol oxidation is decreased only in severe liver disease, and consequently the rate of alcohol elimination cannot be used as a measure of liver function.

In rats with experimental centrolobular necrosis caused by carbon tetrachloride the rates of alcohol elimination have been reported to be normal both in vivo [90] and in vitro [14]. In dogs, pretreatment with carbon tetrachloride seems to decrease the elimination rate [91]. Contrary results, however, have also been obtained [9]. In periportal necrosis caused by phosphorus [90] and in liver damage induced by allyl alcohol [14] the rate of ethanol elimination has been reported to be significantly lower than in controls. In rats, jaundice markedly decreases the rate of oxidation of ethanol [42]. This effect can perhaps be related to the inhibiting influence of bilirubin on the activity of alcohol dehydrogenase [19].

F.   Influence of Ethanol on Glucose Metabolism in Normal and Pathological Livers

Extensive clinical and in vitro studies have established that hypoglycemia following alcohol administration during a state of fasting is a normal reaction in man and experimental animals [15, 27, 62]. According to the present data, alcohol-induced hypoglycemia is caused by the inhibition of hepatic gluconeogenesis, the primary effect being a shift in the $NAD/NADH_2$ ratio [39, 46, 47, 62]. This is confirmed by our perfusion experiments with starved rat livers, in which ethanol caused a marked uptake of glucose from the perfusion medium [25]. On the other hand, ethanol did not influence the glucose concentration of the perfusion medium in experiments with protein-deficient fatty rat livers [83]. As already mentioned, ethanol did not change the redox state of these livers and obviously did not inhibit hepatic gluconeogenesis either.

Recently it has been demonstrated that fasted obese individuals are less vulnerable to the hypoglycemic action of alcohol than fasted normal-weight subjects [3, 2]. The refractoriness of most obese subjects to alcoholic hypoglycemia cannot at present be adequately explained. Hed and Nygren [34] observe that many chronic alcoholics do not exhibit hypoglycemia after alcohol consumption and that most of these patients have a diabetic glucose pattern. Their information about the liver condition of these patients is rather inadequate, however, as regards fatty and cirrhotic changes of the liver. Recently I investigated alcoholic hypoglycemia in chronic alcoholics whose food consumption had been inadequate for long periods [81]. After a fast of 40 hr the patients were given 600 mg of ethanol per kg body weight as a 15% solution. During the following 4 hr, blood samples for glucose estimation were taken every 60 min. In experiments performed immediately after the patient's admission to hospital ethanol did not decrease the level of blood glucose, and these patients did not have a diabetic glucose pattern. After 6 weeks' therapy with a high-protein diet, however, a normal hypoglycemic response to ethanol could be demonstrated (see Figure 4). This observation confirms the results obtained in liver perfusion experiments and indicates that ethanol does not inhibit gluconeogenesis in alcoholics with protein-deficient fatty livers. Perhaps this abnormal reaction of the liver to ethanol explains why chronic alcoholics infrequently have fatal hypoglycemic reactions. In these patients the intravenous galactose tolerance test was used as a measure of the redox state of the liver (to be discussed later). After the patients were admitted to hospital, the galactose tolerance test with ethanol was pathologic; i.e., ethanol did not decrease the elimination rate of galactose (see Figure 5).

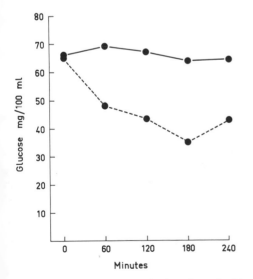

Figure 4. The influence of ethanol on the blood glucose curve of a chronic alcoholic whose food consumption had been inadequate for long periods. Six hundred milligrams of ethanol was given per kilogram body weight after a fast of 40 hours: ●——● blood glucose curve immediately after hospital admission; ●- - -● blood glucose curve after the therapy of six weeks.

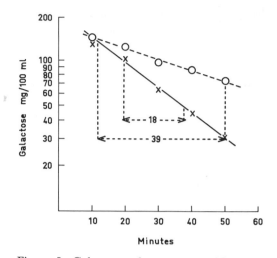

Figure 5. Galactose tolerance test with ethanol immediately after admission to hospital (×——×) and after six weeks' therapy with high protein diet (O- -O).

After 6 weeks' therapy, not only was the galactose tolerance test with ethanol normalized (see Figure 5), but the fatty infiltration of the liver cells in liver biopsy specimens had almost disappeared. It can be concluded that ethanol does not induce hypoglycemia in human alcoholics whose food consumption has been inadequate for long periods and who, in consequence, have choline-deficient fatty livers. In these patients ethanol does not change the redox state of the liver and obviously does not decrease gluconeogenesis either.

G. The Influence of Ethanol on Galactose Metabolism and the Use of the Galactose Tolerance Test for the Early Diagnosis of Fatty Liver in Human Alcoholics

It is believed that the conversion of galactose to glucose proceeds through the following four stages [40]:

1. Galactose + ATP $\rightleftarrows$ galactose-1-phosphate + ADP
2. Galactose-1-phosphate + UDP-glucose $\rightleftarrows$ glucose-1-phosphate + UDP-galactose
3. UDP-galactose $\rightleftarrows$ UDP-glucose
4. UDP-glucose + pyrophosphate $\rightleftarrows$ glucose-1-phosphate + UTP

These reactions are catalyzed by the enzymes galactokinase, galactose-1-phosphate-uridyltransferase, UDP-galactose-4-epimerase, and UDP-glucosepyrophosphorylase, respectively. Recently evidence has been presented of the existence of a new pathway for galactose breakdown in the mammalian liver [11], galactose being converted to galactonolactone by the enzyme galactose dehydrogenase in the presence of NAD. Galactonolactone is further converted to d-xylulose by a series of reactions. The reaction product, $NADH_2$, is a strong competitive inhibitor of galactose dehydrogenase [12].

One of the key reactions in the metabolism of galactose is the third one, involving the conversion of UDP-galactose to UDP-glucose. Maxwell [65] shows that the coenzyme in this epimerization is NAD and that $NADH_2$ is a potent inhibitor of the enzyme.

The redox potentials of biologic redox system in the liver cell can be measured either by quick freezing of liver tissue followed by the determination of the concentrations of metabolites forming redox pairs [35] or by catheterization of the hepatic vein and analysis of the blood concentrations of these metabolites [59]. In vitro the redox potentials can be measured either by analyzing the concentrations of metabolites in the perfusion medium in experiments with isolated perfused livers [85] or by determining the same concentrations from the buffer solution in experiments with liver slices [21]. The metabolites forming redox pairs are readily oxidized or reduced in peripheral tissues. Thus the determination of their ratio from venous blood does not afford an accurate picture of the redox state of the liver cells. Since galactose is mainly oxidized in the liver and its reaction rate depends on the $NADH_2/NAD$ ratio [77], it was assumed that the rate of galactose elimination could be used for estimating changes in the redox potential of the intact liver.

As mentioned before, during ethanol oxidation large amounts of $NADH_2$ are formed, and hence it may be supposed that in the normal liver both pathways for galactose breakdown are inhibited. In fact, in experiments with rat liver homogenate, the capacity of the liver to oxidize galactose has been reported to be diminished in the presence of ethanol [38]. A pronounced impairment of galactose tolerance as a result of ethanol consumption has also been observed in normal individuals [92, 94, 95].

Since ethanol did not affect the redox state of protein-deficient fatty rat livers, the rate of galactose elimination was used as a measure of the redox potential of these livers with and without ethanol [79, 84]. In these experiments ethanol caused almost total inhibition of galactose elimination in normal animals. In protein-deficient rats, however, as expected, ethanol had no effect at all on the rate of galactose elimination. Variations in the proportions of fat and carbohydrate in the diet did not exert any influence on galactose elimination. After the addition of choline to the low-protein, high-fat diet the rate of galactose elimination, both with and without ethanol, was again the same as in the control rats. It could be concluded that the rate of galactose elimination can be used as a measure of the redox state of the liver and that ethanol no longer induces a shift in the redox state of the protein-deficient fatty rat liver, apparently on account of the lack of choline.

These observations led us to study the influence of ethanol on the rate of galactose elimination in chronic alcoholics. It was possible to demonstrate that ethanol does not decrease galactose breakdown or obviously increase the hepatic $NADH_2/NAD$ ratio, either, in chronic alcoholics whose food consumption has for long periods been inadequate with regard to protein and vitamins [88]. In patients with grave malabsorption no response to ethanol can be observed either. Subsequently we have been able to demonstrate that the galactose tolerance test with ethanol is normalized after 6 weeks' therapy with a high-protein diet [82]. In other cases of fatty liver (obesity, diabetes, alcoholism with adequate food consumption, etc.), ethanol decreases the rate of elimination of galactose quite normally [82].

There are two main disadvantages inherent in the existing liver function tests. They are not capable of demonstrating early alterations in liver function during the development of protein-deficient fatty liver, and they do not provide any information about the etiology of hepatic injury. The most valuable diagnostic aids in hepatic steatosis have up to the present been palpation of the liver and liver biopsy [49]. The galactose tolerance test with ethanol can be used in exploring the etiology and nature of the fatty liver. In planning suitable therapy and a follow-up study of an alcoholic patient, the test is quite useful. Recently a technically easier peroral galactose tolerance test with and without ethanol was developed for screening purposes [41].

CONCLUSIONS

It has been established that the change in the redox state of the liver during ethanol oxidation is probably responsible for most of the effects of ethanol on normal liver metabolism. Thus the activity of the citric acid cycle decreases, fatty acid synthesis increases, urea production decreases, breakdown of galactose decreases, serotonin metabolism decreases, and gluconeogenesis from various precursors decreases. In fatty livers produced by a low-protein diet ethanol does not cause a shift in the redox state of the liver. Correspondingly it has been demonstrated in liver perfusion experiments that the influence of ethanol on citric acid cycle activity is decreased during the course of development of the protein-deficient fatty liver. Further ethanol does not decrease the elimination rate of galactose and does not cause hypoglycemia in experiments with rats or human alcoholics with protein-deficient fatty livers. What is the primary reason for the differences mentioned above, how the other metabolic parameters differ from one another in normal and protein-deficient fatty livers and how these changes can be related to the pathogenesis of dangerous, irreversible liver cirrhosis, are questions that remain to be settled. Although definitive answers are not yet available, these observations and questions point to the need for further investigation in this interesting field of liver pathology.

REFERENCES

1. Ahlqvist, J., M. Nyholm, M. Salaspuro, and H. Wallgren, Biochemical and morphological alterations in livers of rats fed high alcohol and high fat diets with ample protein and vitamin supply, *Acta Physiol. Scand.,* **74,** 15A (1968).

2. Arky, R. A., E. A. Abrahamson, and N. Freinkel, Alcohol hypoglycemia: VII. Further studies on the refractoriness of obese subjects, *Metabolism,* **17,** 977 (1968).

3. Arky, R. A., and N. Freinkel, Alcohol hypoglycemia: V. Alcohol infusion to test gluconeogenesis in starvation with special reference to obesity, *New Engl. J. Med.,* **274,** 426 (1966).

4. Asada, M., and J. T. Galambos, Liver disease, hepatic alcohol dehydrogenase activity, and alcohol metabolism in humans, *Gastroenterology,* **45,** 67 (1963).

5. Atwater, W. O., and F. D. Benedict, An experimental inquiry regarding the nutritive value of alcohol, *Med. Natl. Acad. Sci.,* **114,** 501 (1964).

6. Bücher, Th., and M. Klingenberg, Wege des Wasserstoffs in der lebendigen Organisation, *Angew. Chem.,* **70,** 552 (1958).

7. Büttner, H., Äthanolunverträglichkeit beim Menschen nach Sulfonylharnstoffen, *Deut. Arch. Klin. Med.,* **207,** 1 (1961).

8. Büttner, H., Aldehyd- und Alcoholdehydrogenase-Aktivität in Leber und Niere der Ratte, *Biochem. Z.,* **341,** 300 (1965).

9. Campos, I., W. Solodkowska, E. Munoz, N. Segovia-Riquelme, J. Cembrano, and J. Mardones, Ethanol metabolism in rats with experimental liver cirrhosis: I. Rate of combustion of labeled ethanol and rate of decrease of ethanol level, *Quart. J. Studies Alc.,* **25,** 417 (1964).

10. Carpenter, T. M., and R. C. Lee, Die Wirkung von Galaktose auf den Äthylalkoholumsatz beim Menschen, *J. Pharmacol. Exptl. Therap.,* **60,** 254 (1937).

11. Cuatrecasas, P., and S. Segal, Galactose conversion to *d*-xylulose: An alternate route of galactose metabolism, *Science,* **153,** 549 (1966).

12. Cuatrecasas, P., and S. Segal, Mammalian galactose dehydrogenase II: Properties, substrate specificity, and developmental changes, *J. Biol. Chem.,* **241,** 5910 (1966).

13. Dajani, R. M., and J. M. Orten, Utilization of ethanol by way of citric acid cycle in the rat, *J. Nutr.,* **76,** 135 (1962).

14. Evans, E. A., G. Eisenlord, and C. H. Hine, Studies in detoxication by means of the isolated perfused liver, *Toxicol. Appl. Pharmacol.*, **5**, 129 (1963).
15. Field, J. B., H. E. Williams, and G. E. Mortimore, Studies on the mechanism of ethanol-induced hypoglycemia, *J. Clin. Invest.*, **42**, 497 (1963).
16. Fiessinger, N., H. Benard, J. Courtical, and L. Dermer, Combustion de l'alcool éthylique au cours de la perfusion du foie, *Compt. Rend. Soc. Biol.*, **122**, 1255 (1936).
17. Figueroa, R. B., and A. P. Klotz, Alterations of liver alcohol dehydrogenase and other hepatic enzymes in alcoholic cirrhosis, *Gastroenterology*, **43**, 10 (1962).
18. Filip, J., and J. Hoenigová, Rate of ethanol combustion, following intravenous administration, in cirrhotic patients, *Rev. Czech. Med.*, **12**, 82 (1966).
19. Flitman, R., and M. H. Worth, Jr., Inhibition of hepatic alcohol dehydrogenase by bilirubin, *J. Biol. Chem.*, **241**, 669 (1966).
20. Fondal, E., and C. D. Kochakian, In vitro effect of ethyl alcohol on respiration of rat liver and kidney slices, *Proc. Soc. Exptl. Biol. Med.*, **77**, 823 (1951).
21. Forsander, O. A., Influence of the metabolism of ethanol on the lactate/pyruvate ratio of rat-liver slices, *Biochem. J.*, **98**, 244 (1966).
22. Forsander, O. A., Influence of some aliphatic alcohols on the metabolism of rat liver slices, *Biochem. J.*, **105**, 93 (1967).
23. Forsander, O. A., Der Einfluss des Äthanols auf den Stoffwechsel der perfundierten Ratten leber, in *Stoffwechsel der isoliert perfundierten Leber*, W. Staib and R. Scholz (eds.), p. 210, Springer-Verlag, Berlin, 1968.
24. Forsander, O. A., and N. C. R. Räihä, Metabolites produced in the liver during alcohol oxidation, *J. Biol. Chem.*, **235**, 34 (1960).
25. Forsander, O. A., N. Räihä, M. Salaspuro, and P. Mäenpää, Influence of ethanol on the liver metabolism of fed and starved rats, *Biochem. J.*, **94**, 259 (1965).
26. Forsander, O., N. Räihä, and H. Suomalainen, Alkoholoxydation und Bildung von Acetoacetat in normaler und glykogenarmer intakter Rattenleber, *Z. Physiol. Chem.*, **312**, 243 (1958).
27. Freinkel, N., R. A. Arky, D. L. Singer, A. K. Cohen, S. J. Bleicher, J. B. Anderson, C. K. Silbert, and A. E. Foster, Alcohol hypoglycemia: IV. Current concepts of its pathogenesis, *Diabetes*, **14**, 350 (1965).
28. Frieden, C., Glutamic dehydrogenase: II. The effect of various nucleotides on the association-dissociation and kinetic properties, *J. Biol. Chem.*, **234**, 815 (1959).
29. Fritz, I. B., Factors influencing the rates of long-chain fatty acid oxidation and synthesis in mammalian systems, *Physiol. Rev.*, **41**, 52 (1961).
30. Glynn, C. E., H. P. Himsworth, and O. Lindan, The experimental production and development of diffuse hepatic fibrosis ("portal cirrhosis"), *Brit. J. Exptl. Pathol.*, **29**, 1 (1948).
31. Green, D. E., and F. L. Crane, Structure of the Mitochondrial Electron Transport System, in *Proceedings of the International Symposim on Enzyme Chemistry, Tokyo and Kyoto, 1957*, p. 275. Pergamon, London, 1958.

32. Hartroft, W. S., and E. A. Porta, Alcohol, diet and experimental hepatic injury, *Can. J. Physiol. Pharmacol.*, **46**, 463 (1968).

33. Hassinen, I., Hydrogen transfer into mitochondria in the metabolism of ethanol: I. Oxidation of extramitochondrial reduced nicotinamide-adenine dinucleotide by mitochondria, *Ann. Med. Exptl. Biol. Fenniae (Helsinki)*, **45**, 1 (1967).

34. Hed, R., and A. Nygren, Alcohol-induced hypoglycaemia in chronic alcoholics with liver disease, *Acta Med. Scand.*, **183**, 507 (1968).

35. Hohorst, H. J., F. H. Kreutz, and Th. Bücher, Über Metabolitgehalte und Metabolit-Konzentrationen in der Leber der Ratte, *Biochem. Z.*, **332**, 18 (1959).

36. Horn, R. S., and R. W. Manthei, Ethanol metabolism in chronic protein deficiency, *J. Pharmacol. Exptl. Therap.*, **147**, 385 (1965).

37. Isselbacher, K. J., and N. J. Greenberger, Metabolic effects of alcohol on the liver: I, II, *New Engl. J. Med.*, **270**, 351, 402 (1964).

38. Isselbacher, K. J., and S. M. Krane, Studies on the mechanism of the inhibition of galactose oxidation by ethanol, *J. Biol. Chem.*, **236**, 2394 (1961).

39. Kaden, M., N. W. Dakley, and J. B. Field, Effect of alcohol on gluconeogenesis using the isolated liver perfusion technique, *Am. J. Physiol.*, **216**, 756 (1959).

40. Kalckar, H. M., Galactose metabolism and cell "sociology," *Science*, **150**, 305 (1966).

41. Kesäniemi, A., and K. Kurppa, to be published.

42. Kiessling, K. H., and L. Pilström, The effect of bile obstruction on the oxidation rate of ethanol in the rat, *Acta Physiol. Scand.*, **69**, 187 (1967).

43. Klatskin, G., Alcohol and its relation to liver damage, *Gastroenterology*, **41**, 443 (1961).

44. Klingenberg, M., and H. v. Häfen, Wege des Wasserstoffs in Mitochondrien: I, *Biochem. Z.*, **337**, 120 (1963).

45. Koch, O. R., E. A. Porta, and W. S. Hartroft, A new experimental approach in the study of chronic alcoholism: III. Role of alcohol versus sucrose or fat-derived calories in hepatic damage, *Scand. J. Clin. Lab. Invest.*, **18**, 379 (1968).

46. Krebs, H. A., The redox state of nicotinamide-adenine dinucleotide in the cytoplasm and mitochondria of rat liver, *Advan. Enzyme Regulation*, **5**, 409 (1967).

47. Krebs, H. A., R. A. Freedland, R. Hems, and M. Stubbs, Inhibition of hepatic gluconeogenesis by ethanol, *Biochem. J.*, **112**, 117 (1969).

48. Kulpe, W., and H. J. Mallach, Das verhalten des Blutzuckerspiegels bei Lebercirrhosen unter Alcoholwirkung, *Z. Klin. Med.*, **157**, 55 (1962).

49. Leevy, C. M., A study of 270 patients with biopsy proven fatty liver and a review of the literature, *Medicine*, **41**, 249 (1962).

50. Leevy, C. M., Clinical diagnosis, evaluation and treatment of liver disease in alcoholics, *Federation Proc.*, **26**, 1474 (1967).

51. Leloir, L. F., and J. M. Munoz, Ethyl alcohol metabolism in animal tissues, *Biochem. J.,* **32,** 299 (1938).
52. Lieber, C. S., Alcohol and the Liver, in *Progress in Liver Diseases,* H. Popper and F. Schaffner (eds.), vol. 2, chap. II, Grune & Stratton, New York, 1965.
53. Lieber, C. S., Metabolic derangement induced by alcohol, *Ann. Rev. Med.,* **18,** 35 (1967).
54. Lieber, C. S., Metabolic effects produced by alcohol in the liver and other tissues, *Advan. Internal. Med.,* **14,** 151 (1969).
55. Lieber, C. S., and C. M. De Carli, Effect of ethanol on cholesterol metabolism, *Clin. Res.,* **12,** 274 (1964).
56. Lieber, C. S., D. P. Jones, M. S. Losowsky, and C. S. Davidson, Interrelation of uric acid and ethanol metabolism in man, *J. Clin. Invest.,* **41,** 1863 (1962).
57. Lieber, C. S., and R. Schmid, The effect of ethanol on fatty acid metabolism: Stimulation of hepatic fatty acid synthesis *in vitro, J. Clin. Invest.,* **40,** 394 (1961).
58. Lieberman, F. L., The effect of liver disease on the rate of ethanol metabolism in man, *Gastroenterology,* **44,** 261 (1963).
59. Lundquist, F., U. Fugmann, E. Klaning, and H. Rasmussen, The metabolism of acetaldehyde in mammalian tissues, *Biochem. J.,* **72,** 409 (1959).
60. Lundquist, F., N. Tygstrup, K. Winkler, and K. Mellemgaard, Ethanol metabolism and production of free acetate in the human liver, *J. Clin. Invest.,* **41,** 955 (1962).
61. Lundsgaard, E., Alcohol oxidation as a function of the liver, *Compt. Rend. Trav. Lab. Carlsberg, Sèr. chim.,* **22,** 333 (1938).
62. Madison, C. C., A. Lockner, and J. Wulff, Ethanol-induced hypoglycemia II: Mechanism of suppression of hepatic gluconeogenesis, *Diabetes,* **16,** 252 (1967).
63. Majchrowicz, E., and J. H. Quastel, Effects of aliphatic alcohols and fatty acids on the metabolism of acetate by rat liver slices, *Can. J. Biochem. Physiol.,* **39,** 1895 (1961).
64. Majchrowicz, E., and J. H. Quastel, Effects of aliphatic alcohols on the metabolism of glucose and fructose in rat liver slices, *Can. J. Biochem. Physiol.,* **41,** 793 (1963).
65. Maxwell, E. S., The enzymic conversion of uridine diphosphogalactose and uridine diphosphoglucose, *J Biol. Chem.,* **229,** 139 (1957).
66. Mellanby, E., Alcohol: Its absorption into and disappearance from the blood under different conditions, *Medical Research Committee, Special Report Series* 31, His Majesty's Stationary Office, London, 1919.
67. Mikata, A., A. A. Dimakulangan, and W. S. Hartroft, Metabolism of ethanol in rats with cirrhosis, Gastroenterology, 44, 159 (1963).
68. Nikkilä, E. A., and K. Ojala, Ethanol-induced alterations in the synthesis of hepatic and plasma lipids and hepatic glycogen from glycerol-C^{14}, *Life Sci.,* **2,** 717 (1963).
69. Nikkilä, E. A., and K. Ojala, Role of hepatic L-α-glycerophosphate and trigly-

ceride synthesis in production of fatty liver by ethanol, *Proc. Soc. Exptl. Biol. Med.*, **113**, 814 (1963).

70. Nyberg, A., J. Schuberth, and L. Änggård, On the intracellular distribution of catalase and alcohol dehydrogenase in horse, guinea pig and rat liver tissues, *Acta Chem. Scand.*, **7**, 1170 (1953).

71. Piotz, D. G., B. D. Rosenak, and R. N. Harger, Alcohol metabolism in hepatic dysfunction, *Am. J. Gastroenterology*, **34**, 140 (1960).

72. Porta, E. A., O. R. Koch, C. L. A. Comez-Dumm, and W. S. Hartroft, Effects of dietary protein on the liver of rats in experimental chronic alcoholism, *J. Nutr.*, **94**, 437 (1968).

73. Purvis, J. L., and J. M. Lowenstein, The relation between intra- and extramitochondrial pyridine nucleotides, *J. Biol. Chem.*, **236**, 2794 (1961).

74. Quastel, J. H., Effects of aliphatic alcohols on tissue metabolism, *Proc. Intern. Congr. Alcohol Alcoholism, 26th*, Stockholm, 1960, p. 45 (Pub. 1963).

75. Räihä, N. C. R., and M. S. Koskinen, Effect of a non-ionic surface active substance on the activation of alcohol dehydrogenase of rat liver homogenates, *Life Sci.*, **3**, 1091 (1964).

76. Reboucas, G., and K. J. Isselbacher, Studies on the pathogenesis of the ethanol-induced fatty liver: I. Synthesis and oxidation of fatty acids by the liver, *J. Clin. Invest.*, **40**, 1355 (1961).

77. Robinson, E. A., H. M. Kalckar, and H. Troedsson, On the loss of uridine diphosphogalactose-4-epimerase activity in L cell cultures and in tumor cells, *Biochem. Biophys. Res. Commun.*, **13**, 313 (1963).

78. Rosenfeld, G., Inhibitory influence of ethanol on serotonin metabolism, *Proc. Soc. Exptl. Biol. Med.*, **103**, 144 (1960).

79. Salaspuro, M. P., Ethanol inhibition of galactose oxidation as related to the redox state of fatty liver, *Scand. J. Clin. Lab. Invest.*, **18**, *Suppl.* **92**, 145 (1966).

80. Salaspuro, M. P., Application of the galactose tolerance test for the early diagnosis of fatty liver in human alcoholics, *Scand. J. Clin. Lab. Invest.*, **20**, 274 (1967).

81. Salaspuro, M. P., Korreferat, *Therapie Woche, 39*, 2267 (1970).

82. Salaspuro, M. P., and A. Kesäniemi, to be published.

83. Salaspuro, M. P., and P. H. Mäenpää, Influence of ethanol on the metabolism of perfused normal, fatty and cirrhotic rat livers, *Biochem. J.* **100**, 768 (1966).

84. Salaspuro, M. P., and A. E. Salaspuro, The effect of ethanol on galactose elimination in rats with normal and choline-deficient fatty livers, *Scand. J. Clin. Lab. Invest.*, **22**, 49 (1968).

85. Schimassek, H., Der Einfluss der Leber auf den extracellulären Redox-Quotienten Lactat/Pyruvat, *Biochem. Z.*, **336**, 468 (1963).

86. Schlesinger, K., Genetic and biochemical correlates of alcohol preference in mice, *Am. J. Psychol.*, **122**, 767 (1966).

87. Scholz, R., R. G. Thurman, and J. R. Williamson, Control of mitochondrial functions by extramitochondrial redox state, Federation European Biochem. Soc., 6th Meeting, Madrid, 1969, *Abstr. Commun.*, p. 239.

88. Seligson, D., H. H. Stone, and P. Nemir, Jr., The metabolism of ethanol in man, *Surg. Forum,* **9,** 85 (1959).
89. Senior, M. R., Ethanol and liver disease, *Postgrad. Med.,* **41,** 65 (1968).
90. Sirnes, T. B., The blood alcohol curve in zonal necrosis of the liver, *Quart. J. Studies Alc.,* **13,** 189 (1952).
91. $lesinger, C., Belastung der Leber gesunder und kranker Hunde mit Äthylalkohol im Vergleich mit der exkretion des Bromsulphaleins und Bilirubine, *Arch. Exptl. Veterinärmed.,* **19,** 609 (1965).
92. Stenstam, T., Peroral and intravenous galactose tests: A comparative study of their significance in different conditions, *Acta Med. Scand.,* **125,** *Suppl.,* **177,** 84 (1946).
93. Theorell, H., and B. Chance, Studies on liver alcohol dehydrogenase: II. The kinetics of the compound of horse liver alcohol dehydrogenase and reduced diphosphopyridine nucleotide, *Acta Chem. Scand.,* **5,** 112 (1951).
94. Tygstrup, N., and F. Lundquist, The effect of ethanol on galactose elimination in man, *J. Lab. Clin. Med.,* **59,** 102 (1962).
95. Tygstrup, N., and K. Winkler, Galactose blood clearance as measure of hepatic blood flow, *Clin. Sci.,* **17,** 1 (1958).
96. Vallee, B. L., and F. L. Hoch, Zinc in horse liver alcohol dehydrogenase, *J. Biol. Chem.,* **225,** 185 (1957).
97. von Wartburg, J.-P., and H. M. Eppenberg, Vergleichende Untersuchungen über den oxydativen Abbau von 1-C^{14}-Äthanol und 1-C^{14}-Azetat in Leber und Niere, *Helv. Physiol. Pharmacol. Acta,* **19,** 303 (1961).
98. Westheimer, F. H., H. F. Fisher, E. E. Conn, and B. Vennesland, The enzymatic transfer of hydrogen from alcohol to DPN, *J. Am. Chem. Soc.,* **73,** 2403 (1951).
99. Williamson, D. H., P. Lund, and H. A. Krebs, The redox state of free nicotinamideadenine dinucleotide in the cytoplasm and mitochondria of rat liver, *Biochem. J.,* **103,** 514 (1967).
100. Wilson, E. C., Ethanol Metabolism in Mice with Different Levels of Hepatic Alcohol Dehydrogenase, in *Biological Factors in Alcoholism,* R. P. Maickel (ed.), p. 115, Pergamon, New York, 1967.
101. Winkler, K., F. Lundquist, and N. Tygstrup, The metabolism of ethanol in normal man and in patients with cirrhosis of the liver, *Scand. J. Clin. Lab. Invest.,* **18,** *Suppl.* **92,** 78 (1966).
102. Ylikahri, R. H., P. H. Mäenpää, and I. E. Hassinen, Ethanol-induced changes of cytoplasmic redox state as modified by thyroxine treatment, *Am. Med. Exptl. Biol. Fenniae (Helsinki),* **46,** 137 (1968).

Chapter VII

EFFECTS OF ALCOHOL ON CARDIAC AND MUSCULAR FUNCTION

RALPII M. MYERSON

DEPARTMENT OF MEDICINE
THE MEDICAL COLLEGE OF PENNSYLVANIA
MEDICAL SERVICE, THE MEDICAL COLLEGE OF PENNSYLVANIA DIVISION
VETERANS ADMINISTRATION HOSPITAL, PHILADELPHIA

There is convincing clinical, laboratory, and experimental evidence that alcohol exerts a direct toxic effect on both the myocardium and the skeletal muscular system. Although the basic mechanism of this action may be similar in both systems, it is appropriate and convenient to consider alcoholic cardiomyopathy and alcoholic (skeletal) myopathy as separate entities.

A. Alcoholic Cardiomyopathy

1. Historical Aspects

The experimental effect of ethanol on the myocardium has been a popular topic of investigation for over a century. European and American investigators have used a variety of techniques to gather information on the subject. These have included in vitro studies involving tissue slices and homogenates, histochemical and microscopic studies, and acute and chronic in vivo experiments with the oral administration and intravenous infusion of alcohol in both man and animals.

In 1869 Zimmerberg [128] published a dissertation on the topic, and a voluminous amount of literature has accumulated since that time. Early papers describing relatively crude techniques and unscientific parameters resulted in contradictory data [27, 46, 48, 51, 52, 64, 69, 73, 74, 88, 102, 117, 119]. As techniques of experimentation improved, however, more and more evidence was accumulated, indicating that alcohol had a deleterious effect on cardiac function [27, 64].

Relatively little attention was paid, however, to the possible clinical implications of this knowledge. In 1873 W. H. Walshe [121], an English cardiologist, gave passing recognition to the fact that alcoholism may be associated with heart disease. He commented on "cirrhosis of the heart," occurring in the absence of valvular and coronary artery disease. In 1884 Bollinger [14] described cardiac dilatation and congestive heart failure in a group of individuals with a heavy consumption of beer—the so-called "München Bierherz." In 1895 Aufrecht [8] reported "alcoholic myocarditis" in association with albuminuria and liver disease. The term "alcoholic heart disease" seems to have been first used by Mackenzie [71] in 1902. In 1906 Steell [110] noted the association between alcoholism and beriberi heart disease.

The definition of the syndrome of beriberi heart disease and its association with thiamine chloride deficiency was established in the 1920s and 1930s [1, 24, 57, 125]. The syndrome was reported in Europe and the United States in common association with chronic alcoholism and was referred to as "occidental beriberi" [13]. Its frequency in alcoholics was attributed to a relative thiamine deficiency associated with the relatively high concentration of carbohydrate in alcoholic beverages.

Although it was recognized early that many cases of heart disease in alcoholics did not fall into a hyperkinetic pattern [13, 24, 57, 125], there was a tendency to attribute all forms of alcoholic heart disease to beriberi. The confusion that resulted was compounded by reports of cardiac abnormalities associated with general malnutrition [41, 43, 55, 114] and with deficiencies commonly present in chronic alcoholics [127]. In experimental animals, in which it is possible to induce specific deficiencies, myocardial damage was reported secondary to a variety of deficiencies, including niacin [127], pyridoxine [87, 111], vitamin C [11, 76], vitamin D [127], and vitamin E [127].

It soon became apparent, however, that alcoholic cardiomyopathy existed as a distinct entity, resulting from the direct action of alcohol on the myocardium. There was, as mentioned, a substantial amount of experimental evidence to this effect plus a rapidly accumulating body of clinical evidence. For example, many alcoholic patients exhibit a low-output form of cardiac failure rather than the hyperkinetic manifestations seen in beriberi [10, 12, 13, 17, 21, 34, 56, 57, 58]. Distinctive electron microscopic findings have been described in alcoholic cardiomyopathy [6, 53].

An interesting addition to the historical aspects of alcoholic cardiomyopathy has been the recent description of beer drinkers' cardiomyopathy. Outbreaks of a serious form of low-output cardiac failure following heavy consumption of beer have been described in several localities, notably Omaha, Nebraska [77], and Quebec City [9, 15, 78, 79, 80, 81]. The evidence suggests that the syndrome was produced by cobalt, a foam-producing additive to some brands of beer [80]. It is interesting that in a similar episode occurring in beer drinkers in Manchester, England, in 1900, arsenic was implicated, though not convincingly, as the offending agent [33, 101].

Thus it is recognized that several mechanisms may operate in the production of cardiac disease in alcoholics. These include (1) general and specific nutritional deficiencies other than thiamine chloride, (2) beriberi heart disease secondary to thiamine deficiency, and (3) toxic factors, such as cobalt, present in alcohol. Our emphasis, however, is on that form of cardiomyopathy due to the direct effects of alcohol itself.

2. Pathophysiology

This aspect of alcoholic cardiomyopathy is limited to the effects of alcohol on the hemodynamic and functional capacity of the cardiovascular system, particularly the myocardium. The reader is referred to other chapters in this book for a description of the basic metabolic and cellular effects of alcohol.

A. HEMODYNAMIC EFFECTS OF ALCOHOL. There is a voluminous amount of early work on the effects of alcohol on the cardiovascular system. Many of these studies presented presumptive evidence of the depressing action of alcohol on the heart, but measurements were not precise and conditions uncontrolled. In 1924 Sulzer [113], using the Starling heart-lung preparation in dogs, studied the effect of alcohol in concentrations commonly reached in the human blood during intoxication. There was no evidence of any stimulant effect of alcohol on the heart in any doses. With concentrations of alcohol in the blood as low as 0.06% he observed an increase in diastolic and systolic volumes, an effect that became more and more marked as the concentration of the alcohol was increased. With higher concentrations Sulzer noted a diminution in the cardiac output and a rise in venous pressure. He also noted a reduction in coronary blood flow.

In 1927 Visscher [118] confirmed the findings that small quantities of alcohol in the circulating blood caused a marked dilatation of the ventricles of the dog's heart in a heart-lung preparation during a constant workload by the heart. Peters and his associates [93] also reported the fact that alcohol in humans produced cardiac dilatation or increased diastolic volume of the heart. They also demonstrated a decrease in oxygen consumption and cardiac output when diastolic volume was maintained at a constant level.

Using isolated strips of the auricle of the tortoise, Seliskar [108] demonstrated that the rate of conduction of the cardiac impulse was slowed by alcohol. Gimeno and his coworkers [42], using the rat atrium in vitro, demonstrated an almost linear relationship between the concentration of alcohol and a decline in myocardial contractility. Haggard and his associates [47] found that high concentrations of alcohol in the artificially respired rat produced cardiac dilatation and failure. Wakim [120] reported similar findings in the isolated turtle heart, as did Schwarte and Dukes [107] in the pig's heart. Using in vivo dog experiments, Loomis [70] demonstrated cardiac depression by high concentrations of ethanol.

Maines and Aldinger [72] administered 25 percent ethanol orally to rats for 7 months. After 4 months of alcohol administration there was a consistent decrease in potential ventricular contractile force, blood pressure, and cardiac rate. Vitamins afforded no protection against these effects. Cardiac dilatation and arrhythmias were noted.

The studies of Webb and his coworkers [122, 123] also demonstrated that ethyl alcohol given intravenously to lightly anesthetized intact dogs reduced myocardial functional capacity, as judged by Starling-Sarnoff function curves, roughly proportional to the amount administered. They felt, however, that this method of study did not indicate whether the effects were primary on the heart or secondary to metabolic or other effects elsewhere in the body. Accordingly they studied the effects of alcohol, using an isolated heart-lung preparation in the open-chest dog [124]. Under these circumstances ethyl alcohol in concentrations up to 900 mg% was not found to have any appreciable effect on myocardial contractility. These results are difficult to reconcile with those found in the intact human or animal [3].

Regan and his associates studied various hemodynamic parameters in man following the oral ingestion of ethanol [97, 98, 100]. Following the ingestion of 6 oz of alcohol, ventricular function, myocardial blood flow, and metabolism were not significantly elevated. At higher doses there was a progressive decrease in cardiac output accompanied by a rise in end-diastolic ventricular pressure. These changes reverted toward normal after 4 hr [97]. Chronic ingestion of 16 oz of Scotch whisky daily by an alcoholic subject while on a normal diet produced, after 12 weeks, a progressive increase of heart rate and size, accompanied by a prolonged circulation time, an increased venous pressure, and an elevated end-diastolic ventricular pressure. Normal values were restored within 7 weeks after interrupting alcohol [97].

B. METABOLIC DEFECTS AND ALCOHOLIC CARDIOMYOPATHY. Although it is beyond the scope of this chapter to explore in detail the basic metabolic effects of ethyl alcohol [66; see also Chapter 1], it may be pertinent to relate some of these effects to the myocardium.

The influence of alcohol on the neuroamines may have a bearing on the production of myocardial failure by chronic alcoholism. It has been shown that the administration of ethanol results in an increase in the urinary excretion of catecholamines [2, 7, 61, 92, 103]. There seems to be a generalized depression of sympathetic nervous system activity in the chronic alcoholic, and bradycardia and hypotension are common accompaniments of many of the acute and chronic studies on the effects of alcohol. The sympathetic nervous system depression may be a combined effect of a depression of the central nervous system [103] and depletion of circulating catecholamines. There is evidence that intrinsically liberated catecholamines play a role in the contractile strength of the myocardium and that depletion of myocardial catecholamines, particularly norepinephrine, is commonly present in congestive heart failure [16]. This lack deprives the myocardium of the valuable positive inotropic effect exerted by the catecholamines. This may well be an important mechanism by which alcohol exerts a deleterious effect on the myocardium and contributes to congestive heart failure. Wendt and his associates [126] have shown that alcohol has a more depressing effect on the alcoholic with cardiomyopathy than on the alcoholic with an apparently normal heart. Gould and his coworkers [44] studied the cardiac hemodynamics in 15 chronic alcoholic men without obvious evidence of heart or liver disease. On exercising, 13 of the patients showed a significant increase in the left ventricular end-diastolic pressure and mean pulmonary artery pressure. Further, 5 of the patients showed a fall in the stroke index on exercising. This abnormal exercise response indicates the presence of an impairment in cardiac function.

There is also evidence that alcohol results in a decrease in oxidative enzymes in the myocardium and an accumulation of lipid in the myocardial fibers [38, 39] . Electron-microscopic studies of the hearts of patients with alcoholic cardiomyopathy indicate that the mitochondria of the cardiac myofibrils are damaged. Reported changes include swelling and rupture of mitochondria, alterations in the mitochondrial cristae, the presence of dense intramitochondrial inclusions, and swelling of the endoplasmic reticulum [6, 53]. Similar changes have been noted in rat hearts perfused with small amounts of alcohol [83] (see Figures 1 and 2). These findings strongly suggest that alcohol interferes with the production of myocardial energy. The electron-microscopic changes resemble those noted in the liver following acute and chronic excesses of alcohol [60, 94, 95, 115].

Biochemical changes in the myocardium following alcohol administration

Figure 1. Electron micrograph (×32,000) of rat myocardium (*left ventricle*) following 60 min of perfusion with Krebs-Ringer solution. There is a minimal increase in the size and number of mitochondria.

Figure 2. Electron micrograph (×32,000) of rat myocardium (*left ventricle*) following 60 min of perfusion with Krebs-Ringer solution containing 0.003% ethanol. Note marked increase in number of mitochondria. There is enlargement and disorientation of mitochondria. The mitochrondrial cristae are enlarged, separated, and disrupted.

are in support of the histochemical and histological findings above. The in vivo studies of Wendt and his coworkers [126] demonstrated the release of oxidative enzymes from the myocardium of alcoholic patients. Lipid accumulation in heart muscle has been demonstrated as a consequence of acute alcohol ingestion in the experimental animal [96]. A decrease in the myocardial extraction of free fatty acid and an associated increase in plasma lipids may be important determinants in this process [68, 96, 99].

It seems likely that changes in membrane permeability may well be the basic mechanism of the alcohol-induced changes mentioned above [54, 63].

3. Clinical Manifestations

The clinical picture of alcoholic cardiomyopathy has emerged during the past 10 to 15 years.

A. HISTORY. The usual patient is a man between the ages of 30 and 50 years with no manifestations or indications of heart disease of other etiology. The history is one of long-standing heavy intake of alcoholic beverages. A history of general or specific dietary deficiency is usually absent.

Although Evans [35, 36] has emphasized the insidious onset of congestive heart failure in patients with alcoholic cardiomyopathy, the author has been impressed with the acuity with which signs and symptoms may occur.

The hypokinetic hemodynamics of alcoholic cardiomyopathy are reflected in the amanuensis. The usual history is one of left-sided cardiac failure as manifested by dyspnea on exertion followed by orthopnea, cough, palpitations, and episodes of paroxysmal nocturnal dyspnea. Right-sided failure usually follows the onset of left ventricular failure but may occur simultaneously or, rarely, precede it. It is manifested by peripheral edema, which may rapidly progress to involve the scrotum and abdomen. Right upper quadrant abdominal pain due to hepatic congestion is a fairly frequent complaint.

B. PHYSICAL EXAMINATION. On physical examination the patient usually is well nourished and may even be obese. It is unusual to find gross evidence of malnutrition or deficiency syndromes. The patient is usually in acute distress, appearing dypsneic and orthopneic. The pulse is rapid, and the pulse pressure tends to be low because of an elevation of the diastolic blood pressure. It is not unusual to record a blood pressure of 130 systolic, 100 diastolic. The neck veins are distended and a prominent V wave is common. The heart is enlarged to the left, and the heart sounds are of poor quality. A protodiastolic gallop rhythm is almost always present, and an atrial gallop is quite common. A normal sinus rhythm is the rule. An apical systolic murmur due to functional mitral insufficiency secondary to cardiac enlargement is a frequent finding. Rales are present at the lung bases, and pleural effusions may be present. The liver is enlarged and tender in the presence of right-sided failure, and there is a positive hepato-jugular reflux. Other indications of right-sided failure are distension of the neck veins, peripheral edema, and ascites. Cyanosis may be present as a result of arterial oxygen unsaturation and peripheral venous stasis.

C. LABORATORY FINDINGS. The laboratory findings are nonspecific and of no help in establishing the diagnosis of alcoholic cardiomyopathy. There may be a mild leucocytosis. The blood urea nitrogen may be elevated because of chronic passive congestion of the kidneys. Liver function is frequently abnormal but changes are minimal. Mild elevations of serum bilirubin and increases in serum levels of hepatic enzymes are frequent. They tend to improve as passive congestion of the liver decreases, following effective therapy for congestive heart failure.

D. ELECTROCARDIOGRAPHIC CHANGES. The electrocardiographic changes in alcoholic cardiomyopathy have been emphasized by Eliaser and Giansiracusa [31, 32] and by Evans [34]. Eliaser and Giansiracusa described abnormal electrocardiograms in 57.4% of a group of 94 chronic alcoholic persons with an average age of 42 years and in whom there were no other manifestations of heart diseases. The changes noted were those of abnormal left ventricular repolarization simulating a digitalis effect or evidence of left ventricular enlargement. These changes were not present in electrocardiograms made several days after alcohol was discontinued.

Evans [34] described ECG changes in 17 out of 20 patients with alcoholic cardiomyopathy that he considered to be distinctive for the entity. The distinctive deformities were limited to the T wave, which he described as a "depressed dimple" in 8, upright and "cloven" in 7, and "spinous" in 2. Evans also described nonspecific ECG changes in his group of patients consisting of extrasystoles, paroxysmal auricular tachycardia, auricular fibrillation, bundle branch block, and depression of ST segments.

The author has been unimpressed by the specificity of an electrocardiographic finding in alcoholic cardiomyopathy, nor have the changes been transient. The changes noted have been nonspecific, occurring in a variety of other myocardial abnormalities. Left ventricular hypertrophy has been a fairly frequent ECG finding. Other changes noted have been abnormal P waves, left bundle branch block, prolongation of the QT interval, and low, isoelectric, or negative T waves. A variety of arrhythmias has been noted, although normal sinus rhythm has been the rule. Extrasystoles of supraventricular or ventricular origin are seen fairly frequently. Atrial fibrillation may be present. As the disease progresses, there is a tendency for QRS voltage to decrease, while QRS duration increases. The ECG pattern otherwise tends to be relatively static. The changes described have been noted by others [19].

E. ROENTGENOGRAPHIC CHANGES. Roentgenograms of the heart reveal generalized cardiomegaly involving all chambers of the heart. The picture is nonspecific and cannot be distinguished from any other process producing generalized myocardial disease [112]. If cardiac failure is present, the typical pattern of congestive changes radiating from the hila of the lungs is present (see Figures 3 and 4). Because of lymphatic engorgement, the so-called B lines of Kerley are often present. Pleural effusions are common. The roentgenogram may simulate the findings of pericardial effusion. Indeed, on fluoroscopy, the heart appears extremely hypokinetic, again resembling pericardial effusion. A hugely dilated heart may result in the presence of a paradoxical pulse.

F. SPECIAL STUDIES. The venous pressure is elevated, and the circulation time is prolonged. Cardiac catheterization studies reveal low cardiac output and elevation of the end-diastolic pressure. There is no response in cardiac output to thiamine chloride. The hypokinetic hemodynamic state is in contrast with the hyperkinetic state that exists in beriberi heart disease. Although the two diseases may mimic each other clinically, the difference in cardiac output forms a useful differential feature. Although venous pres-

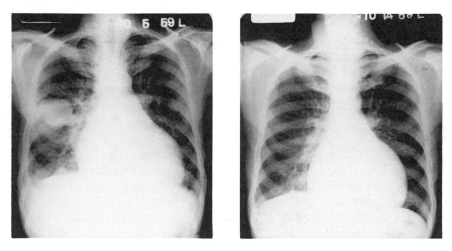

Figure 3   Figure 4

Figure 3. PA chest roentgenogram of a patient with alcoholic cardiomyopathy. There is marked cardiac enlargement and pulmonary congestion. The lesion in the right mid-lung fields is an interlobar collection of fluid.

Figure 4. PA roentgenogram of the chest of the same patient depicted in Figure 3, taken 48 hrs after institution of therapy (digitalis, diuretics, and salt restriction). There has been marked improvement in pulmonary congestion but marked cardiac enlargement persists.

sure is elevated in beriberi, the hyperkinetic state usually results in an apparently paradoxically normal or rapid circulation time.

4. Pathology

The pathological findings in alcoholic cardiomyopathy are nonspecific. Gross examination of the heart reveals marked dilatation of all cardiac chambers. The valves are normal. Patchy areas of endocardial fibroelastic thickening may occur especially in the region of the septum and the left ventricular wall. The myocardium is pale and flabby, and on cut section patchy areas of fibrosis may be noted.

Under light microscopy there is hyalinization, edema, vacuolization, and disruption of myofibrils. Cross striations may be absent. There are prominent nuclear changes consisting of changes in size and pyknosis. Focal collections of inflammatory cells are usually present. Some authors have noted a decrease in the incidence of coronary atherosclerosis in chronic alcoholics. Such observations are difficult to substantiate, inasmuch as a number of other variables may coexist. At any rate, if coronary atherosclerosis is present in the patient with alcoholic cardiomyopathy, it generally does not contribute to the clinical picture.

The findings of histochemical studies and electron microscopy have been previously noted (see pages 188–189). A significant change consists of increased amounts of lipid within the myocardial fibers [39]. Most of the lipid material consists of triglycerides and is deposited in the form of irregular droplets varying in size from 0.1 to 3.0 μ in diameter. A decrease in a number of myocardial oxidative enzymes has been demonstrated, including cytochrome oxidase, succinic dehydrogenase, lactic dehydrogenase, isocitric dehydrogenase, malic dehydrogenase, and DPN-diaphorase [7].

Electron-microscopic changes are prominent in the mitochondria and mitochondrial cristae. Swelling of the sarcoplasmic reticulum has been noted [6, 53].

The changes are those of extensive myocardial cellular damage with prominent mitochondrial disturbances, indicating interference with energy production.

5. Treatment

The therapy of patients with alcoholic cardiomyopathy involves a two-pronged approach. One effort is directed against the congestive heart fail-

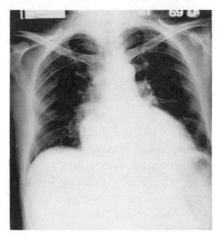

Figure 5

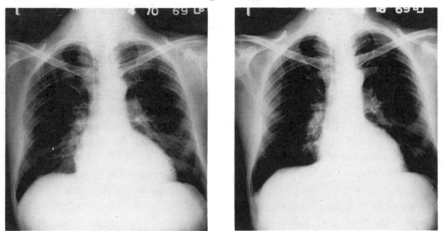

Figure 6   Figure 7

Figures 5, 6, 7. PA roentgenograms of the chest of a patient with alcoholic cardiomyopathy. Figure 6 was taken 3 months after Figure 5 and Figure 7, 8 months after Figure 6. The patient was maintained on a program of prolonged bedrest and showed a slow but steady decrease in the size of his heart.

ure; the other toward the avoidance of further alcoholic intake. The latter is a multidisciplined, multifaceted subject beyond the scope of this chapter.

The therapy of congestive heart failure in alcoholic cardiomyopathy does not differ from that of other low-output types [84]. Bedrest, sodium restriction, digitalization, and diuretics comprise the base of therapy. It is the author's general experience that by the time alcoholic cardiomyopathy reaches clinical significance, the usual therapeutic regimen is relatively ineffective. The heart may remain enlarged, electrocardiographic changes persist, and the congestive heart failure may be relatively resistant to the usual therapeutic modalities. In cases such as this, Burch and coworkers have recommended a carefully outlined program of complete bedrest for periods of 6 to 12 months [20, 21, 22]. Under this regimen, refractory cases may show improvement (see Figures 5, 6, 7). Each case must be individualized, and a regimen adjusted to meet the individual needs of the patient. Administration of thiamine chloride and other supplements is not associated with significant clinical improvement.

6. Differential Diagnosis

It is obvious that many cardiac conditions are associated with cardiac enlargement and congestive heart disease [40]. There is no pathognomonic diagnostic feature of alcoholic cardiomyopathy, and the diagnosis is often one of exclusion.

The relative youth of the patient and the absence of a history of angina pectoris and myocardial infarction is helpful in ruling out arteriosclerotic heart disease. On occasion, however, diffuse coronary sclerosis may produce a diffuse myocardial process mimicking a cardiomyopathy. Valvular heart disease due to rheumatic fever or lues is usually readily ruled out. Hypertensive heart disease in its terminal, "burned-out" phase may simulate alcoholic myocardiopathy. The previous history and remaining stigmata of hypertensive cardiovascular disease are helpful in eliminating hypertension as a factor.

Marked cardiomegaly may suggest pericardial effusion, and the clinical findings may be identical. In such patients it may be necessary to perform cardioangiography with carbon dioxide or radioopaque contrast media to establish the correct diagnosis [67, 89].

There remains a group of disorders that primarily affect the myocardium that may be extremely difficult to differentiate from alcoholic cardiomyopathy. These disorders are classified as primary myocardial diseases (PMD) and include the various forms of myocarditis, infiltrative myocardial disorders that are part of a systemic disease, and a group of myocardial disorders of unknown or uncertain etiology [75].

Generally speaking, the various forms of acute myocarditis of bacterial, viral, fungal, rickettsial, and parasitic etiology are acute processes usually associated with the systemic manifestations of an infectious process. A variety of drugs and allergens have also been associated with an acute toxic myocarditis.

Infiltrative disorders associated with a myocardiopathy include amyloidosis, hemochromatosis, sarcoidosis, neoplasms, and glycogen storage disease. These are usually associated with extracardiac manifestations of the underlying process.

The idiopathic primary myocardial disorders include Fiedler's myocarditis (acute "isolated" myocarditis, isolated interstitial myocarditis, idiopathic myocarditis, granulomatous myocardites), familial cardiomegaly, and idiopathic cardiac hypertrophy. Under certain circumstances these may be impossible to differentiate from alcoholic cardiomyopathy. The age of the patient, familial history, and the history of the patient's drinking habits may afford valuable clues. In regard to the last, a confirmed history of abstinence or of a modest alcoholic intake is of much more diagnostic significance than is a history of heavy alcoholic intake.

B. Alcoholic Skeletal Myopathy

1.   Historical Aspects

In contrast with alcoholic cardiomyopathy, the recognition of a skeletal myopathy secondary to alcohol has been quite recent. Hed and his coworkers [29, 37, 49] in Sweden seem to have been the first to recognize this entity. In retrospect, however, it seems that earlier case reports of acute myopathy and myoglobinuria were undoubtedly secondary to excess alcohol [45, 49]. The studies of Nygren [85, 86], Perkoff and his associates [62, 90, 91], and Lafair and Myerson [65] have clearly confirmed the existence of alcoholic myopathy as a pathologic and clinical entity. In the past few years a number of additional case reports of alcoholic myopathy have appeared in the literature [18, 28, 106, 116].

2.   Pathophysiology

There is little known concerning the pathophysiology of alcohol-induced skeletal myopathy. The evidence suggests that alcohol has a direct toxic action on the myofibril, perhaps inducing changes similar to those in alcoholic cardiomyopathy (see pages 188–189). Basically there seems to be a change in cell membrane permeability, resulting in edema, necrosis, hyalinization, and cellular infiltration. As muscular damage ensues, there is release of muscle enzymes, resulting in increased serum levels of creatine phosphokinase (CPK), aldolase, glutamic oxaloacetic transaminase (GOT), and lactic dehydrogenase (LDH).

Myerson and Lafair infused 5% alcohol intravenously into 12 patients during or following an episode of subclinical alcoholic myopathy [65, 82]. The total dose of alcohol varied between 0.7 and 1.0 g/kg of body weight. Blood alcohol levels following termination of the infusion varied between 0.05 and 0.5 mg/ml. Two to six hours after infusion there was significant elevation of serum CPK in 6 out of 8 patients infused during subclinical myopathy. In 2 out of 4 patients infused after subsidence of an episode of myopathy, there were significant CPK elevations ($p < .05$) (see Table I). No elevations of CPK were noted in this group after control infusions of 5% glucose in water. Similar doses of intravenous alcohol in nonalcoholic patients had no effect on CPK levels.

The pattern of muscle involvement in acute and chronic alcoholic myopathy is of interest. Those groups most frequently and most seriously affected seem to be muscles involved with antigravity functions. Kleine and von Chlond [59] demonstrated a shift from aerobic to anaerobic metabolic path-

TABLE I   Effects of the Intravenous Infusion of 5% Alcohol on the Serum CPK Levels of 12 Patients During or Following an Episode of Subclinical Alcoholic Myopathy

| | CPK levels, units/ml[b] | | Alcohol |
Patient[a]	Preinfusion	Postinfusion	administered, g/kg
1. A.C.	3.7	4.5	1.0
2. W.L.	5.3	8.7	0.77
3. T.R.	2.5	4.1	0.72
4. E.S.	11.8	15.8	0.82
5. J. McC.	6.0	8.6	0.71
6. R.P.	3.6	5.1	0.86
7. T.P.	3.1	3.2	0.80
8. P.H.	7.0	6.8	0.71
9. J.H.	0.0	6.0	0.74
10. V.B.	0.3	4.6	0.74
11. T.M.	0.6	0.6	0.82
12. F.W.	0.4	0.5	0.84

[a] Patients 1 to 8 were infused during acute myopathy; patients 9 to 12, following recovery from acute myopathy.
[b] Normal levels up to 1.5 units/ml—method of Tanzer and Gilvarg [121].

ways in muscles affected by progressive muscular dystrophy and following irradiation and chronic hypoxemia. Since the antigravity "red" muscles use primarily oxidative pathways, they exhibit earlier and more severe damage than do the "white action" muscles, which use both aerobic and anaerobic pathways.

It is possible that alcohol may damage muscular oxidative systems, causing the muscle cell to function with a less efficient anaerobic mechanism. The integrity of the muscle cell may be disturbed, thereby allowing for leakage of energy transport enzymes, such as CPK, from the cell [5, 23, 25, 26, 59].

3.   Clinical Spectrum of Alcoholic Myopathy

Alcoholic myopathy encompasses a wide spectrum of manifestations both with and without overt clinical expression [20, 65, 90]. Clinically both acute and chronic types of myopathy have been described. There is convincing evidence that in the majority of exposed individuals, alcoholic myopathy has no overt clinical expression [65].

A.   ACUTE ALCOHOLIC MYOPATHY. An acute syndrome of muscle pain, tenderness, and edema has been described following acute excesses of alcohol. The proximal musculature of the extremities and the musculature of the thoracic cage are common sites of involvement. Severe cramps and weakness of the affected muscles are common.

Accompanying these clinical manifestations is laboratory evidence of muscle damage as indicated by serum elevations of "muscle enzymes," notably creatine phosphokinase (CPK) and aldolase. Isoenzyme analysis of the CPK elevations in these cases reveals that the enzyme is of skeletal-muscle origin [82]. Glutamic oxaloacetic transaminase (GOT) and lactic dehydrogenase (LDH) levels in the serum are also elevated. These abnormalities of serum enzymes persist for 1 to 3 weeks in most cases.

Acute alcoholic myopathy is usually self-limited and relatively benign. Occasionally, however, severe muscle necrosis may give rise to myoglobinuria, which in turn may result in acute tubular necrosis.

Biopsies of affected musculature reveal fragmentation of myofibrils, edema, necrosis, hyalinization, and cellular infiltration (see Figure 8).

Under the electron microscope significant mitochondrial changes are noted [62] similar to those present in alcoholic cardiomyopathy [6, 38, 53].

B.   CHRONIC ALCOHOLIC MYOPATHY. A syndrome of chronic muscle wasting and weakness, particularly of the proximal muscle groups of the extremities, has been described in chronic alcoholics [29]. The patients deny symptoms

Figure 8   Figure 9

Figure 8. Muscle biopsy (×90) of a patient with acute alcoholic myopathy with overt muscle tenderness and swelling. Note disruption, necrosis, and hyalinization of myofibrils. There is marked cellular infiltration.

Figure 9. Muscle biopsy (×90) of a patient with subclinical alcoholic myopathy. Changes similar to those depicted in Figure 8 are present, but the findings are less marked.

of muscle pain or tenderness, and the course is insidious and progressive. Differentiation from other causes of muscle atrophy and from variants of muscular dystrophy may be difficult. This group of individuals seldom has prominent elevations of serum enzymes, and myoglobinuria is absent.

C. SUBCLINICAL MYOPATHY. There is convincing biochemical and morphologic evidence that alcohol often produces an acute myopathy that is subclinical, that is, without an overt clinical expression [28, 90]. Patients with this entity are usually seen with an acute alcoholic intoxication syndrome or a withdrawal syndrome. Symptoms related to the skeletal musculature are absent or obscured by the presenting syndrome, e.g., delirium tremens, acute alcoholic hallucinosis. Studies of serum enzymes reveal elevations of CPK and aldolase, and examination of randomly taken muscle biopsies reveals changes similar to those noted in overt alcoholic myopathy (see Figure 9).

In a series of 330 patients with acute alcoholic and acute withdrawal syndromes, Myerson and Lafair [82] noted 10 with acute alcoholic myopathy as manifested by muscle pain, tenderness, and cramps. Three manifested myoglobinuria, and one had transient acute tubular necrosis. In 250 out of the remaining 320 patients (78%) there was significant elevation of serum CPK but without overt clinical evidence of myopathy. The incidence was similar in those presenting with acute alcoholic intoxication, acute hallucinosis, "rum fits," or delirium tremens. Muscle biopsies were performed in several patients and confirmed the presence of an acute myopathy, although no focal or localizing signs referable to the muscular system were present.

4. Differential Diagnosis

The diagnosis of acute myopathy is not difficult when overt clinical manifestations of muscle tenderness and edema are present. Differentiation from a wide variety of other forms of acute myopathy may be difficult, especially in the absence of a definite history of an excessive intake of alcohol. The reader is referred to excellent reviews of the subject for a more detailed description of the various forms of acute myopathy [30, 109]. In the light of our current knowledge, it seems likely that many cases of acute myopathy hitherto termed idiopathic or ascribed to other etiologies may indeed have been examples of alcoholic myopathy.

There is nothing distinctive about chronic alcoholic myopathy. It may be difficult, if not impossible, to differentiate it from various forms of primary muscle disorders.

Subclinical alcoholic myopathy is diagnosed on the basis of elevations of serum levels of muscle enzymes following alcoholic intake. Though clinically inapparent, random muscle biopsy yields positive findings. Caution must be used in the interpretation of elevated levels of serum glutamic oxaloacetic transaminase (GOT) following alcohol intake. It is important to recognize that elevations of SGOT result from both muscle and liver injury. The use of more specific tissue enzymes or isoenzymes is necessary to define the tissue source of the enzyme elevation.

It seems likely that as awareness of the entity of subclinical alcoholic myopathy develops, an increasing number of cases will be reported.

5. Therapy

Acute alcoholic myopathy is usually a self-limited disease, subsiding gradually once the patient abstains from drinking. Symptoms, however, may be severe, and the patient may be acutely ill. Bedrest and analgesics form the basis of therapy. Generally speaking, it is wise to avoid the use of narcotics, since many of the patients are prone to addiction. Aspirin or a combination of aspirin and codeine is usually an effective analgesic agent. The author has been impressed with the efficacy of phenylbutazone as an analgesic and apparent anti-inflammatory agent in alcoholic myopathy. The usual dosage is 100 mg qid. Indomethacin has not been effective, nor have any of the "muscle-relaxant" agents. Local compresses may provide symptomatic relief.

It is imperative that fluid and electrolyte balance be maintained. The patient should be carefully monitored by frequent determinations of serum electrolytes and blood urea determinations, and by urinalyses for myoglobin. The complication of myoglobinuria is extremely serious, because it may lead to acute tubular necrosis. Because of the relative paucity of reported cases, it is difficult to evaluate the over-all incidence of this complication, but from the author's personal experience and a review of the literature, myoglobinuria probably occurs in 20 to 25% of cases of acute alcoholic myopathy.

Acute tubular necrosis secondary to myoglobinuria should be treated similarly to acute tubular necrosis due to other causes. Fluids are withheld to a minimum to "rest the kidneys" until natural recovery may occur. Extracorporeal or peritoneal dialysis may be necessary if blood urea nitrogen and serum potassium levels reach high levels in the face of continuing oliguria or anuria.

The patient with acute alcoholic myopathy is a candidate for alcoholic withdrawal syndromes, particularly delirium tremens. There is, in fact, suggestive evidence that alcoholic myopathy itself may occur as a withdrawal phenomenon [65, 82].

Once recovery occurs, there is usually little or no residual muscle incapacity. The patient should be urged to abstain from further use of alcohol in order to prevent recurrences or possible progression to a chronic myopathy.

The therapy of chronic alcoholic myopathy is primarily one of prolonged physical medicine and rehabilitation coupled with abstinence from alcohol. There is no evidence that vitamins or other supplements are useful therapeutic agents. The prognosis for return of muscle function is guarded.

REFERENCES

1. Aalsmeer, W. C. and K. F. Wenckebach, Herz und Kreislauf bei der Biriberi Krankheit, *Wien. Arch. Inn. Med.,* **16,** 193 (1929).
2. Abelin, I., C. Herren, and W. Berli, Über die erregende Wirkung des Alko-

hols auf den adrenalin- und noradrenalinhaushalt des menschlichen organismus, *Helvet Med. Acta,* **25,** 591 (1958).

3. Abelmann, W., H. Kowalski, and W. McNeely, The circulation of blood in alcohol addicts, *Quart. J. Studies Alc.,* **15,** 1 (1964).

4. Alexander, C. S., Idiopathic heart disease: Analysis of 100 cases with special reference to chronic alcoholism, *Am. J. Med.,* **41,** 213 (1966).

5. Alexander, C. S., Alcohol and the heart, *Ann. Intern. Med.,* **67,** 670 (1967).

6. Alexander, C. S., Electron microscopic observations in alcoholic heart disease, *Brit. Heart J.,* **29,** 200 (1967).

7. Anton, A. H., Ethanol and urinary catecholamines in man, *Clin. Pharmacol. Therap.,* **6,** 462 (1965).

8. Aufbrecht, G., Die alkoholische Myocarditis mit nachfolgender Lebenkrankung und zeitweiliger Albuminurie, *Deut. Arch. Klin. Med.,* **54,** 615 (1895).

9. Auger, C. and J. Chenard, Quebec beer-drinkers' cardiomyopathy: Ultrastructural changes in one case, *Canad. Med. Assoc. J.,* **97,** 916 (1967).

10. Benchimol, A. B. and P. Schlesinger, Beriberi heart disease, *Am. Heart J.,* **46,** 245 (1953).

11. Bessey, O. A., M. L. Minten, and C. G. King, Pathologic changes in organs of scorbutic guinea pigs, *Proc. Soc. Exp. Biol. Med.,* **31,** 455 (1934).

12. Blankenhorn, M. A., The diagnosis of beriberi heart disease, *Ann. Intern. Med.,* **23,** 398 (1945).

13. Blankenhorn, M. A., C. F. Vilter, I. M. Scheinker, and R. S. Rustin, Occidental beriberi heart disease, *J. Am. Med. Assoc.,* **131,** 717 (1946).

14. Bollinger, O., Ueber die Haufigkeit und Ursachen der idiopathischen Herzhypertrophie in München, *Deut. Med. Wchnschr,* **10,** 180 (1884).

15. Bonenfant, J. L., G. Miller, and P. E. Roy, Quebec beer-drinkers' cardiomyopathy: Pathological studies, *Canad. Med. Assoc. J.,* **97,** 910 (1967).

16. Braunwald, E., Congestive heart failure in biochemistry and physiological consideration: Combined clinical staff conference at the National Institutes of Health, *Ann. Intern. Med.,* **64,** 904 (1966).

17. Brigden, W., Uncommon myocardial diseases: The noncoronary cardiomyopathies, *Lancet,* **2,** 1179 (1957).

18. Buge, A., P. Autissier, and R. Escourolle, Myopathic myoglobinurique chez un alcoolique, *Bull. Soc. Med. Hop.* (Paris), **118,** 615 (1967).

19. Burch, G. E. and N. P. De Pasquale, Alcoholic cardiomyopathy, *Cardiologia,* **52,** 48 (1968).

20. Burch, G. E. and J. J. Walsh, Cardiac insufficiency in chronic alcoholism, *Am. J. Cardiol.,* **6,** 864 (1960).

21. Burch, G. E., J. J. Walsh, and W. C. Black, Value of prolonged bed rest in management of cardiomegaly, *J. Am. Med. Assoc.,* **183,** 81 (1963).

22. Burch, G. E., J. J. Walsh, V. J. Ferrans, and R. Hibbs, Prolonged bedrest in the treatment of the dilated heart, *Circulation,* **32,** 852 (1965).

23. Cherrick, G. L. and C. M. Leevy, Effect of ethanol metabolism on levels

of oxidized and reduced nicotinamide-adenine dinucleotide in liver, kidney, and heart, *Biochem. Biophys. Acta,* **107,** 29 (1965).

24. Cowgill, G. R., Vitamin B, clinical aspects, *Int. Clin.,* **4,** 54 (1934).

25. Davis, V. E., H. Brown, J. A. Huff, and J. L. Cashaw, Ethanol-induced alterations of norepinephrine metabolism in man, *J. Lab. Clin. Med.,* **69,** 787 (1967).

26. Davis, V. E., H. Brown, J. A. Huff, and J. L. Cashaw, The alteration of serotonin metabolism to 5-hydroxytryptophol by ethanol ingestion in man, *J. Lab. Clin. Med.,* **69,** 132 (1967).

27. Dixon, W. E., The action of alcohol on the circulation, *J. Physiol.,* **35,** 346 (1906).

28. Douglas, R. M., J. D. Fewings, and J. R. Casley-Smith, Recurrent rhabdomyolysis precipitated by alcohol: A case report with physiological and electron microscopic studies of skeletal muscle, *Aust. Ann. Med.,* **15,** 251 (1966).

29. Ekbom, K., R. Hed, L. Kirstein, and F. E. Astrom, Muscular affections in chronic alcoholism, *Arch. Neurol.,* **10,** 449 (1964).

30. Elek, S. D. and H. F. Anderson, Paroxysmal paralytic myoglobinuria, *Brit. Med. J.,* **2,** 532 (1953).

31. Eliaser, M. and F. Giansiracusa, Electrocardiograph Changes Associated with Chronic Alcoholism, in *Premier Congres Mondial de Cardiologie Communications,* vol. 11, p. 307, Balliere, Paris, 1952.

32. Eliaser, M. and F. Giansiracusa, The heart and alcohol, *Calif. Med.,* **84,** 234 (1956).

33. Epidemic of arsenical poisoning in beer-drinkers in the north of England during the year 1900, *Lancet,* **1,** 98 (1901).

34. Evans, W., The electrocardiogram of alcoholic cardiomyopathy, *Brit. Heart J.,* **21,** 445 (1959).

35. Evans, W., Alcoholic myocardiopathy, *Am. Heart J.,* **61,** 556 (1961).

36. Evans, W., Alcoholic myocardiopathy, *Prog. Cardiovas. Dis.,* **7,** 151 (1964).

37. Fahlgren, H., R. Hed, and C. Lundmark, Myonecrosis and myoglobinuria in alcohol and barbiturate intoxication, *Acta Med. Scand.,* **158,** 405 (1957).

38. Ferrans, V. J., R. G. Hibbs, and D. G. Weilbaecher, Alcoholic cardiomyopathy: A histochemical and electron microscopic study, *Am. J. Cardiol.,* **13,** 106 (1964).

39. Ferrans, V. J., R. G. Hibbs, D. G. Weilbaecher, W. C. Black, J. J. Walsh, and G. E. Burch, Alcoholic cardiomyopathy: A histochemical study, *Am. Heart J.,* **69,** 748 (1965).

40. Gefter, W. I., B. H. Pastor, and R. M. Myerson, *Synopsis of Cardiology,* Mosby, St. Louis, Mo., 1965.

41. Gillanders, A. D., Nutritional heart disease, *Brit. Heart J.,* **13,** 177 (1951).

42. Gimeno, A. L., M. G. Gimeno, and J. C. Webb, Effects of ethanol on cellular membrane potentials and contractility of isolated rat atrium, *Am. J. Physiol.,* **203,** 194 (1962).

43. Goodhart, R. and N. Jolliffe, The role of nutritional deficiencies in the pro-

duction of cardiovascular disturbances in the alcoholic addict, *Am. Heart J.,* **15,** 569 (1938).

44. Gould, L., M. Zahir, M. Shariff, and M. DiLieto, Cardiac hemodynamics in alcoholic heart disease, *Ann. Intern. Med.,* **71,** 543 (1969).
45. Gunther, H., Die kryptogenen myopathien, *Ergeb. inn. Med. Kinderheilk.,* **58,** 331 (1940).
46. Gutnikow, O., Über den Einflusz des Alkohols auf die Blütcirculation, *Zeitsch, Klin. Med.,* **21,** 169 (1892).
47. Haggard, H. W., L. A. .Greenberg, L. H. Cohen, and N. J. Rakieton, Studies on the absorption, distribution, and elimination of alcohol: IX. The concentration of alcohol in the blood causing primary cardiac failure, *J. Pharmacol. Exper. Therap.,* **71,** 358 (1941).
48. Hascovec, L., Nouvelles contributions a la question de l'action de l'alcool sur le coeur et la circulation du sang, *Arch. Med. exp. d'anatomie pathologique,* **13,** 539 (1901).
49. Hed, R., H. Larsson, and F. Wohlgren, Acute myoglobinuria: Report of a case with a fatal outcome, *Acta Med. Scand.,* **152,** 459 (1955).
50. Hed, R., C. Lundmark, H. Fahlgren, and S. Orell, Acute muscular syndrome in chronic alcoholism, *Acta Med. Scand.,* **171,** 585 (1962).
51. Hemmeter, J. C., On the effects of certain drugs on the velocity of the blood current, *Med. Rec.,* 292 (1891).
52. Hemmeter, J. C., Recent experiments on the physiological activity of ethylic alcohol, *Trans. Med. Chiruir.* Faculty Maryland, 230 (1889).
53. Hibbs, R. G., V. J. Ferrans, W. C. Black, D. G. Weilbaecher, J. J. Walsh, and G. E. Burch, Alcoholic cardiomyopathy: An electronic microscopic study, *Am. Heart J.,* **69,** 766 (1965).
54. Israel, Y. and H. Kalant, Effect of ethanol in transport of sodium in frog skin, *Nature,* **200,** 476 (1963).
55. Jelinek, E. M., *Alcohol Addiction and Chronic Alcoholism: Effects of Alcohol on the Individual,* vol. 1, Yale University Press, New Haven, 1942.
56. Jones, R. H., Beriberi heart disease, *Circulation,* **19,** 275 (1959).
57. Keefer, C. S., The beriberi heart, *Arch. Intern. Med.,* **45,** 1 (1930).
58. Kesteloot, H., R. Terryn, P. Bosmans, and P. V. Joossens, Alcoholic perimyocardiopathy, *Acta Cardiol.* (Brux), **21,** 341 (1966).
59. Kleine, T. O. and H. von Chlond, Enzyme distribution patterns of healthy human skeletal, heart, and smooth muscles and their pathological changes in progressive muscular dystrophy (Erb) and other conditions, *Clin. Chem. Acta,* **15,** 19 (1967).
60. Kiessling, K. H., L. Lindgren, B. Strandberg, and U. Tobe, Electron microscopic study of liver mitochondria from human alcoholics, *Acta Med. Scand.,* **176,** 593 (1964).
61. Klingman, G. I. and McC. Goodall, Urinary epinephrine and levarterenol excretion during acute sublethal alcohol intoxication in dogs, *J. Pharmacol.,* **121,** 313 (1957).
62. Klinkerfuss, G., V. Bleisch, M. M. Dioso, and G. T. Perkoff, A spectrum

of myopathy associated with alcoholism: II. Light and electron microscopic observations, *Ann. Intern. Med.,* **67,** 493 (1967).

63. Knutson, E., Effects of ethanol on the membrane potential and membrane resistance of frog muscle fibers, *Acta Physiol. Scand.,* **52,** 242 (1961).

64. Kochmann, M., Die Einwirkung des Alkohols auf das Warmblutherz, *Arch. Intern. Pharmacodyn.,* **13,** 329 (1904).

65. Lafair, J. S. and R. M. Myerson, Alcoholic myopathy, with special reference to the significance of creatine phosphokinase, *Arch. Intern. Med.,* **122,** 417 (1968).

66. Leiber, C. S. and C. S. Davidson, Some metabolic effects of ethyl alcohol, *Am. J. Med.,* **33,** 319 (1962).

67. Levy, L. II, R. Fowler, H. Jacobs, J. Leckert, J. Irion, I. Rosen, and H. Chastant, Angiocardiographic confirmation of pericardial effusion, *Am. Heart J.,* **43,** 59 (1952).

68. Lindeneg, O., K. Mellemgaard, J. Fabricuis, and F. Lundquist, Myocardial utilization of acetate, lactate and free fatty acids after ingestion of ethanol, *Clin. Sci.,* **27,** 427 (1964).

69. Loeh, O., die Wirkung des Alkohols auf das Warmblütherz, *Arch. Exp. Path. Pharm.,* **52,** 459 (1904).

70. Loomis, T. A., The effect of alcohol on myocardial and respiratory function, *Quart. J. Studies Alc.,* **13,** 561 (1952).

71. Mackenzie, J., *The Study of the Pulse,* Edinburgh and London, 1902, p. 237.

72. Maines, J. E. and E. E. Aldinger, Myocardial depression accompanying chronic consumption of alcohol, *Am. Heart J.,* **73,** 55 (1967).

73. Martin, N. and L. T. Stevens, *Mem. Biol. Lab.,* Johns Hopkins Univ., **2,** 213 (1887).

74. Marvaud, J. L. A., L'alcool, son action physiologique, Paris, 1872.

75. Mattingly, T. W., Changing concepts of myocardial diseases, *J. Am. Med. Assoc.,* **191,** 33 (1965).

76. McBroom, J., D. A. Sunderland, J. R. Monte, and T. D. Jones, Effect of acute scurvy on the guinea pig heart, *Arch. Path.,* **23,** 20 (1937).

77. McDermott, P. H., R. L. Delaney, J. D. Egan, and J. F. Sullivan, Myocardosis and cardiac failure in men, *J. Am. Med. Assoc.,* **198,** 253 (1966).

78. Mercier, G. and G. Patry, Quebec beer-drinkers' cardiomyopathy: Clinical signs and symptoms, *Canad. Med. Assoc. J.,* **97,** 884 (1967).

79. Morin, Y., Quebec beer-drinkers' cardiomyopathy: Hemodynamic alterations, *Canad. Med. Assoc. J.,* **97,** 901 (1967).

80. Morin, Y. and P. Daniel, Quebec beer-drinkers' cardiomyopathy: Etiological considerations, *Canad. Med. Assoc. J.,* **97,** 926 (1967).

81. Morin, Y. L., A. R. Foley, G. Martineau, and J. Roussel, Quebec beer-drinkers' cardiomyopathy: Forty-eight cases, *Canad. Med. Assoc. J.,* **97,** 881 (1967).

82. Myerson, R. M. and J. S. Lafair, Alcohol muscle disease, *Med. Clin. N. Am.* (in press, 1971).

83. Myerson, R. M., J. S. Lafair, and J. Rabinowitz, Enzymatic and electron

microscopic changes in the rat heart following exposure to alcohol, to be published.

84. Myerson, R. M. and B. H. Pastor, *Congestive Heart Failure,* Mosby, St. Louis, Mo., 1967.

85. Nygren, A., Serum creatine phosphokinase activity in chronic alcoholism, in connection with acute alcohol intoxication, *Acta Med. Scand.,* **179**, 623 (1966).

86. Nygren, A., Serum creatine phosphokinase in chronic alcoholism, *Acta Med. Scand.,* **182**, 383 (1967).

87. Olsen, N. S. and W. E. Martindale, Studies in chronic vitamin B$_6$ deficiency in the rat: I. Changes in the intact animal, *J. Nutr.,* **53**, 317, (1954).

88. Parkes, E. A. and D. Wollowicz, Experiments on the effects of alcohol (ethyl alcohol) on the human body, *Proc. Roy. Soc.* (London), **18**, 362 (1870).

89. Paul, R. E., T. M. Durant, M. J. Oppenheimer, and H. M. Stauffer, Intravenous carbon dioxide for intracardiac gas contrast in the roentgen diagnosis of pericardial effusion and thickening, *Am. J. Roentgenol.,* **78**, 224 (1957).

90. Perkoff, G. T., M. M. Dioso, V. Bleisch, and G. Klinkerfuss, A spectrum of myopathy associated with alcoholism: I. Clinical and laboratory features, *Ann. Intern. Med.,* **67**, 481 (1967).

91. Perkoff, G. T., P. Hardy, and E. Vilez-Garcia, Reversible acute muscular syndrome in chronic alcoholism, *New Engl. J. Med.,* **274**, 1277 (1966).

92. Perman, E. S., Observations on the effect of ethanol on the urinary excretion of histamine, 5-hydroxylindol-acetic acid, catecholamines and 17-hydroxycorticosteroids in man, *Acta Physiol. Scand.,* **51**, 62 (1961).

93. Peters, H. C., C. E. Rea, and J. W. Grossman, Influence of ethyl alcohol on energy metabolism of the mammalian heart, *Proc. Soc. Exper. Biol. Med.,* **34**, 61 (1936).

94. Porta, E. A., B. J. Bergman, and A. A. Stein, Acute alcoholic hepatitis, *Am. J. Path.,* **46**, 657 (1965).

95. Porta, E. A., W. S. Hartroft, and F. A. de la Iglesia, Hepatic changes associated with chronic alcoholism in rats, *Lab. Invest.,* **14**, 1437 (1965).

96. Regan, T. J., G. T. Koroxenesis, C. B. Moschos, H. A. Oldewurtel, P. H. Lehan, and H. K. Hellems, The acute metabolic and hemodynamic response of the left ventricle to ethanol, *J. Clin. Invest.,* **45**, 270 (1966).

97. Regan, T. J., G. E. Levinson, H. A. Oldewurtel, M. J. Frank, A. B. Weisse, and C. B. Moschos, Ventricular function in non-cardiacs with alcoholic fatty liver: Role of ethanol in the production of cardiomyopathy, *J. Clin. Invest.,* **48**, 397 (1969).

98. Regan, T. J., C. B. Moschos, P. Casanegra, G. Koroxenides, and H. K. Hellems, Depression of cardiac function and altered myocardial metabolism after ethanol, *Ann. Intern. Med.,* **60**, 709 (1964).

99. Regan, T. J., H. A. Oldewurtel, C. B. Moschos, A. B. Weisse, and S. K. Asokan, Dominance of lipid metabolism in the myocardium under the influence of 1-norepinephrine, *J. Lab. Clin. Med.,* **70**, 221 (1967).

100. Regan, T. J., A. B. Weisse, C. B. Moschos, L. J. Lesniak, M. Nadimi, and

H. K. Hellems, The myocardial effects of acute and chronic usage of alcohol in man, *Trans. Assoc. Am. Phys.*, **78**, 282 (1965).

101. Reynolds, E. S., An account of the epidemic outbreak of arsenical poisoning occurring in the beer-drinkers in the north of England and the Midland counties in 1900, *Lancet*, **1**, 166 (1901).

102. Rosenfeld, G., *Der Einfluss des Alkohols auf den Organismus*, Wiesbaden, 1901.

103. Rosenfeld, G., Inhibitory influence of ethanol on serotonin metabolism, *Proc. Soc. Exper. Biol. Med.*, **103**, 144 (1960).

104. Tanzer, M. L. and C. Gilvarg, Creatine and creatine kinase measurements, *J. Biol. Chem.*, **234**, 3201 (1959).

105. Tobin, J. R., Jr., J. F. Driscoll, M. T. Lim, G. C. Sutton, P. B. Szanto, and R. M. Gunnar, Primary myocardial disease and alcoholism, *Circulation*, **35**, 4 (1967).

106. Schnack, H., F. Wewalka, and I. Obiditsch-Mayer, Akute Myonekrose nach Alcoholintoxikation, *Deut. Med. Wchnschr.*, **86**, 391 (1961).

107. Schwarte, L. H. and H. H. Dukes, The action of drugs on the cardiovascular mechanism of the pig, *J. Am. Vet. Med. Assoc.*, **79**, 180 (1931).

108. Seliskar, A., The action of alcohol upon conduction in the auricle of the tortoise, *J. Physiol.*, **61**, 294 (1926).

109. Spaet, T. II., M. C. Rosenthal, and W. Dameshek, Idiopathic myoglobinuria in man: Report of case, *Blood*, **9**, 881 (1954).

110. Steell, G., Textbook on diseases of the heart, p. 18, Macmillan, Manchester, 1906.

111. Street, H. R., G. R. Cowgill, and H. M. Zimmerman, Some observations of vitamin B₆ deficiency in the dog, *J. Nutr.*, **21**, 275 (1941).

112. Steiner, R. E., The roentgen features of the cardiomyopathies, *Seminars Roentgen*, **4**, 311 (1969).

113. Sulzer, R., The influence of alcohol on the isolated mammalian heart, *Heart*, **11**, 141 (1924).

114. Suzman, M. M., Premier Congress Mondial de Cardiologie Communications, vol. II, p. 495, Baillerie, Paris, 1952.

115. Svoboda, D. J. and R. T. Manning, Chronic alcoholism with fatty metamorphosis of the liver: Mitochondrial alterations in hepatic cells, *Am. J. Path.*, **44**, 645 (1964).

116. Valaitis, J., C. G. Pilz, H. Oliver, and B. Chomet, Myoglobinuria, myoglobinuric nephrosis and alcoholism, *Arch. Path.*, **70**, 195 (1960).

117. Vernon, H. M., The mode of union of certain poisons with cardiac muscle, *J. Physiol.*, **41**, 194 (1910).

118. Visscher, M. B., The influence of ethyl alcohol upon the oxidative metabolism and the mechanical efficiency of the dog's heart, *Am. J. Physiol.*, **81**, 512 (1927).

119. Vondermuhll, P. and A. Jacquet, Zur pharmacologischen Wirkung des Alcohols, *Correspbl. Schw. Aertze*, **21**, 457 (1891).

120. Wakim, K. G., The effects of ethyl alcohol on the isolated heart, *Federation Proc.*, **5**, 109 (1946).
121. Walshe, W. H., *A Practical Treatise on the Diseases of the Heart and Great Blood Vessels*, p. 359, Smith, Elder, London, 1873.
122. Webb, W. R., I. U. Degerli, W. A. Cook, and M. O. Unal, Alcohol, digitalis and cortisol and myocardial capacity in dogs, *Ann. Surg.*, **163**, 811 (1966).
123. Webb, W. R. and I. U. Degerli, Ethyl alcohol and the cardiovascular system, *J. Am. Med. Assoc.*, **191**, 1055 (1965).
124. Webb, W. R., D. N. Gupta, W. A. Cook, W. L. Sugg, F. A. Bashour, and M. O. Unal, Effects of alcohol on myocardial contractility, *Dis. Chest*, **52**, 602 (1967).
125. Weiss, S. and R. W. Wilkins, Nature of cardiovascular disturbances in nutritional deficiency states (beriberi), *Ann. Intern. Med.*, **11**, 104 (1937).
126. Wendt, V. E., C. Wu, R. Balcon, G. Doty, and R. J. Bing, Hemodynamic and metabolic effects of chronic alcoholism in man, *Am. J. Cardiol.*, **15**, 175 (1965).
127. Wolbach, S. B., Pathological changes resulting from vitamin deficiency, *J. Am. Med. Assoc.*, **108**, 7 (1937).
128. Zimmerberg, H., *Untersuchungen über den Einfluss des Alkohols auf die Thätigkeit des Herzens*, Dissertation, Strassburg, 1869.

Chapter VIII

THE IMPORTANCE OF CONGENERS IN THE EFFECTS OF ALCOHOLIC BEVERAGES

HENRY B. MURPHREE

RUTGERS MEDICAL SCHOOL AND CENTER OF ALCOHOL STUDIES
RUTGERS UNIVERSITY
NEW BRUNSWICK, NEW JERSEY

The difference of action of the alcohols as they follow in their series and as the carbon increases is most striking. The slowness of action, the prolongation of action, step by step, from the lighter to the heavier compounds, is a fact as definite as any in physiology . . . Considering how much of the heavier kind of alcohol is distributed for consumption . . . I think it is possible that the heavier fluids may be the cause of delirium tremens in the human subject, as they are probably the cause of that continued coldness, lassitude, and depression which follow the well-known dinner with "bad wine."

B. W. Richardson, 1869

A. Definition of Congeners

Congeners is a term applied to diverse small molecules other than ethanol present in alcoholic beverages. They mostly have boiling points less than

150°C. Both aliphatic and aromatic compounds are included. More than 300 such compounds have been identified in wines, although most are present in such tiny amounts that all the ingenuity of modern analytical chemistry is needed to detect them. A few of this number are present in quantities large enough to have significant effects on flavor and aroma and possibly, as first suggested by Richardson [59] a century ago, to have appreciable pharmacological actions.

The congeners present in larger amounts include mainly primary alcohols other than ethanol, aldehydes, and esters. A few substances with strong biological activity, such as histamine [56], occur, but these are present in small amounts or are inactivated by digestive processes, so that in general they have no significant role. The kinds and amounts of congeners in different beverages have changed over the years with different production techniques. This has resulted in changes of flavor and aroma. Whether the congeners, as imbibed in ordinary amounts of common beverages, have significant pharmacological actions has remained unclear. Consideration of the evidence is the object of this chapter. Clearly toxic examples, such as oil of wormwood (mainly thujone), an ingredient of absinthe, are omitted.

B.   Historical Background

1.   Early Efforts to Improve Wines

The vast majority of effort to understand congeners has been derived from efforts to improve the flavor and aroma of beverages, especially wines. Such efforts are very old, most likely even antedating history. Wines were first made as long ago as 8000 B.C., and by the time of the ancient Egyptians, wine making had become a highly developed art. Evidently the ancient Greeks made very good wines. They had knowledge of making clay amphorae that were nonporous, so that spoilage and evaporation were reduced. Thus they were able to age their wines. Early Roman amphorae were porous, and wines made in them had to be drunk "young." Later the Romans learned to line their amphorae with pitch, so that by the Augustan age there were "great" wines 100 years old that were treasured.

With the onset of the Middle Ages the art of making amphorae was lost, and people resorted to wooden casks. These let in air, so that spoilage again became a problem. Once more only young wines were practical. When glass bottles became generally available toward the beginning of the Renaissance, these were used only as decanters. The innovation of sealing the bottles with corks for aging the wine was not introduced until the early seventeenth century. Even then spoilage continued to be a recurring problem until the time of Pasteur.

Another solution to the problem of spoilage developed in the Iberian Peninsula. This consisted of fortifying wines with distilled spirits, thereby increasing the alcohol concentration to a point where bacteria cannot survive and convert the ethanol to acetaldehyde and acetic acid. In effect the extra alcohol amounts to a preservative. This of course results in a beverage of altogether different character and thus is apart from the goal of improving the flavor and aroma of ordinary unfortified wines.

Besides attempts to improve wines by aging, the other main path of development has been to try to produce grapes that yield the best wines. Of the 8000 or so varieties of grapes, only about 50 produce first-rate wines. The great wine-bearing grape, *Vitis vinifera,* is the source of wines most admired by most people. The northern fox grape of America, *Vitis labrusca* (wild vine), including Isabella, Concord, and Catawba, gives wines having a distinctive flavor, instantly recognizable to most connoisseurs. This is called "foxy" because of its association with the fox grape. The name has nothing to do with the animal directly. Although some do not mind, or even like this gustatory overtone, most find it to some degree objectionable. Therefore there have been many efforts to breed it out. An early experimenter with viticulture in North America was Thomas Jefferson. He brought wines from Tuscany; these died before yielding even one crop, probably because of fungi and phylloxera. He did succeed, however, in producing a hybrid Catawba that came to be recognized as one of the best native wines of the day. For comprehensive reviews of the history of wine, see Hyams [43], Austin [6], and Amerine [3]. The third kind of grape common in North American is *Vitis rotundifolia,* best represented by the scuppernong. Wines produced from this grape have only local interest.

2. Distillation

Development of distillation techniques brought new challenges for using aging to improve flavor and aroma. Early techniques did not fractionate ethanol very precisely from other substances, so that freshly distilled spirits usually had pungent odor and harsh, raw flavor. White corn (maize) whisky, drunk unaged in parts of the United States, typifies this and fully deserves the epithet "white lightning." As soon as distillation techniques became widespread, distillers came to appreciate the benefits of aging. Unlike wine, the aging of spirits is best done in wooden casks, with a controlled amount of oxidation taking place. Paradoxically some congeners are increased during aging even while flavor and aroma are improving [42]. A great deal of ingenuity has been devoted to attempts at artificial or accelerated aging [55]. None has been notably successful.

As to brandies prepared from grapes, the choice of grape again is important. Grapes that make good cognac or pisco do not make especially good wines, and vice versa. The character of other distilled beverages is similarly affected by the choice of grains or whatever else is fermented [75]. This influence decreases as one produces a "lighter," that is, lower-congener beverage, and well-made vodka is indistinguishable as to source of carbohydrate.

3. Yeasts

Another factor in the production of beverages is the selection of yeast used in fermentation. All yeast used for both brewing and baking is *Saccharomyces cerevisiae*. The different strains are classified according to the breakdown of different disaccharides and the fermentation of different monosaccharides. They also differ in the ratio of alcohol to gas (carbon dioxide) formation, having different enzymes for these. Bakery yeast works fast and produces copious carbon dioxide, which raises the loaf. Some ethanol also is produced by bakery yeast, but most is lost in cooking. Perhaps 0.5% remains to give flavor. Brewery yeast is dark and bitter and, if used for cooking, works slowly and gives a small, dense, bitter loaf. Wine yeasts are of the same species and are commercially named after the district of origin. There have been attempts to transport yeasts from one place to another and thereby reproduce some of the character of the wine of the original place. But these efforts have not met much success, owing to rapid environmental modification of the strain. In usual practice, then, the choice of the strain of yeast has to do more with productivity than with the quality of the beverage. Thus a yeast can be "trained" to accept high concentrations of sugar and alcohol and to withstand higher temperatures. This again is only an environmentally produced change, and the yeast culture modifies quickly under other conditions. Similarly the performance of a yeast can be enhanced by the addition of ammonium salts as a source of nitrogen. This is all the yeast needs to make its own amino acids and proteins. A few yeasts can use nitrates, but not *Saccharomyces cerevisiae*. There are no "essential" amino acids for yeast. Ammonium salts affect congeners also, because they tend to inhibit the production of isoamyl and "active" amyl alcohols from leucine and isoleucine.

4.   Early Chemical Analyses

Because interest in beverages has always been great, as soon as analytic chemistry came into being, people began investigating the composition of wines and liquors. Of course the main ingredient has been known longest. Alcohol was first isolated in Arabia in the ninth century. The Arabic term *al-kuh'l* meant a fine powder applied to the eyelids, hence anything impalpable, as a spirit.

Further developments had to wait for the nineteenth century. Then soon after the beginnings of analytic chemistry the presence of other alcohols was identified. Justus von Liebig isolated from wine a substance that he called "oenanthic ether," to which he gave the empiric formula $C_{14}H_{26}O_2$. Liebig and Pelouze believed that what we now call the ethyl ester of the compound was responsible for the "ethereal, vinous" odor of wine. The name "enanthic acid" is now given to heptanoic (normal heptoic) acid, the seven-carbon compound that amounts to about one-half of Liebig's formula. Much of the odor with which Liebig was concerned comes from "pelargonic ester," another old term, once used to describe a mixture mainly of caprylic and capric esters. Nowadays the term "pelargonic acid" is applied to nonanoic (normal nonoic) acid, esters of which are found in the leaves of geraniums (*Pelargonium*) and allied plants. The ethyl ester is prepared commercially by oxidizing oil of rue (*Ruta graveolens*) and is used as a flavoring for wines and liquors.

5.   Classical Toxicologic Studies of Compounds Related to Ethanol

As soon as knowledge about the organic chemical constituents of alcoholic beverages became available, interest in the pharmacologic and toxicologic properties of these substances arose. The epochal insight of the time was that of Benjamin Richardson [59], who, after studying straight-chain primary alcohols, recognized that the pharmacologic action of these increases in proportion to the number of carbons. He immediately proposed, as quoted at the beginning of this paper, that these other substances, that is, congeners, were responsible for toxic effects, such as hangover. That higher alcohols have greater activity has been confirmed many times, so that the observation has come to be known as Richardson's rule or Richardson's law.

Work in succeeding decades was desultory and was hampered by inadequate analytic techniques and insensitive assay methods. In large part it consisted of trying to test various compounds or beverages for acute toxic effects in various in vitro or in vivo preparations. The work of the first five decades was well reviewed by David Macht [47] in 1921. He also confirmed the law in several preparations.

Richardson's rule has by now been confirmed by a variety of methods, some of which are described below; and modifications have been developed having to do with primary, secondary, and tertiary alcohols, branching, unsaturation, and so on.

6. Early Basic Findings

Three examples of congeners that crop up again and again in publications in the field are methanol, furfural, and "fusel oil." Beverage industries have spent a great deal of effort to try to control or eliminate the occurrence of these substances. As further background, then, a brief consideration of these might be worthwhile.

A. METHANOL. Methanol is "wood-alcohol," the one-carbon compound CH_3OH. It is lighter and more volatile than ethanol (see Table I). The acute toxicity of methyl alcohol is less than that of ethyl alcohol, in accordance with Richardson's rule; that is, one has to drink more to get as drunk. The problem with methanol is the toxicity of its metabolite, formaldehyde. Methanol occurs to some extent in beverages, but the concentrations are generally kept small; and although it is among the more plentiful congeners, the amounts are not nearly so large as those of some others. It is important because of the control exercised over its presence.

B. FURFURAL. Furfural is mentioned frequently in older reports dealing with congeners. An old name for furfural is "artificial oil of ants." It is an oily, colorless liquid used mostly as a solvent. On exposure to air or light, furfural turns yellowish or brownish and resinous. As shown in Table I, furfural is very much more toxic than other congeners. Ingestion or absorption of 60 mg of furfural is said to cause a persistent headache. Because of its relatively high boiling point, 162°C, furfural is easily removed by reasonably careful distillation, and it does not occur in modern distilled beverages.

C. FUSEL OIL. Fusel oil is an old term for the oily-phase residue left on the surface of any beverage after all the ethanol has been removed. This was first noticed in 1785 [73]. The name *fousel,* an old German word meaning bad spirit, was applied to this residue in the early nineteenth century. The substance became the object of extensive chemical study, with several investigators contributing to the finding, in the 1870s, that the main ingredients are isoamyl (3-methyl-1-butanol) and "active" amyl

TABLE I   Characteristics and Industrial Uses of Common Congener Substances

	Boiling point, °C	LD$_{50}$, gm/kg, oral, rat	Uses
Acetaldehyde	21	1.9	Manufacture of paraldehyde, acetic acid, perfumes, flavors, hardening gelatin
Ethyl formate	53–54	4.3	Flavoring for lemonades and essences, artificial rum and arrac; fungicide and larvicide for tobacco, cereals, dried fruits, solvent
Ethyl acetate	77	5.6	Artificial fruit essences; solvent and cleaning fluid; carminative and antispasmodic (dose 1–2 ml); counterirritant
Methanol	64.7	...[a]	Solvent, extractant, antifreeze; fuel; denaturant for ethanol, manufacture of formaldehyde
n-Propanol	97–98	1.9	Solvent
i-Butanol	108	2.5	Solvent; manufacture of esters for fruit flavoring essences
i-Amyl Alcohol	132	4.3[b]	Solvent; dehydrating agent
Furfural	161.8	0.05–0.1	Manufacture of plastics; fungicide, germicide; solvent; reagent in analytical chemistry

[a] Complex toxicity; see text.
[b] Rabbit.

(2-methyl-1-butanol) alcohols. The latter contains an asymmetric carbon and therefore is optically active. Besides these, many other compounds are present in small or trace amounts in fusel oils [72]. Because of its marked and highly disagreeable odor and taste, fusel oil is fractionally removed with great precision from modern commercial beverages. It is used as a crude solvent or as a source for the various alcohols of which it is composed. Despite careful removal of fusel oil, a significant amount of isoamyl alcohol remains in some beverages. For detailed information on fusel oil, see Webb and Ingraham [73].

C.   Industrial Quality-Control Methods

By 1900 the odious character of the substances mentioned above was fully recognized, but industrial quality control was haphazard and mostly non-existent, with notable exceptions. These exceptions arose from pride of product in part and also from farsighted understanding that, given a choice, people prefer a better product to a worse one. A pioneer in this respect was Col. Edmund Taylor, a grandnephew of President Zachary Taylor. He insisted on producing a well-aged product of uniform high quality for the time. In pursuit of this, he played a major part in the passage of the bonding law in 1890 [16]. This law, widely misunderstood, has no direct relationship to quality. It simply specifies conditions under which a distiller can defer paying tax on his product while it is aging. The only guarantee of quality involved is that the final beverage must be 100 proof (U.S.). Also it must be at least 4 years old. Bonding does make sufficient aging to produce a high-quality beverage economically feasible. Whether the distiller pursues this advantage well is up to him. The constraints of competitive marketing are more forceful than the bonding law. These constraints tended to stimulate production of ever improving beverages up to the time of Prohibition in the United States, and elsewhere in unbroken succession up to the present. Prohibition and subsequent Repeal in the United States initiated a change in beverage quality that is still continuing. With Repeal, manufacturers were faced with the need for quickly producing enough beverage for an abruptly large demand while they had only limited backlogs of aged product. One solution was to produce "blends," that is, grain neutral spirits lightly flavored and colored with straight whiskey. This was in accordance with a tradition already common in Scotland and Canada, and advertising was aimed at cultivating a market for "light" whiskies. The trend is continuing and seems to be increasing. The feature secondary to considerations of taste and economics is that these beverages have much smaller congener contents (see Table II). Of course the major considerations still are all important. A master distiller with a modern column still can tailor his "cut" to produce anything from a very high-congener beverage to virtually pure ethanol. But even with very high-congener beverages, such as bourbon whiskey and cognac, the trend seems to be toward less congeners. Using gas chromatography, Carroll [15] compared a pre-Prohibition bourbon with a current bourbon and found that the latter had far smaller amounts of congeners. Beckmann [8] reported in 1905 that a sample of French cognac contained 140 mg% of "amyl alcohol," presumably isoamyl. The concentration in an 1898 Californian cognac was 210 mg%. The amount of isoamyl alcohol in a recent sample of the same brand of French cognac was only 116 mg% [15].

D.   Modern Analytic Methods and Their Implications

Quality control in the production of beverages, as well as analysis for research purposes, has been eased immensely by the advent of gas (vapor-

TABLE II   Amounts of Congeners in Typical Beverages (mg/100 ml, Adjusted to 100 Proof U.S.)[a]

	Vodka	Gin	Canadian blend	Light rum	Scotch whisky	U.S. blend	Cognac	Bourbon	Synthetic alcohol	Grain neutral spirits
Acetaldehyde	0.44	0.33	1.71	4.18	3.14	1.69	7.14	1.98	0.16	0.09
Ethyl formate	0.50	0.40	1.11	1.88	1.55	0.96	3.93	3.14	0.42	0.95
Ethyl acetate	0	0.06	14.70	13.75	32.71	40.70	53.58	96.00	0	0.08
Methyl alcohol	0.49	2.33	2.82	1.44	3.49	1.98	14.76	3.04	0.26	0.48
n-Propyl alcohol	0	0.06	2.19	10.62	14.90	4.54	16.67	12.80	0	1.63
i-Butyl alcohol	1.35	1.17	5.56	4.56	24.40	18.60	39.60	29.10	0	0
i-Amyl alcohol	0.52	0	18.45	23.70	30.25	62.10	116.60	139.50	0	0
Total fusel oil	1.87	1.23	26.20	38.88	69.55	85.24	172.87	181.40	0	1.63
Total congeners	3.30	4.35	46.54	60.13	110.44	130.57	252.28	285.56	0.84	3.23

[a] Adapted from Carroll [15].

phase) chromatography. Earlier workers had to rely on a variety of techniques, such as fractional distillation, titrimetry, and column chromatography. Although some very detailed results were obtained [12, 49, 55, 65] this was extremely tedious. Nowadays not only is rapid, highly accurate analysis possible, but also one can, by means of process vapor-phase chromatography, produce skillfully tailor-made distilled beverages with great precision. This then sharpens the question as to which congeners should be left in beverages for flavor and bouquet and which should be removed because they smell bad, taste bad, or have bad physiological effects. A difficulty is that a given substance may be out of place in one beverage from the esthetic point of view but actually called for in another beverage. The latter may remain true although the substance is fairly toxic. An example is acetaldehyde, which is an important constituent of sherry, so much so that for sherry production, yeasts are carefully chosen that are high acetaldehyde producers [2]. This kind of thing suggests that there may be sharp resistance to some changes based entirely on pharmacologic considerations.

E.   Congener Research and Wine Industry

The wine industry through various institutes in different parts of the world has engaged in extensive studies of congeners. These are directed toward improvement of the quality of beverages. On the one hand, with modern methods of quality control, congeners are not much of a problem. Spoilage is virtually a thing of the past, and fusel oil can be kept at a minimum. Esters of proper kinds and amounts are probably necessary to the maintenance of traditional flavors and aromas, as acetaldehyde is to sherry. Wines of uniform quality can be produced by automated methods in very large quantities. On the other hand, these wines, although quite acceptable in ordinary use and far better than much *vin ordinaire* produced by inferior methods, are not considered to be "great." The pursuit of the elusive qualities encompassed in adjectives such as great continues. Most likely this will never end, because judgments tend to be influenced by factors other than mere flavor and bouquet.

One congener that continues to be a problem, however, is methyl anthranilate. This aromatic ester has a sweet, flowery odor, causing it to be dubbed "artificial oil of orange blossoms." Methyl anthranilate is the substance responsible for the "foxy" flavor of wines obtained from *Vitis labrusca,* as described above. A practical method for controlling concentrations of methyl anthranilate, either by viticultural methods or by some method of processing the wine, would be worthwhile.

F. Biochemical Aspects

1. Biosynthesis

Although methyl anthranilate is a product of the grape itself, as are many other congeners contributing to flavor and bouquet, the troublesome congeners, those which cause bad odor and flavor and possibly have adverse pharmacologic effects, are mostly fermentation products. These result from the uncontrolled deamination of protein material or from bacterial infection resulting in formation of alcohols rather than amino acids from basic carbon skeletons. Production of such substances by bacterial fermentation can be extensive. Indeed *Clostridium acetobutylicum* is used for the commercial preparation of acetone and butanol from blackstrap molasses. Therefore wines produced by "natural fermentation" commonly contain two to three times as much higher alcohols as wines produced from carefully controlled inoculation with selected yeast cultures. Leucine and isoleucine are the most troublesome amino acids, because their deamination by the Ehrlich reaction produces amyl and isoamyl alcohols, the principal ingredients of "fusel oil." These amino acids are especially plentiful in grain, beetroots, and potatoes, as well as the marc of grapes. The production of fusel oil is minimized by the addition of ammonium salts to the ferment, which retards deamination.

2. Metabolic Fate

Extensive work about the metabolic fate of congeners is lacking, although inferences can be made from the compounds that have been studied. Methanol is oxidized to formaldehyde and formate. Formaldehyde is now regarded as the villain in methanol poisoning [18]. Higher primary alcohols similarly are oxidized to corresponding aldehydes and fatty acids [40]. These reactions proceed much more slowly than those of the smaller molecules, and this may account for longer durations of pharmacologic and toxic actions. Also there is the possibility that the metabolism of these compounds is retarded by competition with ethanol for alcohol dehydrogenase, since this enzyme seems to dispose of all these smaller primary alcohols [33]. Third, the higher fatty acids finally formed from the higher alcohols are themselves depressant to the central nervous system [40, 74].

Secondary alcohols can be oxidized only to corresponding ketones, and tertiary alcohols cannot be oxidized biochemically at all. These alcohols then are largely excreted intact and not very rapidly. Secondary and tertiary alcohols do not occur to appreciable extents in normal beverages, however.

The foregoing concerns monohydric alcohols. The most common aliphatic diols are ethylene and propylene glycol. Ethylene glycol, if ingested, is highly toxic. In part, it is oxidized to oxalic acid, which harms renal tubules. The propylene glycols go to pyroacemic or lactic acid and are toxic only in large amounts. Neither of these diols is encountered in normal beverages. With more than two hydroxyl groups, compounds become sweet to taste and lose pharmacologic activity. Of course some polyols are natural foodstuffs or metabolites. Polyphenols occur in wines in small amounts, in which they probably are important in flavor and bouquet.

The aliphatic esters most likely are hydrolyzed. The most prevalent are ethyl esters, and the ethanol thus produced would be treated as the rest of the ethanol in the beverage. The fatty acid moiety similarly would be treated as any other fatty acid. Methyl esters occur much less plentifully, and the amount of methanol produced would be tiny in comparison with the small amount of methanol already present. Aromatic esters would be hydrolyzed with more difficulty or not at all, depending on steric factors.

The third large group of congeners is the aldehydes. Like the higher alcohols, they are mostly undesirable, because they have bad smell and taste. They would be oxidized to the corresponding fatty acids. They are present only in tiny amounts, however, with the single exception of acetaldehyde, which, as mentioned, is considered desirable in sherry. Acetaldehyde is oxidized rapidly to acetate and enters the fatty acid metabolic cycle. Acetaldehyde is also the intermediate in the oxidation of ethanol to acetate. Thus it has the unique position of being both a congener and a metabolite [70]. Ordinarily the rate-limiting step in the metabolism of ethanol is that from ethanol to acetaldehyde. The next step, to acetic acid, proceeds very rapidly, so that concentrations of acetaldehyde remain very small. Disulfuram and some related compounds have been shown to inhibit aldehyde dehydrogenase in vitro. Formerly a large buildup of acetaldehyde was thought to account for the toxic effect of ethanol when the latter is drunk by a person taking disulfuram. More recently doubt has been cast on this possibility. Acetaldehyde is quite toxic, however.

G.   Composition of Current Distilled Beverages

Because the congener content of undistilled beverages is so extensive, diverse, and variable, the rest of this chapter is confined to consideration of distilled beverages.

Carroll [15], using vapor-phase chromatography, conducted studies of the more common distilled beverages in North America. Older studies, using more laborious methods, also have been very well done and have yielded comparable results for beverages commonplace here and elsewhere. Webb, Kepner, and Ikeda [72] and Webb and Ingraham [73] have given exhaustive reviews of "fusel oil." Table II shows concentrations of the most common congeners in several beverages. From this it is clear that isoamyl alcohol (3-methyl-1-butanol) and ethyl acetate are by far the most ubiquitous. Also evident is the great difference in congener contents of gin or vodka versus bourbon whisky or cognac. The moot question then is what pharmacologic or toxicologic effect, if any, these congeners have in the amounts commonly drunk and, corollary with this, what differences, if any, occur from drinking high-congener versus low-congener beverages.

H. Neuropharmacologic Actions of Congeners

Much of the information available about congener substances concerns toxic rather than pharmacologic effects. Many studies have involved acute lethality, and although they yield comparative data, they tell us nothing about the actions of the compounds in sublethal doses, much less the actions of doses approximating common consumption. Many publications have concerned the effects of inhalation of the compounds, because that is the more common kind of exposure in industry, although percutaneous, as well as oral, toxicity is important with some of the compounds. Industrial toxicologic data are summarized well by Elkins [23], Fassett [27, 28], Flury and Klimmer [30], Gross [35], Rowe [61], and Treon [69]. The rest of this chapter concerns reports which may bear on the actions of congeners as imbibed in beverages or which concern comparisons of beverages with each other or with pure ethanol.

A point of major importance is that with few exceptions the substances differ only in regard to potency and time-action curves. They do not differ in their qualitative neuropharmacologic effects. When swallowed, all produce gastrointestinal irritation followed by intoxication typical of ethanol and the volatile general anesthetics: dizziness, light-headedness, and excitement followed by lassitude, then somnolence proceeding to coma as the dose is increased. Headache and nausea and vomiting, as well as respiratory depression, also are common with larger doses.

Ethyl acetate, the second most common congener (see Table II) may have a unique property, that of lowering blood sugar. This possibility is raised by a report [41], confirmed by many unpublished cases, of poisoning with a paint remover–solvent mixture containing 1 part of ethyl acetate to 100 parts of ethanol, along with other solvent substances, none of which has been reported to produce hypoglycemia. The patients had drunk from 0.5 pint to 2 quarts of the mixture. They were admitted in shock with tachypnea and serum carbon dioxide as low as 12 mEq/l probably due to the amount of methanol present (1%). Blood glucose was as low as 13 mg%. The amounts reported to have been consumed contained 24 or more ml of ethyl acetate. Therefore this effect would not be encountered with any ordinary beverage, but it should be kept in mind in poisonings and should be investigated properly. The effect is especially dangerous when associated with ethanol intoxication, since higher blood sugar protects against the acute toxicity of alcohol [38].

1.   Possible Basis for Differences in Effects of Beverages

As stated above, most congener substances do not differ in qualitative neuropharmacologic effect, although they may differ in toxic effects on other systems. Therefore differences in effects of beverages with differing congener contents would be only quantitative. Differences in this respect may be substantial, however, and could be due to any of several possible mechanisms.

Haggard, Greenberg, and Cohen [39], after extensive studies of the actions of congeners concluded that: "The alcohol of different distilled spirits may be metabolized at different rates. This difference results from the presence in various amounts of a congener—or congeners—in the different spirits which exerts an action in slowing the rate of metabolism of alcohol in the body." An echo of this is found in the recent report of Greenberg [33] that in vivo the metabolism of isoamyl alcohol to valeraldehyde and the disappearance of valeraldehyde from plasma are retarded in the presence of ethanol.

This kind of postulation, however, does not explain some of the actions of congeners that are prolonged well after blood alcohol is zero. It might do so if one could assume that tissue concentrations persist longer than blood concentrations. But the reverse is true: blood concentrations tend always to be larger than tissue concentrations [29]. Therefore the actions of congeners may be due to separate actions of their own or to additive or synergistic actions with alcohol. Since true drug synergism is extremely rare, this seems least likely. Since the actions of the congeners are closely similar to those of ethanol, some degree of additive effect might be expected, followed by separate actions of the longer-lasting congeners as the amount of ethanol wanes. Most likely, however, to further our perplexity, a mixture of interactions occurs, including the possibility suggested by Haggard, Greenberg, and Cohen. The data comparing beverages that follow are only empirical, without regard to mechanism.

2. In Vitro Studies

Macht [47] in 1921 gave a review of earlier work and reported studies of his own in several systems. He found that Richardson's law held for the depression of isolated frog heart and pig ureter. In general his in vitro work corroborated that of other investigators as far back as 1885. In 1921 Fühner [31] also reported similar findings for the depression of isolated frog heart.

Romano [60] tested the effects of several fatty acids, ketones, and aliphatic esters on the rat uterus and found them to have no effect.

Beer and Quastel [9] tested the effects of aliphatic aldehydes on the respiration of rat brain cortex slices and rat brain mitochondria. They found that acetaldehyde inhibited potassium chloride stimulation of rat brain cortex slices at 0.005, the concentration at which ethanol had the same effect. These same authors also showed that the inhibition in this preparation obeyed Richardson's law, that is, increased as the length of the carbon chain increased [10].

Rang [57] studied contractility in guinea-pig gut, tissue oxygen consumption (chopped guinea-pig lung), and anaphylactic histamine release. He found that for arithmetic increase of chain length in aliphatic primary alcohols having from one to eight carbons there was a logarithmic decrease in the concentrations required for the effects. Alcohols having more than eight carbons had no effect.

Agin, Hersh, and Holtzman [1] tested the same series of alcohols for their action in blocking membrane depolarization. They found that the logarithm of the minimum blocking concentration varied inversely as the number of carbons up to n-octanol. Similarly they found that the polarizability of their experimental preparation varied directly as the number of carbons.

Thus from a variety of in vitro studies by many investigators for many years, it is clear that higher alcohols have greater pharmacologic potency. When one moves to the comparison of different beverages, the picture is not so clear.

In 1936 Barlow, Beams, and Goldblatt [7] compared the effects of chemically pure ethanol with those of grain ethanol and whisky in a variety of systems, including coagulation of egg white, irritability and conductivity of frog sciatic, and effects on perfused frog heart. They found no differences among the effects of the three.

3. In Vivo Studies of Pure Compounds in Animals

Vernon [71] in 1913 studied the effects of some of these substances on growth rates in tadpoles. Aquatic animals are convenient for such trials, because they can be maintained for long periods in constant solutions and therefore with stable tissue concentrations, Vernon found that the concentrations for narcosis and for death varied greatly with age. When this was taken into account, Richardson's law again held true up to octyl alcohol. Vernon also found that the ethyl esters of aliphatic fatty acids with two to five carbons obeyed the law.

Taylor [68] in 1934 studied the effects of these alcohols on bacterial luminescence and respiration. He found increasing "narcosis of luminescence" as carbon number increased from one to eight. Along with this he found an increase in respiration.

4. In Vivo Studies of Beverages in Animals

Barlow, Beams, and Goldblatt [7], besides the in vitro studies with chemically pure ethanol, grain ethanol, and whisky described above, also carried out several in vivo studies. They compared the effects of the three substances in the following: rabbit ear subcutaneously and cat stomach topically for local irritant action; anesthetic and toxic effects in paramecia, daphnia, goldfish (see comment on Vernon's study above), and earthworms; and growth rate in rats. They also did more conventional determinations of depressant and toxic effects in rats, rabbits, and cats by various routes of administration. They found no instance in which chemically pure ethanol and grain ethanol differed. Whisky had greater irritant effects on rabbit ear and cat gastrointestinal tract. Whisky was more toxic in paramecia, in rats intraperitoneally, in rabbits orally and intravenously, and in cats orally. Whisky's effect on growth rate in rats did not differ from that of the two ethanols.

In 1954 Estable and coworkers in several studies [24, 25, 26, 34] compared the effects of samples of the following: ethanol, caña, grappa, cognac, and whisky. They found no differences of lethal potency among the different substances in fish maintained in aquariums or in mice, guinea pigs, or dogs by the intraperitoneal route. Testing voluntary consumption by white rats, they found that the animals consumed less alcohol than water and less of all the beverages than alcohol. Finally they studied blood alcohol concentration in dogs following equivalent doses of the substances and found no differences. These investigators seem to have had the goal of demonstrating that there was no pharmacological difference among the preparations and that the only substantial differences were matters of flavor and aroma, that is, subjective preference.

Haag and coworkers [36] studied preparations of congeners minus ethanol. They determined the effects of irritation in rabbit eye and LD_{50}'s but did not do any comparative studies. McKennis and Haag [48] also published a review without original data in which they concluded that ". . . small quantities of congeners in proper balance . . . may lessen the undesirable physiologic effects through interaction with ethanol and other constituents of the beverage." Just how they reached this opinion in the face of diverse reports including that of Haag and coworkers [36] that congeners are toxic remains unclear.

In 1962 Di Luzio [21] undertook a comparative study of different beverages on the development of acute fatty liver. He found no contribution by congeners. In a later study the same investigator [22] was comparing the effects of acute and chronic administration of alcohol and alcoholic beverages on tissue triglyceride concentrations. He had carried out many investigations with ethanol-supplemented formula diets in rats as compared with other isocaloric diets. In this study he compared bourbon, vodka, and ethanol, with sucrose as a control. To his surprise 23% of the animals given bourbon died. None of the animals given vodka, ethanol, or sucrose died, nor had he ever encountered any deaths before on ethanol-supplemented diets.

Kiessling and coworkers [46] undertook extensive studies of the effects of ethanol on enzymatic activity and histologic appearance of rat liver. In a study published in 1968 they compared morphologic and functional changes after the prolonged consumption of various alcoholic beverages and pure ethanol. The beverages were cognac, Scotch whisky, vermouth, white wine, and red wine. They examined mitochondrial sizes and shapes, and oxidation, and aerobic glycolysis rates. Also they assayed activities of the following dehydrogenases: isocitrate, α-glycerophosphate, malate, and glyceraldehyde phosphate. They found highly significant differences in effects of the various beverages, but no consistent pattern of differences:

"Some of the observed changes may be interpreted as signs of adaptation to alcoholic beverages continuously present in the organism. Several of the changes seem rather consequences of by-products in the alcoholic beverages than of the ethanol itself."

Ryback [63] compared the effects of vodka and bourbon on sleeping time in mice. He gave mice equivalent doses and then placed them on an inclined screen and compared "fall" time, that is, time to roll off the screen, and times of onset and duration of sleep. He found the "fall" and onset time shorter and the duration longer with bourbon than with vodka.

5. Pharmacologic Studies with Humans

Barlow, Beams, and Goldblatt [7] compared the effects of chemically pure ethanol, grain ethanol, and whisky on motility and emptying time of the upper gastrointestinal tract in human subjects. They found that with these indices of irritation, "straight-run" whisky had greater effect than blends made with either synthetic or grain ethanol and that the blend had more effect than either grain or synthetic ethanol alone. The latter were indistinguishable from each other.

In a somewhat different kind of study, Asmussen, Hald, and Larsen [5] investigated the action of acetaldehyde in humans. They infused acetaldehyde intravenously to increase the plasma concentration to the range of 0.2 to 0.7 mg%, which is about 10 times normal. They found that this caused increases in heart rate and respiratory rate, as well as subjective symptoms referred to as "hangover."

Aschan and coworkers [4], in studying positional nystagmus during and after alcohol intoxication, used whisky and brännvin. They did not attempt, however, to distinguish between the effects of these two beverages in their analysis. Most likely there would have been no difference, because both beverages contain large amounts of congeners.

Murphree, Price, and Greenberg [50] undertook a direct study of the effects of congeners in alcoholic beverages on the incidence of nystagmus. They compared the effects of vodka with those of bourbon and a superbourbon prepared to contain increased amounts of congeners without any greater concentration of ethanol. They found no difference in the blood alcohol concentrations or incidences of nystagmus produced by bourbon and vodka. The superbourbon, however, produced much greater incidence of nystagmus, which persisted well after blood alcohol concentrations had returned to zero.

Murphree and coworkers undertook a comparative study of the effects of different beverages in humans, using electroencephalography. In a report given in 1966 [52] they demonstrated that the characteristic electroencephalographic effect of moderate doses of alcoholic beverages was the appearance of time-serial trends in which alpha activity was reciprocally replaced by slow activity. A subsequent report [51] summarized the earlier work and reported that the incidence of these reciprocal trends was greater after bourbon than after water. The incidence after vodka did not differ significantly from those after water or bourbon; that is, vodka was intermediate in action. Two later reports concern qualitative effects. One is that dosage with bourbon is sometimes followed by a mixture of alpha and fast ("beta") activity similar to that produced by barbiturates [53]. The other is that bourbon may produce unusual parietal activity peaking at 8 to 9 per sec [54]. During this phase, alpha activity is absent. Neither of these effects has been encountered after vodka or controls (water or orange juice).

Another line of investigation [66] concerned prolonged cardiovascular effects of these alcoholic beverages in humans. Both bourbon and vodka produced significant increases in heart rate. These increases did not appear immediately but then lasted 7 hours after dosage. Effects on blood pressure were more complex and may be explained as a mixture of vasodilator and pressor effects, the latter in turn possibly due to catecholamine release. Whether the high-congener beverage differs significantly from the low-congener one is not clear at this writing.

I. Behavioral Studies

The foregoing makes clear that many studies indicate differences in the actions of high-congener and low-congener beverages in diverse life systems. As well, such differences seem to have a solid basis in the comparative studies of different compounds, as undertaken to test Richardson's law. Unfortunately there are difficulties with controls in many of these studies, and such difficulties are multiplied when behavioral studies are undertaken. Basic studies with animals are mostly lacking, and such human studies as have been made often include no attempt at controls. Thus although their conclusions may be correct, the data themselves are not so cogent as might be wished.

1. Behavioral Studies in Animals

Raynes and Ryback [58] compared the effect of alcoholic beverages of low and high congener content on the aggressive response of the Siamese fighting fish (*Betta splendens*). They found that bourbon increased the aggressive display more than did vodka. This is in line with widespread thinking that alcoholic beverages "unleash" aggressions. But this thinking has recently come under sharp criticism [11] as being far too simplistic.

Moreover extrapolation from data about fixed, "wired-in," or "prepro-grammed" responses of simple animals to complex human activity is stretch-ing anthropomorphism.

Ryback [62] compared the effects of ethanol, bourbon, and various etha-nol levels on Y-maze learning in goldfish. Placed in ethanol solutions rather than plain water, the fish demonstrated initial impairment as their tissues reached equilibrium concentrations of ethanol. After 6 or 72 hr, they dem-onstrated adaptation. When placed in bourbon solutions, however, the fish failed to learn even after 2 days of training.

2. Behavioral Studies in Humans

Katkin and Hayes [44] studied the differential effects on reaction time and perceptual motor performance of bourbon and vodka. They tested their human subjects at 1 and 3 hr after dosage for "simple" and "complex" reaction times and a mirror-drawing task. In the 1-hr trials there were no differences in reaction times; the subjects given bourbon did worse on the mirror-drawing task. In the 3-hr trials the findings were reversed: There were no differences in mirror drawing, but the subjects given bourbon showed impaired reaction times.

Katkin and coworkers [45] also studied the effects of the two beverages in a "risk-taking" model task. They found greater incidence of risk taking in young subjects than in old, and in drunk subjects than in sober. As well, they found increased risk taking in subjects given high-congener bever-age as compared with those given low-congener doses.

The foregoing shows well that the evidence of different behavioral effects of beverages having differing congener concentrations, although intriguing and suggestive, is far too small and fragmentary for any firm conclusions.

J. Relevance of Congeners to Clinical Phenomena

1. Acute Intoxication

Ingestion of congener substances as such is clearly toxic, indeed sometimes disastrous. Futcher [32] wrote eloquently of fusel-oil poisoning in 1901. The question is whether these substances have significant effect in the amounts present in ordinary beverages. Many have thought so and have written persuasively on the topic. Examples besides Richardson [59] are Brunton and Tunnicliffe [13] in 1902 and Shorell [64] in 1938. Although they offer no direct data, many of the studies cited above seem to support their view.

Brusch and coworkers [14] conducted comparisons of gin, rum, vodka, and whisky in human subjects, but the objective basis of these comparisons is not made clear in their report. Controls seem to have been lacking, and the bias of the authors is evident. Thus the subjects may well have been influenced by the "placebo" effect. For a discussion, see Haas, Fink, and Härtfelder [37]. The same kind of problem occurs with the studies of Damrau and Liddy [19, 20]. They gave vodka, whisky, and "whisky congeners" prepared by "boiling off" the ethanol, presumably fractional distillation. The subjects were heterogeneous as to age, sex, and drinking experience and habits. Therefore, once again, the data are not impressive even if the conclusions are correct. Much more careful work is needed.

2.   Subacute Intoxication: Hangover

The same problems as discussed above occur with studies of "hangover." Thus most available reports cannot be considered conclusive. In addition, hangover may be compounded by such things as fatigue and emotional factors apart from any actual pharmacologic-toxicologic effects.

Takala, Siro, and Toivainen [67] in 1958 published a report of studies of intellectual functions and dexterity during hangover. They did a variety of experiments in human subjects following intoxication with brandy and beer. They found that subjects performed as well after brandy as did controls. After beer the subjects did better on some tasks and worse on others. No consistent pattern emerged, and no general conclusions could be drawn as to differential effects of the two beverages.

To try to produce an accurate quasiclinical model, Chapman [17] gave human volunteers doses of bourbon or vodka in the evening in a setting intended to resemble a usual social setting. With amounts of beverage containing 1.5 ml/kg of absolute ethanol, significantly more frequent and severe hangover followed the bourbon. Although this study was conceived and performed better than most, it still suffers from possible placebo effects. The idea is widespread that vodka causes less hangover than bourbon, although not everyone believes it. Nevertheless this may have been convincing enough to enough subjects to influence the outcome of the experiment.

3.   Longer-term Effects

Longer-term effects of regular dosage with alcoholic beverages include chronic toxicity and the pharmacologic dependence and withdrawal syndrome. The latter, which culminates in delirium tremens, is now included under the general term "alcohol-barbiturate dependence." Comparative chronic toxicities of the congeners have not been studied. Neither have their proclivities for inducing dependence. Certainly the possibility that they have greater effects in these respects seems reasonable in light of their greater depressant and acute toxic activities. Investigations in this area would be worthwhile. Knowledge of whether high-congener beverages differ substantively from low-congener beverages in these respects would be valuable.

CONCLUSION

Many persons prefer the aroma and flavor of high-congener beverages. No doubt they would continue to do so, even if these beverages were shown to have somewhat greater adverse effects. This is a matter of taste and personal choice, and such considerations are not within the scope of this chapter. Moreover the differences in effect may be insignificant in the relatively small amounts of alcoholic beverages drunk by most people. The differences are of interest to scientists and physicians, because we wish to broaden our knowledge of these beverages as part of our understanding of alcohol consumption and because the differences may become significant in persons who chronically consume large amounts of the beverages.

REFERENCES

1. Agin, D., L. Hersh, and D. Holtzman, The action of anesthetics on excitable membranes: A quantum chemical analysis, *Proc. Nat. Acad. Sci. U.S.*, **53**, 952 (1965).
2. Amerine, M. A. and V. L. Singleton, *Wine: An Introduction for Americans*, University of California Press, Berkeley, 1965.
3. Amerine, M. A., The search for good wine, *Science*, **154**, 1621 (1966).
4. Aschan, G., M. Bergstedt, L. Goldberg, and L. Laurell, Positional nystagmus in man during and after alcohol intoxication, *Quart. J. Stud. Alc.*, **17**, 381 (1956).
5. Asmussen, E., J. Hald, and V. Larsen, The pharmacological action of acetaldehyde on the human organism, *Acta Pharmacol.*, **4**, 311 (1948).
6. Austin, C., *The Science of Wine*, American Elsevier Publishing Company, New York, 1968.
7. Barlow, O. W., A. J. Beams, and H. Goldblatt, Studies on the pharmacology of ethyl alcohol, *J. Pharmacol. & Exper. Therap.*, **56**, 117 (1936).
8. Beckmann, E., Zur Bestimmung des fuselölgehaltes alkoholischer Flussigkeiten, *Zeitschr. Untersuch. Nahr. Genusm.*, **10**, 143 (1905).

9. Beer, C. T. and J. H. Quastel, The effects of aliphatic aldehydes on the respiration of rat brain cortex slices and rat brain mitochondria, *Canad. J. Biochem. Physiol.,* **36,** 531 (1958).

10. Beer, C. T. and J. H. Quastel, The effects of aliphatic alcohols on the respiration of rat brain cortex slices and rat brain mitochondria, *Canad. J. Biochem. Physiol.,* **36,** 543 (1958).

11. Bennett, R. M., A. H. Buss, and J. A. Carpenter, Alcohol and human aggression, *Quart. J. Stud. Alc.,* **30,** 870 (1969).

12. Bleyer, B., W. Diemair, and E. Frank, Bestimmung höherer Alkohol (Fuselöl-Bestimmung), *Zeitschr. Untersuch. Lebensmitt.,* **66,** 389 (1933).

13. Brunton, L. and F. W. Tunnicliffe, Concerning injurious constituents in whiskey and their relation to flavour, *Lancet,* **162,** 1591 (1902).

14. Brusch, C. A., C. M. Cerrato, P. N. Papos, and F. A. Straccia, Clinical and laboratory evaluation of alcoholic beverages, *Amer. J. Proctol.,* **6,** 140 (1955).

15. Carroll, R. B., Gas-liquid chromatography of whiskies by direct injection, *Quart. J. Stud. Alc., Suppl.* 5, in press.

16. Carson, G., *The Social History of Bourbon,* Dodd, Mead, New York, 1963.

17. Chapman, L. F., The experimental induction of hangover, *Quart. J. Stud. Alc., Suppl.* 5, in press.

18. Closs, K. and C. O. Solberg, Methanol poisoning, *J. Am. Med. Assoc.,* **211,** 497 (1970).

19. Damrau, F. and E. Liddy, Hangovers and whiskey congeners: Comparison of whiskey with vodka, *J. Nat. Med. Ass.,* **52,** 262 (1960).

20. Damrau, F. and E. Liddy, The whiskey congeners: Comparison of whiskey with vodka as to toxic effects, *Curr. Therap. Res.,* **2,** 453 (1960).

21. DiLuzio, N. R., Comparative study of the effect of alcoholic beverages on the development of the acute ethanol-induced fatty liver, *Quart. J. Stud. Alc.,* **23,** 557 (1962).

22. DiLuzio, N. R., Comparative evaluation of the acute and chronic administration of alcohol and alcoholic beverages on tissue triglyceride concentrations, *Quart. J. Stud. Alc., Suppl.* 5, in press.

23. Elkins, H. B., *The Chemistry of Industrial Toxicology,* Wiley, New York, 1960.

24. Estable, J. J., J. W. Grezzi, and J. Varela Rodriguez, Toxicidad comparada del alcohol y las distintas bebidas alcohólicas destiladas nacionales sobre peses mantenidos en acuarios, *Arch. Soc. Biol. Montevideo,* **21,** 43 (1954).

25. Estable, J. J. and J. W. Grezzi, Toxicidad comparada del alcohol y las distintas bebidas destiladas A.N.C.A.P. en animales de sangre caliente, *Arch. Soc. Biol. Montevideo,* **21,** 47 (1954).

26. Estable, J. J., J. W. Grezzi, and J. Varela Rodriguez, Acción de la concentración del alcohol y las "impurezas" de las bebidas alcohólicas destiladas, sobre la curva de alcoholemia en el perro, *Arch. Soc. Biol. Montevideo,* **21,** 56 (1954).

27. Fassett, D. W., Esters, in *Toxicology,* D. W. Fassett and D. D. Irish (eds.), chap. 41; vol. II of *Industrial Hygiene and Toxicology,* F. A. Patty (ed.), Wiley—Interscience, New York, 1963.

28. Fassett, D. W., Aldehydes and Acetals, in *Toxicology*, D. W. Fassett and D. D. Irish (eds.), chap. 43; vol. II of *Industrial Hygiene and Toxicology*, F. A. Patty (ed.), Wiley-Interscience, New York, 1963.
29. Forney, R. B. and R. N. Harger, The Alcohols, in *Drill's Pharmacology in Medicine,* J. R. DiPalma (ed.), 3rd ed., p. 216, McGraw-Hill, New York, 1965.
30. Flury, F. and O. Klimmer, Alcohols, Esters, Aldehydes, and Ketones, Ether, Including Plasticizers, in *Toxicology and Hygiene of Industrial Solvents,* K. B. Lehmann and F. Flury (eds.), Williams & Wilkins, Baltimore, 1943.
31. Fühner, H., Die Wirkungsstärke der Narkotika: I. Versuche am isolierten Froschherzen, *Biochem. Zeitschr.,* **120,** 143 (1921).
32. Futcher, T. B., Fusel-oil poisoning with special reference to copper reducing substances eliminated in the urine, *Am. Med.,* **2,** 210 (1901).
33. Greenberg, L. A., The appearance of some congeners of alcoholic beverages and their metabolites in blood, *Quart. J. Stud. Alc., Suppl.* 5, in press.
34. Grezzi, J. W. and J. J. Estable, Influencia de las "impurezas" de las bebidas alcohólicas destiladas en el consumo voluntario de alcohol por la rata blanca, *Arch. Soc. Biol. Montevideo,* **21,** 79 (1954).
35. Gross, E., Other Solvents, in *Toxicology and Hygiene of Industrial Solvents,* K. B. Lehmann and F. Flury (eds.), Williams & Wilkins, Baltimore, 1943.
36. Haag, H. B., J. K. Finnegan, P. S. Larson, and R. B. Smith, Studies on the acute toxicity and irritating properties of the congeners in whisky, *Toxicol. Appl. Pharmacol.,* **1,** 618 (1959).
37. Haas, H., H. Fink, and G. Härtfelder, Das Placeboproblem, *Fortschr. Arzneimittelforsch.,* **1959,** 279–454.
38. Haggard, H. W. and L. A. Greenberg, The effects of alcohol as influenced by blood sugar, *Science,* **85,** 608 (1937).
39. Haggard, H. W., L. A. Greenberg, and L. H. Cohen, The influence of congeners of distilled spirits upon the physiological action of alcohol, *Quart. J. Stud. Alc.,* **4,** 3 (1943).
40. Haggard, H. W., D. P. Miller, and L. A. Greenberg, The amyl alcohols and their ketones: Their metabolic fates and their toxicity, *J. Indust. Hyg. Toxicol.,* **27,** 1 (1945).
41. Hammack, W. J., Solox intoxication, *J. Am. Med. Assoc.,* **165,** 24 (1957).
42. Herstein, K. M. and M. B. Jacobs, *Chemistry and Technology of Wines and Liquors,* 2d ed., Van Nostrand, New York, 1948.
43. Hyams, E., *Dionysus: A Social History of the Wine Vine,* Thames and Hudson, London, 1965.
44. Katkin, E. S. and W. N. Hayes, Differential effects upon reaction time and perceptual motor performance of alcoholic beverages differing in congener content, *Amer. Psychol. Assn.,* Washington, 1967.
45. Katkin, E. S., W. N. Hayes, A. I. Teger, and G. Pruitt, The effects of alcoholic beverages differing in congener content on psychomotor tasks and on level and style of risk taking: Two experiments. *Quart. J. Stud. Alc., Suppl.* 5, in press.
46. Kiessling, K.-H. and L. Pilstrom, Effect of ethanol on rat liver: V. Morphologi-

cal and functional changes after prolonged consumption of various alcoholic beverages, *Quart. J. Stud. Alc.,* **29,** 819 (1968).

47. Macht, D. I., A toxicological study of some alcohols with especial reference to isomers, *J. Pharmacol. & Exper. Therap.,* **16,** 1 (1921).

48. McKennis, H. and H. B. Haag, On the congeners of whisky, *J. Amer. Geriat. Soc.,* **7,** 848 (1959).

49. Mohler, H. and W. Hammerle, Über Kirschwasser: IV. Konstitutionelle und analytische Eigenschaften des Kirschwasserbuketts, *Zeitschr. Untersuch. Lebensmitt.,* **72,** 504 (1936).

50. Murphree, H. B., L. M. Price, and L. A. Greenberg, Effect of congeners of alcoholic beverages on the incidence of nystagmus, *Quart. J. Stud. Alc.,* **27,** 201 (1966).

51. Murphree, H. B., L. A. Greenberg, and R. B. Carroll, Neuropharmacological effects of substances other than ethanol in alcoholic beverages, *Fed. Proc.,* **26,** 1468 (1967).

52. Murphree, H. B. and L. M. Price, Effectos electroencephalográficos de algunas bebidas alcohólicas, *Arch. Biol. Med. Exper. Suppl.,* **3,** 68 (1969).

53. Murphree, H. B., Effects of Alcoholic Beverages Containing Large and Small Amounts of Congeners, in *Biochemical and Clinical Effects of Alcohol Metabolism,* V. M. Sardesai (ed.), pp. 259–265, Charles C. Thomas, Springfield, Ill., 1969.

54. Murphree, H. B., R. E. Schultz, and A. G. Jusko, Electroencephalographic effects of high congener intake by human subjects, *Quart. J. Stud. Alc., Suppl.* 5, in press.

55. Piriz MacColl, C. R. and R. Balcárcel, *Añejamiento de Bebidas Alcohólicas Destiladas: Revision Crítico Bibligrafico,* Administracion Nacional de Combustibles, Alcohol, y Portland, Montevideo, 1954.

56. Quevauviller, A. and M. A. Mazière, Recherche et dosage biologique de l'histamine dans les vins, *Ann. Pharmac. Franc.,* **27,** 411 (1969).

57. Rang, H. P., Unspecific drug action: The effects of a homologous series of primary alcohols, *Brit. J. Pharmacol.,* **15,** 185 (1960).

58. Raynes, A. E. and R. S. Ryback, The effects of alcoholic beverages of low and high congener content on the aggressive response of Betta splendens, *Quart. J. Stud. Alc., Suppl.* 5, in press.

59. Richardson, B. W., Physiological research on alcohols, *Med. Times & Gaz.,* **2,** 703 (1869).

60. Romano, C., L'Attività biologica di alcuni acidi, chetoni ed esteri alifatici, *Arch. Sci. Biol., Napoli,* **39,** 304 (1955).

61. Rowe, V. K., Glycols, in Toxicology, D. W. Fassett and D. D. Irish (eds.), chap. 35; vol. II of *Industrial Hygiene and Toxicology,* F. A. Patty (ed.), Wiley-Interscience, New York, 1963.

62. Ryback, R. S., Effect of ethanol, bourbon and various ethanol levels on Y-maze learning in the goldfish, *Psychopharmacologia,* **14,** 305 (1969).

63. Ryback, R. S., The effects of vodka and bourbon on sleeping time in mice, *Quart. J. Stud. Alc., Suppl.* 5, in press.

64. Shorell, I. D., New views on alcoholic beverages in health and disease: Medical aspects of comparative toxicities based on congeneric content, *Med. Rec.,* **14,** 145 (1938).
65. Snell, C. A., The congener content of alcoholic beverages, *Quart. J. Stud. Alc.,* **19,** 69 (1958).
66. Starr, M. B., H. B. Murphree, and R. E. Schultz, Prolonged cardiovascular effects of alcoholic beverages, *Fed. Proc.,* **24,** 274 (1970).
67. Takala, M., E. Siro, and Y. Toivainen, Intellectual functions and dexterity during hangover: Experiments after intoxication with brandy and with beer, *Quart. J. Stud. Alc.,* **19,** 1 (1958).
68. Taylor, G. W., The effect of narcotics on respiration and luminescence in bacteria with special reference to the relation between the two processes, *J. Cell. Comp. Physiol.,* **4,** 329 (1934).
69. Treon, J. I., Alcohols, in *Toxicology,* D. W. Fassett and D. D. Irish (eds.), vol. II of *Industrial Hygiene and Toxicology,* F. A. Patty (ed.), Wiley-Interscience, New York, 1963.
70. Truitt, E. B., Discussion in *Biochemical and Clinical Aspects of Alcohol Metabolism,* V. M. Sardesai (ed.), Charles C. Thomas, Springfield, Ill., 1969.
71. Vernon, H. M., The changes in the reaction of growing organisms to narcotics, *J. Physiol.,* **47,** 15 (1913).
72. Webb, A. D., R. E. Kepner, and R. M. Ikeda, Composition of a typical grape brandy fusel oil, *Anal. Chem.,* **24,** 1944 (1952).
73. Webb, A. D. and J. L. Ingraham, Fusel oil, *Adv. Appl. Microbiol.,* **5,** 317 (1963).
74. White, R. P. and F. E. Samson, Effects of fatty acid anions on the electroencephalograms of unanesthetized rabbits, *Am. J. Physiol.,* **186,** 271 (1956).
75. Willkie, H. F. and J. A. Prochaska, *Fundamentals of Distillery Practice,* Joseph E. Seagram & Sons, Louisville, 1943.

Chapter IX

TOLERANCE TO, AND DEPENDENCE ON, ETHANOL

HAROLD KALANT and A. EUGENE LEBLANC

DEPARTMENT OF PHARMACOLOGY
UNIVERSITY OF TORONTO

ROBERT J. GIBBINS

ADDICTION RESEARCH FOUNDATION OF ONTARIO
TORONTO, CANADA

A. Introduction

Common experience and clinical observation have both revealed two important phenomena in relation to the use of ethyl alcohol by humans, apart from the immediately recognizable pattern of acute effects. The first, which has been known for centuries, is the tendency for regular drinkers to become more resistant to the intoxicant effect of alcohol, so that they can tolerate larger amounts on repeated exposure. The second, which has been identified much more recently, is the occurrence of clinical pictures of varying degrees of severity, characterized by manifestations of hyperexcitability of the nervous system, on reduction or termination of a period of sustained intoxication. Although these hyperexcitable states have also been known for centuries, controversy continued until less than 20 years ago as to whether they were signs of chronic intoxication or of alcohol withdrawal. In this instance, common experience proved to be superior to many older clinical judgments, because alcoholics have long known that the signs can be abolished by the ingestion of more alcohol and are manifestations of physical dependence on it.

Experimental studies of the factors influencing the development and loss of tolerance and dependence, in relation to ethanol as well as to other neurotropic drugs, have been described sporadically for more than a century. Significant progress could not be made, however, until reliable methods had been developed for the production and measurement of tolerance and dependence in experimental animals, so that the influence of various factors could be studied quantitatively. Some methods have been available for about 30 years, but the most reliable objective ones have been developed only during the past decade.

Finally, experimental analysis of the fundamental biological mechanisms of tolerance and of dependence and their relation to each other must still be considered rudimentary. A number of physiological and biochemical processes in brain and other tissues have been shown to change in a way that coincides roughly, in time and magnitude, with the changes in tolerance and dependence. The exact relationship of these various processes to the integrated function of the nervous system, however, is far from clear. Therefore it is not yet possible to know which of the changes are causally related to the development of tolerance and dependence, which are consequences, and which are concomitant results of the same basic mechanisms.

The purpose of this chapter is to summarize the present knowledge concerning each of these topics in turn and to indicate important questions that have not yet been answered.

B. Tolerance

1. Definition

The term *tolerance,* as used in relation to ethanol or any other drug, has two different connotations. The first is that of spontaneous or "initial tolerance," as expressed by the amount of a drug that the subject must receive on the first exposure to it, to produce a designated degree of effect.

This tolerance, sometimes incorrectly called "innate tolerance," reflects a variety of congenital and environmental factors that contribute to the broad range of differences in tolerance between individuals, sexes, species, age groups, and dietary and other treatment groups. The second connotation is that of an "acquired change in tolerance" within the same individual as a result of repeated exposure to the drug, so that an increased amount of drug is required to produce the same specified degree of effect or less effect is produced by the same dose of drug. There is no evidence that an individual's capacity for increase in tolerance is proportional to his initial tolerance. In this chapter, therefore, initial tolerance is not considered, and *tolerance* is used synonymously with *acquired increase in tolerance*.

This definition of tolerance carries no implications with respect to mechanisms. Possible mechanisms can be divided into two classes, viz., dispositional tolerance and functional tolerance. The first includes those changes in drug absorption, distribution, excretion, and metabolism that might lead to a reduction in the intensity and duration of contact between a given drug and the tissue on which it exerts its characteristic action ("target tissue"). The second includes those changes in the properties and functions of the target tissue that render it less sensitive to the same degree of exposure to the drug. In the case of ethanol the target tissue with which we are primarily, though not necessarily exclusively, concerned is the nervous system. Both types are considered below.

2.   Measurement of Tolerance

A.   PHYSIOLOGICAL TESTS. Since the measurement of tolerance involves measurement of the change in the relation between the dose of ethanol and its effect, any method suitable for measuring the acute effect should theoretically be suitable for measuring the acquisition of tolerance. Various physiological measures, such as the effects of ethanol on the human EEG [44, 143], on critical flicker fusion frequency [142], and on electroshock seizure threshold in rats [2], as well as the minimum dose for death by respiratory failure [78], have been used for this purpose. There is no reason why positional alcohol nystagmus or ethanol effects on peripheral blood flow, secretion of vasopressin or oxytocin, or spinal reflexes (for specific references to these and other acute effects, see Ref. 55) could not be used for the same purpose, although no one seems to have done so.

There are two objections, however, to the use of some of these phenomena for the study of tolerance. The first objection is that some, such as LD_{50}

measurement, involve doses that are much above those used for the development of tolerance. For obvious reasons, one cannot challenge an animal with near-lethal doses of ethanol daily. This may be one reason why very little increase in the minimum lethal dose was found after chronic treatment with smaller doses [78]; another explanation is suggested in Section D.2. The second objection is that some of the measurement procedures require surgical intervention that makes it impossible to study the same animal more than once. Tolerance must then be assessed by comparing the measured effects of ethanol in different groups of animals, before and after chronic exposure to ethanol. Such a process increases both the difficulty of the experiment and the variability of results.

For these reasons, most investigators have preferred to use simple behavioral tests which are affected by ethanol in the same dose range as that used in the chronic treatment to produce the tolerance and which can be applied repeatedly to follow the development of tolerance in the same subject.

B. BEHAVIORAL TESTS. Many different tests have been used to measure the acute effects of ethanol in man and experimental animals. They may be classified roughly as tests of motor performance, sensory acuity, perception and discrimination, complex intellectual function, emotional responses, and subjective mood ratings. It is beyond the scope of this chapter to examine these methods in detail. The only point that is noted here is the difference between those tests with quantal responses and those with continuously variable responses.

Quantal, or "all-or-none," responses are obtained in those tests in which only a single end point is possible. The rota-rod test of motor performance in rats or mice [14], for example, involves placing the animal on a thick rod that rotates about its longitudinal axis at constant speed. The test runs for a set time, and the animal is scored as either staying on the rod for the full time or falling off. To establish a dose-response curve, therefore, it is necessary to have a sufficiently large number of animals at each dose to permit a statistically valid estimate of the proportion at each dose that falls off.

In contrast, a recent modification of the rota-rod test [53] consists of applying a constant acceleration to the motor that rotates the rod, so that each animal eventually reaches a point at which it falls off and this point can be rated on a continuous scale of time or speed of rotation. This kind of measurement permits more flexibility and economy of tests in establishing a dose-response relationship, and most recent workers have preferred such techniques.

Much valuable information, with respect to acute effects of ethanol as well as to tolerance, was obtained by Newman and his colleagues [102–105] by the use of what may be called a quasi-quantitative technique that provided results in the form of apparently continuously variable behavioral scores. The observers became expert at discriminating different degrees of motor impairment in dogs, ranging from slight unsteadiness of gait to complete inability to stand. They ranked these in order of increasing severity, assigned numerical ratings from 1 to 10, and used these numerals as scores to be plotted against alcohol dose or alcohol concentration in the blood. This procedure assumes that each step up the rating scale represents an equal increment of impairment of the motor system, but this was never shown to be true.

Among the more widely used techniques that do use continuous rating scales are the measurement of duration of sleep produced by ethanol [72, 78], measurement of spontaneous motor activity [97, 130], and the inclined-plane test [3, 57]. The most recent method, which is also the most sensitive in terms of its ability to discriminate between the effects at small dose intervals, is the motor-driven-treadmill test [29]. These three procedures have the merit of covering three different dose ranges, with some overlap, so that they are complementary to one another.

3. Identification of Type

As noted in Section B.1, the measurement of tolerance gives little or no clue concerning its cause. To differentiate dispositional tolerance from functional tolerance, it is necessary to relate the effect to the concentration of alcohol in the blood or brain, rather than to the administered dose. Earlier chemical methods of alcohol analysis required samples of a size which could be conveniently and repeatedly obtained from dogs by venupuncture but which could be obtained from rats only by cardiac puncture or decapitation. Enzymatic [8, 126] and gas-chromatographic [73] measurements of ethanol in blood, however, are so sensitive and accurate that they can be performed repeatedly on a single rat during one period of intoxication and during the development of tolerance [74].

4. Dispositional Tolerance

A. ABSORPTION, DISTRIBUTION, AND EXCRETION. The literature on this topic has been reviewed recently [56, 139]. It is abundantly clear that ethanol can be absorbed through any mucosal or serosal surface by simple diffusion and is rapidly distributed throughout all body water in the same way. Absorption from the small intestine is more rapid than from the stomach, so that delay in gastric emptying tends to slow the absorption. In subjects treated chronically, the rate of ethanol absorption from the gastrointestinal tract is at least normal and may even be increased, perhaps because of less delay in gastric emptying [22, 23, 102, 133, and LeBlanc et al., unpublished]. It is one of the most clearly decided matters, that altered absorption does not contribute to ethanol tolerance. In any case, much of the experimental work is done with parenterally administered ethanol.

With the exception of Mapother [86] no one has considered it probable that tolerance might arise through reduced entry of ethanol into the brain and other target tissues. In fact, direct measurements have shown equal concentrations of ethanol in the brain of normal and tolerant animals, after the administration of equal doses [77 and LeBlanc et al., unpublished].

Similarly, increased elimination of ethanol in the urine, breath, and sweat cannot be invoked as an explanation of tolerance. Elimination by these routes is also a process of simple physical diffusion [56, 139] and is therefore a function of the blood ethanol level. Excretion rates in tolerant subjects have been found to be either normal or reduced [106, 115]. Reduction could be explained by an increased rate of metabolism of ethanol, with a corresponding reduction of the total area under alcoholemia-time curve; this possibility is considered below.

B. METABOLISM. A number of excellent reviews on the metabolism of ethanol have appeared in the past few years [79, 83, 122, 137], as well as in Chapter 1 of the present work, to which the reader is referred for detailed information. Our concern here is only with the question of the role that changes in metabolism might play in the production of tolerance.

1. An increase in the rate of ethanol metabolism as a result of prolonged administration has been reported by many investigators; many others have found no change or a decrease (for references, see Ref. 39). The controversy has continued, but recent work [63, 80, 136] tends to confirm the view that the chronic ingestion of ethanol leads to an increase in the rate of its metabolism unless overt liver disease supervenes.

Since the alcohol dehydrogenase activity of the liver cytoplasm has long been considered the major determinant of the rate of ethanol metabolism, it is not surprising that the same disagreement exists about the effect of chronic ethanol treatment on alcohol dehydrogenase activity as on the rate of ethanol metabolism [39, 100, 138]. The explanation of the disagreement may be the same as that noted above. An alternative explanation is suggested by the recent finding [136] that dinitrophenol increases the rate of ethanol metabolism in slices of normal rat liver but does not enhance further the increased rate found in slices from rats made tolerant to ethanol. In the latter the increase in the rate of metabolism may result, at least in part, from an increase in the rate of $NADH_2$ oxidation by liver mitochondria as the final stage of the alcohol dehydrogenase pathway. Our concern at this point, however, is with the extent, rather than with the mechanism, of increase.

The maximum increases reported in all these studies have been about 60 to 100% of the control rate. On this basis the concentration of ethanol in the blood after a given dose in tolerant subjects would be expected to return to zero in one-half to two-thirds of the time required in normal subjects. Other things being equal, the total duration of exposure of the nervous system, and of the period of intoxication, should be shortened accordingly. Because of the rapidity of absorption, however, the typical blood alcohol curve in the fasting subject [56, 139] shows its maximum concentration at 30 to 60 min after the ingestion of a small or moderate dose and up to 120 min or later after a large dose. In the rat, metabolizing ethanol at a normal rate of about 275 mg/kg-hr, a 100% increase would mean a rate of about 0.5 g/kg-hr, so that one-fourth of a 2 g/kg dose could be metabolized by the time the peak level would normally be reached. This should result in a slightly lower and earlier peak level than in the previously untreated animal and could thus contribute to a slight reduction in observed behavioral effects. The larger the dose, the lower would be the proportional reduction in peak height. After intraperitoneal injection of 2 g/kg or less the peak blood alcohol level is reached within minutes, and the maximum behavioral impairment on the treadmill test appears at 10 to 15 min [74]. Under these conditions, increased metabolism would make no appreciable difference to the maximum effect, since even a 100% increase would mean that not more than 0.1 g/kg could be metabolized in this time.

In summary, increased rate of ethanol metabolism could decrease a little the peak effect measured after oral administration of small doses of ethanol but would be a negligible factor in the degree of tolerance found after larger doses or after parenteral administration of ethanol.

2. Possible changes in the pathways of ethanol metabolism are of interest for another reason. It has long been known that, in the absence of ethanol, ethanol-tolerant subjects also show tolerance to barbiturates, volatile anesthetics, and a variety of other drugs with more or less similar effects on performance. Recently it has been proposed that this cross-tolerance may

result from the ability of hepatic microsomal enzyme systems to metabolize both ethanol and the other drugs in question [80, 81, 107, 119] and to be induced by chronic treatment with either ethanol or these other drugs. In support of this view it has been reported that not only pentobarbital and meprobamate [99] but also tolbutamide and various other drugs [64] are metabolized more rapidly after the chronic intake of ethanol.

Several other groups [46, 66, 118] have presented evidence, however, suggesting that the metabolism of ethanol by liver microsomes is an arte-factual result of tissue homogenization and does not occur in vivo. Other reports are consistent with this suggestion, since inhibitors and inducers of drug metabolism were found to have no effect on the rate of ethanol disappearance in vivo [65, 68, 131] and chronic ethanol pretreatment did not affect pentobarbital metabolism in vivo or by liver slices [62]. The apparent contradiction may be explained in part by the fact that the report by Kater et al. [64] concerns human alcoholics, rather than subjects given alcohol experimentally. Devenyi and Wilson [12] found that a substantial proportion of alcoholics were also heavy users of other drugs, some of which may be very effective microsomal inducers. Further the metabolism of tolbutamide involves one step catalyzed by liver alcohol dehydrogenase [91]; if the latter is increased by chronic alcohol administration, it might account for the faster disappearance of tolbutamide.

In summary the bulk of evidence presently available suggests that ethanol is not metabolized to a significant extent by liver microsomal enzyme systems and that mutual induction of this system is not a major factor in cross-tolerance between ethanol and barbiturates and related drugs.

5. Functional Tolerance

A. INTRODUCTION. The term *functional tolerance* is used here in preference to the more conventional "tissue tolerance" in order to avoid the implication of a difference between physiological or biochemical tolerance of the nervous system and so-called psychological or behavioral tolerance. Many writers in this field have made this distinction, but we believe such a mind-body dichotomy to be unwarranted scientifically, for reasons to be given in Section B.5c.

In the preceding sections, tolerance has been understood to develop on prolonged or repeated exposure to ethanol, but no assumption has been made about the length or number of exposures required. Jellinek [49] enunciated most authoritatively the commonly held view that tolerance is built up over years of repeated heavy consumption of alcohol and persists for a long time after the cessation of alcohol intake. Work to be cited below shows that this is wrong and that the time base can be measured in days or weeks. On the other hand the literature contains many reports of tolerance developing during the course of a single exposure to ethanol, with a time base measured in hours. This acute tolerance has generally been considered a separate phenomenon, related in some undefined way to chronic tolerance. Both are reviewed in turn, in an attempt to clarify this relation.

B.   ACUTE TOLERANCE. Mellanby [93] was the first to report that the degree of impairment was greater at a given ethanol concentration in the rising portion of the blood alcohol curve than at the same concentration in the descending part of the curve. This has been confirmed repeatedly, with a wide range of physiological and behavioral measures of alcohol effect [4, 6, 31, 129]. Harger and Forney [38] point out that Mellanby measured ethanol levels in venous blood from the arm. During the rising phase of the alcohol curve, i.e., while absorption and distribution are still proceeding, skin and muscle equilibrate with the blood much less rapidly than the brain does (for references, see Ref. 56), and the venous blood in the limbs has a lower alcohol concentration than arterial blood or brain. They believe, therefore, that the "Mellanby phenomenon" results from this imbalance of alcohol distribution rather than from acute tolerance.

The same objection could also be raised to the observations [5, 15, 60, 84, 103] that a greater degree of functional disturbance is produced at a given blood ethanol concentration when this concentration is reached rapidly than when it is reached slowly. By infusing the same total dose of ethanol intravenously at different rates, Gostomzyk et al. [36] showed that the arteriovenous concentration difference in the limbs was greater, the more rapid the infusion.

This criticism does not apply, however, to certain other experiments. Maynert and Klingman [90] found clear evidence of acute tolerance in dogs, even when alcohol was measured in jugular venous blood, which is rapidly equilibrated with the brain [56]. Eggleton [16] found that secretion of vasopressin was inhibited only while the concentration of ethanol in the blood was rising. When the level was kept high but steady by repeated small doses, the inhibition disappeared. Similarly Mirsky et al. [98] made repeated intravenous injections of ethanol into hepatectomized rabbits, in which metabolism was virtually abolished, so that the blood alcohol level could be kept practically constant for a long time. They found that ear drop and nystagmus gradually disappeared despite the continuing alcohol level. A new injection produced a new plateau, with the return of the signs of intoxication followed by the gradual disappearance again, despite blood alcohol concentrations of up to 400 mg/100 ml. Heidelmann et al. [40] report that the cutaneous vasodilatation produced by ethanol is also seen only during the rising part of the blood alcohol curve.

Loomis and West [82], studying the effect of ethanol on human performance in a simulated driving test, concluded that there was no evidence of a Mellanby phenomenon in relation to the objective measures of performance but that the subjective effects in some cases were perceived to be less intense after 3 to 5 hr at a maintained blood alcohol level. Examination of their data indicates, however, that the blood alcohol level was held relatively stable in 36 out of 40 separate trials, and in 14 of these, such as in their Figure 1, there was some indication of improved performance, practically the same proportion as that reporting subjective improvement. Difficulties arise in the interpretation of human studies of this kind, because it is almost impossible to control the level of motivation. As the authors point out, the measured performance is subject to the influence of sleepiness and loss of interest, which are common aftereffects of alcohol. When the subjects know that errors of performance in a simulated task cannot harm them, it is difficult to be certain how much of the later effect represents the direct action of alcohol.

Subjective ratings are possibly less liable to this influence, and it is interesting that Goldberg [32] presents data suggestive of acute tolerance in relation to them. Intensity of subjective effects at the time of the maximum blood alcohol concentration was plotted against this concentration for each subject in separate experiments involving low and high doses of ethanol. The regression line relating peak concentration to effect was different in the two experiments, less effect being noted at the same blood alcohol level in the high-dose experiment. Since more time was required to reach the maximum level in the high-dose experiment, the findings are consistent with the idea that there was more opportunity for acute tolerance to develop under these conditions.

The most direct proof of acute tolerance, however, is provided by correlation of effects with actual concentration of ethanol in the brain. In unpublished work in our laboratory, rats were trained to perform the treadmill test [29] and were then tested at various times after the injection of various doses of ethanol. Each animal was given a single 2-min test under ethanol and immediately afterward was decapitated and the brain removed for analysis of ethanol concentration. Animals tested during the first 10 min after injection showed significantly worse performance at a given brain alcohol level than those tested at 30 or 60 min. The data are strongly indicative of the rapid development of acute tolerance.

C.   CHRONIC TOLERANCE

Definition. Chronic tolerance can be defined as tolerance developing after more than one dose of ethanol. Since the question of acute tolerance has usually been examined separately, chronic tolerance has been studied by comparing either the maximum effect after each dose of alcohol or the effect at a fixed time after each dose following various periods of alcohol administration.

Speed of production. Different investigators have described the development of tolerance after widely differing periods of alcohol exposure. Newman and Lehman [105], for example, observed it after 7 months of treatment in dogs. Other groups have observed it after 2 to 3 weeks in humans [1, 44, 94, 143], dogs [85], and rats [74, 140]. Still others have found it to develop within a few days [41]; one group [17] reported it after only 1 day but did not present the actual experimental data on which the claim is based.

Despite the range of times noted, it is clear that tolerance develops rapidly. Some of the differences between these results may depend on differences in alcohol dose, in species, and in the test used. These and other factors are considered further in the following sections.

Extent of tolerance. Although the degree of tolerance produced by chronic ethanol treatment has varied in different studies, it is far less than that which can develop toward the opiates. The graphic representation of ethanol tolerance, in terms of dose-effect function, is a parallel shift of the dose-effect curve toward the higher end of the dose scale. The degree of tolerance can be expressed either as the vertical separation of the two regression lines, i.e., the difference in effect at a given dose, or the horizontal separation, i.e., the difference in dose required to produce a given effect. The percentage of change can vary considerably, depending on which method of comparison and what points on the curves are selected (see Figure 1). On theoretical grounds, since we are dealing with a horizontal displacement of the curve, it is more valid to express tolerance in terms of horizontal separation at a fixed reference point on the response axis. The only two studies in which complete dose-response curves have been shown are those of Newman and Lehman [105] and LeBlanc et al. [74]. In both, the increase in dose required for half-maximal effect was about 30 to 50%.

Effect of alcohol dose. No valid conclusion can be drawn from the results above concerning the effect of dose on the rate or magnitude of tolerance development. Since different species have different degrees of tolerance

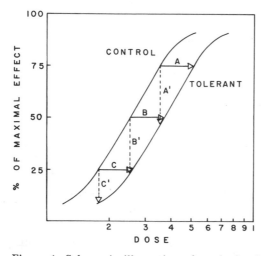

Figure 1. Schematic illustration of methods of expressing the degree of tolerance. If tolerance is expressed as the increase in dose required to produce a given degree of effect, the tolerance as shown by the shift in log [dose]-response curve at A, B, and C is 0.17 log units in each case. However, this corresponds to dose increases of 42, 59, and 83%, respectively. If tolerance is expressed as the decrease in effect produced by a given dose, the tolerance at A^1, B^1 and C^1 is 37, 56, and 66%, respectively. Many apparent differences in the degree of tolerance to ethanol reported by different investigators are probably attributable to the use of a single test dose at an unknown place in the dose-response curve for the function being examined.

to ethanol, with respect to a given criterion of performance, each dose should be expressed in ratio to the threshold dose for the species used. There is not enough information available to permit such an analysis of the data in the literature. Partial results in a single species (unpublished work in this laboratory), however, make it clear that tolerance develops more rapidly with higher doses. Rats trained on the treadmill test developed maximum tolerance within 19 to 22 days on a schedule of increasing daily dosage rising gradually from 3 to 9 g/kg during the whole period [74]. Other rats, performing the same test, developed the same maximum tolerance in 13 to 16 days when given 6 g/kg-day from the outset. It would be desirable, however, to have this question studied more systematically with different dosages and in various species.

Duration and carry-over. On cessation of alcohol treatment, tolerance was found to revert gradually to normal during a period of 2 to 3 weeks

[74]. This seemed to be at variance with the clinical observation that human alcoholics with a pattern of intermittent bout drinking show high tolerance during the bouts, even when these are separated by months of abstinence. The apparent discrepancy can be explained, however, by the following observations on the effects of repeated cycles of alcohol administration.

Groups of rats trained on the treadmill test were submitted to a regimen of daily dosage with ethanol 6 g/kg. Of this amount, 2.2 g/kg was injected intraperitoneally immediately before testing on the treadmill every third day, and the balance of the dose was given by gastric tube on completion of the test. One group was given a single 16-day period of this treatment; other groups got two, three, or four cycles separated by 17-day intervals without ethanol. During the first cycle for each group, tolerance increased progressively to a maximum by the thirteenth to sixteenth day. In the groups getting more than one cycle of treatment the same maximum tolerance was reached by the tenth day in the second cycle, day 4 to 7 in the third cycle, and day 2 to 4 in the fourth cycle. In other words an animal that has once been made tolerant retains or "carries over" to the next exposure an increased ability to reacquire tolerance. In rats this hysteresis was found to persist for as long as 3 months after the end of a cycle of alcohol treatment. In humans this effect could conceivably last even longer. On this basis the apparent retention of tolerance by intermittent drinkers from one drinking bout to another, even when these are separated by rather long intervals, could be explained by enhanced ability to reevoke tolerance rapidly in each bout.

Generalization of tolerance. In most of the work mentioned above, tolerance has been studied in relation to a single behavioral test or physiological measure. A few studies, however, have involved several different measures. Goldberg [31] used a battery of psychomotor, sensory, and physiological measures, but he was comparing alcoholic patients with moderate drinkers and nondrinkers, rather than the same subjects before and after heavy drinking. Isbell et al. [44] and Mendelson [94] and his collaborators did study the same subjects before and after several weeks of heavy drinking, using a wide variety of tests. In both of these studies, however, the subjects were alcoholics or drug addicts who had been abstinent for a few months by virtue of confinement to a hospital or prison. In view of present knowledge concerning carry-over effects the conclusions of these studies may not be completely applicable to all instances of tolerance.

If tolerance represents a fundamental change in the effect of the drug on the organism, rather than a highly specific functional compensation for individual kinds of impairment, one might predict that tolerance should develop simultaneously to all the central effects produced by a specified dose of ethanol. This would be in keeping with common human experience, as well as with observation of the spontaneous behavior pattern of chronically treated laboratory animals. Animal experiments do not seem to bear out this prediction consistently. Hogans et al. [41] report that tolerance developed more rapidly to the overt behavioral impairment produced in monkeys by ethanol than to the effects on the EEG. They used a rather crude assessment of behavioral impairment, however, and did not give quantitative results. Experiments in this laboratory have shown that tolerance acquired by rats on one test does carry over to another. Rats were trained on both the treadmill test and the circular maze [7]. They were then given daily intoxicating doses of ethanol, and the development of tolerance was monitored with the treadmill test only. When tolerance was maximal, they were tested in the circular maze under the influence of ethanol and were found to be tolerant as judged by this test also. The circular-maze test involves different sensory and motor requirements from the treadmill test, as shown by the absence of facilitation of learning of one test by previous learning of the other. The reason for the apparent discrepancy between these findings and those of Hogans et al. [41] may lie in the methods used. There is need for more work in this area, to follow in detail in the same subjects the kinetics of acquisition and loss of tolerance, by several different measures based on different components of behavior or nervous system function.

Tolerance and learning. As noted in Section 5a, many writers have distinguished between physiological tolerance and psychological or "learned" tolerance. Chen [7] reports an experiment that seems to justify this distinction. Three groups of rats were trained during 4 successive days to perform correctly in the circular maze that he designed. One group received an injection of ethanol immediately before each training session. A second group received the same dose of ethanol after each training session. The third group received no ethanol at all. After the 4 days of training, all groups were tested under the influence of ethanol. The first group was much less impaired than the other two groups, which did not differ significantly from each other. Chen's results have been verified in our laboratory, with both the treadmill and the circular-maze tests. Chen interpreted his findings as evidence that the first group had developed psychological tolerance rather than physiological tolerance, on the grounds that any physiological adaptation should have occurred equally in the second group.

The work has been extended in our laboratory, however, by continuing the training schedule for more than 2 months, on the following basis. The three groups were trained to the same criterion of performance on the circular maze without any injections. They were all tested once under ethanol to show that they were comparably sensitive and then were started on the following schedule. One group (ES) received an injection of ethanol immediately before each training session and an injection of saline immediately after. The second group (SE) received saline before training sessions and ethanol after. The third group (SS) received only saline before and after. All groups received a cycle of three training days, followed by a test under ethanol on the fourth; this cycle was repeated without interruption for a total of 16 test days. The difference between ES and SE groups proved to be only a matter of the rate of development of tolerance: after the second cycle the SE group was also significantly more tolerant than the SS. The ES group reached maximal tolerance after 3 cycles, the SE group after 5; the SS group continued unchanged through 11 cycles. Daily intubation with ethanol, 6 g/kg, at the end of each training or test session, was then started; it did not increase further the tolerance of the ES or SE groups, but it rapidly brought the SS group up to the same level of tolerance as the others.

From this work it seems that "learned tolerance" is essentially the same as "physiological tolerance," except that it is acquired somewhat more rapidly. In other experiments we have found it to show the same carry-over effect as described in Section 5c, and to bear the same relationship to physical dependence, to be discussed in Section C. For this reason we prefer to call it "behaviorally augmented tolerance," emphasizing the similarity rather than the minor difference.

C. Dependence

1. Definition

Just as in the case of tolerance, so also has it been traditional to distinguish between "physical" dependence and "psychic" or "psychological" dependence on alcohol and other mood-modifying drugs. The distinction is incorporated into the definition of drug dependence by the Expert Committee of the World Health Organization [145]. As Oswald et al. [108] observe, this mind-body dichotomy will become increasingly untenable as the physiological and biochemical bases of psychological function become better known. For the present, however, the distinction is operational, because there is no experimental evidence, of the kind noted in Section B.5c, to relate the two kinds of dependence.

Dependence is itself an operationally defined term. It is a state of discomfort produced by the withdrawal of a drug from a subject who has been chronically exposed to it, and alleviated by renewed administration of this drug or of another with similar pharmacological actions. The discomfort may consist of a nonspecific dissatisfaction giving rise to a desire, ranging from a mild wish to intense craving, for the perceived effects of the drug; this is called psychological dependence and may persist with varying intensity for a long time after drug withdrawal. The discomfort may also include a more specific set of physiological disturbances of varying intensity and related in a fairly characteristic way to the dosage and pharmacological actions of the drug; this is called physiological dependence and is usually confined to the first few days or weeks after drug withdrawal.

2. Psychological Dependence

Until recently a major difficulty in the study of psychological dependence on ethanol has been the lack of an adequate model in experimental animals. Many investigators have approached the problem with a preconception that the essential role of ethanol in dependent humans is that of reduction of anxiety or internal conflict and have attempted to create "alcoholism" in experimental animals by exposing them to situations involving noxious stimuli or "stress." The classic work of this kind is that of Masserman and Yum [89], who reported that cats consuming ethanol, mixed with milk to mask its aversive taste, showed a reduction in the severity of pathological behavior evoked by a conflict situation in which an attempt to obtain food caused the animal to receive a blast of air in its face. Since then many investigators have used other techniques, such as electric shock, strong noise, or conditioned avoidance of electrical shock, to induce states of stress with the expectation that this would increase the consumption of solutions of ethanol that were available to the animals. Many of these studies are reviewed by Lester [76] and Schuster and Thompson [123]. It is perhaps sufficient for our purposes to summarize Lester's comments: although these studies did indicate that stressed animals increased their intake of alcohol solution, there is no evidence that most of them consumed enough to obtain a significant pharmacological effect, that the increased consumption was correlated in a consistent manner with the timing of exposure to stress, or that the increase persisted in a manner suggestive of psychological dependence.

A clearly different result was obtained when the drinking of ethanol solution was made the instrumental response by which a rat could prevent electric shock [144]. By this method, rats were readily induced to maintain a high daily intake of ethanol, with clear signs of intoxication. This did not prove to be related specifically to shock avoidance, however, because similar results were obtained when alcohol consumption was made the instrumental response for obtaining food [67, 114, 124]. Further the pharmacological effect of the ingested ethanol was not in itself reinforcing, because when the rats could obtain food by drinking either ethanol in saccharine solution or saccharine solution alone, they chose the latter [67].

A different approach, also related to food intake, was devised by Lester [75]. Food-deprived rats, trained to bar-press to obtain small pellets of food at intervals of about 1 to 1.5 min, consume an astonishing quantity of water together with the pellets [21]. Lester found that they would consume a dilute alcohol solution in the same way, to the point of gross intoxication, and would persist in this behavior for many weeks of trials. This has been confirmed by others [20]. An operant response by the rat proved to be unnecessary, however, because "free" presentation of pellets at fixed intervals was just as effective in promoting ethanol ingestion [20, 67]. Further when saccharine solution was available as an alternative, the rats did not drink alcohol [67]. Finally evidence has been presented that any preference for ethanol over water in these conditions is probably a consequence of the caloric value of the ethanol, rather than its intoxicant properties [25]. The same consideration seems to apply also to rats with lesions in the ventromedial hypothalamus [87], of the kind that produces hyperphagia and obesity. These animals became obese but with varying amounts of replacement of calories from solid food by calories from alcohol. Again there was no evidence of intoxication or of any reinforcement of intake by the pharmacological effect of ethanol.

One further approach, without any theoretical rationale, is the repeated administration of minute amounts of ethanol solution by cannula directly into the lateral ventricles of the brain. Myers [101] reports that such treatment caused a lasting increase in the preference for ethanol over water. Again the amounts of ethanol ingested were not large, and there was no evidence that the animals became intoxicated. Others have been unable to find any effect of this treatment on alcohol consumption by monkeys [70] or dogs [53].

This brief survey is meant only to point out the main shortcomings of the various experimental models mentioned above in relation to the concept of psychological dependence in man. Some of the methods have not been shown to lead to the ingestion of intoxicating amounts of alcohol. Those which do, such as the operant techniques or food-contingent drinking, do not depend on the pharmacological effect of alcohol as the reinforcing factor. The only method that does depend on this factor is the intravenous self-administration technique [141] originally developed for studies on opiate dependence (for references and descriptions, see Refs. 11, 132). By this method the animal is first exposed to the effects of the drug by injection through an indwelling venous cannula and is then enabled to self-administer the drug through the same route by pressing a bar that activates an injection pump. The effect of the drug is the sole reinforcer, and the experimenter can study the effects of various environmental and physiological manipulations on the pattern of self-administration by the animal.

So far very scant reference has appeared to the effectiveness of ethanol in this situation [11, 132]. A number of groups are now working with the technique, however, and it is probable that much new information will appear shortly.

3. Physical Dependence

A. SIGNS AND SYMPTOMS OF ALCOHOL WITHDRAWAL. The signs and symptoms of alcohol withdrawal in man are so well known that they require little description here. Excellent descriptions are to be found in the human experimental studies by Isbell et al. [44] and Mendelson and his colleagues [94] and in the reviews of clinical experience by Victor and Adams [135] and Victor [134]. It is sufficient to point out here that the various clinical pictures fall on a continuum of increasing severity from the mildest picture of tremulousness, sleeplessness, and irritability, increasing through hallucinatory states and seizures, to the severest kind, delirium tremens. All of these states are characterized by varying degrees of hyperexcitability and hyperactivity of all parts of the nervous system—central, peripheral somatic, and autonomic. In general the signs and symptoms are the opposite to those characterizing the picture of acute intoxication.

Similar pictures have been produced in several species. Tremor, convulsions, and peculiar behavior suggestive of responses to hallucinatory stimuli have been noted in dogs [19] and monkeys [18]. In mice a similar picture, with gross tremor and convulsions, has been produced [26], and the threshold for electroshock seizures is reduced [92]. In contrast the rat does not seem to develop nearly so severe a picture. Rats made maximally tolerant to ethanol [74] showed, on withdrawal, only hyperirritability on being handled or receiving mild electric shock to the feet [30]. Spontaneous convulsions have not been reported. This apparent species difference has not yet been explained.

B. RELATION TO ALCOHOL LOAD. The schedule of alcohol intake or administration used to produce these pictures has been quite varied. In the human experiments Isbell et al. [44] gave an average total daily dose of roughly 4 to 5.5 g/kg for 7 to 87 days; Mendelson and his collaborators [94] gave approximately the same dosage for about 3 weeks. Essig and Lam [19] gave their dogs roughly the equivalent of 76 g of absolute ethanol daily for 54 days. Since the weights of the dogs are not given, one can offer only a guess that the dosage was about 7 to 8 g/kg-day. No blood alcohol concentrations are given, but the animals were grossly intoxicated throughout the ethanol treatment period. In Freund's study [26] the mice consumed an average of 12 to 13 g/kg-day for 4 to 5 days. Ellis and Pick [18] used 4 to 8 g/kg-day in divided doses and terminated the treatment when fine tremor of the monkeys' fingers appeared before each dose on two consecutive days; this happened in 10 to 18 days. Gibbins et al. [30] used a schedule of incremental dosage rising in 1-g steps from 3 to 7 g/kg over 19 days. In view of the relation, noted in Section B.5, between dosage schedule and the development of tolerance it is a reasonable speculation that the speed and intensity of the development of physical dependence will also be found to depend on the dosage. No one has yet studied the relationship systematically, although McQuarrie and Fingl [92], using a constant dosage of 6 g/kg-day, state that the fall in electroconvulsive threshold on withdrawal was proportional to "the intensity and, to a lesser extent, to the duration" of the alcohol treatment.

C. MEASUREMENT OF DEPENDENCE. This measurement has been almost entirely a matter of visual observation and assessment of the severity of the overt signs by experienced observers. Only a few studies have used objectively quantifiable methods. In animal studies the measurement of electroconvulsive threshold [92] has already been mentioned; Gibbins et al. [30] measured the threshold for the production of a startle reaction by electroshock to the feet. In a clinical study of human alcoholics Sereny and Kalant [125] used a battery of objective tests, including photoelectric measurement of hand tremor and electrical conductance of the skin. More detailed studies of the kinetics and mechanisms of development of dependence will probably require the development of additional quantitative techniques.

D. RELATION TO TOLERANCE. The experimental studies in man [44, 94] showed that during sustained high intake of ethanol the degree of behavioral impairment gradually decreased unless the dose was suddenly increased [94]. At the same time, withdrawal signs began to appear in the intervals between doses, although major signs did not occur in most cases until alcohol intake was curtailed or stopped. Similarly in animal studies [18, 19] signs of withdrawal began to appear in the longer intervals between doses, suggesting that the duration of the effect of each dose was diminishing.

These observations indicated that tolerance and physical dependence were developing in a roughly parallel manner. This relation was demonstrated quantitatively by Gibbins et al. [30]. By measuring the startle thresholds either 30 min after the preceding dose of ethanol, when the blood alcohol concentration was high, or 23 hr after, when the level was negligible, they showed that tolerance and dependence developed in parallel during the same period as that in which tolerance had been found to develop in the treadmill test [74].

D. Mechanisms of Tolerance and Physical Dependence

1. Hypothetical Models

Explanations of tolerance and dependence that have been advanced so far are entirely speculative. Nevertheless they are useful in orienting future investigation. For present purposes we consider first the broad theories relating tolerance and dependence and then specific proposals concerning the possible mechanisms involved.

A. PHYSIOLOGICAL VERSUS PSYCHOLOGICAL TOLERANCE. The first hypothesis must be introduced with a major point of theoretical dispute concerning the distinction between physiological and psychological tolerance, discussed in Section B.5. A major argument in favor of this differentiation has been the demonstration of "state-dependent" learning in relation to ethanol and other drugs [35, 50, 109–112, 121, 128]. Essentially this work shows that an animal that learns to perform a task while under the influence of a drug can subsequently perform the task much better in the drug state than in the drug-free state. The interpretation is that the action of the drug modifies the subject's perception of both internal and external stimuli and that these modified cues constitute the specific constellation or "gestalt" in which the task is learned. Consequently the task is not performed properly until this constellation is produced again by administration of the drug.

The observations have been greatly refined by Kubena and Barry [71], who were able to show that a task learned under the influence of small doses of alcohol could also be performed under equivalent doses of drugs with similar effects (pentobarbital or chlordiazepoxide) but not under drugs with different pharmacological actions. "Learned tolerance" to ethanol [7] can be interpreted as arising from the ability of the subject, which had previously learned a task, such as the treadmill test, in the drug-free state, to relearn it in relation to the new constellation of drug-related stimuli. The tolerance curve would be seen simply as a new learning curve. Cross-tolerance between alcohol and barbiturates would depend on the perceived resemblance of one drug state to the other [71]. Physiological tolerance would be seen as a separate process involving cellular adaptation and relating to basic physiological processes involved in consciousness and survival rather than in performance.

Against this view, however, is the evidence given in Section B.5c, which indicates that the only difference detectable between learned tolerance and physiological tolerance is one of rate. In addition the demonstration that an animal can acquire control of heart rate and other "autonomic" functions by instrumental learning [13, 95, 96] makes it difficult to accept a differentiation between learning and basic neurophysiological processes. We propose, therefore, that drug-dependent learning is simply one specific manifestation of functional tolerance.

In this view the stimulus to the development of tolerance is not the concentration of drug itself, but the degree of functional disturbance that it produces. Obviously the degree of disturbance is related to the functional demand made on the organism. An animal that is forced to perform a task under the effect of ethanol experiences more demand and more impairment of function than one that is left to sleep in its cage while the drug is metabolized. Therefore the stimulus to the development of tolerance and the rate of its development are correspondingly greater. It will be possible to test this hypothesis experimentally by administering the drug under several different conditions of functional demand.

B. ACUTE AND CHRONIC TOLERANCE. A second hypothesis that can be made is that acute tolerance and chronic tolerance involve the same adaptive process in the nervous system and that the effect of repeated doses is to increase the rate, intensity, and duration of the adaptive process. This hypothesis could be tested experimentally by a study of the time course of drug effect after each dose and the magnitude of acute tolerance as these change during the course of repeated administration. Tentative support is provided by the occurrence of rebound fall in electroconvulsive threshold after either a single dose or repeated doses of ethanol [92], as well as by the observations on carry-over in repeated cycles of drug administration (see Section B.5c).

C. RELATIONSHIP BETWEEN TOLERANCE AND PHYSICAL DEPENDENCE. The time relation between tolerance and physical dependence suggests strongly that the two phenomena derive from the same adaptive change in the nervous system. In essence it is postulated that this change results in increased excitability of the nervous system, offsetting the depressant effects of the alcohol and thus producing tolerance. In the absence of alcohol, or a decrease in its concentration, the increased excitability gives rise to withdrawal signs, i.e., physical dependence. There is no way of testing this relationship further until specific cellular mechanisms of tolerance and physical dependence are identified and shown to be either the same or distinct. The fact, however, that withdrawal signs are largely the reverse of the signs of intoxication and that summation of the two would result in the picture of drug tolerance is at least consistent with this hypothesis.

2. Specific Mechanisms

A. PROPOSED MECHANISMS. At the present there is no hypothesis concerning specific mechanisms of tolerance and dependence that can draw on any body of experimental evidence to back it. Goldstein and Goldstein [33, 34] proposed an "enzyme induction" theory based on the idea that ethanol or any other drug producing similar dependence inhibits the synthesis of some substance essential for neuronal function and that the reduction in concentration of this substance leads to de-repression of the enzymes that synthesize it, thus causing tolerance. On withdrawal of the drug, excessive synthesis of the substance would lead to withdrawal overactivity.

Collier [9] proposed a variant of this idea, in which the induced synthetic system is that which produces receptor sites for a neurotransmitter substance. Interference by the drug with either the release or the action of the transmitter would, in this scheme, induce a synthesis of new receptors until the probability of a normal frequency of combination with the reduced concentration of transmitter molecules was restored, i.e., tolerance resulted. On withdrawal of the drug, the increased probability of combination between a normal concentration of transmitter substance and the increased concentration of receptors would lead to overstimulation of the cell bearing the receptors. This suggestion is a refinement of the disuse or "denervation supersensitivity" hypothesis [47, 48], also based on the premise that drugs, such as ethanol, barbiturates, or opiates, block the release of some neurotransmitter substance, leading to oversensitivity of the receptors for this substance. Although this concept originally derived from observations of denervation supersensitivity in structures innervated by peripheral autonomic fibres, Friedman et al. [27] have recently shown that a similar phenomenon can be produced by anticholinergic blockade at cholinergic synapses in the central regulatory mechanism for body temperature.

An alternative hypothesis relating to neurotransmitters [113] is that the drug may prevent the release of neurotransmitter, leading to an increase in its concentration within the nerve ending. When the concentration becomes high enough, a "breakthrough" release would occur, and normal function would be evident even in the presence of drug, i.e., tolerance. On removal of the drug, uninhibited release of the large stock of transmitter would cause overactivity in the postsynaptic cells. An argument against this hypothesis, however, is the fact that ethanol in concentrations that inhibited the release of acetylcholine from brain slices in vitro did not significantly raise the content of bound acetylcholine in the slices [58]. Presumably the level of acetylcholine in the nerve endings provides feedback control of the rate of synthesis.

Although these hypotheses are attractive, they cannot be tested until specific enzymes, substances, or neurotransmitters are proposed as the targets for the initial action of ethanol or the other drugs in question. These can then be examined critically with respect to their relation to tolerance and dependence. If one or more biochemical changes are found to coincide consistently with the development of tolerance, paralleling it in both time and degree, and to disappear progressively with the disappearance of signs of dependence, then these changes may be classed as "biochemical correlates" of tolerance and dependence [120]. It will still remain to be proved by experimental manipulation whether they are causes of tolerance, effects of it, or parallel results of some other more fundamental change.

B. EXPERIMENTAL SUPPORT. Among the cellular mechanisms that might be related in some way to alcohol tolerance the only one that has been studied in enough detail to qualify to some extent as a biochemical correlate is that of active transport of sodium and potassium ions across the cell membrane. Ethanol has been shown to inhibit this process in a variety of tissues [56, 59, and Chapter II of this volume]. Since active transport is essential for the maintenance of a normal resting potential across the cell membrane, inhibition of it would be expected to reduce the ability of the cell to maintain a high frequency of response. In animals made tolerant to ethanol the rate of active transport of cations in brain tissue and the activity of Na,K-dependent adenosine triphosphatase in brain were found to be significantly increased when measured in the absence of ethanol [45]. This change reverted to normal by 2 weeks after withdrawal of ethanol. In the same study, active transport by erythrocytes from hospitalized alcoholic patients was found to be higher than in healthy controls. This is a most promising start, but much work is required to clarify the relation between the biochemical changes and the behavioral phenomena.

As noted above, the release of acetylcholine by rat brain cortex slices in vitro was found to be inhibited by ethanol [58, 61], and an increase in the concentration of acetylcholine-like material in the brain and heart of rats under the influence of a large single dose of ethanol has been reported [42, 43]. These findings are in agreement with a large body of evidence that any drug or condition that decreases neuronal activity also inhibits the release of acetylcholine, but they do not prove a cause-and-effect relation. Smyth and Beck [127] report that the chronic intake of ethanol solutions by rats was accompanied by a fall in the concentration of coenzyme A in the brain and later by decreases in acetylcholine levels and in the activity of the enzyme systems for biosynthesis and degradation of acetyl-choline in brain. These findings are cited in support of the hypothesis [88] that ingestion of ethanol leads to impairment of acetylcholine synthesis and release and that this in turn leads to a compensatory fall in cholinester-ase activity and induction of acetylcholine receptors as proposed by Collier [9].

This hypothesis would not explain, however, the finding that brain slices from ethanol-tolerant animals released acetylcholine in vitro at the same rate as control slices in the absence of ethanol but no longer showed inhibi-tion by ethanol [58]. All the findings would be consistent with the view that ethanol, by decreasing neuronal activity by some other mechanism, decreases both the energy metabolism and the acetylcholine release in the brain. With chronically reduced neuronal activity the relevant enzymatic pathways might decrease as a result of feedback control until the develop-ment of tolerance caused a return to normal activity (Smyth and Beck did not show that their animals had actually become tolerant to ethanol). Gage [28] presents evidence that the direct action of ethanol on motor nerve endings in isolated nerve-muscle preparations leads to an increase in the amount of acetylcholine released per impulse. If this is so, it is even more probable that the effects on brain noted above are secondary to a reduction of total activity by some other means.

Acute effects of ethanol on several other possible neurotransmitters have been studied in some detail. Catecholamines, 5-hydroxytryptamine, and gamma-aminobutyric acid have received almost equal attention, and the results of the numerous investigations do not yet yield a very clear picture (see Chapters II and III). We have not seen any studies in relation to chronic ethanol administration that could provide a plausible hypothesis for a role of these substances in the development of tolerance and de-pendence. A recent suggestion [10], discussed more fully in Chapter III of this book, is that acetaldehyde, derived from the oxidation of ethanol, competitively blocks the oxidation of the aldehyde derivative of dopamine. This derivative can condense with another molecule of dopamine to form tetrahydropapaveroline (THP), which can in turn be converted to the morphine precursor, normorphine. It is suggested that this may be the substance to which tolerance and dependence actually develop. Raskin and Sokoloff [116] showed the presence, in rat brain, of a minute amount of alcohol dehydrogenase activity and have recently reported [117] that this activity increases by about 50% after 2 weeks of ingestion of 15% ethanol solution. Conceivably an increased local generation of acetaldehyde in the brain could increase the probability of the THP pathway being followed.

This hypothesis is ingenious and should be readily testable. If it is correct, nalorphine or another opiate antagonist should precipitate a withdrawal reaction in animals made tolerant to ethanol. It seems rather unlikely, however, because there is cross-tolerance between ethanol and barbiturates [24], but the latter are metabolized by a different enzyme system that does not yield acetaldehyde or an equivalent intermediate. Further the characteristic "writhing" pattern seen in rats during morphine withdrawal is not a feature of alcohol withdrawal reactions in this species. Finally it is worth noting that this hypothesis does not offer an explanation of the mechanisms of tolerance and dependence; it merely shifts the onus for initiating these processes from ethanol to a different substance.

One final hypothesis that deserves mention is that relating alcohol withdrawal reactions to sleep disturbances. Ethanol, in a dose of 1 g/kg given during the evening, has been found to decrease the fraction of the first few hours of sleep that is spent in the phase of rapid eye movements (REM sleep) associated with dream activity [37]. Yules et al. [146] and Knowles et al. [69], using the same dose of ethanol, observed that the reduction in REM sleep during the first half of the night was offset by an increase during the second half. When a dose nearly twice as large was used [69], however, the amount of REM sleep remained low throughout the night. It was suggested that prolonged suppression of REM sleep might result in anxiety and irritability, which the alcoholic attempted to treat by ingestion of more alcohol and which might contribute to the symptoms of the withdrawal reaction. A puzzling aspect, however, is that similar suppression of REM sleep is apparently caused by amphetamines [108], which give rise to a very different kind of clinical picture on drug withdrawal. In addition Johnson et al. [51] studied the pattern of REM and non-REM sleep in alcoholics at the end of a drinking bout and during withdrawal and observed that the change in clinical state correlated with a composite index of "goodness of sleep" rather than with the amount of REM sleep.

They concluded that the sleep pattern was a reflection rather than a cause of the clinical state. This area must still be regarded as one for extensive investigation rather than as the basis of a strong plausible hypothesis.

E.   Relation to Alcoholism

It is obviously quite beyond the scope of this chapter to deal in depth with the implications of experimental studies of tolerance and dependence for the clinical problems of human alcoholism. It may be appropriate to refer, however, to two specific questions that are of very great interest.

1.   Etiology of Alcoholism

The etiology of alcoholism is now generally accepted to involve a complex of psychological, social and, physiological factors related to the individual and his total environment apart from the pharmacological actions of ethanol itself. The development of tolerance, however, causes an increase in the amount and frequency of alcohol consumption required to reach either the limit of socially accepted behavior or the desired level of perceived effect. With increasing tolerance there is also increasing probability of physical dependence, as noted in earlier sections. At some point in the drinking history the symptoms arising from the development of physical dependence can become an important contributing etiological factor to the extent that drinking may become a response to the threat of a withdrawal reaction rather than to the original causal factors. Russell [120] proposes a scheme relating both the original causes and the acquired tissue changes to the development and maintenance of alcoholism, as well as to the precipitation of relapses some time after withdrawal.

2.   Treatment of Withdrawal Reactions

The treatment of alcohol withdrawal reactions has involved a wide range of drugs with varying degrees of effectiveness and hazard [134]. The most effective drugs, however, have been those which most nearly resemble ethanol in their pharmacological effects [54] and show cross-tolerance to it. The treatment is therefore a form of substitution therapy, in which the objective becomes successful withdrawal of the substitute drug in place of the withdrawal of ethanol. If the problem is couched in these terms, the risk of transfer of dependence becomes more obvious, and the role of the substitutes is seen as a palliative one of very limited duration. The possibility of preventing the development of tolerance and dependence or of rapidly reversing them by biochemical intervention must remain a more distant objective that may become attainable when their mechanisms are better understood.

ACKNOWLEDGMENT

The authors are indebted to Mr. E. Polacsek, Director of the Archive Section of the Addiction Research Foundation, for aid in the bibliographic search and location of the necessary reference material.

REFERENCES

1. Adams, A. E. and H. Hubach, Hirnelektrische Korrelate der Wirkungen zentraldämpfender chemischer Substanzen im normalen EEG des Erwachsenen, *Deut. Z. Nervenheilk.,* **181,** 71 (1960).
2. Allan, F. D. and C. A. Swinyard, Evaluation of tissue tolerance to ethyl alcohol by alterations in electroshock seizure threshold in rats, *Anat. Rec.,* **103,** 419 (1949).
3. Arvola, A., L. Sammalisto, and H. Wallgren, A test for level of alcohol intoxication in the rat, *Quart. J. Studies Alc.,* **19,** 563 (1958).
4. Aschan, G., M. Bergstedt, L. Goldberg, and L. Laurell, Positional nystagmus in man during and after alcohol intoxication, *Quart. J. Studies Alc.,* **17,** 381 (1956).
5. Caspers, H., Die Beeinflussung der corticalen Krampferregbarkeit durch das aufsteigende Reticulärsystems des Hirnstammes: II. Narkosewirkung, *Z. Ges. Exp. Med.,* **129,** 582 (1958).
6. Caspers, H. and G. Abele, Hirnelektrische Untersuchungen zur Frage der quantitative Beziehungen zwischen Blutalkoholgehalt und Alkoholeffekt, *Deut. Z. Ges. Gerichtl. Med.,* **45,** 492 (1956).
7. Chen, C.-S., A study of the alcohol-tolerance effect and an introduction of a new behavioral technique, *Psychopharmacologia,* **12,** 433 (1968).
8. Ciotti, M. M. and N. O. Kaplan, DPN Determination by Alcohol Dehydrogenase (ADH), in *Methods in Enzymology,* S. P. Colowick and N. O. Kaplan (eds.), vol. 3, p. 891, Academic, New York, 1957.
9. Collier, H. O. J., A general theory of the genesis of drug dependence by induction of receptors, *Nature,* **205,** 181 (1965).
10. Davis, V. E. and M. J. Walsh, Alcohol, amines, and alkaloids: A possible biochemical basis for alcohol addiction, *Science,* **167,** 1005 (1970).
11. Deneau, G. A., Psychogenic Dependence in Monkeys, in *Scientific Basis of Drug Dependence,* H. Steinberg (ed.), p. 199, Churchill, London, 1969.

12. Devenyi, P. and M. Wilson, Abuse of barbiturates in an alcoholic population, *Canad. Med. Assoc. J.,* **104,** 219 (1971).
13. DiCara, L. V. and N. E. Miller, Instrumental learning of systolic blood pressure responses by curarized rats: dissociation of cardiac and vascular changes, *Psychosom. Med.,* **30,** 489 (1968).
14. Dunham, N. W. and T. S. Miya, A note on a simple apparatus for detecting neurological deficit in rats and mice, *J. Am. Pharm. Assoc.,* **46,** 208 (1957).
15. Eggleton, M. G., The effect of alcohol on the central nervous system, *Brit. J. Psychol.,* **32,** 52 (1941).
16. Eggleton, M. G., The diuretic action of alcohol in man, *J. Physiol.,* **101,** 172 (1942).
17. Eickholt, T. H., L. J. Schillaci, and S. A. Searcy, Possible ethanol-induced tolerance in rats, *J. Pharm. Sci.,* **56,** 275 (1967).
18. Ellis, F. W. and J. R. Pick, Experimentally induced ethanol dependence in Rhesus monkeys, *J. Pharmacol. Exp. Therap.,* **175,** 88 (1970).
19. Essig, C. F. and R. C. Lam, Convulsions and hallucinatory behavior following alcohol withdrawal in the dog, *Arch. Neurol.,* **18,** 626 (1968).
20. Everett, P. B. and R. A. King, Schedule-induced alcohol ingestion, *Psychonom. Sci.,* **18,** 278 (1970).
21. Falk, J. L., Production of polydipsia in normal rats by an intermittent food schedule, *Science,* **133,** 195 (1961).
22. Fleming, R. and E. Stotz, Experimental studies in alcoholism: I. Alcohol content of the blood and cerebrospinal fluid following oral administration in chronic alcoholism and the psychoses, *Arch. Neurol. Psychiat.,* **33,** 492 (1935).
23. Fleming, R. and E. Stotz, Experimental studies in alcoholism: II. The alcohol content of the blood and cerebrospinal fluid following intravenous administration of alcohol in chronic alcoholism and the psychoses, *Arch. Neurol. Psychiat.,* **35,** 117 (1936).
24. Fraser, H. F., A. Wikler, H. Isbell, and N. K. Johnson, Partial equivalence of chronic alcohol and barbiturate intoxications, *Quart. J. Studies Alc.,* **18,** 541 (1957).
25. Freed, E. X. and D. Lester, Schedule-induced consumption of ethanol: calories or chemotherapy? *Physiol. Behav.,* **5,** 555 (1970).
26. Freund, G., Alcohol withdrawal syndrome in mice, *Arch. Neurol.,* **21,** 315 (1969).
27. Friedman, M. J., J. H. Jaffe and S. K. Sharpless, Central nervous system supersensitivity to pilocarpine after withdrawal of chronically administered scopolamine, *J. Pharmacol. Exp. Therap.,* **167,** 45 (1969).
28. Gage, P. W., The effect of methyl, ethyl and *n*-propyl alcohol on neuromuscular transmission in the rat, *J. Pharmacol. Exp. Therap.,* **150,** 236 (1965).
29. Gibbins, R. J., H. Kalant, and A. E. LeBlanc, A technique for accurate measurement of moderate degrees of alcohol intoxication in small animals, *J. Pharmacol. Exp. Therap.,* **159,** 236 (1968).
30. Gibbins, R. J., H. Kalant, A. E. LeBlanc, and J. W. Clark, The effects of

chronic administration of ethanol on startle thresholds in rats, *Psychopharmacologia*, **19**, 95 (1971).

31. Goldberg, L., Quantitative studies on alcohol tolerance in man. The influence of ethyl alcohol on sensory, motor and psychological functions referred to blood alcohol in normal and habituated individuals, *Acta Physiol. Scand., Suppl. 16*, 5 (1943).

32. Goldberg, L., Behavioral and physiological effects of alcohol on man, *Psychosom. Med.*, **28**, 570 (1966).

33. Goldstein, A. and D. B. Goldstein, Enzyme Expansion Theory of Drug Tolerance and Physical Dependence, in *The Addictive States*, A. Wikler (ed.), chap. 19, *Res. Publ. Ass. Nerv. Ment. Dis.*, **46**, Williams and Wilkins, Baltimore, 1968.

34. Goldstein, D. B. and A. Goldstein, Possible role of enzyme inhibition and repression in drug tolerance and dependence, *Biochem. Pharmacol.*, **8**, 48 (1961).

35. Goodwin, D. W., B. Powell, D. Bremer, H. Hoine, and J. Stern, Alcohol and recall: State-dependent effects in man, *Science*, **163**, 1358 (1969).

36. Gostomzyk, J. G., B. Dilger, and K. Dilger, Untersuchungen über die arteriovenose Differenz der Alkoholkonzentration im Blut und ihre Beziehung zum Alkoholgehalt des Gehirns, *Z. Klin. Chem.*, **7**, 162 (1969).

37. Gresham, S. C., W. B. Webb, and R. L. Williams, Alcohol and caffeine: Effect on inferred visual dreaming, *Science*, **140**, 1226 (1963).

38. Harger, R. N. and R. B. Forney, The Aliphatic Alcohols, in *Progress in Chemical Toxicology*, A. Stolman (ed.), vol. 1, p. 90, Academic, New York, 1963.

39. Hawkins, R. D., H. Kalant, and J. M. Khanna, Effects of chronic intake of ethanol on rate of ethanol metabolism, *Can. J. Physiol. Pharmacol.*, **44**, 241 (1966).

40. Heidelmann, G., H. Petzold, and B. Taschen, Untersuchung über die Nikotin- und Alkoholwirkung auf die akrale Arteriolenfunktion, *Deut. Arch. Klin. Med.*, **199**, 431 (1952); abstract in *Quart. J. Studies Alc.*, **14**, 642 (1953).

41. Hogans, A. F., O. M. Moreno, and D. A. Brodie, Effects of ethyl alcohol on EEG and avoidance behavior of chronic electrode monkeys, *Am. J. Physiol.*, **201**, 434 (1961).

42. Hosein, E. A. and T. Y. Koh, The influence of deep narcosis on the content of substances with acetylcholine-like activity in the heart of the rat, *Rev. Canad. Biol.*, **25**, 25 (1966).

43. Hosein, E. A. and T. Y. Koh, Acetylcholine-like activity of acetyl-L-carnityl CoA in subcellular particles of narcotized brain homogenates, *Arch. Biochem. Biophys.*, **114**, 94 (1966).

44. Isbell, H., H. F. Fraser, A. Wikler, R. E. Belleville, and A. J. Eisenman, An experimental study on the etiology of "rum fits" and delirium tremens, *Quart. J. Studies Alc.*, **16**, 1 (1955).

45. Israel, Y., H. Kalant, A. E. LeBlanc, J. C. Bernstein, and I. Salazar, Changes

in cation transport and (Na + K)-activated adenosine-triphosphatase produced by chronic administration of ethanol, *J. Pharmacol. Exp. Therap.*, **174**, 330 (1970).

46. Isselbacher, K. J. and E. A. Carter, Ethanol oxidation by liver microsomes: Evidence against a separate and distinct enzyme system, *Biochem. Biophys. Res. Comm.*, **39**, 530 (1970).

47. Jaffe, J. H. and S. K. Sharpless, The rapid development of physical dependence on barbiturates, *J. Pharmacol. Exp. Therap.*, **150**, 140 (1965).

48. Jaffe, J. H. and S. K. Sharpless, Pharmacological Denervation Supersensitivity in the Central Nervous System: A Theory of Physical Dependence, in *The Addictive States*, A. Wikler (ed.), chap. 17, *Res. Publ. Ass. Nerv. Ment. Dis.*, **46**, Williams & Wilkins, Baltimore, 1968.

49. Jellinek, E. M., *The Disease Concept of Alcoholism*, Hillhouse, New Haven, Conn., 1960.

50. John, E. R., State-Dependent Learning, in *Mechanisms of Memory*, chap. 5, Academic, New York, 1967.

51. Johnson, L. C., J. A. Burdick, and J. Smith, Sleep during alcohol intake and withdrawal in the chronic alcoholic, *Arch. Gen. Psychiat.*, **22**, 406 (1970).

52. Jones, B. E., C. F. Essig, and W. Creager, Intraventricular infusion of ethanol in dogs: Effect on voluntary alcohol intake, *Quart. J. Studies Alc.*, **31**, 288 (1970).

53. Jones, B. J. and D. J. Roberts, The quantitative measurement of motor in-co-ordination in naive mice using an accelerating rotarod, *J. Pharm. Pharmacol.*, **20**, 302 (1968).

54. Kaim, S. C., C. J. Klett, and B. Rothfeld, Treatment of the acute alcohol withdrawal state: A comparison of four drugs, *Am. J. Psychiat.*, **125**, 1640 (1969).

55. Kalant, H., Effects of Ethanol on the Nervous System, in *International Encyclopedia of Pharmacology and Therapeutics, Section 20, Alcohols and Derivatives*, J. Trémolières (ed.), vol. 1, chap. 8, Pergamon, Oxford, 1970.

56. Kalant, H., Absorption, Distribution and Elimination of Alcohols. Effect on Biological Membranes, in *The Biology of Alcoholism*, B. Kissin and M. M. Begleiter (eds.), vol. 1, *Physiology and Biochemistry*, Chap. 1, Plenum, New York, 1971.

57. Kalant, H. and C. Czaja, The effect of repeated alcoholic intoxication on adrenal ascorbic acid and cholesterol in the rat, *Canad. J. Biochem. Physiol.*, **40**, 975 (1962).

58. Kalant, H. and W. Grose, Effects of ethanol and pentobarbital on release of acetylcholine from cerebral cortex slices, *J. Pharmacol. Exp. Therap.*, **158**, 386 (1967).

59. Kalant, H. and Y. Israel, Effects of Ethanol on Active Transport of Cations, in *Biochemical Factors in Alcoholism*, R. P. Maickel (ed.), p. 25, Pergamon, Oxford, 1967.

60. Kalant, H., R. D. Hawkins, and C. Czaja, Effect of acute alcohol intoxication on steroid output of rat adrenals in vitro, *Am. J. Physiol.*, **204**, 849 (1963).

61. Kalant, H., Y. Israel, and M. A. Mahon, The effect of ethanol on acetylcholine synthesis, release, and degradation in brain, *Canad. J. Physiol. Pharmacol.*, **45**, 172 (1967).

62. Kalant, H., J. M. Khanna, and J. Marshman, Effect of chronic intake of ethanol on pentobarbital metabolism, *J. Pharmacol. Exp. Therap.*, **175**, 318 (1970).

63. Kater, R. M. H., N. Carulli, and F. L. Iber, Differences in the rate of ethanol metabolism in recently drinking alcoholic and nondrinking subjects, *Am. J. Clin. Nutr.*, **22**, 1608 (1969).

64. Kater, R. M. H., P. Zeive, F. Tobon, G. Roggin, and F. L. Iber, Accelerated metabolism of drugs in alcoholics, *Gastroenterology*, **56**, 412 (1969).

65. Khanna, J. M. and H. Kalant, Effects of inhibitors and inducers of drug metabolism on *in vivo* ethanol metabolism, *Biochem. Pharmacol.*, **19**, 2033 (1970).

66. Khanna, J. M., H. Kalant, and G. Lin, Metabolism of ethanol by rat liver microsomal enzymes, *Biochem. Pharmacol.*, **19**, 2493 (1970).

67. Keehn, J. D., "Voluntary" consumption of alcohol by rats, *Quart. J. Studies Alc.*, **30**, 320 (1969).

68. Klaassen, C. D., Ethanol metabolism in rats after microsomal metabolizing enzyme induction, *Proc. Soc. Exp. Biol. Med.*, **132**, 1099 (1969).

69. Knowles, J. B., S. G. Laverty, and H. A. Kuechler, Effects of alcohol on REM sleep, *Quart. J. Studies Alc.*, **29**, 342 (1968).

70. Koz, G. and J. H. Mendelson, Effects of Intraventricular Ethanol Infusion on Free Choice Alcohol Consumption by Monkeys, in *Biochemical Factors in Alcoholism*, R. P. Maickel (ed.), p. 17, Pergamon, Oxford, 1967.

71. Kubena, R. K. and H. Barry, III, Generalization by rats of alcohol and atropine stimulus characteristics to other drugs, *Psychopharmacologia*, **15**, 196 (1969).

72. LeBlanc, A. E., *Methodological Studies on the Measurement of Ethanol Intoxication and Acquired Tolerance in Rats*, M.Sc. thesis, University of Toronto, 1968.

73. LeBlanc, A. E., Micro-determination of alcohol in blood by gas liquid chromatography, *Canad. J. Physiol. Pharmacol*, **46**, 665 (1968).

74. LeBlanc, A. E., H. Kalant, and R. J. Gibbins, Acquisition and loss of tolerance to ethanol by the rat, *J. Pharmacol. Exp. Therap.*, **168**, 244 (1969).

75. Lester, D., Self-maintenance of intoxication in the rat, *Quart. J. Studies Alc.*, **22**, 223 (1961).

76. Lester, D., Self-selection of alcohol by animals, human variation, and the etiology of alcoholism, *Quart. J. Studies Alc.*, **27**, 395 (1966).

77. Lévy, J., Contribution à l'étude de l'accoutumance expérimentale aux poisons: II. Alcoolisme expérimentale: Fixation d'alcool sur les tissus de l'organisme accoutumé a cette substance, *Bull. Soc. Chim. Biol.*, **17**, 27 (1935).

78. Lévy, J., Contribution à l'étude de l'accoutumance expérimentale aux poisons: III. Alcoolisme expérimentale: L'accoutumance à l'alcool peut'elle

être considérée comme une conséquence de l'hyposensibilité cellulaire? *Bull. Soc. Chim. Biol.,* **17,** 47 (1935).

79. Lieber, C. S., Metabolic derangement induced by ethanol, *Ann. Rev. Med.,* **18,** 35 (1967).

80. Lieber, C. S. and L. M. De Carli, Ethanol oxidation by hepatic microsomes: adaptive increase after ethanol feeding, *Science,* **162,** 917 (1968).

81. Lieber, C. S. and L. De Carli, Hepatic microsomal ethanol-oxidizing system. *In vitro* characteristics and adaptive properties *in vivo, J. Biol. Chem.,* **245,** 2505 (1970).

82. Loomis, T. A. and T. C. West, The influence of alcohol on automobile driving ability, *Quart. J. Studies Alc.,* **19,** 30 (1958).

83. Lundquist, F., Enzymatic Pathways of Ethanol Metabolism, in *International Encyclopedia of Pharmacology and Therapeutics, Section 20, Alcohols and Derivatives,* J. Trémolières (ed.), vol. 1, Chap. 4, Pergamon, Oxford, 1970.

84. MacLeod, L. D., The controlled administration of alcohol to experimental animals, *Brit. J. Addict.,* **45,** 112 (1948).

85. Malméjac, J. and P. Plane, Étude expérimentale sur l'influence nerveuse général de faibles doses d'alcool, *Bull. Acad. Nat. Méd.,* **140,** 38 (1956).

86. Mapother, E., Aetiology of alcoholism, *Proc. Roy. Soc. Med.,* **21,** 1346 (1928).

87. Marfaing-Jallat, P., C. Larue, and J. Le Magnen, Alcohol intake in hypothalamic hyperphagic rats, *Physiol. Behav.,* **5,** 345 (1970).

88. Martin, G. J., A concept of the etiology of alcoholism, *Exp. Med. Surg.,* **23,** 315 (1965).

89. Masserman, J. H. and K. S. Yum, An analysis of the influence of alcohol on experimental neurosis in cats, *Psychosom. Med.,* **8,** 36 (1946).

90. Maynert, E. W. and G. I. Klingman, Acute tolerance to intravenous anesthetics in dogs, *J. Pharmacol. Exp. Therap.,* **128,** 192 (1960).

91. McDaniel, H. G., H. Podgainy, and R. Bressler, The metabolism of tolbutamide in rat liver, *J. Pharmacol. Exp. Therap.,* **167,** 91 (1969).

92. McQuarrie, D. G. and E. Fingl, Effects of single doses and chronic administration of ethanol on experimental seizures in mice, *J. Pharmacol. Exp. Therap.,* **124,** 264 (1958).

93. Mellanby, E., Alcohol: Its absorption into and disappearance from the blood under different conditions, *Special Report Series,* no. 31, Medical Research Committee, London, 1919.

94. Mendelson, J. H. (ed.), Experimentally induced chronic intoxication and withdrawal in alcoholics, *Quart. J. Studies Alc.,* suppl. 2 (1964).

95. Miller, N. E. and L. V. Di Cara, Instrumental learning of heart-rate changes in curarized rats: Shaping, and specificity to discriminative stimulus, *J. Comp. Physiol. Psychol.,* **63,** 2 (1967).

96. Miller, N. E. and L. V. Di Cara, Instrumental learning of urine formation by rats; changes in renal blood flow, *Am. J. Physiol.,* **215,** 677 (1968).

97. Milner, G., Modified confinement motor activity test for use in mice, *J. Pharm. Sci.,* **57,** 1900 (1968).

98. Mirsky, I. A., P. Piker, M. Rosenbaum, and H. Lederer, "Adaptation" of the central nervous system to varying concentrations of alcohol in the blood, *Quart. J. Studies Alc.*, **2**, 35 (1941).

99. Misra, P. S., A. Lefevre, E. Rubin, and C. S. Lieber, Effect of ethanol ingestion on ethanol, meprobamate, and pentobarbital metabolism, *Gastroenterology*, **58**, 308 (1970).

100. Mistilis, S. P. and A. Birchall, Induction of alcohol dehydrogenase in the rat, *Nature*, **223**, 199 (1969).

101. Myers, R. D., Alcohol consumption in rats: effects of intracranial injections of ethanol, *Science*, **142**, 240 (1963).

102. Newman, H. W., *Acute Alcoholic Intoxication,* Stanford University Press, Stanford, 1941.

103. Newman, H. W. and M. Abramson, Relation of alcohol concentration to intoxication, *Proc. Soc. Exp. Biol. Med.*, **48**, 509 (1941).

104. Newman, H. and J. Card, Duration of acquired tolerance to ethyl alcohol, *J. Pharmacol. Exp. Therap.*, **59**, 249 (1937).

105. Newman, H. W. and P. J. Lehman, Nature of acquired tolerance to alcohol, *J. Pharmacol. Exp. Therap.*, **62**, 301 (1938).

106. Newman, H. W., R. H. L. Wilson, and E. J. Newman, Direct determination of maximal daily metabolism of alcohol, *Science,* **116**, 328 (1952).

107. Orme-Johnson, W. H. and D. M. Ziegler, Alcohol mixed function oxidase activity of mammalian liver microsomes, *Biochem. Biophys. Res. Comm.*, **21**, 78 (1965).

108. Oswald, I., J. I. Evans, and S. A. Lewis, Addictive Drugs Cause Suppression of Paradoxical Sleep with Withdrawal Rebound, in *Scientific Basis of Drug Dependence,* H. Steinberg (ed.), p. 243, Churchill, London, 1969.

109. Overton, D. A., State-dependent or "dissociated" learning produced with pentobarbital, *J. Comp. Physiol. Psychol.*, **57**, 3 (1964).

110. Overton, D. A., State-dependent learning produced by depressant and atropine-like drugs, *Psychopharmacologia,* **10**, 6 (1966).

111. Overton, D. A., Differential responding in a three choice maze controlled by three drug states, *Psychopharmacologia,* **11**, 376 (1967).

112. Overton, D. A., Dissociated Learning in Drug States (State Dependent Learning), in *Psychopharmacology: A Review of Progress 1957–1967,* D. Efron (ed.), p. 918, Public Health Service Publ. No. 1836, USPHS, Washington, 1968.

113. Paton, W. D. M., A Pharmacological Approach to Drug Dependence and Drug Tolerance, in *Scientific Basis of Drug Dependence,* H. Steinberg (ed.), p. 31, Churchill, London, 1969.

114. Persensky, J. J., R. J. Senter, and R. B. Jones, Induced alcohol consumption through positive reinforcement, *Psychonom. Sci.*, **11**, 109 (1968).

115. Pringsheim, J., Chemische Untersuchungen über das Wesen der Alkoholtoleranz, *Biochem. Z.*, **12**, 143 (1908).

116. Raskin, N. H. and L. Sokoloff, Brain alcohol dehydrogenase, *Science,* **162**, 131 (1968).

117. Raskin, N. H. and L. Sokoloff, Adaptation of alcohol dehydrogenase activity in brain to chronic ethanol ingestion, *Neurology*, **20**, 391 (1970).
118. Roach, M. K., W. N. Reese, and P. J. Creaven, Ethanol oxidation in the microsomal fraction of rat liver, *Biochem. Biophys. Res. Comm.*, **36**, 596 (1969).
119. Rubin, E., F. Hutterer, and C. S. Lieber, Ethanol increases hepatic smooth endoplasmic reticulum and drug-metabolizing enzymes, *Science*, **159**, 1469 (1968).
120. Russell, R. W., Behavioral Effects of Psychoactive Drugs, in *Experimental Approaches to the Study of Drug Dependence*, H. Kalant and R. D. Hawkins (eds.), p. 1, University of Toronto Press, Toronto, 1969.
121. Ryback, R. S., State-dependent or "dissociated" learning with alcohol in the goldfish, *Quart. J. Studies Alc.*, **30**, 598 (1969).
122. Sardesai, V. M. (ed.), *Biochemical and Clinical Aspects of Alcohol Metabolism*, Charles C Thomas, Springfield, Ill., 1969.
123. Schuster, C. R. and T. Thompson, Self-administration of and behavioral dependence on drugs, *Ann. Rev. Pharmacol.*, **9**, 483 (1969).
124. Senter, R. J., F. W. Smith, and S. Lewin, Ethanol ingestion as an operant response, *Psychonom. Sci.*, **8**, 291 (1967).
125. Sereny, G. and H. Kalant, Comparative clinical evaluation of chlordiazepoxide (Librium) and promazine in treatment of alcohol withdrawal syndrome, *Brit. Med. J.*, **I**, 92 (1965).
126. Smith, M. E. and H. W. Newman, Rate of ethanol metabolism in fed and fasting animals, *J. Biol. Chem.*, **234**, 1544 (1959).
127. Smyth, R. D. and H. Beck, The effect of time and concentration of ethanol administration on brain acetylcholine metabolism, *Arch. Int. Pharmacodyn.*, **182**, 295 (1969).
128. Stewart, J., Differential responses based on the physiological consequences of pharmacological agents, *Psychopharmacologia*, **3**, 132 (1962).
129. Story, J. L., E. Eidelberg, and J. D. French, Electrographic changes induced in cats by ethanol intoxication, *Arch. Neurol.*, **5**, 565 (1961).
130. Svensson, T. H. and G. Thieme, An investigation of a new instrument to measure motor activity of small animals, *Psychopharmacologia*, **14**, 157 (1969).
131. Tephly, T. R., F. Tinelli, and W. D. Watkins, Alcohol metabolism: role of microsomal oxidation in vivo, *Science*, **166**, 627 (1969).
132. Thompson, T. and R. Pickens, Drug Self-Administration and Conditioning, in *Scientific Basis of Drug Dependence*, H. Steinberg (ed.), p. 177, Churchill, London, 1969.
133. Troshina, A. E., On the mechanism of habituation of the organism to alcohol [Russian], *Sborn. Trud. Ryazansk. Med. Instit.*, **4**, 1 (1957); Abstract in *Quart. J. Studies Alc.*, **20**, 783 (1959).
134. Victor, M., The Treatment of Alcoholism, in *International Encyclopedia of Pharmacology and Therapeutics, Section 20, Alcohols and Derivatives*, J. Trémolières (ed.), vol. 2, p. 413, Pergamon, Oxford, 1970.

135. Victor, M. and R. D. Adams, The effect of alcohol on the nervous system, *Res. Publ. Ass. Nerv. Ment. Dis.,* **32,** 526 (1953).

136. Videla, L. and Y. Israel, Factors that modify the metabolism of ethanol in rat liver and adaptive changes produced by its chronic administration, *Biochem. J.,* **118,** 275 (1970).

137. Von Wartburg, J. P., Metabolism of Alcohol in Alcoholics and Normals and Mechanisms of Action of Alcohol Dehydrogenase, in *Biology of Alcoholism,* vol. 1, *Biochemistry,* B. Kissin and H. Begleiter (eds.), Chap. 2, Plenum, New York, 1971.

138. Von Wartburg, J.-P. and J. Papenberg, Biochemical and Enzymatic Changes Induced by Chronic Ethanol Intake, in *International Encyclopedia of Pharmacology and Therapeutics, Section 20, Alcohols and Derivatives,* J. Trémolières (ed.), vol. 2, Chap. 12, Pergamon, Oxford, 1970.

139. Wallgren, H., Absorption, Diffusion, Distribution and Elimination of Ethanol: Effect on Biological Membranes, in *International Encyclopedia of Pharmacology and Therapeutics, Section 20, Alcohols and Derivatives,* J. Trémolières (ed.), vol. 1, Chap. 7, Pergamon, Oxford, 1970.

140. Wallgren, H. and R. Lindbohm, Adaptation to ethanol in rats with special reference to brain tissue respiration, *Biochem. Pharmacol.,* **8,** 423 (1961).

141. Weeks, J. R., Experimental morphine addiction: Method for automatic intravenous injections in unrestrained rats, *Science,* **138,** 143 (1962).

142. Weiss, A. D., M. Victor, J. H. Mendelson, and J. La Dou, Experimentally induced chronic intoxication and withdrawal in alcoholics: Part 6. Critical flicker fusion studies, *Quart. J. Studies Alc.,* Suppl. 2, 96 (1964).

143. Wikler, A., T. F. Pescor, H. F. Fraser, and H. Isbell, Electroencephalographic changes associated with chronic alcohol intoxication and the alcohol abstinence syndrome, *Am. J. Psychiat.,* **113,** 106 (1956).

144. Williams, D. R. and P. Teitelbaum, Control of drinking behavior by means of an operant conditioning technique, *Science,* **124,** 1294 (1956).

145. World Health Organization Expert Committee on Drug Dependence, 14th Annual Report, *W.H.O. Tech. Rep. Series,* No. 312 (1965).

146. Yules, R. B., D. X. Freedman, and K. A. Chandler, The effect of ethyl alcohol on man's electroencephalographic sleep cycle, *Electroenceph. Clin. Neurophysiol.,* **20,** 109 (1966).

Chapter X

EXPERIMENTALLY[1] INDUCED INTOXICATION IN ALCOHOLICS: A COMPARISON BETWEEN PROGRAMMED AND SPONTANEOUS DRINKING[1]

NANCY K. MELLO AND JACK H. MENDELSON

NATIONAL CENTER FOR THE PREVENTION AND CONTROL OF ALCOHOLISM
NATIONAL INSTITUTE OF MENTAL HEALTH
CHEVY CHASE, MARYLAND

A. Introduction

One of the many unanswered questions concerning the behavioral and biological effects of alcohol on alcoholics is the extent to which correlates of drinking are a consequence of the pharmacological properties of alcohol per se or of the pattern in which it is consumed. This question has both theoretical and pragmatic implications. If ingestion of 1 quart of alcohol within a 24-hr period induced predictable and comparable effects, irrespective of the pattern of ingestion, then the many behavioral efforts to simulate real-life drinking patterns would be unnecessary [24, 30, 32], and the application of traditional programmed dosage research paradigms to studies of alcoholism would be justified. If the pattern of administration of equivalent doses of alcohol does significantly alter behavioral and biological concomitants of drinking, however, then a reexamination of the potential significance of the usual research strategies used in psychopharmacology for the study of alcoholism is indicated.

Our studies of the effects of alcohol on biochemical and physiological variables in the alcohol addict have used two basic paradigms of alcohol administration: (a) a programmed administration regimen in which alcohol is administered in divided doses once every 4 hr [27, 34, 36] and (b) some variant of free-choice administration in which the subject is allowed to determine the periodicity and volume of his own alcohol intake, constrained only by the total volume potentially available during the defined drinking period [24, 30, 32]. One obvious advantage of the programmed mode of administration is that precise control of the amount and time of administration makes it possible to construct time–dose-response curves relevant to the variables in question. The free-choice mode of administration does not yield dose-response relationships according to predetermined temporal intervals but does have the advantage of more closely simulating real-life drinking behavior.

In this study we compared the effects of programmed and free-choice alcohol administration in the same subjects during identical periods of time. Observations are reported on behavioral and biological changes during and following each drinking sequence of 20 days and compared with predrinking measures. We were primarily concerned with examining how pattern of drinking affected (a) physiological and behavioral effects of alcohol, (b) withdrawal signs and symptoms, (c) sleep behavior, and (d) catecholamine excretion (38).

Although there is anecdotal evidence that the pattern of drinking determines the severity and expression of withdrawal symptoms, there have been no previous attempts to examine this question with each subject as his own control.

The effects of alcohol on sleep patterns in alcoholics have received relatively little experimental study [10, 12] despite the accumulating evidence on the interrelation of sleep disturbances and behavioral disorders [6, 13].

Consequently during the free-choice alcohol administration paradigm, 24-hr observations of sleep behavior were made.

Although there is abundant evidence that alcohol ingestion may affect catecholamine excretion in experimental animals and man, all data obtained to date have been in studies of acute administrations of alcohol [1, 2, 8, 17, 39, 44]. Moreover no dose-response relationships have been established between blood ethanol levels and excretion of catecholamines and their metabolites. The large volume of catecholamine data obtained and the special relevance of these findings, however, require that this material be presented in a separate publication [38].

B.   Methods

1.   Subjects

Eight male volunteers, selected from the alcoholic patient population at the Saint Elizabeths Hospital, were subjects for this experiment. These men either had been committed to the hospital for treatment following public-drunkenness-related offenses or were voluntary patients. No subject was under any legal constraint during the course of this study. Each subject had abstained from alcohol for at least 7 days prior to admission to the Alcohol Research Ward of NIMH National Center for Prevention and Control of Alcoholism at Saint Elizabeths Hospital.

These subjects ranged in age from 37 to 45 and had a history of alcoholism of 12 to 27 years' duration. A summary description of each subject's reported socioeconomic history, drinking history and usual drinking pattern is presented in Table I. No subject had completed high school, and all had been sporadically employed at a variety of semiskilled and nonskilled jobs. Only two subjects (RG and TC) had a relatively stable home situation. All subjects were spree drinkers, and six out of the eight reported that cessation of drinking often resulted in withdrawal signs and symptoms that ranged from mild tremulousness to overt delirium tremens.

Before their participation in these experiments each subject was given a complete physical examination and mental-status assessment. All volunteers selected were in good health and none had a history of neurological disease; seizure disorder; hepatic, renal, pulmonary, cardiac, or gastrointestinal disease; nutritional or metabolic disorder. All subjects received a bromsulphalein clearance test (BSP) before and after the experimental drinking period. No subject showed any evidence of hepatic disease as measured by this test. No subject had a history of drug addiction, and

TABLE I   Subject's Reported Socioeconomic History, Drinking History, and Usual Drinking Pattern

Sub-ject	Age	Drinking history			Usual drinking pattern			Socioeconomic history						WAIS I.Q.[a]
		Years of alco-holism	Withdrawal	Frequency	Type and amount	With whom	Where	Education	Employment	Marital status	Family history alcoholism	Religion	Commit-ment	
ED	45	26	Tremulous, hallucinosis, tactile hallucinosis	Daily	Beer, Wine, ½-whisky	On job In group	Outside	9th grade	Gardener, truck driver & mover	Divorced	Father heavy drinker	Catholic	Voluntary	Not tested
JS	42	26	Tremulous, hallucinosis	Daily	Whisky & wine	Group	Outside	10th grade	None SEH[b] patient	Single	Uncle(s)	Catholic	Court	Not tested
AW	41	16	Tremulous, hallucinosis	Daily	1 pt. whisky	Group	Outside	9th grade	None SEH[b] patient	Separated	None	Protestant	Court	Not tested
DC	37	12	Tremulous, hallucinosis	Daily	Wine & whisky	On job, In group	Outside	10th grade	Painter	Divorced	Father heavy drinker	Catholic	Voluntary	100
TC	43	26	Delirium tremens	Daily & spree	Wine	Group	Outside	5th grade	Waiter	Married	Father heavy drinker	Protestant	Court	89
JL	41	17	Tremulous, hallucinosis, blackouts	Sprees	Whisky & beer	Alone	Home	6th grade	Bartender	Divorced	Wive(s)	Protestant	Voluntary	103
RG	46	27	NO	Daily-evenings	1 pt. whisky	Wife	Home	8th grade	Cook	Married	NO	Protestant	Voluntary	100
EH	37	20	NO	Sprees	Wine	Group	Outside	11th grade	Laborer	Divorced	Brother heavy drinker	Protestant	Court	Not tested

[a] Wechsler Adult Intelligence Scale.
[b] Saint Elizabeths Hospital.

no subject was using any form of medication at the time of this study. Two of the subjects, JL and ED, had had a subtotal gastrectomy approximately 10 years prior to their participation in this study. A more complete description of the screening assessment procedures used for subject selection is available in a previous report [27].

Throughout the experiment the medical status of the patients was monitored daily by a resident physician. Caloric intake was recorded, and subjects were encouraged to eat all their meals. Subjects were given multiple-vitamin capsules daily. Subjects attended group-therapy sessions with a resident staff psychiatrist during all phases of the study.

After completion of the study each subject was offered an opportunity to remain at the Saint Elizabeths Hospital on a halfway-house basis. Psychotherapy was available from the resident staff psychiatrist during this period. The social service department and the rehabilitation unit arranged for job placement or vocational training.

2. Ward Facilities

Subjects were studied in groups of four. Each subject had a private bedroom and access to a dayroom that contained a variety of recreational facilities, e.g., television, games, shuffleboard. No other patients were present on the research ward. The subjects were restricted to the research ward for the duration of this study and were not allowed to have visitors or telephone calls. An alcohol dispenser was located on the wall of the dayroom, and subjects were allowed to drink only in the dayroom.

3. Experimental Procedures

The over-all sequence of the experiments for each group of four men was as follows:

A. PROGRAMMED ALCOHOL ADMINISTRATION. On admission, the men were observed for a base-line period of 5 days, followed by a programmed alcohol-administration phase that lasted for 20 days. During this 20-day period, subjects were given beverage alcohol (bourbon) in divided doses every 4 hr around the clock at 6, 10, and 2 A.M. and P.M. Alcohol dosage was gradually increased, and during the first 3 days the six daily doses were as follows: 0.5, 1.0, and 1.5 ml/kg of 43% alcohol. This dosage resulted in the following approximate daily totals: 8, 16, and 24 oz. Subjects were maintained for 14 days on the maximum daily dosage of 2.0 ml/kg unless gastritis or other intercurrent illness necessitated lowering the dosage. This maximum dose resulted in daily totals ranging between 26 and 32 oz. During the final 3 days of the drinking period the alcohol dosage was gradually reduced in 0.5 ml/kg decrements to 1.5, 1.0, and 0.5 ml/kg on consecutive days. A period of 10 nonalcohol recovery days then intervened before the free-choice drinking paradigm. Maximum expression of withdrawal symptoms usually occurs within 72 hr after the cessation of drinking [43].

B.   FREE-CHOICE ALCOHOL SELECTION. During the free-choice drinking period each subject was given 33 tokens each day that he could spend at any time during the 20-day alcohol phase. Each token purchased 1 oz of alcohol that was directly dispensed from an apparatus located on the wall of the dayroom. A possible alcohol intake of 33 oz/day was selected to approximate the programmed dosage maximum of the heaviest subject and to ensure that the observation of spontaneous free-choice drinking patterns would not be limited by artificial constraints on the amount of alcohol available. To purchase alcohol, subjects inserted tokens into an automated alcohol dispenser. There were no constraints as to how much alcohol a subject could buy at any one time. After 20 days of free-choice drinking, alcohol was no longer available to the subjects, and they remained on the research ward for a minimum of 10 days.

4.   Experimental Assessments

Throughout the course of the experiment the following assessments were made:

A.   BLOOD ALCOHOL LEVELS. Before, during, and after each drinking period, blood alcohol levels were determined three times daily at 8 A.M., 4 P.M., and 12 midnight with an instrument designed to measure the concentration of ethanol in the breath (Breathalyzer, Stephenson Corp., Red Bank, N.J.). Blood alcohol levels were measured during the nonalcohol periods to ensure that subjects were not obtaining alcohol from any outside source. In order to assess the accuracy of these blood alcohol measurements, breath alcohol values were compared with serum alcohol determinations carried out by an enzymatic method [3]. The breath sample values showed no greater variance than plus or minus 10 mg/100 ml from the blood alcohol levels as determined by enzymatic techniques.

B.   SLEEP BEHAVIOR. Twenty-four-hour phenomenological observations of sleep behavior were made on all subjects during the free-choice drinking period. These observations were subjective ratings by the nursing staff. They indicated whether a subject had been awake or asleep for most of the preceding hour, once each hour.

c. WITHDRAWAL SIGNS AND SYMPTOMS. A neurological and mental-status examination was completed daily on each subject by the attendant physician.

C. Results

In the presentation and subsequent discussion of data obtained in this study a number of terms relating to the phenomena of tolerance are used that are best described at the outset. Tolerance can be defined as follows: After repeated administration, a given dose of alcohol tends to produce a decreasing effect, or an increasing dose must be used to produce effects formerly obtained with a lower dose. The mechanisms underlying tolerance are unknown, but two general factors have been suggested: (a) metabolic tolerance, which would reflect an enhanced rate of the metabolic degradation of ethanol, and (b) tissue tolerance, which would reflect an increased degree of cellular adaptation to ethanol in the central nervous system (CNS) and other organs.

Tolerance is usually defined behaviorally by the severity of intoxication and the ability to perform accurately on a specified task. Degree of metabolic tolerance may be determined by serial measurements of blood alcohol levels in subjects during the course of drinking.

1. Drinking Patterns

The amount of bourbon consumed each day and the average daily blood alcohol level attained for each subject during the programmed (dotted line) and free-choice (solid line) alcohol drinking period are presented in Figures 1a, b, and c. A comparison of the amount of alcohol available during the programmed and free-choice drinking period and the number of days that each subject exceeded the intended maximum intake are presented in Table II. The following general findings were obtained for all subjects:

a. All subjects drank more alcohol during the free-choice than during the programmed alcohol-administration phase for at least 33% of the time available. Although more alcohol was available during the free-choice period, these data are surprising, since five of the subjects could not sustain ingestion of the programmed maximum dose of alcohol (2 ml/kg) because of gastritis and vomiting (ED, JS, DC, TC, and EH). Consequently the programmed alcohol dosage was reduced to a level that each subject could tolerate comfortably. During the free-choice drinking period, however, these five subjects drank more than their previously intolerable programmed maximum dosage for 9, 6, 10, 15, and 6 days respectively.

All subjects except AW showed considerable day-to-day fluctuation in alcohol intake during the free-choice drinking period. There was no striking concordance in periodicity of volume changes within either group. All subjects except JS also exceeded the intended free-choice daily maximum for some period of time (cf. Table II).

b. During the free-choice drinking period, all subjects maintained blood alcohol levels that were two to three times as high as those measured during

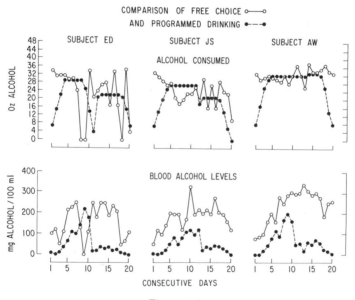

Figure 1A

Figure 1, *a, b, c.* A comparison of alcohol intake and blood alcohol levels during the free-choice and programmed alcohol administration periods are presented for individual subjects. Each drinking period lasted for 20 days. Ounces of alcohol consumed in each 24-hr period during free-choice (open circles) and programmed (closed circles) drinking is displayed in the top row of each figure. Daily mean blood alcohol levels (mg/100 ml) obtained every 8 hrs during free-choice (open circles) and programmed (closed circles) drinking are shown in the bottom row of each figure.

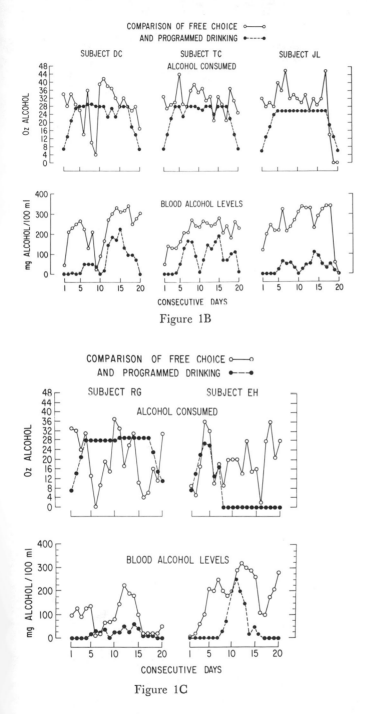

Figure 1B

Figure 1C

Figure 1. (Continued)

TABLE II Comparison Between Alcohol Available and Consumption During Free Choice and Programmed Alcohol Administration

Subject	ED	JS	AW	DC	TC	JL	RG	EH
Daily maximum programmed administration	29 oz	27 oz	32 oz	28 oz	28 oz	26 oz	28 oz	26 oz
Daily increase available during free choice administration	4 oz	6 oz	1 oz	5 oz	5 oz	7 oz	5 oz	7 oz
Number of days free choice alcohol intake exceeded programmed daily allotment (2 ml/kg)	9	6	7	10	15	16	7	6
Number of days free choice alcohol intake exceeded free choice daily allotment (33 oz.)	4	zero	7	7	6	6	1	2
Programmed drinking: 20 days Blood alcohol levels (mg/100 ml) ($\bar{X} \pm$ S.D.)	47.69 ±60.23	48.25 ±40.96	61.24 ±52.80	77.39 ±79.21	90.45 ±59.81	41.34 ±38.44	15.97 ±21.44	30.08[a] ±67.92
Programmed drinking: 14 days constant dosage Blood alcohol levels (mg/100 ml) ($\bar{X} \pm$ S.D.)	67.16 ±63.74	63.76 ±37.70	81.47 ±49.32	97.45 ±81.12	110.00 ±48.95	55.10 ±35.52	21.43 ±22.68	45.79 ±80.12
Free choice drinking: Blood alcohol levels (mg/100 ml) ($\bar{X} \pm$ S.D.)	159.90 ±94.23	175.32 ±81.50	226.60 ±113.16	222.46 ±101.07	205.57 ±68.80	241.15 ±109.93	85.08 ±80.46	184.92 ±106.98

[a] Based on 9 days of drinking.

the programmed drinking period. It is important to note that in those instances in which the daily volume consumed during the free-choice period was comparable with that consumed during the programmed drinking period, e.g., AW, JS and TC, significantly higher blood alcohol levels were observed.

During the free-choice drinking period, subjects tended to consume more alcohol during a concentrated period of time even when daily totals were comparable. Consequently subjects attained higher peak blood alcohol levels because of the difference in their pattern of drinking. The contribution of a possible coincidental correspondence of peak alcohol intake and breath-alyzer measures is attenuated somewhat by the fact that daily average values are presented.

The research-ward staff's subjective assessments of inebriation during the two drinking periods were concordant with the blood alcohol level differences.

2.   Tolerance

An indication of metabolic tolerance to alcohol can be inferred from low blood alcohol levels during a period of heavy drinking. Examination of blood alcohol levels during the programmed drinking phase reveals the following patterns:

1. Some subjects maintained consistently low blood alcohol levels throughout the course of the study. Subject RG is of particular interest, since, on admission, he estimated his usual daily alcohol intake at 1 pint of whiskey after work and denied experiencing withdrawal signs and symptoms. He was able, however, to sustain a daily intake of 28 oz of alcohol in divided doses for the entire 20-day drinking period. Despite his relatively high alcohol consumption he maintained consistently low blood alcohol levels, rarely exceeding 50 mg/100 ml. A comparable pattern was shown by JL. Three subjects (ED, JS, and AW) appeared to develop increasing metabolic tolerance throughout the course of. the programmed drinking period. During the final 7 days of maximal alcohol dosage each of these subjects showed a disproportionately low blood alcohol level despite sustained high alcohol intake.

2. Frequently fluctuations in blood alcohol levels were unrelated to changes in the volume of alcohol ingested. It seems that these volume-independent variations in blood alcohol levels are related both to the degree of metabolic tolerance developed by the subject and to the subject's food intake or gastrointestinal symptoms. Previously we have observed that gas-

trointestinal symptoms were accompanied by marked elevations in blood alcohol levels during a period of invariant programmed drinking [33]. In the present study, subject DC's blood alcohol levels were lowest at the beginning of the programmed drinking period when his alcohol intake was highest and then increased dramatically after day 11. On day 11, DC was disturbed by an incident on the ward and told the staff that he was going to stop eating in order to get more effect from his alcohol. Reduction of food intake did result in a threefold increase in his blood alcohol level, and he appeared more inebriated than at any time during the first 10 days of drinking.

3. Blood alcohol level was rarely an adequate predictor of behavior. No objective measures of behavioral tolerance were made during these studies. Clinical observations of the subjects, however, showed the expected correlation between inferred metabolic tolerance and degree of inebriation only during the programmed-drinking period. All subjects appeared more inebriated during the free-choice drinking period, even when the amount of alcohol ingested approximated that taken during the programmed drinking period. Some subjects showed marked signs of disordered behavior with relatively low blood alcohol levels during both phases of the study. It seemed, however, that when subjects were allowed to determine their own pattern of alcohol ingestion, they tended to drink larger quantities of alcohol at a time than was possible during programmed administration. Consequently they achieved higher blood alcohol levels and appeared more inebriated to staff observers during the free-choice drinking period.

3. Withdrawal Signs and Symptoms

A summary of the kind and duration of withdrawal signs and symptoms of each subject following the programmed and the free-choice drinking period is shown in Figure 2.

All subjects showed withdrawal signs and symptoms on cessation of drinking. After free-choice drinking, all subjects showed more varied and persistent withdrawal symptoms than after programmed drinking. The relative importance of several interacting variables affecting withdrawal symptoms is difficult to specify. One factor that seemed to contribute to the observed differences is the greater volume of alcohol consumed during the free-choice drinking period. Both the number and duration of withdrawal signs and symptoms were greatest in those subjects (AW, JS) who maintained the most consistent high alcohol intake during the free-choice period (cf. Figure

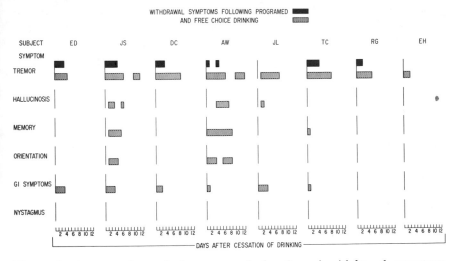

Figure 2. A comparison of the type and duration of withdrawal symptoms observed following cessation of drinking in the programmed and free-choice alcohol administration paradigms are shown for individual subjects.

1). According to clinical observations, AW and JS exhibited the most severe behavioral disruption during the withdrawal period.

Another factor that is often thought to enhance withdrawal signs is abrupt, as opposed to gradual, termination of drinking. Abrupt cessation of drinking cannot account for the observed increases in withdrawal signs and symptoms, since three subjects (JS, ED, and JL) tapered drinking at the end of the free-choice phase and all subjects gradually reduced their alcohol intake at the end of the programmed drinking period. The behavioral act of increasing or decreasing volume of alcohol consumed, however, was not the sole determinant of blood alcohol levels. Although subject DC progressively decreased his alcohol intake at the end of the free-choice phase, his blood alcohol levels remained high (between 275 and 325 mg/100 ml). On the other hand, subject RG increased his alcohol intake during the last 5 days of the free-choice drinking phase, but his blood alcohol levels remained quite low (less than 150 mg/100 ml). Consequently it seems that insofar as withdrawal symptoms are related to the absolute level of blood alcohol levels and the rate of fall in blood alcohol levels, an alcoholic cannot effectively manipulate either variable by his drinking behavior alone.

When considered as independent factors, neither volume ingested nor blood alcohol levels reliably predict the severity and duration of withdrawal signs and symptoms. Rather the crucial factor may be the rate of fall in blood alcohol levels considered in the context of the magnitude and variance of blood alcohol levels through time. This notion is consistent with the observation that many subjects exhibited partial withdrawal signs during the drinking period when blood alcohol levels were falling. Partial withdrawal symptoms were characterized by the appearance of tremulousness, sweating, tachycardia, and anxiety and agitation that abated when subjects ingested more alcohol. Partial withdrawal phenomena did occur when blood alcohol levels remained above 100 mg/100 ml. Therefore a relative decrease rather than an absolute blood alcohol level also seems to be a significant determinant of partial withdrawal signs within a drinking spree.

4. Sleep Patterns

Twenty-four-hour analysis of sleep patterns before, during, and after the free-choice drinking period are presented in Figure 3. The distribution of consecutive hours of sleep for each subject during each period are presented. These data show the percentage of total hours of sleep that is accounted for by the number of consecutive hours of sleep during each successive experimental period. During the predrinking base-line period, all subjects except JS showed an essentially bimodal distribution with a clear primary peak between 4 and 8 hr. The primary peak represents a night's sleep, and the lower secondary peak at 2 to 4 hr represents a nap. The predrinking distribution constitutes the "normal" sleep pattern for each subject and is the basis for subsequent comparisons of his sleep patterns.

On initiation of drinking, the distribution of consecutive hours of sleep changed for all subjects. For three of the subjects (AW, TC, JS) most of the total sleeping time was distributed into shorter blocks of time relative to the predrinking base line. This is shown most dramatically for subject AW as a shift in the primary peak from 6 to 3 hr. This peak shift can be described as an alcohol-induced fragmentation of sleep, since subjects tended to sleep in shorter blocks of time. The remainder of the subjects showed an over-all flattening of the distribution of consecutive hours of sleep. Two subjects (DC and JL) slept in blocks of 1 hr and 10 hr with approximately equal frequency, and their sleeping pattern could not be described as fragmented but rather periodic alcohol-induced somnolence. The other three subjects (ED, EH, and RG) showed a predominantly fragmented sleep pattern insofar as more than half of their total sleep

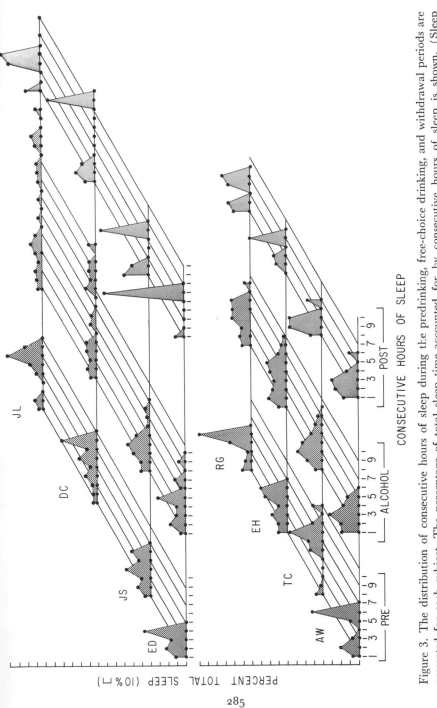

Figure 3. The distribution of consecutive hours of sleep during the predrinking, free-choice drinking, and withdrawal periods are presented for each subject. The percentage of total sleep time accounted for by consecutive hours of sleep is shown. (Sleep distributions were calculated by summing the total hours of sleep during an experimental period and determining what percentage of the total sleep time was accounted for by discrete episodes of sleep lasting one hour, two hours, and so on.)

285

time was spent in blocks of time shorter than their normal sleep pattern. These subjects differed from AW and TC, however, in that some percentage of their sleeping time was also spent in consecutive hours of sleep longer than observed in their normal sleeping pattern. Mean sleep duration during the base-line and drinking periods and daily total hours of sleep during withdrawal are presented for each subject in Table III. No subject slept significantly less during the drinking period than during the base-line period. Two subjects (AW and TC) slept for slightly less time, and six subjects slept slightly longer on the average during the drinking phase. These data indicate that the observed fragmentation of sleep, expressed as a shift in the distribution of consecutive hours of sleep, cannot be accounted for by a relative decrease in total sleep time.

There was no consistent relation between fluctuation in volume of alcohol consumed and hours of sleep. Analysis of peak consumption and direction of change in total sleep time as compared with the immediately preceding day showed a decrease in total hours of sleep 61% of the time. Discrete low-consumption days were accompanied by increases and decreases in hours of sleep with equal frequency.

It is important to distinguish between insomnia, or lack of sleep, and fragmentation, or multiple episodes of sleep. Since many subjects slept as much or more during drinking (cf. Table III), it is the sporadic quality of sleeping rather than sleeplessness that seems to characterize an alcoholic's sleep pattern during inebriation.

This distinction is particularly important in analyzing sleep patterns during alcohol withdrawal. Most clinical descriptions of the effects of alcohol

TABLE III   Sleep Duration, Hours per Day

Subject	Base line		Drinking		Withdrawal, sequential days				
	$\bar{X}$	Range	$\bar{X}$	Range	1	2	3	4	5
Ed	6.8	6–8	8.1	2–17	6	6	8	7	12
AW	9.4	6–13	8.1	5–12	8	14	10	6	6
DC	6.8	5–8	10.8	1–17	5	13	1	6	5
RG	7.6	5–9	8.8	5–14	6	7	3	6	7
TC	9.0	7–12	7.6	1–14	14	12	9	3	10
JL	8.2	5–11	14.8	0–21	2	5	4	4	5
JS	5.6	3–8	9.4	5–16	3	1	7	10	11
EH	8.0	6–11	10.5	4–16	8	6	7	8	12

abstinence on sleep-wakefulness behavior have emphasized the occurrence of insomnia as a concomitant of the withdrawal state [42, 43]. Only two out of the eight subjects (JS and JL) were initially insomniac relative to their base-line sleep pattern (see Table III). Three of the five subjects showing the most prolonged and severe withdrawal signs and symptoms (DC, TC and AW) slept about as long as during the predrinking base line (cf. Table III).

Examination of the distribution of consecutive hours of sleep during the withdrawal period shows that four out of the five subjects exhibiting the most severe withdrawal signs and symptoms (TC, JL, AW and DC) showed fragmentation of sleep patterns. For subjects AW and TC, this represented a persistence of the pattern of fragmentation observed during the drinking period. Subject JS also showed some shift toward shorter blocks of sleep.

Three subjects (RG, ED and EH), with only mild to moderate withdrawal signs and symptoms, showed indications of a return to a more normal sleep pattern during the withdrawal period. It is of interest to note that subject TC, who evidenced severe withdrawal signs and symptoms, slept longer during the first 48 hr of withdrawal than during the preceding 72 hr of the drinking period.

Consequently these data suggest that fragmentation of sleep patterns, independent of changes in the amount of time spent sleeping, is a reliable correlate of alcohol ingestion and a frequent accompaniment of alcohol withdrawal.

D.   Discussion

1.   Physiological and Behavioral Effects of Alcohol

What factors may have accounted for intersubject differences in blood alcohol levels observed during programmed alcohol administration?

A.   ADEQUACY OF HEPATIC FUNCTION. Although some subjects had consistently low blood alcohol levels during the course of the programmed dosage study, although they were ingesting considerable amounts of alcohol, not all subjects showed evidence of metabolic tolerance to alcohol. It is reasonable to postulate that the degree of tolerance is related to the adequacy of hepatic function, since alcohol is primarily metabolized in the liver [15]. Factors relating to liver function could significantly influence the rate of alcohol metabolism and consequently affect blood alcohol levels.

Although no subjects in this study showed evidence of liver disease as determined by physical examination and laboratory studies, the BSP and other liver-function tests provide only an index of hepatic reserve. Considerable liver derangement may be present in subjects with completely normal liver-function tests. Consequently those subjects who did not show evidence of metabolic tolerance may have had some degree of hepatic impairment that was not detected by clinical or laboratory methods.

B.   ENDOCRINE FACTORS. Even if tolerance does occur in alcoholics who have adequate hepatic reserve and function, it is unlikely that this is a steady-state phenomena. We observed marked fluctuations in blood alcohol levels that were not correlated with the volume of alcohol ingested. Such fluctuations presumably reflect a summation of those factors which regulate the absorption and metabolism of alcohol. One factor that may be of considerable importance is the magnitude of the adrenocortical response to ethanol ingestion.

In previous studies we found that alcohol induces an enhancement of adrenocortical activity [34], and it is well known that the glucocorticoids exert a major role in the regulation of carbohydrate metabolism. Thus the rate of ethanol metabolism may be affected by alterations in adrenocortical as well as adrenal medullary function, although the specific determinants and the time course of such modifications are difficult to determine accurately. For example, if the metabolism of alcohol is affected by adrenocortical activity, which, in turn, is affected by alcohol ingestion plus emotional responsivity, it would be expected that, through time, major variations in ethanol metabolism would occur and would be highly dependent on subject-environmental stress factors. The complex interaction of subject-environmental stress factors with the pharmacological effects of alcohol on the CNS probably preclude accurate predictions of the effects of alcohol on a given behavioral parameter and may account for the finding that blood alcohol levels are rarely a reliable correlate of a subject's affective, aggressive, or regressive behavior [23].

What factors may have contributed to higher blood alcohol levels observed during free-choice drinking?

Even when subjects consumed amounts of alcohol during the free-choice drinking study that were equivalent to amounts ingested during the programmed study, blood alcohol levels were considerably higher in the free-choice experiment. We feel that this phenomena cannot be entirely explained by sampling factors, since blood alcohol values were measured three times daily and the final values are an average of these measures. Moreover, during the programmed study, alcohol was administered at 6, 10, and 2;

breathalyzer readings were taken at 8, 4, and 12 and should therefore correspond to peak blood alcohol values for each subject.

The erratic pattern of food intake might explain the higher blood alcohol levels during the free-choice study. In general, caloric intake from food sources other than alcohol was smaller during the free-choice study than the programmed-dose study. Reduction of caloric intake significantly reduces the rate of alcohol metabolism. A number of animal studies have shown that the rate of ethanol metabolism is reduced in fasted or starved rats [7, 41]. Recent studies carried out in our laboratory indicate that the reduction of caloric intake with controlled maintenance of alcohol dosage is associated with a significant decrease in the rate of alcohol metabolism [29].

It is possible that alcoholics learn that eating less food effectively enhances the intoxicating properties of a given dose of alcohol. In this study we observed a deliberate reduction of caloric intake by one subject in a conscious maneuver to enhance his degree of intoxication. If free-choice drinking, as observed in this study, is analogous to patterns of alcohol consumption that occur in real-life conditions, patterns of eating may also be concordant.

What factors may have accounted for differences in subjects' capacity to tolerate alcohol between the programmed and free-choice drinking paradigms?

The unexpected finding that subjects were able to tolerate large quantities of alcohol under free-choice conditions better than smaller doses of alcohol administered on a programmed basis may have a number of unique determinants. One possibility is that the sequential order of the two alcohol administration paradigms was paralleled by an alteration in some aspect of tolerance.

C.   TOLERANCE. Since the programmed-dosage study was carried out before the free-choice experiment, some adaptive change in metabolic tolerance may have occurred as a consequence of the programmed drinking experience. It has been shown that metabolic tolerance may increase after chronic ethanol intake [36] perhaps as a function of an adaptive increase in alcohol dehydrogenase [31], or adaptive changes in hepatic microsomal enzyme systems [19]. The duration of an alcohol-induced increase in metabolic tolerance is unknown, but even if such a process were long-lasting, it could not adequately account for the differences observed in subjects' physiological responsivity in these two studies.

It is important to distinguish between metabolic and tissue tolerance [35]. Alterations in metabolic tolerance would not explain the high incidence of gastrointestinal symptoms during programmed administration as contrasted with the relatively low incidence of these phenomena during free-choice drinking. Development of tissue tolerance, however, could account for a decrease in gastrointestinal symptoms during free-choice drinking.

D.   PATTERN-RELATED EFFECTS. An alternative explanation for the relative alcohol intolerance and frequent occurrence of gastrointestinal disorders during programmed drinking is that small, frequently administered doses of alcohol are more toxic than higher doses that are more widely spaced. No data concerning the relative toxicity of ethanol in intermittent versus continuous administration studies have been reported by other investigators. Examination of the possible significance of dose periodicity, however, may clarify the administration-specific effects of alcohol on behavioral and biological processes.

Man can metabolize alcohol at a rate of about 1 oz/hr [46]. During programmed administration the amount of alcohol delivered every 4 hr produced peak blood alcohol levels that should have been significantly reduced before the administration of the next dose. Consequently subjects were exposed to six ascending and descending blood alcohol levels each day for 20 days, although during free-choice drinking, subjects could sustain a blood alcohol level and avoid a series of abrupt changes within 24 hr if they so choose.

An abrupt rate of change in blood alcohol levels during programmed administration may have produced a variety of unspecified toxic effects. There are data that suggest that ascending blood alcohol levels have a different effect on behavioral and physiological indices than descending blood alcohol levels. Behavioral studies have shown that greater decrements in performance occur at equivalent blood alcohol levels during the ascending as contrasted with the descending limb of the blood alcohol curve [9]. Physiologic data indicate that alcohol-induced diuresis is more significantly related to ascending blood alcohol levels than to maintained high blood alcohol levels. Diuresis seems to occur only when blood alcohol levels are rising and does not persist once stable, although high, blood levels are achieved [37]. It is possible that a repeated challenge to systems responsive to ascending blood alcohol levels gradually exhausts their potential for an adaptive response.

The variability in blood alcohol levels is reflected in the ratio of standard deviation to mean values for blood alcohol levels. The standard deviation for the 14 days of programmed drinking at a constant dosage was proportionately larger than in the free-choice drinking study (cf. Table II). During the programmed drinking phase the standard deviation approximated or exceeded the mean value in four subjects and was greater than 50% of the mean value in two subjects, although, in the free-choice drinking, the standard deviation was close to 50% of the mean blood alcohol value except for subject RG. These data support the interpretation that pulsed dosage during the programmed-administration paradigm was associated with relatively greater variability in blood alcohol levels than occurred during the free-choice study. Further studies would be required to separate the relative contribution of blood alcohol variability from tissue tolerance factors in order to explain a subject's capacity to tolerate alcohol.

2.   Withdrawal Signs and Symptoms

The occurrence of withdrawal signs and symptoms, on cessation of drinking, is one of the major pharmacological criteria of alcohol addiction. We have reviewed studies of the biochemical and behavioral correlates of alcohol withdrawal and discussed some conceptual models of physical dependence elsewhere [25]. We concluded that the determinants of withdrawal symptoms remained unspecified and the biological mechanisms underlying the expression of alcohol withdrawal phenomena were unknown.

Some clarification of the determinants of withdrawal phenomena are provided, however, by observations presented in this chapter. These data testify to the importance of the pattern of drinking as opposed to duration of drinking as a critical determinant of withdrawal duration and severity. Seven out of the eight subjects drank large volumes of alcohol for a period of 20 days under each experimental condition; the free-choice drinking period, however, was followed by more varied and severe withdrawal signs and symptoms. It is important to reemphasize that the mode alone cannot account for the differences in severity of withdrawal signs and symptoms observed in the free-choice and programmed studies (cf. Figure 1, JS, ED, JL). This finding is not inconsistent with the generally held notion that the gradual reduction of alcohol intake may be effective in decreasing the incidence and severity of the alcohol withdrawal syndrome. As will be discussed later, however, the expression of partial withdrawal symptoms is difficult to predict on the basis of the magnitude, as opposed to rate, of change in blood alcohol levels.

Since all subjects drank more alcohol during the free-choice than during the programmed drinking period, it is difficult to isolate the contribution of the pattern of drinking and the over-all volume ingested in precipitating the observed withdrawal syndromes. Two subjects (JS and AW), however, drank very similar quantities of alcohol during the two periods (cf. Figure

1), and both these subjects showed the most varied, severe, and prolonged withdrawal syndromes after free-choice drinking. This observation suggests that pattern of ingestion may be more significant than volume of ingestion in accounting for the consequences of cessation of drinking.

This impression is qualified by the fact that multiple determinants relate both pattern of drinking and volume ingested to blood alcohol levels measured. Since all subjects had higher blood alcohol levels during the free-choice drinking period, this may be of primary importance in determining the expression of withdrawal signs and symptoms. Since there was no instance of comparable blood alcohol levels during the free-choice and programmed drinking, the relative importance of drinking pattern and blood alcohol levels cannot be separated out. Neither can we differentiate the relative contribution of consistent high blood alcohol levels as opposed to high terminal blood alcohol levels. Only one subject (RG) had comparable terminal blood alcohol levels, but his withdrawal syndromes were comparable with subjects who maintained high blood alcohol levels throughout the free-choice drinking phase.

We are certain that the difference in withdrawal phenomena after the two drinking patterns is not a function of the sequential drinking experience insofar as this might produce a general decrease in physical health or intercurrent illness. Most problems with gastritis and intercurrent illness occurred during the initial programmed drinking phase, and all subjects were better able to tolerate drinking during the second, spontaneous drinking period.

A history of alcohol withdrawal seems to be the best predictor of alcohol withdrawal phenomena. Subjects' reports of duration of alcoholism, however, was not correlated with appearance or severity of withdrawal symptoms in this study (cf. Table I, Figure 2). The complex interactions of the behavioral and biologic correlates of withdrawal signs and symptoms in alcoholics do not lend themselves to facile speculations about the biochemical determinants of the abstinence syndrome [cf. 25, 28].

Our understanding of the determinants of alcohol abstinence is somewhat complicated by the observation that alcoholics may experience withdrawal symptoms during a drinking episode if their blood alcohol level falls rapidly, although this fall may be relatively small. The phenomena of partial withdrawal has received relatively little experimental attention since the initial observations of Isbell et al. [14] on alcohol intoxication of morphine addicts and the later studies of Mendelson [27] on alcohol addicts. These data suggest the futility of trying to establish a critical blood alcohol level, since a small decrease from initial values of 300 mg/100 ml may evoke withdrawal phenomena that are just as severe as a small decrease from levels of 100 mg/100 ml. Perpetuation of drinking by alcoholics may be, in part, an attempt to reduce or abate distressful symptoms associated with partial alcohol withdrawal. Such a notion would be consistent with a concept of physical dependence that attempts to ascribe motivation for drinking to a biological or physiological need. The generality of this notion, however, remains to be demonstrated.

3. Alcohol-induced Disruption of Sleep Patterns

The observation of sleep fragmentation as a consequence of alcohol ingestion may be related to other behavioral and affective changes usually associated with sustained inebriation. For example, it has been consistently observed that alcohol produces increases in anxiety and depression in the alcoholic, as contrasted with the nonalcoholic individual [22, 23, 27]. The affective discomfort reported by these alcoholic subjects during chronic intoxication is strikingly similar to that reported by subjects deprived of stage 1 rapid eye movement (REM) activity [5]. It is not known whether alcohol-induced sleep fragmentation is associated with changes in over-all stage 1 REM activity; observations on morphine-induced decreases in REM activity changes in human addicts [16], however, would be consistent with this speculation. Also it has been shown that alcohol tends to decrease stage 1 REM activity in normal subjects [11, 18, 47, 48]. This effect is not unique to alcohol but has been observed for a variety of barbiturates, antidepressants, and tranquilizers [4].

There is increasing evidence that changes in sleep patterns are associated with alterations of steroid and endocrine activity. In particular, concomitants of endocrine activity during REM suggest that the REM state may represent a unique level of central-nervous-system arousal. A biphasic change in urine volume output and osmolality during REM sleep has been reported [21], and increased urinary excretion of 3-methoxy-4-hydroxymandelic acid (VMA) during REM epochs has also been observed [20]. These data converge with reports of increases in plasma 17-hydroxycorticosteriod levels during REM [45] to suggest that activation of endocrine output may correlate with frequency and duration of REM epochs during sleep. We have consistently observed that serum cortisol levels increase significantly during chronic ethanol ingestion [33, 34]. Although it is more parsimonious to ascribe increases in cortisol levels to direct activation of the CNS-pituitary-adrenal axis by ethanol rather than to secondary effects related to fragmentation of sleep and possible changes in REM time and frequency, the interaction between sleep and endocrine patterns is an intriguing question.

The observation that sleep fragmentation rather than insomnia may correlate with severe alcohol withdrawal signs and symptoms is contrary to most clinical reports of insomnia during withdrawal [14, 42]. Our data suggest that withdrawal symptoms may correlate with a disruption of sleep pattern but not necessarily with changes in total hours of sleep. These impressions have subsequently been confirmed in observations of 40 alcoholics in withdrawal [26].

Several investigators have attempted to relate changes in sleep activity to hallucinosis and delusions during withdrawal. Sleep fragmentation as a concomitant of hallucinosis during alcohol withdrawal was observed by Isbell et al. [14]. Alcohol hallucinosis is a frequent concomitant of withdrawal and is sometimes associated with difficulty in discriminating between sleeping and waking states. Although it has been speculated that hallucinosis and dreaming may be associated with increases in stage 1 REM sleep, there have been relatively few studies of electroencephalogram (EEG) correlates of sleep pattern in alcoholics [12, 10]. Among the many problems in studying EEG patterns in withdrawal has been the difficulty of obtaining adequate base-line sleep measures and discriminating among the effects of alcohol abstinence, intercurrent illness, and acute hospitalization.

CONCLUSIONS

We conclude that the pattern of drinking produces discernible differences in physiological and behavioral correlates of intoxication and withdrawal. The magnitude of these differences suggests that the traditional time–programmed-dosage research paradigm may give a very different picture of the alcoholic's response to alcohol than a paradigm that allows spontaneous alcohol consumption. Results obtained with programmed alcohol administration may be of more limited generality for understanding the biological and behavioral aspects of alcoholism as expressed in real life.

All subjects showed idiosyncratic free-choice drinking patterns, but all were able to drink more alcohol with less adverse reactions than during the programmed drinking period. We have discussed the possible contribution of tolerance, hepatic function adequacy, endocrine factors, pattern specific toxicity, and food intake to the observed differences.

Pattern of drinking during free-choice alcohol administration with concomitantly greater blood alcohol levels and decreased food intake consistently produced the most severe, varied, and prolonged withdrawal signs and symptoms. Pattern of drinking seems to be more important than duration of drinking in accounting for the expression of the alcohol abstinence syndrome.

Finally the fragmentation of sleep during free-choice drinking and the absence of insomnia during withdrawal are inconsistent with the usual clinical impressions. Alcohol-induced sleep fragmentation may be related to the affective changes observed during drinking.

REFERENCES

1. Abelin, I., C. Herren, and W. Berli, Ueber die erregende Wirkung des Alkohols auf den adrenalin-und noradrenalin-haushalt des menschlichen Organismus, *Helv. Med. Acta,* **25,** 591 (1958).
2. Anton, A. H., Ethanol and urinary catecholamines in man, *Clin. Pharmacol. Therap.,* **6,** 462 (1965).
3. Bucher, T. and H. Redetzki, Eine spezifische photometrische Bestimmung von äthylalkohol auf fermentativem Wege, *Klin. Wochenschr.,* **29,** 615 (1951).
4. *Current Research on Sleep and Dreams,* Public Health Service Publication 1389, U.S. Department of Health, Education, and Welfare, Washington, D.C. (1966).
5. Dement, W. C., The effect of dream deprivation, *Science,* **131,** 1705 (1960).
6. Feinberg, I. and E. V. Evarts, Some Implications of Sleep Research for Psychiatry, in *Neurobiological Aspects of Psychopathology,* Proceedings of the 58th Annual Meeting of the American Psychopathological Association, J. Zubin and C. Shagass, (eds.), **XXV, 334,** Grune & Stratton, New York, 1969.
7. Forsander, O. A., N. Raiha, M. Salaspuro, and P. Maenpaa, Influence of ethanol on the liver metabolism of fed and starved rats, *Biochem. J.,* **94,** 259 (1965).
8. Garlind, T., L. Goldberg, K. Graf, E. S. Permans, T. Strandell, and G. Strom, Effect of ethanol on circulatory, metabolic, and neurohormonal function during muscular work in man, *Acta Pharmacol. Toxicol.,* **17,** 106 (1960).
9. Goldberg, L., Quantitative studies on alcohol tolerance in man: The influence of ethyl alcohol on sensory, motor and psychological functions referred to blood alcohol in normal and habituated individual, *Acta Physiol. Scand.,* **5,** suppl. **16,** (1943).
10. Greenberg, R. and C. Pearlman, Delirium tremens and dreaming, *Am. J. Psychiat.,* **124,** 133 (1967).
11. Gresham, S. C., W. B. Webb, and R. L. Williams, Alcohol and caffeine: Effect on inferred visual dreaming, *Science,* **140,** 1226 (1963).
12. Gross, M. M., D. Goodenough, M. Tobin, E. Halpert, D. Lepore, A. Perlstein, M. Serota, J. DeBeanco, R. Fuller, and I. Kishner, Sleep disturbance and hallucinations in the acute alcoholic psychoses, *J. Nervous Mental Disease,* **142,** 493 (1966).
13. Hartmann, E., *The Biology of Dreaming,* Charles C Thomas, Springfield, Ill., 1967.
14. Isbell, H., H. F. Fraser, A. Wikler, R. E. Belleville, and A. Eisenman, An

experimental study of the etiology of "rum fits" and delirium tremens, *Quart. J. Studies Alc.,* **16,** 1 (1955).

15. Isselbacher, K. J. and N. J. Greenberger, Metabolic effects of alcohol on the liver, *N. Engl. J. Med.,* **270,** 351 (1964).

16. Kay, D. C., R. B. Eisenstein, and D. R. Jasinski, Morphine effects on human REM state, waking state and NREM sleep, *Psychopharmacologia,* **14,** 404 (1969).

17. Klingman, G. I. and McC. Goodall, Urinary epinephrine and levarterenol excretion during acute sublethal alcohol intoxication in dogs, *J. Pharmacol. Exp. Therap.,* **121,** 313 (1957).

18. Knowles, J. B., S. G. Laverty, and H. A. Kuechler, Effects of alcohol on REM sleep, *Quart. J. Studies Alc.,* **29,** 342 (1968).

19. Lieber, C. S. and L. M. DeCarli, Ethanol oxidation by hepatic mocrosomes: Adaptive increase after ethanol feeding, *Science,* **162,** 117 (1968).

20. Mandell, A. J., P. L. Brill, M. P. Mandell, J. Rodnick, R. T. Rubin, R. Sheff, and B. Chaffey, Urinary excretion of 3-methoxy-4-hydroxymandelic acid during dreaming sleep in man, *Life Sci.,* **5,** 169 (1966).

21. Mandell, A. J., B. Chaffey, P. Brill, M. P. Mandell, J. Rodnick, R. T. Rubin, and R. Sheff, Dreaming sleep in man: Changes in urine volume and osmolality, *Science,* **151,** 1558 (1966).

22. McNamee, H. B., N. K. Mello, and J. H. Mendelson, Experimental analysis of drinking patterns of alcohols: Concurrent psychiatric observations, *Am. J. Psychiat.,* **124,** 1063 (1968).

23. Mello, N. K., Some aspects of the behavioral pharmacology of alcohol, in *Psychopharmacology: A Review of Progress 1957–67,* Proceedings of the Sixth Annual Meeting of the American College of Neuropsychopharmacology, D. Efron (ed.), Public Health Service Publication **1836,** 787, U.S. Government Printing Office, Washington, D.C., 1968.

24. Mello, N. K., H. B. McNamee, and J. H. Mendelson, Drinking Patterns of Chronic Alcoholics: Gambling and Motivation for Alcohol, in *Clinical Research in Alcoholism,* J. O. Cole (ed.), Psychiatric Research Report **24,** 83, American Psychiatric Association, Washington, D.C., 1968.

25. Mello, N. K. and J. H. Mendelson, Alterations in States of Consciousness Associated with Chronic Ingestion of Alcohol, in *Neurobiological Aspects of Psychopathology: Proceedings of the 58th Annual Meetings of the American Psychopathological Association,* J. Zubin and C. Shagass (eds.), vol. XXV, 183, Grune & Stratton, New York, 1969.

26. Mello, N. K. and J. H. Mendelson, Behavioral studies of sleep patterns in alcoholics during intoxication and withdrawal, *J. Pharmacol. Exp. Therap.,* **175,** 94 (1970).

27. Mendelson, J. H., (ed.), Experimentally induced chronic intoxication and withdrawal in alcoholics, *Quart. J. Studies Alc.,* suppl. 2, (1964).

28. Mendelson, J. H., Biochemical pharmacology of alcohol, in *Psychopharmacology: A Review of Progress 1957–1967,* Proceedings of the Sixth Annual Meeting of the American College of Neuropsychopharmacology, D. Efron

(ed.), Public Health Service Publication **1836,** 769, U.S. Government Printing Office, Washington, D.C., 1968.

29. Mendelson, J. H., Biological concomitants of alcoholism, *N. Engl. J. Med.* **283,** 24–32, 71–81 (1970).
30. Mendelson, J. H. and N. K. Mello, Experimental analysis of drinking behavior of chronic alcoholics, *Ann. N.Y. Acad. Sci.,* **133,** 828 (1966).
31. Mendelson, J. H., N. K. Mello, C. Corbett, and R. Ballard, Puromycin inhibition of ethanol ingestion and liver alcohol dehydrogenase activity in the rat, *J. Psychiat. Res.,* **3,** 133 (1965).
32. Mendelson, J. H., N. K. Mello, and P. Solomon, Small Group Drinking Behavior: An Experimental Study of Chronic Alcoholics, in *The Addictive States,* Proceedings of the Association for Research in Nervous and Mental Disease, New York, 1966, A. Wikler (ed.), **46,** 399. Williams & Wilkins, Baltimore, 1968.
33. Mendelson, J. H., M. Ogata, and N. K. Mello, Adrenal function and alcoholism: I. Serum Cortisol, *Psychosom. Med.,* **33** (No. 2), 145 (1971).
34. Mendelson, J. H. and S. Stein, Serum cortisol levels in alcoholic and nonalcoholic subjects during experimentally induced ethanol intoxication, *Psychosom. Med.,* **28,** 616 (1966).
35. Mendelson, J. H., S. Stein, and M. T. McGuire, Comparative psychophysiological studies of alcoholic and nonalcoholic subjects undergoing experimentally induced ethanol intoxication, *Psychosom. Med.,* **28,** 1 (1966).
36. Mendelson, J. H., S. Stein, and N. K. Mello, Effects of experimentally induced intoxication on metabolism of ethanol-1-C^{14} in alcoholic subjects, *Metab. Clin. Exp.,* **14,** 1255 (1965).
37. Ogata, M., J. H. Mendelson, and N. K. Mello, Electrolytes and osmolality in alcoholics during experimentally induced intoxication, *Psychosom. Med.,* **30,** 463 (1968).
38. Ogata, M., J. H. Mendelson, N. K. Mello and E. Majchrowicz, Adrenal function and alcoholism: II. Catecholamines, *Psychosom. Med.,* **33** (No. 2), 159 (1971).
39. Perman, E. S., The effect of ethyl alcohol on the secretion from the adrenal medulla in man, *Acta Physiol. Scand.,* **44,** 241 (1958).
40. Perman, E. S., The effect of ethyl alcohol on the secretion from the adrenal medulla of the cat, *Acta Physiol. Scand.,* **48,** 323 (1960).
41. Smith, M. E. and H. W. Newman, The rate of ethanol metabolism in fed and fasting animals, *J. Biol. Chem.,* **234,** 1544 (1959).
42. Victor, M., Treatment of alcoholic intoxication and the withdrawal syndrome: A critical analysis of the use of drugs and other forms of therapy, *Psychosom. Med.,* **28,** 636 (1966).
43. Victor, M. and R. D. Adams, The effect of alcohol on the nervous system, *Res. Publ. Assoc. Res. Nervous Mental Disease,* **32,** 526 (1953).
44. Wartburg, J. P. von, W. Berli, and H. Aebi, Der Einfluss langdauernder Athylakolholbelastung auf die Katecholamin-ausscheidung im harn der Ratte, *Helv. Med. Acta,* **28,** 89 (1961).

45. Weitzman, E. D., H. Schaumberg, and W. Fishbein, Plasma 17-hydroxycorti-costeroid levels during sleep in man, *J. Clin. Endocrinol. Metab.*, **26**, 121 (1966).
46. Westerfeld, W. W. and M. P. Schulman, Metabolism and caloric value of alcohol, *J. Amer. Med. Assoc.*, **170**, 197 (1959).
47. Yules, R. B., D. X. Freedman, and K. A. Chandler, The effect of ethyl alcohol on man's electroencephalograph sleep cycle, *Electroencephalog. Clin. Neurophysiol.*, **20**, 109 (1966).
48. Yules, R. B., M. E. Lippman, and D. X. Freedman, Alcohol administration prior to sleep: The effect on EEG sleep stages, *Arch. Gen. Psychiat.*, **16**, 94 (1967).

Chapter XI

APPETITE FOR ALCOHOL

NATIVIDAD SEGOVIA-RIQUELME,
ANIBAL VARELA, and JORGE MARDONES

INSTITUTO DE INVESTIGACIONES SOBRE ALCOHOLISMO
UNIVERSIDAD DE CHILE
SANTIAGO

A. Historical Introduction

In spite of the fact that human appetite for alcohol has been known since the most remote antiquity, the experimental approach to the study of this problem in laboratory animals is rather recent.

It seems that the first attempt in this line was performed in 1926 by Richter [92], who observed that rats drink indifferently water or alcohol solutions as high as 8% v/v when both fluids are offered in self-selection conditions and that the consumption of calories from solid diet decreased proportionally to the energy obtained from the alcohol solution. Around 1940 the same author and his coworkers included the study of the self-selection of alcohol in a general research plan concerning the ability of the rat to choose instinctively a well-balanced diet. They showed [96] that rats recognize alcohol solutions in concentrations as weak as 1.8% and prefer 2 to 5% alcohol to water.

Our group entered into the study of this problem in 1941 with the idea that the appetite for alcohol should increase when rats were fed on diets deprived of thiamin. This idea originated in the observation by Richter et al. [97] that rats deprived of vitamin B complex select a diet richer in fat than in carbohydrates and in the fact that the thiamin requirement per calorie of nutrient is lower for ethanol than for carbohydrates. This study showed that either the deprivation of thiamin or of a new factor, called N, induced an increase in voluntary alcohol intake by rats [55].

The research group headed by R. J. Williams, in Austin, Texas, confirmed our results and extended this study to other single vitamin deprivations [140].

Independently Williams et·al. [130] and Mardones et al. [54] reported on the importance of individual variations in the voluntary intake of ethanol by rats. Based on the mentioned facts, Williams [138] formulated the hypothesis of the genetotrophic origin of alcoholism. It would be better indeed to talk about the genetotrophic origin of the appetite for alcohol. The group in Austin gave up the genetical study of the problem; our group started in 1948 [58] a selection by inbreeding and is still continuing it. We have obtained two strains of rats: "nondrinker" (UCh-A) and "drinker" (UCh-B); but in spite of 36 and 30 generations of inbreeding respectively, we have not obtained a pure line of any of these strains.

The appetite for alcohol has also been studied in mice. Loiseleur and Petit [46] observed that this species exhibits a high appetite for ethanol and that they are able to distinguish it from methanol. Mirone [71] reported on genetic influences in alcohol appetite in this species. Subsequently other authors, mainly McClearn, Rodgers, and coworkers (see Section D.1), studied this probelm on highly inbred strains of mice.

The studies on the effect of stress in alcohol appetite were initiated by Massermann et al. [65] in cats.

Since the 1950s, the number of papers on alcohol appetite in experimental animals increased gradually. The problem has been the subject of successive review by Mardones [52], Rodgers [100], Lester [44], and Triksson [26].

B.   General Methodology

The general method used for the study of the appetite for alcohol consists basically in offering to laboratory animals a free choice between water and alcohol solutions, measuring the daily intake of both fluids.

In some experiments a definite alcohol concentration is used, and daily ethanol intake is refered to body weight. Other experiments are designed with the purpose of knowing the preference of the animal for solutions of variable concentrations of ethanol in comparison with water.

It is convenient to discuss briefly the significance of both methods; each of them has been considered the best by different authors, even polemically [79]. The appetite for a food or a drug can be measured either as an instantaneous preference in relation to another one or by the amount of the substance spontaneously consumed. Everyday experience shows that after consuming a sufficient amount of a very desirable food, the appetite for it decreases and even disappears. For this reason the study of the relative amount of water and different solutions of alcohol ingested in a free-choice condition cannot be considered as revealing the actual appetite for alcohol, since its results are affected by the ingested amount of alcohol and water. Obviously the alcohol ingested is higher for the same volume of fluid as the ethanol concentration increases; the limiting effect of the amount of fluid previously ingested is more important as the concentration of alcohol decreases. Accordingly this method gives results suitable only for estimating the daily amount of ethanol that the animals desire when the concentration of offered solutions ranges between limits where alcohol is recognized and not rejected and the amount ingested is not affected by the appetite for fluids. Concentrations of about 10% v/v fulfill these requirements.

On the other hand a comparison of the preference for solutions of variable concentrations is the only useful method for the knowledge of the concentration threshold where alcohol is recognized or rejected.

When the preference of ethanol solutions of variable concentration is studied, it seems convenient to avoid the error induced by the natural tendency of each animal to select a certain position (right or left), through the rotation of the bottle position. We have observed that this precaution is unnecessary, and even disturbing, when an alcohol solution of constant concentration is offered, because in this case the position of the alcohol solution bottle is another element of learning.

In some experiments ethanol is added to natural fluids, such as milk or fruit juices, or its flavor is changed by the addition of sweetening agents.

In the evaluation of the total intake of ethanol in experiments in which this substance is offered in high concentrations (30 to 40%) it is necessary to take account of the fact that alcohol concentration decreases in the surface of contact with the air and that rats learn how to drink by licking the surface of the drop, where alcohol concentration is lower than in the rest [125].

C.   Interspecies Variations of the Appetite for Alcohol

Appetite for alcohol, as every quantitative attribute, exhibits variations among species, strains, and individuals.

Several species of laboratory animals have been studied concerning the appetite for ethanol, namely, rat (*Rattus norvegicus*), mouse (*Mus musculus*), deer mouse (*Peromiscus californicus*) [23], cotton rat (*Sigmodon hispidus*) [23], golden hamster (*Mesgricetus auratus*) [4, 23, 31], guinea pig (*Cavia porcellus*) [3], rabbit (*Lepus cuniculus*) [3], hedgehog (*Ermaceus europeus*) [3], rhesus monkey (*Macaca nemestrina, M. Mulata*) [2, 18, 29, 67], orangutan (*Simia satyrus*), and chimpanzee (*Antropopythecus niger*) [29].

Rats and mice have been the most extensively used in this kind of experiments. On the contrary experiments with other species are rather scarce, the samples very small, and the ranges of variation very wide. Consequently the mean of these experimental results cannot be considered so good an estimate of the central value corresponding to the respective species.

The daily intake of ethanol varies in normal rats from zero to about 1.0 ml of absolute ethanol per 100 g of body weight and that of mice ranges from 0 to 1.4 ml/100 g. The weight of a rat is about 10 times that of a mouse, but its metabolic rate per weight unity is about half that of the mouse. If the comparison is performed by body surface, the average daily intake of the rat seems to be about 24 g/m^2 and that of the mouse about 22 g/m^2.

Concerning the appetite for alcohol among human populations, the only one giving suitable information about its distribution is that reported by Ledermann [42] performed in France, a country in which daily consumption of alcoholic beverages is the rule, and there are practically no abstemious. This study shows that the distribution of the alcohol consumption is asymmetric, the mode being about 30 ml/day, the median about 60 ml/day, and the mean about 80 ml/day. Considering an average body surface of 1.75 m^2, the mean daily intake would be about 37 g/m^2 of ethanol i.e., a figure slightly higher than that of rats and mice.

D.   Genetic Influences on Alcohol Appetite

The amplitude of the intraspecies variations of the appetite for alcohol is an indication of the eventual influence of major genetic factors. Evidences of this genetical influence are coming from studies about strain differences, artificial selection, and hybridization.

1. Strain Differences

The importance of strain differences in the appetite of alcohol was observed by Reed [91] in six strains of rats. An isolated observation by Richter [95] showed that a wild rat consumed abnormally high amounts of alcohol, and Eimer and Senter [22] confirmed that wild rats exhibited higher appetite for alcohol than hooded rats. Myers [75] reported that G-4 rats strain drink more alcohol than Wistar.

The same problem was studied in highly inbred strains of mice by McClearn and Rodgers [48] and subsequently confirmed by several authors. These studies show that C57BL mice exhibit the highest preference for alcohol, BALB and DBA drink very little ethanol, and other strains, such as RIII and C_3H, occupy an intermediate position.

2. Artificial Selection

In 1948 we initiated a selection by inbreeding of rats exhibiting low or high voluntary intake of alcohol when fed with a purified diet deprived of factor N_1 (see Section I.3.d). At the present we are studying the thirty-seventh-generation of the nondrinker strain (UCh-A) and the thirty-first of the drinker one (UCh-B). This selection started from rats of the colony maintained in the Instituto Bacteriológico de Chile, which probably was the result of a hybridization of Wistar and Rockefeller. Figures 1 and 2 summarize the pedigree of both strains. As it can be seen, we have not yet obtained a pure line, suggesting that each of the phenotype drinker and nondrinker could correspond to more than one genotype. A study of the frequency distribution of both phenotypes in the two pedigrees [53] showed that it can be explained by the presence of at least two major gene loci, assuming that nondrinkers are recessive homozygotes in one locus.

A similar selection has been performed by Eriksson [25] on Wistar rats of the ALKO colony in Helsinki, following a procedure including outbreeding in the first four generations and alternating inbreeding and outbreeding in the following ones. In contradistinction with our strains the appetite for alcohol was studied in rats fed on complete stock diet. The distribution of the phenotypes drinker and nondrinker until the eighth generation shows that drinker rats are also observed among the nondrinker strain and vice versa.

The heredity coefficient studied in our strains in the third to seventh

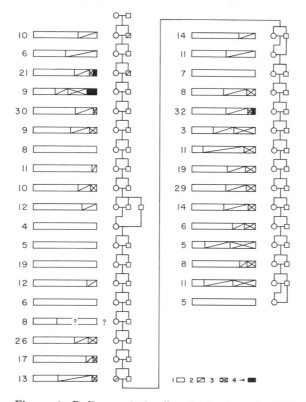

Figure 1. Pedigree of the "nondrinker" strain UCh-A. Alcohol consumption in ml/100 g body weight and day: $1 = <0.20$; $2 = 0.20$ to 0.39; $3 = 0.40$ to 0.59; $4 = 0.60$. The figures represent the number of siblings from their respective parents.

generations was $r = +0.42 \pm 0.05$ (58), and in the eighth generation of ALKO strains $r = +0.75 \pm 0.15$ (25)—both highly significant.

3. Hybridization

The studies concerning the appetite for alcohol of hybrids from drinker and nondrinker parents have been performed mainly on mice.

McClearn and Rodgers [49] reported that the appetite for alcohol of the F_1 generation from parents belonging to mice strains with different alcohol appetite is generally intermediate between those of the parents.

Fuller [33] observed that the offspring of crossing mice of median (A or C_3H) with low appetite (DBA) for alcohol exhibited an intermediate one, but closer to the low one, and those of the crossing of A or C_3H

with mice of high appetite for alcohol (C57BL) exhibited also an inter-mediate appetite, but closer to the high one. The crossing of DBA with C57BL as well as the crossing of A with C_3H resulted in median appetite.

Thomas [130], studying the hybrids of C57BL and DBA observed an intermediate alcohol appetite in the F_1 generation with certain dominance of DBA; but in the F_2 generation the appetite revealed a tendency to be high, the individuals with low one being rather scarce.

We have also started experiments of hybridization between rats of our strains UCh-A and UCh-B. The data (unpublished) of the F_1 generation from parents drinking daily 0.4 to 0.6 ml of ethanol per 100 g b.w. or 0.0 to 0.1 includes 53 offspring, whose mean daily alcohol consumption was 0.30 ± 0.022 ml/100 g b.w., i.e., an intermediate value between that of both parents.

In a review of the data available in 1966 Rodgers [100] points out that the genetic material responsible for high alcohol preference is not widely distributed across inbred strains of mice and is therefore probably limited to only few allelic forms.

Summarizing, it can be stated that the experiments of hybridization show,

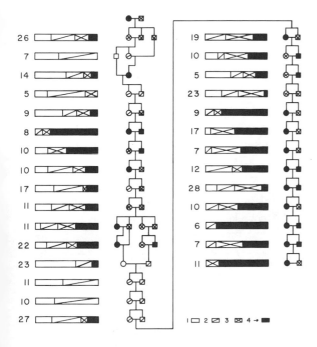

Figure 2. Pedigree of the "drinker" strain UCh-B. (See legend to Figure 1.)

in general, that the appetite for alcohol of hybrids is intermediate between that of the parents, suggesting that various loci are involved. If a certain degree of dominance may exist in some genes, it seems to be of minor importance and not clearly established.

4.   Conclusions

The known facts allow us to state with a high degree of security that in rats and mice the appetite for alcohol is genetically determined and that this heredity seems to be polygenic.

In the case of the rat it seems that there are at least two autosomic major genes and that the recessive homozygotes in one of them would be drinker.

Sex-linked genes probably do also exist in some strains (see Section G). This is evident in the Wistar strain studied by Eriksson, but it does not appear in our strains UCh-A or UCh-B. These strains are originated in rats from the same colony in such a way that if all the members of this colony were homozygotes for this gene, its influence could not be revealed in the progeny. If this gene is located in the X chromosome, it carries an attribute that increases the appetitite for alcohol, since the females studied by Eriksson consume more alcohol than males.

Concerning mice, it seems also that the heredity is polygenic. Some observations suggest a certain degree of dominance of both high and low preference and that the allelic forms for high preference seem to be less prevalent.

E.   Metabolic Differences Linked to Variable Alcohol Appetite

Since ethanol is oxidized in the body system in such a way that the metabolism of other substrates interferes, it is reasonable to think that the variable appetite for alcohol could be related to the metabolic traits of the individuals. Following this idea, the correlations between the degree of alcohol appetite and the rate of different metabolic pathways have been investigated. These studies concern mainly the metabolism of ethanol, carbohydrates, and fat. Other variables, such as the susceptibility of the central nervous system and the liver to the effect of alcohol, have also been studied.

1.   Ethanol Metabolism and Alcohol Appetite

Our studies concerning the metabolic rate of ethanol, measured by the recuperation of the activity of ethanol labeled with ^{14}C either in C_1 or

C_2 [113, 114] in the expired CO_2, have not shown significant differences between rats of the drinker (UCh-B) and nondrinker (UCh-A) strains.

Rodgers and McClearn [101], using a similar method in mice did not observe differences in the metabolic rate of ethanol between C57BL (high alcohol preference) and BALB or DBA (low alcohol preference). Schlesinger et al. [111], using the same method, reported that the maximum oxidation rate of ethanol was slightly but significantly higher in C57BL than in DBA mice when ethanol was administered in small doses (≤ 1.19 g/kg), and there was no difference with higher doses (2.21 g/kg).

Another approach to this problem is the study of the rate of disappearance of injected ethanol from the blood. Rodgers [100] reported no significant difference in this parameter between mice from strains of high (C57BL), median (C_3H), or low (DBA) alcohol preference, the mean being somewhat higher in the mice of low preference. Equivalent results were reported by Kakihana et al. [38], studying C57BL and BALB mice.

All these results allow us to conclude that the higher preference for alcohol by rats and mice does not seem to be correlated with a higher rate of the oxidation of this drug.

Concerning the activity of enzyme systems involved in ethanol metabolism, Rodgers et al. [103], comparing the activity of liver alcohol dehydrogenase (ADH) of mice from six strains exhibiting different alcohol preference, found a significant direct correlation between alcohol preference and liver ADH activity.

Sheppard et al. [123] studied the activity of acetaldehyde-dehydrogenase (ALDH), an enzyme acting on the second step of ethanol oxidation, in the liver of mice with low (DBA) and high (C57BL) alcohol preference and their hybrids. The results showed that the liver ALDH activity of C57BL mice was three times higher than that of the DBA; that of the hybrids was intermediate. In the same line, Schlesinger et al. [112] reported that blood acetaldehyde after the same dose of ethanol was lower in C57BL than in DBA mice. Disulfiram increased acetaldehyde blood level in mice of both strains, but the level at 2 hr was significantly higher in C57BL than in DBA mice.

2.   Carbohydrate Metabolism and Alcohol Appetite

Studies concerning differences in the metabolism of some sugars between rats from our nondrinker (UCh-A) and drinker (UCh-B) strains [115] showed that the rate of recovering the activity of an overload of glucose-1-^{14}C in expired CO_2 was higher in males of the drinker strain than in those of the nondrinker one. Furthermore the rate of recovering the activity of tracer doses of gluconate-1-^{14}C in CO_2 was also significantly higher in rats of both sexes from the drinker strain than in those of the nondrinker one. Both results suggest that the pentose cycle way of glucose metabolism is more rapid in drinker than in nondrinker rats. Recently [36] we have observed that the metabolic rate of a fructose-U-^{14}C overload of 10 mM/kg was significantly higher in rats of both sexes of the drinker strain than in those of the nondrinker one.

We have also reported the absence of strain differences concerning the metabolic rate of glucose-6-^{14}C and of some metabolites, such as pyruvate labeled in carbons 1, 2, or 3 and acetate lebeled in carbons 1 or 2 [114, 115, 116, 117].

In all these studies it is possible that the observed differences were either genetical or secondary to the voluntary alcohol intake, because in spite of the fact that the experiments were performed after a period without access to alcohol, the possibility of long-lasting enzyme disturbances induced by the previous alcohol ingestion cannot be ruled out.

Roach and Williams [99] observed that, after injecting labeled glucose, the activity found in brain was higher in sirian hamsters with high preference for alcohol than in those with low preference. In the same paper the authors report that ethanol intoxication enhances the transport of labeled glucose to the brain; thus it is possible that this difference between drinker and nondrinker hamsters was acquired rather than congenital.

3. Alcohol Appetite and Fat Metabolism

Forsander and Salaspuro [32] studied the urinary excretion of ketonic bodies in rats of both sexes fed on a fat-rich diet exhibiting different voluntary ethanol consumption and observed a negative correlation between ethanol preference and this excretion. The change of redox potential of liver induced by this diet was also smaller in rats of high than in those of low alcohol preference [30]. These differences do not seem to be the consequence of previous alcohol intake, because the experiments were performed a long time after the study of alcohol appetite.

Solodkowska and coworkers [data published in Segovia-Riquelme et al., 118] observed that the lipid content of liver tissue was higher in male rats of the drinker strain than in those of the nondrinker one; no significant difference was observed in females. These experiments were performed on rats fed on complete stock diet and not having received alcohol previously. The same group of authors [127] recently reported that the rate of in vitro incorporation of labeled ethanol or acetate into fatty acids by adipose tissue slices of drinker rats was significantly higher than that of nondrinker ones, both groups fed with stock diet and having free access to ethanol 10 % v/v and water.

4. Alcohol Appetite and Tolerance of CNS to Ethanol

Strain differences concerning the tolerance of the central nervous system to the effect of alcohol were first studied by McClearn et al. [47] on mice with high (C57BL) and low alcohol preference (BALB). They observed no difference in the time for inducing sleep, but its duration was three times higher in BALB than in C57BL mice. These results were confirmed by Kakihana et al., [38] who studied in the same strains the alcohol content in brain after a standard dose of ethanol and found significantly lower values in BALB mice. The alcohol blood level at waking was significantly higher in C57BL mice; but 3 to 4 hr after the injection, when all the rats were awake, no significant difference in alcohol blood level was observed.

In vitro studies on the effect of ethanol on the respiration of brain cortex slices stimulated by potassium, performed by Mendelson and Mello [68], showed no difference between male hooded rats exhibiting high or low alcohol preference.

5. Fatty Liver and Alcohol Appetite

Rodgers et al. [100] observed that C57BL mice drinking great amounts of alcohol did not show pathological changes in the liver, but when sucrose was added to the alcohol solution during a long period, they increased the ingestion of this solution and exhibited fatty infiltration and inflammatory focuses of the liver similar to those observed in human alcoholic hepatitis. These lesions were not observed in C57BL mice having access only to alcohol or sucrose solutions. In contradistinction, mice from strains with low alcohol preference (BALB and DBA) showed more vulnerability to the sucrose than to the sucrose plus alcohol solution, the latter being consumed in small amounts.

6. Lethal Doses of Ethanol and Alcohol Appetite

Whitney and Whitney [137] reported that C57BL mice were more sensitive to the toxic effects of ethanol than BALB, DBA, or A/ALB, since the proportion killed by a dose of 0.4 ml of ethanol 50 % v/v was respectively 92, 73, 63, and 57%. The lethality among the hybrids was intermediate.

7. Morphine Dependence and Alcohol Appetite

Through selective inbreeding, Nichols and Hsiao [83] obtained two strains of rats with different susceptibility to morphine dependence: one very susceptible and another resistant. The F_3 generations differed also in the voluntary alcohol intake after a period of forced administration, the strain more liable to morphine dependence exhibiting a higher appetite for alcohol than the resistant one.

F.   Age Influence on Alcohol Appetite

Studies concerning the influence of age on voluntary alcohol intake have been performed on rats and mainly on males. The procedure used plays an important role in the interpretation of the results. When the preference for alcohol solutions of different concentrations is compared at different ages, the results are affected by the changes of total fluid intake occurring during development. This problem has been studied by Eriksson [26], who states that when the results are analyzed according to the daily alcohol intake by body weight, all the reported results agree in showing that it increases with age. This analysis confirms the initial results reported by Wallgren and Forsander [135] and shows that the decrease in the preference for alcohol solutions reported by Goodrik [34] in Sprague Dawley males and by Parisella and Pritham [84] in Wistar males is not actually accompanied by a decrease in the daily ethanol intake.

The results obtained by the last-mentioned authors [84] in experiments in which rats received simultaneously a glucose solution are difficult to interpret because of the known interference of a third choice of a sugar solution on the voluntary alcohol intake (see Section I.4).

Concerning primates, Fitzgerald et al. [29] reports that male chimpanzees drink significantly more alcohol after the fourth decade of life than before.

G.   Influence of Sex on Alcohol Appetite

There is no agreement in the results reported by different authors concerning the influence of sex on the appetite for alcohol in the rat. Shadewald et al. [122] observed in a group of Sprague Dawley rats that the alcohol intake was significantly ($p < 0.02$) higher in males than in females. The same difference between sex was reported by Clay [19] in a study including 55 males and 40 females from different strains and colors, selected at random from her laboratory colony. In contradistinction, Eriksson et al. [28] reported that in the ALKO colony of Wistar rats the alcohol intake of females was higher than that of males. We have studied (unpublished data) the eventual sex difference in our nondrinker (UCh-A) and drinker (UCh-B) strains at several stages of the artificial selection, and we have never found a significant difference in the voluntary alcohol intake between females and males. Similar results were obtained by Zarrow et al. [144] in a study on Sprague Dawley rats.

The great majority of the authors who have studied different strains of mice have not observed significant sex difference in alcohol appetite [39, 48, 72, 102]. Recently Eriksson and Pikkarainen [27] performed an extensive study on C57BL and DBA mice and observed a significantly higher alcohol consumption in females C57BL than males of the same strain; no sex difference was apparent in DBA. Parallel to the higher intake of alcohol, the activity of liver ADH was also higher in C57BL females than in males.

Arvola and Forsander [4] report that male hamsters drink more alcohol than females.

The problem has also been studied in monkeys by Fitzgerald et al. [29] through offering to chimpanzees and orangutans of both sexes fruit juices with or without alcohol. Male chimpanzees drank more alcohol than females ($p < 0.01$) ; no sex difference was observed amoung orangutans.

As we have discussed above (see Section D) strain differences may explain the contradictory observations reported by the different authors.

H. Endocrine Influences on Alcohol Appetite

1. Gonades

Some authors reported no significant effect of gonadectomy on alcohol appetite in rats of any sex [Mardones and Segovia, 56; Aschkenasy-Lélu, 5]; Shadewald et al. [122] observed a slight decrease of alcohol intake in males and an increase in females.

Estradiol and diethylstilbestrol decrease the alcohol intake of gonadectomized rats of both sexes [5, 56]. Emerson et al. [23] reported the same effect in intact deer mice. This is in agreement with a decrease in alcohol intake during estrus observed by Aschkenasy-Lélu [5] in rats.

Neither progesterone [23] in intact and gonadectomized deer mice nor testosterone [5, 56] in intact and gonadectomized rats has shown a significant effect on alcohol appetite.

Carved [15] reports that alcohol intake decreases in the hamster 1 to 3 days before delivery and during lactation.

2.   Thyroid

The results concerning the influence of thyroid hormone on alcohol appetite are controversial. Mardones and Segovia [56] did not observe changes in the alcohol intake of rats during a period of daily administration of 50 to 100 μg of thyroxin. Richter [93] reported that the addition of 0.04 to 0.1% of thyroid powder to the diet decreased the alcohol intake of rats; lower proportions did not modify it. Prieto et al. [88] observed a significant increase of alcohol consumption by rats of drinker and non-drinker strains when 0.5% of thyroid powder was added to the diet. Aschkenasy-Lélu [7] reported that thyroidectomy apparently decreased the alcohol intake of rats after a transient period of increase; Richter [95] observed an increase in one rat.

The addition of propylthiouracil to the diet of rats was reported by Zarrow and Rosenberg [143] to increase alcohol intake, but this result could be the consequence of a decrease in the consumption of solid diet due to the bitter taste of the drug.

Feeding an iodine-deprived diet to C57 mice, Mirone [70] reported a decrease in alcohol consumption. In contradistinction, Mäepää and Forsander [50] observed in Wistar rats that the shift of a balanced diet to an iodine-deprived one induced an initial decrease of alcohol intake, followed by a gradual increase to values higher than the basic one; after reestablishment of the balanced diet alcohol intake returned to the basic levels.

3.   Insulin

Insulin induces an increase of alcohol intake in rats [31, 56]. Pancreatectomy [56] or alloxan diabetes decreases it [31]. Carbutamide, an oral antiabetic drug, increases alcohol appetite [31]; others, such as chlorpropamide, phenbutamide, and metrahexamide, reduce it [110], possibly because they induce a disulfiram-like effect when administered together with alcohol.

4. Adrenals

Concerning the influence of adrenals on the appetite for alcohol in experimental animals, Mardones in his 1960 review [52] points out that this problem has received little attention, since only a paper of Mardones and Segovia [56] reports that in rats the alcohol intake increases during the second to twelfth days after the removal of the adrenals, and subsequently it decreases to the basic level. The situation is the same in 1970, in spite of the fact that the effect of stress situations has been the subject of several studies (see Section L).

I. Nutrimental Influences on Alcohol Appetite

1. Food Restriction

Assuming that an increase in alcohol appetite induced by thiamin deprivation (see Section I.3.a) could be the consequence of a decrease in food intake, Westerfeld and Larrow [136] studied the effect of food restriction on alcohol appetite in rats. They reported that a decrease of the offered food to 75% of the amount voluntary consumed did not affect alcohol appetite; a decrease to 50%, induced a significant increase in alcohol intake. The extra alcohol consumed corresponded to about 40% of the suppressed calories.

Royer et al. [109], restricting the ad libitum diet of rats to 12 hr/day, observed an increase in the free choice of alcohol. In the same line, Marfaing-Jallat [63] observed an increase in alcohol intake in rats submitted to food restriction, this increase being higher in those exhibiting basic high than low alcohol intake.

Aschkenasy-Lélu [6] observed that fasting increased the alcohol intake of rats; but when the fasting period was prolonged or when rats were submitted to successive periods of fasting, alcohol appetite tended to decrease.

All these results show that rats are able to learn that ethanol may replace the restricted food.

2. Organic Composition of the Diet

In 1955 we reported [61] that changes in the organic composition of the diet of rats fed on a purified solid diet supplemented with the known vitamins did not change the voluntary alcohol intake. The proportions in these experimental diets ranged from 29 to 81% carbohydrates, 6 to 28% fat, and 9 to 39% proteins.

Subsequent studies by other authors did not agree with the absence of effect of organic composition of the diet on voluntary alcohol intake. Lester and Greenberg [45] reported a higher alcohol intake of rats fed on a diet containing 46% than 63% of carbohydrates. Le Magnen and Marfaing-Jallat [43] reported that rats fed on a fat-rich diet (39%) consumed significantly less ethanol solution than controls receiving a balanced diet. Eriksson [26] studied this problem, using diets containing exclusively protein and carbohydrate or protein and fat. In both diets protein represented 25% of the total calories. His results show that the alcohol intake was appreciable lower with the fat diet; rats fed on the carbohydrate diet consumed equivalent amounts than controls with a balanced stock diet.

Mirone [70] reported that in mice alcohol intake increased when a balanced diet was shifted to a high-protein (60%) and low-carbohydrate (18%) one and that it decreased when fed on a fat-rich (45%) and low-carbohydrate (23%) diet.

The analysis of all the known facts in this line allows us to state that when rats or mice are fed on a diet sufficiently rich in fat, the voluntary alcohol intake decreases and that other changes in the diet induce less constant results.

3. Influence of Vitamin Deprivation

A. THIAMIN. The first results concerning the influence of vitamin deprivation on the voluntary alcohol intake of experimental animals were reported by Mardones and Onfray in 1942 [55]. These authors observed that rats fed on a purified diet in which the source of B vitamins was autoclaved yeast highly increased the alcohol intake but that subsequent supplement of thiamin, alone or together with other pure vitamins of the B complex, did not return the intake to normal levels. Furthermore we reported [51] that when the experiments were started with the mentioned diet supplemented with thiamin, no increase of the alcohol intake was observed (see Section I.3.d). Beerstecher et al. [9] confirmed the increase of alcohol intake of rats fed on a thiamin deprived diet. Mirone [70] reported that in C57 mice, exhibiting high preference for alcohol, thiamin deficiency did not increase the alcohol intake; Brown [12] observed that in mice from a strain of low preference for alcohol, LA/Bw, thiamin deficiency increased the alcohol intake of females but did not modify it in males.

The results of experiments in which thiamin was given in the alcohol solution [Senter et al., 120] are difficult to interpret, because the choice of the alcohol solution is affected by the search for the vitamin.

B. OTHER SINGLE VITAMIN DEFICIENCIES. In the above-mentioned paper Beerstecher et al. [9] also reported that single deprivation of riboflavin, pyridoxine, or pantothenate induced a significant increase of alcohol intake in rats; deficiency of biotin, choline, or vitamin A did not induce significant changes.

The study of Mirone [70] on C57 mice did not show an effect of pyridoxine or pantothenate deficiency on alcohol consumption. The experiments on LA/Bw mice performed by Brown [12] showed that pantothenate deprivation did not change alcohol intake; pyridoxine deficiency induced a significant increase in females but not in males. The same experiments showed that niacin deficiency induced a very significant increase of alcohol intake in mice of both sexes.

C. INFLUENCE OF MULTIPLE VITAMIN DEFICIENCY. Brady and Westerfeld [10] and Williams et al. [141] in rats, and Mirone [70] in C57 mice, have reported that a diet lacking simultaneously several vitamins of the B complex induced an increase in alcohol appetite. Delore and Berry [21] observed that rats fed on a purified diet without any vitamin supplement increased the alcohol intake, which returned to the basic level after shifting to a stock diet.

D. FACTOR N_1. The evidence that the deprivation of an unknown factor increases the alcohol appetite has been obtained in rats fed on a purified diet supplemented with autoclaved yeast. Under these experimental conditions [55] rats increased the voluntary alcohol intake and simultaneously lost weight; when a supplement of thiamin was then given, the animals recovered their weight, but the alcohol intake remained at the same levels. In contradistinction, when autoclaved yeast was shifted to an untreated one, the alcohol intake decreased to the basic level simultaneously with the gaining of weight and improvement in the general appearance. This unknown substance contained in untreated yeast was called factor N.

Afterward we observed [57] that rats fed on a diet supplemented with both autoclaved yeast and thiamin did not increase alcohol intake. Furthermore when rats that had reached a high-level alcohol intake after being fed a purified diet supplemented with autoclaved yeast were given a supplement of thiamin during several weeks, the alcohol consumption decreased slowly, reaching the basic level after 7 to 10 weeks. These facts show that factor N is actually formed by thiamin plus an unknown substance partially thermolabile that we named factor N_1. Table I summarizes the results obtained in the experimental conditions mentioned. The data show that

TABLE I   Effect of Various Supplements to a Purified Diet on the Voluntary Alcohol Intake of Rats[a] (groups of 4 to 6 rats)

Supplement	Number of groups	Alcohol intake, ml/day of 95% ethanol (mean ± standard error)	
		Per rat	Per 100 g b.w.
Untreated yeast	50	0.18 ± 0.02	0.13 ± 0.01
Autoclaved yeast	164	0.70 ± 0.02	0.64 ± 0.02
Autoclaved yeast plus thiamine (4 μg/100 g b.w.)	9	0.21 ± 0.05	0.13 ± 0.03
Pure B vitamins[b]	16	0.57 ± 0.04	0.35 ± 0.03

[a] Data from J. Mardones, N. Segovia, and A. Hederra, Complejidad del factor N, Bol. Soc. Biol. Santiago (Chile), 5, 27 (1948).
[b] Daily per 100 g body weight: thiamine, 4 μg; riboflavine, 25 μg; calcium pantothenate, 10 μg; pyridoxine, 10 μg; niacin, 0.5 mg; and choline chloride, 1.0 mg.

even when all the known vitamins were supplemented in doses covering with excess the requirements, alcohol appetite increased in the absence of yeast.

We have not yet succeeded in the isolation of factor N_1, because several circumstances have made this goal difficult. First, an important proportion of the drinker rats obtained by artificial selection are refractory to factor N_1 supplement; i.e., they maintain their high alcohol intake in spite of receiving dry liver in doses sufficient to decrease it to basic levels in others. This is an important handicap for the bioassay. Second, the content of factor N_1 in cattle liver, which is the raw material that we use for the isolation, varies very much from sample to sample. Third, it is not impossible that factor N_1 is not a single substance, which is another handicap for the isolation. Concerning the last point, two substances have been observed to reduce alcohol intake in N_1-deprived rats, namely, thioctic acid and glutamine; but in both cases the alcohol intake did not reach the lowest level, and the addition of a supplement of dry liver decreased it further. Finally, the activity of our research group has been directed to some other lines that emerged during the work and seemed more promising.

E.   THIOCTIC ACID. Since thioctic acid is a factor needed by certain microorganisms for the utilization of glucose or pyruvate but not acetate, we tested its effect on the voluntary alcohol intake of rats fed on a factor N_1–free diet [60]. Thioctic acid given in oral doses ranging from 62.5 to

750 µg per 100 gm of body weight during 4 to 10 days induced a slow decrease of the alcohol consumption, which was statistically significant 11 to 20 days after starting the supplement. The subsequent administration of dry liver induced a more marked decrease of alcohol intake. The effect of thioctic acid was not observed when it was given simultaneously with sulfasuxidine, suggesting that it could be mediated by the intestinal flora [59].

F. GLUTAMINE. Ravel et al. [90] reported that the toxicity of alcohols on *Streptococcus faecalis* was prevented by glutamine. Rodgers et al. [106, 107] observed that this nutrient decreased the voluntary alcohol intake of rats by 34 or 38% and that some related substances, such as glutamic acid, monosodium glutamate, asparagine, and glycine, did not change it. We have tested glutamine in rats fed on N_1-free diet and observed a small (14 to 25%) but significant decrease in the alcohol consumption [52].

4.   Influence of Offering a Third Choice of Nutrients on Alcohol Intake

In order to know whether the alcohol appetite of rats is similar to that of alcoholic patients, Lester and Greenberg [45] studied the changes of the alcohol intake in rats under free choice of water and alcohol solution, when a "third choice" of sucrose solution, fat emulsion, or saccharine solution was offered. The results of this experiment show that during the third-choice period the alcohol intake decreased significantly. Mardones et al. [61] confirmed these results concerning the third choice of sucrose and glucose solutions of variable concentrations. The results concerning the influence of a third choice of solid sucrose and of saccharine solution are not so clear [52].

The effect of a third choice points out the idea that the voluntary alcohol intake observed in rats is not actually a craving, and thus it is not exactly equivalent to the compulsive drive to alcohol observed in alcoholic patients, whose appetite for alcohol cannot be satisfied with sugar solutions or other nutrients.

J.   Pharmacological Influences on Alcohol Appetite

1.   Effect of Forced Intake of Ethanol

Since the behavioral signs of human alcoholism generally appear after long time of excessive drinking, the effect of a period of forced administration of ethanol on the subsequent alcohol intake under free-choice conditions has been studied in experimental animals, following different procedures.

The studies in which the period of forced ingestion of ethanol was given after establishing the basic appetite allow the comparison of the voluntary intake after and before this period.

Richter in 1953 [94, 95] did not find changes in the voluntary alcohol intake of laboratory rats even after very long periods—6 to 15 months—of the administration of alcohol solutions ranging from 8 to 24% as only source of fluid. Prieto et al. [87] reported no changes in the alcohol intake after periods ranging from 1 to 5 weeks, during which the only source of fluid was ethanol solutions at 10, 20, or 30% v/v.

In the same group of studies may be included the experiment performed by Eriksson [26] with rats genetically drinker and nondrinker, because in spite of the fact that the basic consumption was not studied, the expected one was known. In this experiment the level of the free choice of alcohol after a period during which 5% ethanol was the only source of fluid was equivalent to the expected one.

In another experiment, Eriksson [26], working with rats selected at random, without studying the basic consumption, observed that after a forced administration of 5% ethanol the level of free-choice intake was higher than that of the controls. The variance analysis, considering the alcohol intake in each of the 20 days of observation by every rat, showed that the intake of the group with previous forced administration of ethanol was significantly higher than the untreated controls. Nevertheless since the number of rats in each experimental group was rather small, the statistical analysis should consider that the random selection was performed on a group of rats with variable basic alcohol appetite, and thus the actual degrees of freedom are smaller than those corresponding to each daily intake. A new statistical analysis considering this situation cannot be performed with the published data.

The last-mentioned results are in agreement with those reported by Mirone [69], who observed that the prior administration of 5% alcohol solution to CF1 and DBA mice resulted in a higher alcohol appetite in subsequent free-choice conditions than their littermates who received water in the pretesting period.

Another kind of experiment on the influence of previous administration consists in offering to mice different concentrations of alcohol and water and studying their preference. Following this procedure, Thomas [130] compared the preference when concentrations are given in an ascending sequence from 10^{-10} to 30% and in descending order between the same limits. She observed no difference in the selection under both orders of administration in DBA and RIII mice, and a significant higher preference for the 10% alcohol solution of C57BL mice when it was preceded by 30% than by 1% ethanol solution.

Veale and Myers [134] studied the influence of a period of administration of 12% ethanol as the only source of fluid on the preference of alcohol solution ascending from 3 to 30%. They observed that these rats showed lower preference for any alcohol solution than the control receiving water during 10 days prior to the starting of the preference test. In the same paper these authors compared the total alcohol intake of rats submitted to consecutive sequences from 3 to 30% alcohol solutions and observed that the total alcohol intake was generally higher during the second than the first sequence, and during the third than the second one. When the second sequence was replaced by ad libitum water, the following sequence was not different from the third one of the control group; but when the second sequence was replaced by ad libitum 15% alcohol without water, the total alcohol intake observed during the subsequent sequence was significantly lower than the third one of the controls. The interpretation of these results is rather difficult. In fact in the same paper the authors reported that when successive sequences (3 to 30%) were given, the mean total alcohol intake increased from the first to the third sequence and afterward remained enough constant. This is in agreement with the idea that a learning process requiring a certain time is involved. This fact makes difficult the interpretation of the results obtained during the first experiences of experimental animals with alcohol solutions.

The offering of a weak solution of ethanol (2 to 4%) as the only source of fluid does not result in a real forced alcohol intake, because in this condition the limiting factor of the ingestion is the appetite for fluid, and thus the ingestion of ethanol is rather small. Thus it is not surprising that Rick and Wilson [98] reported that when 2 or 4% ethanol solutions were given as the only source of fluid, no significant changes were observed when water was offered as a second choice; when a 16% alcohol solution was given as the only source of fluid, the total alcohol intake significantly decreased when a second choice of water was offered.

Another factor making the interpretation of the results difficult is the interposition of periods of total deprivation of fluids between two experimental conditions.

Summarizing, it can be stated that the experimental results show in general that when a steady level of alcohol intake has been reached after a period of learning, the interposition of a period of forced alcohol intake does not alter the free choice in the subsequent period; but that the forced ingestion of alcohol previous to the learning period may either shorten or disturb it.

2.   Drugs Acting on Ethanol Metabolism

Assuming that alcohol appetite may be related to its use as a source of energy, the effect of drugs interfering with its metabolism on the voluntary intake of ethanol has been studied.

Koe and Tenen [40] observed that n-butyraldoxime, an alcohol dehydrogenase (ADH) blocking drug, induced a marked and lasting decrease of alcohol preference in C57BL mice. This drug also blocks aldehyde dehydrogenase in vivo, increasing blood acetaldehyde after ethanol administration, and thus the effect on alcohol preference could be also related to this disulfiram-like activity (see below).

The influence of metronidazol, another ADH blocking agent acting also on other steps of ethanol metabolism, has been studied. Campbell et al. [13] administered 125 mg/kg of this drug to rats having a free choice of 5% ethanol and water and observed an average significant decrease of alcohol intake, which returned to the basic one after discontinuing the drug. This effect was observed in 12 out of 18 rats; the other 6 did not change their alcohol intake during the metronidazol period. Valle-Anex et al. [132] studied the same problem in 10 rats from our drinker (UCh-B) strain under free choice of water and 10% v/v ethanol solution. The administration of 5 mg/kg of this drug during 10 days decreased significantly the alcohol intake in 3 rats; the group average decrease was nonsignificant ($-12.5 \pm 6.8\%$). Thus it seems that in some rats the appetite for alcohol was decreased by metronidazol; in others the drug seemed to be ineffective.

Disulfiram, a drug that blocks the oxidation of acetaldehyde and, when given together with alcohol, induces a toxic syndrome, has been reported to decrease the alcohol intake of rats [35] and mice [112]. Analogs of disulfiram induce an equivalent effect, exhibiting variable activity [35].

3.   Drugs Acting on Central Nervous System

Different drugs acting on CNS have been studied concerning their effect on the free choice of alcohol by rats, either untreated or submitted to stress.

No significant effect of amphetamine [73], methylphenidate, chlorpromazine, azacyclonol, meprobamate, pipradol, LSD, and reserpine [105] on alcohol appetite has been observed. Promazine [105] induces an increase in ethanol intake associated with a decrease of food consumption, perhaps due to the change of the taste of the diet.

Myers and Cicero [78] reported no changes in the alcohol intake of hooded rats submitted to different stressing situations, after receiving tybamate, a meprobamate analog.

4. Hepatotoxic Drugs

In 1953 Sirnes [124] reported that rats chronically intoxicated with carbon tetrachloride induced both liver cirrhosis and increase of appetite for alcohol. Campos et al. [14] showed that this increase of alcohol appetite was related to a higher rate of decrease of blood alcohol level, without an increase of the oxidation of ethanol to CO_2. Solodkowska et al. [126] reported that during this chronic intoxication the rate of in vitro incorporation of labeled ethanol into fat by adipose tissue slices, but not by liver slices, increased.

Since fatty liver can be produced experimentally in rats by adding 1% orotic acid to the diet [128], Muñoz et al. [74] studied the influence of this drug on the alcohol intake of rats exhibiting a wide range of basic alcohol intake and observed a significant increase of alcohol appetite in rats with a basic low or median intake and decreased it significantly in rats exhibiting abnormally high consumption. In the same group of rats the incorporation of labeled ethanol into fat by adipose tissue slices was significantly higher than in untreated controls; the incorporation into fat by liver slices was not different in experimental and control rats.

All these facts lead us to think that the rate of decrease in blood alcohol level by its incorporation into fat in the adipose tissue could be a factor in alcohol appetite.

5. Drugs Acting on Catecholamines or Serotonin Metabolism

The increasing interest in the effect of alcohol on catecholamines and serotonin metabolism, discussed by Davis and Walsh in this book, will motivate more studies of the effect of drugs acting on the metabolism of these amines on alcohol appetite. The data available today are rather scarce.

The effect of nialamide, a monoamine oxidase inhibitor, on alcohol intake was studied by Prieto et al. [89] in drinker and nondrinker rats. They observed that the administration of this drug decreased significantly the alcohol appetite in drinker and nonsignificantly in nondrinker rats.

Myers et al. [81] reported that α-methyl tyrosine, a drug that decreases brain catecholamines, slightly diminished the alcohol preference of rats. They also observed that p-chlorphenylalanine, an inhibitor of the production of serotonin in CNS, decreased the preference for alcohol during a period that lasted for 1 month after discontinuing the drug; the level of serotonin in brain was recuperated 2 weeks before.

6. Other Drugs

The effect of some glutamine antagonists has been studied by Rodgers et al. [108]. Azaserine induced a slight decrease of alcohol intake; methionine sulfoximide induced an immediate and long-lasting increase in alcohol consumption. This effect was not counteracted by simultaneous administration of glutamine.

Concerning sulfa drugs Nash et al. [82] observed that sulfadiazine increased the alcohol intake in 4 out of 13 rats. Mardones et al. [59] reported no change in the alcohol intake of rats fed on a N_1-free diet after the administration of sulfasuxidine.

The effect of diuretics (hydrochlorothiazide and Hygroton) was studied by Eriksson [24], who reported that although the total fluid intake was significantly increased, the alcohol intake remained unchanged.

K.   Effect of Physical Agents on Alcohol Appetite

The effect of environmental temperature on alcohol preference was studied by Myers [75] on Wistar and G-4 rats. He reported that the preference for ethanol solutions was higher at 27°C than at 18°C.

Since it is known that ethanol protects mice against the deleterious effect of irradiation [20, 85], Peacock and Watson [86] studied its effects on alcohol preference in C57BL mice and observed that during the 4 days after irradiation the alcohol intake significantly decreased without changing the total fluid intake, but after 2 days the alcohol intake recovered the preirradiation level.

L.   Influence of Stress on Alcohol Intake

In general the experiments on the effect of different stressing conditions on the voluntary intake of alcohol show that they increase alcohol appetite.

The first experiments in this line were performed by Masserman and coworkers [65] on cats submitted to conflicts inducing experimental neurosis. The results showed that under these stressing conditions cats preferred milk containing alcohol better than without alcohol, under free choice of both fluids.

Different stressing conditions have been studied on mice, rats, and monkeys. Noxious sounds in rats [41] and rotation of the cage in mice [11] have been reported to increase alcohol consumption. The effect of electric stimulation is irregular. Casey [16] has reported that rats submitted to this stress did not change alcohol intake during the time in which the electric stimulation was applied, but during 20 days after the shock period the alcohol intake increased, as if discontinuation of stress would induce a state of anxiety that increases the appetite for alcohol. Myers and Holman [80] did not observe any change in alcohol intake during a period of electric shocks applied to the footpads of Wistar rats. Mello and Mendelson [67] observed an increase of alcohol intake in one out of four monkeys submitted to electric shocks; in the other three no change was observed.

The increase of the number of mice in each cage has been reported [11, 130] to decrease alcohol intake; other experiments [104] did not show influence of this kind of stress.

Various stressing conditions used together have also been reported to increase alcohol appetite [19, 66, 119, 121].

Experiments on the influence of the learned avoidance of electroshocks on alcohol intake showed that it increased during the avoidance period in Wistar rats [1] and rhesus monkeys [18].

Concerning the psychological conditions related to alcohol consumption, Tobach [131] reports that rats exhibiting signs of timidity drink more alcohol than others.

M. Influence of Central Nervous System Injuries on Alcohol Appetite

The influence of the local administration of ethanol in the CNS on the alcohol preference of rats has been studied by Myers [76], who observed that the chronic administration of weak ethanol solutions in the cerebral ventricles increased the alcohol preference and that this effect was related to the dose. The same author [77] reported that the intraventricular injection of acetaldehyde, paraldehyde, or methanol solutions increased the preference of ethanol; the intraventricular injection of saline solution did not change this preference.

Marfaing-Jallat et al. [64] recently reported that female adult Wistar rats submitted to bilateral electrolytic lesions placed stereotaxically in the ventromedial hypothalamic area, offering free choice of water and 8% wt/v alcohol solutions and either ad libitum or with limited access to solid food, significantly increased their alcohol intake. These rats expressed their hyperphagia by increasing alcohol consumption and became obese. The maximum intake of pure alcohol did not exceed the maximum rate of oxidative capacity.

N. Appetite for Alcohol in Humans

Although appetite for alcohol in experimental animals can only be recognized through the amount consumed under free choice, in the case of humans it is possible to obtain information about the subjective phenomena involved.

Varela [133] systematically explored the subjective phenomena driving to the use of alcoholic beverages, either in normal individuals or in excessive drinkers and alcoholics. He proposed a classification of the alcohol appetite in three forms that can be easily distinguished, although borderline cases do also exist. These forms have been called the physiological, pharmacological, and pathological appetite for alcohol.

1.   Physiological Appetite for Alcoholic Beverages

The concept of a physiological appetite for alcohol has been postulated independently by Forsander et al. [31] and Mardones and Varela [62] as a form of appetite for drinking alcoholic beverages that does not involve the desire of experiencing its pharmacological effects on CNS.

This form of appetite is expressed, for instance, in individuals who like wine as a beverage with meals, who prefer to appease thirst with beer rather than with other drinks, or to consume small amounts of liquor before or after dinner.

It is possible that the small amounts of alcohol consumed under these conditions could induce some effects in the propioceptive system that may represent either absolute or conditioned stimuli of neurovegetative reflex evoking pleasant sensations.

It seems that the alcohol appetite observed in rats and mice is physiological.

2.   Pharmacological Appetite for Ethanol

Pharmacological appetite is defined as the desire of experiencing the effects of alcohol on the central nervous system.

In its higher degree the desired effect is an overt inebriety, as a way of impairing self-consciousness in order to avoid the awareness of unpleasant situations. This degree of pharmacological appetite is rather uncommon, even among alcohol dependents, and it is generally associated with severe personality disturbances.

A minor degree of pharmacological appetite is more common. Many people drink because they like the enhancement of self-esteem, the satisfaction with their own performances and the feeling of well-being induced by alcohol. This kind of appetite is very prevalent, even among individuals who can be considered normal concerning their drinking behavior.

It is convenient to state that the pharmacological appetite is not equivalent to psychic dependence but always accompanies it. As a matter of fact, psychic dependence is not defined by the degree of the desired pharmacological effect but by the frequency and the overpowering character of this desire, which conform to a characteristic behavior. An individual who attends a cocktail party and drinks rapidly until feeling "high" clearly expresses a pharmacological appetite, but he is not necessarily psychically dependent unless this appetite is overpowering and repeated or permanent.

Apparently this minor degree of pharmacological appetite for alcohol is more prevalent in liquor-drinker countries; physiological appetite is more common in wine- or beer-drinking populations. This could explain the different focusing of social drinking by authors from different countries. The excellent papers of P. Bailly Salin (France) [8] and M. Chafetz (United States) [17] in the Jellinek Memorial Symposium are good examples of these different criteria.

It is difficult to decide whether or not pharmacological appetite is present in laboratory animals who prefer alcohol solutions to water under free-choice conditions. The fact that rats decrease significantly the alcohol consumption when a third choice of a sugar solution is offered (see Section I.4) supports the absence of this kind of appetite, since it should not occur if a pharmacological effect were desired. It is possible that the self-administration of intravenous injections of alcohol solutions by monkeys under adequate experimental conditions may express a pharmacological appetite [142].

3. Pathological Appetite for Alcohol

It is commonly accepted that there are two forms of alcoholism in which the main behavioral traits reveal an abnormal appetite for alcohol, i.e., a pathological one. These behavioral traits are loss of control over drinking and inability to abstain.

The loss of control over drinking is characteristic of the so-called "intermittent alcoholism," for which Jellinek coined the name gamma alcoholism [37]. The individuals suffering from this form experience an overpowering desire to continue drinking after a first drink, that can even be taken for complying with social rules, without clear desire. This pathological appetite induces the patient to drink repeatedly until reaching an overt and maintained drunkenness. The drinking episode commonly ends by gastrointestinal disturbances, compelling him to stop drinking and bringing about withdrawal symptoms, such as intense tremor and, in some cases, consciousness disturbances, delirium, and convulsive seizures.

In contradistinction, inability to abstain characterizes the so-called "inveterate alcoholism" (delta alcoholism, according to Jellinek, Ref. 37). Patients suffering from this form are compelled to drink alcoholic beverages in variable doses repeated during the day and sometimes also during the night. A few hours after a drink, an overpowering appetite for a new one comes forth, apparently related to slight withdrawal symptoms, such as anxiety, discomfort, tremor, or autonomic disturbances, which are alleviated by the new drink. The appetite for alcohol in this condition is so overpowering that these patients are unable to abstain from alcoholic beverages, even when they are clearly aware of the severity of the organic, psychic, and social damages involved. These patients are commonly able to control the amounts ingested each time and to prevent or promote drunkenness at will.

The pathological appetite involved in any of these forms of alcoholism appears commonly after years of excessive drinking, either continuous or intermittent, but it is not exceptionaly observed after shorter periods, even less than 1 year. In some individuals both forms of alcoholism are observed in different periods of their life.

Apparently these two main forms of pathological appetite are the consequence of organic disturbances induced by the previous effect of alcohol, in a similar way to the withdrawal syndrome observed after continuous use of opiates or barbiturates. It seems also that an individual predisposition to acquire this pathological appetite may exist, since it is not observed in every heavy drinker and many of the patients exhibiting a short period of excessive drinking before pathological appetite emerges commonly belong to families with a heavy load of alcoholism.

As far as we are aware, nothing equivalent to a pathological appetite has been observed in experimental animals.

Very little is known about the intimate mechanism involved in the genesis of these three forms of appetite for alcohol. Thus they represent a matter widely open to exciting research.

REFERENCES

1. Adamson, R. and R. Black, Volitional drinking and avoidance learning in the white rat, *J. Comp. Physiol. Psychol.*, **52**, 734 (1959).
2. Anderson, W. D. and O. A. Smith, Jr., Taste and volume preferences for alcohol in Macaca nemestrina, *J. Comp. Physiol. Psychol.* **56**, 144 (1963).
3. Arvola, A. and O. Forsander, Comparison between water and alcohol consumption in six animal species in free-choice experiments, *Nature,* **191**, 819 (1961).
4. Arvola, A. and O. Forsander, Hamsters in experiments of free choice between alcohol and water, *Quart. J. Studies Alc.,* **24**, 591 (1963).
5. Aschkenasy-Lélu, P., Rélation entre l'effet inhibiteur des oestrogènes sur la consommation d'alcool du rat et leur action génitale, *Arch. Sci. Physiol.,* **14**, 165 (1960).
6. Aschkenasy-Lélu, P., Disparition de la préférence du rat pour l'alcool après des periodes succesives d'inanition suivies de réalimentation, *Compt. Rend. Soc. Biol.,* **156**, 1791 (1962).
7. Aschkenasy-Lélu, P., L'action inhibitrice des oestrogènes sur la consommation élective d'alcool du rat passe-t-elle par un relais thyroidien? *Arch. Sci. Physiol.,* **16**, 203 (1962).
8. Bailly-Salim, P., Clinical forms of alcoholism prevalent among wine drinkers. In *Alcohol and Alcoholism,* R. Popham (ed.), pp. 117–120, University of Toronto Press, Toronto, 1970.
9. Beerstecher, E., Jr., I. G. Reed, W. D. Brown, and L. J. Berry, The effect of single vitamin deficiencies on the consumption of alcohol by white rats, *Texas University Publishing,* **5109**, 115 (1951).
10. Brady, R. A. and W. W. Westerfeld, The effect of B-complex vitamins on the voluntary consumption of alcohol by rats, *Quart. J. Studies Alc.,* **7**, 499 (1947).
11. Brown, R. V., Effects of stress on voluntary alcohol consumption in mice, *Quart. J. Studies Alc.,* **28**, 555 (1967).
12. Brown, R. V., Vitamin deficiency and voluntary alcohol consumption in mice, *Quart. J. Studies Alc.,* **30**, 592 (1969).
13. Campbell, B., J. I. Taylor, and W. K. Haslett, Anti-Alcohol properties of metronidazol in rats, *Proc. Soc. Exp. Biol. N.Y.,* **124**, 191 (1967).
14. Campos, I., W. Solodkowska, E. Muñoz, N. Segovia-Riquelme, J. Cembrano, and J. Mardones, Ethanol metabolism in rats with experimental liver cirrhosis: I. Rate of combustion of labled ethanol and rate of decrease of blood ethanol level, *Quart. J. Studies Alc.,* **25**, 417 (1964).
15. Carved, J. W., J. B. Nash, G. A. Emerson, and W. T. Moore, Effect of pregnancy and lactation on voluntary alcohol intake of hamster, *Federation Proc.,* **12**, 309 (1953).
16. Casey, A., The effect of stress on the consumption of alcohol and reserpine, *Quart. J. Studies Alc.,* **21**, 208 (1960).

17. Chafetz, M. E., Clinical syndromes of liquor drinkers. In *Alcohol and Alcoholism*, R. Popham (ed.), pp. 111–116, University of Toronto Press, Toronto, 1970.
18. Clark, R. and E. Polish, Avoidance conditioning and alcohol consumption in rhesus monkeys, *Science*, **132**, 223 (1960).
19. Clay, M. R., Conditions affecting voluntary alcohol consumption in rats, *Quart. J. Studies Alc.*, **25**, 36 (1964).
20. Cole, E. J. and M. E. Ellis, Decreased X-ray sensitivity of mice following the administration of ethanol, *Amer. J. Physiol.*, **170**, 724 (1959).
21. Delore, P. and H. Berry, Carence alimentaire et récours à l'alcool, *Press Med.*, **63**, 1591 (1955).
22. Eimer, E. O. and R. J. Senter, Alcohol consumption in domestic and wild rats, *Psychosom. Sci.*, **10**, 319 (1968).
23. Emerson, G. A., R. C. Brown, J. B. Nash, and W. T. Moore, Species variation in preference for alcohol and the effect of diet or drugs on this preference, *J. Pharmacol. Exp. Therap.*, **106**, 389 (1952).
24. Eriksson, K., Effect of two diuretics drugs on liquid consumption and free choice of alcohol in albino rats, *Nature*, **213**, 316 (1967).
25. Eriksson, K., Genetic selection for voluntary alcohol consumption in the albino rats, *Science*, **159**, 739 (1968).
26. Eriksson, K., Factors affecting voluntary alcohol consumption in the albino rats, *Ann. Zool. Fennici*, **6**, 227 (1969).
27. Eriksson, K. and P. H. Pikkarainen, Differences between the sexes in voluntary alcohol consumption and liver ADH-activity in inbred strains of mice, *Metabolism*, **17**, 1037 (1968).
28. Eriksson, K. and K. K. Malmström, Sex differences in consumption and elimination of alcohol in albino rats, *Ann. Med. Exp. Fennica*, **45**, 389 (1967).
29. Fitz-Gerald, F. L., M. A. Barfield, and R. J. Warrington, Voluntary alcohol consumption in chimpanzees and orangutans, *Quart. J. Studies Alc.*, **29**, 330 (1968).
30. Forsander, O., Metabolism of rats as related to voluntary alcohol consumption, *Psychosom. Med.*, **28**, 521 (1966).
31. Forsander, O., J. Kohonen, and H. Soumalainen, Physiological alcohol consumption, *Quart. J. Studies Alc.*, **19**, 379 (1958).
32. Forsander, O. and M. Salaspuro, Voluntary ethanol consumption as related to ketone bodies metabolism in rats, *Life Sciences*, **1**, 467 (1962).
33. Fuller, J. L., Measurement of alcohol preference in genetic experiments, *J. Comp. Physiol. Psychol.*, **57**, 85 (1964).
34. Goodrick, C. L., Alcohol preference of the male Sprague-Dawley albino rats as a function of age, *J. Gerontol.*, **22**, 369 (1967).
35. Harkness, W. D., C. D. Johnston, and G. Woodard, Methods to evaluate in rats the antipathy to alcohol produced by antabuse and related compounds, *Federation Proc.*, **12**, (1953).
36. Jara, N., N. Segovia-Riquelme, and J. Mardones, Fructose metabolism in drinker and nondrinker rats, *Arch. Biol. Med. Exp.*, **7**, 47 (1970).

37. Jellinek, E. M., *The Disease Concept of Alcoholism,* Hillhouse, New Haven, 1960.
38. Kakihana, R., D. R. Brown, G. E. McClearn, and I. R. Taberhhaw, Brain sensitivity to alcohol in inbred mouse strains, *Science,* **154,** 1574 (1966).
39. Kakihana, R. and G. E. McClearn, Development of alcohol preference in BALB/c mice, *Nature,* **199,** 511 (1963).
40. Koe, B. K. and S. S. Tenen, Inhibiting action of *n*-butyral-doxime on ethanol metabolism and on natural ethanol preference of C57BL mice, *J. Pharmacol. Exp. Therap.,* (in press).
41. Korman, M., I. J. Knopf, and R. L. Leon, Alcohol as a discriminative stimulus; a preliminary report, *Texas Rep. Biol. Med.,* **20,** 61 (1962).
42. Ledermann, S. C., *Alcool, Alcoolism, Alcoolisation,* Cahier no. 29, Institut National d'Etudes Démographiques, Paris, 1956.
43. LeMagnen, J. and P. Marfaing-Jallat, L'interaction entre les consommations spontanées d'alcool éthylique et de divers regimen alimentaires chez le rat blanc, *Arch. Sci. Physiol.,* **16,** 179 (1962).
44. Lester, D., Self-selection of alcohol by animals: Human variations and the etiology of alcoholism, *Quart. J. Studies Alc.,* **27,** 395 (1966).
45. Lester, D. and L. A. Greenberg, Nutrition and the etiology of alcoholism: The effect of sucrose, fat and saccharine on the self-selection of alcohol by rats, *Quart. J. Studies Alc.,* **13,** 553 (1952).
46. Loiseleur, J. and M. Petit, L'éthylisme experimental de la souris, *Compt. Rend. Soc. Biol.,* **141,** 568 (1947).
47. McClearn, G. E., Genetic differences in the effect of alcohol upon behavior of mice, *Proc. Third internat. Conf. Alc. Road Traffic,* pp. 153, 1962.
48. McClearn, G. E. and D. A. Rodgers, Differences in alcohol preference among inbred strains of mice, *Quart. J. Studies Alc.,* **20,** 691 (1959).
49. McClearn, G. E. and D. A. Rodgers, Genetic factors in alcohol preference of laboratory mice, *J. Comp. Physiol. Psychol.,* **54,** 116 (1961).
50. Mäenpää, P. K. and O. A. Forsander, Influence of iodine deficiency on free choice between alcohol and water in rats, *Quart. J. Studies Alc.,* **27,** 530 (1966).
51. Mardones, J., On the relationship between deficiency of B vitamins and alcohol intake in rats, *Quart. J. Studies Alc.,* **16,** 563 (1951).
52. Mardones, J., Experimentally induced changes in the free selection of ethanol, *Intern. Rev. Neurobiol.,* **2,** 41 (1960).
53. Mardones, J., Pharmacogénétique de l'alcoolisme, *Actualités Pharmacologiques,* **21,** 1 (1968).
54. Mardones, J., A. Hederra, and N. Segovia, Fluctuaciones individuals del consumo de alcohol en ratas carenciadas, *Bol. Soc. Biol.* (Santiago), **7,** 1 (1949).
55. Mardones, J. and E. Onfray, Influencia de una substancia de la levadura (elemento del complejo vitamínico B?) sobre el consumo de alcohol en ratas en experimentos de autoseleccion, *Rev. Chilena Hig. Med. Prevent.,* **4,** 293 (1942).
56. Mardones, J. and N. Segovia, Adquisiciones del alcoholismo experimental y

sus proyecciones en el alcoholismo humano, Fundación Lucas Sierra, Chile, *Jornadas Clin. de Verano,* **5a,** 378, 1951.

57. Mardones, J., N. Segovia, and A. Hederra, Complejidad del factor N, *Rev. Med. Aliment.,* **7,** 27 (1947).

58. Mardones, J., N. Segovia, and A. Hederra, Heredity of experimental alcohol preference in rats: II. Coefficient of heredity, *Quart. J. Studies Alc.,* **14,** 1 (1953).

59. Mardones, J., N. Segovia, A. Hederra, and F. Alcaíno, Influence of sulfasuxidine on the effect of α-lipoic or thioctic acid on the voluntary alcohol intake of rats depleted of factor N_1, *Acta Physiol. Latinoamer.,* **3,** 140 (1953).

60. Mardones, J., N. Segovia, A. Hederra, and F. Alcaíno, Effect of synthetic thioctic or alpha lipoic acid on the voluntary alcohol intake of rats, *Science,* **119,** 735 (1954).

61. Mardones, J., N. Segovia-Riquelme, A. Hederra, and F. Alcaíno, Effect of some self-selection conditions on the voluntary alcohol intake in rats, *Quart. J. Studies Alc.,* **16,** 425 (1955).

62. Mardones, J. and A. Varela, Enfoque farmacológico de las toxicomanías en especial del alcoholismo, *Rev. Psiquiat.* (Chile), **21,** 83 (1956).

63. Marfaing-Jallat, P., Differences interindividuelles de la consommation spontanée d'éthanol par le rat blanc dans diverses situations expérimentales, *J. Physiol.* (Paris), **55,** 296 (1963).

64. Marfaing-Jallat, P., C. Larue, and J. LeMagnen, Alcohol intake in hypothalamic hyperphagic rats, *Physiol. Behav.,* **5,** 345 (1970).

65. Masserman, J. H., K. S. Jum, and M. R. Nicholson, Neurosis and alcohol, *Am. J. Physiol.,* **101,** 389 (1944).

66. Mello, N. K. and J. H. Mendelson, Operant performances by rats for alcohol reinforcement, *Quart. J. Studies Alc.,* **25,** 226 (1964).

67. Mello, N. K. and J. H. Mendelson, Factors affecting alcohol consumption in primates, *Psychosom. Med.,* **28,** 529 (1966).

68. Mendelson, J. H. and N. K. Mello, Potassium-stimulated respiration of cerebral cortex: Effect of ethanol on tissues from alcohol preferring and nonpreferring animals, *Quart. J. Studies Alc.,* **25,** 235 (1964).

69. Mirone, L., The effect of ethyl alcohol on growth, fecundity and voluntary consumption of alcohol by mice, *Quart. J. Studies Alc.,* **13,** 365 (1952).

70. Mirone, L., Dietary deficiency in mice in relation to voluntary alcohol consumption, *Quart. J. Studies Alc.,* **18,** 552 (1957).

71. Mirone, L., The effect of ethyl alcohol on growth and voluntary consumption of alcohol of successive generations of mice, *Quart. J. Studies Alc.,* **19,** 388 (1958).

72. Mirone, L., Water and alcohol consumption by mice, *Quart. J. Studies Alc.,* **20,** 24 (1959).

73. Moore, W. T., B. M. Moore, J. B. Nash, and G. A. Emerson, Effect of amphetamine sulfate on voluntary choice of alcohol in albino rat, *Texas Biol. Med.,* **10,** 406 (1952).

74. Muñoz, E., R. Alvarado-Andrade, W. Solodkowska, and Mardones, J., Effect of orotic acid on voluntary alcohol intake and alcohol metabolism by liver and adipose tissue slices in rats (to be published).

75. Myers, R. D., Alcohol choice in Wistar and G-4 rats as a function of environmental temperature and alcohol concentration, *J. Comp. Physiol. Psychol.*, **55**, 606 (1962).

76. Myers, R. D., Alcohol consumption in rats: Effects of intracranial injections of alcohol, *Science*, **142**, 240 (1963).

77. Myers, R. D. and W. L. Veale, Alterations in volitional alcohol intake produced in rats by chronic intraventricular infusion of acetaldehyde, paraldehyde or methanol, *Arch. Int. Pharmacodyn.* (in press).

78. Myers, R. D. and T. J. Cicero, Effects of tybamate on ethanol intake in rats during psychological stress in an avoidance task, *Arch. Int. Pharmacodyn.*, **176**, 290 (1968).

79. Myers, R. D. and K. Eriksson, Ethyl alcohol consumption valid measurement in albino rats, *Science*, **161**, 76 (1968).

80. Myers, R. D. and R. B. Holman, Failure of stress of electric shock to increase ethanol intake in rats, *Quart. J. Studies Alc.*, **28**, 132 (1967).

81. Myers, R. D. and W. L. Veale, Alcohol preference in the rat. Reduction following depletion of brain serotonin, *Science*, **160**, 1469 (1968).

82. Nash, J. B., W. T. Moore, and G. A. Emerson, Effect of sulfonamides on voluntary choice of 10% V/V alcohol by albino rats, *J. Pharmacol. Exp. Therap.*, **106**, 408 (1952).

83. Nichols, J. R. and S. Hsiao, Addiction liability of albino rats breeding for quantitative difference in morphin drinking, *Science*, **157**, 561 (1967).

84. Parisella, R. M. and G. H. Prithman, Effect of age on alcohol preference by rats, *Quart. J. Studies Alc.*, **25**, 248 (1964).

85. Peterson, E. and J. J. Matthews, Protective action of ethyl-alcohol on irradiated mice, *Nature*, **168**, 1126 (1951).

86. Peacock, L. J. and J. A. Watson, Radiation induced aversion to alcohol, *Science*, **143**, 1262 (1964).

87. Prieto, R., A. Varela, and J. Mardones, Influencia de un período de consumo forzado de alcohol sobre el consumo voluntario de alcohol en ratas, *Asoc. Latinoam. Cienc. Fisiol*, **1**, Reunión Punta del Este, Uruguay, Res. Trab. pp. 146, 1957.

88. Prieto, R., A. Varela, and J. Mardones, Influence of oral administration of thyroid powder on the voluntary alcohol intake by rats, *Acta Physiol. Latinoam.*, **8**, 203, (1958).

89. Prieto, R., A. Varela, and J. Mardones, Influencia de la nialamida en el consumo voluntario de alcohol en ratas. *Simp. Panam,* Inhibición enzimática y su aplicación terapéutica, Guanajuato, México, p. 74, 1960.

90. Ravel, J. M., S. Felsing, E. M. Landsford, Jr., R. H. Trubey, and W. Shive, Reversal of alcohol toxicity by glutamine, *J. Biol. Chem.*, **214**, 497 (1955).

91. Reed, J. G., A study of the alcoholic consumption and amino acid excretion

patterns of rats of different inbred strains, *Texas University Publishing,* **109,** 144 (1951).

92. Richter, C. P., A study of the effect of moderate doses of alcohol on the growth and behavior of the rat, *J. Exp. Zool.,* **44,** 397 (1926).

93. Richter, C. P., Loss of appetite for alcoholic beverages produced in rats by treatment with thyroid preparations, *Endocrinology,* **59,** 472 (1956).

94. Richter, C. P., Alcohol, beer and wine as food, *Quart. J. Studies Alc.,* **14,** 523 (1953).

95. Richter, C. P., Production and control of alcoholic craving in rats. In *Neuropharmacology Transactions of the Third Conference,* H. A. Abramson (ed.), pp. 39–146, Princeton, N.J., 1956, New York.

96. Richter, C. P. and K. H. Campbell, Alcohol taste thresholds and concentrations of solution preferred by rats, *Science,* **91,** 507 (1940).

97. Richter, C. P. and C. D. Haukes, The dependence of the carbohydrate, fat and protein appetite of rats·on the various components of the vitamin B complex, *Am. J. Physiol.,* **131,** 639 (1941).

98. Rick, J. T. and C. W. M. Wilson, Alcohol preference in the rat and its relationship to total fluid consumption, *Quart. J. Studies Alc.,* **27,** 447 (1966).

99. Roach, M. K. and R. J. Williams, Impaired and inadequate glucose metabolism in the brain as an underlying cause of alcoholism: An hypothesis, *Proc. Nat. Acad. Sci.* (Wash.), **56,** 566 (1966).

100. Rodgers, D. A., Factors underlying differences in alcohol preference among inbred strains of mice, *Psychosom. Med.,* **28,** 498 (1966).

101. Rodgers, D. A. and G. E. McClearn, Alcohol preference of mice, in *Roots of Behavior,* E. L. Bliss, (ed.), pp. 68–95, Hoeber, New York, 1962.

102. Rodgers, D. A. and G. E. McClearn, Mouse strain differences in preference for various concentrations of alcohol, *Quart. J. Studies Alc.,* **23,** 26 (1962).

103. Rodgers, D. A., G. E. McClearn, E. L. Bennett, and M. Herbert, Alcohol preference as a function of its caloric utility in mice, *J. Comp. Physiol. Psychol.,* **56,** 666 (1963).

104. Rodgers, D. A. and D. D. Thiessen, Effect of population. density on adrenal size behavioral arousal and alcohol preference of inbred mice, *Quart. J. Studies Alc.,* **25,** 240 (1964).

105. Rogers, L. L. and R. B. Pelton, Effect of behavior-altering drugs on alcohol consumption by rats, *Texas Rep. Biol. Med.,* **16,** 133 (1958).

106. Rogers, L. L., R. B. Pelton, and R. J. Williams, Voluntary alcohol consumption by rats following administration of glutamine, *J. Biol. Chem.,* **214,** 503 (1955).

107. Rogers, L. L., R. B. Pelton, and R. J. Williams, Aminoacid supplementation and voluntary alcohol consumption by rats, *J. Biol. Chem.,* **220,** 321 (1956).

108. Rogers, L. L., R. B. Pelton, and R. J. Williams, Effect of some glutamine antagonist on alcohol consumption by rats, *Federation Proc.,* **16,** 238 (1957).

109. Royer, R., G. Debry, and M. Lamarche, Recherches experimentales sur les réactions vasomotrices a l'alcool après administration de quelques sulfamides hypoglicemiants, *Thérapie,* **17,** 989 (1962).

110. Royer, R., M. Lamarche, and G. Debry, Comparison de la consommation

spontanée d'alcool chez le rats sous l'influence de quelques sulfamides hypoglicemiants, *Compt. Rend. Soc. Biol.,* **157,** 161 (1963).

111. Schlesinger, K., E. L. Bennett, and M. Herbert, Effect of genotype and prior consumption of alcohol on rats of ethanol 1-^{14}C metabolism in mice, *Quart. J. Studies Alc.,* **28,** 231 (1967).

112. Schlesinger, K., R. Kakihana, and E. Bennett, Effect of tetraethylthiouramdisulfide (antabuse) on the metabolism and consumption of ethanol in mice, *Psychosom. Med.,* **28,** 514 (1966).

113. Segovia-Riquelme, N., J. J. Vitale, D. M. Hegsted, and J. Mardones, Alcohol metabolism in "drinking" and "nondrinking" rats, *J. Biol. Chem.,* **223,** 399 (1956).

114. Segovia-Riquelme, N., I. Campos, W. Solodkowska, G. González, R. Alvarado, and J. Mardones, Metabolism of labeled ethanol, acetate, pyruvate and butyrate in "drinker" and "nondrinker" rats, *J. Biol. Chem.,* **237,** 2038 (1962).

115. Segovia-Riquelme, N., I. Campos, W. Solodkowska, I. Figuerola-Camps, and J. Mardones, Glucose and gluconate metabolism in "drinker" and "nondrinker" rats, *Med. Exper.,* **11,** 185 (1964).

116. Segovia-Riquelme, N., I. Figuerola-Camps, I. Campos-Hoppe, N. Jara, E. Negrete, and J. Mardones, Influencia del sexo, el linaje y la administración de etanol sobre el metabolismo de los carbonos 1 y 6 de la glucosa en la rata, *Arch. Biol. Med. Exp.,* **2,** 74 (1965).

117. Segovia-Riquelme, N., I. Figuerola-Camps, I. Campos-Hoppe, and J. Mardones, Metabolismo del etanol y acetato en ratas bebedoras y no bebedoras en ausencia de sobrecarga de substrato, *Arch. Biol. Med. Exp.,* **3,** 43 (1966).

118. Segovia-Riquelme, N., A. Hederra, M. Anex, O. Barnier, I. Figuerola-Camps, I. Campos-Hoppe, N. Jara, and J. Mardones, Nutritional and genetic factors in the appetite for alcohol, in *Alcohol and Alcoholism,* R. Popham (ed.), pp. 86–96, University of Toronto Press, Toronto, 1970.

119. Senter, R. J. and J. J. Persenky, Effect of environment on the alcohol consumption in rats after conditioning, *Quart. J. Studies Alc.,* **29,** 856 (1968).

120. Senter, R. J. and J. D. Sinclair, Thiamin-induced alcohol consumption by rats, *Quart. J. Studies Alc.,* **29,** 337 (1968).

121. Senter, R. J., F. W. Smith, and S. Lewin, Ethanol ingestion as an operant response, *Psychosom. Sci.,* **8,** 291 (1967).

122. Shadewald, M., G. A. Emerson, W. T. Moore, and B. M. Moore, Voluntary preference for alcohol of white rats after gonadectomy, *Federation Proc.,* **12,** 364 (1953).

123. Sheppard, J. R., P. Albersheim, and G. E. McClear, Aldehydedehydrogenase and ethanol preference in mice, *Proc. XXVIII Internat. Congress Alcohol Alcoholism* (Wash.), **1,** 110 (1968).

124. Sirnes, T. B., Voluntary consumption of alcohol in rats with cirrhosis of the liver: A preliminary report, *Quart. J. Studies Alc.,* **14,** 3 (1953).

125. Sohler, A. D., P. Burgio, and P. Pellerin, Changes in drinking behavior in rats in response to large doses of alcohol, *Quart. J. Studies Alc.,* **30,** 161 (1969).

126. Solodkowska, W., R. Alvarado-Andrade, E. Muñoz, and J. Mardones,

Ethanol metabolism in adipose tissue from rats chronically exposed to carbon tetrachloride: In vitro oxidation to CO_2 and incorporation into fatty acids and insaponifiable fraction, *Med. Exp.,* **18,** 331 (1968).

127. Solodkowska, W., R. Alvarado-Andrade, and J. Mardones, Comparison of metabolic pathways of ethanol-1-^{14}C and acetate-1-^{14}C in adipose tissue of rats, *Pharmacology,* (in Press).

128. Stranderfer, S. B. and P. Handler, Fatty liver by orotic acid feeding, *Proc. Soc. Exp. Biol. Med.,* **90,** 270 (1955).

129. Thiessen, D. D. and D. A. Rodgers, Alcohol injection grouping and voluntary alcohol consumption of inbred strains of mice, *Quart. J. Studies Alc.,* **26,** 378 (1965).

130. Thomas, K., Selection and avoidance of alcohol solutions by two strains of inbred mice and derived generations, *Quart. J. Studies Alc.,* **30,** 849 (1969).

131. Tobach, E., Individual differences in behavior and alcohol consumption in the rat, *Quart. J. Studies Alc.,* **18,** 19 (1957).

132. Valle-Anex, M., O. Barnier, and N. Segovia-Riquelme, (Unpublished data).

133. Varela, A., The role of personality in alcohol abuse. In: Alcohol and Alcoholism, R. Popham (ed.), p. 160, University of Toronto, Press, Toronto, 1970.

134. Veale, W. L. and R. D. Myers, Increased alcohol preference in rats following repeated exposures to alcohol, *Psychopharmacol.,* (Berl.), **15,** 361 (1969).

135. Wallgren, H. and O. Forsander, Effect of adaptation to alcohol and of age on voluntary consumption of alcohol by rats, *Brit. J. Nutr.,* **17,** 453 (1963).

136. Westerfeld, W. W. and J. Lawrow, The effect of calorie restriction and thiamin deficiency on the voluntary consumption of alcohol by rats, *Quart. J. Studies Alc.,* **14,** 378 (1953).

137. Whitney, C. D. and I. Whitney, Ethanol toxicity in the mouse and its relationship to ethanol selection, *Quart. J. Studies Alc.,* **29,** 44 (1968).

138. Williams, R. J., The etiology of alcoholism; a working hypothesis involving the interplay of hereditary and environmental factors, *Quart. J. Studies Alc.,* **7,** 567 (1946–1947).

139. Williams, R. J., L. J. Berry, and E. Beerstecher, Jr., Biochemical individuality: III. Genotrophic factors in the etiology of alcoholism, *Arch. Biochem. N.Y.,* **23,** 275 (1949).

140. Williams, R. J., L. J. Berry, and E. Beerstecher, Jr., Individual metabolism pattern, alcoholism, genetotrophic disease, *Proc. Nat. Acad. Sci. U.S.A.,* **35,** 265 (1949).

141. Williams, R. J., L. J. Berry, and E. Beerstecher, Jr., Genetotrophic diseases: Alcoholism, *Texas Rep. Biol. Med.,* **8,** 238 (1950).

142. Yanagita, T., G. A. Deneau, and M. H. Seevers, Evaluation of Pharmacologic Agents in the Monkey by Long Term Intravenous Self or Programmed Administration, in *XXIII Int. Congress of Physiol. Sci.* (Tokyo), 1965.

143. Zarrow, M. X. and B. Rosenberg, Alcoholic drive in rats treated with propylthiouracil, *Am. J. Physiol.,* **141,** 151 (1953).

144. Zarrow, M. X., H. Aduss, and M. E. Denison, Failure of the endocrine system to influence alcohol choice in rats, *Quart. J. Studies Alc.,* **21,** 400 (1960).

Chapter XII

GENETIC ASPECTS OF ALCOHOLISM

RICARDO CRUZ-COKE

GENETIC SECTION HOSPITAL J. J. AGUIRRE
UNIVERSITY OF CHILE, SANTIAGO

A. Introduction

Because alcoholism can be considered a modern disease only since its existence was first traced in 1804 by Trotter [48], the studies on its heredity component are very recent. The first one who studied this problem formally was Legrain [34] in Paris in 1889. This author found that one-third of the near relatives of alcoholics carried signs and symptoms of excessive drinking or alcohol addiction. But since the disease concept of alcoholism was not developed until Jellinek [27] in the middle of this century, no significant statistical study on the biological basis of alcoholism in man was performed until the classical monograph of Åmark in 1951 [2]. Using a psychiatric approach to study the morbidity risk for alcoholism among relative of alcoholics, this author studied 349 brothers, 265 sisters, 186 fathers, and 200 mothers of 203 male alcoholic probands. He found the following expectancies of morbidity risk: 21% for brothers, 26.2% for fathers, and only 2% for mothers and 0.9% for sisters. The morbidity risk for alcoholism among male siblings with only one alcoholic parent was 33.3% and with two nonalcoholic parents, only 17.1%. From these data it was clear that alcoholism was seen more in men than in women and that a significant familial factor was present.

The analysis of the concordance and discordance of alcoholism prevalence in monozygotic and dizygotic twins is a useful method to evaluate a genetic component. Important researches on detecting genetic factors in alcoholism by the twin method have been performed by Kaij [29] and Partanen et al. [43]. Kaij [29], in 1960, studying 174 twin pairs found a significant difference in the morbidity concordance between identical or monozygotic and dizygotic twins, suggesting an important heredity factor in the etiology of the disease. An impressive investigation of the inheritance of drinking behavior by Partanen et al. [43] in a large sample of 902 twins found hereditary differences between individuals in all variables describing drinking behavior. These authors concluded that the existence of hereditary differences between individuals with respect to alcoholism was a complex problem, because different definitions and operational indicators may be used. For instance, if the indicators of alcoholism are based on drinking behavior and dependence on alcohol, the presence of hereditary factors seems highly plausible, but if the criteria of alcoholism are based on social consequences of drinking, there is no evidence of hereditary factors.

The genetic study of alcoholism by the method of the "marker" genes is very recent. Lester [36] has reviewed the literature and showed that scant data are inconclusive. In 1958 Achté [3] found no difference in the distribution of the ABO system between 212 alcoholics and 1383 controls in Helsinki, Finland. A similar study of Nordmo 1959, in Colorado, was inconclusive. Peeples, in 1962, studied the inability to taste phenylthiocarbamide (PTC) in 52 alcoholics and 70 controls and found among the alcoholics a significantly greater proportion of nontasters, supporting an association between the recessive gene "t" and alcoholism. Lester [36] considers that these kinds of researches are at present the only way to hold up the possibility that genetic factors are involved in a predisposition to alcoholism.*

An important study by a pedigree approach method was performed by Kroon [32] in 1924. This author, impressed by the strong male prevalence of alcoholism, studied a large family, the progenitors of which were not alcoholics, and composed of subjects living in different places and belonging to different social and economical strata. He studied carefully this pedigree

---

* An association between alcoholism and ABH group substances and secretor status has been reported by Camps, et al., *Brit. Med. J.,* **4,** 457 (1969).

along five generations and found that alcoholism appeared only in males and that the mothers operated as the carriers of a supposed alcoholic hereditary character. Kroon concluded that in this pedigree alcoholism behaved as a sex-linked hereditary (or sex-limited trait), not influenced by the multiple cultural factors.

The first experimental evidence of the existence of a biological basis of the appetite for alcohol was shown by Richter and Campbell [44], who in 1940 reported that rats exhibited alcohol taste threshold for preferred solution. In 1949 Williams et al. [54] studied individual patterns of ethanol consumption in rats. Mardones and coworkers [39] studied, from 1942, the nutritional and genetic influences on alcohol appetite in rats, showed the importance of individual variations in voluntary alcohol intake, and demonstrated the genetic origin of these variations, allowing them to obtain through artificial selection, two strains of rats, one "drinker" and the other "nondrinker." In a recent review on the pharmacogenetic of alcoholism, Mardones [40] analyzed his material on a two-locus basis and suggested the hypothesis that nondrinker rats had a dominant gene in two loci, that drinker rats were recessive homozygous for one locus, and that rats with two recessive loci were lethal. These findings opened an important approach to one of the most important variables in the biology of alcoholism, the alcohol appetite.

In 1964 Cruz-Coke [7] reported the discovery of a strong gene disease association that was four times greater than any other between the genetic marker "color blindness" and alcoholic cirrhosis. Before analyzing this study and the following researches on this subject, it is very important to discuss some basic concepts of the genetic study of common diseases and of color vision and color blindness.

B.   Genetic Study of Common Diseases

The theoretical basis of the study of the hereditary components of common diseases in man have been posed recently by Morton [41], Edwards [16], and Falconer [17]. Because alcoholism can be considered a common disease, it is very important to discuss briefly the genetical methods used in the specific study of its hereditary component. In the next paragraphs some basic concepts and definitions in this controversial subject are summarized.

According to Edwards [16], almost all diseases in man are familial, in the sense that they are more likely to attack a person with an affected relative than someone with an equivalent set of unaffected relatives. All disorders are genetic in the sense that we could anticipate drastic changes in their incidence by selective breeding within the same environment. Where the pattern of inheritance is not consistent with a single factor, it is impossible to discriminate in the pattern of familial distribution between the genetic constitution and characteristics determined through other features showing familial similarities, such as nutrition, infection, housing, occupation, education, and in sibships the common uterine and noenatal experience.

1.   Multifactorial Inheritance

The fundamental difficulty of devising genetic models in common diseases with no explicable single genetic pattern lies in the nature of the complex phenotypic distribution. A classical explanation assumes that multiple factors, both inherited and acquired, acting independently, lead to a distribution that is correlated in families, so that we can measure the intensity of the familial concentration. This concept is known as the model of multifactorial or polygenic inheritance.

But it is possible that major genes may influence the continuous phenotypic distribution. Morton [41] considers that the effect of a gene on a character may be called "microphenic" if small as compared with phenotypic standard deviation and "megaphenic" if large. Consequently variation due to the interaction of microphenic effects and environment is called "continuous," avoiding the term "multifactorial" or "polygenic." On the contrary a gene has a megaphenic effect on a given phenotype, causing discontinuous variation. But every gene with only one primary specificity has multiple megaphenic and microphenic effects, the discoverable number of these effects being limited only by the patients and the technique of the investigator. So it is possible that major genes cause a significant proportion of the variation of defects in common diseases of obscure etiology, which are supposedly controlled by multifactorial kinds of inheritance.

2.   Heritability

Falconer [17] considers that the best way to study the genetic causation of a common disease that is not simply inherited is to determine the relative importance of heredity as a causative agent. The method consists in the analyses of the amount of variation, i.e., the variation between individuals that causes some to be affected and some not. The fraction of this variation attributable to genetic difference between individuals is called "degree of genetic determination." Unfortunately this fraction cannot be estimated directly from human data, unless possibly by the twin method. But a related quantity, heritability, can be estimated.

Heritability expresses the extent to which the phenotypes exhibited by parents are transmitted to their offspring and therefore determines the correlation between relatives. Because heritability can be estimated from the degree of resemblance between relatives through the correlation coefficient, Falconer has devised a method for converting the information contained in the disease incidences to an estimate of the correlation between relatives. He supposes that there is an underlying gradation of some attribute related to the causation of the disease, referred to as the "liability" to the disease. The term "liability" is extended to express not only the innate tendency of the individual to develop the disease, i.e., his susceptibility, but also the whole combination of external circumstances that makes him more or less likely to develop the disease.

This author illustrates this concept with an example. In the case of an infectious disease the individual's susceptibility in the usual sense depends on his immunological defenses, but the liability includes also the degree of exposure to the infective agent. Now whether an individual is affected or not depends on whether his liability exceeds or falls short of a fixed threshold. The correlation of liability between the relatives leads to an estimate of the heritability of liability, which estimates the relative importance of hereditary factors as causes of differences of liability between individuals.

A special graph for estimating the heritability of liability from two observed incidences of the disease, between the general population and the relatives of affected individuals, is given by Falconer [17]. Applying this graph to the figure given by Åmark [4] of 3.4% of alcoholics in the general population of males and 21.1% in the brothers of alcoholics, the heritability reaches a high figure of 90%. The figure for the sisters of alcoholics is lower, with a heritability of 42%. There is an important sex difference in the inheritance of liability of alcoholism. Figures given by Falconer on the heritability values of other diseases are 46% for renal stone disease, 37% for peptic ulcer, and 79% for congential pyloric stenosis. Consequently, using the method of Falconer [17], the hereditary factor seems to be a very strong component of the causes of differences of liability to alcoholism between individuals.

3.   Association

An association of a given disease with characteristics known to be inherited in a single gene would seem to support a biological factor in the etiology of a disease. If we consider a case in which multiple influences affect the phenotype so that a proportion of individuals show some sign that can be scored, then we may suppose that this difference in incidence denotes a difference in the susceptibility in persons with different genetic characters. Nevertheless the biological meaning of an observed correlation between a genetic character and a disease is not always obvious. Many environmental influences can explain the association, together with biased samples and inappropriate stratification.

Quoting Clarke [6], it is very important to differentiate an "association" from a "linkage." Linkage is purely a mechanical arrangement of genes in the same chromosome. In association, characters appear more frequently together in the same individual patient than would be expected by chance. The importance of this association from the medical point of view is that it may throw light on the etiology of the diseases. For example, the association of group O with duodenal ulcer might be due to the H antigens on mucosal secreting cells of 0 individuals conferring less protection against ulcerogenic agents than the A antigen on A cells.

During the last decade a large number of gene-disease associations have been investigated. Clarke [6] has recently summarized the situation. The strongest association between blood groups ABO used as genetic markers and the disease duodenal ulcer has a relative prevalence of only 40%. This genetic or predisposing risk is small, considering that the relative risk of lung cancer with cigarette smoking is between 800 and 900% greater among smokers than nonsmokers.

Edwards [16] has proposed a model for the interpretation of association between blood groups and disease in terms of variance partitioning. He expresses the association by reference to the difference between the mean of two constituent normal curves of variation of liability to diseases that are assumed to be of equal variance. Applying this method, it is possible to estimate that the contribution of the ABO genetic system to the total variance of gastrointestinal diseases, as duodenal ulcer or cancer of the stomach, is only 1%. According to Edwards the genetic component of duodenal ulceration, marked with the ABO system, is very small and weak.

C.   The Genes for Color Vision

The color-vision system of the human species is controlled by a large, complex, and evolving groups of genes, interacting with environment and culture. We are just beginning to understand the meaning of the existence of this wonderful biological system. Defective color vision is not an innocent trait, neutral in relation to the existence of man, but highly related to his biological and cultural evolution and his diseases. Few sentences may give some basic information on the interesting controversy of the features of this crucial problem in the study of biology of man.

The color-vision genes are located in the X chromosome and consequently are named sex-linked genes. These genes have been detected in the short arm of this chromosome, together with other classic X-linked genes, as hemophilia, blood group Xg, glucose-6-phosphate dehydrogenase, ichtiosis, and serum system Xm [28]. Most recent genetic studies [5] suggest that the color-vision system is located in the middle of this short arm, distributed in two possible places or "loci": protan and deutan loci.

After the recent discoveries of Waaler [51] of the normal genes of the blue and green regions of the spectrum, the total known number of color-vision genes has mounted up to 10, probably grouped in five places or loci. Table I shows a comparison between the classical notation and a new molecular classification of these genes, according to Waaler [52]. There is no correspondence between both classifications in the Tritan region, which is related to the blue-yellow lines of color blindness. Waaler [52] suggests that the Tritan and possible Tetartan genes belong to the families of the normal color-vision genes B1, B2, G1 and G2. Then the number of genes would be only 8. In any case from this table it is possible to observe that the color-vision system in human beings is large, multiple, and complex and located in the X chromosome.

TABLE I   Classical and Molecular Classification of Color-Vision Genes

Classical notation (Wright-Kalmus)			Molecular notation (Waaler-Linkz)			
Locus	Genes	Male phenotype	Male phenotype pure color	Spectrum locus, nm	Genes	Locus
Normal	cv+	Normal vision	Low blue	479	B1	
			High blue	487	B2	
			Low green	515	C1	
			High green	525	G2	
						Cistron
Protan	cvp	Protanomaly	Low yellow	583	P1	
	cvP	Protanopia	Red anopia	563	PP	
Deutan	cvd	Deuteranomalia	High yellow	583	D1	
		Deuteranope	Green anopia		DD	
Tritan	cvt	Tritanomalia	(Blue anopia)			
	cvT	Tritanopia				

The biological characteristics of this color-vision system can be summarized as follows: (a) it is a large system controlling the interaction of retina with the spectrum of electromagnetic radiation between 400 to 700 nm; (b) it is organized according to multiple individual genes, having different degrees of genetic dominance, i.e., the less severe defects are dominant over strongest defects; (c) the genes control directly the three basic color pigments *eritrolabe* (red-catching), *chlorolabe* (green-catching), and *cyanolabe* (blue-catching), which are responsible for all the color mixing possibilities; and (d) the color-vision defects arise from the pigments deficiencies named "anomalies" (protanomaly, deuteranomaly, and tritanomaly), and the pigments abscences "anopias"; protanopia (red-lacking), deuteranopia (green-lacking), and tritanopia (lacking the *cyanolabe* pigment).

The tritanopia gene is an exception in this system, because, according to the studies of Kalmus [28], it is an autosomal gene (non-sex-linked) and very rare, less than 0.001% in the general population.

The six abnormal mutant genes sustain the phenotype known as "color blindness," which was discovered by John Dalton in 1798. The fact that color blindness is more frequent in males is the consequence of a basic mechanism of sex-linked inheritance. Genotypes of females behave as an autosomal inheritance with two homozygotes and one heterozygote. On the contrary, males show only two different genotypes, because they have only one X chromosome. Sex-linked inheritance at the individual level affects mainly the heterogametic or hemizygous sex, leaving females less affected by color blindness. But the distribution of color blindness in a population of males and females is controlled by the vision genes which are grouped in the human population under a biological system named "genetic polymorphism."

Color blindness is the expression of a genetic diversity that reaches a high incidence in a human population, the same as the diversity of different types of blood groups. People who are color-blind show a type of variation with sharply distinct qualities that coexist as normal members of a population. This biological condition has been considered by Ford [21] as a genetic polymorphism and defined as "the occurrence together in the same habitat of two or more discontinuous forms of a species in such proportions that the rarest of them cannot be maintained merely by recurrent mutation." This definition excludes geographical or racial continuous variation of metrical characters and the segregation of major genes when responsible for rare diseases maintained by recurrent mutation (hemophilia). Color blindness fulfills this definition, because (a) the color-vision genes are discontinuous and common; (b) the color-vision defects are multiple and graded in severities in a series of multiples alleles (classes of genes); and (c) probably color-vision defects are evolving under the influence of powerful selective forces.

The normal and abnormal color-vision genes are detected through different types of subjective tests. The less efficient tests are the pseudoisochromatic plates of Ishihara and Hardy-Rand-Ritter. With best efficiency and good selectivity ranks the Farnsworth-Munsell 100 Hue test [19], which detects significant low discrimination ability along all the spectrum loci. The most efficient tests are the anomaloscopes of Nagel and Pickford, which in the hands of a skilled observer allow us to detect even the slightest color deficiency. Unfortunately color blindness is commonly explored with the less efficient tests, and consequently the true figures of color-blindness frequencies among human populations are not really known.

Nevertheless the Ishihara test, which was introduced in 1926 in Western countries, has been used among human populations throughout the world. According to the results of this test, the frequency of color blindness has a wide range of variation, from the absence in most primitive populations up to 8 to 9% in most acculturated peoples in Europe and the United States. This difference could be explained by the flow of mutant genes of Western men into primitive regions or by a selection relaxation mechanism, as proposed by Post [42]. This author suggests that 5000 years ago, before the agriculture revolution, color-blindness genes were very rare and maintained in the population by a classical balance between mutation and natural selection. Color blindness may be a serious handicap in primitive cultures of hunters and food gatherers and thus subject to selection. The agriculture revolution changed these conditions, and probably natural selection against the color-vision mutant genes relaxed to zero, and color-vision mutants started to increase by unchecked mutations.

Questioning this hypothesis, Ford [21] suggested that it is not possible to consider mutation as the sole force balancing the handicap of color blindness in primitive people. Any rare genetic system can reach the status of polymorphism throughout the association with advantages as well as disadvantages, and consequently the color-vision mutants could have increased the frequency in human populations under the support of an adaptative advantage in a new habitat.

D. Association of Color Blindness with Alcoholism

Although color blindness was the first genetic polymorphism described, studies relating this phenotype to disease susceptibility began only after the report of Cruz-Coke in 1964 [7]. In that year a highly significant association between color blindness and alcoholic cirrhosis of the liver was found in a Chilean hospital sample of 900 consecutive admissions.

In October 1963 Cruz-Coke begun to study formally the genotypic basis of common diseases in all consecutive admissions to Division B of Medicine of the University Hospital J. J. Aguirre in Santiago. The experiment was designed according to the prospective disease association method suggested by Li. The conditional probability $P(z|y)$ of having a disease z, given the individual carries the genetic character y, was calculated according to the equation $P(z|y) = N(zy)/(N(y)$, where $N(zy)$ represents the number of patients with disease z who carry the genetic character y and $N(y)$ the total number of patients who carry y. The relative risk x of a common disease in a given genetic character was determined by the relation between two conditional probabilities, with and without the genetic character.

During the first week in the hospital, every patient was "marked" with the following genetic systems: (a) blood groups ABO; (b) blood groups MN; (c) PTC taste sensitivity; and (d) color-vision test with the Ishihara and Hardy-Rand-Ritter pseudoisochromatic plates. The statistical significance of the differences in the incidence of each genetic character with each common disease was determined by the χ^2 test. Table II shows the 40 tests performed between 10 common diseases and the 4 genetic systems. A highly impressive association between color blindness and cirrhosis of the liver was discovered. For one degree of freedom the χ^2 test reached the impressive value of 65.68, with P less than 10×10^{-12}. The relative risk x of a color-blind subject to became cirrhotic was found to be 6.51, that is, 551% greater than a normal-color-vision individual, and four times greater than in any known association between blood groups and diseases.

In order to estimate the importance of the association discovered, we can use the analysis of genetic variance with the method of Edwards [16]. This analysis shows that the contribution of the color-vision loci to the variance of liability of alcoholic cirrhosis is 13.6% in males, 5.9% in females, and 10.4% in both sexes. It seems that color blindness is an important source of variation in the liability to alcoholic cirrhosis disease.

After this discovery, Cruz-Coke increased the sample up to 900 patients and published in 1965 the first general results [8]. The frequency of color blindness in males was found to be 9.8%, versus only 4.7% among Chilean male students and 3.5% among sailors of the Chilean navy. The study shows similar distribution of the types protan, deutan, and undetermined and their intensity (mild, moderate, strong) among patients with color defectiveness either with or without cirrhosis. Clinical data and laboratory findings were also similar in color-blind and noncolor-blind cirrhotic patients. In this preliminary series Cruz-Coke found respectively 84 and 85% of alcoholics among cirrhotics with and without color blindness.

TABLE II   Values of χ^2 Test with One Degree of Freedom Obtained in the Comparison Between 10 Common Diseases and 4 Genetic Polymorphic Systems in a Prospective Sample of 727 Inpatients. After Cruz-Coke [11]

		Characters			
		Blood groups		PTC	Color
Common diseases	N	ABO	MN	test	blindness
Hypertension	76	0.89	1.12	1.83	1.34
Nephritis	66	0.13	0.68	2.93	0.07
Rheumatic disease	65	0.13	0.91	0.41	4.69
Liver cirrhosis	75	0.02	0.23	3.22	65.68[a]
Cardiosclerosis	50	0.006	4.73	2.03	3.93
Diabetes	31	1.38	0.20	0.01	3.80
Hepatitis	11	3.14	0.03	0.17	0.18
Obstructive jaundice	25	0.003	0.02	0.93	0.24
Pulmonary tuberculosis	36	0.10	0.14	0.18	0.50
Cholecystitis	41	0.007	2.10	1.63	0.10

ABO   = O versus non-O
MN   = MM versus non-MM
PTC   = nontasters versus tasters
Color blindness = color blind versus normal

[a] $P < 0.000001$; $r = 0.30$,
   relative risk $x = 6.51$

Because in the studied group the association between cirrhosis and alcoholism was similar among patients exhibiting color blindness and normal color vision, Cruz-Coke and Varela [10] tried to disclose the association between color blindness and alcohol addiction. They studied a sample of 100 male alcoholics and found 18 color-blind subjects. Using a control group of 633 male students of the same urban area, 30 of whom were color-blind [10], a highly significant association was found with the method of Woolf: $x = 4.41$; $\chi^2 = 55.9$; $P < 0.001$. This result suggests that the association between color blindness and cirrhosis could be due to alcoholism itself.

It is very important to stress the fact that Cruz-Coke [8] and Cruz-Coke and Varela [10] did not specify the type of color blindness associated with alcoholism or alcoholic cirrhosis. In both studies half of the color defectives belonged to the unclassified type as detected, and they did not conclude that color blindness among alcoholics was of the red-green type.

After these researches the association discovered was confirmed in other populations. Saraux et al. [46] in France studied 40 alcoholic patients with the F-M 100 Hue test and found a high proportion with very low discrimination ability in the blue-yellow zone, and also on both protan and deutan regions. Dittrich and Neubauer [14] studied 120 inpatients in a hospital in Vienna, using anomaloscope, Ishihara and Farnsworth dichotomous-15 tests, and found a highly significant association between alcoholic cirrhotics and yellow-blue defectiveness. In a small sample of 50 inpatients in the hospital in Arica, in northern Chile, with a significant proportion of Aymara-speaking people, Cruz-Coke [9] found also a highly significant association between color blindness and alcoholic cirrhosis.

Some authors have published results in which such association was not statistically significant. Using Ishihara plates, Gorrel [23] studied 4.177 patients in a hospital in Birmingham and, surveying 55 alcoholics, found only 3 color-blind subjects. Thuline [57] could not find a statistically significant association in a sample of 172 alcoholics in a Veteran Administration Hospital in United States, but the χ^2 test for the deutan group was 3.4, which is near the significant $P = 0.05$. Reid et al. [45] studied 100 patients with cirrhosis and 100 controls in a hospital in Baltimore; 4 color-blind were found in the control group and 13 in the cirrhotic patients, but the difference was significant only at the 5% level (χ^2 with the Yate's correction = 4.1). Among the 39 Negro cirrhotic patients 9 were color-blind, and among the 61 white cirrhotic patients only 4 were color-blind. The trend seems to be toward an increase in color blindness in Negro cirrhotics (χ^2 with Yate's correction = 4.37; $P < 0.05$).

Fialkow et al. [20] studied in Seattle 24 male and 22 female alcoholics and found 20 color-blind subjects, that is, 41%. This investigation reveals an association between color-vision defects and Leannec's cirrhosis or alcoholism. However, when retested during convalescence 7 of the "defective" patients were now scored as normal. This fact is explained because 5 false defectives were first tested in inappropriate mental conditions and 12 of the 20 defectives were classified with a mild undetermined defect by missing plate 3 of the H-R-R test. In any case, among the males, 13% remained color-blind during convalescence, a figure that is higher than the 6.1% found in 5.263 school children of the state of Washington. According to Fialkow the possibility that these patients have slightly increased frequency of classic X-linked color blindness cannot be excluded until larger series are tested.

Table III summarizes all the surveys performed in world population

TABLE III   World Surveys of Color-Vision Defectiveness Among Male Cirrhotic and Alcoholic Patients (1964–1969)

Year	Country, City	Disease	Total patients	Color-blind		Test	Type of predominant defect	Reference
				N	%			
1964	Chile, Santiago	Cirrhosis	63	21	33.3	HRR	U RG	8
1965	Chile, Santiago	Alcoholism	100	18	18.0	HRR	U RG	10
1966	Chile, Arica	Cirrhosis	8	5	62.5	HRR	U RG	9
1966	France, Paris	Alcoholism	40	9	22.5	FM	RG?	46
1966	U.S., Seattle	Cirrhosis	24	3	12.5	HRR-IS	U RG	20
1967	Austria, Vienna	Alcoholism	49	34	69.3	FM-IS-AN	RG BY	14
1967	U.S., Seattle, Wash.	Alcoholism	172	10	5.8	HRR	RG	57
1967	U.K., Birmingham	Cirrhosis	55	3	5.4	IS	RG	23
1967	U.K., Birmingham	Alcoholism	26	2	7.7	IS	RG	23
1968	U.S., Baltimore	Cirrhosis	58	9	15.5	HRR-IS	RG	45
1968	Mexico, Mexico, D.F.	Cirrhosis	32	6	18.8	HRR-IS	U RG	37
1968	Italy, Rome	Cirrhosis	16	7	43.7	HRR-IS-FM	BY	4
1969	Chile, Santiago	Alcoholism	65	33	50.7	FM-HRR-IS	BY	50
1969	Chile, Santiago	Alcoholism	149	58	38.9	FM-HRR-IS	BY	49
			857	219	25.6			

HRR = Hardy Rand Ritter; IS = Ishihara; FM = Farnsworth-Munsell; AN = Anomaloscope.
U = undetermined; RG = Red-Green; BY = Blue-Yellow.

among cirrhotics and alcoholic patients. An over-all estimate of the incidence of color blindness of all types reached in males the very high figure of 25.4% versus a mean world value of 5.0%.

All these researches, with either significant or not significant results, were performed in small samples, but always, preliminary estimates have shown at least an increase or excess of color-blind individuals in the alcoholic population. Consequently, after 6 years of a worldwide color-vision survey in alcoholic cirrhotics it seems that an association between a genetic marker and a common disease has been established. Now a second stage of research has begun in order to solve three basic problems: (a) the determination of the type of color-vision deficiency; (b) the determination of the nature of the defect, acquired or genetic; and (c) the relationship among color vision, cirrhosis of the liver, and alcoholism.

E.   Acquired Color Defectiveness

The most simple explanation of the existence of this association is that cirrhosis of the liver or alcoholism tends to interfere with the formation of the eye pigments needed for color vision and to produce secondarily an "acquired" color blindness. In his original paper Cruz-Coke [8] discarded this idea, because the clinical and laboratory findings were similar in cirrhotic patients with and without color blindness; the type and intensity of defective color vision were similar among cirrhotic and noncirrhotic patients, and other common diseases of the liver, such as viral hepatitis or obstructive jaundice, were not associated with color blindness.

Fialkow et al. [20] suggested that the majority of color-vision defects in alcoholic patients with cirrhosis could reasonably be considered secondary to the disease. The impaired mental status and poor attention span seen in decompensate cirrhosis or consequent to acute and chronic alcoholism interfere with color vision perception, at least in a testing situation. Considering the researches of Laroche [34] on the modifications of color vision under the influence of drugs, vitamins, and alcohol, Fialkow raised the possibility that the color-vision abnormalities seen in his patients were secondary to alcohol intake, to malnutrition with vitamin deficiency, and that their reversal to normal with convalescence may be due to vitamin therapy given in the hospital.

The problem of the nature, acquired or genetic, of the color defectiveness is related directly with the type or class of color defect. Before discussing the findings and interpretations of Cruz-Coke and of Fialkow, we must consider some basic information about the concept of acquired color blindness.

By definition color blindness is a hereditary character. But other color-vision disturbances may emerge as secondary complications of serious diseases of the eye or the nervous system. According to François and Verriest [22], the frequency of these acquired color-vision disturbances is relatively small, probably less than 2% of the total color-vision defectives. Roughly there are two kinds of acquired deficiencies: the red-green type and the yellow-blue type. All diseases of the eye can affect color vision at the prereceptorial, within the receptors, or at the postreceptorial level. This disease seems to develop in three stages: first, there is an abnormal trichromatic condition; in the second stage a dichromatic state appears, with the suppression of one color receptor; and at the end of the process the monochromatic condition and complete blindness develop. Kelekom [30] has studied the distribution of the types of color-vision deficiencies according to the morphological sources of the optical lesions. It seems that yellow-blue defects are more common in retinal diseases and red-green defects in the optic nerve involvement.

Yellow-blue deficiencies have been found in advanced stages of hypertensive retinopathy and at the early stages of diabetic retinopathy. Moreover François and Verriest [22] gave a long list of drugs and chemical substances that can produce acute intoxication affecting transitorily color vision in man. According to Saraux et al. [46], chronic alcohol intoxication probably involves the optic nerve causing some inespecific disturbances in color vision. But up to the present it seems that not any one common disease, without ocular involvement, has been known to originate a color-vision disturbance.

From these facts it is clear how important it is to determine the specific type of color-vision disturbance. The classical Ishihara plates are not suitable for detecting these minor defects. The invention, in 1943, of the Farnsworth-Munsell 100 Hue Test [19] facilitates the study of these minor defects along all the spectrum color, by the recognition of the type and extent of an acquired reduction of color discrimination. Consequently according to the studies of Saraux et al. [46] and Dittrich and Neubauer [14], blue-yellow defects detected with the F-M 100 were interpreted as the expression of acquired color defectiveness, since they appear in alcoholic patients. Nevertheless this statement has not been supported by the color-vision study of each patient before the onset of alcoholism or liver disease.

In order to differentiate hereditary and acquired color defectiveness, it is possible to follow two methods: (a) the analysis of the evolution of the defectiveness and (b) the study of the prevalence of color blindness in nonalcoholic relatives of alcoholics. Now, according to the first method, it is clear that when the supposed cause is suppressed and the color-vision defectiveness disappears, an acquired condition can be diagnosed. This was the interpretation of Fialkow [20], discussed above, when they observed that in some cases of liver cirrhosis the errors of plate 3 of the H-R-R test disappeared during convalescence.

This observation indicates the necessity to analyze more carefully this plate 3. According to Lakowski [33], plate 3 of the H-R-R test presents a very small difference of saturation between the colored signs and the grey background. According to the experience of the author, there are some cases who failed plate 3 in the first test but performed a correct answer in a second or third retest. An error in plate 3 should be considered a small alteration in either the red-green or the blue-yellow discrimination ability that could be better detected by the F-M 100 Hue test when an error in this plate was not observed in a second test of the H-R-R. Consequently plate 3 was a sensitive and transitorily test to detect minor defectiveness. Probably an important proportion of the color defectiveness of alcoholics detected by Cruz-Coke [8] and Fialkow et al. [20] through this plate belonged to the blue-yellow type of color blindness.

In order to clarify the relationship between color blindness and alcoholic liver damage, Ugarte et al. [49] studied 149 male alcoholics with routine liver tests and hepatic biopsy and submitted this sample to Ishihara, Hardy-Rand-Ritter, and F-M 100 Hue tests. The high prevalence of color blindness in the blue-yellow zone (58 cases) was confirmed, but no significant correlation between this disturbance and histological findings, abnormalities in the laboratory test, or duration of drinking habit was found. These results suggest (a) that blue-yellow defectiveness is related to alcoholism itself and not to the induced liver damage; (b) that the alteration of color vision does not seem to be associated to a possible genetic susceptibility to develop liver disease induced by alcohol abuse; and (c) that a reasonable doubt is raised on the idea that color-vision defectiveness in the blue-yellow zone is an acquired condition, secondary to either alcohol abuse or liver disturbances.

After questioning the classical interpretation of the acquired color defectiveness secondary to alcoholism, we can enter directly in the genetic analysis of the problem.

F.   Supporting a Genetic Hypothesis

On discovering the association between color blindness and alcoholic cirrhosis, Cruz-Coke [8] suggested the possibility that this correlation could be explained on genetical basis. As a working hypothesis it was supposed that alcoholic cirrhosis might be a common trait inherited by an X-linked mechanism or that an X-linked gene might control some metabolic pathways in the pathogenesis of the disease. A similar suggestion was postulated by Kroon [32] 45 years ago starting from a pedigree approach.

There are two basic aspects to be considered on studying the possibility that alcoholism and color defectiveness are biologically related to the X chromosome. The first one is that alcoholism should be a disease condition controlled mainly by a gene located in the X chromosome, or second that alcoholism should be the disease or physiological character that has operated during historic times as an agent of natural selection increasing the prevalence of color blindness in human populations.

To analyze the first point, we study the following evidences and significant experiments that support a biological association between color blindness and alcoholism: (a) the relative sex prevalence; (b) the familial aggregation; (c) the fertility advantage; and (d) the common genetic polymorphism.

1. Sex Prevalence in Human Populations

A significant biological characteristic of alcoholism in the human species is the marked difference of its prevalence among men and women. A basic population study by Helgason [26] in Iceland showed that the expectancy of alcoholism was over 10 times higher in men than in women, irrespective of social class, birth place, and residence areas. A recent analysis of this problem by Winokur and Clayton [56] suggested that certain kinds of biological factors may make men more likely to develop the illness and women more resistant to it. They agreed with Cruz-Coke and Varela that perhaps an X-linked recessive gene is implicated in alcoholism, if not as the sole factor, at least as a significant one.

The first step in detecting X-linked inheritance in a common disease is to study the relative frequency of affected males and affected females [13]. If the trait is recessive, the frequency of affected females will be the square of the frequency of affected males. In 1955 Marconi, Varela, and coworkers [38] performed a survey of the prevalence of alcoholism among the adult population of a suburb of Santiago, Chile. In a sample of 905 males and 1071 females, 75 alcoholic males and only 7 alcoholic females were found. These figures represent 8.29 and 0.65% respectively, and a genetic analysis performed by Cruz-Coke and Varela [10] showed that they were consistent with an X-linked recessive trait (Table IV).

This idea has also been analyzed by Winokur [55], using a general population sample studied by Helgason [26] in Iceland. This investigator found an expectancy of alcoholism of 6.51% for men and 0.42% for women. According to a genetic equilibrium for sex-linked traits, the square of the male frequency (0.0651) should approximate the observed female frequency (0.0042). This is a perfect fit of the expected female frequency. The figures given by Åmark [2] show that the prevalence of alcoholism in the general population of Sweden was 3.40% for men and 0.11% for women, which agreed in a perfect fit with the expected female frequency (0.115%). These studies showed clearly that the different sex prevalence rates of alcoholism in three general population samples agreed with impressive fits to an X-linked hypothesis.

2. Family Aggregation

An elementary approach to the families of alcoholics is to study the prevalence of color blindness in their first-degree relatives of both sexes. Varela et al. [50] studied 65 male alcoholic patients from the Department of Psychiatry of the University Hospital, 41 relatives of them (18 males and 23 females) as well as nonalcoholic controls (53 males and 44 females), who were submitted to the Farnsworth-Munsell 100 Hue test. As a very sensitive test the F-M 100 is able to detect minor defects in the axis of confusion of the chromaticity diagram: protan, deutan, tritan, and the postulated "tetartan."

Results of this investigation are summarized in Table V and showed that (a) alcoholic patients exhibited a significant lower discrimination ability around the blue-yellow than nonalcoholic male controls; (b) nonalco-

TABLE IV Gene Frequencies and Phenotypic Distribution by Sex of Alcoholic Trait q on Supposition of X-Linked Inheritance in a General Population Sample of 905 Males and 1071 Females in Santiago[a]

Supposed parameter	Observed males	Expected females[b]	Observed females
Frequency of normal allele (p)	0.9171	0.9171	0.9192
Frequency of mutant allele (q)	0.0829	0.0829	0.0808
Supposed phenotype			
Normals	(p) 0.9171	(p^2) 0.8409	0.8436
Carriers		($2pq$) 0.1522	0.1499
Alcoholics	(q) 0.0829	(q^2) 0.0069	0.0065
Total	1.0000	1.0000	1.0000

[a] Marconi et al. Ref. 38.

[b] χ^2 0.025. q = pooled $(2q_{xx} + q_x)/3 = 0.0815$.

TABLE V   Distribution of the Mean Error of Scores of Farnworth-Munsell 100 Hue Test in the Different Spectral Zones in the Group of Alcoholics, Their Relatives, and Control (number of cases with mean error per capita lower and higher than 1.5)

	Row	Protan	Deutan	Tritan	"Tetartan"
Males:					
Alcoholics	1	48–17	46–19	41–24	32–33
Controls	2	46–7	46–7	48–5	48–5
Relatives	3	17–1	17–1	15–3	15–3
Females:					
Relatives	4	19–4	20–3	13–10	16–7
Controls	5	43–1	43–1	42–2	42–2
χr^2 rows 1 and 2		2.27	1.79	10.46[a]	20.99[b]
χr^2 rows 2 and 3		0.005	0.65	0.16	0.16
χr^2 rows 1 and 4		0.31	1.59	0.09	2.07
χr^2 rows 4 and 5		3.02	1.47	13.00[b]	6.62[a]

[a] $P < 0.01$.
[b] $P < 0.001$.

holic female relatives of alcoholic patients showed also a lower discrimination ability than female controls around the same axis; and (c) nonalcoholic male relatives exhibited a discrimination intermediate between controls and alcoholics, without significant differences from either groups. Consequently these results strongly suggest the presence of a sex-linked familiar correlation in color-vision defects between alcoholic patients and their female relatives.

In this research Varela et al. [50] confirmed the striking sex differences in the discrimination ability of the patient's offspring observed in a preliminary investigation by Cruz-Coke and Varela [10]. This agreed with the X-linkage hypothesis on the supposition that females are the carriers of both alcohol defectiveness and the color-vision defect. Moreover these authors were able to determine the specific part of the spectrum where defectiveness is predominant among alcoholics in agreement with the results reported by Saraux et al. [46] and Dittrich and Neubauer [14]. The defect correlation between patients and female relatives is established on the same region of the blue-yellow discrimination ability.*

Recent investigations from our group in samples of female alcoholics, with the aid of a Pickford anomaloscope, a very sensitive device able to

* Recently supported by Sassoon et al., Lancet, ii, 367 (1970).

detect minor blue-yellow disturbances, has confirmed a high prevalence of blue-yellow defectiveness in female alcoholics as well as their nonalcoholic first-degree female relatives (daughters and sisters).*

3. Fertility Advantage

If we assumed that alcoholism is a disease controlled mainly by a mutant X-linked gene, it could be considered, as is color blindness, as an example of genetic polymorphism. Maintenance of polymorphism depends on natural selection operating in favor of the heterozygote. Now if the alcoholism gene is X-linked, only females could be heterozygous, as is shown in Table IV, and the selectional balance must be maintained by some fertility advantage operating on them. To sustain the X-linked hypothesis, we should have to demonstrate a fitness advantage in the mothers of alcoholics, i.e., the supposed heterozygote carriers of the mutant alcohol allele.

Studying the relationship between birth order and family size in a sample of alcoholics from the general population of Ontario, Canada, Smart [47] was able to find that the percentage of alcoholics who came from large families was significantly greater than expected. He discovered that the observed percentage of alcoholics was greater than expected in the sibships sizes 5 and over (15.8 versus 9.3%). This result suggests that mothers of alcoholic patients may be more fertile than other women. Discussing his research, Smart could not explain this significantly higher fertility.

Cruz-Coke and Varela [13] estimated the fertility difference of color blindness and alcoholic cirrhosis in the same hospital sample where the association was discovered. Table V shows clearly that in both traits the heterozygous women, mothers of alcoholic male patients and of male color-blind patients, were significantly more fertile. This table is preliminary and tentative, because it is very difficult to ascertain the normal nonalcoholic and the noncolor-blind subjects and the true male fertility. But in any case it shows that the genetic X-linked model could explain the excess of fertility detected by Smart and confirmed by Cruz-Coke and Varela [13].

4. A Common Genetic Polymorphism

The discovery of Smart [47] confirmed by Cruz-Coke and Varela [13] supports the theory of the existence of a heterozygous advantage in the mothers of alcoholics and color-blind subjects. According to Table VI the

* Cruz-Coke et al., Rev. Med. Chile, 99, 118 (1971).

supposed alcohol mutant has virtually the same frequency in both sexes. Heterozygous advantage is limited to the homogametic sex (female), but fertility differences between the two hemizygous (male) types would affect the equilibrium frequency or the relatives frequencies in males and females if equilibrium had not been attained. Alcoholic males are less fertile than normal, and this affects the equilibrium of the females. This fact makes it very difficult to study the detection of sex-linked genetic polymorphism and determine the number of generations required to achieve the equilibrium frequency on its asymptote line.

In a preliminary estimation Cruz-Coke and Varela [13] calculated the evolution of color blindness and the supposed alcoholic polymorphism. Using the equation of Haldane and Jajakar [25] and applying to Table IV the female fitness in Table VI, the equilibrium condition of the alcoholic gene for both sexes is attained with nearly equal values (0.178 in eggs and 0.164 in spermatozoa). A new estimation, using the method of Kirkman [31] with the same basic data, both polymorphic systems reach the equilibrium frequencies at higher levels, by the order of 0.40.

Figure 1 shows the theoretical curves of rising polymorphic systems of females reaching their respective asymptotes; the color-vision mutant at the level of 0.41 in 66.8 generations, and the alcoholic mutant at 0.47

TABLE VI Preliminary Estimates of Fertility Differences on Supposition of X-Linked Inheritance of Color Defectiveness and Alcoholism in 900 Patients [13]

Genotype	Females			Males	
	AA	Aa	aa	A	a
Phenotype	Normal[a]	Carrier[b]	Affected[c]	Normal[a]	Affected[c]
Alcoholism:					
Number	20	61	9	328	40
Mean age	60–69	70	47	43	50
Mean progeny number	4.63	6.24	2.33	4.46	4.07
Fitness (AA,A/= 1)	1.000	1.347	0.500	1.000	0.912
Color defectiveness:					
Number	20	42	13	328	40
Mean age	60–69	70	47	43	64
Mean progeny number	4.63	6.02	2.92	4.46	4.37
Fitness (AA,A/= 1)	1.000	1.300	0.630	1.000	0.979

[a] Nonalcoholics with normal color vision.
[b] Mothers of alcoholic male patients.
[c] Alcoholic cirrhotic patients.

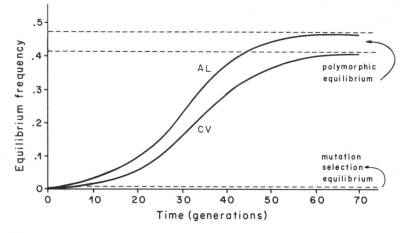

Figure 1. Estimated approaches to polymorphic equilibrium of a color-vision defective gene (CV) and a supposed alcoholism mutant gene (AL). (After Cruz-Coke [11].)

in 63.1 generations. This figure shows clearly that the two polymorphic systems are evolving in a common path in the Chilean population, rising at a very fast rate of 1% each generation. If we estimated the distance between two generations in the Chilean population as 21 years, the present frequencies of the alcoholic and the color-vision mutants have been reached in less than 500 years, by the time the European invaders came to the New World. Also this calculation agrees with the increased prevalence of alcoholism in Chile, estimated by the change in the mortality rate of alcoholic cirrhosis from 5 to 25 per 100,000 during the last 50 years [13].

This and the previous supporting evidence suggest strongly that the color-blind and alcoholic traits are phenotypes belonging to a common or similar genetic polymorphic system. The two traits are associated in female relatives according to an X-linked model, but this does not necessarily mean that they are genetically linked.

G.   Evolution and Alcoholism

If we analyze together the basic ideas that have supported the discussion of the genetical hypothesis of a sex-linked genetic component in the etiology of alcoholism, we arrive immediately to touch a most important problem in the relationship between biology and medicine: the evolutionary concept of disease.

From a biological point of view, diseases are the most important evolutionary agents in shaping the genetic structure of the human population [24]. Before the neolithic revolution, man had little opportunity to establish genetic systems of resistance to infectious diseases in small groups. But with the advent of agriculture, large groups permitted the extension of epidemics and natural selection begun to operate. An infectious disease has a strong genetic impact, killing genetically susceptible individuals before the age of reproduction. It is possible that genetic polymorphism may owe its existence to the selective action of infectious epidemic diseases. Consequently according to the model proposed by Haldane [24], common disease may be also selective agents in the dynamics of the evolution of man.

Diseases are not only phenotypic expression of underlying specific genotypes but also a cultural component related to the physical environment where man has built up civilization. Diseases may be conceived as a link between the fields of biological and cultural evolution, because they are not independent random events but the expression of the interaction of biological and cultural factors. In any case it is very difficult to consider together the multiple evolutionary, genetic, ecological, and cultural factors that influence the emergence of a disease in the existence of human species.

Different models of biological and cultural interaction have been devised. Wiesenfeld [53] sees a disease as a biological solution to a cultural problem. Adams et al. [1] considers that environmental resources limit and orientate the course of cultural evolution, which indirectly but ultimately influences genetic adaptation of the human species to the changing world. Dobshansky [15] has pointed out that human evolution may be considered a unified process, because culture is also part of the biology of man. Cruz-Coke and Varela [13] have suggested that color blindness and alcoholism are also associated in cultural groups and that the disease emerges as a disturbing factor in the process of cultural evolution. They consider that color blindness could not have reached the status of a polymorphism unless the genes responsible for the condition were associated with advantages and disadvantages. They demonstrated in their samples that color blindness is not a neutral trait from a fertility point of view and that the color blindness–alcoholism association is consistent. As it is shown in Table VII, their results of the study of color-vision defectiveness and alcoholism in a primitive population (Aymará-speaking people) living at present in various stages show a significant correlation among the prevalence of color blindness, the prevalence of alcoholism, the typology of alcohol consumption, and the degree of cultural evolution and Caucasian admixture. This multiple association agrees with the suggestion of Fallding [18] that alcohol-drinking patterns have evolved from the "independent-ornamental symbolic type

TABLE VII Correlation Between Prevalence of Color Defectiveness and Alcoholism in Males in a Contemporary Cultural Gradient of Alcohol Consumption in an Aymará-Speaking People in Northern Chile

Villages	Cultural level	Fallding types[a]	N of men in sample	Caucasian admixture, %	% defectives		
					Color vision	Alcoholism	Both
Huallatire	Semi-nomade	I	65	9.0	1.6	0.0	0.0
Chapiquiña	Rural	II	33	2.0	6.0	3.0	0.0
Belen	Rural	II-III	70	9.0	5.7	2.8	0.0
Molinos	Rural	II-III	37	2.0	0.0	0.0	0.0
Azapa	Advanced rural	III	70	15.0	2.8	1.4	0.0
Arica (hospital)	Urban	IV	50	47.0	18.0	16.0	10.0

[a] See text.

I" of primitive societies to a "dependent-retaliation type IV" of urban civilization. The gene-disease association appears only in the last stage of cultural evolution.

These basic concepts in the evolutionary dynamics of alcoholism may be considered elementary guidelines to new researches in the biology of the disease. But also they support for the hypothesis that alcoholism is a disease strongly related to the genetics and ecology of the color-vision system of man and consequently associated with its polymorphism discovered by Dalton. Alcoholism seems to be a complex disease, evolving under the influence of strong environmental and cultural factors but also with a genetic component operating from the X chromosome. We cannot exclude other major genes with megaphenic effects controlling the predisposition to the disease, but at present the only evidence of a clear and significant relationship with a gene is that of the X-linked model that we have discussed here.

H. Epidemiological Perspective

Although our study of the genetic component of alcoholism and the discussion on its eventual inclusion in a hypothetic evolutionary system of the biology of the human species is highly theoretical, it is possible to obtain some practical conclusions in order to apply them to the prevention of the disease. In fact, alcoholism is a typical disease problem that contemporary man must face with new methods of detection and prevention.

At present it is impossible to detect the alcoholic disease in a given individual before the onset. Moreover it is very difficult to differentiate the excessive drinkers from the true alcoholic addicts at early stage. Unfortunately the influence of the drinking patterns of parents operates strongly during the second decade of life, the period in which the beginning of drinking habits of the individual begin. There are no available methods to protect in that crucial period the vulnerable individuals who are prone to become alcoholics. In fact only a small proportion of teenagers are liable to develop the disease, and consequently educators and preventive physicians could not supress completely alcohol drinking in all young people in order to protect the unknown carriers from alcoholic predisposition.

We think that the gene-disease-association methodology could solve at least some basic barriers to overcome this problem. We have proved that yellow-blue defectiveness is a marker gene system that could be easily detected in a general survey in a population, with simple aids, such as the Farnswort-Munsell 100 Hue test and the Pickford anomaloscope.

The theoretical probability basis of the detection of the vulnerable groups

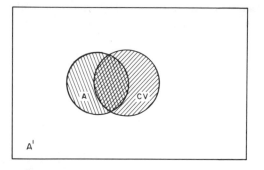

Figure 2. Euler-Venn diagram. A: alcoholism; CV: color-vision defectiveness.

predisposed to alcoholism can be explained by a classical model of the Euler-Venn diagrams of the set theory. Figure 2 shows the total population sample S, which is the sum of a subset of A alcoholic individuals, and complementary A' nonalcoholic subjects. To detect the subset A, we put inside the sample S one marker gene system, CV for color-vision defectiveness. The phenotype CV with a frequency of 9.7% has a large intersection with subset A. The probability of occurrence of events A and CV are given by the equations

$$P(A) = \frac{N(A)}{N(S)} \text{ and } P(CV) = \frac{N(CV)}{N(S)} \tag{1}$$

and the probability that event A occurred given the intersects with CV is

$$P(A|CV) = \frac{P(A \cap CV)}{P(CV)}.$$

The relative risk x to develop the event A (alcoholic disease), given the carriers a genetic character CV, is determined by the relation between the two conditional probabilities, with and without the genetic character CV:

$$x = \frac{P(A|CV)}{P(A|\text{non-}CV)}.$$

Applying these equations to our data it is possible to observe that the intersection of CV with A is 33%, which gives a relative risk four times higher ($x = 4.0$) than in the noncolor-blind individuals. Then it is possible to conclude that the population with positive CV marker genes (color-blind) is situated at a very high risk level to intersect with subset *A* and, consequently, prone to develop alcoholic disease.

Consequently the analysis of these probability models gives us the possibility to use powerful color-vision tests, to detect an important proportion of the human population predisposed to alcoholism.

REFERENCES

1. Adams, M. S. and J. D. Niswander, Birth weight of North American Indians, *Human Biol.,* **40,** 226 (1968).
2. Amark, C. A., Study in alcoholism: Clinical social psychiatric and genetic investigations, *Acta Psychiat. Neurol. Scand. Suppl.,* **70** (1951).
3. Achte, K., Correlation of ABO blood groups and alcoholism, *Duodecim,* **74,** 20 (1958).
4. Carta, F., E. Vincinguerra, and E. Barrea, Indazine sul senso chromatic degli epatopatici, *Ann. Ottal.,* **93,** 350 (1967).
5. Carter, C. O., An ABC of medical genetics, *Lancet* (1969).
6. Clarke, C. A., *Genetics for the Clinician,* Blackwell, Oxford, 1965.
7. Cruz-Coke, R., Colour blindness and cirrhosis of the liver, *Lancet,* **ii,** 1064 (1964).
8. Cruz-Coke, R. Colour blindness and cirrhosis in the liver. *Lancet,* **i,** 1113 (1965).
9. Cruz-Coke, R., Asociación entre la oportunidad para la selección natural de los defectos de visión de colores y el alcoholismo crónico en diversas poblaciones humanas, *Arch. Biol. Med. Exp.,* **3,** 21 (1966).
10. Cruz-Coke, R. and A. Varela, Colour blindness and alcohol addiction, *Lancet,* **ii,** 1348 (1965).
11. Cruz-Coke, R., El componente genético de las enfermedades comunes, *Rev. Med.* (Chile), **96,** 420 (1968).
12. Cruz-Coke, R., A. P. Cristoffanini, M. Aspillaga, and F. Biancani, Evolutionary forces in human populations in an environmental gradient in Arica, Chile, *Human Biol.,* **38,** 421 (1968).
13. Cruz-Coke, R. and A. Varela, Inheritance of alcoholism, *Lancet,* **ii,** 1282 (1966).
14. Dittrich, M. and O. Neubauer, Störungen des Farbisehens bei Leberkrankeiten, *Munch. Medizin. Wochenscrift,* **109,** 2690 (1967).
15. Dobzhansky, T., Mankind evolving, Yale University Press, New Haven, 1962.
16. Edwards, J. H., The meaning of the association betweeen blood groups and disease, *Ann. Human Genet.,* **29,** 77 (1965).
17. Falconer, D. S., The inheritance of liability to certain diseases estimated from the incidence among relatives. *Ann. Human Genet.,* **29,** 51 (1965).
18. Falding, H. Q., The source and burden of civilization illustrated in the use of alcohol, *Quart. J. Studies Alc.,* **16,** 714 (1964).

19. Farnsworth, D., The Farnsworth-Munsell 100 hue test and dichotomous test for color vision, *J. Opt. Soc. Am.*, **33**, 568 (1943).
20. Fialkow, P. J., H. C. Thuline, and F. Fenster, Lack of association between cirhosis of the liver and the common types of color blindness, *N. Engl. J. Med.*, **275**, 584 (1966).
21. Ford, E. B. *Genetic Polymorphism*, M.I.T. Press, Cambridge, 1965.
22. François, J. and G. Verriest, On acquired deficiency of colour vision, *Vision Res.*, **1**, 201 (1961).
23. Gorrel, G. J., A study of defective colour vision with Ishihara test plates, *Ann. Human Genet.*, **31**, 39 (1967).
24. Haldane, J. B. S., Disease and Evolution, *La Ricerta Scientifica*, **19**, 68 (1949).
25. Haldane, J. B. S. and S. Jayakar, Equilibria under natural selection at a sex linked genes, *J. Genet.*, **59**, 29 (1964–66).
26. Helgason, T., Epidemiological studies of alcoholism in Iceland, *Acta Psychiat. Scand.*, **173** (1964).
27. Jellinek, E. M., *The Disease Concept of Alcoholism*, Hillhouse, Highland Park, New Jersey, 1960.
28. Kalmus, H., *Diagnosis and Genetics of Defective Color Vision*, Pergamon, Oxford, 1965.
29. Kaij, L., *Studies on the Etiology and Sequels of Abuse of Alcohol*, University of Lund, Lund, 1960.
30. Kelekom, J., Les dyschromatopsies acquises, *Arch. Ophthal.* (Paris), **23**, 15 (1963).
31. Kirkam, H. N., Properties of X-linked alleles during selection, *Am. J. Human Genet.*, **18**, 424 (1966).
32. Kroon, H. N., Die Erblichkeit der Trunksucht in die familie X, *Genetica* **6**, 391 (1924).
33. Lakowski, R., A critical evaluation of color vision test, *Brit. J. Physiol. Opt.*, **23**, 186 (1966).
34. Laroche, J., Modification de la vision de couleurs chez l'homme sous l'action de certain substances médicamenteuses, *Ann. Oculist.* (Paris), **200**, 275 (1967).
35. Legrain, M., Heredité et alcoolisme, Paris, 1889.
36. Lester, D., Alcohol self selection and human variation, *Quart. J. Studies Alc.*, **29**, 406 (1968).
37. Lisker, R., M. Trujeque, A. Barrera, J. Villalobos, Cirrosis del hígado y ceguera al color, *Acta Cient.* (Venezolana), **19**, 202 (1968).
38. Marconi, J., A. Varela, E. Rosenblatt, G. Solari, I. Marchesse, R. Alvarado, and W. Enriquez, A survey on the prevalence of alcoholism among the adult population of a suburb of Santiago, *Quart. J. Studies Alc.*, **16**, 438 (1955).
39. Mardones, J. Experimental induced changes of the free choice of ethanol, *Int. Rev. Neurobiol.*, **2**, 41 (1960).
40. Mardones, J. Pharmacogenetique de l'alcoolisme, *Actualité Pharmacol.*, **21**, 1 (1968).
41. Morton, N. E., The detection of major genes under additive continuous variation, *Am. J. Human Genet.*, **19**, 23 (1967).

42. Post, R. H., Population differences in red and green color vision deficiency; a new and a query on selection relaxation, *Eugen. Quart,* **9,** 131 (1962).
43. Partanen, J., K. Brunn, and T. Markannen, *Inheritance of Drinking Behaviour,* Finnish Foundation for Alcohol Studies, Helsinki, 1966.
44. Richter, C. P., and K. M. Campbell, Alcohol taste threshold and concentration of solutions preferred by rats, *Science,* **91,** 507 (1940).
45. Reid, N. C. R. W., P. W. Brunt, W. B. Beas, W. R. Maddrey, B. A. Alonso, and F. L. Iber, Genetic characteristic and cirrhosis: A controlled study of 200 patients, *Brit. Med. J.,* **i,** 463 (1968).
46. Saraux, H., R. Lahet, and B. Biais, Aspects actuelles de la nevrite optique de l'éthylique, *Ann. Oculist,* **199,** 943 (1966).
47. Smart, R. G., Alcoholism birth order and family size, *J. Abnorm. Psychol.,* **66,** 17 (1963).
48. Trotter, T., *An Essay Medical Philosophical and Chemical on Drunkness and its Effect on the Human Body,* 2nd ed. London, 1804.
49. Ugarte, G., H. Altschiller, R. Cruz-Coke, and L. Rivera, Relations of color blindness to alcoholic liver damage, *Pharmacology,* **4,** 308 (1970).
50. Varela, A., L. Rivera, J. Mardones, and R. Cruz-Coke, Color vision defects in nonalcoholic relatives of alcoholic patients, *Brit. J. Addict.,* **64,** 67 (1969).
51. Waaler, G. N. M., Heredity of two types of normal color vision, *Nature,* **215,** 406 (1967).
52. Waaler, G. H. M., *New Facts in the Genetics of Colour Vision Besides Ideas of the Colour Perception,* Universitetsforlaget, Oslo, 1968.
53. Wiesenfeld, S. L., Sickle cell trait in human biological and cultural evolution, *Science,* **157,** 1134 (1967).
54. Williams, R. J., L. Berry, and E. Beerstecher, Jr., Individual metabolic patterns: Alcoholism genetotrophic diseases, *Proc. Nat. Acad. Sci. U.S.,* **35,** 265 (1949).
55. Winokur, G., X-borne recessive genes in alcoholism, *Lancet,* **ii,** 466 (1967).
56. Winokur, G. and P. J. Clayton, Family history studies: IV. Comparison of males and females alcoholics, *Quart. J. Studies Alc.,* **29,** 885 (1968).
57. Thuline, H. C., Inheritance of alcoholism, *Lancet,* **i,** 274 (1967).

Chapter XIII

NUTRITIONAL FACTORS IN ALCOHOLISM AND ITS COMPLICATIONS

CARROLL M. LEEVY, ERLINDA VALDELLON, and FRANCIS SMITH

DIVISION OF HEPATIC METABOLISM AND NUTRITION,
DEPARTMENT OF MEDICINE
NEW JERSEY COLLEGE OF MEDICINE, NEWARK

A. Introduction

Evaluation of the mechanism responsible for tissue injury in the alcholic requires consideration of the role of (a) nutritional defects resulting from abnormal intake, absorption, or assimilation of food; (b) direct injury from ethanol, acetaldehyde, congeners, or contaminants of ingested alcoholic beverages; and (c) untoward effects of ethanol on intermediary metabolism, including NADH or lactate accumulation and release of catecholamines or other endogenous substances (see Figure 1). Regardless of the causative mechanism, repair of cell damage in the alcoholic increases the need for nutrients; failure to supply extra protein, vitamins, and minerals contributes to chronic tissue injury. An overlap in etiologic factors is common; however,

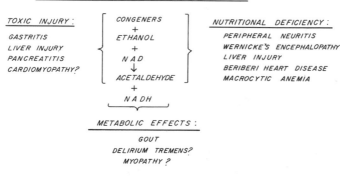

Figure 1. Possible mechanisms of tissue injury in alcoholism.

it seems that nutritional deficiency is of primary importance in the development of peripheral neuritis [16], Wernicke's encephalopathy [47], cirrhosis [26], beriberi heart disease [30], and macrocytic anemia [15]. Malnutrition may also increase susceptibility to toxic or immunologic injury in alcoholics with gastritis [38], some phases of liver injury [22], pancreatitis [6], and perhaps cardiomyopathy [1]. Nutrient deficits by altering production or activity of ethanol-oxidizing enzymes may be of importance in the development of gout [40], delirium tremens [37], or acute myopathy [45].

B.   Influence of Ethanol on Nutrient Intake and Absorption

Inadequate food intake, secondary to alcoholism, is the chief cause of nutrient deficiency among civilized people with adequate food supplies. Clinical and laboratory evidence of malnutrition occurs in the majority of persons who consume sufficient ethanol to interfere with work and social responsibilities on a continuing basis [29]. There is usually a decrease in appetite and food intake during heavy consumption of ethanol; moreover, alcoholic beverages cause a marked change in diet composition by virtue of their high caloric content [21]. Dietary patterns in both the nonalcoholic and alcoholic are determined by economic status, geographical location, religious indoctrination, and ethnic background. Dietary inadequacy was encountered in each of 3000 low-income persons admitted to a large municipal hospital because of medical complications of alcoholism. Deficient dietary intake occurred during periodic bouts of excessive alcoholic intake in 40%, prolonged dietary deficiency alternating with a marginal or normal diet during periods of abstinence was present in 25%, and continuous dietary deficiency, except during periods of hospitalization for complications of alcoholism. was characteristic of 35% [33].

Decreased absorption of dietary fats, calcium, magnesium, and selected vitamins is common in alcoholics with fatty liver, steatosis, and cirrhosis. Malabsorption in these instances may result from altered intestinal, pancreatic, or liver function. Intestinal dysfunction may result from ethanol toxicity, protein deficiency, or both. Subjects given large quantities of ethanol develop mucosal damage with back diffusion of hydrogen ion into the lumen of the stomach. There is loss of fine filamentous surface found on normal gastric mucosa [19]. Alcohol-induced changes appear important, since ethanol may inhibit intestinal transport of folic acid [14], thiamine [56], vitamin B_{12} [43], and amino acids [2, 17, 18]. Illustrative are studies of the absorption of ^{35}S-thiamine hydrochloride, whose intestinal transport is rate-limited in normal subjects. Twenty-five percent of the patients given 1.5 g/kg of ethanol before receipt of ^{35}S-thiamine hydrochloride exhibited a 40 to 60% reduction in absorption of this vitamin. Either oral or parenteral ethanol reduced absorption, suggesting that metabolic effects of ethanol are principally responsible for encountered changes (see Figure 2).

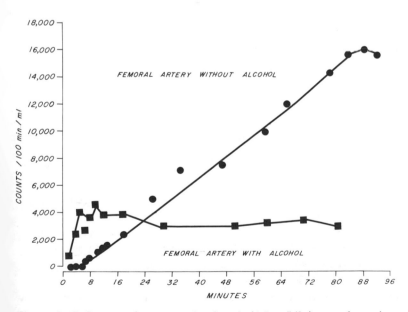

Figure 2. Influence of parenteral ethanol (1.5 g/kilo) on absorption of orally administered ^{35}S-labeled thiamine hydrochloride. Thiamine was given 1 hr after receipt of ethanol. Ethanol caused a significant reduction in absorption of ^{35}S thiamine reflected in serum radioactivity [56].

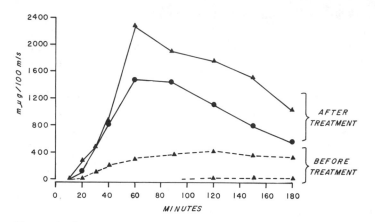

Figure 3. Serum radioactive thiamine after oral administration of ^{35}S thiamine hydrochloride in a malnourished thiamine-repleted alcoholic before treatment (*lower lines*) and after a 6-week period of nutritious diet (*upper lines*).

Protein-depleted alcoholics with fatty liver exhibit a similar decrease in absorption of ^{35}S-thiamine that is not altered by correcting associated vitamin deficiency and persists until fat is mobilized and protein is repleted [56]. Combined umbilical-hepatic vein catheterization studies indicate that the defect is at the intestinal level in these patients (see Figure 3). Ethanol in the setting of malnutrition causes a further reduction in absorption of thiamine hydrochloride and may also interfere with absorption of folic acid, whose transport is not rate-limited in the range tested (14).

C.   Influence of Ethanol on Nutrient Balance

An infusion of ethanol or consumption of large quantities of alcoholic beverages over a 24 to 48 hr period has little effect on nutrient balance in well-nourished subjects. In contrast the alcoholic who ingests large quantities of ethanol without food for several days exhibits negative nitrogen, vitamin, and mineral balance. Loss of these nutrients, except zinc [53], is diminished with threatened body depletion. Once significant tissue damage occurs, a catabolic phase is begun that may lead to progressive nutrient depletion despite cessation of alcoholism.

Volunteers who develop steatonecrosis when fed 1 to 2 pints of vodka daily in the setting of a normal or protein-deficient diet exhibit low circulating levels of vitamin E, vitamin C, folate, vitamin B_6, thiamine, nicotinic acid, and riboflavin. This is expected. Alpha tocopherol or other antioxidants diminish the enhanced peroxidation of liver lipids that occur during heavy ethanol intake [5]. Ascorbic acid is required for collagen synthesis [7], and increased folic acid, vitamin B_{12}, and vitamin B_6 are necessary for cell replication [23]. Investigations of folate metabolism during the feeding of ethanol provided the first direct evidence that the alcoholic requires increased quantities of a specific nutrient. An alcoholic with hereditary elliptocytosis fed 1 to 2 pints of vodka daily developed steatonecrosis. This was associated with a lowering of serum folate levels, appearance of bone marrow megaloblastosis, and inappropriate increase in in vitro hepatic DNA synthesis [39] (see Figure 4). Despite an increase in the amount of ingested ethanol and progression of the severity of liver injury, DNA synthesis and regenerative capacity returned to normal when extra folate was provided.

Malnourished alcoholics are more susceptible to ethanol-induced injury. A deficiency of critical nutrients interferes with the production of enzymes and cofactors required for the oxidation of ethanol and, thereby, contributes to its toxicity. Animal studies indicate that protein or folate deficiency, by interfering with the production of alcohol dehydrogenase, may reduce ethanol oxidative capacity [36]. In addition it has been shown that a decrease in ethanol clearance may also occur in patients with a marked deficiency of nicotinic acid or riboflavin, which are necessary for electron transport and ethanol oxidation [23]. Prolonged deficiency of thiamine,

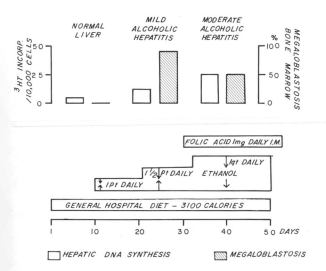

Figure 4. Influence of ethanol-induced injury on bone marrow megaloblastosis and *in vitro* hepatic DNA synthesis [39].

biotin, vitamin B$_6$, magnesium, or zinc may also alter ethanol oxidation, since these vitamins are required for adaptive increments in mitochondrial and microsomal enzymes [39].

D.   Nutrition in Specific Medical Complications of Alcoholism

1.   Neurologic Disorders

Neurologic disorders constitute the most direct relationship between nutrient deficiency and a medical complication of alcoholism [47]. Most alcoholics with peripheral neuritis have multiple vitamin deficiencies. Therapeutic studies indicate that thiamine depletion is principally (80%) responsible for this condition [10]; however, a deficiency of vitamin B$_6$, nicotinic acid, or pantothenic acid may produce identical signs of peripheral neuropathy (see Figure 5). Despite the identification and correction of thiamine and other vitamin deficiencies, peripheral neuropathy in the alcoholic may persist because of irreversible neurologic damage or inability to use administered vitamins. Protein malnutrition and severe liver disease are regularly associated with malutilization of vitamins.

Recent studies indicate that alcoholics with Wernicke's encephalopathy, which has been classically attributed to thiamine depletion, also have multi-

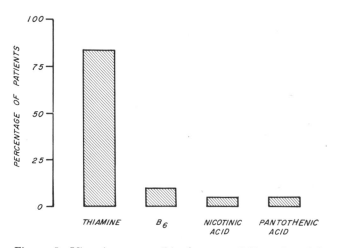

Figure 5. Vitamins responsible for reversibility of peripheral neuropathy in 50 alcoholics.

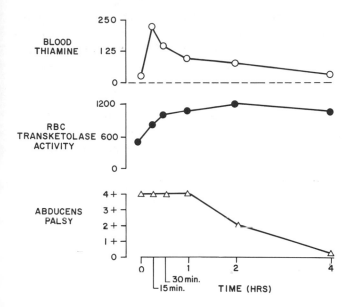

Figure 6. Responsiveness of extraocular palsy to thiamine therapy in a patient with Wernicke's encephalopathy and fatty liver; 12 to 44 hrs were required for an identical response in patients with cirrhosis [4].

ple nutrient deficiencies that influence therapeutic response. Ocular palsy in this syndrome usually disappears rapidly after administration of intravenous thiamine; however, the time of response depends, in part on the ability to convert thiamine into its metabolically active form [4]. Thus only 4 to 6 hr are usually required for the disappearance of ocular palsy in subjects with normal liver histology; 24 to 48 hr are often needed for response in patients with cirrhosis (see Figure 6). This sign may be refractory to thiamine in patients with defective DNA and RNA synthesis attendant to nutritional deficiency despite the presence of a normal blood thiamine and red blood cell transketolase. Correction of deficits of other key nutrients is necessary for response in these instances.

Special attention has been focused on the role of nutrient deficiency in convulsive disorders encountered among alcoholics. Approximately 10% of alcoholics have electroencephalographic evidence of cerebral dysrhythmia, which may become accentuated with nutrient deficiency. Such persons often exhibit hypoglycemia or laboratory evidence or vitamin B_6, thiamine, and magnesium deficiency, and occasionally there is abatement of symptoms after replacement therapy [37].

Neuropsychiatric syndromes in the alcoholic are not currently believed to be due to mineral or vitamin deficits. Despite a dramatic decrease of hallucinations and hyperkinesis in some patients with delirium tremens after the parenteral administration of magnesium, thiamine, nicotinic acid, or vitamin B_6, controlled therapeutic studies did not show a reduction in recovery time after such therapy [58]. An increase in spinal fluid lactate and pyruvate is characteristic of delirium tremens and is often accompanied by a reduction in body stores of thiamine and magnesium and alteration of acid-base balance [55]. Although correction of these abnormalities may have no influence on cerebral glycolysis and oxidative metabolism, replacement therapy is indicated, since transient inadequate utilization of key minerals or vitamins may precipitate or aggravate this condition.

2. Liver Disease

The relative role of nutritional deficiency and ethanol toxicity in pathogenesis of liver disease in alcoholics has been debated for over a century. An appropriate answer to this query must include consideration of the various morphologic phases of liver injury of the alcoholic: fatty metamorphosis, alcoholic hepatitis, cirrhosis, and hepatoma. Also it is necessary to reconcile the fact that approximately 70 to 90% of chronic alcoholics, many of whom subsist on an inadequate diet, fail to develop chronic liver disease despite the ingestion of large quantities of ethanol. Resistance to chronic liver disease has been attributed to the periodic interruption of alcoholism and variation in constitutional or genetic background [28].

Concepts of the mechanism of liver injury in alcoholics have been largely based on studies of fatty liver. Since identical degrees of fat accumulate in the liver in diabetes, obesity, and pancreatitis, where nutrient imbalance is present, it has been assumed that nutrition is an important factor in its development in alcoholics. On the other hand, fat may accumulate in the liver of volunteers fed alcoholic beverages despite the receipt of a "normal" diet, interpreted as evidence that ethanol per se may contribute to hepatic steatosis [51]. Hepatic steatosis after the receipt of ethanol has been attributed to the increased mobilization of triglycerides from peripheral stores, increased synthesis or altered oxidation of liver fat, and inadequate transport of fat from the liver to the periphery. Nutrient deficiency could play a key role in fat accumulation from either of these mechanisms. It has been found that the degree of fatty liver after ethanol ingestion may be diminished by a high-protein diet and androgenic-anabolic steroids [20] and often disappears despite continuing alcohol intake if the "normal"

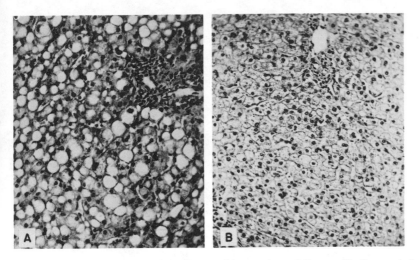

Figure 7. Development of fatty liver after receipt of "normal" diet and 1 pt of ethanol in the form of vodka for 12 days (A). Normal liver with continuation of vodka plus androgenic-anabolic steroids for an additional 10 days (B) [20].

diet is continued (see Figure 7) or if medium-chain triglycerides are substituted for long-chain triglycerides [41].

Little is known about the cause of steatonecrosis or alcoholic hepatitis, demonstrated to be a direct precursor of cirrhosis. Patients with this lesion who subsequently develop cirrhosis usually have a history of gross dietary inadequacy while consuming large amounts of alcoholic beverages [27]. This lesion is not specific, since hyaline bodies, characteristic of alcoholic hepatitis, occur in children with cirrhosis in India. These bodies contain histones and are often associated with endoplasmic reticulum [48]. Studies in our laboratory indicate that ethanol or autologous liver homogenate added to cultures of lymphocytes from patients with alcoholic hepatitis stimulates their transformation [52]. This suggests that immunologic hyperactivity of a delayed hypersensitivity type may contribute to the development or perpetuation of this lesion. Regardless of its cause, the recognition and correction of nutritional deficiency are essential in the treatment of alcoholic hepatitis [34]. Of particular importance is the provision of nutrients needed for nucleic acid synthesis: protein, folic acid, vitamin B_6, vitamin B_{12}, and zinc (see Figure 8).

Prospective studies of cirrhosis of the alcoholic in our clinic showed a direct relationship between nutritional deficiency and transformation of a noncirrhotic to a cirrhotic liver. Each of 26 malnourished alcoholics who

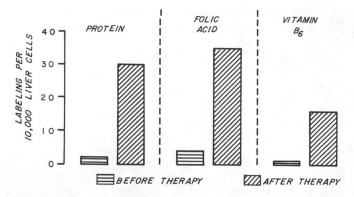

Figure 8. Influence of protein, folic acid, and vitamin B₆ therapy on in vitro incorporation of H³T into DNA by percutaneous liver biopsies in malnourished alcoholics with a deficit of these nutrients.

developed cirrhosis over a 2 to 8 year period had principally ingested carbohydrate containing foods while consuming alcoholic beverages [35]. Serial studies of in vitro nucleic acid synthesis by percutaneous liver biopsies show that liver damage is accompanied by increased replication of mesenchymal cells [23]. Mesenchymal cell proliferation leads to fibrosis and the alteration of the microcirculation of the liver and the eventual distortion of lobular architecture. Once cirrhosis develops, clinical and laboratory evidence of nutritional deficiency is often accentuated because of reduced food intake and intestinal malabsorption. Nutrient imbalance interferes with the functional of uninjured cells and delays the repair of damaged liver cells, thereby contributing to complications of cirrhosis, including ascites, a bleeding tendency, mental changes, and hypogonadism. Increased iron often accumulates in the liver, pancreas, skin, heart, and endocrine glands in the alcoholic. Excess iron per se does not cause or aggravate liver injury in pancreatic disease in experimental animals; however, it seems to be deleterious in man, for dramatic clinical improvement is often noted when the iron overload is decreased by phlebotomy or chelating agents [44].

3.   Pancreatic Disease

Pancreatitis is present in approximately one-third of alcoholics who succumb to medical complications of alcoholism [59]. Pancreatic dysfunction contributes to nutritional deficiency by interfering with the absorption of fat, protein, or carbohydrate. Body depletion of zinc has been attributed to its increased loss in pancreatic secretions [54]. Nutritional alterations play a key role in the genesis of pancreatitis: (a) hyperlipemia induced by ethanol may stimulate pancreatic secretion and lead to pancreatitis [60]; (b) protein deficiency leads to shrinkage and atrophy of acinar cells, diminution of secretory granules, and fibrosis of the parenchyma of the pancreas [57].

4. Heart Disease

Beriberi heart disease with a high cardiac output is occasionally seen, and cardiomyopathy with reduced cardiac output is a common problem among alcoholics. It has been suggested that different functional and morphologic characteristics of beriberi heart disease and alcoholic myocardiopathy may represent phases of the same underlying process that results from alcoholism and malnutrition [8]. Ethanol toxicity may be responsible for myocardiopathy, since it depresses the function of both the normal and diseased heart. An alcoholic with cardiomyopathy fed ethanol while maintaining a normal diet had a recurrence of gallop rhythm and congestive failure after the prolonged receipt of ethanol under controlled conditions [50]. This was attributed to ethanol; however, as in the case of experimental liver injury, it is equally possible that malutilization of essential nutrients or development of a hypersensitivity reaction may be of critical importance in the genesis of myocardial changes.

5. Myopathy

Changes in the structure and function of skeletal muscles have been attributed to ethanol toxicity. It has been suggested that alcohol alters membrane permeability and allows the escape of intracellular enzymes into the extracellular fluids and serum [46]. In our experience such patients regularly exhibit clinical and laboratory evidence of protein, vitamin, and mineral deficits; however, similar changes are present in alcoholics without myopathy, so that a cause-and-effect relationship is difficult to establish.

6. Hematological Abnormalities

Nutrition is of key importance in hematological abnormalities encountered in alcoholics. Iron-deficiency anemia is quite common and due, in

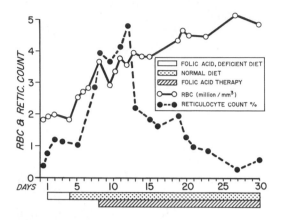

Figure 9. Response of folate deficiency anemia in a malnourished alcoholic to a normal diet and to folic acid therapy.

most instances, to an inadequate diet coupled with blood loss attendant to menses or gastrointestinal hemorrhage. An equal number of alcoholics exhibit macrocytic anemia due to a deficiency of folic acid, which is not provided as a food supplement or contained in most commercially available multivitamin preparations [24]. Anemia in these instances is associated with leukopenia and thrombocytopenia and an increased susceptibility to infections (see Figure 9). Less commonly alcoholics exhibit anemia due to vitamin B_6, vitamin B_{12}, ascorbic acid, or protein deficiency.

E.   Recognition of Nutrient Deficiency

Classic features of beriberi, pellagra, and scurvy are often encountered in alcoholics. Glossitis represents the most readily recognized clinical sign of nutritional deficiency in the absence of these conditions. Isolated deficits of nicotinic acid, riboflavin, folic acid, vitamin B_6, vitamin B_{12}, biotin, iron, or protein may each produce this sign, which also occurs in patients with dentures in the absence of nutrient depletion. Availability of simple and reliable methods to detect a deficiency of micronutrients in biological fluids and tissues has made it possible also to recognize subjects with subclinical deficiency syndromes. Randomly conducted survey wth these methods indicate that chronic alcoholics with poor dietary intake each have serum protein disturbances, hypovitaminemia, and varying degrees of mineral depletion [29]. We have, therefore, evaluated routinely serum proteins, potassium, folic acid, vitamin B_6, and thiamine in our alcoholic patients.

Magnesium, zinc, other vitamins, and red blood cell transketolase have also been obtained when warranted.

F. Nutritional Therapy in the Alcoholic

A program of nutritional rehabilitation is of prime importance to the succcess of any effort to interrupt alcoholism. Success depends on a multidiscipline approach, involving physicians, nutritionists, psychologists, social workers, and occupational therapists, with emphasis on prevention and correction of physical illness as well as psychological and social problems [31]. Development of regular mealtimes in the home is a key to the control of alcohol intake in the ambulant patient, since this contributes to family cohesiveness and diminishes psychological and social difficulty. Ingestion of nutritious meals and complete abstinence from ethanol permits successful social rehabilitation in 70% of alcoholics [32, 49].

Intensive diet therapy is required in malnourished alcoholics with tissue injury. Extra protein, vitamins, and minerals are needed to correct malnutrition, provide daily dietary requirements, and furnish additional nutrients needed for new cell formation. The diet and food supplements should be given in a manner that ensures maximum absorption. Frequent, small, appetizing feedings are desirable to provide a balanced diet with sufficient calories. It may be necessary to modify carbohydrate, protein, and fat intake in patients with liver and pancreatic disease. Loss of hepatic or pancreatic regulatory mechanisms makes it desirable to adjust carbohydrate intake to amounts that can be readily assimilated. Parenteral glucose is indicated to rapidly correct ethanol-induced hypoglycemia, which may result from the inhibition of gluconeogenesis [13]. Excess protein should be avoided in alcoholics with liver failure and mental changes; antibiotics are indicated to increase protein tolerance in such patients [30]. Medium-chained triglycerides, which are more readily absorbable than long-chained triglycerides, are valuable in alcoholics with steatorrhea [42].

Vitamins should be initially given parenterally to correct overt evidence of a depletion syndrome. Stigmata of hypovitaminosis persist despite corrective therapy in approximately one-fourth of patients with active liver disease because of the decreased ability of the injured liver to convert vitamins into their metabolically useful form [11]. Administration of all vitamins is desirable; intravenous vitamins should, therefore, be followed by a nutritious diet with oral vitamin supplements (10 to 20 times the established daily minimum). Patients in whom the control of alcoholic intake is impossible should be instructed to eat and ingest vitamin supplements when body tissues and fluids are free of ethanol. Vitamin congeners with the greatest

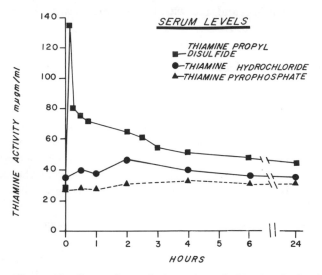

Figure 10. Comparison of absorption of thiamine hydrochloride, thiamine propyl disulfide, and thiamine pryophosphate.

absorbability should be used to ensure adequate tissue levels (see Figure 10).

Trace-metal and electrolyte imbalance should also receive urgent attention. Electrolyte imbalance is usually recognized from routine admission laboratory study. Vigorous therapy should be provided for hypokalemia, hyponatremia, and hypocalcemia. A good diet is usually needed in patients with chronic neurologic, hepatic, pancreatic, or cardiac disease to permit the gradual correction of trace-metal deficiency.

SUMMARY AND CONCLUSIONS

1. Nutritional deficiency is of etiologic and therapeutic importance in the medical complications of alcoholism. Malnutrition is of primary importance in the development of peripheral neuritis, Wernicke's encephalopathy, cirrhosis, and macrocytic anemia in the alcoholic. Nutrient deficits may also alter the susceptibility to tissue injury attributed to the toxic, immunologic, or metabolic effects of ethanol.

2. Malnutrition in the alcoholic results from inadequate food intake, malabsorption of ingested foodstuffs, reduced ability of damaged tissues to convert absorbed nutrients into useful forms, and excess utilization or

loss of available nutrients because of tissue injury. Recognition and correction of nutrient deficiency in the alcoholic has been facilitated by the laboratory measurement of micronutrients in biological fluids and tissues.

3. The alcoholic needs extra nutrients to correct protein, vitamin, and mineral deficits and to repair tissue damage. Special attention should be focused on eating regular meals within a family setting to facilitate the social rehabilitation of the alcoholic. Alcoholics in whom abstinence is impossible should be instructed to eat when body tissues and fluids are free of ethanol to ensure the absorption of ingested nutrients.

REFERENCES

1. Alexander, C. S., Idiopathic heart disease: I. Analysis of 100 cases with special reference to chronic alcoholism, *Am. J. Med.,* **41,** 213 (1966).
2. Chang, T., J. Lewis, and A. J. Galazko, Effect of ethanol and other alcohols on the transport of amino acids and glucose by everted sacs of rat small intestine, *Biochem. Biophys. Acta,* **135,** 1000 (1967).
3. Cherrick, G. R. and C. M. Leevy, The effect of ethanol metabolism on levels of oxidized and reduced nicotinamide adenine dinucleotide in liver, kidney, and heart, *Biochem. Biophys. Acta,* **107,** 29 (1965).
4. Cole, M., A. Turner, O. Frank, H. Baker, and C. M. Leevy, Extraocular palsy and thiamine therapy in Wernicke's encephalopathy, *Am. J. Clin. Nutr.,* **22,** 44 (1969).
5. DiLuzio, N. R. and A. D. Hartman, Role of lipid peroxidation in the pathogenesis of the ethanol-induced fatty liver, *Federation Proc.,* **26,** 1436 (1967).
6. Dreiling, D. A., A. Richman, and N. F. Fradkin, The role of alcohol in the etiology of pancreatitis: A study of the effect of intravenous ethyl alcohol on the external secretion of the pancreas, *Gastroenterology,* **20,** 636 (1952).
7. Dunphy, J. E., K. N. Udupa, and L. C. Edwards, Wound healing: A new perspective with particular reference to ascorbic acid deficiency, *Ann. Surg.,* **144,** 304 (1956).
8. Evans, W., Alcoholic cardiomyopathy, *Am. Heart J.,* **61,** 556 (1961).
9. Evans, W., *Alcoholic Myocardiopathy: Progress in Cardiovascular Disease,* Vol. 7, Grune and Stratton, New York, 1964, p. 151.
10. Fennelly, J., O. Frank, H. Baker, and C. M. Leevy, Peripheral neuropathy of the alcoholic: I. Etiologic role of thiamine and other B-complex vitamins, *Brit. Med. J.,* **2,** 1290 (1964).
11. Fennelly, J., O. Frank, H. Baker, and C. M. Leevy, Red blood cell transketolase activity in malnourished alcoholics with cirrhosis, *Am. J. Clin. Nutr.,* **20,** 946 (1967).
12. Flax, M. H. and W. A. Tisdale, An electron microscopic study of alcoholic hyaline, *Am. J. Pathol.,* **44,** 441 (1964).
13. Freinkel, N., D. L. Singer, R. A. Arky, S. J. Bleicher, J. B. Anderson, and

C. K. Silbert, Alcohol hypoglycemia: I. Carbohydrate metabolism of patients with clinical alcohol hypoglycemia and the experimental reproduction of the syndrome with pure ethanol, *J. Clin. Invest.,* **42,** 1112 (1963).

14. Halsted, C. H., R. C. Griggs, and J. W. Harris, The effect of alcoholism in the absorption of folic acid (H³ PGA) evaluated by plasma levels and urine excretion, *J. Lab. Clin. Med.,* **69,** 116 (1967).

15. Herbert, V., R. Zalusky, and C. S. Davidson, Correlation of folate deficiency with alcoholism and associated macrocytosis, anemia, and liver disease, *Ann. Int. Med.,* **58,** 977 (1963).

16. Hornabrook, R. W., Alcoholic neuropathy, *Am. J. Clin. Nutr.,* **9,** 398 (1961).

17. Israel, Y., I. Salazar, and E. Rosenmann, Inhibitory effects of alcohol on intestinal amino acid transport in vivo and in vitro, *J. Nutr.,* **96,** 499 (1968).

18. Israel, Y., J. E. Valenzuela, I. Salazar, and G. Ugarte, Alcohol and amino acid transport in the human small intestine, *J. Nutr.,* **98,** 222 (1969).

19. Ito, S. and R. J. Winchester, The fine structure of the gastric mucosa in the bat, *J. Cellular Biol.,* **16,** 541 (1963).

20. Jabbari, M. and C. M. Leevy, Protein anabolism and fatty liver of the alcoholic, *Medicine,* **46,** 131 (1967).

21. Koch, O. R., E. A. Porta, and W. S. Hartroft, A new experimental approach in the study of chronic alcoholism: III. Role of alcohol *versus* sucrose or fat derived calories in hepatic damage, *Lab. Invest.,* **18,** 379 (1968).

22. Leevy, C. M., Fatty liver, a study of 270 patients with fatty liver on biopsy with a review of the literature, *Medicine,* **41,** 249 (1962).

23. Leevy, C. M., *In vitro* studies of hepatic DNA synthesis in percutaneous liver biopsy specimens from man, *J. Lab. Clin. Med.,* **61,** 761 (1963).

24. Leevy, C. M., Folic acid metabolism, *Am. J. Clin. Nutr.,* **20,** 570 (1967).

25. Leevy, C. M., Observations on Hepatic Regeneration in Man, in *Advances in Internal Medicine,* W. Dock and I. Snapper (eds.) p. 97. Year Book, Chicago, Ill., 1967.

26. Leevy, C. M., Clinical diagnosis, evaluation, and treatment of liver disease in alcoholics, *Federation Proc.,* **26,** 1474 (1967).

27. Leevy, C. M., Cirrhosis in Alcoholics, in *Medical Clinics North America,* vol. 52, 1445, 1968.

28. Leevy, C. M., Hard liquor and cirrhosis, *Proc. Thule International Symposium,* in press.

29. Leevy, C. M., L. Cardi, O. Frank, R. Gellene, and H. Baker, Incidence and significance of hypovitaminemia in a randomly selected municipal hospital population, *Am. J. Clin. Nutr.,* **17,** 259 (1965).

30. Leevy, C. M., W. Y. Chey, P. Arts, C. L. Mendenhall, and M. Howard, Protein tolerance in liver disease, *Am. J. Clin. Nutr.,* **10,** 46 (1962).

31. Leevy, C. M., C. L. Cunniff, D. Walton, and M. Healey, Organization and function of a clinic for the alcoholic patient with liver disease, *Quart. J. Studies Alc.,* **15,** 537 (1954).

32. Leevy, C. M., E. Davidson, and H. Jeghers. Acute alcoholism in the general hospital, *Hosp. Med.,* **2,** 24 (1965).

33. Leevy, C. M., W. tenHove, Pathogenesis and Sequelae of Liver Disease in Alcoholic Man, in *Biochemical Factors in Alcoholism,* R. P. Maickel, (ed.), p. 151, Pergamon, New York, 1967.

34. Leevy, C. M. and F. Smith, Alcoholism and liver injury, *Proc. VIII International Symposium on Nutrition,* 1969, in press.

35. Leevy, C. M., F. Smith, C. Tamburro, W. tenHove, and M. Howard, The natural history of cirrhosis of the alcoholic, to be published.

36. Leevy, C. M., C. Tamburro, and W. tenHove, Ethanol Oxidizing Enzymes and Response to Liver Injury, in *Liver Research,* J. Vandenbroucke, J. DeGroote, and L. I. Standaert (eds.), p. 71, Tydschrift voor Gastroenterologie, Antwerp, 1967.

37. Leevy, C. M., C. Tamburro, M. Kirkland, and C. Cabansag, Biochemical Alterations in Delirium Tremens, in *Biochemical and Clinical Aspects of Alcohol Metabolism,* by W. Sardesai (ed.), p. 241, Charles C Thomas, Springfield, Ill., 1969.

38. Leevy, C. M., A. K. Tanribilir, and F. Smith, Biochemistry of Gastrointestinal and Liver Disease in Alcoholism, in *Biology of Alcoholism, Vol. 1, Biochemistry,* Plenum, New York, in press.

39. Leevy, C. M., A. D. Thomson, and H. Baker, Vitamins and liver injury, *Am. J. Clin. Nutr.,* **23,** 493 (1970).

40. Lieber, C. S., D. P. Jones, M. S. Losowsky, and C. S. Davidson, Interrelation of uric acid and ethanol metabolism in man, *J. Clin. Invest.,* **41,** 1863 (1962).

41. Lieber, C. S., A. Lefevre, N. Spritz, L. Feinman, and L. M. DeCarli, Difference in hepatic metabolism of long and medium chain fatty acids: The role of fatty acid chain length in the production of the alcoholic fatty liver, *J. Clin. Invest.,* **46,** 1451 (1967).

42. Lincheer, W. G., J. F. Patterson, E. W. Moore, R. J. Clermont, S. J. Robins, and T. C. Chalmers, Medium and long chain fat absorption in patients with cirrhosis, *J. Clin. Invest.,* **45,** 1317 (1966).

43. Lindenbaum, J., B. Rybak, C. D. Gerson, E. Rubin, and C. S. Lieber, Effects of ethanol on the small intestine of man, *Clin. Res.,* **18,** 385 (1970).

44. McDonald, R. A., *Hemochromatosis and Hemosidersosis,* Charles C Thomas, Springfield, Ill., 1964.

45. Perkoff, G. T., M. M. Dioso, V. Bleisch, and G. Klinkerfuss, A spectrum of myopathy associated with alcoholism: I. Clinical and laboratory features, *Ann. Int. Med.,* **67,** 481 (1967).

46. Perkoff, G. T., P. Hardy, and E. Velez-Garcia, A reversible acute muscular syndrome in chronic alcoholism, *N. Engl. J. Med.,* **274,** 1277 (1966).

47. Phillips, G. B., M. Victor, R. B. Adams, and C. S. Davidson, Study of nutritional defect in Wernicke's syndrome, *J. Clin. Invest.,* **13,** 859 (1952).

48. Porta, E. A., B. J. Bergman, and A. A. Stein, Acute alcoholic hepatitis, *Am. J. Pathol.,* **46,** 657 (1965).

49. Powell, W. J., Jr. and G. Klatskin, Duration of survival in patients with Laennec's cirrhosis, *Am. J. Med.,* **44,** 406 (1968).

50. Regan, T. J., G. Koroxenidis, C. B. Moschos, H. A. Olde-Wurtel, P. M. Lehan,

and H. K. Hellems, The acute metabolic and hemodynamic responses of the left ventricle to ethanol, *J. Clin. Invest.,* **45,** 270 (1966).

51. Rubin, E. and C. S. Lieber, Alcohol-induced hepatic injury in nonalcoholic volunteers, *N. Engl. J. Med.,* **278,** 869 (1969).

52. Sorrell, M. and C. M. Leevy, Alcoholic hepatitis and immunologic reactivity, *Clin. Res.,* **18,** 388 (1970).

53. Sullivan, J. F. and H. G. Lankford, Zinc metabolism and chronic alcoholism, *Am. J. Clin. Nutr.,* **17,** 57 (1965).

54. Sullivan, L. N. and Y. K. Liu, Suppression of hematopoiesis by ethanol., *J. Clin. Invest.,* **45,** 1078 (1966).

55. Tamburro, C. and C. M. Leevy, Lactate elevation in delirium tremens, to be published.

56. Thomson, A. D., H. Baker, and C. M. Leevy, Patterns of ^{35}S-thiamine hydrochloride absorption in the malnourished alcoholic, *J. Lab. Clin. Med.,* in press.

57. Veghelyi, P. V., T. Kemeny, J. Pozsonyi, and J. Sos, Dietary lesions of the pancreas, *Am. J. Dis. Child.,* **79,** 658 (1950).

58. Victor, M., The role of nutrition in the alcoholic neurological diseases, *J. Clin. Invest.,* **39,** 1037 (1960).

59. Woldman, E. E., D. Fishman, and A. J. Segal, Relation of fibrosis of the pancreas to fatty liver and/or cirrhosis: An analysis of one thousand consecutive autopsies, *J. Am. Med. Assoc.* **169,** 1281 (1959).

60. Zieve, L., Relationship Between Acute Pancreatitis and Hyperlipemia, in *Medical Clinics North America,* Vol. 52, p. 1493, 1968.

Chapter XIV

THE PSYCHOLOGICAL AND PHARMACOLOGICAL BASIS FOR THE TREATMENT OF ALCOHOL DEPENDENCE

EBBE CURTIS HOFF

BUREAU OF ALCOHOL STUDIES AND REHABILITATION,
VIRGINIA STATE HEALTH DEPARTMENT,
DEPARTMENTS OF PSYCHIATRY AND PHYSIOLOGY,
MEDICAL COLLEGE OF VIRGINIA
HEALTH SCIENCES DIVISION, VIRGINIA COMMONWEALTH UNIVERSITY,
RICHMOND

A.   Introduction

In speaking of the treatment of alcohol dependence, we mean those therapeutic enterprises which we set up to help a *person* who is a victim of alcohol dependence. This is an important distinction to make, because it brings into focus what we should always keep in mind, namely, that alcohol problems are problems of people and not solely problems inherent in the chemical upon which they are dependent. Like other psychoactive drugs, alcohol is variable in its effects on different people, depending on their personality, biochemical individuality, and their aims, endeavors, and expectations so far as the alcohol use is concerned. The Cooperative Commission on the Study of Alcoholism, set up in 1961 by a grant from the National Institute of Mental Health of the United States Department of Health, Education, and Welfare, devoted much attention to problem drinking as a comprehensive and important human problem [11]. For the purposes of the report of this Commission published in 1967, "problem drinking" has been defined as a repetitive use of beverage alcohol causing physical, psychological, or social harm to the drinker or to others. In thinking about this definition, we see that it stresses the disturbance of functioning rather than any particular or specific type of drinking behavior. Thus the actual amount, frequency, or pattern of alcohol use is not considered a primary criterion. Problem drinking, then, is rather widely defined to cover all persons who drink repetitively and are victims thereby of harm. The Commission in its report defined "alcoholism" as a condition in which an individual has lost control over his alcohol intake in the sense that he is consistently unable to refrain from drinking or to stop drinking before getting intoxicated. Thus an alcoholic is a problem drinker who in addition to being a victim of problems by reason of his drinking has also lost control over drinking and is unable to refrain from drinking consistently or to stop drinking before he becomes drunk. Obviously no definition is entirely adequate in this field, but the definition of the alcoholic as set forth by the Commission does bring out this characteristic loss of control which does seem to apply to a large proportion of problem drinkers and sufficiently so that it may be used fairly adequately as a criterion for what we may call alcoholism. One value of differentiating the terms *problem drinking* and *alcoholism* is that we are hereby able to gather together under the term *problem drinker* a large number of persons who are in need of help but who may not have reached a stage of consistent loss of control. Treatment enterprises may be different for the one than for the other, and we are in a better position to recognize the fact that no two problem drinkers are alike as to behavior, biochemical responses, or psychological structure. The definitions enable us to discern in the population many people who need help but who cannot be labeled as alcoholics indefinitely. This should enable us in our therapeutic efforts to be more successful in drawing into the area of therapeutic concern many people who are in trouble but who otherwise would not be able to accept the need for or be accepted for treatment. The need for early recognition of prealcoholic behavior is great, and earlier recognition of prodromal symptoms would do much to render therapy more successful.

It is obvious that an important goal in the field of drinking problems is to enhance our success in prevention. Prevention of drinking problems, although extraordinarily important, is at the same time extremely difficult. Several approaches may be taken, and one of these is to try to change drinking practices in the population so as to reduce harmful drinking. This may be done through various educational procedures both in schools as well as colleges and through the public media. There are nonspecific devices among which helping to create a better society is notable, and also the promotion of healthy families is a significant venture. An extraordinarily potent way of reducing problem drinking consists in the detailed research study of problem drinking, including alcoholism, with the goal of uncovering more fully the varied etiological factors in the constellation of causes leading to problem drinking and alcoholism. Through such clinical research we are placed in a better way to recognize vulnerable segments of the population and thus be more successful in very early intervention at a time when problem drinking is nonexistent or at a very primary stage. There will undoubtedly develop various psychological and biochemical criteria by which we can sooner or later recognize early vulnerability to problem drinking, and this may indeed stand us in good stead in providing special protection for such vulnerable persons.

As we think about the psychological and pharmacological basis for the treatment of alcohol dependence, it is quite useful to remember that treatment must be devised according to the needs of the particular patient and his family and that therefore the first step in sound treatment is an accurate diagnosis. This includes psychiatric diagnosis, medical investigation as well as social and cultural evaluation. Psychological diagnostics are essential in most cases, and the degree of our success in planning therapy is determined by our success in understanding the person who is the victim of the illness in question. We are convinced at the present time that the treatment of problem drinkers must be comprehensive, that is to say, it must include attention to all significant aspects of the person's life. Treatment also, it seems to me, is most successful if it involves an interdisciplinary approach by a skillful therapeutic team; nor can we treat only the patient himself in isolation but must be concerned with his family and must bring in his relations to the community and the community to him as well as his job relations, family associations, and many other aspects. There has been a tendency in the past, unfortunately, to treat so-called alcoholics in an episodic manner, as it were, handling the most vividly presenting acute problems, such as drunkenness, and then abandoning the patient until his acute symptoms flair up again. Nothing could be less successful. The only adequate way of treating problem drinkers is to devise and provide a therapeutic plan that is continuing, comprehensive, and based on a realistic understanding of the wide range of the patient's problems and his characteristics as a person. It is a mistake also to think that a one-sided treatment approach that deals only with limited issues, such as biochemical defects, can be successful in the present state of our knowledge. With this brief introduction we may now proceed to a discussion of some of the essential elements in initiating and continuing treatment.

B.   Initiation of Therapy

1.   Principles

We shall consider in the present chapter the condition of patients who have been drinking but may not be so acutely intoxicated as to be incapable of making decisions for themselves and who may arrive in the treatment situation in a state of withdrawal from recent drinking [5]. They may alternatively be free of alcohol in the blood on entry into therapy or when they become motivated to ask for help. We shall not discuss in detail the detoxification of the acutely intoxicated person, but it may be appropriate to consider those who are in a state of withdrawal or who have been recently using alcohol harmfully. The procedures for bringing a patient to care are extremely critical and important. Problem drinkers and frank alcoholics may find it hard to seek treatment, and yet the willingness to do so is essential. Problem drinkers can profit by an urgent sense of necessity for care. This has been called "hitting bottom" and does play a valuable part in the beginning of treatment. Many patients do benefit by an imposition of pressure. Thus a person may be faced with the necessity to enter into therapy by the imminent threat of the loss of his job, particularly if the job is a good one with tenure. When we say that a person seeks therapy voluntarily, we do not rule out the fact that there are many forms of pressure to which he may respond and may respond in quite a healthy manner. Motivation then to accept therapy does not rule out such forms of pressure that may impose on the prospective patient the recognition that his defenses and rationalizations are failing.

2.   Intake

Those who are victims of problem drinking and in particular of alcoholism may properly be described as sick people. Thus we may appropriately speak of "treatment" of alcohol dependence, as we have done in the title of this chapter. There is manifest illness in the course of the acute phases of problem drinking and also of withdrawal from a heavy and stormy drinking episode. The manifestations of alcoholism extend beyond drunkenness and its complications and include mental, emotional, and physical conditions that exist even during periods of the patient's "dry" states. One of the characteristic complications of problem drinking is very often the difficulty that the victim experiences in recognizing effectively his need for treatment. Although this is not limited to problem drinkers but is found as a part of other illnesses, nevertheless difficulties of denial and inadequate motivation are so important that they require special consideration at the very start of any attempt to help problem drinkers. It has sometimes been said that alcoholics are more accessible to treatment when they are actually in the middle of a drinking episode or at any rate going through the withdrawal symptoms and other sufferings associated with the spree. Sometimes this is true, but there is also the difficulty that a person suffering from withdrawal may simply be looking for relief of immediate symptoms and troubles. When these are assuaged, the motivation for continuing therapy for full rehabilitation may vanish.

Intake, therefore, is a process that requires skill on the part of staff who work with alcoholics and great consideration and wisdom by members of family, employers, and so forth. Sometimes it is essential to "pull the rug out from under" the prospective patient, and sometimes this is done to him without any deliberate intention to do so. Much has been made of the phenomenon of surrender in which rationalizations give way and the prospective patient sees himself powerless and helpless over his condition and that he must avail himself of treatment for a rehabilitation that goes beyond simply getting dried out. There are those that feel that no effort at therapy is of any avail until this experience of surrender has been realized. Motivation for rehabilitative therapy can be assisted by skilled persons, and it is of importance to use whatever motivational techniques are likely to work so as to bring the patient to help as soon as possible. Sometimes, unfortunately, a patient becomes motivated, his denial mechanisms break down, but there has been so much brain damage and deterioration, say, of liver function that recovery becomes unlikely in spite of motivation.

It is well if therapy for an alcoholic can be initiated on a voluntary basis. Enforced treatment by legal commitment is, I believe, fraught with difficulty. For example, the resentment of a patient who has been legally committed to a hospital is often extraordinarily vivid and may entail a long-standing unwillingness ever again to undertake a rehabilitative program. On the other hand there are forms of pressure that have been applied to alcoholics by their employers, families, friends, or by themselves that sometimes have marked the beginning of effective treatment. A man, for example, who has important stakes in a skilled job may be responsive to the realistic threat that his job may or probably will be lost if his drinking continues and if his effectiveness in his work continues to deteriorate.

Intake into therapy varies in its processes and procedures according to the community and various customs throughout the world. In our Bureau of Alcohol Studies and Rehabilitation of the Virginia State Health Department, our patients are referred from several sources as follows: self-referrals 7.2%; relatives 9.1%; friends 9.4%; courts 7.4%; social agencies 3.9%; physicians 34.6%; spouses 6.7%; clergy 3.6%; Alcoholics Anonymous 8.2%; old patients of the bureau 4.7%; and others 7.9%. There are presently in our bureau 11 outpatient clinics specializing in the treatment of alcohol problems and located in centers of population throughout the state. Most of our referrals come from these clinics, and when patients have completed their hospitalization phase of treatment, they return to the clinic of origin for outpatient follow-up. We maintain a public information program that encourages patients with drinking problems to apply for treatment as early as possible in the course of their condition. Actually the outpatient clinics of our bureau constitute the first line of the intake process, and in these clinics an alcoholic or any person who believes that he may have a problem with alcohol can freely discuss his difficulties with a member of a staff in the clinic who may recommend therapy either as an outpatient or referral for hospitalization in the bureau's hospital facilities at the Medical College of Virginia, Health Sciences Division of the Virginia Commonwealth University at Richmond, Virginia, or at the University of Virginia School of Medicine at Charlottesville. We have found that patients referred from social agencies, physicians, Alcoholics Anonymous, and old patients tend to have the best success rates by criteria that include abstinence records, improvement of family situations, and job stability. Patients referred from spouses tend to have a rather low record.

Patients may enter therapy in our bureau sober and without symptoms or sober with withdrawal symptoms or in an acutely intoxicated state. About half of the patients are either sober and without symptoms or in withdrawal state and with a zero alcohol blood level. The rest of the patients have some degree of acute alcohol intoxication. We do not find it true that patients who are intoxicated tend to do better than those who are not.

Every patient who is seen for admission into the program of our bureau is seen by a skilled member of our intake team. The prospective patient has an opportunity to express his problems of whatever sort and to indicate what he is seeking in terms of rehabilitation. The patient has an opportunity to hear from the intake staff member that the program of our bureau is not primarily concentrated on simply "drying out" but that treatment involves not only hospitalization but also the continuation of treatment in one of our outpatient clinics for a year or more. We also stress with patients the importance of the problem and help the patient, as far as he is able, to evaluate his situation at the time of asking for help. The attitude of the intake staff is one of helpfulness, absence of punitive attitude, and yet recognition of the seriousness of the situation and expression of a realistic appraisal of the kinds of action that are required.

The patient is helped to deal with his denial problems, and he is offered reasonable hope of recovery. We recognize that many problems from which alcoholics and their families suffer are problems compounded by neglect. If possible and if the prospective patient is willing, we like to have a member of the family present at an intake interview, and members of the family are encouraged to take part in the treatment situation, particularly in helping them to recognize and deal with their own personal, emotional, and other problems. We stress this rather than emphasizing what the wife, for example, can do to keep her husband sober. It seems to us important that the privilege of maintaining sobriety is a privilege that belongs to the patient himself. On the other hand, members of the family can, through a better understanding, themselves, be more helpful family members. In many cases earlier entry into therapy may have prevented many difficulties, especially if treatment had been undertaken before irreversible physical and mental damage had been done. As can be seen then, one of the most pertinent issues in intake process is how and in what manner to motivate patients to accept and continue therapy at as early a stage as possible in the process of their illness. Unfortunately we usually begin too late. We find that an all too common difficulty is that in the earlier stages the victim of problem drinking is indeed making a valiant effort to continue to secure what he conceives to be the rewards of his drinking, whatever these may be, in the fervent hope that he may not have to pay too much in terms of unwanted illness. Often a patient will tolerate self-destructive behavior and personal and economic loss, because it is so difficult for him to accept the fact that he is indeed powerless over alcohol and that his life, as has been said in the first step of AA, has become unmanageable. Alcoholics find the practice of a regime of abstinence is characterized often by the vista of a bleak and unattractive future. It is an unpleasant reality to have to come face to face with the realization that they can no longer support life situations and still drink. This can be depressing and even intolerable. Many alcoholics spend years moving through a variety of rationalizations and compromises that one by one let them down.

In the intake process, however long it may require—one interview or several—the process must be honest, straightforward, and in full concordance with facts. It is also needful that the patient be helped to reach a covenant or agreement with the helping agents. The time before admission is the time to clarify the terms of treatment, how long it will last in all probability, what it will involve, and what help will be needed through Alcoholics Anonymous, the patient's employers, his family, and his community. The value of voluntary entry into therapy may be vitiated by accepting for therapy a patient without his having come to some such clear-cut agreement.

Although our knowledge of the illness of alcoholism is incomplete, we do recognize alcoholism as a multiplex of etiological factors that are physiological, psychological, social, and economic. We believe that a patient must deeply feel the need to recover in a broad sense and such recovery really cannot be accomplished without skillful help [9]. A patient cannot really do it by himself alone, although we are indeed aware of apparently spontaneous restoration of abstinence. Recovery is indeed a matter of abstinence, that is to say, an alcohol-free life. It is also partly a reestablishment of human relationships.

As we have said, the first goal in the care of an alcoholic is to bring him therapy and to help him to continue in a well-planned program of rehabilitation seen as a long-term project. The intake problem is complicated by the fact that many alcoholics cannot really see themselves in this condition, because it often attacks the victim subtly. Often without understanding how this has happened, an alcoholic discovers himself involved in symptoms of loss of control, harmful alcohol use characterized by the attendant family, jobs, social, economic, and health problems. Alcoholics sometimes only imperfectly recognize that they use alcohol as a kind of psychotherapeutic drug. We find it hardly surprising that alcoholic patients so often resort to rationalization and to denial of the precise realities of the problems and, even when denial is no longer possible, an alcoholic may attempt to misinterpret or misevaluate his symptoms and problems and misconstrue his necessary course of action. Many alcoholics do seek to control their alcohol intake by rigid enforcement of self-discipline or "willpower," only to fail again and again. The fact that the patient comes to therapy with a history of failure and that members of the family seek help for him with the same history of repeated failure may make it difficult to initiate therapy in the truer sense of the word.

That alcoholics may fall into various patterns of misuse of alcohol is sometimes a point that the intake staff member must deal with early in the intake process. Many alcoholics, even when they have come so far as to seek help, find it impossible to accept as a fact that their alcohol use is indeed out of control and follows a pathologically deviant pattern.

It is not always easy for an alcoholic clearly to relate to alcohol use the harm that is being done in his life, nor can he accurately perceive that he is using alcohol as a means of holding life together as a self-medication with a psychoactive drug. Although many alcoholics realize that things are going wrong, they cannot face the need to stop drinking, because, whether they recognize it or not, alcohol has become a necessity without which they cannot function unless life is changed drastically in a way that the applicant cannot presently plan for. Thus the intake process is important, and many decisions have to be made.

Alcohol does give the alcoholic many rewards, although ultimately unhealthy ones. It does allow him to escape quickly and temporarily from his own sense of isolation or defeat. It may pull him together when he is in a state of panic, and it may indeed invite him to withdrawal into his own world of fantasy, where he can for a short time at least be protected from the pain of living in a world that he sees only too clearly was not created solely for him. For an alcoholic, life may be so overwhelming that without some form of medication he cannot begin to face it effectively. Alcohol is his own highly compelling form of medication and one that many alcoholics cannot abandon because they know no other. The trouble with the alcoholic then is partly that he has in alcohol hit on a psychopharmacological agent that is actually defective but has a great appeal, although he may not be willing to express this.

As a problem drinker's difficulties become more and more sharply focused, he is pressed in various ways by his family, his friends, his employer, and the circumstances of his own living to abandon his drinking. He is, however, appalled by the prospect of an existence without the support of alcohol, because, as we have said, he is not aware of any other technique that has proved as effective in handling some of his life situations. To face the prospect of years and years without the chemical comfort that alcohol gives is insupportable. Members of the family, whether of a man or a woman alcoholic, finally reach their wit's end, and these family members in their harrassment propose what seem to them to be reasonable solutions and often suggest the use of willpower and other devices by which the unfortunate victim ought to be able to abstain from something that is so apparently destructive to him. In the intake process where the family comes into the picture, we must recognize that the family quite typically goes through a series of experiences characterized first by unbelief and in a way denial. Members of the family find it difficult, as does the alcoholic, to recognize what has happened or what is happening, although they may realize that something has gone wrong even before the victim himself does.

The first phase of the family's confrontation with the alcoholic member's difficulty is often one of frank unbelief and an attempt at "business as usual." This is partly because the onset of the difficulty for the victim can be subtle and gradual. There is often a succeeding state of shock associated with family disorganization and functional breakdown. The family may itself react by denial as a defense against panic. The family does its best to maintain its functional integrity in the hope that the problem will "go away by itself." Both alcoholics and their families are not unaware of the usefulness of denial in dealing with minor problems. Therefore it is not surprising that denial is used in so serious a condition as progressive alcoholism. A feature of this denial process is the tendency not only of the victim himself but also of the family to underestimate the severity of the condition. When this fails, as it inevitably does, the family begins to mobilize itself in various ways to mount a kind of therapeutic assault on the difficulty. We often see family members come to seek advice for therapy of their alcoholic spouse, parent, or child when the family therapeutic approach has failed. Families sometimes attempt to "wall off" the family from others and to become more isolated. They also isolate the victim himself within the family, and there occurs a reorganization of power structure within the family, so that the victim becomes a kind of supernumerary member. This walling off within the family and establishment of new power structures are both such a failure that it is often at this point that family members seek help. Members of the family who seek help for the victim when their own efforts have failed often present themselves as highly angry, hostile, and full of blame. Their tendency may be to reject the sick member, and yet this is not completely possible, because a sick member intrudes himself so irritatingly and pervasively into the family situation. Thus a spouse may come to the intake staff member, angrily speaking of divorce. Sometimes, if the alcoholic is the wife, the last act of the nonalcoholic husband may be to turn the patient over to a therapeutic agency and then abandon the wife.

The problems that will be uncovered by contact with the family members during the intake process will depend partly on the stage which the family has reached. Sometimes the family can be an extremely helpful unit. Sometimes, unfortunately, there is little to be achieved through attempts at family reunion. The more the alcoholic member remains a problem to the family members, the more likely there is to be hostility, despair, and guilt. Sometimes one sees the complete reorganization of the family with more or less successful restructure and maintenance. Sometimes there is a secondary disorganization within the family and the appearance of symptoms of illness and decompensation in the nonalcoholic members. It may be at this point that family members seek help, not only for the patient's sake, but also in recognition of their own need for guidance from outside the family.

By the time an alcoholic seeks help, even under pressure, he may see what is happening to himself almost as well as his family does. It may be that, as he talks with the intake officer, he may be able to share his despair that the family suggestions seem empty, unhelpful, excessively critical, and useless. He may react to his family's responses by feeling hurt, angry, or guilty. He may accept their ideas, for example, that his drinking is a weakness or a bad habit that he can control through the disciplined exercise of his will. He may try very hard to do this, only to fail repeatedly. For the alcoholic who eventually recovers and who establishes an alcohol-free way of life, there is something quite remarkable that happens from which he may forever after date all the events and circumstances of his life. This is often an experience within the fellowship of AA and is characterized by a self-awareness experienced in different ways by different patients. For all those who experience it, it is a serious and even desperate crisis that pulls the alcoholic up short and reveals to him a future that holds nothing but despair and hopelessness within the situation of drinking. For some alcoholics who come for help this experience has already been lived through before the patient comes to the interviewer or interviews. As we see it, the patient recognizes that his life has failed and that there is nothing to look forward to but pain and misery as long as he continues to use alcohol. His coming for therapy is a cry of help. This surrender has been a useful concept suggested by the 12 steps in AA and is made use of in the practice of many skilled therapists. Even at the beginning of the intake experience the patient can see his actual condition quite clearly, and the surrender process is not considered a mobilization of willpower but a recognition that he has lost the battle. A sensitive investigation of patients who recover does reveal very often the association of this surrender experience with a conversion, namely, pulling oneself up to a halt and turning around to a new direction. Sometimes this happens as a result of the patient's own internal experiences and sometimes as a result of the loss of a good job, loss of a spouse by divorce, or any number of catastrophic experiences. We do know enough about the experience of hitting bottom in men who come for therapy; however, we are not sure at all what happens to those who hit bottom and who never actually come for help. I am certain that the experience can be devastating. They may become deeply and irreversibly depressed and may commit suicide. We need more study of the techniques by which motivation may be guided right at the start and the applicant's motivation may be assisted in the direction of health. To be content to wait passively for the patient to reach such a "bottom" may be a faulty interpretation of the phenomenon of surrender.

In assisting the patient toward effective motivation [9], especially at the onset, as therapists we can be of help by the frankness and honesty with which we relate ourself to the prospective patient and his family by refusing to condemn or to permit the patient to manipulate us and so prolong the pathological situation. Patients do hit bottom repeatedly during recurring crises. The surrender experience is not necessarily permanent, and the motivation arising from the experience of crisis can be erased as the patient senses his early temporary improvement. There is thus a kind of "false cure" that may be experienced even within a few days after entering into therapy. What seemed to be intolerable crises may evaporate within a week or two. Thus we ought to help our patient to be aware of this and help him to understand that the real therapeutic endeavor is joined as the patient recognizes the so-called "false cure." Many patients are most vulnerable to drinking relapse and other relapses when their depression, for example, has been ameliorated. At the start the patient should be helped to know that his therapy in order to be successful must be planned rather than sporadic and continuing rather than episodic [4]. Such episodic intermittent so-called treatment based only on carrying the patient through drinking sprees cannot but fail. It is often the case that alcoholic patients are frequently unwanted in hospitals and doctors' offices, partly because the emphasis in treatment has for so long and too often been solely on symptomatic relief of crisis problems. We feel that as long as help for the alcoholic patient is limited to the periodic management of acute episodes, whether in the hospital, in the office, or through home visit with no on-going, planned, rehabilitative program, it is highly unlikely that much progress will be made. There are, of course, other crises besides acute alcoholic ones through which the patient may be helped to enter effective therapy. It is also worth knowing that family members and the patient himself can learn to recognize symptoms of nervousness, irritability, depression, panic, and others which may foretell a drinking bout and for which a patient may profitably seek help before the drinking occurs and within the setting of an on-going treatment program.

We have said that alcoholics are ill, that they are overwhelmed by a highly complex disorder, not fully understood, and that they move often within a family situation that has become quite disordered. We have found in the intake experience that by the time an alcoholic reaches some therapeutic confrontation, other members of the family may be even more sick than the alcoholic himself, either because of or from causes prior to the patient's alcoholism. Ideally, therefore, some accurate evaluation must be made of the family members and their situation as a family group. Such evaulation must include the strength, resources, and stability of the family, its capacity to readjust as the patient moves along in therapy, and ways in which they may be most effectively helped to handle their own problems and those arising out of alcoholism within the family. Living with an alcoholic can never be entirely free from some problems even when the alcoholic is sober and remains so for years. We are aware that, as therapy proceeds, the patient's own progress in recovery may create some kinds of new disturbances within the family because of resulting adjustments in the family interpersonal relationships. We not infrequently see a case in which an alcoholic under therapy or having profited by therapy for some time may no longer be an acceptable partner to a spouse. It may also be the case that members of the family may over the patient's drinking years have so adjusted themselves to the drinking alcoholic's behavior pattern that it may be difficult or even impossible to accept the alcoholic person as a maturing person facing reality in a sober way of life. It is for these reasons that family members need help to understand as clearly as possible the nature of the alcoholic member's illness and their own problems that arise from it. In this way there may be fostered within the family an environment that is hopefully therapeutic to all. As an alcoholic becomes sober and starts to travel the long road of rehabilitation, many realignments of family relationships and function have to occur. Room must be made for the alcoholic member to take up again his place within these relationships. This is sometimes difficult because of the uncertainty of his sobriety and his capacity to sustain a new and cooperative role. Occasional sprees and slips may mean that the family will have quickly to adjust to allow for the patient's unpredictably changing status. This uncertainty of the patient's capacities from week to week or month to month is in itself confusing to the family. Some but not all of these matters can be discussed in the initial interviews with the family, and certainly as therapy proceeds the alcoholic and his family both can profit by an understanding of what is happening when it occurs. Certainly in the initial interviews the family can be helped to understand that through all this recovery endeavor to be undertaken there must be established and strengthened the family's resources within a setting that is as far as possible conducive to recovery. Perhaps the most significant of all is that members of the family should be helped to relinquish their own self-imposed responsibilities as therapists and see themselves more and more in the natural family roles as fathers, mothers, children, and so forth.

In our discussion of initiation into therapy we have spoken so far of the applicant who is reasonably well motivated or at least sufficiently well motivated to come and engage in dialogue with the admitting staff member. This, it seems to me, is the most hopeful initiation process but cannot always be counted on. Many patients enter the area of the therapeutic environment for a serious acute drinking emergency. Sometimes all we can do is to hospitalize our patient, knowing very little about him from his own lips. Dealing with an intoxicated patient can be difficult; however, with modern sedative medication the grosser difficulties can be obviated. Tranquilizers, such as chlordiazepoxide, either by mouth or intramuscularly, can sometimes be used to good effect to help the patient to a state in which he can talk and discuss his problems to some extent at least. In any case it is often all one can do to admit the patient to the hospital, in which he receives sound physiological and pharmacological treatment for his acute intoxication, reserving for some hours later a discussion of his motivations, and so forth. In spite of what we try to accomplish in this direction we sometimes find that the patient may sign himself out if he is admitted on a voluntary basis or may find himself unable to benefit by therapy because of his sense of having been forced into the situation. In the management of intake process of the acutely intoxicated patient it is always wise to treat him with courtesy, firmness, consistency, and without blame or recrimination. Also it is well if his wife or other significant member of the family can take part in such an intake to help to relieve the panic that almost inevitably is associated with an acute intoxication experience by the alcoholic member.

3.   The Settings for Treatment of Problem Drinkers and Their Families

A.   THE GENERAL PRACTITIONER. A certain number of problem drinkers have done well under the care of their own general practitioner. In smaller communities especially, this may be effective. General physicians have in fact borne the brunt of a high proportion of all the alcoholics. Especially now that there are community mental health centers, alcoholism programs, both inpatient and outpatient, and other assistances and resources available to the physician, it is certainly true that the work of the doctor in general practice can be rewarding. General practitioners know the families in their community and often are in close touch with not only the alcoholic member of the family but also others in the family. The doctor's effectiveness can be enhanced by the device of creating a team within his own community. This may consist of a clergyman who is clinically trained as a counsellor and who appreciates the problems of alcoholism and also by keeping in touch with public health nurses, employers, and others. Sometimes the general practitioner may choose to handle an acute episode of drinking in the home, and this may be the procedure of choice if a well-motivated family member can help with the acute situation. More often these days, however, the local general hospital can be more helpful, and fortunately more and more community hospitals are becoming willing to accept alcoholics as such with a primary diagnosis of alcohol dependency. One of the most effective features of the care by the general medical practitioner is that he can see the patient for continuing visits for many months or a year or so. Sometimes the medical practitioner refers his patient to a community mental health center or an inpatient or outpatient program of a state alcoholism division in which comprehensive interdisciplinary treatment can be made available. In our own Bureau of Alcohol Studies and Rehabilitation, as has been stated, approximately one-third of our patients come from general medical practitioners. Although we continue to follow up such patients, we also find it helpful if the physician who made the initial referral also takes part in the ongoing treatment. The local doctor and the clinic staff of specialists working together are usually able to provide better care than if either tries alone. I have personally come to know many general practitioners in Virginia who have worked closely with Alcoholics Anonymous and various agencies and who keep in touch with our Bureau of Alcohol Studies and Rehabilitation of the State Health Department. Sometimes the general practitioner sets up a weekly group-therapy meeting, and the patients of such practitioners become sources of referral from others whom the doctor may wish to work with himself or refer them on to our bureau or some other appropriate therapeutic setting.

The usefulness of the general practitioner is a pertinent example of how important it is to mobilize all the community resources. Many young physicians, especially in general practice, have found working with alcoholics rewarding. The general practitioner, far from finding his own practice adversely affected by his work with alcoholics, discovers that his experiences with alcoholics and their families can help him with virtually all categories of patients that he encounters in his practice.

The general practitioner is in an ideal position to set up therapeutic relationships with the rest of the family. As a perceptive physician, he may be the most knowledgeable person regarding alcoholism and its distribution of anyone in the whole community. The same may be said also for clinically trained clergymen and experienced members of Alcoholics Anonymous. Often one of the most successful therapeutic plans consititutes a team consisting of a general practitioner, a clergymen, and a member of Alcoholics Anonymous helping to bring the alcoholic and his family to treatment in a special setting, such as our bureau or the community hospital, and then following this up by well-planned coordinated work with members of the team and the alcoholic and his family. It is important for the members of such teams to respect their own competence and to realize that their expertise extends often far beyond simply referring to specialists or to AA alone. Moreover when a physician or clergyman or a member of AA refers to our alcoholism center or a mental health center, he is not surrendering his interest in or responsibility for the patient and the family. His responsibility continues, and his referral to the specialized center is often simply the beginning of his relationship with the patient and the family.

As has been said, we have found that referrals to our bureau from professional persons, such as physicians, clergymen, members of AA, and so forth, are usually attended by a higher degree of success than from any other referral source. This is partly because of the professional's competence in matching the patient with the treatment setting and also in his understanding of the need for treatment and in his willingness to explain to the prospective patient and the family the exact nature of the treatment needs and proposed plans.

The general practitioner who surrounds himself with a team is in an ideal position to exemplify the principle of comprehensive treatment, an interdisciplinary team, and concern for rehabilitation of the family as a whole [6]. The general practitioners should make themselves acquainted with competent members of AA in their community, with fellow practitioners who are similarly interested in alcohol problems, and with clergy who are well trained and well motivated. They should also be on terms of close acquaintance with the staff of local hospitals and specialized centers within effective working distance of the patients whom they are likely to refer and work with afterwards.

B. THE GENERAL HOSPITAL AND THE TEACHING MEDICAL CENTER. The increasing awareness that persons suffering from problem drinking are ill even when not currently in an acute alcoholic state has helped to change the attitude of general hospitals and teaching medical centers toward the admission of such patients. In the past and unfortunately even now, it is difficult or even impossible to secure admission to a general hospital except through a fictitious diagnosis. Emergency rooms in general hospitals and teaching centers do offer acute detoxification, and the quality of such care varies from hospital to hospital. Many hospital administrators find it relatively unrewarding simply to take in the acutely intoxicated brought in off the streets from police, and many emergency room physicians find the provision of care for the acutely intoxicated an unwanted complication in what they might regard as the legitimate function of the emergency service. As time goes on, detoxification procedures are becoming more and more effective, and the milieu and staffing set up in such a way that procedures are more likely to be successful. It must be recognized, however, that the acutely intoxicated patient who is brought into the emergency services of a general hospital does not necessarily represent a person with a good prognosis. In many general hospitals, however, such patients may be retained in a special medical ward after they have become medically sober and can then be seen by social workers and other staff of the psychiatric service if there is one or a specialized alcoholism unit if it is available in the community or in the hospital itself. In our own Bureau of Alcohol Studies and Rehabilitation, many patients who are alcoholics are referred from various units of the Department of Medicine or the Department of Neurology, and there is a frequent interchange of patients between the Bureau of Alcohol Studies and the Department of Psychiatry.

To secure cooperation in caring for alcoholics in a general hospital, it is necessary that all concerned persons be involved. This includes members of the administrative staff as well as senior medical personnel and the interns and residents. I sincerely trust that the time is not far off when no general hospital will be regarded as adequately serviced and staffed unless it does have provisions for the care of alcoholics, both in the acute phase or subacute withdrawal phase and for more prolonged hospitalization, offering group psychotherapy and individual psychotherapy and other therapeutic modalities that are indicated by the diagnosis. What we are saying is that alcoholics should be admissable to general hospitals under the same general principles of good practice that apply to all persons who are ill. The diagnosis should be carried out in a sound fashion, and admission should be based on the diagnosis and the expectations for treatment and the capabilities of the general hospital in question to handle the therapeutic planning.

In the matter of therapeutic planning and milieu in the general hospital it ought to be stated that adequate hospitalization care of alcoholics should go far beyond simply keeping the patient isolated in a hospital bedroom. I have unfortunately run into general hospitals in which people are, so to speak, sequestered in the hospital, oversedated and isolated. This unfortunately happens too often with persons of considerable means who enter the hospital under a spurious diagnosis and who are lonely, sluggish, and frustrated until they leave the hospital, only to return to drinking again. This is not to say that such persons are not well diagnosed but they certainly do not have the benefit of a group milieu in the hospital in which they can share their problems with other patients. Thus the general hospital, after the administrative and clinical staff have decided that it is a proper milieu for the care of alcoholics and their families, should carefully set up structure and function in such a way that these patients are treated in accordance with the most modern and up-to-date social, psychological, and psychiatric principles and that sedation is a modality of therapy linked with group work, work with the families, and so forth.

The teaching medical center is a special case that should receive careful attention. In teaching medical centers, problem drinkers may be found in most of the major departments and this is proper. Thus alcoholics are to be encountered in the departments of medicine, surgery, psychiatry, neurology, physical medicine, and others. Certainly the large clinical center of a medical school with its university affiliations has tremendous opportunities for taking leads in clinical and basic research and in moving ahead the field of therapy and that of prevention. I believe that every teaching medical center should have a division of alcohol studies and rehabilitation as part of the institution and that there should be free and liberal exchange of consultation and referral from one department to the other as may be indicated. Outpatient clinics, well staffed, should be a part of the treatment provided for problem drinkers in the medical center. In addition to this the teaching center provides opportunity for instruction of medical students as well as others in training, notably, nurses, externs, interns, and residents. Both predoctoral and postdoctoral students should have opportunity for learning about alcohol problems in a practical way, not only in the emergency room, but also in long-term rehabilitation programs. Wherever possible, community mental health centers and specialized alcoholism outpatient clinics should be closely geared to the programs of the medical school and the university hospitals, and also the university setting should be operating in close coordination with a number of other agencies of the community, for instance, welfare, correctional agencies, and so forth.

C. PRIVATE SANATORIA AND HOSPITALS. Private sanatoria and hospitals vary greatly in quality, cost of services, and therapeutic approaches. At their best these institutions are a valuable resource in the community, and certainly it would be difficult to do without them. They are a source of support to many alcoholics who could or would not avail themselves of other programs. At their worst, some of these institutions are simply rather poor drying-out centers with antiquated methods. Even so, in the present state of our service network, the private sanatoria and hospitals offer much. Perhaps one of the greatest advantages is that patients can be admitted to such services with a minimum of waiting. Many private sanatoria make no more elaborate claim than that they do deal effectively with acutely intoxicated patients or patients in withdrawal. Such sanatoria and hospitals are likely to continue to function, and effort should be made by the staff of such agencies to upgrade, update, and enhance the quality of their service. Where it seems unlikely that they can set up outpatient programs, they should in any case refer leaving patients to outpatient clinics in the area, so that continuity of treatment can be maintained. There are efforts now being made in some private hospitals to set up well-rounded, comprehensive treatment programs for alcoholics with their wives or other family members. This is a remarkable step forward.

D. COMMUNITY MENTAL HEALTH CENTERS. These centers and other agencies with the avowed mission of bringing treatment close to where people live and work are of great potential value for the future as well as for the present. The functional organization of the centers should be such that there are staff who make it their concern to see that alcoholics are not neglected in selection and continuing treatment. It can happen very easily that alcoholic patients as it were "sign themselves out" of treatment. Both in the general hospitals and the teaching medical centers it is important that there be a special organizational setup by which alcoholic patients' needs are recognized. The same applies to private sanatoria and hospitals, although there is less danger in these institutions that the alcoholics are neglected, since such a high proportion of their patient clientele often consists of problem drinkers. As community mental health centers grow in service and function, their effectiveness in the network for helping alcoholics will benefit by special planning by which alcoholics and their families are not neglected.

E. STATE HOSPITALS. The tradition of state hospitals in the earliest time of their inception tended toward the philosophy of isolating those whose behavior rendered them unacceptable in the social situation. A large proportion of state-hospital patients have been admitted either on commitment or more recently more frequently on a voluntary basis. This latter trend is to be encouraged. Also to be promoted is the increasing tendency to provide special settings within state mental hospitals for alcoholics, so that they are not thrown into a general hospital milieu in which persons of all kinds of mental and emotional diagnoses are gathered together. State hospitals in recent years have provided opportunities for the special treatment of alcoholic patients, and the influence of the state hospitals has been enhanced as time has gone along. Special buildings, wards, and staff have been set up in state hospitals for alcoholics, so that their particular needs can be more adequately cared for. This is in the direction that it should be. For some, the state mental hospital remains the only effective or potentially effective program. State hospitals have set up group-therapy programs and have enhanced the meaning of the therapeutic community.

A defect still remains that patients emerging from state hospitals do not always have available to them or make available to themselves continuing outpatient clinic treatment in the community in which or near which they live.

F. ALCOHOLISM PROGRAMS. In the United States [10] and Canada and in other parts of the world there have been established state alcoholism programs that in different degrees have provided not only hospitalization but also outpatient clinic treatment. Such programs in their more advanced and sophisticated development have provided not only inpatient services but also ongoing treatment. Some state programs have been defective in the quality of treatment, but where attention to this has been emphasized, the state alcoholism programs have indeed provided a comprehensive inter-disciplinary approach to both alcoholics and their families. I feel that the alcoholism program network is an essential part of the entire therapeutic milieu and that one of the main services that the alcoholism programs of states and provinces can provide is to keep the important subject of alcohol problems alive in the concerns of the citizenry.

Alcoholism programs initiated by states or provinces have had a history of variation in their establishment. Some have been importantly influenced by Alcoholics Anonymous and the concern of citizens who wish to provide treatment where this has been neglected. Alcoholism programs do often provide the needed outpatient care where this is not available elsewhere. As in the case of other agencies that wish to help alcoholics and their families, it should be stressed that alcoholism programs, state, provincial, or local, must never forget that their function is to be shared with other agencies and that one of their major missions is to see to it that such sharing does occur. There is no one agency in any community that has an exclusive concern or an exclusive responsibility for alcohol problems. The question of the setting within the administrative milieu of the alcohol-ism programs is one that has been answered variously in different parts of the United States, Canada, and the rest of the world. Isolated, specialized commissions for alcoholism seem to be waning, and the tendency now is to place such programs in either the department of mental hygiene and hospitals or the department of health. In any case, wherever the program is established administratively, it is vital that the alcoholism programs func-tion to keep alive and in public view the concern for alcoholics and their families and that the programs combat the rather unwholesome idea that, simply because there is an alcoholism program in a community (state, local, or provincial), this does not mean that all other agencies must and should cease their action. In fact the very opposite should be the case.

One of the major functions of the alcoholism programs is that they should help to mobilize all the potential helping agencies.

In our discussion of the milieu for the treatment of alcoholics we have stressed the importance of ongoing care. The quality of any of the milieus is measured in large proportion by the degree to which the patients are given the opportunity and privilege of continuing rehabilitative treatment. Nothing is more important than to make clear that problem drinking is a chronic, progressive disorder that cannot be adequately cared for simply by the episodic treatment of alcoholic crises alone. An alcoholic is often no less in need of care when he is sober than when he is drinking. Moreover there are other emergencies that the alcoholic and his family experience apart from the acute drinking episode. In establishing and maintaining the milieus for rehabilitation for alcoholics and their families, it is essential that these patients be given the opportunity to receive appropriate ongoing care in accordance with their needs. Nothing less is adequate. Too long we have confined ourselves to caring for the drinking episodes, to "drying out" patients and neglecting the all-important aspect of continuing rehabilitative procedures.

C.   The Hospital Phase of Treatment

1.   Handling Acute Emergencies

Patients entering therapy in many milieus go through the experiences of remorse, depression, fear, acute anxiety, nervousness, and a sense of being overwhelmed by the problems in which they find themselves enmeshed. Patients who have been drinking heavily and who are emerging from the acute effects of alcohol, especially on the brain, are responding to inevitable neurological overactivity, particularly in the limbic system, which means that they are overreactive in a number of ways [3]. There may be tremor, fear, anxiety, guilt, and many other responses that are in part, at any rate, the result of a backlash of overactivity following sedation of the central nervous system by alcohol. This higher cerebral overactivity can account for many of the symptoms of the alcoholic patient in withdrawal. It is essential that treatment for such conditions be undertaken with due regard for diagnosis and appropriate prognosis. We have found it appropriate to provide certain standing orders and to modify these as the internist in charge of patients considers that this is desirable. All patients who are in a withdrawal state receive ascorbic acid, approximately 100 mg by mouth four times a day, and also multivitamin capsules by mouth also four times a day. Benadryl, 50 mg by mouth at bedtime as required, is a valuable aid to relaxation and sleep and as a nighttime sedative. If necessary, this may be repeated in 3 hr. For sober patients with withdrawal symptoms, chlordiazepoxide (Librium), 25 mg every 4 hr by mouth as required, is regularly prescribed. Patients who have an appreciable alcohol blood level but who are suffering from withdrawal symptoms as well are given a multivitamin formula, 1 cm^3 intramuscularly four times a day for approximately 3 days, and ascorbic acid, 100 mg by mouth 4 times a day. Multivitamin capsules by mouth are also made available once a day. It has been our experience that chloral hydrate, 1.0 g by mouth 4 times a day as required for the first 3 days, is a valuable daytime sedation. Chlordiazepoxide (Librium), 50 mg intramuscularly every 4 hr as required, is also useful. After the third day Librium, 25 mg by mouth every 4 hr as required, may be administered.

2.   Diagnosis and Prognosis

Perhaps one of the most glaring defects in the care of alcoholics is that one does not make available to them the best in diagnosis and prognosis. No two alcoholics are alike, and no two alcoholics require the same treatment. The hospital is the setting in which an accurate diagnosis must be made and a prognostic formulation be worked out. The interdisciplinary team made available to the patient should always consist of skillful internists, psychiatrists, and psychologists as well as social workers.

3.   Planning

One of the main reasons why the patient is brought into the hospital is to help him and members of his family to make plans for his future therapy. The phase of hospitalization must be considered not the whole of treatment but simply a threshold of rehabilitative enterprise. Many alcoholics come into the hospital service with a history of failure. The interdisciplinary staff must be ready to recognize this and to establish a new programatic endeavor that offers an approach that may have a better chance for success. In the hospital, psychopharmacological help will be initiated in accordance with the diagnostic formulations and therefore the needs of the patient in question. Also, in whatever ways can be devised, patients should be given the opportunity of looking at their problems more realistically, and this is often most effectively done by a combination of group therapy, including psychodrama, and individual confrontations with members of the staff: psychiatrists, internists, vocational rehabilitation counsellors, social workers, and others. Psychotherapy, as well as other modalities of therapy, begins as soon as the patient enters the therapeutic environment. In general, alcoholic patients do respond to group therapy. One of the difficulties of alcoholics coming into the treatment program is that they are depressed, paralyzed, and unable to act effectively without help. There seems to settle over such patients a kind of ennui, lethargy, and inability to make choices and carry out decisions. Whatever methods are available to handle such situations should be undertaken, whether this includes the use of antidepressant drugs or skillful group and individual psychotherapy and social therapy. The hospital is an environment in which such treatment can be effectively prosecuted, and the effective establishment of a therapeutic community setting is of tremendous value. Here the importance of properly trained nurses cannot be overestimated. Very often the nurses' attitudes and actions can make the difference between success and failure. Many alcoholics exhibit themselves in the initial phases of hospital treatment as hopeless and beyond help. They may respond to psychotherapy by a kind of unrealistic philosophical set rather than by beginning to handle their problems in a practical way. For example, they may wish the nurse or the social worker or their own spouse to handle their problems for them. For example, the patient is not himself willing or able to call his boss to let him know that he is in the hospital but requires someone else to do this. Whether or not the patient should be asked to make such contacts with the boss depends on the situation. Wherever possible, however, the patient should be encouraged to act effectively on his own initiative.

4. Special Therapeutic Enterprises to be Initiated in the Hospital Phase

In the hospital the staff have many demands made on their own resourcefulness, and likewise they have many opportunities to mobilize the resourcefulness of their patients. All members of the team who are brought into a particular case work together to deal in so far as possible with acute emergencies. It is remarkable that emergencies that seem so overwhelming at the beginning of the hospital phase tend to fade out as time goes on, although they are not solved. In such cases it is important that the vocational rehabilitation counsellor and the social worker as well as the psychiatrist help keep the need for dealing with important acute issues in proper focus. Sometimes it is inevitable that patients may remain in the hospital so long that they find themselves cut off from acute needs that seemed so important at first. When this happens, or if it happens, an important change in policy is necessary. If possible, such a situation should be avoided.

We believe that generally the phase of hospitalization should last only as long as is necessary to make an accurate diagnosis, to establish a prognosis, and to introduce a plan. If hospitalization lasts beyond this, it can become distherapeutic. The social worker and other members of the team see essential members of the family and also the employer or other significant person who may and should be drawn into the situation. The degree to which others should be drawn in is an important issue in deciding the subsequent composition of the interdisciplinary team that works with the patient after he leaves the hospital. Often it may be that some members of the family are more disturbed than the primary patient himself. This may apply to the spouse as well as the children in the family. It should always be remembered that the relation of the primary patient to his family may be different from one case to the next. The family members may be cooperative or hostile and rejecting, depending on the experiences that they have had before the patient's coming into the therapeutic program. Where the family can become therapeutically helpful, this must always be encouraged. Most of all, it seems that the family should be encouraged to assume and to maintain their functions as members of the family rather than as therapists. In all this interdisciplinary work at the beginning of treatment in the hospital, it must be remembered that the situations can change very rapidly from day to day or from week to week in the hospital. Issues that seemed quite vital and critical on the second or third day in the hospital may fade into unimportance by the first or second week. Conversely issues of vast importance may not emerge before several days after hospitalization has been initiated. The skillful therapist is sensitive to such changes in emphasis and ready to take advantage of any need for change in plans. What is important is that the therapeutic team working together must be resourceful, flexible, and alert to the need for deviation in plans.

As the patient settles down in hospital and as his family begin to be more free in expressing their needs, feelings, and problems, there comes a time in hospitalization when valid and important plans can be made. Vocational rehabilitation counseling may appropriately be withheld for a certain number of days, pending a real appreciation of what the patient's needs are. The bringing into the situation of the employer must be timed accurately, so that his help and cooperation may be elicited at the best time possible.

5. The Therapeutic Community

Alcoholics tend to become, if they were not so before their illness, isolated persons in spite of their great dependency. Therefore the inpatient phase of the long-term comprehensive rehabilitation efforts must include opportunities for reorientation of relations with others on a healthy basis. This enterprise must begin early in the period of hospitalization; in fact, as early as the patient is able to get out of bed. In our Bureau of Alcohol Studies and Rehabilitation we move patients from the intensive-care area, in which patients are in bed or in their rooms during the day, to a group-therapeutic community setting, in which the patients live in self-care units, with the furniture and other appointments set up something like a college dormitory in which there are sofa beds that open out at night as beds and can be used during the daytime as sofas. Patients eat with one another and are encouraged to take advantage of the opportunity of maximum group participation. Patients may dine in their own rooms or in other parts of the service in larger or smaller aggregations. Patients living in the group community setting spend virtually all their morning in inpatient group therapy and part of their afternoons in inpatient individual therapy, psychodiagnostic tests, and medical and psychiatric evaluations. Every day there is a staff conference in which patients are seen briefly, and day-to-day discussions of their needs, plans, and prognosis are held.

It should be said as a preamble to a discussion of the therapeutic community living that about half of the patients are admitted from the out-patient clinics of our bureau in an alcohol-free condition at the time of admission; the remainder are in a state of post-alcoholic withdrawal or acute intoxication. We have found that the prevalence of delirium tremens, hallucinosis, convulsions, and other acute complications of alcoholism is relatively low, since the emphasis of the inpatient program is not on "drying out" but on cooperating with the patient and reaching a diagnosis and working out a plan of rehabilitation on a long-term basis.

Group therapy is an integral part of the comprehensive rehabilitation program and is an essential component of community living. The formal aspects of group therapy are supplemented by informal discussions that patients have with each other and with the nurses who take leadership within the group of patients. Clearly the therapeutic community within the inpatient service is closely knit, and the community is continually changing and modifying itself through new admissions and through the discharge of patients as they reach the end of their hospitalization period. It should be said that there is no standardized time during which patients stay in the hospital, and the duration of hospitalization is determined by the individual needs of the patient himself. There is an ongoing relationship and interaction among the patients themselves and, of course, between the patients and the staff. Within this setting, which is generally free and in which there is a minimum of rules and regulations, the formalized inpatient group sessions serve in the first place to make available to patients accurate, understandable information about the programs and procedures of the bureau, the day-to-day activities, and the roles and functions of various members of the staff. This didactic objective of group work is carried out, for example, by 0.5-hr television tape presentations 3 days a week exhibited to patients in their recreation room. In this tape staff members are introduced and speak of their particular work and how the bureau operates in both its inpatient and outpatient phases. The tape presents a warm and cordial introduction to the service and is tied together by comments by the medical director. It has been found that the patients generally like to view this tape more than once, and it provides an orderly and reassuring source of information about life in the ward. This didactic and introductory video tape is supplemented by several teaching films regularly scheduled throughout the week on such subjects as the nature and course of alcoholism, the use of Antabuse, and so forth. The film "Profile of a Problem Drinker" (Addiction Research Foundation, Ontario), which is a narrative story of a young man and his wife who seek help, is presented regularly. It has been our experience that such didactic material presented on video tape or on films tends to serve to evoke specific discussion in the formal inpatient groups and in the informal groups in which patients gather around for coffee by themselves, unsupervised by members of the staff. Sometimes the most useful group activities are exemplified by the sessions in which patients and nurses play games of cards and other games and in which discussions may come up quite informally and the nurses apply their therapeutic skill in handling such questions raised. We have found that clear, simple, accurate, neuropsychological and physiological teaching at strategic moments during group-therapy sessions has value in encouraging patients to express psychologic, family, and other problems. Also neuropsychologic and physiological explanations serve to reassure patients as to exactly what is happening to them in their lives. Thus didactic functions of group work are not lost sight of and are often incorporated into psychodramatic groups and other modes of group activity.

It has been our experience that the morale generated and fostered by the inpatient group sessions creates a kind of contagion that draws new patients into the ward community. It has been our experience that the milieu of the group sessions often seems to be less threatening, especially for new patients, than individual sessions and allows for group interaction and intragroup support in which patients can express their feelings of depression, fear, guilt, anger, and confusion. It is found that in inpatient groups, as well as in outpatient groups, patients are quite frequently motivated to seek special individual sessions with staff afterward and to ask for conferences with members of their family, their employers, and other significant persons.

A meaningful objective of group therapy, whether in the outpatient setting or in the inpatient phase, is to enhance the quality of motivation for sobriety and a more satisfying, effective way of life. The therapeutic plan that does not give high priority to the objective of sobriety cannot really succeed. In both the inpatient and outpatient group sessions, particularly the outpatient groups, in which the continuity of the group is more typical, there can and should develop a growing understanding of motivation resulting from continuity of contact. Even in the inpatient group work, in which there is a more rapid turnover, it is possible and, indeed, to be expected that intergroup relationships develop. It is quite remarkable that the measure of group relationships is not simply the length of time during which patients are together but rather the quality of such relationships. It is sometimes noted that even a single group session may have profound and enduring meaning to a patient. Even so, we see group work as a part of a spectrum of continuing therapy that patients who particularly find inpatient group work meaningful should continue in the more stable group sessions of the outpatient phase. Also, the group setting, whether in the inpatient phase or in the outpatient situation, seems to be favorable in assisting patients to make plans, take inventory, and develop talent in some of the major principles of orderly problem solving. Group work, whether inpatient or outpatient, has limitations, and patients should learn to share these and recognize them. The patients' own expectations for the group should be assessed and freely aired in the group, and in general patients should be encouraged to look on group therapy as simply a part of the total therapeutic program in which, for example, individual sessions have values and present opportunities not available in the group and vice versa.

The therapeutic community would not be complete without the opportunity for night care and day care. In the matter of night care, this in our practice gives an opportunity for those who are nearing the end of their hospitalization phase to go out to work during the day, come back in the evening for special therapy, and spend the night. Such night care enables patients to bridge the gap between full 24-hr hospitalization each day and discharge into the community. Sometimes abrupt discharge into the community can be an anxiety-producing experience, and this is especially the case when patients have remained in the hospital for rather longer than the usual time and may have become dependent on the hospital setting. We also have provisions for day care. In our use, day care applies to the program of admitting for hospitalization during the daytime hours. In such situations patients may come into the hospital in the morning after they have taken their children to school and leave the hospital somewhere between 4:30 and 5 o'clock in the afternoon. As might be expected, most of those who take advantage of such opportunities are women or retired men. Mostly these are patients who have been in the hospital before and who will benefit from group therapy and other intensive programs during the day but who can go to their own homes at night and then return the next day. Such partial hospitalization in the day-care program has special uses, and it is important that these special values should not be abused.

Day care under these circumstances is no substitute for drying out patients who are suffering from acute alcoholic intoxication but who are admitted on a day-care basis in the absence of available beds.

The therapeutic community of the hospital may merge with subsequent care in a halfway house. A great deal could be said about halfway houses in the social, psychological, and economic therapy of alcoholics. Their great strength is that they provide an interim home for alcoholics who have or will get a job shortly and who can provide for the cost of their stay in the halfway house. Halfway houses vary greatly throughout the world in their quality and strength. Some halfway houses allow patients to live in the house for many weeks or months, and some require that this be the case. Virtually all halfway houses make sobriety a condition of admission and retention, and there are programs associated with Alcoholics Anonymous and various forms of group living and group discussion. One of the weaknesses of the halfway houses is that they are sometimes forced to operate on a rather tenuous economic basis. Another weakness is that the organization and management of halfway houses may leave something to be desired. Halfway houses should be encouraged, however, and there is some advantage that such houses be a part of the governmental provisions for helping alcoholics.

6. Antabuse

We shall complete this section by discussing the pharmacological agent, disulfiram (Antabuse), which is perhaps the only specific therapeutic modality available to alcoholics and which, in our opinion, should be used

only in conjunction with and adjunctive to a broad spectrum of comprehensive therapy [1]. In our bureau we have used Antabuse since November
1948. Up to the present we have afforded comprehensive treatment to
just under 11,000 patients, and of these approximately 50 to 60% have
used Antabuse at one time or another. In one study between June 1949
and August 1954 we made Antabuse available as an adjunct in the treatment of 1187 patients who volunteered to use this drug. Of these we made
a detailed study of 1020 (922 males and 98 females) admitted to the
service between June 1949 and November 1953 and 484 control alcoholic
patients (421 males and 63 females). These were all accepted in the service
during the same period and were all exposed to the same therapeutic plan
except that the controls did not receive Antabuse [1]. In our experience
with Antabuse, all patients have been technically voluntary and were not
given Antabuse unless they so requested. All the patients in this study
presented histories of progressively serious difficulties related to uncontrolled
drinking and had usually had such difficulties for many years. Most had
previous treatment for alcohol problems in private sanatoria, state hospitals,
or from private physicians. Most had been drinking heavily within a day
prior to admission. In this series, 31.1% were referred by physicians; 23.1%
by courts, social agencies, clergymen, and Alcoholics Anonymous; and
35.8% by family, friends, or others; 10% were self-referred. Our therapeutic
plan for these patients included initial hospitalization for 1 or 2 or more
weeks followed by outpatient clinic care for at least 1 year. All the patients
in this series received medical, psychological, psychiatric, and social workup
as indicated. Therapy was on a comprehensive basis and included necessary
medical care as well as group therapy during the hospital stay and individual psychotherapy and other care in the outpatient clinic. Job placement
and other elements of vocational and social rehabilitation were initiated
when needed, and members of the family, employers, clergy, or other concerned persons were drawn into the treatment program when this was
deemed desirable and the patient was accepting.

   In our experience over the years we have observed that Antabuse has
been used in the treatment of alcoholics with a variety of objectives. One
method, indeed, is to try to build a "pharmacological fence" around the
patient and so to transfer from him to the drug the responsibility for abstinence. Our experience with this theory of treatment is that it is less
than successful. We have come more and more to believe that the alcoholic
patient can never delegate to any other person or modality the privilege
and responsibility of his own decision about abstaining. Therefore in our
use of Antabuse throughout the years we have encouraged the patient
to take the drug each day in the amount of 250 mg, usually in the evening

only after he has in the quiet of his own room specifically reexamined and reexperienced his acceptance of the fact that he could not drink safely and after he has chosen to accept another day of an alcohol-free life. The patient then takes the medication unsupervised and is free from any other further decision about the matter until the next day at the same time. If the patient has any doubt about his acceptance of his powerlessness over alcohol or wish to undertake another day of sobriety, he is counselled not to take the Antabuse but to contact his clinic physician at once.

In the earlier history of the use of Antabuse the contraindications were rather sharply spelled out. It was our practice not to offer Antabuse to patients with serious kidney, liver, heart, pulmonary, or metabolic diseases, and we also eliminated from the Antabuse series any patient with obvious mental deterioration or psychoses.

Our earlier procedure was to initiate Antabuse in the hospital. In the early years of our program with Antabuse we conducted an Antabuse-alcohol reaction test. In our schedule at that time, Antabuse was given in the amount of 1.5 g initially usually about the fifth or sixth day after admission, 1.0 g the next day, and 0.5 g on the third and fourth days. With this dosage, side reactions were absent or very moderate. On the fourth day after starting Antabuse the patient was placed on his back for 0.5 hr in bed and then given a dose of 86 to 96 proof whisky. In our earlier use of Antabuse we gave as much as 50 or 60 cm^3, but the reactions were so severe as to make it desirable that patients remain in the hospital thereafter for 1 or 2 days longer than usual. We accordingly reduced the doses to 30 cm^3 or less, which gave what we considered to be a satisfactory reaction. A physician or nurse remained with the patient during the entire reaction, checking blood pressure, pulse, and respiration every 5 min. We never followed the plan of administering the Antabuse-alcohol reaction in groups, nor were there any formalized therapeutic contacts with the patient during the reaction. The meaning of the reaction experienced with the patient was, however, interpreted in subsequent therapeutic planning for him. As the years have gone on, we have found that patients who do not receive the Antabuse-alcohol reaction, but simply have it explained to them have a success rate as good as those who do take the reaction. Therefore we have eliminated it in our service, and it has been eliminated generally throughout the world. This has permitted us and many other clinics to initiate Antabuse as an outpatient clinic procedure. Thus in any setting in which adequate medical, psychological, psychiatric, and social diagnosis can be made, Antabuse can be started and continued, although the patient may not be in the hospital or may not ever come into the hospital setting at all.

Each patient, when he leaves the hospital, carries with him a card stating that he is taking Antabuse and directing anyone who sees him ill to take him immediately to the emergency service of a hospital. Reactions induced by patients have been very rare in our program, probably because the pressure to take Antabuse is minimal and because patients tend to stop taking Antabuse if they plan to drink. Generally speaking, we have found that those patients who do permit themselves a self-induced Antabuse-alcohol reaction tend to have lower than usual prognosis for eventual abstinence. In our formal study the Antabuse group of 1020 patients differed in a number of particulars from the 484 control patients. The former were a younger group than the control. The peak for the Antabuse patient was in the 35-to-39-year age category; that for the controls was in the 40-to-44-year-old group. This shift to the left of the Antabuse population distribution curve may result from our selection procedures in which younger, possibly healthier, more courageous, and more highly motivated patients accepted an adjunct that was rejected by or denied to older patients with more profound medical and possibly psychologic deterioration.

Evaluation of the therapy of alcoholics has always presented a number of problems. Some of the most realistic criteria of success elude objective and mathematical handling and thus are of somewhat limited value. In our evaluation studies throughout the years we have used abstinence as a criterion and have also used such criteria as job record and family adjustment. The criterion of abstinence has defects and possibly overbalances the emphasis on drinking in the patient's total problem. Just as drinking is a sign of alcoholic disturbances, however, so abstinence and reduction of the frequency and intensity of drinking are a sign of recovery.

Using abstinence as a criterion, we found that 27.4% of the Antabuse cases maintained complete abstinence for 1 year or more as compared with 23.0% in the controls. We found that 76.5% of the Antabuse patients as a whole had received benefit by treatment, although they had not maintained unmitigated sobriety or abstinence. Fifty-five percent of the controls were classified as improved by the same criteria. The follow-up record in the Antabuse cases is better than in the control group in the clinic. Of the Antabuse cases only 1.0% broke treatment early, whereas 8% could not be traced. Of the controls 16.7% discontinued treatment early, and an additional 13.5% broke contact.

The differences between the Antabuse and the control abstinent groups, that is, the completely abstinent groups, are questionably significant by t tests, whereas the differences for improved versus unimproved are highly significant. Thus a t test of significance of the difference between the scores of 76.5% of the improved in the Antabuse group and 55.0% in the controls gives a t value of 8.3 and p of less than 0.01. Antabuse patients, therefore, do significantly better in general than the controls.

In the Antabuse group of our series men patients did significantly better than the women. Of the male Antabuse patients 77.4% were improved and 67.3% of the Antabuse women showed improvement ($t = 2.1$; p is less than 0.05). The difference in performance and clinical progress in the control males and the control females is not significant. A test of significance of the difference between the improvement scores of the Antabuse males versus the control males is highly significant. The difference between the improvement scores of the Antabuse women versus the control women is also significant.

In earlier studies we found consistently poorer results for patients under 30 in both the Antabuse and the control groups. Our more complete, longer-term studies indicate that the patients under 30 have nearly but not quite so good a record as the total group. In the Antabuse group 71.1% of the total of 114 patients under 30 were benefited. In the control group 11 out of 26 under 30 showed improvement. The Antabuse age groups below 40 are somewhat poorer than the total group in percentage of improvement; the Antabuse age groups over 40 are somewhat better. Of the age categories where significant percentages can be derived, it seemed that the Antabuse groups between the ages of 40 and 45 made the best score (79.4% improved out of 219 cases). Among control patients the percentages of improved in each age category do not indicate any clear trend. The 40 to 44 age group has the best score, with the 64.1% improved out of 92 patients, but they are only slightly better than the 30s to the 34s and the 50s to the 54s. At the extremes of both the Antabuse and control age-group curves, the number of cases is too small to provide significant data.

Antabuse seems to be most effective in those patients who have had one relapse or more but who seem to have established a stable alcohol-free pattern eventually. Inspection of our statistics at once exposes the fact that the Antabuse group has a much better record of follow-up and contact with the clinics than do the controls. A major function of Antabuse may, therefore, be to differentiate more highly from less highly motivated patients and to select those who will continue to respond and to attend treatment more faithfully and provide additional incentive for the continuation of treatment. If we eliminate from both the Antabuse and control groups those who discontinued treatment and those who could not be classified, we find that out of 928 such Antabuse cases compared with 333 such control patients 84.1% of the Antabuse group may be listed as improved; 79.8% of the controls are so listed. If we analyze the significance of this difference we derive $t = 1.7$ and p between 0.10 and 0.05, which is not considered clearly significant.

We have conducted a further analysis that seems important. In earlier studies we found a difference in performance between those controls who are denied Antabuse and those who rejected it, the former having a much better subsequent record than the latter. Specifically we found that out of 69 patients who were denied Antabuse on physical or psychological grounds none of these discontinued treatment early, and 62% were improved. Out of 152 patients who declined the medication 31% discontinued treatment early, and only 44% showed improvement. Thus it seems that the group who are denied Antabuse were apparently a more highly motivated group who may have accepted the condition that disqualified them as a challenge to discover a new approach to an alcohol-free life.

A further comment on pharmacological approaches to therapy during the inpatient period remains to be discussed briefly. It is primarily a research aspect and deals with investigations of the possible therapeutic effects of LSD in the treatment of alcoholics. A considerable literature has developed in this field, and there is some evidence that patients treated adjunctively with LSD experiences may show enhanced subsequent improvement over the controls. It is important that such factors as the greater attention given to such patients be carefully sorted out. In any case the clinical use of LSD in the therapy of alcoholics should be investigated by highly competent teams and the results analyzed in a sophisticated manner.

D. Outpatient Treatment

There can be no doubt that, although hospitalization in a specialized service or in the general hospital or in a psychiatric program may be extremely valuable, its value is limited if treatment does not continue after hospitalization is completed. For this reason it is felt that long-term, continuing outpatient care is essential to a well-balanced comprehensive program [7]. Care may and should in many instances include not only the primary patient himself but also members of his family, as may be needed. It is usually well that the outpatient should work with the same therapist, throughout, at least a year and sometimes this should be longer. The principal outpatient therapist should be alert in drawing in other members of the treatment team—a social worker, other physicians, a clergyman, other counsellors, or whoever may serve at a particular time of need. It is important that the leader of the team be a person of resource and ready for the benefit of the patient to take advantage immediately of changes in the situation as they may develop. In some instances it is well that a psychiatric member of the group take over the major handling of the case and working with the patient. In other cases this may not be required.

It is always important that the therapist remember that the patient may have ups and downs and that he may have drinking crises, although these may be infrequent. Some patients may never drink again, and some maintain sobriety after one or two or more "slips." The therapist takes advantage of the values to the patient of Alcoholics Anonymous, the church, the gradually adjusting family, and so on. Sometimes the family has difficulty in adapting to the primary patient's rehabilitation. It sometimes happens that the primary patient has over the years of his active abnormal drinking become a kind of supernumerary member of the family, as it were, like another child. Decisions and family responsibilities have been taken over by other members of the family, say, the nonalcoholic spouse and one of the older children. As the alcoholic patient returns more and more to a more healthy way of living, he may resent his own lack of authority and may try to recover it. Sometimes those who have been working as leaders of the family for years are not understanding about turning the reins of the family back to the alcoholic; also if they do, sometimes the patient may drink again, and the old status has to be restored, at least temporarily. These ups and downs are frustrating, difficult, and disturbing to members of the family, including the alcoholic himself. A part of therapy is to help both the family and the primary patient to know that the road to recovery is not necessarily smooth and that sobriety in itself does not necessarily take care of the whole problem of readjustment and growth in the family. Some alcoholics may be "dry" and yet intolerable to live with. Sometimes nonalcoholic members of the family may find it excessively difficult to live with a dry alcoholic, partly because the difficulties that exist can no longer be ascribed to drinking. In such cases we sometimes discover that severe maladjustment in the family may become exacerbated after sobriety has been achieved, and sometimes divorces occur at such a time. It sometimes occurs that the alcoholic member who is "doing well" receives inordinate praise from his boss, his friends, and within the church or other helping groups, whereas the wife may feel alone, forgotten, and by herself. These possibilities stress the importance of Alanon (an organization linked with Alcoholics Anonymous but not a part of it). In Alanon, spouses and other relatives of alcoholics learn to explore their own problems of living not only with a drinking alcoholic but also with one who is consistently or periodically sober. If there is an Alanon group within the community, it is often possible and, I believe, always wise that the nonalcoholic spouse should make contact with the group. The function of Alanon is far from constituting a forum in which nonalcoholic spouses "gripe" about their drinking husbands or wives.

All this brings out the importance of the outpatient period of therapy, which should go on a year or more. The outpatient period should be a time of growth, insight, understanding, and a continuing adventure in understanding oneself. As an alcoholic continues his sobriety, it is not surprising that he may find himself gradually becoming more and more efficient in his work, and also in handling his emotional, intellectual, and other problems. Many patients say that during their first 6 months of sobriety they were not able to function so effectively as, say, after the second 6 months. This may partly be due to the gradual but genuine recovery from disturbed brain function and a general improvement in health.

Outpatient care does not ever really come to an end. If the outpatient therapist and the patient have decided that formal treatment is no longer necessary at the time, the therapist should assure the patient that the relationship is not permanently broken but that the patient may feel free at any time to seek help if he needs it. It is a mistake, in my opinion, to say to the patient that he is "graduated" and that the clinic therefore has nothing more to offer him.

In our Bureau of Alcohol Studies and Rehabilitation at the Medical College of Virginia, Health Sciences Division of the Virginia Commonwealth University, in Richmond, Virginia, we have been working for the last 4 or 5 years with an outpatient group of men and women who meet every week in an attractive conference room for special outpatient-clinic group therapy. All the members of the group are or have been working individually with other members of the staff of the outpatient clinic of the bureau. The only condition of entry into this group is an outpatient's personal wish to do so and an agreement to remain in the group for at least 6 months. Patients also agree to report by telephone in advance if they must for some reason be absent from a meeting. At any time after 6 months a patient may withdraw voluntarily from the group. Thus the outpatient group session is a semiclosed group, and, as it turns out, the turnover is rather slow. We have generally set a maximum of 10 patients for the group, but in the past year we have found that more than this number generally attend. At present there are approximately 12 who participate regularly in the group. There is a corps of old members, and on the whole the group organization is quite stable. Some patients in the group have worked as long as the group has been in existence.

In certain particulars the outpatient group work differs from the inpatient group activity. In the first place the continuity of the discussion from week to week is more specific than in the inpatient group. The outpatient group at the time of its organization evolved the concept that therapy would be by the group as a whole for the members of the group, and this objective has been quite consistently followed. Usually each member of the group or at least certain members of the group report on incidents that have happened during the previous week and how they have been getting along in their day-to-day living. Ordinarily at every meeting each week some one patient or possibly two bring up special matters on which they desire the counsel of the group. This may be a serious problem at home, a problem at work, or some other difficulty in which the patient seeks the help of the group. In this kind of transaction it turns out that one or two members take leadership in counseling, but it is rare for anyone to maintain silence if a member of the group seeks help. The sessions are quite informal, and although existential issues are ordinarily uppermost in the discussion, it frequently happens that many basic questions on the cause, course, and treatment of alcoholism as well as principles of problem solving come up.

From time to time the members of the outpatient group stand ready to help new patients in the inpatient service. Some of the outpatient group members visit the inpatient service at such times as they may get off from work. One member, for example, is now working out a plan to take inpatients on visits to the local museums, and so on. Sometimes members of the outpatient group find work for another outpatient. In various situations a new inpatient may seek and find an opportunity of talking with members of the outpatient group, and very often certain members rally round such new inpatients to help them with, say, a place to stay when they leave the ward. The outpatient group often considers its work a training program for acting as nonprofessional aids under the guidance of the leader in carrying out such help. The outpatient group sometimes discusses what goes on in the inpatient group and stands ready to come into the inpatient group for special helping presence. In general the inpatients welcome outpatients who take such an interest and are frequently encouraged by the fact that members of the outpatient group can share their experiences of attempts at sobriety.

We have found that the outpatient group does not tend to resort to psychodramatic techniques but from time to time discusses and offers suggestions for inpatient role playing and other psychodramatic approaches. On some occasions members of the outpatient group have come into the inpatient group and assumed roles when they were free to do so.

The outpatient group has other projects that it may undertake. Thus presently an instructional film is being prepared, and many of the members of the outpatient group have indicated that they are willing to share their experiences in making this film.

The adjunctive use of pharmacological therapy in the outpatient phase of the treatment has already been discussed in terms of Antabuse. In other aspects of psychopharmacology the physician in charge of an outpatient in the clinic uses his skills and judgment as well as his understanding of the psychiatric and medical needs of his patient. He is resourceful in this and remembers that psychoactive drugs may be needed but likewise keeps in mind that an aim of therapy in the outpatient clinic is to enable the patient to function adequately in the absence of drugs or with their conservative and minimal use. It is impossible to say how long and if a patient should receive psychopharmacological aid. This must depend on the patient's condition and progress. It is also essential to recall that alcoholic patients can transfer their dependency from alcohol to other pharmacological agents, and this should be guarded against.

Many alcoholics, in addition to other disturbances, are sensitive to autonomic dysfunction; that is to say, they may react excessively to affective and other manifestations of disturbances of the higher cerebral levels of visceral and emotional control. Just what may be the psychological and somatic causative factors we do not know [2]. Studies in our own laboratories during the past several years, however, have established the existence both in animals and in men of cortical and subcortical representation of visceral control and of affective behavior. Specifically stimulation of the limbic system may result in alteration of systemic blood pressure, changes in intracardiac dynamics, and modifications of peripheral circulation as well as functional and vascular changes in the kidney, gut, and other organs. Acute and chronic changes in pulmonary, coronary, and bone marrow circulation have been discerned, and it has been shown that limbic stimulation modifies the activity of epinephrine and norepinephrine as well as salivation. In man, particularly, such disturbances of visceral function may be intimately associated with anxiety, fear, anger, and other affective disturbances. We may hypothesize that there is an overlapping as well as integration of central visceral and somatic control systems and that these systems are related to neurological mechanisms of behavior and emotional responses. Therefore neurotropic or psychotropic drugs do have a definite value in protecting patients who respond unduly to stresses by higher cerebral overresponse. A value of neurtropic or psychotropic drugs may be to modulate overresponses of automatic mechanisms and render patients more available to psychotherapy. Thus such drugs may be of use as adjuncts in the therapy of alcoholics who, as we have stated, are often vulnerable to psychosomatic overreaction [8].

We have compared the action of intravenously administered alcohol and chlordiazepoxide on autonomic responses evoked in animals by threshold stimulation (with controlled parameters) of isocortical loci and loci in the limbic system [3]. Stimulation with stereotaxically placed electrodes causes pressor responses, cardiac arrhythmias (nodal and ventricular extrasystoles and ventricular tachycardia with indications of coronary insufficiency), and mydriasis and inhibition of the motility of the pyloric sphincter and the ileum. Salivation has also been elicited as well as retraction of the nictitating membrane. Chlordiazepoxide was found greatly to attenuate the pressor responses from all brain areas studied. Centrally induced cardiac arrhythmias were blocked by the chlordiazepoxide, but alcohol had no blocking action on these responses except in a very few cases. Neither compound showed any activity against centrally evoked salivation, mydriasis, or gastrointestinal inhibition.

Thus alcohol as measured by its effects on centrally induced autonomic responses seems to be a defective tranquilizing agent. In fact its central actions on higher nervous function seem to be a complicated combination of excitatory and inhibitory effects. This seems to stem from the fact that in earlier phases of the effects of alcohol on the nervous system a predominant action may be inhibition of inhibitory circuitry. As the alcohol blood level rises, there is eventually a generalized depression of central nervous function. Although alcohol thus seems to be an imperfect attenuator of centrally generated autonomic activity, chlordiazepoxide acts effectively to protect the visceral systems from harmful cerebral autonomic malfunction. This brings out the point that alcohol is undesirable as a psychological medication. If a person needs a tranquilizing substance, alcohol is contraindicated.

The stabilizing action of chlordiazepoxide on higher cerebral autonomic control systems as well as visceral and emotional control systems has led us to explore during a number of years its use, as well as diazepam, in not only the inpatient phase of treatment of alcoholics but also in the outpatient phase. It has been found that both of these substances, when used for appropriate indications and supervised regularly in the outpatient clinic, have been valuable psychopharmacological agents in the armamentarium of the therapist. These drugs as well as all other tranquilizing or antidepressant substances used for the therapy of problem drinkers ought always to be evaluated at regular and frequent intervals. Also in keeping with the philosophy of the comprehensive approach to the treatment of alcoholics, the psychopharmacologic regime ought to be coordinated with psychotherapy, job rehabilitation, work with the family, and all aspects of rehabilitation.

A discussion of the psychological and pharmacological basis for the treatment of alcohol dependence is not complete without at least a brief reference to the necessity of evaluation of the results of treatment. It is obvious that in alcohol dependence, about which we know less than we should like, we should be constantly exploring the effects of our intervention. We need to study various ways of measuring the outcome of treatment, and this in itself is a complicated subject. The criteria of successful treatment need to be examined in more detail and with greater skill than we have done already. We are not sure exactly what our therapy does and if it does anything how it does it. Thus it is essential that we continue to make evaluation a component of all our therapeutic endeavors.

REFERENCES

1. Hoff, E. C., The use of disulfiram (Antabuse) in the comprehensive therapy of a group of 1020 alcoholics, *Conn. St. Med. J.*, **19**, 793 (1955).
2. Hoff, E. C., The etiology of alcoholism, *Quart. J. Studies Alc.*, **1**, 57 (1961).
3. Hoff, E. C., The use of pharmacological adjuncts in the psychotherapy of alcoholics, *Quart. J. Studies Alc.*, **1**, 138 (1961).
4. Hoff, E. C., A comprehensive approach to the rehabilitation of alcoholics, *Missouri Med.* p. 958 (1962).
5. Hoff, E. C., Initiation of Long-Term Therapy for the Alcoholic, in *The First Hahnemann Symposium on Psychosomatic Medicine,* J. H. Nodine and J. H. Moyer, (eds.), Chap. 101, Lea & Febiger, Philadelphia, 1962.
6. Hoff, E. C., Comprehensive rehabilitation program for alcoholics, *Arch. Environ. Health,* **7,** 460 (1963).
7. Hoff, E. C., Clinical treatment of alcoholics, *Rehabilitation Record,* **6,** 37 (1965).
8. Hoff, E. C., Current research in treatment of alcoholism, *Indust. Med. Surg.,* **35,** 867 (1966).
9. Hoff, E. C., Motivating the Alcoholic to Accept Rehabilitative Therapy, in *Biochemical Factors in Alcoholism,* R. P. Maickel, (ed.), p. 241, Pergamon, New York, 1966.
10. Hoff, E. C., A new plan for the study and comprehensive treatment of alcoholics in Virginia, *Virginia Med. Monthly,* **94,** 515 (1967).
11. Plaut, Thomas F. A., *Alcohol Problems: A Report to the Nation,* by the Cooperative Commission on the Study of Alcoholism, Oxford, New York, 1967.

Chapter XV

THE EPIDEMIOLOGY
OF ALCOHOLISM

JAN DE LINT and WOLFGANG SCHMIDT

ALCOHOLISM AND DRUG ADDICTION RESEARCH FOUNDATION
TORONTO, CANADA

Generally speaking, epidemiologists seek to establish the prevalence and explain the variation in the rates of occurrence of a disease or a behavioral disorder. In the case of alcoholism it has not been possible to establish rate differences on the basis of actual counts. Its defining characteristics—the craving for alcohol, the loss of control, the repetitive intake of alcohol usually in large quantities, the damaging consequences to health—are too imprecise to allow the identification of every alcoholic in a population. How much craving, which quantity of alcohol consumed and in what frequency, what kind of damage to health define alcoholism? The elusive nature of this condition is perhaps best illustrated by the way in which alcoholics differ from nonalcoholics with respect to individual quantities consumed.

A. The Distribution of Alcohol Consumption

Individual consumption ranges from very small quantities to near lethal amounts. Within this range each consumption level occurs with a certain

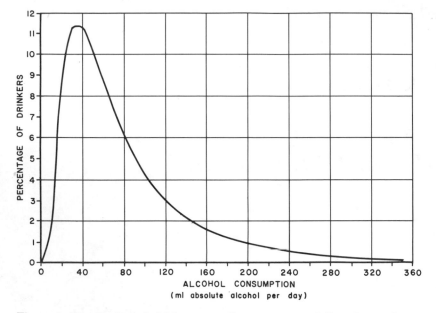

Figure 1. Distribution of drinkers according to average daily volume of consumption in a population with an annual consumption per drinker of 30 liters of absolute alcohol.

frequency. It has been demonstrated for a variety of populations that the distribution of consumption levels closely approximates a smooth, skewed curve known as the logarithmic normal curve [7, 24]. Thus in a population with an average consumption of 30 liters of alcohol the distribution is as shown in Figure 1.

Presumably alcoholics are located in the upper ranges. The transition from moderate to excessive quantities is very gradual, however, and, therefore, a definition of alcoholism on the basis of consumption levels is inevitably arbitrary. For example, should the consumption be defined as alcoholic when in excess of 150, or when in excess of 200 ml of absolute alcohol daily? Similar difficulties pertain to a definition of alcoholism based on craving, loss of control, and physical damage attributable to alcohol use. The close association of these characteristics with levels of consumption [17, 25, 26, 32] suggests that they too are distributed in a gradual manner.

Thus it seems that alcoholism belongs in the category of diseases and behavioral disorders that differ only in degree from the normal state of health or conduct.

B.   Rate Variation in Alcoholism

In the absence of a "real definition" two possible approaches remain to establish rate variation in alcoholism. First, alcoholism can be arbitrarily defined, and the definition then used to obtain direct counts of cases or to estimate prevalence. Indeed such a procedure is quite common in the epidemiology of behavioral disorders [50]. Second, indices that reflect the magnitude of the alcoholism problem can be used.

With reference to the first approach one arbitrary definition that reasonably agrees with clinical and popular notions of alcoholism is to define alcoholic drinking as consumption in excess of a daily average of 150 ml of absolute alcohol. This approximates very closely the range of consumption typically reported by patients in alcoholism clinics [26, 44, 54].

Although it would be difficult in practice to count such drinkers, their

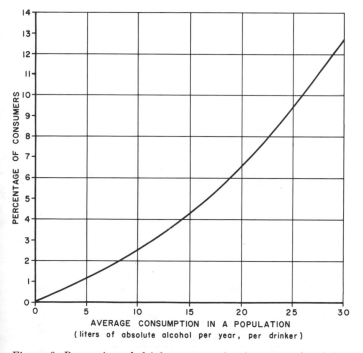

Figure 2. Proportion of drinkers consuming in excess of a daily average of 150 ml of absolute alcohol by average consumption of the drinking population; e.g., in a population with an average annual consumption per drinker of 30 liters of absolute alcohol about 13% of the drinking population consumes in excess of a daily average of 150 ml.

number can be indirectly estimated on the basis of the logarithmic normal distribution of consumption. Thus if the per drinker consumption is known, the percentage of persons consuming in excess of 150 ml can be derived.[1] In Figure 2 the relationship between per drinker consumption and the frequency of those who drink in excess of 150 ml of absolute alcohol daily is shown.

A more common approach to establish rate variation in alcoholism is to use an index rather than estimates. The most widely used are per capita alcohol consumption and mortality from cirrhosis of the liver. The use of the latter quantity rests on the observation that the rate of death from this cause among alcoholics is disproportionately high [19, 28, 43, 51]. Although it has been noted that some of the variation in these rates may be attributable to factors unrelated to alcohol use, nevertheless a close relationship obtains between per capita consumption and liver cirrhosis mortality [33, 45], as given in Table I.

[1] To arrive at an estimate of per drinker consumption, the annual sales volume of beverage alcohol is converted into units of absolute alcohol to which estimates of illicitly produced beverage alcohol are added. This sum is then divided by the estimated number of users of beverage alcohol in a population. The over-all consumption level is usually expressed as the annual alcohol consumption per drinker.

TABLE I   Temporal and Regional Correlations Between Rate of Liver Cirrhosis Mortality and per Capita Alcohol Consumption in Various Countries[a]

Country	Series	Correlation coefficient	Probability
Australia	1938–1959	.65	< .005
Belgium	1929–1959 (less 1940–1945)	.75	< .001
Canada	1927–1960	.88	< .001
Canada	9 provinces, 1955	.81	< .01
Finland	1933–1957	.78	< .001
France	1925–1958	.62	< .001
France	23 departments, 1950	.76	< .001
Holland	1927–1958	.57	< .001
Sweden	1926–1956	.45	< .05
U.S.A.	46 states, 1957	.86	< .001

[a] Correlation studies of these two variables have been reported previously for all the series shown [36]. In all instances, liver cirrhosis mortality was expressed as an unstandardized rate: deaths per 100,000 population aged 20 and older; and the measure of alcohol consumption comprised sales of alcoholic beverages expressed as imperial gallons of absolute alcohol per capita of population aged 15 and older.

Other indices of alcoholism prevalence found in the literature are arrests for drunkenness, hospital admissions, deaths from alcoholism, and deaths from alcohol poisoning. Unfortunately admission and arresting procedures differ considerably from region to region. For instance, skid row alcoholics in some large cities in the United States are much less likely to be admitted to alcoholism clinics or arrested for drunkenness than their counterparts in Canadian cities of similar size.

Parenthetically alcohol poisoning as a cause of death is an ambiguous diagnosis, and the kinds of deaths attributed to it vary among jurisdictions. It is felt, therefore, that at present the most useful indices are liver cirrhosis mortality and per capita consumption.

C. International Variation in Alcoholism Prevalence

In Table II estimates and indices of alcoholism prevalence are given for a number of countries. Their selection was determined simply by the availability of the required statistical data.

It is apparent that these countries vary greatly in alcoholism prevalence. These differences have been explained in a number of ways. For instance, in countries ranking highest in over-all level of alcohol consumption and rates of death from liver cirrhosis (France, Italy, Portugal) viniculture has traditionally played an important role in the life styles of the inhabitants. Drinking of wine is typically an incidental part of everyday living, and this pattern of use is facilitated by the reluctance of the governments of these countries to impose heavy taxes or pass other measures aimed at restricting the production and consumption of wine. Thus the simple ranking of countries according to alcoholism prevalence suggests certain relevant sociocultural factors: traditions related to the production and consumption of alcoholic beverages, patterns of use, governmental alcohol legislation. Evidently a comparison of this kind cannot identify all the relevant sociocultural factors, nor can it provide much information as to their relative importance; for example, what factors explain a gradual increase of alcoholism prevalence in certain urban areas? In an effort to answer such questions epidemiological studies tend to become more selective with respect to the populations compared.

D. Drinking Practices

One of the first epidemiological questions to be raised concerned the relationship between customary drinking practices and alcoholism prevalence; for example, the low prevalence of alcoholism among Jews in North

TABLE II   Annual per Drinker Consumption in Liters of Absolute Alcohol, Estimated Rates of Alcoholism and Rates of Death from Liver Cirrhosis

Country	Per drinker consumption (1966 or 1967)[a]	Estimated rates of alcoholism per 100,000 population aged 15 and older[b]	Rate of death from liver cirrhosis per 100,000 population aged 15 and older 1963, 1964, or 1965)[c]
France	25.9	9405	45.3
Italy	20.0	5877	27.3
Portugal	19.5	5652	42.7
Spain	17.1	4635	24.3
Austria	16.0	4212	35.0
W. Germany and W. Berlin	16.0	3978	26.7
Switzerland	15.8	3901	19.7
Luxembourg	12.5	2988	34.2
Hungary	12.4	2952	12.9
U.S.A.	12.0	2198	18.4
Czechoslovakia	11.4	2655	13.1
Canada	11.1	2272	10.0
England and Wales	10.9	1946	3.7
Rep. of Ireland	10.9	1946	4.5
Denmark	9.4	1848	10.2
Belgium	9.3	2052	12.9
Poland	9.0	1752	8.6
Sweden	8.4	1515	7.9
Netherlands	7.7	1456	4.9
Finland	5.9	945	4.6
Norway	5.9	945	4.7

[a] Alcohol consumption data were taken from the 1968 Annual Report of the Dutch Distillers' Association [37].

[b] Alcoholics are defined here as drinkers of daily averages in excess of 150 ml. of absolute alcohol. Their numbers were tabulated on the basis of data provided in J. Hyland and S. Scott, Alcohol consumption tables: An application of the Ledermann equation to a wide range of consumption averages [14].

[c] Demographic Yearbook of the United Nations, 1966 [52].

America has been attributed to their strong disapproval of drunkenness and the use of alcoholic beverages in their religious observances:

"In the circumcision ceremony a benediction is said over a cup of wine; a few drops are placed on the infant's lips and the godfather drinks the remainder. After the Bar Mitzvah the Jewish equivalent of the Christian confirmation rite, wine is drunk at the feast of celebration. In the marriage ceremony, the bride and groom drink wine from a common cup; and in the old days one of the rites performed at funerals consisted in washing the head of the corpse with wine" [34].

In contrast the drinking practices of the Irish have been characterized as predominantly utilitarian; for example, the use of liquor to alleviate physical and emotional discomfort [1]. The allegedly high rates of alcoholism among them have been attributed to this attitude. The Italian custom of drinking with meals [29] is said to be conducive to a low prevalence of alcoholism, whereas the high rate of alcoholism in France has been attributed to the custom of drinking on many occasions throughout the day.

Although it may seem from these and similar studies that certain drinking customs are typically associated with high or low rates of alcoholism, such a conclusion is not always justified. First, the assumed rates of alcoholism for these cultural groups are not always supported by estimates based on consumption and liver cirrhosis mortality data (see Table II). In the case of Italy both these measures indicate a very extensive alcoholism problem. Conversely these same measures show that the Irish in Ireland have relatively low rates of alcoholism. Apparently the Italian custom of drinking wine at meal time does not prevent alcoholism. Similarly the Irish habit of seeking intoxication on most drinking occasions does not necessarily result in high rates of alcoholism. Second, most of the investigations of drinking practices and alcoholism ignore the crucial role of volume of consumption. It has been demonstrated repeatedly that the over-all level of alcohol consumption in a population is intimately related to alcoholism prevalence [24, 36, 44]. It follows, therefore, that any factor that affects the volume of consumption inevitably affects the alcoholism prevalence rate and vice versa. Clearly the French habit of using alcoholic beverages on many occasions implies a high level of over-all consumption. Accordingly such drinking practices are accompanied by high rates of alcoholism.

On the other hand, drinking practices that typically involve seeking intoxication do not necessarily imply a high volume of consumption if the drinking occasions are relatively infrequent. Thus in Finland drunkenness is quite prevalent but annual consumption and rates of alcoholism are relatively low [20].

For these reasons it is unfortunate that most studies of specific cultural groups have failed to investigate the relationship between customary drinking practices and the over-all levels of consumption.

E.   Accessibility

An obvious factor in the epidemiology of alcohol use and alcoholism is the accessibility of alcoholic beverages. Thus in countries with a high per capita consumption, alcoholic beverages are readily available and quite inexpensive. Indeed it would be difficult to envisage alcoholic beverages as an incidental part of everyday living if they were expensive and difficult to obtain. Conversely high cost and low accessibility result in a low level of consumption; for example, during prohibition in the United States the over-all level of alcohol use, based entirely on illicitly procured and distributed beverages, and the rates of liver cirrhosis mortality were much reduced [19, 33].

The effect of less drastic government measures regulating the number and kind of outlets, hours of sale, and other conditions relating to the consumption of alcoholic beverages is more difficult to evaluate. It is evident that in countries with a high level of consumption both public drinking places and stores in which alcoholic beverages can be bought are very numerous. It is therefore surprising that in North America and the United Kingdom no relationship was found in time or space between per capita consumption and the number of public drinking places [35]. Whether these observations are attributable to temporal and regional variation in the amount of home consumption, in size of public drinking places, the use of the automobile, which renders distance between consumer and outlet less important, or other factors is not clear.* At any rate in rural Finland, where liquor outlets are quite rare, the introduction of government stores for beer and wine in some selected communities on a trial basis led to a marked increase in the consumption of all legally sold alcoholic beverages, particularly of wine and beer [21]. More recently the Finnish Government allowed beer to be sold in a wide variety of stores and eating places. Within a year after the introduction of the measure alcohol consumption increased approximately 50% [22, 23]. Unfortunately there are no recent data available that would show the effect of decreased accessibility, short of total prohibition, on alcohol consumption.

---

* Perhaps under these conditions the number of public drinking places per population unit has no significant effect on a person's access to beverage alcohol.

F.   Cost

Access to alcoholic beverages is also affected by their cost. Because they can be produced and distributed quite inexpensively, variation in price among countries and from period to period is largely attributable to differences in taxation policies. These policies have a long history. Originally they reflected the concern of legislators over the allegedly high incidence of drunkenness among the working classes during the nineteenth and early twentieth century [6, 39, 40]. At present the relatively high taxes on alcoholic beverages in many countries still tend to be considered an important method of controlling alcoholism and other alcohol problems.

It has been observed that spatial and temporal variations in the price of alcohol relative to average disposable income correlate inversely with level of consumption [30, 31, 47]. In Figure 3 the remarkably close association between these variables is shown graphically for Ontario. Unfortunately in these investigations the temporal series usually covered periods during which price relative to income had decreased and consumption had increased. One would like to know whether this relationship would also hold as consistently in a reverse situation, e.g., under a gradual increase of prices.

Most important, alcohol taxation and thus the cost of beverage alcohol tend to reflect the degree of acceptance of alcohol use. Accordingly variation in consumption should not be attributed to differences in the cost factor alone.

G.   Urbanism

In North America the incidence of liver cirrhosis mortality and per capita sales rise and fall with the extent of urbanism [16]. These differences may to some extent be attributable to reporting artifacts. For example, the quality of diagnostic facilities, rates of autopsy, and the nature of the relationship between the diagnostician and the family of the deceased have been singled out as factors influencing the accuracy of reporting deaths from this cause. Furthermore alcohol is produced illicitly in many regions in rural North America, and, consequently, alcohol consumption in these regions is higher than sales statistics indicate. The observed rural-urban differences in levels of alcohol use and rates of alcoholism, however, are too large to be fully explained by such factors. Rather it has been proposed that these differences in part reflect the presence of strong temperance sentiments in many parts of rural North America. In fact in these areas a relatively large proportion of the population voted against the repeal of prohibition [46].

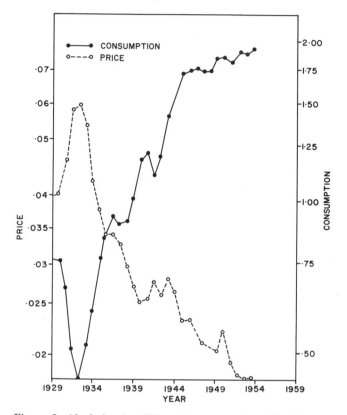

Figure 3. Alcohol price (P) and consumption (C). Ontario, 1929–1958: $P =$ the price of an average gallon of absolute alcohol expressed as a fraction of average disposable income; $C =$ consumption in gallons of absolute alcohol per person 20 years and older.

A more speculative interpretation refers to the "input overload" in modern cities. Specifically it has been proposed that high population density implies a mutual overstimulation that may result in various collective pathologies such as alcoholism [46].

With reference to the latter suggestion it is important to note that these differences are by no means universal. For example, in France, liver cirrhosis rates and consumption averages do not vary with urbanism [24]. Of course in France in both urban and rural areas, acceptance of drinking is high, and alcoholic beverages are very accessible. This observation suggests that the urban environment per se does not necessarily imply higher rates of alcoholism.

H. Occupation

In the epidemiology of diseases and behavioral disorders the work environment has always been of interest. In the case of alcoholism it was known since the early nineteenth century that rates of death from liver cirrhosis tend to be relatively high among publicans and employees of drinking establishments [2]. In Table III occupational groups with the highest and the lowest mortality from cirrhosis of the liver are shown for the United

TABLE III   A Selection of Occupations with High and Low Mortality Ratios from Cirrhosis of the Liver, United States 1950[a],[b]

Occupation	Estimated population	Standardized mortality ratios[e]
Waiters, bartenders, and counter workers	347,941	392
Longshoremen and stevedors	71,853	342
Transportation laborers, except railroad	109,447	314
Cooks, except private household	209,031	286
Musicians	79,384	278
Meat cutters, except slaughter and packinghouse	170,219	258
Authors, editors, and reporters	70,062	222
Bakers	106,920	219
Other service workers, except private household	352,566	209
	.	.
	.	.
	.	.
Accountants and auditors	324,997	87
Mail carriers	164,736	84
Insurance agents and brokers	272,770	73
Foremen	539,147	55
Farmers and farm managers	3,834,661	51
Carpenters	947,908	49

[a] Men aged 20 to 64 years.
[b] From Ref. 12.
[e] Mortality of total labor force = 100.

States [12]. Mortality is presented in terms of standardized ratios that compare the observed number of deaths with the number that would be expected if the mortality experience of the total population (the male labor force 20 to 64 years of age) had prevailed in the particular occupational group.

Evidently the low rate among farmers was to be expected, since temperance attitudes are still much stronger in rural than in urban North America. The unusually high rates among waiters bartenders, and cooks agree with observations from other countries [2, 8, 12, 38]. Undoubtedly they can be attributed to a ready access to beverage alcohol as well as a traditionally high acceptance of its use among these groups.

It is somewhat more difficult to explain the other very high and very low rates of liver cirrhosis mortality. One would need to consider all the socioeconomic factors affecting the selection of these occupations as well as the circumstances related to their practice.

I.   Specific Beverage Consumption

It has frequently been argued that the consumption of distilled spirits is more likely to lead to alcoholism than the consumption of the lighter beverages [13, 41]. For this reason the sales of distilled spirits are generally subjected to more legal restrictions and higher taxation than other kinds of beverage alcohol [53].

The alleged importance of distilled spirits in the development of alcoholism seems to draw support from the observation that this beverage leads more rapidly to intoxication than the consumption of identical amounts of ethanol in the form of wine and beer [11]. It should be noted, however, that only a little more time and effort are required to achieve intoxication with beer and wine. More important, there is no evidence that the speed at which intoxication is achieved is relevant in the development of alcoholism.

In this context it is of interest that the beverage preference of alcoholics does not depart much from that of the drinking population at large. For example, in Australia and southern Germany, beer is the most commonly used beverage, and according to clinical reports, also the beverage of choice of most alcoholics [27, 54].

Perhaps the best evidence against the notion that the consumption of distilled spirits is more likely lead to alcoholism than the consumption of the lighter beverages comes from a comparison of countries according to estimated rates of alcoholism and the contribution of distilled spirits to the total consumption (see Table IV). Clearly many countries in which

TABLE IV   Estimated Rates of Alcoholism and Contribution of Distilled Spirits to Total Consumption for Various Countries 1966–1967

Country	Estimated rates of alcoholism per 100,000 population aged 15 and older[a]	Percentage of contribution of distilled spirits consumption to total alcohol consumption[b]
France	9405	13.5
Italy	5877	12.6
Portugal	5652	4.1
Spain	4635	20.7
Austria	4212	18.2
W. Germany and W. Berlin	3978	21.2
Switzerland	3901	17.7
Luxembourg	2988	13.0
Hungary	2952	21.8
U.S.A.	2198	46.0
Czechoslovakia	2655	17.4
Canada	2272	36.0
England and Wales	1946	14.2
Rep. Ireland	1946	34.4
Denmark	1848	17.2
Belgium	2052	15.0
Poland	1752	61.2
Sweden	1515	54.0
Netherlands	1456	37.0
Finland	945	46.7
Norway	945	45.8

[a] See footnote b to Table II.
[b] Alcohol consumption data were taken from the 1968 Annual Report of the Dutch Distillers' Association [37].

a large proportion of alcohol is consumed in the form of beer and wine rather than distilled spirits have high rates of alcoholism.

It may be argued that in some of the countries in which the contribution of distilled spirits to total alcohol consumption is large, e.g., Finland, the predominant drinking pattern consists of occasional consumption, e.g., once or twice a month, of intoxicating amounts. Indeed the prevalence of such a drinking pattern may be somewhat reduced by a program of promoting the use of beer and wine. The problem of occasional intoxication, however, should not be confused with alcoholism.

J. Sex

All available indices of alcohol abuse—liver cirrhosis mortality, consumption data, drunkenness arrests, and hospital admissions—show a difference between men and women in the prevalence of alcoholism. In Canada and the United States the ratio is about six male to one female alcoholic [49]. Although international differences have been observed in the size of this ratio [15], the higher rate among males seems to be a general phenomenon. It has been suggested that the difference is a reflection of the double moral standard in Western societies. Thus it is generally less acceptable for a woman to drink heavily than a man. Particularly drunkenness among women is regarded with great disapproval. This explanation is supported by an apparent absence of sex differences in other disturbances, such as neurotic conflicts, anxiety states, or personality disorders [34].

In view of the apparently fixed relationship between the total volume of alcohol typically consumed in a population and the prevalence of alcoholism, it follows that a similar sex difference should be found in per capita consumption. Indeed the results of a number of drinking surveys [5, 10, 21] seem to support this contention.

K. Age

Many years of drinking typically precede the onset of alcoholism [17]. Hence the prevalence of alcoholism in the younger age groups must be quite low. For example, about 80% of Ontario alcoholics were between 30 and 55 years of age at the time of their first admission to a clinic (see Figure 4).

Apart from the question of the representativeness of this sample of clinically treated alcoholics, it must be noted that the length of time between the onset of alcoholism and the first admission may vary considerably from patient to patient [42]. Therefore it would not be possible to establish accurate prevalence rates by age groups on the basis of these data. Nevertheless it is quite apparent that alcoholism is most prevalent among the middle-aged. This raises the question as to why, at a period in life when most persons would be expected to have stabilized their pattern of alcohol intake, some continue to gravitate toward the tail end of the distribution curve (see Figure 1).

L. Psychological Factors

Some attempts have been made to explain rate variation in alcoholism on the basis of differences among populations in the prevalence of emotional

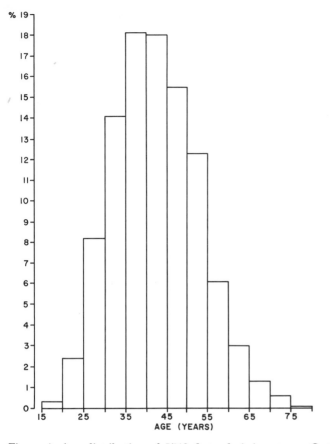

Figure 4. Age distribution of 5743 first admissions to an Ontario alcoholism clinic during the period 1951–1961.

disturbance. In essence it is argued that in sociocultural environments that produce a great deal of inner stress and tolerate "utilitarian drinking," e.g., drinking to unwind, as a mode of adjustment to such stress, high rates of alcoholism occur [1, 4].

This theory raises a number of questions. First, it is difficult to develop useful indices of the mental health of a population. For example, how would one compare the mental health of the Swedish nation to that of the French? At best, such a comparison would involve highly arbitrary definitions and procedures. Second, if high rates of alcoholism were in part attributable to a high rate of emotional disturbance and to utilitarian drinking as a mode of adjustment, we should have to conclude that in countries such as France, Portugal or Italy these factors must be relatively common. Clearly there is no evidence that would support this notion.

In the so-called vulnerability acceptance theory" emotional disturbances are linked with the acceptance of alcohol use. In societies that have a low degree of acceptance of large daily amounts of alcohol, mainly those are exposed to the risk of addiction who, on account of high psychological vulnerability, have an inducement to go against the social standards. But in societies that have an extremely high degree of acceptance of large daily alcohol consumption the presence of any small vulnerability, whether psychological or physical, suffices for exposure to the risk of addiction [18]. Indeed it is reasonable to assume that there is considerable variation from country to country in the rate of severity of emotional disturbance among alcoholic drinkers, i.e., those who consume in excess of a daily average of 150 ml of absolute alcohol. Where the over-all level of consumption is low, drinkers of alcoholic quantities comprise a relatively small segment of the population, and their drinking deviates drastically from the drinking norm. It is then not surprising that such drinkers typically are persons who also deviate in other respects. Conversely in high-consumption countries, drinking in excess of 150 ml of absolute alcohol daily is much more common, and therefore, one would expect the rate of emotional disturbance to be lower among excessive drinkers.

M.   Mortality of Alcoholics

In addition to environmental factors contributing to alcoholism, the consequences of such behavior for health also fall within the province of the epidemiologist. A common approach compares the mortality experiences of samples of alcoholics with that of the population at large. These studies show that the rate of death of alcoholics is more than twice the expected [3, 9, 43, 51]. The excess mortality is largely attributable to the following causes: neoplasms of the upper digestive and respiratory tract; alcoholism; heart disease; pneumonia; cirrhosis of the liver; suicides; other violent causes. Explanation for the high mortality of alcoholics usually refers to the acute and chronic effects of alcohol, the relatively high prevalence of emotional disturbance, and a general state of neglect frequently encountered among alcoholics.

Another line of investigation relates variation in levels of consumption among populations to mortality. For example, it has been shown for some countries that variation over time in excess mortality of males over females in the age groups 35 to 60 correlates with variation in alcohol consumption. Accordingly it has been suggested that the generally much higher alcohol consumption of males explains in part why men have higher rates of death than women [25]. A further example is the correlation over time and space between liver cirrhosis mortality and consumption rates. Invariably a high per capita consumption implies a high rate of death from liver cirrhosis (see Table I).

N. The Prevention of Alcoholism

Programs aimed at the reduction or prevention of alcoholism include total and partial prohibition of the sale of alcoholic beverages, the control of the number and kind of liquor outlets, taxation of beverage alcohol, the dissemination of information on alcohol and alcoholism, the encouragement of the use of low-content alcoholic beverages, and penal sanctions for drunkenness. Roughly these measures fall into two groups. Some aim at the reduction of the over-all level of alcohol consumption, whereas others try to encourage "desirable" modes of drinking.

Current epidemiological findings lend strong support to the former approach. Since rates of alcoholism rise and fall with the over-all level of alcohol use in a population, a reduction in the per capita alcohol consumption must lead to lower rates of alcoholism. For this reason the taxation of beverage alcohol and, in general, all control measures that reduce accessibility seem to be effective, particularly if there is also a wide acceptance of the public health value of such controls.

The merits of programs that aim at the bringing about of so-called desirable drinking patterns are questionable. For example, those seeking to encourage the use of beer and wine and to discourage distilled spirits consumption through differential taxation or other means; to promote drinking with meals or at other regular occasions, may well lead to a reduction in the rate of intoxication relative of all drinking occasions. All evidence to date, however, indicates that such drinking patterns also lead to high over-all levels of consumption [22, 23, 48] and to higher rates of alcoholism.

A final question concerns the apparently fixed relationship among the various consumption levels. Is the quasi-mathematical connection between alcoholism prevalence and per capita consumption unalterable? A priori the possibility of a quite different distribution of consumption levels cannot be rejected.

REFERENCES

1. Bales, R. F., Cultural differences in rates of alcoholism, *Quart. J. Studies Alc.,* **6,** 480 (1946).

2. Bertillon, J., De la morbidité et de la mortalité professionnelles, *Annuaire Statistique de la Ville de Paris,* 186, 1889.
3. Brenner, B., Alcoholism and fatal accidents, *Quart J. Studies Alc.,* **28,** 517 (1967).
4. Brunn, K., The social and cultural background of alcoholism, *Alkoholpolitik,* **22,** 81–82 (1959).
5. Cahalan, D., I. Cisin, and H. Crossley, *American Drinking Practices,* Report No. 3, Social Research Group, George Washington University, Washington, D.C., 1967.
6. Coffey, T. G., Beer street; gin lane: Some views of the 18th century drinking, *Quart. J. Studies Alc.,* **27,** 669 (1966).
7. de Lint, J. and W. Schmidt, The distribution of alcohol consumption in Ontario, *Quart. J. Studies Alc.,* **29,** 968 (1968).
8. Febvay et Aubenque, La mortalité par catégorie professionnelle. *Études statistiques* (I.N.S.E.E.), **3,** 39 (1957).
9. Gabriel, E., Über die Todesursachen bei Alkoholikern. *Z. ges. Neurol. Phychiat.,* **153,** 385 (1935).
10. Gadourek, I., *Riskante Gewoonten,* Wolters, Groningen, Holland, 1963.
11. Goldberg, L. A., The definition of an intoxicating beverage, *Quart. J. Studies Alc.,* **16,** 316 (1955).
12. Guralnick, L., Mortality by occupation and industry among men 20 to 64 years of age, United States 1950. *Vital Statistics,* Special Reports vol. 53, no. 2, p. 49, 1962.
13. Haggard, H. W., and E. M. Jellinek, *Alcohol Explored,* p. 75 Doubleday, Garden City, N.Y., 1942.
14. Hyland, J. and S. Scott, Alcohol consumption tables: an application of the Ledermann equation to a wide range of consumption averages, ARF Mimeo, 1969.
15. Jellinek, E. M., The Problems of Alcohol, in Alcohol, Science and Society, *J. Studies Alc.,* (New Haven), Lecture 2, 13, 1945.
16. Jellinek, E. M., Recent trends in alcoholism in alcohol consumption, *Quart. J. Studies Alc.,* **8,** 1, 1947.
17. Jellinek, E. M., Phases of alcohol addiction, *Quart. J. Studies Alc.,* **13,** 673 (1952).
18. Jellinek, E. M., International Experience with the Problem of Alcoholism, MS. of Paper Presented to the Alcoholism Research Symposium, *Fifth International Congress on Mental Health,* Toronto, 1954.
19. Jolliffe, N., and E. M. Jellinek, Vitamin deficiencies and liver cirrhosis. VII. Cirrhosis of the liver, *Quart. J. Studies Alc.,* **2,** 544 (1941).
20. Kuusi, P., *Suomen viinapulma: Gallup—tutkimuksen valossa,* p. 156, Otava, Helsinki, 1948.
21. Kuusi, P., *Sales Experiment in Rural Finland,* p. 117, The Finnish Foundation for Alcohol Studies, 1957.
22. Kuusi, P., Alkoholkonsumtionens nya nivå, *Alkoholpolitik,* **2,** 45 (1969).

23. Kuusi, P., Fredlig start, *Alkoholpolitik,* **1,** 1, (1969).

24. Ledermann, S., "Alcool-Alcoolisme-Alcoolisation; Données Scientfiques de Caractère Physiologique Économique et Social," Institut National d'Études Démographiques, Travaux et Documents, Cahier No. 29, Presses Universitaires de France, 1956. p. 123 ff., 137–139, 158.

25. Ledermann, S., Alcool-Alcoolisme-Alcoolisation; Mortalité, Morbidité Accidents du Travail, Institut National d'Études Démographiques, Travaux et Documents, Cahier No. 41, Presses Universitaires de France, 1964, p. 417 ff.

26. Lelbach, W. K., Leberschäden bei chronischem Alkoholismus, *Acta Hepato-Splenol.,* **13,** 321 (1966).

27. Lelbach, W. K., Zur leberschädigenden Wirkung verschiedener Alkoholika, *Deut. Med. Wochenschrift,* **6,** 233 (1967).

28. Lipscomb, W. R., Mortality among treated alcoholics: A three year follow-up study, *Quart. J. Studies Alc.,* **20,** 596 (1959).

29. Lolli, G., E. Serianni, G. M. Golder, P. Luzzatto-Fegiz, *Alcohol in Italian Culture,* Monogr. No. 3, Yale Center of Alcohol Studies, Free Press, The Free Press, Glencoe, Illinois, 1958.

30. Mikolaj, T., The policy of pricing versus rising consumption of alcohol, *Problemy Alkoholizmu,* **4,** 7 (1969).

31. Nielsen, J., and E. Strömgren-Risskov, Über die Abhängigkeit des Alkoholkonsums und der Alkoholkrankheiten vom Preis alkoholischer Getränke, *Akt. Fragen Psychiat. Neurol.,* **9,** 165 (1969).

32. Pequignot, G., Investigation on dietetic conditions of alcoholic cirrhosis in France, *Bull. Inst. Nat. Hygiene* (Paris), **13,** (1958).

33. Popham, R. E., The Jellinek alcoholism estimation formula and its application to Canadian data, *Quart. J. Studies Alc.,* **17,** 559 (1956).

34. Popham, R. E., Some social and cultural aspects of alcoholism. *Canad. Psych. Assoc. J.,* **4,** 222 (1959).

35. Popham, R. E., The urban tavern: Some preliminary remarks. *Addictions,* **9,** 2, 1962.

36. Popham, R. E., Indirect methods of alcoholism prevalence estimation: A critical evaluation, in *Alcohol and Alcoholism* p. 294, University of Toronto Press, Toronto, 1970.

37. Produktschap voor Gedistilleerde Dranken, *Verslag over het jaar 1968.* Schiedam, April 1969.

38. The Registrar-General's Decennial Supplement, England & Wales, 1951, *Occupational Mortality,* part II, vol. I, Her Majesty's Stationery Office, London, 1958.

39. Reuss, C., *History of Beer Consumption in Belgium 1900–1957,* Institut de Rechêrches Économique et Sociales de l'Université de Louvain, Louvain, 1959.

40. Sariola, S., *Prohibition in Finland 1919–1932: Its Background and Consequences,* Finnish Foundation for Alcohol Studies, Helsinki 1951.

41. Sariola, S., *Drinking Patterns in Finnish Lapland,* p. 23, Finnish Foundation for Alcohol Studies, Helsinki, 1956.

42. Schmidt, W., R. G. Smart, M. K. Moss, *Social Class and the Treatment of*

Alcoholism, Addiction Research Foundation Monograph No. 7, University of Toronto Press, Toronto, 1968.

43. Schmidt, W., and J. de Lint, Mortality experiences of male and female alcoholic patients, *Quart. J. Studies Alc.,* **30,** 112 (1969).
44. Schmidt, W., and J. de Lint, Estimating the prevalence of alcoholism from alcohol consumption and mortality data, *Quart. J. Studies Alc.,* **31,** 957 (1970).
45. Seeley, J. R., Alcoholism prevalence: An alternative estimation method, *Quart. J. Studies Alc.,* **21,** 500 (1960).
46. Seeley, J. R., The Ecology of Alcoholism: A Beginning, in *Society, Culture and Drinking Patterns,* D. J. Pittman and C. R. Snyder (eds.), Chap. 18, J. Wiley, New York, 1962.
47. Seeley, J. R., Death by liver cirrhosis and the price of beverage alcohol, *Canad. Med. Assoc. J.,* **83,** 1361 (1960).
48. Skala, J., Some characteristic signs of alcoholism in Czechoslovakia, vol. 1, pp. 21–34, Selected Papers presented at the 12th International Institute on the Prevention and Treatment of Alcoholism, Prague, 1966.
49. Snyder, C. R., A Sociological View of the Etiology of Alcoholism, in *Alcoholism: An Interdisciplinary Approach,* Chap. III, D. J. Pittman (ed.) Charles C Thomas, Springfield, Ill., 1959.
50. Srole, L., T. S. Langner, S. T. Michael, M. K. Opler, and T. A. C. Rennie, *Mental Health in the Metropolis: The Midtown Manhattan Study,* vol. 1. McGraw-Hill, New York, 1962.
51. Sundby, P., *Alcoholism and Mortality,* Universitetsforlaget, Oslo, and Rutgers Center on Alcohol Studies, New Brunswick, N.J., 1967.
52. United Nations, *Demographic Yearbook 1966,* Eighteenth Issue, Mortality Statistics, Statistical Office of the United Nations, Dept. Economic and Social Affairs, United Nations, New York, 1967.
53. van Niekerk, J. A. H., *A Survey of the Control of Alcoholic Beverages in Other Countries,* Brewer's Institute of South Africa, Johannesburg, 1958.
54. Wilkinson, P., J. Santamaria, J. Rankin, and D. Martin, Epidemiology of alcoholism: Social data and drinking patterns of a sample of Australian alcoholics, *Med. J. Aust.,* **1,** 1020 (1969).
55. World Health Organization, *Manual of Statistical Classification of Diseases, Injuries, and Causes of Death,* 7th Revision, 1955.

INDEX